Personality

ANALYSIS AND
INTERPRETATION OF LIVES

Personality

ANALYSIS AND
INTERPRETATION OF LIVES

———— ❖ ————

David G. Winter
University of Michigan

Boston, Massachusetts   Burr Ridge, Illinois   Dubuque, Iowa
Madison, Wisconsin   New York, New York   San Francisco, California   St. Louis, Missouri

McGraw-Hill

A Division of The **McGraw·Hill** *Companies*

PERSONALITY
Analysis and Interpretation of Lives

Acknowledgments appear on pages A1–A4.

This book is printed on acid-free paper.

 4 5 6 7 8 9 10   FGRFGR   9 9 8 7

ISBN 0-07-071129-1

This book was set in Palatino by The Clarinda Company.
The editors were Brian L. McKean, David Dunham, and
Ty McConnell, who supervised the final revision and production;
Anne Manning efficiently supervised the photographs and artwork;
the production supervisor was Annette Mayeski.
The cover was designed by Amy Becker.
R. R. Donnelley & Sons Company was printer and binder.

Cover: Self Portrait, Judith Leyster. National Gallery of Art, Washington, DC.
 Gift of Mr. and Mrs. Robert Woods Bliss, © 1995 by the Board of Trustees.

Library of Congress Cataloging-in-Publication Data

Winter, David G., (date).
    Personality: analysis and interpretation of lives / David G.
    Winter.
        p.   cm.
    Includes bibliographical references and index.
    ISBN 0-07-071129-1
    1. Personality.   I. Title.
BF698.W523   1996
155.2—dc20
                                            95-15697

About the Author

———————— ❖ ————————

David G. Winter was born and raised in Grand Rapids, Michigan. He graduated from Harvard University, majoring in Social Relations. As a Rhodes Scholar, he studied philosophy, politics, and economics at Oxford. He received a Ph.D. from Harvard University in 1967, in Social Psychology.

He taught for twenty years at Wesleyan University, in Middletown, Connecticut. He is currently a Professor of Psychology at the University of Michigan. He has been a visiting faculty member at Harvard University, Massachusetts Institute of Technology, the University of Amsterdam, and the College of the Holy Cross.

Besides the psychology of personality, his principal academic interest is political psychology, especially the study of personalities of public officials at a distance and by indirect means, and the psychological aspects of war and peace. His research interests include the study of power motivation and how it can be controlled, the nature of authoritarian ideology, and the relationships between personality and culture.

He is married, with two children, and lives in Ann Arbor, Michigan. His hobbies include travel, cooking, classical music, and reading historical novels.

To Abby, Nick, and Tim

Contents

———— ❖ ————

$\mathcal{P}$reface

❖

In this introduction to the psychology of personality, I try to give a comprehensive account of the main lines of personality theory and research. Most psychological research on personality has been carried out in the last fifty years, since World War II, by Americans; much of it is based on studies of college students (whose participation is often part of a psychology course requirement), typically white and middle-class, disproportionately male (see Carlson, 1984; Schultz, 1969). Let me state my conviction at the outset, therefore, that the topic of personality is much broader than such studies, so that the study of personality should go beyond a review of recent American psychological research. In this book, I try to set the study of personality psychology in a much broader context. I believe that we can best understand the psychology of personality by drawing on as many different kinds of information and wisdom as we can, and the approach I take in this book reflects that belief.

Accordingly, I have not limited myself to the traditional personality research literature. You will also find citations of the plays of Shakespeare and other great literary works, as well as brief excursions into history, sociology, anthropology, political science, and even philosophy. For example: How did personality assessments help President Jimmy Carter to negotiate peace between Israel and Egypt at Camp David (Chapter 1)? What does the hostility of boys in the Trobriand Islands toward their *uncles* (rather than their fathers) teach us about the Oedipus complex (Chapter 4)? What do authoritarians in contemporary Russia believe (Chapter 7)? What dimensions of trait usage are shared by collegiate slang, two poems by John Milton, and Henry Kissinger's descriptions of world leaders (Chapter 11)? What does Gilbert and Sullivan's *Pirates of Penzance* demonstrate about Virginia Woolf's family and childhood (Chapter 17)?

Many of these topics and examples reflect my liberal arts college background and my professional interest in political psychology (a field that surveys the effects of psychological factors on the political process, and vice versa). For example, because of my own interest in studying American presidents, I emphasize indirect methods of assessing personality—methods that can be applied from a distance to study prominent persons and historical figures.

CONCEPTUAL FRAMEWORK

This book is organized around four major elements of personality: (1) motivation, (2) cognition (including the "self"), (3) traits and temperament, and

(4) the social context. These four elements, in turn, may be organized along two underlying dimensions, as shown in the accompanying figure. In the left column of the figure are the personality elements that are *subjective or private* (inner thoughts and emotions), versus the *objective or public* (external, observable behavior) elements in the right column. The rows distinguish elements that *endure across situations* (top row) from elements that are *situation-dependent* (bottom row). The resulting four-fold classification is the main conceptual framework for this book. It is used to group personality theories and research concepts.

Many theorists and theories are easily classified as concerned with one element (e.g., Freud, neo-Freudians, and Murray as motivational; Kelly as cognitive; Jung and Eysenck as trait-oriented; and Mischel, Bandura, Skinner, and Erikson as contextual). Some theorists use elements from more than one domain. For example, Allport focuses on values (cognition) and traits, Rogers on actualization (motive) and self (cognition).

	Inner, Private, Subjective	Outer, Public, Objective
Enduring and typical across situations	COGNITIONS Examples of variables: Beliefs, attitudes, values, self-concept Major theorists: Kelly, Rogers	TRAITS, TEMPERAMENT Examples of variables: Extraversion, energy level Major theorists: Allport, Jung, Eysenck
Situation-dependent	MOTIVATION Examples of variables: Motives, defenses, psychic structure Major theorists: Freud, Murray, McClelland	SOCIAL CONTEXT Examples of variables: Habits, models, culture, class, ethnicity, gender Major theorists: Mischel, Erikson, Stewart

The major elements of personality.

The central argument of *Personality: Analysis and Interpretation of Lives* is that while theories and variables from each element can contribute to our understanding, a complete account of human personality requires all four domains. That is, any adequate account of personality must include elements of motivation and emotion, cognition, temperament, and social-cultural context. Stretching a single theory to cover all four domains of behavior (e.g., trying to explain everything with *only* motives, habits, beliefs, or temperament) is inadequate, and only provokes familiar criticisms about the limited explanatory power of personality theories and variables.

Most personality textbooks try to integrate theory and research. Because it provides a common analytical framework, the four-element conceptual organization makes possible a deep and comprehensive integration of personality theory, research, and assessment. Thus for each element of personality, I trace the origins of the principal concepts and issues back to the classical theories and forward to the most recent research questions and controversies.

HISTORICAL CASE STUDIES

Like the authors of many textbooks, I illustrate concepts and theories with examples drawn from college life. I have learned, however, that students can easily grow tired of such examples. Sometimes they are so obvious that they trivialize important concepts of personality rather than illustrating them. And college students are not all alike: they live many different kinds of lives. Therefore, I have concentrated on developing case studies of historical figures to illustrate the concepts and processes of the four elements of personality. Each case is chosen to be particularly appropriate for one of the elements of personality: former U.S. President Richard Nixon for motives, blind and deaf writer and activist Helen Keller for cognitions, physicist Albert Einstein for temperament, and African-American writer Maya Angelou and English novelist Virginia Woolf for social context. For each case study, I use extensive quotations from published autobiographies to illustrate and also to raise questions about the concepts, theories, and problems of the corresponding personality element.

SPECIAL TOPICS AND EMPHASES

I have tried to give up-to-date coverage of important recent controversies in personality psychology. Examples include: feminist thinking and the critique of psychoanalytic theory, including a new interpretation of the Oedipus complex; moral reasoning, including the debate between Kohlberg and Gilligan about "principles" versus "caring" morality; a discussion of the uses *and* limitations of the five-factor model of traits (the "Big Five"); and a critical analysis of genetics of personality and recent attempts to link personality to modern evolutionary theory. In recounting the situationist critique of personality by Mischel and others, I include a detailed discussion of the many improvements in personality research that resulted from this debate (Chapter 16).

I include many topics ignored or treated only briefly in personality textbooks. Examples include: authoritarianism and social attitudes (Chapter 7), research on possible selves and narcissism (Chapter 9), and moral reasoning and concerns for justice (Chapter 10). Most texts make only a brief reference to the idiographic method of personality description. Since this method is important for the interpretation of individual persons, I feel that a more extensive description and examples are in order (Chapter 12). And since Jung's typology of persons is the basis of the Myers-Briggs Type Indicator, one of the most widely used personality tests in the world, I present a detailed description in this book (also in Chapter 12).

PERSONALITY IN ITS SOCIAL CONTEXT

One of the most novel topics of this book is the extensive converage of the social context of personality in Part Four (especially Chapter 17). This includes the relationships between personality and social structure, institutions, and culture. With this coverage, I hope to place the book on the cutting edge of recent efforts to bring psychology back into contact with the other social sciences. The discussion of gender relations incorporates some perspectives of feminist theory, bringing together the effects of gender, social class, and racial oppression on personality under the unifying concept of *hegemonic relations.* An extensive analysis of what it means to say "it's culture," instead of (or in addition to) "it's personality," introduces the study of cultural variation in the meaning and structure of personality variables. With case study examples and many kinds of research data, I also illustrate the personality implications of history and a person's generation.

PLAN OF THIS BOOK

After an introductory chapter, this book is organized into four parts, one for each element of personality. Starting with motives in Part One, it proceeds clockwise around the figure to cognitions (Part Two), traits (Part Three), and social context (Part Four). Within each part, the first chapter defines the element, gives examples from everyday life, presents a few classic and modern research studies, and introduces the historical figure to be used as a case study for that element. Next, major theories are presented, in this or the next chapter. Finally, the remaining chapters of each part explore research, issues, and applications of that personality element.

AN INVITATION

I invite you to join in the fascinating exploration of human personality. We begin with the topic of motives and motivation, which leads to Freud and psychoanalytic theory in Chapter 3. Freud's work is an appropriate starting point for our understanding of the psychology of personality, since so many writers after Freud were trying to agree with, support, revise, disprove, or reconsider his ideas. From there, we move on to the study of cognition (Chapters 6–10), traits and temperament (Chapters 11–14), and social context (Chapters 15–17). In the final Chapter 18, I suggest three ways in which the four elements can be put together to form an integrated, unified conception of personality.

ACKNOWLEDGMENTS

In writing this book, I want to acknowledge an enormous debt of gratitude to many other people—colleagues, mentors, students, and others. First and foremost is my debt to Abby Stewart, with whom the basic structure of this book was first conceived in a dinner-table discussion long ago. In the years since, her ideas, suggestions, encouragement, and arguments have been a major force in giving life to this conception.

My many debts to those who taught me personality are obvious. David McClelland has been my earliest and most enduring mentor. His breadth of theoretical vision, and his capacity for asking unusual questions and then answering them in unorthodox ways, have been an inspiration to me for over three decades. This book also reflects the influence of many other college and graduate school teachers—by no means all of them psychologists. I also thank members of the Society for Personology, who in our annual meetings have stressed that personality psychology is, in the end, about persons. I am grateful for the comradeship of many colleagues, past and present, at the University of Michigan: Joseph Veroff, Nancy Cantor, David Buss, Randy Larsen, Donald Brown, Andrea Hunter, Janet Landman, Christopher Peterson, George Rosenwald, and John Atkinson. And during an exciting year in Berkeley, I enjoyed the stimulating perspectives of Jack Block, Oliver John, Ravenna Helson, Kenneth Craik, Philip Tetlock, and William McKinley Runyan. My students and teaching assistants at Wesleyan and Michigan have through their responses guided me in developing and elaborating the text. Todd Shackelford played a major role in creating the Instructor's Manual, to which Cheryl Rusting also added helpful advice and criticism.

Any successful textbook owes a lot to editors and publishers. Here I record my debt to Mary Falcon, who originally encouraged me to develop this framework; to Christopher Rogers, who helped the project along; and finally to Brian McKean and David Dunham, who supervised the final revision and production. Many other people at McGraw-Hill worked on various aspects of

the editorial and production process. I am indebted to a large number of
reviewers who made helpful comments on early drafts of several chapters:

Hal Arkowitz, University of Arizona
Joel Aronoff, Michigan State University
Robert T. Croyle, University of Utah
Adrienne Gans, New York University
Leon Gorlou, Pennsylvania State University
Sharon Rae Jenkins, University of North Texas
Nadia Webb, LaSalle University

The comments of Cele Gardner, of McGraw-Hill, were especially helpful. Since
I didn't always follow all of their advice, the responsibility for what follows
naturally remains mine.

Finally, a special word of gratitude to Nick and Tim, who provided their
own special kind of encouragement.

David G. Winter

Personality

ANALYSIS AND
INTERPRETATION OF LIVES

1

Introducing Personality

❖

You are about to begin the systematic study of personality. As a field of psychology, personality is new to you. As a word, however, "personality" is quite familiar. What is personality? Sometimes the word is used as if it means something that varies in quantity or amount ("She has lots of personality"; "He has no personality"). Often we use the word "personality" as an evaluation ("She has a great personality"), particularly in making a contrast to physical appearance ("He may not

1

be good-looking, but he has a great personality"). People with "good" person-alities are typically described as happy, outgoing, energetic, fun to be with, interesting, honest, genuine, agreeable, easy-going, and polite. In contrast, people with "bad" personalities are seen as abrasive, annoying, rude, crude, boring, having nothing to say, and not fun to be with. For many college stu-dents, the ultimate put-down is to compare someone's personality to an inani-mate object ("He has all the personality of a doorknob"—or a brick wall, rock, wet noodle, tree stump, etc.).

In any case, the word "personality" is familiar to most Americans. Accord-ing to ABC news anchor Peter Jennings, "No country in the world is so driven by personality as this one," and Americans' appetite for news reflects their "hunger to identify with larger-than-life personalities" ("Only spectacular crimes," 1994).

BUT WHAT IS PERSONALITY?

Personality as a Mask

The word "personality" is derived from the ancient Greek word *persona*, a mask worn by an actor in a play. (*Per sona* means "sound through": characters spoke or "sounded through" their masks.) The masks served to conceal the actors as they presented their characters. In psychology, this concealment per-spective can be seen in book titles such as *The Presentation of Self in Everyday Life* (Goffman, 1959) and *Beneath the Mask* (Monte, 1991), and in dramaturgical conceptions of personality as a series of roles enacted on a stage for a real or imagined audience (Snyder, 1987; see Buss & Briggs, 1984, for a thoughtful discussion and critique of the dramaturgical perspective on personality).

In a sense, however, among the ancient Greeks masks were intended to enhance and intensify rather than to conceal, to convey to the audience a clear conception of the character being portrayed. In wearing the mask, the actor *became* the character, just as in some religions the person wearing the mask of a deity is believed to become that deity. In the ancient Greek sense, then, your personality is a mask that displays, rather than hides, the essential you.

Psychological Conception of Personality

To a psychologist, personality means the ways in which general "laws" of physiology, perception, memory, learning, motivation, and social influence—which are assumed to apply universally, to all people—are integrated and expressed in individual persons, each of whom is unique. Thus, for example, our eyes and ears all follow the same laws of sensation, and our nervous sys-tems and brains all operate by the same principles of information processing; yet we are unique individuals, each of us different from all the others. We each have our own unique perceptions, memories, goals, and social background. To adapt a famous formulation by Kluckhohn and Murray (1953, p. 53), every person is in certain respects (1) like all other people, (2) like some other people, and (3) like no other people. The personality psychologist tries first to describe this combination of universality and uniqueness, and then to explain how it functions and how it develops.

The Field of Personality Psychology

Personality psychology has three parts. First, psychologists construct *theories* about the nature, structure, and development of personality. Many of these psychological theories of personality have roots in various philosophical, religious, and ideological views of human nature. The psychoanalytic theories of Sigmund Freud, for example, drew upon both the ideas of the nineteenth-century German philosopher Friedrich Nietzsche and the Jewish mystical tradition (Bakan, 1958). The humanistic ideas of Carl Rogers were undoubtedly shaped by his study for the liberal Protestant Christian ministry before he turned to clinical psychology (Rogers, 1966). And the theories of Erich Fromm (1941, 1947) reflect ideas of Karl Marx that link personality to economic conditions.

Second, psychologists carry out *research* on personality. They identify and develop measures of its important elements or variables, relate these variables to behavior, and study their origins, structure, and organization. Personality psychologists use research to evaluate theories of personality and to improve ways of measuring personality.

Finally, psychologists make *assessments,* or formal descriptions, of people's personalities, not only to carry out personality research but also to identify people's psychological problems and to design a program of treatment for them. Personality assessment methods include quite a range of procedures: interviews; case studies; indirect methods such as the Rorschach test, in which the person interprets inkblots, and the Thematic Apperception Test (TAT), in which the person tells stories about vague or ambiguous pictures; omnibus questionnaire inventories such as the Minnesota Multiphasic Personality Inventory (MMPI) and the California Personality Inventory (CPI), which measure many variables at once; and more limited questionnaires that measure one or more specific personality variables. All of these methods require direct access to the people being assessed, either one-to-one or in groups. This need for direct access often severely constrains personality assessment. Many important people, whose personalities may affect millions of people, are not available for direct assessment: for example, political leaders, authors, cultural and entertainment figures. Can you imagine walking into the Oval Office of the White House to give a psychological test or interview to the President of the United States?[1] And most historical figures are dead, so that their Oedipus complexes or achievement motives are beyond the reach of the standard techniques for personality assessment.

---

[1]A 1967 movie, *The President's Analyst,* is based on the premise that any psychologist who had such access to the president would quickly be sought after by every national (and multinational) spy agency. It's a funny movie, available in many video rental stores and on late-night television.

In this book, I emphasize indirect methods of assessing personality, that is, methods that can be applied from a distance to study prominent people and historical figures. These methods have been developed over the past 30 years by Hermann (1980b), Simonton (1990), Winter (1991a, 1992a), and other political psychologists. In political psychology, these are often the only way to study political leaders. And even when access for direct assessment is possible, problems can arise. Psychological tests can make some people anxious, defensive, and suspicious. They may try to present themselves in the most favorable light, they may give the answers they think the psychologist wants, they may agree with everything the tester says, or they may answer randomly. These factors are called *response sets* or *response styles* (Anastasi, 1982; Merydith & Wallbrown, 1991); they interfere with the accuracy of psychological tests. In contrast, indirect methods used to measure personality at a distance are *nonreactive*. People being measured do not react to them because they do not "take" them in the same way they take standard personality tests. Instead of presenting people with test situations and stimuli, psychologists who study personality at a distance try to analyze samples of people's ordinary, natural behavior, especially their verbal or written behavior. Because such at-a-distance methods do not arouse reactions, they have advantages for assessing people even when direct access is possible (Winter, 1991a, p. 71; see also Webb, Campbell, Schwartz, & Sechrest, 1966, on indirect or unobtrusive measures). Of course at-a-distance measures have problems, too: they often require more time and training to score than do questionnaires, they may have certain biases, and some psychologists have raised questions about their reliability and validity credentials (see Chapter 5).

Many textbooks separate the theory, research, and assessment parts of personality psychology. Some books focus on theory, while others emphasize research results. Sometimes personality assessment is left to advanced courses in clinical psychology. This book covers all three parts of the field, not as separate topics but rather as integrated parts of a whole, namely the study of persons and personality.

Person-Centered versus Variable-Centered Approaches

Some personality psychologists study individual people, tracing how their personalities developed out of early experience and are reflected in the whole course of life. This approach is called the *study of lives* (White, 1981), *life history, personology*[2] (Murray, 1938, p. 4), or the *idiographic approach*[3] (Allport, 1937, 1962; Carlson, 1971, 1984). When applied at a distance to historical figures, this approach is also called *psychobiography* (Greenstein, 1969/1987, chap. 3; McAdams & Ochberg, 1988; Runyan, 1981, 1984, 1988). In this approach, the emphasis is on *interpretation*, or "making sense of," the individual's life. The

---

[2]In a footnote to his definition of the word "personology," Murray suggested that "as here defined, [it] is what all men, except professional psychologists, call psychology" (1938, p. 4n).

[3]Splitting the word "idiographic" into two parts gives us "idio-," refering to individuality (as in "idiosyncracy"), and "graph," meaning a visual representation or chart of form and shape. Thus "idiographic" refers to the charting or representing of a person's individuality.

personality psychologist looks for coherent themes and patterns that unify people's actions, words, and concerns over the whole course of their lives.

Most personality psychologists, however, try to identify fundamental dimensions applying to all people—dimensions along which individuals differ—and then construct general laws about these dimensions. To use an analogy from chemistry, these dimensions, or *variables,* can be thought of as a relatively small set of "elements" that combine into an almost unlimited number of possible "compounds" (see Murray, 1938, pp. 142–143). This focus on variables is often called the *nomothetic* or *dimensional approach* to personality (Allport, 1962). In the nomothetic approach, the personalities of particular individuals can be described by their scores on measures of general personality variables. The emphasis is on the *analysis* of unique persons and lives and into their component elements and variables, much as a chemist analyzes a wide variety of unique and complex substances and breaks them down into a few simpler chemical elements.[4]

I try to combine both approaches—hence this book's subtitle, "Analysis and Interpretation of Lives." We will use theories and concepts of personality psychology to interpret or understand unique lives in all their complexity. At the same time, we will introduce the major variables of personality and use them to analyze or simplify lives into some of their major universal components. Each approach has value. I have selected five historical figures to use as "case studies" for interpretation and analysis, to illustrate principles and concepts, and to raise questions and challenges. Each case is especially useful for illustrating certain elements of personality: for motives, there is former U.S. President Richard Nixon (1913–1994); for cognitions, blind and deaf social activist Helen Keller (1880–1968); for traits, scientist Albert Einstein (1879–1955); and for social context, two authors: African American poet and autobiographer Maya Angelou (b. 1928) and British novelist and critic Virginia Woolf (1882–1941).

Each of these five people wrote an autobiography or autobiographical essays, from which I quote extensively. Since they are all available in paperback,[5] I encourage you to read more in order to understand and to analyze the psychological concepts of personality. Does a psychological analysis of personality help you to interpret and understand real people? You may then want to ask whether Virginia Woolf's critique of modern fiction (1919/1925) can also be applied to personality psychology:

[4]In medicine, these same two approaches are engaged in a debate about whether useful generalizations can be made beyond the individual case. Hippocrates, the ancient Greek physician honored as the founder of medicine, reflected the idiographic approach in his claim that "there are no diseases, only sick people" (Temkin, 1981, p. 261).

[5]Nixon wrote three autobiographies: *Six Crises* (1962), *RN: The Memoirs of Richard Nixon* (1978), and *In the Arena: A Memoir of Victory, Defeat, and Renewal* (1990). Keller wrote *The Story of My Life* (1903b), covering the years through college, and *Midstream: My Later Life* (1929), an account of her middle years. Einstein wrote some brief "Autobiographical Notes" for an edited book about him (Einstein, 1949/1979), as well as several personal and philosophical reflections collected in two books, *Out of My Later Years* (1950) and *Ideas and Opinions* (1954). Angelou has written several volumes of autobiography, the first and best-known of which is *I Know Why the Caged Bird Sings* (1970). Woolf's essay, "A Sketch of the Past," and other autobiographical writings have been collected by Schulkind under the title *Moments of Being* (1985).

Whether we call it life or spirit, truth or reality, this, the essential thing, has moved off, or on, and refuses to be contained any longer in such ill-fitting vestments as we provide. Nevertheless, we go on perseveringly, conscientiously, constructing our two and thirty chapters after a design which more and more ceases to resemble the vision in our minds. (p. 188)

Of course, people's autobiographies are not literal transcriptions of events, but rather their efforts to make sense of their lives at a particular point and for a particular purpose. Thus Richard Nixon wrote *RN: The Memoirs of Richard Nixon* shortly after resigning the presidency in disgrace. Helen Keller wrote the original version of *The Story of My Life* as an assignment for a college writing class. Einstein's brief autobiographical essay was written in response to an editor's request. Maya Angelou began the first volume of her story at the urging of friends, when she changed careers from acting to writing. Virginia Woolf wrote "A Sketch of the Past" less than a year before her suicide; it "was clearly intended to provide relief from particularly taxing literary commitments and from the deepening gloom of the second world war" (Schulkind, 1985, p. 11).

INTRODUCING THE ELEMENTS OF PERSONALITY

I think of personality as having at least four elements or domains: motivation, cognition, traits and temperament, and social context (see Figure 1.1). These four elements, in turn, are based on two fundamental dimensions. The vertical columns distinguish the subjective (internal or private) from the objective (external or public) elements of personality. Motives and cognitions are both private, or subjective. They exist only in people's minds, and can be observed only indirectly by asking or through some other indirect means. Traits and social contexts, in contrast, are more public and observable (though they also have internal aspects).

Labeling the horizontal rows is more difficult. Cognitions and traits tend to be relatively independent of the situation. If they do change, it is usually slowly. Thus they are well-suited to explaining broad and enduring regularities of behavior. They are often measured by asking about people's "typical" or "usual" characteristics. In contrast, motives and social contexts are much more dependent on immediate past, present, and future situations. Their measurements are likely to vary according to the situation of measurement. Thus they are elements of personality especially useful in explaining behaviors that are more specific, constantly changing, and often surprising and unusual. In Figure 1.1, therefore, I have labeled the rows "Enduring and typical across situations" (cognitions and traits) and "Situation-dependent" (motives and social contexts), though as with the columns, the difference is only one of degree.

This conception of personality helps to bring together a wide range of theories (as shown by the placement of major theorists in Figure 1.1), and an

	Inner, Private, Subjective	Outer, Public, Objective
Enduring and typical across situations	COGNITIONS Examples of variables: Beliefs, attitudes, values, self-concept Major theorists: Kelly, Rogers	TRAITS, TEMPERAMENT Examples of variables: Extraversion, Energy level Major theorists: Allport, Jung, Eysenck
Situation-dependent	MOTIVATION Examples of variables: Motives, defenses, psychic structure Major theorists: Freud, Murray, McClelland	SOCIAL CONTEXT Examples of variables: Habits, models, culture, class, ethnicity, gender Major theorists: Mischel, Erikson, Stewart

FIGURE 1.1
The major elements of personality.

almost bewildering assortment of personality variables and research. Each part of this book is devoted to one of the four elements, with all four elements drawn together in the final chapter. At this point I will only give a brief introduction to each element; more extensive treatments will be given in the chapter that begins each part.

The rest of this book is organized around the framework presented in Figure 1.1. Starting with motives in Part One, we will proceed clockwise around the figure to cognitions, traits, and social context in Parts Two through Four. Then in the last chapter, we will consider how these four elements are combined or integrated into a unified conception of personality.

Motives or Goals

We often find it necessary to describe people's actions in terms of their goals, intentions, or motives. A *goal* is a future state of affairs that we first imagine or anticipate and then try to bring about. This "trying to bring about" is often felt consciously as an *intention*. The whole sequence of orientation toward a goal, anticipation of the goal, conscious resolve to pursue the goal, and action to bring about the goal is a *motive*. *Approach motives* guide and direct our actions so as to move us closer to the anticipated goal; *avoidance motives* move us away from some aversive state of affairs.

Motives are flexible and variable, in two different ways. First, they increase and decrease over time, as a result of satisfaction or lack of satisfaction. Thus eating a big meal usually reduces the hunger motive to zero temporarily, while going without food for a long time increases it.

Second, the appropriate actions to reach any particular goal will vary greatly according to the circumstances. For example, imagine that you are hungry (your motive). Think about the specific actions you would take to get food (your goal) in each of the following circumstances: (1) at home in your kitchen, (2) in your favorite restaurant, or (3) on the streets of a foreign city where you do not know the language and have no phrase book. Your actions are likely to be different in each case—the more so during the initial phase of searching for food, the less so during the final phase of starting to eat. However, the motive and goal remain the same; in all three cases, you might describe yourself as "looking for food" (your intention). Of course if there were no food available (say, you were on a five-hour airplane flight with no meal service), then at that moment your hunger motive might not be expressed in action at all. Motives are thus a kind of mental gyroscope, guiding behavior toward the goal in question (in the example, food). Thus motives are different from *habits*, which are inflexible or stereotyped reactions to stimuli we have encountered before; for example, whenever I see a red light while driving, I habitually move my foot to the brake pedal.

Often our motives are in conflict with each other. To handle these conflicts and thereby to integrate different motives into a smooth-functioning flow of behavior, we develop several personality structures and mechanisms. The concept of the ego and the defense mechanisms of psychoanalytic theory are examples. These too can be considered as part of the domain of motives, so we will consider them also in Part One.

Cognitions

Our minds are filled with all sorts of mental furniture. We have *beliefs* (Why do things turn out the way they do? Is the world a threatening place or a safe place?), *values* (What is the good life? Is freedom more important than equality?), and *attitudes* or *opinions* (What do I think about abortion? Which presidential candidate do I prefer?). I use the term *cognitions* to refer to all these different concepts because they are all based on cognitive processes: perception, categorization, enduring storage in long-term memory, and judgment and decision making. Many psychologists have used the term *schema* as a generic term for cognitions. Presiding over all cognitive processes or schemas is the self-concept, self-schema, or identity—that is, who we think we are to ourselves. The self-concept is our single most important cognition: a serious challenge to it can undermine the entire integrity of our personality.

Like motives, cognitions guide behavior, but in a different way. Cognitions are normally independent of the immediate situation, whereas motives wax and wane as a result of internal states and anticipated external situations. Beliefs, values, and self-concept, in contrast, tend to endure regardless of variables such as the weather, our goals of the moment, or the immediate situation we are in. The distinction between motives and cognitions is discussed further in Chapters 5 and 10.

Traits and Temperament

To other people, our personalities express themselves most directly through consistent individual differences in observable behavior: some people are "bouncy," with a high energy level, while others are quiet and withdrawn; some are stable and dependable, others erratic and flighty; some refined, others crude. These regularities of behavior or style that are visible to others make up the domain of *traits*. (Some psychologists use the term *temperament* for traits assumed to be partly biological.) Traits are the part of personality closest to our everyday understanding of what personality is. Most words that we ordinarily use to describe personality—outgoing, quiet, generous, stingy, boring—actually refer to traits.

Some personality psychologists have used the term "trait" in a very broad way, to include almost all personality variables. This is because in the early days of scientific personality research, Gordon Allport (1931; Allport & Allport, 1921) proposed the concept of "trait" as the basic unit or variable of personality. Later, however, Allport (1937, 1961) realized that traits and motives were quite different kinds of personality elements, though he still referred to them both as traits; what we are calling traits he called "stylistic traits," and what we are calling motives he called "dynamic traits." Similarly, Guilford (1959) defined "trait" so broadly that it could include any personality variable: "any distinguishable and relatively enduring way in which one individual differs from others" (p. 6). However, he too went on to distinguish several different kinds of traits: needs and interests (motives), attitudes (cognitions), and temperaments (traits). Since I believe motives and cognitions are fundamentally different from traits and from each other, I want to consider them in this book as three different elements of personality. Hence I reserve the term "trait" for what Allport called "stylistic traits" and Guilford called "temperaments."

Social Context

Personality does not exist in isolation. From birth, our personalities grow and develop in social contexts. We continually select, incorporate, and rearrange features of those contexts. Over time, they become internalized as aspects of our personalities, and at every moment social contexts channel the expression of personality. Some psychologists go so far as to claim that our personalities are nothing but the accumulated social contexts in which we have lived. We shall examine this claim in Chapter 16.

I deliberately use the term "social context" to cover a broad range of phenomena. At one extreme is the *immediate situation*, a short-lived microcontext that consists of those rapidly changing forces that are acting on behavior right now, in the short run. For example, as I am writing these words the sun is shining, it is almost lunch time, I am getting over jet lag from a long trip, and today is a national holiday. Each of these microcontexts interacts with the elements of my personality to affect my behavior at the moment. In a typical psychology laboratory experiment, the experimenter manipulates certain features of the microcontext and observes the responses of the research participants. Microcontexts change rapidly, giving way to other microcontexts. Some personality psychologists, especially those with a learning or experimental psychology perspective, find it useful to think of people's personalities as their accumulated series of microcontexts from birth onward, but most find this level of analysis too confining.

At the other extreme, social context refers to the long-term, enduring *social structures* in which personality is embedded. These can be called macrocontexts. For example, personality always exists in a social structure in which *gender* plays an important part: each person is usually classified as either female or male, but not both, and only rarely changing from one to the other. "Gender" is not the same as "sex" in the sense of the anatomical and physiological differences between women and men; rather, gender is the elaborate system of cognitions and social relations that are constructed on the basis of sex (see Deaux, 1985, on this distinction). In Part Four I will argue that the macrocontext of gender has enormous consequences for the development and organization of personality.

Similarly, many other macrocontexts have important consequences for personality: social class (the individual's position in an economically stratified social structure), religion, ethnicity, nationality, culture, and even historical period.

While American psychology has always paid a great deal of attention to the influence of microcontexts on personality, its concern with the effects of macrocontext has been more variable. In the 1930s and 1940s, the flourishing "culture and personality" movement tried to integrate personality psychology with sociology and anthropology (see, for example, Honigman, 1967; Kluckhohn, Murray, & Schneider, 1953). Later, as a result of conceptual and methodological criticism (Inkeles, 1953; Inkeles & Levinson, 1954), difficulties of measuring cultural differences in personality, and a changed academic climate that emphasized separate, autonomous disciplines and sharp departmental boundaries (Jencks, 1968), culture and personality studies withered away. Instead, personality psychology followed a trend toward identifying universal mechanisms that apply to all human beings. In recent years, however, there are signs that personality psychologists are again taking culture seriously (Berry, Poortinga, Segall, & Dasen, 1992; Church, 1987; Markus & Kitayama, 1991; Yang & Bond, 1990).

*P*ERSONALITY ELEMENTS AS ADAPTIVE CONSTANCIES

Our world is constantly changing; everything is in flux, and we never really encounter the exact same situation twice. If we are to adapt—to think, feel, plan, and act as humans—in the face of this ebb and flow of experience, then we need mechanisms or systems that preserve a sense of continuity and coherence. I suggest that personality is such a *self-regulating internal system or set of systems, with the function of preserving a constant (or at least a reasonably orderly and integrated) state.* Personality is therefore a psychological analogy to the self-regulating physiological systems of our bodies. Such systems are said to maintain *homeostasis* (from the Greek words for "same state"). By homeostasis, I do not mean that personality always stays the same and never changes, but rather that continuity, coherence, and integration are maintained during change—call it a "dynamic homeostasis" or a "changing equilibrium." Thus personality enables us to function as human beings in a complex and changing world. (Of course, sometimes homeostasis breaks down, with the effect of rapid and dramatic personality change or disintegration.) Homeostatic conceptions were important in the work of Murray (1938) and Stagner (1937), two founders of the field of personality psychology, and they continue to be influential in recent years (see Carver & Scheier, 1981; Strelau & Eysenck, 1987).

The four elements of personality—traits, social context, motives, and cognitions—described in the previous section can be thought of as four components of a general homeostatic personality system, each designed or evolved to maintain certain specific stabilities or constancies. For example, our basic *traits* such as activity level and sociability maintain a *constancy of energy*. This constancy of energy acts as a kind of thermostat in the midst of ever-changing input from the environment. If things get too hectic, we slow down, especially if our characteristic activity level is low. If things get boring, we liven up a bit, especially if we have a characteristically high activity level.

Second, *social contexts* create *constancies of reaction to stimuli that have previously occurred,* or constancies of habit. If we are to get along in any social context, our behavior has to be predictable to others. Consequently, we have to learn and obey the social rules. Thus we learn our culture's "rules" of gender behavior, our social class's rules of taste and manners, and our college's rules of appropriate dress, behavior, and attitudes.

Third, *motives* keep us oriented toward goals; that is, they are *constancies of anticipated future stimuli.* If conditions change and the goal "moves" or the path toward it becomes blocked, then our motive leads to a corresponding adjustment of our behavior to keep us headed toward the goal.

Finally, *cognitions* are enduring *constancies of internal mental structure.* Once we have created cognitive categories for organizing our experiences of the world, society, other people, and ourselves, we can act more efficiently because we don't have to relearn everything each time we encounter a given situation again. And by using abstract and complex categories, we can generalize from past experience to new situations never before encountered. The most abstract and complex cognition is that of the self, enduring through time and physical changes. Once we have achieved this cognition, we can weather the most extraordinary vicissitudes and changes, including even the certainty of our own death. In the most abstract sense, the self as a concept is immortal, living on in the form of descendants and contributions to society. In some religions, the concept of the self has been developed into the ultimate abstraction as a self that truly lives forever, an immortal soul (see Rank, 1930/1961).

PERSONALITY THEORY AND THE ELEMENTS OF PERSONALITY

The Classic Theorists

I believe that most important classic theories and theorists of personality can be classified into one or more of the four elements that we have been discussing. For example, Sigmund Freud and his many psychoanalytic followers were principally theorists of motivation, so their theories are discussed mostly in Part One. The fit is not perfect, since Freud also wrote about cognitive structures such as the ego and superego, but these develop to handle problems resulting from motives and especially conflicts among motives. The theory of Carl Rogers also involves more than one element of personality. His concept of an actualization motive is presented in Part One (Chapter 4), while his ideas about the self are definitively cognitive and so are discussed in Part Two (Chapter 9).

Other theorists are easier to place in the discussion of just one personality element. Henry Murray, who was primarily a motivational theorist, is discussed in Chapters 4 and 5 of Part One. George Kelly was clearly a cognitive theorist, so his ideas are discussed in Part Two, especially Chapter 6. In different ways, Gordon Allport, Carl Jung, and Hans Eysenck are trait theorists; they are discussed in Part Three. Walter Mischel and Albert Bandura combine skepticism about traditional personality concepts with a commitment to social-learning principles, so they are discussed in Part Four. Since they have given increasing attention to cognitive processes, they could also be characterized as "social-cognitive" theorists.

While Erik Erikson is usually thought of as a psychoanalytic or neo-Freudian theorist, I believe his most characteristic and important work involves not internal motivational forces as such, but rather the ways in which society and social contexts are integrated or brought into harmony with internal forces, resulting in the development of a stable identity. Therefore I discuss Erikson's identity concept in connection with the self (Chapter 9), and his more general psychosocial developmental approach in Chapter 18 of Part Four.

Range of Convenience and Focus of Convenience

The main principle of this book is that any full description of personality, whether "personality" in the abstract or the personalities of particular people, requires the use of all four elements. Descriptions that concentrate on only one or two elements will be limited and biased, though they may be useful for some purposes. Thus psychoanalysis, while offering a detailed account of people's motives and conflicts among motives, does not take much account of their traits or their social contexts. As a result, psychoanalysis tends to be at its best in explaining surprising or unusual thoughts, actions, and mistakes. In contrast, the trait theories of Eysenck and the "five-factor" theorists (Chapter 12) are effective at explaining people's observable everyday behavior, but they don't have as much to say about their inner goals, their cognitive experiences, their social contexts, or their surprising and unusual behaviors. To use a term of George Kelly (1955), each theory seems to have a "focus of convenience," in which it is at its best and most useful, and a "range of convenience," in which it works fairly well.

Plan of This Book

The rest of this book is organized around the four elements. Starting with motives in Part One, we will proceed clockwise around the figure to cognitions (Part Two), traits (Part Three), and social context (Part Four). The first chapter of each part contains a definition of the element to be discussed in that part, examples of its functioning from everyday life, some important classic and modern research studies illustrating the nature and effects of that element, and the historical figure to be used as a case study. Then a major theory or theories are presented—depending on space, either in this same chapter or in the next chapter of the part. The remaining chapters of each part are devoted to important research, issues and problems, and applications of concepts and variables related to that element of personality. In the final chapter, we will consider various ways of combining or integrating these four elements into a unified conception of personality.

You may think that beginning with motivation is a strange way to proceed, since in the final chapter I will argue that personality development begins with traits and temperament and proceeds clockwise, through context to motives and finally cognitions. Of course you can read this book, and instructors can cover the four elements, in any order. I have chosen, however, to start with motives because that means starting with Freud and psychoanalytic theory. Before they take a course, many students believe that this is what the psychology of personality *is*. Of course there is more, much more, but these students are correct, in at least two different ways. First, most of modern personality psychology does proceed from Freud's work—as a further development, a modification, or a reaction and rejection. Thus it makes sense to start with Freud. Second, and more broadly, the concept of motive (or intention) is the core organizing principle of narrative or story-telling. Narrative, in turn, is a basic mode of understanding, a "primary cognitive instrument," an "irreducible form of human comprehension, an article in the constitution of common sense" (Mink, 1978, pp. 131–132; see also Bruner, 1986, pp. 17–19, and McAdams, 1985). To begin with motives, then, is to begin with Freud and at the same time to begin with one of our most basic ways of understanding our experience. And so I begin this book as I begin my own personality course, with Freud and motivation.

WHY STUDY PERSONALITY?

Practical Reasons: Career and Living

Why should you want to study the psychology of personality? You are likely to find it useful for many advanced psychology and social science courses. For example, understanding the nature and structure of normal personality is an important foundation for understanding how and why things go wrong (abnormal psychology), as well as how they might be remedied (clinical psychology and psychotherapy). In other words, personality is a kind of basic science prerequisite for many intervention "technologies."

Other fields that require an understanding of personality include business, advertising, law enforcement, politics, teaching, medicine, and sports. In each case, the goal is to understand how and why different people act differently, to get them to do something (buy something, vote for someone, carry out simple directions, and so forth). In each case, results vary according to the personalities of the people involved. Thus anyone planning a career in these fields would find a knowledge of the psychology of personality important. In fact, almost any service or management career involves the need to size up and deal with different kinds of people and adjust your own behavior accordingly.

Personal Reasons

Regardless of our careers, all of us encounter many situations in everyday life in which an accurate appraisal of someone else's personality is essential. Do I have what it takes to succeed in this career? What would this person be like twenty years from now, as my life partner? How will my child respond to this day-care center or that teacher? Can I trust this real estate or automobile sales person? What are the presidential candidates really like as people? As a juror, what kind of person do I think the defendant is? As a defendant's lawyer, what kind of person do I think this prospective juror is? Last but not least, who am I, and what do I really want?

Social-Policy Reasons

Social policies involving such matters as economic development and international relations, as well as health care, welfare, and the criminal justice system all reflect policymakers' implicit theories of personality or their *lack* of such theories (see Lemann, 1994). For example, reforms of the health care, welfare, or criminal justice systems presume knowledge of how people will respond to particular examples, incentives, and threats. The evidence is clear that different people respond to all of these in different ways. The preferences and expectations of legislators and administrators are not always shared by those who are the objects of their lawmaking and administration—patients and doctors, unemployed workers and business owners, welfare clients and caseworkers, or criminals and police. Programs are often designed as if one size fits all, but this is no more true of public policy than it is of clothing. Thus designing and administering effective social policies require an understanding of individual differences in personality.

This general point can be illustrated with specific examples from several different policy fields.

The impact of individual motivation on economic development. Achieving national goals such as economic growth and "competitiveness" is usually considered to be a matter of rational economic calculation. Yet even John Maynard Keynes (1936), whose economic theories are the foundation of many governmental policies, acknowledged that personality forces were more fundamental than any "rational" factors:

> A large proportion of our positive activities depend on spontaneous optimism rather than on a mathematical expectation. . . . Our decisions to do something positive . . . can only be taken as a result of animal spirits—of a spontaneous urge to action rather than inaction, and not as the outcome of a weighted average of quantitative benefits multiplied by quantitative probabilities. . . . Thus if the animal spirits are dimmed and the spontaneous optimism falters, leaving us to depend on nothing but a mathematical expectation, enterprise will fade and die. (pp. 161–162)

Personality psychologists have defined Keynes's "animal spirits" in terms of certain specific personality variables such as high achievement motivation (McClelland, 1961; McClelland & Winter, 1969) or low levels of pessimistic reflection about bad events (Zullow, 1991).

Preventing war and encouraging peace: Jimmy Carter at Camp David. Historians and political scientists often explain war and peace as the result of vast, impersonal forces of history or complex government institutions. These forces do not exist in a psychological vacuum, however, but are affected by what the British historian James Joll (1968) called "unspoken assumptions" and "mentalities." "It is only by studying the minds [of people]," he concluded, "that we shall understand the causes of anything" (p. 24). The political scientist Fred Greenstein (1969/1987, chap. 2) noted that individual political leaders often act in accord with their own beliefs, emotions, and unconscious goals in new or unstructured situations, when people's expectations are unclear—conditions that are especially true of international crises. Two recent collections of essays by psychologists and psychologically minded political scientists (Glad, 1990; White, 1986) discuss a wide range of personality factors that can tip a disagreement or crisis either toward war or toward peace (see also Winter, 1992b, 1993c).

In managing crises, leaders could often be helped by a knowledge of the personalities of other leaders with whom they must interact. This was certainly the experience of U.S. President Jimmy Carter, who in 1979 was able to bring together Egyptian President Anwar Sadat and Israeli Prime Minister Menachem Begin at Camp David to negotiate and then sign the first peace treaty between Israel and an Arab state. Here is how Carter described the task in his memoirs (1982):

> I was poring over psychological analyses of [Sadat and Begin] which had been prepared by a team of experts within our intelligence community. This team could write definitive biographies of any important world leader, using information derived from a detailed scrutiny of events, public statements, writings, known medical histories, and interviews with personal acquaintances of the leaders under study. I wanted to know all about Begin and Sadat. What had made them national leaders? What was the root of their ambition? What were their most important goals in life? What events during past years had helped to shape their characters? (p. 320)

Carter then summarized the personality sketch of Sadat:

> Sadat would be much more willing to strive for a comprehensive agreement, while Begin would probably want to limit what might be achieved. . . .
> Sadat was strong and bold, very much aware of world public opinion and of his role as the most important leader among the Arabs. . . . [He saw himself as] inheriting the mantle of authority from the great pharaohs and . . . [was] convinced that he was a man of destiny. (p. 328)

Know your enemy: Assessing Hitler. At the height of World War II in the spring of 1943, General William J. Donovan, head of the U.S. Office of Strategic Services (forerunner to the Central Intelligence Agency) commissioned psychiatrist Walter Langer to do a personality portrait of the German dictator Adolf Hitler. U.S. policymakers disagreed about what Hitler was like and how he might respond to various events. There was an urgent need for more reliable sources of guidance than either German propaganda or journalists' impressions. With the following instructions, Donovan commissioned Walter Langer to do a study of Hitler (Langer, 1972):

> What we need is a realistic appraisal of the German situation. If Hitler is running the show, what kind of a person is he? What are his ambitions? . . . What is he like with his associates? What is his background? And most of all, we want to know as much as possible about his psychological make-up—the things that make him tick. In addition, we ought to know what he might do if things begin to go against him. (p. 10)

After a careful study of Hitler's writings, the historical record of his life, and interviews with people who had met him, Langer concluded that a particular sexual preference lay at the core of Hitler's personality: "an extreme form of masochism in which [he] derives sexual gratification from the act of having a woman urinate or defecate on him" (1972, p. 134). On the basis of this inference, Langer went on to explain Hitler's anti-Semitism, his aggressive oratory, and even his vegetarianism.

The OSS wanted to know what Hitler would do as the tide of battle turned against him. Langer predicted that Hitler would first become even more aggressive but in the end would probably commit suicide:

> Each defeat will shake his confidence still further. . . . In consequence he will feel himself more and more vulnerable to attack from his associates, and his rages will increase in frequency. He will probably try to compensate for his vulnerability by continually stressing his brutality and ruthlessness. . . . It is not wholly improbable that in the end he might lock himself into [a] symbolic womb and defy the world to get him. (p. 212)

Langer's prediction turned out to be quite accurate, though you might ask how it could logically follow from his speculative diagnosis of Hitler's sexual proclivities. In the months just before Germany's final defeat in 1945, Hitler ordered his country's destruction before the advancing Allied armies: "Germany is not worthy of me; let her perish." At the very end, on April 30, 1945, Hitler did in fact commit suicide in his underground bunker in Berlin (Waite, 1977, pp. 411–426). Although Langer's predictions were largely correct, his personality portrait and analysis of Hitler raised quite a controversy among historians (see Waite, 1972).

Personality assessments conducted at a distance are not always so accurate. When the FBI decided to move against David Koresh and his followers in the Branch Davidian compound near Waco, Texas, in April 1993, they were said to have been assured by psychologists who had studied Koresh at a distance that he would not order a mass suicide in response to an assault. Several hours and over seventy fiery deaths later, these apparent predictions were proved wrong ("Reno approved," 1993).[6]

Liberal Arts Reasons

While personality psychology may have many practical applications, there are also compelling intellectual reasons for studying it, reasons that go to the heart of the liberal arts tradition. What is it to be human? What are the possibilities and limits of human nature? How are we different from each other? Attempts to answer such questions have been made by thinkers in every culture, in every intellectual tradition, for thousands of years. One answer, familiar to many people in the Western tradition, is contained in the words of Psalm 8:

> What are human beings that you are mindful of them,
> mortals that you care for them?

---

[6]Actually, there is some dispute about whether the assessment was wrong, or correct but ignored by FBI officials and then withheld from the Justice Department officials who reviewed the operation ("Outside review criticizes," 1993).

Yet you have made them a little lower than angels,
and crowned them with glory and honor.
You have given them dominion over the works of your hands;
you have put all things under their feet.

(Psalm 8:5–7, New Revised Standard Version)

Another answer is reflected in the theory of the human being as rational actor, which is the foundation of most economic theory and analysis (Becker, 1976):

> The economic approach is a comprehensive one that is applicable to all human behavior, be it . . . rich or poor persons, men or women, adults or children, brilliant or stupid persons, patients or therapists, businessmen or politicians, teachers or students. . . . All human behavior can be viewed as involving participants who maximize their utility from a stable set of preferences and accumulate an optimal amount of information and other inputs in a variety of markets. (pp. 8, 14)

Political ideologies supply still other answers. Thomas Jefferson (1779/1944), for example, argued that:

> Almighty God hath created the mind free, and manifested his supreme will that free it shall remain by making it altogether insusceptible of restraint; that all attempts to influence it by temporal punishments, or burthens, or by civil incapacitations, tend only to beget hypocrisy and meanness. (p. 48)

In contrast, Mao Zedong, the longtime Communist leader of the People's Republic of China, said that humans *are* subject to civil and social constraints (1966):

> In class society everyone lives as a member of a particular class, and every kind of thinking, without exception, is stamped with the brand of a class. (p. 8)

Yet a still different view of the nature of humanity can be found in other cultural traditions, such as the following legend of the Plains Indian people (Storm, 1972):

> Each Man, Woman, and Child Upon the Earth is a Living Fire of Power and Color. The Powers I Speak of here are Cold, Heat, Light, and Darkness. They are a Living, Spinning Fire, a Medicine Wheel. And these Colors from this Living Wheel of Fire can be Seen by all Men, and Each can learn from them. . . . In the Time of the many Colors of the Earth, these all Come Together, and the Sisters sit in a Common Lodge. . . . It is a time when things are Equal. (pp. 221–222)

To the perennial question of what it is to be human, the field of personality psychology has its own set of answers. Many classic theories of personality (such as those of Freud, Kelly, and Rogers) are actually theories of human nature, different from but comparable to those of the psalmist, the economist, and Chairman Mao. Moreover, as we will see in the remaining chapters of this book, the more narrowly defined concepts and "variables" of personality psychology also, in a sense, reflect theories about the nature and possibilities of human beings.

DOUBTS AND DANGERS IN STUDYING PERSONALITY

As you study the psychology of personality, you may have doubts or misgivings. You may even wonder whether it is dangerous; whether, for example, interpreting lives and analyzing people will interfere with being friends or getting along with them. I do not believe that the study of something is necessarily a threat to enjoying it or responding to it in other ways. After all, the scientific study of plants does not keep a botanist from enjoying beautiful flowers, a professional musician can still respond emotionally to music, and a biologist can fall in love! Some other concerns can be addressed now, at the beginning of the book.

Personality Psychology: It's Not Science!

If you have taken a lot of science courses, you may find yourself questioning the claim that personality psychology is a science. We will devote considerable time and space to discussing personality theories that conflict with one another. In any "real" science, surely, researchers would by now have disproved many old theories; these would be forgotten instead of filling the pages of an introductory text. In personality psychology, though, many old theories live on. Others have simply become obsolete on account of changing intellectual fashions rather than as a result of systematic testing and disproof. In fact, there are few if any scientific "laws" of personality psychology, expressed in mathematical terms. We do not yet have a single, universally accepted list of personality elements and variables, analogous to the periodic table in chemistry. How then is personality psychology a science?

To understand the essence of science, we must be prepared to ignore superficial features such as mathematical symbols or words such as "law." Science is a systematic way of organizing and accumulating knowledge, all the while refining and extending that knowledge by repeatedly comparing its structure with the real world. At a certain stage, mathematics is useful as a formal way of representing structures of knowledge. At some point, a consensus emerges about the nature and arrangement of the elements, but this is an *accomplishment* rather than a *prerequisite* of scientific thinking. In the years before 1869, when Dmitri Mendeleyev developed the familiar periodic table of the elements, chemistry was still a science, though Mendeleyev's accomplishment greatly advanced the pace of discovery in chemistry. The psychology of personality *is* an organized field of knowledge, in which current ideas are systematically compared to real-world experience. Progress is slow, because the individuality and variation of human beings are much more complicated than even the most complex organic molecules; but it is science nonetheless.

Personality Psychology: It's Too Scientific!

Some of you may feel that the psychology of personality is *too* scientific, trying to capture the infinite variation of human experience by fitting people into a few—far too few—convenient cubbyholes. You may even feel that a genuine understanding of our unique individualities can only be achieved by inspiration and intuition, the methods of art, rather than through scientific inquiry.

In fact this observation has merit, for personality description is surely an art as well as a science. Even the most precise and objective measurements cannot replace clinical insight or an intuitive grasp of a personality (see Allport, 1962, pp. 543–544). And I know of no evidence that personality psychologists as individuals are conspicuously successful at understanding and getting along with other people. As Allport put it (1938/1960):

> [Psychologists], in spite of their profession, are no better than anyone else in understanding people. They are not exceptionally shrewd, nor are they always able to give advice on problems of personality. . . . I should go further and say that, because of their habits of excessive abstraction and generalization, many psychologists are actually inferior to other people in their comprehension of the *single* lives that confront them. (p. 12)

Still, we must confront the basic reality that human beings are different from each other. If classifying and putting people's personalities into cubbyholes has problems, treating everybody alike is also degrading and unfair. If we are to be sensitive and effective in our help, our policies, and our everyday life, then we need to understand as much as possible about the range of individual difference. For this task, we can use all the intuition *and* systematic knowledge we possess.

Personality Psychology Blames the Victim

We must take care when we describe other people or trace links between personality and behavior. To say that personality is related to behavior and the life course is not to say that it is the only cause, or even the most important cause. Nor does such an analysis prove that changing personality is the only way to change behavior. Consider poverty and economic development. It is certainly true that being poor and having little social power both affect personality (see Chapter 17). In a few carefully defined circumstances, it may even be true that changing people's personalities improves their economic situation (see McClelland & Winter, 1969). On the other hand, in many circumstances, changing policies and structures may be a more effective way to change people's economic behavior—and their personalities as well (see Lemann, 1994; Veroff, 1983).

In studying the psychology of personality, it is easy to focus so much on individual variation that we forget that people's personalities develop in a larger social context and that the expression of personality is always constrained by that context. Pointing to personality as the cause—the only cause—of poverty or other misfortune is often a form of "blaming the victim" (Ryan, 1971).

AN INVITATION

As a text of personality psychology, this book is an inventory of the theories, models, mechanisms, variables, and findings about personality developed by scientific psychology by the end of the twentieth century. At the same time, I hope this book can contribute to your thinking about some broader questions:

What do people want?
Is behavior under the control of beliefs or biology?
How would I be different if I had grown up in a different culture? With a different gender? In a different social class or race?
How can we best describe individual lives?
What kind of government is best fitted to human nature?
How do people with different personalities affect how governments and institutions function? And how do institutions change different people's personalities?

While covering the field of personality, therefore, I also intend to explore fundamental topics and questions about people and differences among people in diverse social contexts.

I invite you to join in that exploration. We begin in the next chapter with the topic of motives and motivation, which leads to Freud and psychoanalytic theory in Chapter 3. As I suggested above, Freud's work is an appropriate starting point for our understanding of the psychology of personality, since so many writers after Freud were trying to agree with, support, revise, disprove, or reconsider his ideas. From there, we move on to the study of cognition (Chapters 6–10), traits and temperament (Chapters 11–14), and social context (Chapters 15–17). In the final chapter, Chapter 18, I will suggest three ways in which everything that has gone before may be put together to form an integrated portrait of personality.

For at least two thousand years, artists have painted Venus (the Roman goddess of love) and Mars (the god of war), drawing on the story of their affair in Book VIII of *The Odyssey*. How they depict the relation between the two reflects their conception of the relation between the two important social motives of affiliation and power. The version shown here is from the wall of a house in Pompeii (the ancient city that was buried by a volcanic eruption in A.D. 79). Venus and the forces of love seem to be in charge, as the infant Cupid plays with the armor of Mars (Museo Nazionale, Naples). Similarly, Sandro Botticelli's *Mars and Venus* (1485, National Gallery, London) shows Venus as calmly triumphant over the sleeping Mars. However, other artists have viewed this relationship quite differently. For example, Bartolomeo Manfredi's *Cupid Chastised* (ca. 1605–1610, Art Institute of Chicago) shows power triumphant, as Mars lashes the child Cupid while Venus looks on helplessly. Finally, Peter Paul Rubens's allegorical painting of *Peace and War* (ca. 1629, National Gallery, London) suggests that only *wisdom* (represented by the goddess Minerva)—not love—is able to restrain power and so protect the infant figure of peace.

Mars and Venus, *wall painting, Museo Nazionale, Naples*

PART ONE

--- ❖ ---

Psychoanalytic Theories and Motives: Freud, Murray, and McClelland

2

Understanding Motives in Everyday Life

❖

WHY STUDY MOTIVES?

We begin the study of the elements of personality with motivation. As shown in Figure 2.1, motives are internal or within the person, not directly observable in actions. Thus we infer the presence of motives rather than observing them

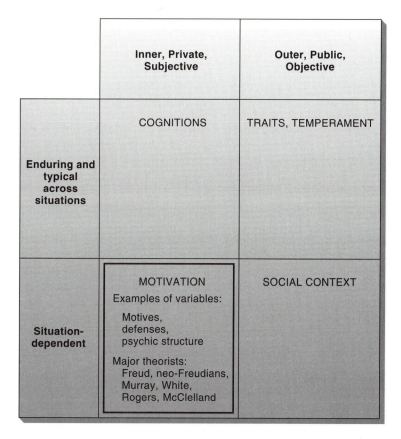

FIGURE 2.1
Motivation and the elements of personality.

directly. Motives and goals also vary according to the situation, in two ways. First, the strength of any given motive varies as a complex function of the length of time since it was last satisfied. No matter how good my appetite generally is, I am unlikely to eat right after a big meal. Second, the behaviors associated with a motive vary according to the characteristics and opportunities of the situation. While I can be hungry at any time and in any place, what I do about my hunger will depend upon where I am, whether there is food available, and many other variables such as whom I am with, my manners and patience, and so forth.

In everyday language, people's motives are their intentions, goals, or reasons for their actions. When we try to figure out people's motives, we are trying to understand why they acted in a certain way. Yet people do not always know their own motives, and even if they did, they might not want to tell others. This means that we may need to use indirect methods to discover people's motives. As a result, there may not be an infallible way to measure motives: in any particular case, different observers, each reasonable and conscientious, may disagree.

Since motives are both subtle and complex, we will analyze a few examples of motivated behavior before turning to the psychological study of motives later in the chapter.

An Example: Lee Harvey Oswald's Motives

For all the difficulties in answering it, often the most important question we can ask about an action is, Why? Our decisions about people's motives are the foundation for understanding their behavior. In the following vivid historical example, notice the variety of motive explanations that are given, and the consequences that follow from each different explanation. On November 22, 1963, President John F. Kennedy was shot and killed in Dallas, probably by Lee Harvey Oswald. Exhaustive technical investigations have revealed many facts about what happened, but a full understanding of what "really" happened there and then depends on our understanding Oswald's motive (assuming, of course, that he was indeed the assassin). Many people have suggested possible motives, but after more than three decades, we have no satisfactory answers. No doubt this is one reason for the continued popularity of conspiracy theories about the Kennedy assassination, such as that presented in Oliver Stone's film, *JFK*.

The Warren Commission, established by presidential order to investigate all aspects of the assassination, concluded the following after a 47-page discussion of every motive they could think of (United States, Warren Commission, 1964):

> No one will ever know what passed through Oswald's mind during the week before November 22, 1963. . . . Many factors were undoubtedly involved in Oswald's motivation for the assassination, and the Commission does not believe that it can ascribe to him any one motive or group of motives. (pp. 421, 423)

At the other extreme, one of the commission's early critics argued against the report precisely because of the problem of Oswald's motives (Meagher, 1967):

> The complete absence of any motive was a main factor in the doubt of Oswald's guilt that flourished all over the world after the assassination. The Warren Commission has not resolved this problem. . . . [Oswald] was without a personal or political motive for assassinating the President, and he was not irrational, disturbed, or psychotic. (pp. 243, 246)

Fifteen years after the Warren Commission report, a House of Representatives committee reviewed the evidence and concluded—rather haltingly—that Oswald's motives were political (House of Representatives, 1979):

> Although no one specific ideological goal that Oswald might have hoped to achieve . . . can be shown with confidence, it appeared to the committee that his dominant motivation, consistent with his known activities and beliefs, *must have been* a desire to take political action. (p. 63; italics added)

Oswald's biographer, however, suggested a mixture of political and personal motives (McMillan, 1977):

> The way Lee saw it . . . fate had singled him out to do the dangerous but necessary task which had been his destiny all along, and which would cause him to go down in history. . . . [Also] he would be achieving in life and in death a one-ness with the man he was destroying. For it is clear that Oswald's motives were not purely political. (pp. 459, 462)

A scholar of political assassinations completely dismissed any political motive (Clarke, 1982):

> Oswald's motive in the assassination was personal and compensatory rather than political. He hoped to prove his value to the Cubans . . . he would also even the score with the FBI . . . and in the process he would leave his wife, who had turned him away, with a nagging sense of guilt for what he did. (p. 126)

Those who knew Oswald best were puzzled. His brother decided that Lee had acted out of sibling rivalry, his wife couldn't understand the charges against him, and his mother grasped for any motive that might redeem his act:

> BROTHER: On the three dates when I was most aware of my good fortune [career success, happy marriage, birth of a son], Lee tried to gain the world's attention through violence and destruction. (Oswald, 1967, p. 240)
>
> WIFE: But he liked Kennedy! (McMillan, 1977, p. 466)
>
> MOTHER: It is possible that my son was chosen to shoot him in a mercy killing for the security of the country. And if this is true, it was a fine thing to do and my son is a hero. (Stafford, 1966, p. 12)

Oswald's own words give almost no clue as to his motives. In one of his few recorded comments between the assassination and his own murder two days later, he explicitly denied many of the motives attributed to him by others: "I am not a malcontent; nothing irritated me about the president" (Summers, 1980, p. 129).

As we might expect, psychologists and psychiatrists have weighed in with their own contributions. A psychiatrist who had seen Oswald about a school truancy problem over ten years before, but had not seen him since, offered a rich array of conclusions that left few theoretical stones unturned (Hartogs & Freeman, 1965):

> The act of assassination may have been founded on fantasies in Oswald's mind that made it the murder of an unknown father. It may also have been a boy killing a stepfather he hated. Or a brother killing his big brothers. Or it may have stemmed from his early childhood fantasies about his mother. It may also have been the act of a man who felt sexually inadequate and was trying to assert his masculinity through violence. Or an act rooted in homosexual impulses, natural to all men, but deeply repressed in Oswald. (pp. 195–196)

Lee Harvey Oswald. In custody he said, "I am not a malcontent; nothing irritated me about the president" (Summers, 1980, p. 129). So what was his motive, if indeed he assassinated President Kennedy?

At this point, if you have followed all of the speculations, you may throw up your hands: only a Sherlock Holmes could unravel this mystery of motives! And, in fact, even the legendary detective (as resurrected by an imaginative British professor) applied his talents of logical analysis and deductive methods to the problem of Oswald's motives (Aubrey, 1980):

> Oswald was involved in a conspiracy whose nature and extent he did not fully comprehend . . . the perfect "patsy." He was solitary, easily flattered by attention, he had a degree of cunning, and he was impoverished. He would be told only what he needed to know for his part in any plan. (pp. 213, 216)

Lessons from the Oswald Example

As we have seen, many different answers have been given to the question of Oswald's motive in assassinating President Kennedy (if, indeed, he did so). We have learned several things from these answers.

1. First, nearly *everyone asks the question*. No study of the assassination is complete without some speculation about Oswald's motives. Figuring out motives is something we feel a strong urge to do, particularly for actions that are especially important or significant.

2. Next, the different motive explanations *vary widely*, and even contradict each other.

3. Finally, inferences about motives are based on many *different sources of information*. Some people try to observe or reconstruct the action itself along with what happened before and after. In the Oswald case, a lot of information is forever missing, and many of the "facts" are in dispute. And even if we could reconstruct Oswald's life on November 22, 1963, down to the last detail, we still might have only the dimmest, most fleeting glimpse into his purposes or goals.

Other interpreters have tried to "read" the motives in Oswald's mind by paying special attention to his words: words spoken after his arrest, recollected conversations before November 22, and the few meager scraps of his writings. Of course Oswald's own words would not be taken at their face value: he might be lying or concealing, he might not know his own motives, he was probably confused or in conflict. To learn anything from Oswald's words, we would probably have to interpret or "decode" them.

To fill gaps in these two sources of information, many interpreters have postulated motives on the basis of their own point of view, their personal needs, their ideology, or their theoretical orientation. If assassins in general (or people in general) have certain motives, the argument runs, then Lee Harvey Oswald must have acted out of these motives.[1]

With Oswald dead, it is difficult to imagine any facts that could possibly prove—or disprove—any of the motive explanations we have reviewed. This case shows the problems of inferring motives from behavior, of using the judgments of experienced observers, of examining the person's own words, and of relying on general theories. In the course of the next three chapters on motivation, we will come to understand these problems more fully and learn some of the ways that can be used to overcome them.

For the figure of Oswald, however, the question of motivation will always remain an enigma. You may wonder why we bother trying to answer it, since speculation about motives will not undo the terrible act or its sad consequences. To most Americans alive in 1963, the assassination of President Kennedy was a bitter tragedy; but it was not a random, meaningless act. There had to be a reason: any act with such emotional and political significance had to have *meaning*, whether as a dark conspiracy, a political protest, or the crazy deed of a disturbed person. (The role of "meanings" in personality will be discussed in Part Two, and the connection between cognitive meanings and

---

[1]For example, you can read interpretations of Oswald based on Freudian theory (Katz, 1967; Rothstein, 1966), Adlerian theory (Ansbacher, Ansbacher, Shiverick, & Shiverick, 1967), Jungian theory (Progoff, 1967), and even rational-emotive theory (Ellis, 1965).

motives is elaborated in Chapter 10.) Thus explanations of Oswald's motives are attempts to create meaning, so as to lay these painful and discordant events finally to rest in the vaults of history.

Judgments of motives are also important in the present. For example, imagine that Lee Harvey Oswald had lived to stand trial for the assassination. Each of the explanations of Oswald's motives given above, if proved to the jury, would affect their verdict about guilt or a judge's decision about length of sentence. Each explanation would have a different effect on the Secret Service's plans for protecting the president. Finally, each explanation would affect your own image of the American political system in quite different ways.

Importance of Motives in Everyday Life

To illustrate some important features of motives, we have considered a striking example of unusual behavior. But motives are important in understanding ordinary actions and events as well. When something good happens, we feel pride and happiness if we can connect the good outcome to some prior purpose or intention on our part—that it wasn't accidental, that we tried to do it and succeeded. When other people do something nice for us, our gratitude is enhanced if we think that they *wanted* or intended to be nice—that their action wasn't accidental or random.

Imagine that someone smiles, gives you a gift, yells angrily at you, or turns to you and dissolves in tears. How you will respond depends on your assessment of the person's motives. How you evaluate yourself in a competitive situation also depends on your motives. If you want to do the *best* possible job, then a spectacular failure would be devastating (though you might learn from your mistake and so do better in the long run). But if you were trying to have a big *impact* on other people, then a really spectacular failure might be almost as good as a success, because it would draw the attention of others. Finally, if you were primarily motivated by *love and friendship*, your reaction would depend on how well your friends did in the competition.

Religion, morality, and our legal system also involve questions of motivation. In common with many other religious leaders, Jesus argued in the Sermon on the Mount that morality was based on people's *intentions* more than on their *actions:*

> You have learned that our forefathers were told, "Do not commit murder; anyone who commits murder must be brought to judgment"[focus on action]. But what I tell you is this: Anyone who nurses anger against his brother [focus on motive] must be brought to judgment. . . . You have learned that they were told, "Do not commit adultery" [action]. But what I tell you is this, If a man looks on a woman with a lustful eye [motive], he has already committed adultery with her in his heart. (Matthew 5:21–22, 27–28, New English Bible)

Similarly, studies of moral development show that the higher people's level of moral development, the greater the role considerations of motives (rather than action) play in their moral judgments (see Piaget, 1932/1966; Rest, 1986).

In the criminal justice system, the defendant's perceived motives or intentions affect judgments about the degree of guilt and the appropriate punishment. Often they even affect the judgment of whether a crime occurred in the first place. For example, the theme of conflict between ordinary laws and people who act from "higher" motives runs through thousands of years of Western culture. Thus in Sophocles' play *Antigone* (441 B.C.), Antigone was forbidden by royal decree from burying the body of her slain brother. She defied the prohibition: "If I must die, I say that this crime is holy." In a dialogue with King Creon, she explained her reasons:

CREON: And yet you dared defy the law.

ANTIGONE: I dared. It was not God's proclamation. That final justice
That rules the world below makes no such laws.
Your edict, king, was strong,
But all your strength is weakness itself against
The immortal unrecorded laws of God.

(scene 2, D. Fitts and R. Fitzgerald, trans.)

Over 2,400 years later, the Reverend Martin Luther King, Jr. (1963/1986) articulated the same theme of a higher motive in the struggle for civil rights:

I submit that an individual who breaks a law that conscience tells him is unjust, and who willingly accepts the penalty of imprisonment in order to arouse the conscience of the community over its injustice is in reality expressing the highest respect for law. (p. 294)

Thus the language of motivation—intentions, motives, reasons, and goals—is a natural, even inevitable way of describing actions and outcomes. We readily view ourselves, our past, and other people and their past in terms of goals, things we are trying to accomplish. Thus motives and motivation are good topics with which to begin the systematic study of personality.

The topic of motivation also leads to Sigmund Freud's ideas. As we shall see in Chapter 3, motivation is at the core of Freud's conception of personality. From the psychoanalytic perspective, disturbed functioning and pathology arise from conflicts and confusions of *motives*, and a therapeutic cure involves clarification and awareness of one's own motives. Together with additions, revisions, and opposition, Freud's ideas are the foundation of personality psychology. Any complete theory, model, or conception of personality, therefore, has to say something about motives.

*E*XPLAINING BEHAVIOR BY MOTIVES

Our systematic study of personality, then, begins with questions that are fundamental to classical personality theories and also important to our everyday life: What do we want? What are the purposes or goals of our actions?

Since Lee Harvey Oswald's motives were complex and uncertain, let us turn to a simple example to bring out the important features of the concept of *motive* (see also Winter, 1973, chap. 2): "Why did Jane cross the street?" A typical answer to this question might suggest a reason or motive: "To go to the library to get a book," or "Because she wanted to get a book." The first thing to notice is that we are trying to explain a *change* in behavior, a change that is voluntary and not compelled. Jane was walking along the sidewalk (or standing, or sitting, or doing something else); *then* she crossed the street. We notice a change in the flow of her behavior, and mark it out with words as a separate, identifiable action. Probably there was no obvious external force to account for this action or change of behavior, such as a construction barrier on the sidewalk or a request from a police officer to cross the street. If there were, we would explain Jane's street-crossing behavior in terms of these forces rather than her motive. Of course in such cases we might invoke some other motive in Jane, such as "to avoid running into construction barriers" or "to comply with police requests." We might also ask about the motives of the officer who called to Jane or the person who put up the barrier.

Goal Explanations

Assume that we agree that Jane crossed the street to get a book from the library. This explains her behavior by linking it to a *goal*. The goal is a series of future behaviors (entering the library, going to the book stacks, and so forth) that lead to a "final" behavior—in this case getting (and probably reading) a book. If our motive explanation is correct, then we will be able to predict Jane's future behavior, at least up to the point that she gets the book. For example, if the book is already checked out of the library, she may try to borrow it from someone else or get the information she wants from some other book. If she stops on the way to the library to talk with some friends, then she will eventually continue on to the library or at least feel she ought to do so. In contrast, if Jane's original motive in going to the library was to meet friends, then in this latter case we would predict that she will stay and talk with these people and *not* go on to the library. Once Jane has satisfied her present motive (whether reading the book or seeing friends), however, we would need to know her next motive in order to predict her behavior.

If we go beyond Jane's immediate motive and ask about her longer-term motive or goal (for example, "Because she wants to write an excellent honors thesis"), then we can predict Jane's future behavior over an even longer time span. Tomorrow (and next week) she will probably get more books; she will discuss her thesis with professors and friends; she may cut short telephone calls and avoid watching television; she is likely to get anxious about deadlines and feel alternating pride and doubt about her work, and so forth.

Habit Explanations

We can also explain Jane's behavior by learning: that is, she crossed the street "because she has learned to cross streets." In more technical terms, we might say that her street-crossing responses have been reinforced in the past. Notice how this learning or habit explanation focuses on *present or past stimuli* (the street) rather than on *anticipated future stimuli* (getting the book or writing the thesis) to explain Jane's behavior. To some psychologists, such a learning explanation seems more "scientific" and attractive, but it simply will not cover the present case. Jane doesn't *always* cross streets whenever she sees them— only on certain occasions, such as now when she wants a book from the library, which happens to be across the street. Of course we can expand the description of the immediate stimulus situation: "In certain situations [stimulus-pattern = honors thesis work + lack of book + perception of library across the street], Jane has learned to cross streets." Actually, it is doubtful that Jane has ever encountered this exact complex stimulus situation before, so that even this expanded "explanation" doesn't really explain at all. Moreover, this cumbersome expansion is not satisfactory because Jane could have reached her goal in an indefinitely large number of ways: by going to the library via alternate routes that don't cross this street at this point, by asking another student about the information, or even by using a computer terminal in her dorm room to call up the information on the Internet from some library or database halfway around the world. If one of these behaviors works (that is, reaches the goal of getting information), then Jane would not be likely to carry out any of the others. Trying to broaden the nature of Jane's so-called learned response to cover all of these possibilities gives us, in effect, an awkward and unwieldy motive explanation of her behavior.

Motives Are Constant and Variable

To summarize: motives involve both constancies and variabilities. A motive is a disposition, internal to the person, which is used to explain *variable* behavior. As conditions change and opportunities and obstacles come and go, motives guide behavior in intelligent ways. However much the actions may change, they are always oriented toward this future goal, which functions like an internal gyroscope. This *linking of present action to a desired future state of affairs is the essential feature of a motive explanation of behavior.* Thus motives are constant, while their associated behaviors depend on the situation and so are variable. Yet in another sense, motives also vary over time because they wax and wane as they are aroused and then satisfied. In a third sense, though, motives are dispositions that are relatively stable within individuals and different across people. Thus when we speak of a person's dominant or characteristic motives, we do not mean motives that are always aroused and active at every moment in that person. Rather, we are referring to motives that are (1) more frequently aroused and active, (2) to a higher or stronger level, (3) in a broader range of circumstances in that person as compared to other people. Atkinson (1982)

presents a formal model of how stable motive dispositions can lead to fluctuations in aroused motive strength over time. Because this third sense of the
motive concept involves stable individual differences, it is the one that is most
important for the psychology of personality.

PSYCHOLOGICAL STUDIES OF THE CHARACTERISTICS OF MOTIVATED BEHAVIOR[2]

As we have seen in the Jane example, motives and goal-directed behavior
show several characteristics.

1. Motives display a *pattern of rising and falling over time*, as particular
   motives are satisfied and become less important, then grow again in
   strength.

2. Motivated behavior shows *intelligent variation* according to changing
   conditions, so that behavior becomes increasingly predictable as the
   goal is approached. A potentially infinite variety of specific response
   elements can be integrated into a single goal-seeking tendency. The
   closer Jane's thesis is to being done, the more predictable her behavior
   is likely to be with respect to this goal. Once reaching that goal and temporarily having satisfied that motive, however, Jane's behavior can only
   be predicted by knowing about her other motives.

3. Motivated behavior is *persistent*, energetic, and efficient. Jane overcomes
   difficulties and distractions and is likely to make better use of her study
   time than does a student who is just fooling around. Of course, if motivation is too strong, efficiency may actually decline. At times Jane may
   become so involved with her work that she needs to take a break in
   order to stay alert and work effectively. And if her thesis goal conflicts
   with other goals, then her efficiency might suffer.

4. Motivated behavior has an *associated network of cognitions*—images and
   anticipations of the goal and heightened perception of things relevant
   to it, including difficulties and obstacles. In her mind, Jane often pictures the completed thesis. When talking to friends, she is quick to
   connect many topics that come up in the conversation to her thesis
   work.

5. Motivated behavior has *emotional or affective consequences*. Jane feels
   intense pleasure and pride at the prospect of completing her thesis and
   anxiety about not finishing on time or not doing a good job. Often she

---

[2]This section draws together several classic theories and research studies into a few general con-
clusions. It is based on the following sources: Atkinson (1958), Brody (1983), Klinger (1966),
McClelland (1951, pp. 478–521, 1985), Melton (1952), Murray (1938, pp. 54–129), Tolman (1932),
Weiner (1980, pp. 327–404), and Young (1961).

verbalizes a *need* to reach her goal: "I want to get it done, and done well, so much!" We can imagine how she will feel when she actually does complete the thesis.

These characteristics of motivated behavior can also be seen in some classic experimental studies of motivated behavior.

Early Studies by Lewin and His Students

During the 1920s, Kurt Lewin and his students at the University of Berlin carried out some studies of human motivation that are even today landmarks in the field (summarized by Marrow, 1969, pp. 244–259). (After Hitler's rise to power in the early 1930s, Lewin settled in the United States at the University of Iowa, where his interests turned toward group dynamics and social psychology.) Each of the Berlin studies focused on a specific aspect of behavior, such as persistence or memory, and compared people in whom a specific motive had been experimentally aroused or reduced with people whose motives were not experimentally modified. This experimental design is quite powerful, because the presence of a motive does not depend on intuition or clinical judgment, but rather can be objectively and precisely defined as being the experimental instructions and other procedures that were carried out with the motive-aroused group.

Maria Ovsiankina (1928), for example, studied the relationship between motivation and persistence. When people working on a task were "acciden-

Kurt Lewin, whose students in Berlin demonstrated experimentally many effects of motivation. "The point of departure . . . was the investigation of the measurement of the will" (Lewin, 1935, p. 239).

tally" interrupted, they usually resumed that same task later. This suggests that they had a motive or goal to complete the task; after interruptions, that motive led them to resume work on it. However, when the experimenter described the interruption as a sign that the purpose or goal of the task had been accomplished (an experimental satisfaction or reduction of the motive), fewer people resumed the task later. Since persistence varied as a function of experimental manipulations of the motive to complete the tasks, we can conclude that motivation is related to persistence.

In one of the most famous experimental paradigms in human psychological research, Bluma Zeigarnik (1927) studied the influence of motivation on memory. Her experiments began with a simple observation at the *Schwedische Cafe* (Swedish Cafe), across the square from the Psychological Institute of the University of Berlin. Lewin's students often gathered there in the long afternoons to discuss psychology. As they talked, they ordered coffee, cakes, more coffee, and so forth. When they called for the bill, the waiter easily remembered what everyone had eaten. Half an hour later, Lewin asked the waiter to write down the check again. The waiter replied, "I don't know any longer what you people ordered. You paid your bill" (Marrow, 1969, pp. 26–27). This incident, when it was brought into the laboratory and precisely defined and

The *Opern Cafe Unter den Linden*, on the Berlin site of the former *Schwedische Cafe*, where Bluma Zeigarnik, a student of Lewin's, discovered the Zeigarnik effect by noticing the waiter's extraordinary memory for what people ordered—until after they paid their bill. (Photo by Anne Tschida and William Fleeson)

manipulated, led to the concept of the *Zeigarnik effect,* or the tendency for incomplete tasks (for which the motivation is presumably still unsatisfied and high) to be remembered better than completed tasks. The Zeigarnik effect demonstrates two important points about motives: they affect memory (wanting payment, the waiter could remember the orders), and they fluctuate over time (after getting payment, the waiter's motive—and memory—decreased). Later research has shown that the existence and magnitude of the Zeigarnik effect also depend on many other factors within the person, the tasks, and the overall situation.

After completing her work with Lewin in Berlin, Zeigarnik returned to her native Russia where she taught at the University of Moscow for several decades. Ovsiankina and Tamara Dembo followed Lewin to the United States. Dembo also used the technique of interrupting people while they were carrying out "motivated" tasks in order to study the effects of motivation on the emotions (Dembo, 1931). Not surprisingly, she found that interruptions produced anger. When people had no chance to resume their original task, they engaged in a variety of substitute actions, including daydreaming. Other Lewin students explored the effects of different substitute actions on people's tendency to resume the original task. Such studies could establish the functional equivalence of different goals—that is, goals that can be substituted for each other—and thus help to draw the boundaries of different classes of goals or motives. Still other Lewin students studied the effects of satiation (repeated attainment of a goal) and results (success or failure at the task) on motivated behavior over time.

Motivation, Learning, and Performance

In the 1930s and 1940s, most American psychologists were interested in learning. They came to distinguish *learning* (the acquisition of new connections between stimuli, or between a stimulus and a response) from *performance* (likelihood of a particular response occurring in a particular situation). Motivation is crucial to this distinction. While simple contiguity (co-occurrence) of two stimuli is probably sufficient to explain learning, motivation (incentive, reinforcement) is necessary for the performance of responses, either during the learning process or after they have already been learned. Many of the research studies relating motivation to performance involve experimental manipulation of the hunger, thirst, and fear drives in animals. One example, Birch's (1945) study of the effects of hunger on learning and performance in six young chimpanzees, illustrates some of the complexities of the motivation-performance relationship.

Birch presented the chimpanzees with a series of problems, each of which required "insightful" learning. For example, a desirable food object was set on a table far enough away from the bars of the animal's cage so that it could be reached only with a stick (or a stick attached to a piece of string that had to be pulled first so as to bring the stick within grasping range, and so on). Birch

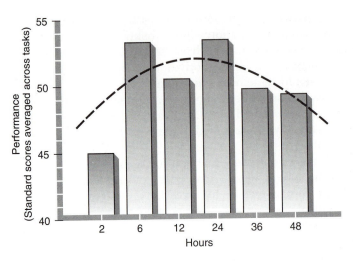

FIGURE 2.2
Effects of motivation level on insightful behavior.

systematically varied the hunger motive by controlling the number of hours a chimp had gone without food: 2, 6, 12, 24, 36, or 48 hours. As shown in Figure 2.2, when the chimps were moderately motivated (6, 12, or 24 hours without food), they performed significantly better than when they were *either* unmotivated (2 hours' deprivation, which is hardly any deprivation at all), or extremely motivated (36 or 48 hours without food).[3] The relationship shown in Figure 2.2 resembles an upside-down or inverted letter U, as sketched in the dotted line of the figure. It is a classic example of the Yerkes-Dodson law, which states that there is an inverted-U shaped relationship between quality of performance (for example, speed of learning) and motivation (see Yerkes & Dodson, 1908).

In Birch's experiment, the animals with low motivation were not very interested in getting food. Consequently they were easily distracted and spent most of their time wandering around the cage, playing with their neighbors, or grooming themselves. If they failed to get the food, they tended to give up. Sometimes they came over to the experimenter as if to get help. The highly motivated animals, in contrast, were so focused on the food that they tended to ignore other parts of the situation (sticks, strings) which were essential to getting the food. And if they failed, they tended to persist rigidly at the same responses that were unsuccessful in the first place. Sometimes they also screamed or had tantrums.

[3]The 12-hour deprivation condition actually meant the inactive early morning hour before eating, without a chimp's having missed any regular meal. The 6-hour condition involved missing the major midday meal and a full day of activity. Birch suggests that from the point of view of the animals' feeding and activity habits, the 12-hour condition was actually *less* of a deprivation than the 6-hour condition. If this is true, then the relationship shown in Figure 2.2 would be even more significant.

At first, the parallels between Birch's chimpanzees and the effects of motivation in our daily lives seem obvious. In college, for example, it helps to be moderately motivated when taking an exam or writing a paper. Too little motivation, and we might wander around the dorm room; too much, and we might clutch up with anxiety instead of preparing for the exam or writing the paper. Actually, however, the Yerkes-Dodson law gives fairly imprecise predictions. The law implies that moderate motivation gives the quickest learning and the best performance, but "moderate" is only defined in relative and not absolute terms—as less than high motivation and more than low.

In fact, the optimal "moderate" level of motivation depends on the complexity or difficulty of the task to be learned or the problem to be solved, and this further depends on the ability of the person (or animal) performing the task. A study by Broadhurst (1957) provides a particularly vivid demonstration of this interaction between motivation and task difficulty. One hundred twenty albino rats were required to learn how to escape from an underwater maze. The maze was Y-shaped, with one "choice point" or turn to be learned, and it came in three versions: easy, medium, and difficult. The rats' motivation was, of course, the need for air, which Broadhurst manipulated by detaining them underwater for four different intervals, ranging from 0 to 8 seconds. Broadhurst took the proportion of "correct" trials as a measure of speed of learning, and analyzed this in terms of the effects of motivation and maze difficulty.[4]

As you would expect, task difficulty itself was important: that is, the rats learned the easy maze more quickly than the hard maze. However, task difficulty also interacted with motivation. For the easy maze, the higher levels of motivation had little decremental effect on performance; but for the most difficult maze, the optimal level of motivation was quite low (2 seconds delay), and performance deteriorated sharply at both higher and lower levels. The more motivated rats usually swam faster, but in this study faster swimming did not always mean quicker learning. Thus Broadhurst's results suggest a more complex version of a familiar proverb: "Haste makes waste—but especially so on difficult tasks."

Experimental Arousal of Motives by McClelland and His Associates

While the work of Lewin's group demonstrated the effects of motivation on action, the research of David McClelland and his associates at Wesleyan, Harvard, and the University of Michigan in the years shortly after World War II was concerned with how motivation affects mental processes such as perception, thinking, and imagination. In the first study (McClelland & Atkinson, 1948), they unobtrusively aroused the hunger motive in one group of navy

---

[4]Since only three rats died, the rest presumably either made the correct discrimination or else were rescued by the experimenter after their mistakes.

submarine trainees by having them miss breakfast (for reasons seemingly unrelated to the experiment), with the result that they had gone without food for 16 hours. These trainees were tested in the early afternoon, together with another group of submarine trainees who had eaten breakfast but had not yet had lunch (4 hours hungry) and a third group who had had breakfast and had eaten an early lunch (1 hour hungry). All trainees were told that the study was concerned with visual perception under low illumination, a topic that was "very important in submarine work." McClelland and Atkinson went to great lengths to disguise the fact that hunger was being studied in order to arouse only the hunger motive, while not affecting other motives and factors that might come into play if the trainees had known they were participating in a study of hunger.

In the tests, trainees were given 20 seconds to look at each of 12 slides, under very low illumination. For some slides, they were asked to name the objects, identify the actions, or describe the feelings that the slides portrayed, while for others they were given no prompting and simply told to report what they "saw." In fact, all slides were blank, though some had smudges or shadows. The main result of this study was as follows (McClelland & Atkinson, 1948):

A reliable increase in the number of "instrumental" food responses [for example, dish, spoon, plate, salt] as hours of deprivation increased, while the number of "goal object" responses [for example, milk, bread, apple, candy] stayed practically the same. (pp. 211–213)

In a second study (Atkinson & McClelland, 1948), similar groups of sailors wrote stories about a series of ambiguous pictures—for example, pictures of four tramps resting, a restaurant balcony scene, or a woman looking into a room. This procedure is a modification of the Thematic Apperception Test, which has since become a major method of measuring human motives (see Chapter 5). The stories written by the men who were 16 hours hungry had more themes of food deprivation, more explicit statements of a character in the story wanting food, and more instrumental activity toward getting food than did the stories of the other groups. They did not, however, contain more references to people actually eating.

After these initial studies, McClelland and his associates turned to studying social motives, such as achievement and affiliation, that are more central to personality functioning. This work will be discussed in Chapter 5. For present purposes, their early work with the hunger motive demonstrates how motivation affects perception and thought. At the levels of motivation used by McClelland and Atkinson, the hunger motive leads to instrumentally oriented perception and imagination, making people more alert for things that are useful for reaching the goal of food. This suggests that McClelland and Atkinson were primarily manipulating the sailors along the rising left-hand part of the Yerkes-Dodson inverted-U curve. Perhaps at higher levels of arousal, hunger would increase thoughts and visions about the food goal itself. In a state of extreme motive arousal, as in the falling part of the Yerkes-Dodson curve, distortion might set in, until people begin to refashion their perceptual world and imaginative fantasies into a delusional system.

The Expression of Motivation in Action

Motivated behavior is persistent. So long as the level of motivation is not too high for the task at hand, motivated behavior also shows intelligent variation and is therefore more likely to be successful. When blocked, it seeks substitute gratifications. Motivated behavior is accompanied by anticipations and emotions, as well as desires and plans. Figure 2.3 shows how many of these characteristics of motivated behavior would fit together in the concrete situation of Jane working on her thesis.

In actual life, of course, motives are more complicated than this. Most people have several different goals and motives, often in conflict with each other.

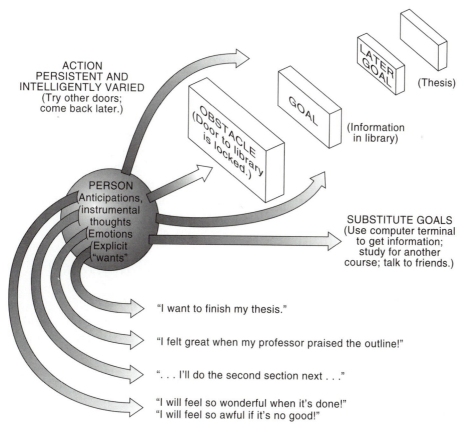

FIGURE 2.3
Characteristics of motivated behavior in Jane's situation.

Sometimes the goal is something we fear, so our behavior is directed toward *avoiding* it rather than *approaching* it. Sometimes we are ambivalent, with both approach and avoidance tendencies toward the same goal. At any one time, then, we are usually pursuing several different goals. Any particular action is likely to be a compromise among motives that are partly in harmony with each other and partly in conflict.

Lewin conceptualized three different kinds of motive conflict (1935, pp. 66–135; see also Miller, 1959). In an *approach-approach conflict*, we are torn between two attractive alternatives. For example, Jane wants to work on her thesis, but she may also want to be with her friends. As soon as she moves toward one of these goals, however, the conflict should diminish, at least for awhile. This is because the relative attractiveness of the goal that is approached increases as it becomes closer. In an *avoidance-avoidance conflict*, we are caught between two unattractive choices. For example, Jane may have to choose between staying up late and losing sleep or being unprepared for class. In an *approach-avoidance conflict*, the same alternative has both attractive and aversive qualities. For example, perhaps Jane is really ambivalent about her thesis, experiencing it as a source of pleasure and also anxiety. These last two conflicts are not so easy to resolve, because any movement toward or away from one goal does not reduce the sense of conflict.

Like the rest of us, Jane probably experiences many conflicts of motive. In addition to her desire to write a good thesis, she also has friends, enjoys music, likes to organize political campaigns, and fears nuclear war; she is ambivalent about her family, uncertain about her career plans, sometimes can't decide what she really wants, and even occasionally dislikes her thesis work. Thus it might be hard for even a trained and expert observer to identify the goals or motives underlying any particular behavior of hers. Still, most people can recognize and understand many instances of their own motivated behavior. The more we can accurately identify our own and others' motives, the better we can understand the role they play in our personality, behavior, experience, and the course of our lives.

A CASE STUDY OF MOTIVATION: IDENTIFYING RICHARD NIXON'S MAJOR MOTIVES

As explained in Chapter 1, each of the four elements of personality will be illustrated and discussed in the life of a well-known and interesting public figure. We begin our case study of motivation by trying to identify motives in the life of Richard Nixon, the thirty-seventh president of the United States.

The Paradoxes of Nixon

I have chosen Nixon to study motives because many of his actions were confusing and paradoxical, raising deep questions about his real goals, and at the same time creating problems for any theory of personality or motivation. As

With his family standing behind him, Richard Nixon made his nationally
televised farewell remarks to the White House staff, just before his August 1974
resignation. Why did Nixon try to cover up the Watergate break-in? Why didn't
he destroy the tapes of his conversations, tapes that became the "smoking gun"
that eventually forced his resignation?

the writer-journalist Norman Mailer put it after the 1972 Republican convention: "Freud is obsolete. To explain Nixon, nothing less than a new theory of
personality can now suffice" (1972, p. 202). For example, why did Nixon at age
10 announce to his mother that "I would like to become a lawyer—an honest
lawyer, who can't be bought by crooks" (Kornitzer, 1960, p. 19)? Fifty-one
years later, he resigned the presidency in the face of indisputable evidence that
he was involved in the biggest political scandal in American history and guilty
of several specific felonies (yet maintaining, at a nationally televised news conference, that "I am not a crook"). How can we explain this ironic contradiction?

Another example: On graduation from college, Nixon described his political thinking as "very liberal, almost populist" (Nixon, 1978, p. 17). Why, then,
did he launch his political career ten years later by attacking a liberal oppo-
nent and hunting down communists? Finally, as president twenty-five years
after that, he visited China and toasted its communist hero, Mao Zedong, in
Beijing's Great Hall of the People. How can we explain all these twists and
turns of political belief and practice?

Another example: After losing elections for the presidency in 1960 and the
governor of California in 1962, how and why did Nixon manage to get elected
president in 1968, and then reelected in 1972 with the biggest electoral vote
margin in American history up to that time?

Yet another example: In May 1970, Nixon widened the Vietnam war by
ordering an invasion of Cambodia. In response, thousands of American college students descended on Washington, D.C., to protest. On May 8, after a
press conference in which he aggressively defended his actions, Nixon made
fifty-one telephone calls over the next seven hours and then drove to the Lin-

coln Memorial at 4:35 A.M. to visit with the protesting students. He told them, "I want you to know that I understand just how you feel," but after only a very brief mention of the Vietnam war, he then went on to talk about travel, Native Americans, architecture, and college football (Nixon, 1989; Safire, 1975, pp. 202–212). How can we explain such a bewildering variety of Nixon behaviors in such a short time?

And of course there is a final set of paradoxes: Why did Nixon try to cover up the Watergate break-in? Why did he make tapes of his conversations? And since these tapes were to provide the evidence that finally forced his resignation, why didn't he destroy them?

Judging Nixon's Motives from His Words

Richard Nixon is now dead and, like other historical figures, is not available for us to ask these questions directly. Unlike the case of Lee Harvey Oswald, however, we do have access to a lot of Nixon's spoken and written words. Three times Nixon wrote about his life, his actions, and his goals. *Six Crises* (1962) is an autobiographical account of certain events in his adult political life, written shortly after he lost the 1960 presidential election to John F. Kennedy. *RN: The Memoirs of Richard Nixon* (1978) is an autobiography written three and a half years after his resignation. *In the Arena* (1990) offers further reminiscences and musings about his life, organized by theme rather than by chronology. Even by the standards of American presidents, Nixon talked and wrote a lot about himself. But like all political autobiographies, his self-revelations are selective, self-censored, and self-justifying. If we want to measure his motives and goals from these words, we may need to interpret and sometimes even discount them.

We shall explore Nixon's own account of his early life up to 1942 when at age 29 he left practicing law to join the Navy at the beginning of American involvement in World War II (Chapter 1 of *RN*). To understand Nixon's motives, we shall examine his words, noting what goals he sought with persistence and intelligence, what made him happy or sad, and what he tried to avoid. What follows here is my own interpretation, broadened and checked by several class discussions with students, of the strength of three Nixon motives: achievement, affiliation, and power. If you are interested in Nixon, you may want to study his autobiography and work out your own interpretation. Keep in mind Nixon's challenge to our efforts: "I always find it amusing when psycho-historians I have never met conclude that I have what they consider to be a warped personality" (1990, p. 79). (In what follows, all page numbers are from the hardbound edition of *RN*.)

Success and Achievement, without Joy

The most striking theme in Nixon's account of his early years is *energetic hard work* directed towards overcoming obstacles to goals of *success and achievement*. The first few sentences of the book set the achievement stage in the southern

California of the 1920s: "for those who were willing to work hard . . . a place and time of almost unlimited opportunity." And Nixon did work hard. As a teenager, he got up at 4 in the morning to buy the "best" produce at a "good price" for the family market—"not an easy life, but a good one" (p. 5). In high school and college, he "continued to plug away at my studies. . . . I needed the steady discipline of nightly study to keep up with all my courses and reading" (p. 15). One of his major extracurricular activities was debate, "a serious pursuit and a highly developed art" which demanded "thorough" research (p. 17). From his football coach at Whittier College, Nixon learned that "if we worked hard enough and played hard enough, we could beat anybody. . . . He drilled into me a competitive spirit and the determination to come back after you have been knocked down or after you lost" (p. 20). After college, there was Duke University Law School, "a fast competitive track." Confronted with demanding courses and brilliant classmates, Nixon "sometimes despaired of pulling the memorized facts together into any meaningful knowledge of the law." An encouraging upperclass friend reassured him: "You have what it takes to learn the law—an iron butt" (p. 20). To Nixon, his education was "first-rate" and "excellent" (pp. 17, 21).

Nixon's early years were filled with achievements. Having learned to read at home, he skipped second grade. He finished third in his high school class and won oratorical and all-around student awards. At Whittier College, he was president of the student body. In law school, he was third in his class, held a competitive scholarship, and was on the Law Review. Later, back in Whittier as a partner in the city's oldest law firm, he was also president of four local clubs and the youngest member of the Whittier College Board of Trustees. Altogether, an impressive record for someone only 29 years old. Nixon was certainly entitled to feel pleased with himself. Yet curiously enough, he mentions very little personal pleasure, happiness, or pride in all of these accomplishments. For example, he wrote that his graduation from law school was "a proud day" for his family, since he finished third in his class and was elected a member of the national legal honor society, but he said nothing about his own feelings (p. 22). Instead, he seemed almost to relish austerity, self-denial, and a Spartan lifestyle. For example, at Duke it was "exciting and adventurous" to live with three friends out in the woods, in a one-room shack that lacked heat and indoor plumbing (pp. 20–21).

Perhaps related to this preference for austerity is a didactic or pedantic quality in Nixon's talking and writing about himself. Sometimes he speaks of himself in the third person (p. 24), and often he seems to be analyzing, evaluating, or "coaching" his own behavior even as he describes it. For example, "young lawyers trying to get business for their firms are expected to join local clubs, so I began to participate extensively in community affairs" (p. 22). Here we see Nixon soberly calculating means-ends relationships and talking to himself as he does it: Is this the right way to get what I want? How am I doing? Should I be doing this, or that?

Themes of achievement sometimes arouse anxiety and pain in Nixon. When he thought that he had failed the California bar exam, he shut himself in the bathroom to open the envelope from the examiners so that his family would not see his distress (p. 22). (In fact, he had passed.) Of his father, Frank Nixon, Richard wrote: "Throughout his life, my father tried to better himself through work" (p. 5), but the combination of family illnesses, lack of education, and his own tempestuous temper always seemed to hold him back so that by 1930, "the family finances had been stripped to the bone." As a result, Richard could not even afford to accept a tuition scholarship to Yale, but had to attend hometown Whittier College (p. 15). Perhaps Richard Nixon's concern with success grew out of a desire to redeem his father's failures, for "my success in politics meant to him that everything he had worked for and believed in was true; that in America, with hard work and determination a man can achieve anything" (p. 7). Considering this remark along with Nixon's recollection of his law school graduation as a "proud day" for his family, we may wonder whether his strong work and achievement motives were related to other goals involving family love and friendship.

Love and Affiliation, Endangered

To many, Richard Nixon had the reputation of being an aloof person, keeping to himself. It may be surprising, therefore, to notice how often he described his early years in terms of the pleasure, happiness, and enjoyment of *affiliation or intimacy with others*. When he was 12, Nixon was sent to live with an aunt and uncle in order to take music lessons. "My parents came to bring me home [six months later] . . . I was happy to see them after what seemed a very long time" (p. 9). He "loved to listen" when his mother, aunts, and grandmother would slip into the plain speech—"thee" and "thou"—that is a special sign of intimacy in Quaker families (p. 13). What he really liked about being on the college football team was "the spirit, the teamwork, the friendship" (p. 19), a theme echoed in the "great time" he had living with his friends in the shack in the woods during law school. After his marriage to Pat Ryan, "our life was happy, and full of promise." On a Caribbean cruise just before the war, "we enjoyed what turned out to be our last vacation in years" (p. 25). After joining the Navy in 1942 and being assigned to an air station in Iowa instead of a ship at sea, his initial disappointment was overcome "by the warmth and friendship of our new neighbors" (p. 27).

Yet for all their importance, love and friendship were not motives that Nixon could satisfy directly and easily in his early years. His parents, whatever their real feelings, did not make it easy for a child to feel loved. In his father Frank, for example, "it was his temper that impressed me most as a small child. . . . He was a strict and stern disciplinarian, and I tried to follow my mother's example of not crossing him when he was in a bad mood" (p. 6). Hannah Nixon, his mother, "was intensely private in her feelings and emotions"; in fact, the entire family had "reticence about the display of affection" (pp. 8, 9). In 1990, Nixon wrote that "in her whole life, I never heard her say to me or to anyone else, 'I love you,'" though he went on to rationalize this by claiming that "her eyes expressed the love and warmth no words could possibly convey" (1990, p. 87).

Richard Nixon with his daughter and parents in 1952, right after being named the Republican vice-presidential candidate. "In her whole life, I never heard [my mother] say to me or to anyone else, 'I love you' . . . [although] her eyes expressed the love and warmth no words could possibly convey" (Nixon, 1990, p. 87).

Nixon's early years, moreover, were filled with major losses and threats to love. When Richard was 12, his younger brother Arthur died, unexpectedly and from a rare and mysterious cause. "For weeks after Arthur's funeral, there was not a day that I did not think about him and cry" (p. 10). Five years later, Richard wrote a paper for a college composition course about what Arthur meant to him. After lovingly recounting his memories of Arthur as a baby and little boy, he concluded with deep feelings of loss at Arthur's death: "And so when I am tired and worried, and am almost ready to quit trying to live as I should, I look up and see the picture of a little boy with sparkling eyes, and curly hair" (p. 11).

Eight years after Arthur's death, when Richard was a junior in college, his older brother Harold died after a ten-year struggle with tuberculosis. "The long, losing fight left its tragic mark on our whole family" (p. 11), involving for Richard not just the loss of an older brother but also an extended separation from his mother. Three years before, Hannah had moved with Harold to a tuberculosis colony in Prescott, Arizona. "To make ends meet she took care of three other bedridden patients" (p. 11). During these years Richard lived with his father Frank and only saw his mother and older brother during school vacations. There had been earlier separations. For six months, Richard lived at an aunt's house so that he could take music lessons. During Arthur's brief illness, "because Arthur required constant care and attention, Don [younger brother] and I were sent to stay with my aunt" (pp. 9–10).

It is easy to imagine that such periods of "exile" from family would arouse fears, worries, and unhappiness in any adolescent. For example, he might have wondered whether his mother preferred Harold, or even the three other tubercular patients for whom she cared. Richard did not admit to having such feelings, but some hints do slip out. In discussing Hannah's reactions to the deaths of these three patients, he revealingly wrote that "I could tell that she felt their deaths as deeply *as if they had been her own sons'*" (p. 11, italics added). These themes of separation from mother, her possible preference for a sibling, and feelings of pain all come together in Nixon's first conscious memory, dating from age 3:

> My mother was driving us in a horse-drawn buggy, holding my baby brother Don on her lap while a neighbor girl held me. The horse turned . . . at high speed, and I tumbled onto the ground. I must have been in shock, but I managed to get up and run after the buggy while my mother tried to make the horse stop. (p. 4)

In the face of these exiles, deaths, dangers, and a family atmosphere of rage and reticence, Richard Nixon nevertheless asserted his unshakable conviction that "my mother loved me completely and selflessly" (p. 13) and that his father's outbursts were "just his way of putting life into a discussion" (p. 6). As readers and interpreters, we might conclude that he was simply denying the conflict between his affiliation motive and reality, perhaps by adjusting his perceptions after the fact so that they fit his needs. When we examine the autobiography more closely, however, we can see that Nixon's motive for affiliation, while threatened or blocked, also sought satisfaction in some indirect and unusual ways.

For example, it was difficult for Richard to get close to his father because of Frank Nixon's love of argument and terrible temper. Perhaps partly in imitation of his father, therefore, Richard threw his energies into the debate team, and debating brought a kind of curious closeness with his father. "He would often drive me to the debates and sit in the back of the room listening closely." Yet even this closeness was curiously mixed with a pedantic scrutiny, a trait that in the form of self-scrutiny was to become an important part of Nixon's adult style (see the previous section on achievement): "On the way home he would dissect and analyze each of the arguments" (p. 6). In later years, Nixon's political career had the same effect on Frank. "My father's interest in politics made him the most enthusiastic follower of my career from its beginnings. . . . I sent home copies of the daily *Congressional Record*. He read them cover to cover" (p. 7). Argument, competition, debate, politics—all tinged with ruthless self-scrutiny and self-analysis—were thus ways that Richard gained whatever closeness and intimacy with his father he was able to get.

Later on, he used this same technique with other older men. For four years, he doggedly stuck it out on the Whittier College football team, though "I hardly cut a formidable figure on the field," and in fact rarely played in an actual game. The reason for his persistence was affiliative. "I loved the game— the spirit, the teamwork, the friendship." "College football at Whittier gave me the chance to get to know the coach." "He drilled into me a competitive spirit and determination." "I admired him more . . . [than] any man I have ever known aside from my father" (p. 19).

From his father, Nixon may have learned another indirect and unusual way of obtaining friendship and intimacy. In his speeches and autobiography, for example, Nixon sometimes introduced a new topic by mentioning personal clumsiness or awkwardness or by dwelling on his failures and embarrassments. Because of the fall from the buggy at age 3, "years later, when the vogue of parting hair on the left side came along, I still had to comb mine straight back to hide a scar" (p. 4). Memories of high school are introduced with the sentence, "I suffered my first political defeat in my junior year." His first experience acting in a school play was "sheer torture," because a tender scene on stage evoked "catcalls, whistles, and uproarious laughter" from the audience, while ill-fitting shoes made the whole experience "agony beyond description and almost beyond endurance" (p. 14). When dancing was finally permitted at Whittier College, he tried to learn how to dance. His girlfriend "and several other coeds were very patient with me, but I fear that many new pairs of slippers were scuffed as a result of my attempts to lead my partners around the dance floor" (p. 19). His first-year college basketball team "had a perfect record for the year: we lost every game." And after a collision with another player, "the only trophy I have to show for having played basketball is a porcelain dental bridge" (p. 19).

These personal revelations of "Nixon as klutz" seem calculated to arouse sympathy, disarm opposition, and perhaps even charm others. An incident in 1947, when Frank and Hannah Nixon visited Richard and Pat in New York City, provides a clue as to how Nixon developed this unusual style of gaining friendship. Frank loved musical comedies, so Richard had bought the best seats in the house for the hit show *Oklahoma!* Frank was partly deaf; somehow he left his hearing aid in the hotel room. Richard remembered "how intently he followed the play and how he laughed and applauded . . . so that we would think he was having a good time, even though he could not hear a single word or a single note" (p. 7). Many of you would see Frank's "mistake" as awkward, embarrassing, perhaps even hostile, but Richard Nixon related the story as an example of "the love beneath his brusque and bristling exterior that I remember best" (p. 7). Within the Nixon family, then, being a klutz was apparently one way—to be sure, an extraordinary one—of showing and gaining love.

Nixon described his family as stern and reticent about showing affection. On a few occasions, though, love and intimacy *were* openly expressed; if we study these incidents carefully, we can uncover yet another indirect and unusual way in which he sought affection both within his family and in later life. As a first-year college student, Richard wrote that "two days before my brother's [Arthur] death, he called my mother into the room. He put his arms around her and said that he wanted to pray before he went to sleep" (p. 11). An hour before his death, brother Harold asked his mother "to put her arms around him and hold him very close" (p. 12). During the last stages of his illness, Harold had asked to see the desert that lay over the mountains from their house in Whittier. Richard recalled that "my father dropped everything to make ready for the trip" (p. 12). Thus it seems that only in the face of death could a Nixon boy have physical closeness to his mother and his father. Small wonder, then, that death and affection became linked in Richard's mind. If death means finally attaining warmth and love, then small "deaths" such as failure, exile, and loss are not defeats or signs of loss but rather signs that the affiliation goal is near. Thus to fail is, in a small way, to die—and so finally to be loved.

Richard concluded his composition course paper about Arthur's death with such a wish: "And so when I am tired and worried, and am almost ready to quit trying . . . I remember the childlike prayer ['If I should die before I wake']; *I pray that it may prove true for me as it did for my brother Arthur*" (p. 11, italics added). In this passage, "it" can mean the prayer, or dying before waking, or even being "held very close" by mother.

Over forty years later, Nixon resigned the presidency as a consequence of the Watergate scandal and his disastrous handling of it. In a final disjointed and emotion-filled speech to the White House staff, broadcast live on national television, he echoed this same theme of death and affection. First, he talked about the small size but "great heart" of the White House, the rewards of government service, and his father's business failures. Next he talked about his mother, twice repeating that "nobody'll ever write a book, probably, about my mother." Then he quoted former President Theodore Roosevelt's diary entry after the death of his young wife:

> Fair, pure and joyous to the maiden: loving, tender, happy. . . . And by a strange terrible fate, death came to her. And when my heart's dearest died, the life went from my life forever.

Finally, Nixon (1974) added his own conclusion about failure. (After reading Chapter 3, you may want to return to this passage to interpret the landscape symbolism.)

> The greatness comes not when things go always good for you, but . . . when sadness comes, because only if you've been in the deepest valley can you ever know how magnificent it is to be on the highest mountain. (p. 632)

Power, with Reluctance

To his critics, Richard Nixon was driven by an all-consuming desire for *power or impact on other people*. In fact, however, power and impact are not very prominent themes in the first chapter of his autobiography. Even when they do occur, they are usually mentioned with some ambivalence. Thus while his older brother Harold and many other people responded to Frank Nixon's angry temper by fighting back, Richard developed an "aversion to personal confrontations" (p. 6). In describing his brief pre-Navy war experiences as a Washington bureaucrat, Nixon wrote disapprovingly of career government workers who "became obsessed with their own power and seemed to delight in kicking people around" (p. 26). Even the power represented by his winning the election for college student body president conflicted with the goal of

Richard Nixon as a child (at right), with his parents and brothers Harold and Donald. "It was [my father's] temper that impressed me most as a small child . . . I tried to follow my mother's example of not crossing him when he was in a bad mood. Perhaps my aversion to confrontation dates back to these early recollections" (Nixon, 1978, p. 6).

affiliation toward his rival: "We were good friends and did not feel much enthusiasm for running against each other" (p. 18). In connection with college football, Nixon did write that "I have a highly competitive instinct," but he developed this theme in a way that suggests *watching* power rather than seeking it directly: "I find it stimulating to follow the great sports events" (p. 19). In fact, just about the only time in the first chapter that Nixon writes of having an impact on other people without at the same time feeling ambivalence or conflict is when he disclosed two great unfulfilled ambitions: "to direct a symphony orchestra and to play an organ in a cathedral." Yet even these are elaborated in an achievement way: "I think that to create great music is one of the highest ambitions man can set for himself" (p. 9).

Here is a paradox. Richard Nixon built a long career on the basis of political competition. Three times he sought and twice he won election to one of the most powerful offices in the world. Many of the most famous actions and events of his career seem to reflect obvious concerns for power—persecuting anyone of the American political left whom he presumed to be a "communist," continuing the Vietnam war for four years (including the invasion of Cambodia and the vicious Christmas 1972 bombing of Hanoi), and finally constructing the edifice of "Watergate" (and related illegal activities) to protect his own secrets and steal those of the opposition. You may wonder how we can say that Richard Nixon was not strongly motivated by power goals.

Perhaps he really was concerned with power, and I have just missed the relevant themes and images in the first chapter of *RN*. (Read for yourself Nixon's writings!) Perhaps he really was concerned with power, but purposely edited these goals out of his autobiography in order to disguise his true motives and appear more attractive to readers. Perhaps he really was concerned with power, but was not aware of this motive because in some part of his mind he censored and distorted any thoughts of power. You may want to keep these possibilities in mind as you read through the next three chapters about motives and how they operate.

There is, however, another possibility: that our analysis of Richard Nixon's motives in the themes in the first chapter of *RN* is correct. In other words, Nixon may really have had strong affiliation and achievement goals, but only average (and conflicted) motives for power. In that case, actions that at first seem to be power-related might actually be the result of affiliation and achievement motives. We have already suggested this possibility in discussing Nixon's curious verbal connections between competition, debate, failure, and death, on the one hand, and the search for love, on the other. In this chapter, our analysis of Nixon's motives through his words has been informal and impressionistic. In the last part of Chapter 5, we shall return to the question of Richard Nixon's motives, but with an objective technique for measuring motives in verbal material.

WHAT HAVE WE LEARNED FROM THE NIXON CASE?

The case of Richard Nixon underlines an important point about motivation that has been discussed throughout this chapter. *Motives and behavior are different.* There is no direct, one-to-one relationship between a person's goals and the acts taken to reach those goals. Any particular action can be the result of several different motives (in combination or conflict), and any given motive can lead to several different actions. Some of these actions may be surprising and unusual, but close scrutiny can reveal their connection to the underlying motive.

This conclusion immediately raises an important problem for the study of motivation: if there is no close connection between motives and actions, then it will be difficult to determine a person's motives. Recall the question of whether Nixon had high, low, or medium power motivation. To answer that question, it won't help to make statements such as "Nixon had a strong power motive, because he showed a lot of power behaviors." This statement is circular; the concept of "motive" as it is used here adds nothing to the explanation of "behaviors," because it is based solely on the behaviors that it tries to explain. But if motives are different from behavior, and Nixon's seeming "power behaviors" do not necessarily indicate a strong power motive, then we must find another way to diagnose and measure his motives, a way that is independent of behavior itself.

I have framed the case study of Richard Nixon's motives in terms of three motives—achievement, affiliation, and power. You may wonder whether these are the most important or useful motives for understanding Nixon. Surely there must be others. This raises the question of how many different motives human beings have, and what they are.

All these issues—the number and nature of human motives, the relationship between motives and behavior, and the measurement of motives—are the major concerns of the next three chapters, which review theories and research on the role of motivation in personality.

3

Motives in Freud's Psychoanalytic Theory

❖

Sigmund Freud (1856–1939) was born in what is now the Czech Republic. He spent almost all his working life in Vienna but died in London, a Jewish refugee from Nazi anti-Semitism. Trained as a physician specializing in neurology, he developed the theory and practice of psychoanalysis as a way of treating mental illnesses for which there was no apparent physical basis. Over time, though, psychoanalysis developed into a general theory of personality, and even became a broad philosophical worldview. Psychoanalytic theory is the starting point for most modern personality theory and research, and psychoanalysis is built on the foundation of a theory of motives.[1]

Freud classified human motives into two broad groups, the nature and names of which changed over the course of his career. Before about 1920, he spoke of the *self-preservation motives* and the *libidinal motives* (or libido). After 1920, he revised this classification, combining self-preservation and libidinal motives into a single group, called the ego or life instincts, and adding a new group of aggressive or death instincts. All these terms appear in discussions of psychoanalytic theory.

*T*HE SELF-PRESERVATION MOTIVES

In the self-preservation motive group, Freud included all ordinary bodily needs: food, water, air, elimination, and avoidance of pain. Freud never discussed these motives in detail, because they are relatively easy to gratify—for-

---

[1]Freud's German term, *Trieb,* is usually translated into English as "instinct," which suggests inherited biological motives. While Freud did believe that human motives originated from somatic or bodily sources, he used the term *Trieb* in ways far broader than the way "instinct" is used by modern biologists. This gives Freud's writings on instincts a peculiar, out-of-date flavor that they do not really deserve. I prefer to use the word "motive" as a translation of *Trieb* in discussing Freud's concept of the forces that impel and direct behavior.

See translator James Strachey's general preface to *The Standard Edition of the Complete Psychological Works of Sigmund Freud* (vol. 1, pp. xxiv–xxvi), published 1953–1974 by the Hogarth Press, London, and his preface to Freud's paper on instincts (1915a, XIV, pp. 111–116).

For simplicity, in this book all references to Freud's writings will be in modified American Psychological Association form, including only the date of the original German publication, and then the volume and page numbers of the English translation in the *Standard Edition.*

Sigmund Freud (1856–1939), founder of psychoanalysis. "I have made many beginnings and thrown out many suggestions. Something will come of them in the future, though I cannot myself tell whether it will be much or little. I can, however, express a hope that I have opened up a pathway for an important advance in our knowledge" (Freud, 1925a, XX, p. 70).

tunately so, because their gratification is essential for life itself. For example, we can go without air for only a few minutes, without water for only a few days, and without food for only a few weeks. That's it. Most self-preservation needs cannot be blocked or transformed; they simply must be met. For this reason, most of the self-preservation motives remain in their original form and so are not very interesting for the study of personality.

Pain Avoidance

The pain-avoidance motive, however, was of great interest to Freud. Any behavior, plan, or thought that might arouse "unpleasure" will, he believed, be rejected or vetoed by the action of this motive, fulfilling its function of avoiding pain (Freud, 1916–1917, XVI, p. 349). What behaviors lead to unpleasure? Any unsuccessful action will arouse frustration (mild unpleasure), while actions that are punished will arouse stronger pain. Eventually, even thinking about such actions arouses painful anticipations or fears. In our society, Freud suggested, behaviors arising from libidinal motives (discussed below) are the ones most likely to be frustrated, punished, and controlled by other people and society as a whole. Thus the libidinal motives come into conflict with the self-preservation motive of pain avoidance. As a result of this conflict, the libidinal motives are modified and transformed into the major motives and structures of adult personality. Indirectly, then, one of the self-preservation motives does play an important role in personality development.[2]

An "Activity Motive"?

Freud added a tantalizing but undeveloped speculation about the self-preservation motives, writing that they include "in all probability, [the functions] of muscular excitation and sensory activity" (1913a, XIII, p. 181). Here Freud seems to anticipate an idea that figures prominently in the work of humanistic and cognitive theorists such as White, Rogers, Maslow, and Kelly (see Chapters 4 and 6); that sensory and muscular activity are sought for their own sakes, as a need for exercising our capacities and potentials. How different Freud's theory of personality would be if he had followed up this intriguing idea that he casually mentioned only once!

THE LIBIDINAL MOTIVES

Freud's second class of human motives, the libido or *libidinal motives*, are his most familiar and most significant contribution to the psychology of motivation. In Latin, *libido* simply means "I want" or "I desire." Freud originally used libido to mean sexual desire in the ordinary sense, the way it is still used by physicians. Later, he expanded the conception of "sexual" far beyond this ordinary meaning. Did Freud really believe that (apart from self-preservation) all our motives are sexual? Is it true that he "reduced everything to sex"? In fact, Freud's theory is a good deal more complicated than these simple formulas. His fullest statement of libido theory was first published in 1905 as *Three Essays on the Theory of Sexuality*[3] (1905c, VII), a book he kept revising and adding to over the years. Let us work through his ideas, step by step.

First, the libido is not a unitary thing, but rather a *series or bundle of component motives* that all share the characteristic of being sexual in the broadest

---

[2]The self-preservation motives, especially pain avoidance, necessarily involve establishing and maintaining close connections with the real world (Freud, 1916–1917, XVI, p. 355). When Freud later developed the concept of the ego as the mental "structure" or system that managed these connections (through perception, memory, judgment, and choice), he referred to these motives as the "ego motives."

[3]The English title varies in different editions; this is the official *Standard Edition* title.

sense of the word. This includes every desire or goal that is capable of participating in sexual satisfaction. The most obvious example is *genital sexual intercourse* itself, "the union of the genitals in the act known as copulation, which leads to a release of sexual tension and a temporary extinction of the sexual instinct" (Freud, 1905c, VII, p. 149). Also included are any other goals or aims that are normally a part of the act of love, as preliminary actions or foreplay: touching, looking, and kissing (though in the latter case "the parts of the bodies involved do not form part of the sexual apparatus but constitute part of the digestive tract," Ibid., p. 150).

The libidinal motives are further expanded when we include aims and actions that are linked to sexual behavior in unusual cases: variations in the sexual object (for example, one's own sex, children, or animals) or aim (for example, nongenital parts of the body, fetishes or objects associated with a sexual object, and fixations—that is, exclusive concentration on some action that is usually part of a sequence ending in intercourse). Freud argued that anything that *can* participate in sexual satisfaction (even when society labels it a perversion) *is* therefore sexual, even when it occurs in normal behavior. In other words, perversions simply make unmistakably clear the sexual roots of such actions.

Do these extreme cases have anything to do with ordinary behavior and personality? Freud believed there was no sharp distinction between normal and perverted behavior. For example, he suggested, we can see unmistakably sexual behaviors among ordinary children if we will only look honestly: sucking, playing with feces, masturbation, exhibitionism and voyeurism, and cruelty. In terms of their potential, children are "polymorphously perverse" (1905c, VII, p. 191), but as the demands and prohibitions of reality increase, most of these component motives are either transformed into seemingly nonsexual and recognizable features of adult personality or else retained as part of the sequence of mature loving sexuality.

To many of his contemporaries, Freud's views about sexuality in children were shocking. This was especially true of early twentieth-century Americans, who viewed children as innocent symbols of human progress and perfectibility. In 1913, for example, a leading American popular magazine deplored Freud's "improbable and revolting explanations"; a few years later during World War I, it hinted at Freud's "decadent German pansexualism" (quoted in Hale, 1971, pp. 272). One leading Philadelphia doctor complained:

> What must we think of the wounding of the feelings of a sensitive and innocent nature when to a loving son or daughter is suggested an incestuous love for the mother? What injury can be greater than to give to one of the most beautiful relations in human life the most shocking and vile of interpretations? (Ibid., p. 299)

Component Motives of the Libido

Freud never provided a complete and ordered list of these components of the libidinal group of motives, but the following specific examples can be extracted from his works. They are listed in Table 3.1 and will be discussed in the approximate order of their appearance or prominence during development. (The numbers refer to the table.)

(L-1) Touching and being touched. Freud wrote that "a certain amount of touching is indispensable (at all events among human beings) before the normal sexual aim can be obtained. And everyone knows what a source of pleasure . . . is afforded by tactile sensations of the skin of the sexual object" (1905c, VII, p. 156). (To Freud, a sexual object is the object of *any* of the libidinal motives.) In the view of the *object relations school* of psychoanalytic thought (Bowlby, 1969; Fairbairn, 1952; Klein, 1948), this is one component motive that is fully present and very important at birth. It underlies the process of attachment, or the "bonding" of infants with their parents and caretakers—a process that is the basis of all later social relationships, as well as the foundation for adult personality. Studies of the attachment process demonstrate the importance of sheer physical contact (Ainsworth, 1969; Mahler, Pine, & Bergman, 1975). Harlow (1958, 1971) even showed that touching was important for normal social development among rhesus monkeys.

(L-2) Seeing or looking and being looked at. "Visual impressions remain the most frequent pathway along which libidinal excitation is aroused. . . . Curiosity seeks to complete the sexual object by revealing its hidden parts" (Freud, 1905c, VII, p. 156). Like many other bodily organs, the eyes serve a dual purpose: for the self-preservation motives, they perceive alterations in the environment—information that is important to life; for the libidinal motives, they perceive the charms of a loved object (1910b, XI). When highly developed and generalized, this motive manifests itself as a special pleasure in looking, or *scopophilia* (a combination of the Greek roots for "look" and "pleasure"). Voyeurism and exhibitionism, the compulsive desires to see and show the genitals, respectively, are two perverse manifestations of this motive.

TABLE 3.1 FREUD'S CATALOG OF MAJOR HUMAN MOTIVES

Libidinal motives	*Aggressive motives ("death instincts")*
L-1 Touching and being touched	A-1 Mastery (after 1920)
L-2 Seeing or looking and being looked at	A-2 Cruelty (after 1920)
L-3 Sucking or incorporation	A-3 Destructiveness
L-4 Mastery-control	A-4 Property and possessions
L-5 Cruelty	A-5 Observation, monitoring and control
L-6 Childhood genital sexuality	A-6 Critical judging
L-7 Mature, mutual sexuality	A-7 Rewarding and punishing
L-8 Research	A-8 Nurturance and help

(L-3) Sucking or incorporation. The mouth is also used for gratifying self-preservation motives (obtaining nourishment) and libidinal motives. For Freud, "sensual sucking" was the classic example of childhood sexuality (1905c, VII, p. 182):

> No one who has seen a baby sinking back satiated from the breast and falling asleep with flushed cheeks and a blissful smile can escape the reflection that this picture persists as a prototype of the expression of sexual satisfaction in later life.

The object may be the mother's breast, a bottle, a pacifier, a thumb, or some other part of the child's own body. As the infant becomes aware of the difference between self and not-self, sucking expresses the desire to incorporate or take in good or pleasurable things from outside. *Grasping,* a kind of rhythmic tugging with the hand, often makes its appearance along with sucking. *Biting* is a further development, combining sucking and grasping with the mastery and cruelty motives (Abraham, 1924).

(L-4) Mastery-control. The mastery motive appears most strikingly as children learn to retain and then eliminate (in short, to control) their feces, although it can also be detected earlier, in feeding and play. As Freud described it (1905c, VII, p. 186):

> Children [hold] back their stool till its accumulation brings about violent muscular contractions and, as it passes through the anus, is able to produce powerful stimulation of the mucous membrane. In so doing it must no doubt cause not only painful but also highly pleasurable sensations.

(L-5) Cruelty. Before 1920, Freud believed that the cruelty motive somehow arose from mastery, from the simultaneous pleasure and pain we experience as we simultaneously master something and are mastered by something, as in the example of elimination above. In its active form (sadism), cruelty is aggressive and seeks to inflict pain on others, while in its passive form (masochism), the self seeks to have pain inflicted on it. Often sadism and masochism alternate in the same person. Mastery and cruelty are listed twice in Table 3.1, because Freud later changed his mind and grouped them with aggressive, not libidinal motives.

(L-6) Childhood genital sexuality. Since this motive involves the sexual organs, it is closer to what we ordinarily think of as sexuality, but it is by no means identical. Before puberty, the desire for genital stimulation *may* occur in connection with some real or fantasied partner, as in the case of young children playing doctor. In young children, however, this motive is experienced more as an autoerotic stimulation of one's own genitals (masturbation) than as a true *union* of genitals between two partners. Displaying his characteristic male-centeredness, Freud referred to the former as phallic sexuality, reserving the term "genital" for *(L-7) Mature, mutual sexuality.*

(L-8) Research. Finally, Freud discussed the instinct for knowledge or research as a higher-level fusion of mastery and scopophilia, two elementary motives (1905c, VII, p. 194). Originally the child's research motive is directed toward highly practical interests. For example, the birth of a younger brother or sister may raise questions about where babies come from or the differences between boys and girls. Freud believed that the desire for knowledge is a delicate motive; because it is originally tied to answering sexual questions, any blocking or punishment associated with sexual matters will also inhibit the child's developing curiosity and desire for knowledge. Freud used the concept of "research motive" in a study of Leonardo da Vinci (1910a, XI), a famously curious and knowledge-seeking person.

Active and passive pairs. Notice that several of the libidinal components occur as natural pairs, one active and one passive: touching and being touched, looking and being looked at, sadism and masochism. In a later theoretical development, Freud suggested that in their play, children often repeat, in an active form, pleasant *and* unpleasant experiences they earlier endured in a passive mode. This switch from passive to active is actually an expression of the mastery motive, since "they can master a powerful impression far more thoroughly by being active than they could by merely experiencing it passively" (1920, XVIII, p. 35).

Development of Personality: The Psychosexual Stages

Many component motives seem tied to particular regions of the body, at least in their earliest appearance. For example, sucking involves the mouth, elimination and retention (mastery) the anus, and so forth. Freud called these regions erotogenic (that is, "arousing sexual desire") zones. Any part of the body can become an erotogenic zone, even the eye in the case of scopophilia (1905c, VII, p. 184). The point in development when a component motive tied to a body region first becomes prominent is called a *psychosexual stage.* The stages are named according to their corresponding body zones. Thus we have the *oral stage,* in which sucking and biting are especially important; the *anal stage,* in which mastery first emerges; and the *phallic stage,* during which the child displays aggression and rivalry, culminating in the Oedipus complex (see Chapter 4). The phallic stage is followed by *latency,* a time when strong feelings are muted and the child turns to developing skills.

During the period when a motive first appears, or is especially prominent, excessive frustration or punishment can produce *fixation,* in which the motive becomes rigidly fixed in primitive modes of expression. Fixation at any stage produces enduring effects on adult character: thus Freud spoke of oral, anal, and phallic adult *character types,* the result of fixation at the corresponding developmental stages. The anal character type, Freud theorized, combined the traits of orderliness, stubbornness, and parsimony or stinginess (1908a, IX), the result of fixation at the anal stage. Because of excessive frustrations and punishments, Freud believed, the child's mastery motives of retention and control (originally of feces) became fixated. As that child grows up, the primitive modes of a strong retention-control motive are widely generalized to adult objects: *retaining* money (stinginess), *holding on to* one's own beliefs and opinions (stubbornness), and carefully arranging or *controlling* possessions, schedules, and other people (orderliness).

A critical review of the theory of character types can be found in Fisher and Greenberg (1977).

What Is Sexual about the Libido?

After looking at the different components of the libido, you may well wonder in *what* sense all these motives are sexual. Freud believed that they are all sexual because they all involve a certain kind of satisfaction or pleasure, a pleasure that can be seen most clearly in the case of the sexual motives. Viewed from the outside, this pleasure involves conditions such as warmth, rhythmic or mechanical agitation, possibly muscular exertion (especially with the mastery motive), strong emotions, and (by associative learning) images or ideas (1905c, VII, pp. 209–212). Viewed from the inside, there is both a sensation of tension, unpleasure, or stimulation and then a feeling of pleasure, release, and abolition of tension—all in all, a complex orchestration of tension and release, unpleasure and pleasure. Orgasm is the most obvious example, but to illustrate this end-state of pleasure, Freud also quoted the words of an adult who enjoyed "sensual sucking" such as thumb sucking (E. H., 1920; see also Freud, 1905c, VII, p. 181):

> You cannot put into words what a warm and wonderful feeling flows through your whole body. You are simply out of this world—completely satisfied and unbelievably happy. It is a glorious feeling: you desire nothing but peace—a peace that shouldn't ever be interrupted. It is simply wonderful beyond words: you feel no pain or sorrow, and—ah!—you are transported into another world. (p. 164)

Thus in Freud's view, the libidinal motives all echo sexual arousal and orgasmic satisfaction, though in a muted and modified form. Such echoes survive in some everyday figures of speech and metaphors: dedicated students "love" to "lose themselves" in their studies; an alcoholic is "irresistably driven" to yet another drink; achievement success gives a "warm glow" of satisfaction; some politicians have a "lust" for power; and the tourist industry would have us "love New York." In contrast, ordinary breathing, drinking, or eating just happen, without our being aware of any special satisfaction.

Sometimes breathing, drinking, or eating do take on a libidinal quality, especially if we have been seriously deprived and the incentives are good—a bracing breath of clean, cold air after hours in a stale, smoke-filled room; a glass of ice water on a hot and dusty day; or a spicy pizza when we are especially hungry. In these special cases, self-preservation and libidinal motives seem to be fused together. Such fusions come about because the libidinal motives often first seek the same objects (*cathexes*, in Freudian terms) that gratify self-preservation motives, and the two groups of motives often involve some of the same parts of the body. Thus we eat not only to stay alive but also to get a special, "libidinal" pleasure from the incorporation of food (and also from seeing, smelling, and tasting the food; from being with friends, and so forth).

The fact that these libidinal motives often reinforce our self-preservation motives probably conveys an important evolutionary advantage: with these "surplus" motives, we will be sure to "want" to do the things that we need to do in order to stay alive. There is also a negative side to this fusion of self-preservation and libidinal motives, because the conflicts, disturbances, and compulsions of our libidinal motives may spill over into disturbances in our self-preservation functions—hyperventilation (excessive breathing), anorexia (avoidance of food), compulsive eating, or chronic constipation.

Tension, Tension Release, and Pleasure

Many psychologists refer to Freud as a "tension-release" or "tension-reduction" theorist on the grounds that he believed that pleasure meant the reduction or abolition of tension. This is a great oversimplification: Freud's ideas about the relationship between tension and pleasure are more complicated, because he changed them several times.

At first, Freud suggested that everything worked according to a simple mechanism of tension reduction: "Now in every individual there exists a tendency to diminish this sum of [nervous system] excitation once more, in order to preserve his health" (1893, III, p. 36). While such a mechanism might work for hunger or thirst, it clearly will not do for sexual excitement and satisfaction, which involve a mixture of tension *and* release. Freud soon recognized this problem (1905c, VII):

> If, however, the tension of sexual excitement is counted as an unpleasurable feeling, we are at once brought up against the fact that it is also undoubtedly felt as pleasurable. In every case in which tension is produced by sexual processes it is accompanied by pleasure. . . . How, then, are this unpleasurable tension and this feeling of pleasure to be reconciled? (p. 209)

Freud's 1905 solution involved the concept of *fore pleasure*: we initially seek and get a small increment in pleasure, which leads to a bigger increase in tension, and so on, until we reach a final, highest *end pleasure* that brings with it a great reduction of tension. (Freud called this small initial fore-pleasure that gets us going and keeps us going an "incentive bonus.") Thus, Freud concluded, "sexual tension and pleasure can only be connected in an indirect manner" (1905c, VII, p. 212).

In later years, Freud recognized problems with this revised formulation. For example, with many motives the *increase* of tension is more prominent than any final decrease. Thus the sexual instincts often work *against* falling levels of stimulation by introducing fresh tension (Freud, 1923, XIX, p. 47). By 1924, Freud admitted the distance still to be traveled and suggested a more complex approach (1924b, XIX):

> It cannot be doubted that there are pleasurable tensions and unpleasurable relaxations of tension. . . . Pleasure, and unpleasure, therefore, cannot be referred to an increase or decrease of a quantity . . . it appears that they depend, not on this quantitative factor, but on some characteristic of it which we can only describe as a qualitative one. If we were able to say what this qualitative characteristic is, we should be much further advanced in psychology. Perhaps it is the rhythm, the temporal sequence of changes, rises and falls in the quantity of stimulus. We do not know. (p. 160)

He repeated this conception fifteen years later in the *Outline of Psychoanalysis*, his final theoretical statement published shortly after his death: "What is felt as pleasure or unpleasure is not the *absolute* height of this tension but something in the rhythm of the changes in them" (1940, XXIII, p. 146).

From this brief survey, I hope you agree that Freud was anything but a simple tension-reduction theorist! Libidinal "pleasure" involves a special kind of arousal and satisfaction, mixing increases and decreases of tension in complex temporal patterns.

THE AGGRESSIVE MOTIVES OR DEATH INSTINCTS

Freud believed that our motives were not all of the same kind, and so as we have seen he grouped motives into two classes. After about 1920, however, he radically revised his earlier grouping. Self-preservation (ego) motives and libidinal motives were now combined into a single group called *Eros*, or the life instincts, in opposition to the aggressive, destructive, or "death instincts," later termed *Thanatos*, from the Greek word for death, by other writers.

Freud did not make such a fundamental change in his thinking casually or quickly. Back in 1908 in a dispute with Alfred Adler (an errant disciple whose "mistake" was to stress the importance of an aggressive will to power), Freud explicitly stated, "I cannot bring myself to assume the existence of a special aggressive instinct alongside of the familiar instincts of self-preservation and of sex, and on equal footing with them" (1909a, X, p. 140). By 1920, however, Freud had accumulated several reasons for proposing such a "special aggressive instinct." First, the separation of self-preservation and libido had begun to break down. We have already seen how these two kinds of motives share the same objects and are often fused, as in the case of the "extra pleasure" of a gourmet meal. The phenomenon of *narcissism* indicated even more profound connections between the two original motive groups. Narcissism is a condition in which the ego or self is the sole object of the libidinal motives,[4] so self-

---

[4] In the Greek myth, Narcissus was in love with himself. While gazing fondly at his own reflection in a pool of water, he fell in and drowned.

preservation and libidinal motives almost completely overlap (see Chapter 9). Given Freud's principle that the structure of the normal is revealed by extreme and unusual cases, then the ego must be the *original* object of the libidinal motives for everyone. In the course of normal development, libidinal motives are directed outward, as *object choice;* but after stress, loss, or illness, they often withdraw back into the self. In Freudian terms, object choice regresses to narcissism. These considerations led Freud to the conclusion that there was no fundamental distinction between the two original motive groups. Still, he felt "a kind of conviction, for which I was not as yet able to find reasons, that the instincts could not all be of the same kind" (1930, XXI, p. 118).

Freud's second reason for rearranging his classification of motives stemmed from the problem presented by sadism, or the desire to inflict pain on another person, and its passive counterpart masochism, or the desire to have pain inflicted on one's self. To be sure, sadism often has a sexual tinge, but its real aim seems to be quite different from that of libidinal motives. As Freud put it, sadism "could not hide its close affinity with instincts of mastery which have no libidinal purpose" (1930, XXI, p. 117).

Freud's third reason involved people's compulsion to repeat obviously painful experiences. Examples include repeated traumatic dreams by people who have suffered accidents, reproduction of painful experiences by patients in therapy, and even people's love of watching tragedy on the theatrical stage. While Freud's reasoning is difficult to follow, Freud discerned in these cases the work of a new motive force: a person's desire to "work over" an overwhelming experience in order to master it after the fact. Freud viewed this desire as an inherent urge *to restore an earlier state of things,* and argued that such a motive ultimately leads us back toward the inorganic state that preceded life itself—that is, toward death. Thus for Freud, the life instincts and death instincts were complementary motives, psychological analogues of the complementary biological processes of anabolism and catabolism (building up and tearing down of living cells).

Finally, Freud's thoughts in 1920 about a death instinct were deeply influenced by World War I, through which he had just lived. Like so many people in Europe, Freud had greeted the outbreak of war in 1914 with enthusiasm and a burst of patriotism. "All my libido is given to Austria-Hungary," he wrote to his Hungarian colleague Sandor Ferenczi on August 23, shortly after the Austro-Hungarian invasion of Serbia that began the war (quoted in Jones, 1953–1957, vol. 2, p. 192). Four years of war brought disillusionment. Like many other European thinkers, Freud emerged from these years of stalemate, privation, and previously unimagined human carnage with a strong commitment to peace. In an exchange of public letters with Albert Einstein, Freud wrote (1933c, XXII, p. 213):

> We react to war in this way because everyone has a right to his own life, because war puts an end to human lives that are full of hope, because it brings individual men into humiliating situations, because it compels them against their will to murder other men, and because it destroys precious material objects which have been produced by the labors of humanity.

Invasion, slaughter, destruction, and atrocity now seemed so prominent that they surely must reflect some fundamental human motive. Freud wrote, "I can no longer understand how we can have overlooked the ubiquity of nonerotic aggressivity and destructiveness and can have failed to give it due place in our interpretation of life" (1930, XXI, p. 120).

Freud's idea of a death instinct aroused even greater opposition than his earlier ideas of childhood sexuality. Some later psychoanalytic theorists have given aggressive and destructive instincts a prominent place in their ideas (see Klein, 1948; and members of the object relations school, for example, Fairbairn, 1952), but many others have had serious doubts about the concept. You may therefore wonder why it is worth studying today.

When he separated the death or aggressive instincts from the libidinal or love instincts, Freud was really suggesting that human social motives were of two kinds. One kind involves love or positive ties between people; the other is based on relations of mastery or control. Freud's distinction between aggressive and libidinal motives, when expressed in these more general terms, is very much alive in contemporary personality psychology under the labels of "agentic" and "communal," or "power" and "affiliation," motives. (These will be discussed in the next two chapters.) While Freud's particular label of "death instinct" may not be fashionable,[5] his basic insight that our aggressive and control motives are fundamentally different from our loving or affiliative motives *is* very much in fashion.

Freud's writings on the death instinct or death instincts are speculative and sketchy. Though he never worked out a detailed series of components, as with the libido, we can extract some description of the major forms of this mysterious group of motives from scattered references in his writings (see Table 3.1).

(A-1) Mastery and (A-2) cruelty. Clearly, mastery and cruelty now belong in the group of death instincts. Often these two motives are involved in love, sex, and other libidinal actions, but this is only because many libidinal and aggressive motives are fused together in varying proportions, or alloys. As we have seen, sadism is an alloy of childhood genital sexuality and cruelty, and the instinct for research is a socially useful alloy of scopophilia and mastery.

(A-3) Destructiveness. This is probably the purest form of the death instinct. Directed inward, it produces pain and even death (as by suicide); directed outward, it leads to killing other people (or animals) and destroying objects. In all cases, the goal is to tear down, to change what is alive into something that is not alive, to reduce organized structures to a random jumble.

---

[5]Freud's original labels may even be consistent with recent biological research on a "death gene" that carries out programmed cell death as a necessary consequence of sexual reproduction (see Margolis, 1994).

(A-4) Property and possessions. For Freud, the desire for property originates in desires for mastery and control of feces at the anal stage. Later, private
property becomes a strong instrument of human aggression, often displayed
in "the indifference and the arrogance of the well-to-do" (1930, XXI, p. 113).

(A-5) Observation, monitoring, and control and (A-6) critical judging.
These are outgrowths of mastery. Turned inward, they lead to harsh self-
criticism and self-denial; turned outward, they produce a critical, "negative"
personality. (Couch and Keniston, 1960, later described and measured this
negative or "nay-saying" style.)

(A-7) Rewarding and punishing. Depending on which way the critical
judgment goes, reward or punishment follows as a further form of control.
You will probably agree that punishment involves mastery or even cruelty, but
the ability to reward people also implies having some control over them.

(A-8) Nurturance and help. Nurturance and help usually sustain life.
When you read that Freud considered them components of an aggressive
motive or a death instinct, you may feel that we have reached the point of
absurdity. You may wonder whether, in psychoanalytic theory, *everything* turns
out to be its opposite! There is, however, one subtle way in which nurturance
or helping others *does* show a disguised trace of mastery and aggressive
motives. When we take care of other people, we are affecting or controlling
their behavior. We may call it "guidance" and believe that it is for their own
good; yet giving someone guidance means that their behavior, at least in part
and for the moment, is a function of our wishes rather than theirs. In a small
way, the other person is inanimate—an object rather than a living being. And
for Freud, such a result is a sign of an aggressive motive, fused with libidinal
motives and directed outward.

Of course the moment of giving help passes, and if we really want to keep
helping, we will encourage the other person to take back control; this is called
"empowering" them. Yet even here some aggressive roots of helping can often
be seen. What starts out as help or protection "for their own good" can easily
end up as overprotection and domination. Think about people who receive
help: sometimes they respond not with the gratitude that the helper expects,
but rather with feelings, words, and actions that would be expected in
response to others' power or mastery attempts.

When we *really* want to help other people, then, we must get out of their
way. From a Freudian perspective, this removing ourselves could be seen as
the death instinct turned back inward and experienced as a "duty to die" (in
the controversial words of a former Colorado governor; see "Gov. Lamm
asserts," 1984; also Kass, 1983), in order to leave room and resources for the
next generation. This connection between death and growth, which is prominent in Indian philosophy, was also introduced by the Russian psychoanalyst
Sabina Spielrein in a paper entitled "Destruction as the Cause of Being" (1912).

ORGANIZATION OF MOTIVES

Freud's basic list of fourteen motives (Table 3.1) can be organized in a two-dimensional framework, as shown in Figure 3.1. The aggressive motives or death instincts are the vertical axis, while the libidinal motives are the horizontal dimension (arrows at the end of solid lines). Various combinations or alloys of the two classes of motives are indicated as vectors coming out from the central point of origin in different directions (arrows at the end of dotted lines). Such a two-dimensional arrangement of motives was actually anticipated by Freud when he quoted a suggestion of the physicist G. C. Lichtenberg that the two basic human motives of "bread" (self-preservation) and "fame" could be arranged as the four main points of a compass. All other motives could then "be arranged like the thirty-two winds [points of the compass] and might be given names in a similar way: for instance, 'bread-bread-fame' or 'fame-fame-bread'" (Freud, 1905b, VIII, p. 86; see also 1933c, XXII, p. 210). Thus in Figure 3.1, I have located the nurturance motive as a combination of both the libido and the aggression or mastery motives, while outright killing is an alloy of aggression and *low* (or "negative") libido. We will return to this circular

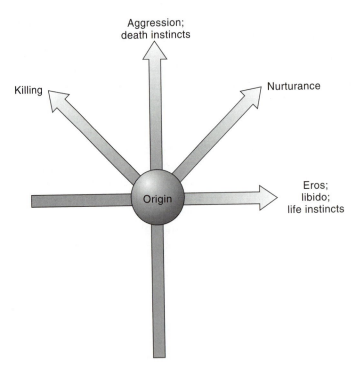

FIGURE 3.1
Two-dimensional organization of Freud's major motives.

arrangement of Freud's two groups of motives over the next two chapters, in discussing other theories and research.

TRANSFORMATIONS OF LIBIDINAL AND AGGRESSIVE MOTIVES

You can easily think of many actions that don't seem to stem from any of these fourteen motives: the musical genius of Mozart, the dedicated scientific curiosity of Marie Curie, or the strange mixture of altruism and love of adventure that led German businessman Oskar Schindler to save over 1,000 Jews from the death camps of the Nazi Holocaust. If the motives of Freud's list are really intended to give an adequate explanation of all these behaviors, then these motives will have to be considerably transformed and modified—perhaps so much that they may not even be recognizable at first.

Did Freud believe that *all* behavior is motivated? Is no act left to chance, or too trivial to be worth explaining? Like most scientists, Freud began with the assumption that everything has a cause. He then applied this assumption systematically, even relentlessly, to all of human behavior. No action was too obscure or too trivial to be exempt from the analysis of motives: people's errors or lapses of memory, slips of the tongue, bungled actions, free associations and stream of thought, choices, and interests (1901, VI); their daydreams and night dreams (1900, IV-V); their jokes (1905b, VIII) and bizarre symptoms (1905a, VII; 1909c, X); the form and content of their works of art (1907a, IX); and the beliefs and rituals of their religion and culture (1913b, XIII). Freud believed that all these are expressions, however disguised, of people's underlying motives.[6]

If we claim that all behavior is motivated, we must admit that the motives are often not obvious. People give a lot of strange answers to the question, "Why did you do that?" If an action is trivial, they are likely to deny having any motive at all. Moreover, people do not like to acknowledge selfish, unworthy, or "bad" motives. Instead, they suggest motives that put their behavior and themselves in the best possible light, no matter how implausible the explanation becomes. Often people simply answer, "I don't know." In such cases, therefore, if people's actions really are motivated, then the motives are not known to them and not obvious to an observer. If there are motives, in short, they must be *unconscious* ones. To understand how motives could be unconscious, we must introduce the psychoanalytic concepts of anxiety and the subsystems of personality.

---

[6]Actually Freud did limit his search for motives to those actions and outcomes over which the person has some control. For example, Freud was once driven to the wrong house by a cab driver. What did it mean? "I of course explain the occurrence as an accident without any further meaning" (1901, VI, p. 257). Without any meaning, at any rate, so far as *Freud's* motives are concerned; but he might have tried to determine the *cab driver's* motives for the "mistake," or even, to push it further, why he himself did not notice that the driver was taking him to the wrong address.

Anxiety

Most of our goals are inherently unrealistic. Freud believed that all motives originally seek pleasure without limit or constraint of reality, only for selfish ends and never for the sake of another. Now in almost any realistic world, with competing claims on limited physical and psychological resources, such motives will quickly fail and lead to pain. Thus many of our desires will go unsatisfied for lack of resources. Further, we are likely to encounter rivals (originally, perhaps, a sibling or same-sex parent) for the most prized resources (originally, perhaps, the opposite-sex parent). We quickly discover that some desires are punished rather than rewarded. Thus our original motives inevitably lead to more pain than pleasure, to anxiety as the anticipation of pain rather than anticipations of happiness.

Id, Ego, and Superego: Freud's Subsystems of Personality

Originally, Freud divided the mind into conscious, unconscious, and preconscious regions. He believed that motives that aroused anxiety remained in the unconscious. Other motives were in the preconscious, until the person's focused attention made them conscious. By about 1923, however, Freud suggested that three personality subsystems or processors develop in order to alleviate this anxiety, to square motives with reality, and to achieve some pleasure without too much pain. These are the id, ego, and superego, to use the Latin words employed by Freud's English translators. Freud's most complete account of these three systems is given in his *New Introductory Lectures on Psychoanalysis* (1933b, XXI, pp. 57–80). The three subsystems are illustrated in Figure 3.2.

The *id* represents our original, unmodified motives. Since it is usually barred from becoming conscious, we experience it as an alien and impersonal force—hence Freud's German term *das Es* or "the it." The id operates according to the *primary process*—solely by the expression of impulse, desire, and pleasure. This means that perceptions and memory traces "float" as random images, connecting themselves only by similarity and association rather than according to sequence, logic, cause-and-effect, or any kind of organized structure. The id has no sense of time or negation.

A person equipped only with an id system could not long survive in the world, since the id cannot distinguish hallucinations from reality. Through contact with the external world, however, part of the id develops into the *ego*. (Nowadays most psychoanalytic theorists believe that the ego is actually present at birth.) Although some parts of the ego are not conscious, it is the seat of our conscious awareness—hence Freud's German term *das Ich* or "the I." The ego operates according to the *secondary process*, which includes language, cognition and judgment, organized memory, time, causality, and negation. Because the ego is in contact with reality, it can recognize dangers, anticipate pain and punishments, modify motives, and direct action. Thus the ego functions as a kind of executive, securing as much gratification as possible for id

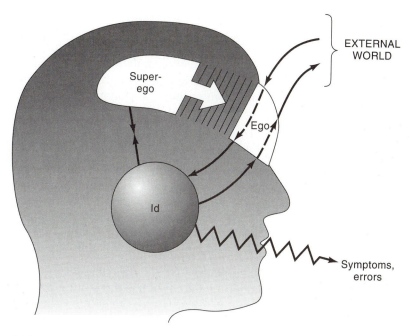

FIGURE 3.2
Id, ego, and superego subsystems of personality. As suggested by the figure, the *id* is not in touch with external reality, except (to some extent) in cases of slips and errors, or extreme cases of delusions and symptoms. The *superego* opposes id desires. While originally formed and later modified by the taking in of external models, it is (usually) neither conscious nor in touch with external reality. The *ego* mediates among the desires of the id, the prohibitions of the superego, and the opportunities and dangers of external reality. It is the seat of consciousness, though many of its operations are unconscious.

impulses while avoiding as much pain as possible. Freud compared the relation between the ego and the id with that between a rider and a horse (1933b, XXII):

> The horse supplies the locomotive energy, while the rider has the privilege of deciding on the goal and of guiding. . . . But only too often there arises between the ego and the id the not precisely ideal situation of the rider being obliged to guide the horse along the path by which it [the horse] itself wants to go. (p. 77)

The efficiency of the ego is greatly improved when, after some experience with pain and punishment, it sets up an internal model of the external rewarding and punishing forces. Freud called this system the *superego* (in German, *Über-ich* or "over-me"). Usually, the superego is constructed on the model of parents, but teachers, authorities, peers, public opinion, and even abstract ideals may be added to or even replace this original model.

Using the energy of several aggressive motives (for example, the observing, judging, rewarding and punishing component motives discussed above), the superego operates as a conscience, monitoring both the wishes of the id and the behavior of the ego. It scrutinizes our fantasies, wishes, and intentions as well as our actions. It punishes when these violate its rules and prohibitions and gives out rewards when these are consistent with its ideals. We are usually not consciously aware of superego functioning, though we sometimes experience it as a voice of conscience from without. We often experience its effects on the ego in the form of the emotions of anxiety, shame, guilt, and occasionally pride. Thus the superego is an efficient way of avoiding anxiety from external punishment, but only at the cost of arousing internal anxiety as a warning signal. For Freud, anxiety can take any of three forms: reality anxiety (stemming from failure or punishment in the real world), moral anxiety (from the punishment of the superego), and neurotic anxiety (from the ego's own fear of the id; 1933b, XXII, pp. 81–94).

Thus the ego's real task is to coordinate id desires, superego prohibitions and ideals, and the opportunities and constraints of reality. In terms of Freud's horse-and-rider analogy, a single rider tries to control three horses, each heading in a different direction! With sufficient *ego strength,* these conflicting demands can be managed and anxieties avoided; but without sufficient ego strength or with an impossibly difficult external world, the ego is vulnerable to being overwhelmed and breaking down in the form of neurosis or psychosis.

Defensive Functioning of the Ego

Figure 3.2 illustrates how the id, ego, and superego systems function and how they are related to each other. The id is not ordinarily in contact with external reality, though occasionally it may slip out in the form of hallucinations, symptoms, or intense daydreams. The superego, gradually shading off from the ego and suppressing id impulses and desires, is also not in contact with reality. The ego, in order to defend against anxiety, transforms any motives that might arouse anxiety by means of *defense mechanisms.* Defense mechanisms can alter either the ways in which motives are expressed or the way the ego functions (as by affecting perception or memory). Either way, they work to avoid or "defend against" anxiety. If they fail, then the ego is flooded with anxiety. It may then seize upon other defense mechanisms the way emergency workers pile up sandbags against a flood. When defenses function well, however, life seems safe and the ego goes about everyday tasks of perception and action free of anxiety.

THE BASIC DEFENSE MECHANISMS

All defense mechanisms share two characteristics: they are operations of the ego, and they transform either motives or perceptions and memories associated with motives so that these motives or perceptions are no longer available to consciousness and so cannot arouse anxiety. And to be successful, the defense mechanisms themselves have to operate outside of consciousness. While many different defense mechanisms have been identified, in practice it is sometimes difficult to distinguish among them because they overlap and work in combination. Freud himself used a variety of terms, in loose and overlapping ways, to describe particular mechanisms. Later Anna Freud (1895–1982), his daughter, constructed a more systematic and thorough account that has become a classic (1937/1946). Cramer (1991) gives an up-to-date review of theoretical and research developments on the topic of defense mechanisms.

Repression

The first defense mechanism identified by Freud is *repression*, the most basic and most thoroughly studied mechanism. The ego simply bars or obliterates from consciousness the anxiety-arousing wishes, memories, or feelings. While

Anna Freud (1895–1982), who developed our understanding of the mechanisms used by the ego to defend against anxiety. "But the ego is victorious when its defensive measures effect their purpose [of restricting] the development of anxiety . . . thereby establishing the most harmonious relations possible between the id, the super-ego, and the forces of the outside world" (A. Freud, 1937/1946, p. 193).

repression may be effective, it is usually quite inefficient, for the amount of energy needed by the ego to repress something must be equal to the amount of id energy behind that material. Even when successful, therefore, repression drains the ego of energy that might be available for other, more constructive activities. Any decrease in the total energy available to the ego (due to fatigue, sleep, or the influence of alcohol or drugs), or any increase in the demands on the ego (due to distraction or stress), tends to jeopardize and break down previously successful repressions. The result could be a bungled action or speech (popularly called a "Freudian slip") or a sudden eruption of a repressed wish, memory, or feeling that obliterates normal consciousness and control for a time. Dreams are a more familiar example of weakened repressions. According to Freud, dreams result from the following process: Sleep relaxes repressions, so previously repressed wishes are able to push forward with greater energy. Still, they are transformed in other ways by the ego (in what Freud called the "dream work") so as to prevent anxiety and preserve sleep. If these further transformations fail, then the dreamer wakes up with the experience of a nightmare (Freud, 1900, IV–V; see especially chapter 6).

It is important to realize that we do not consciously decide to repress something. The act of repression is itself repressed so that we are simply unaware of any defensive processes at work. (When we are aware that we are trying to avoid saying or thinking something, we are using *suppression* rather than repression.)

Somaticization

Sometimes repressed wishes or feelings seem to be converted into physical or somatic expressions, for example, apparent "symptoms" without any underlying organic problem. In these cases, *somaticization* has replaced repression as a defense. This mechanism was especially common among Freud's earliest patients, many of whom suffered from conversion hysteria (a physical symptom such as paralysis, coughing, a tic, or a disturbance of vision or hearing for which there was no organic or physical basis). Originally, Freud believed that conversion involved the actual switching of energy from "mental" nerve cells to "motor" nerve cells, but over time he emphasized *symbolic* connections between the repressed thought and the physical symptom. In other words, the physical serves as a metaphor for the repressed mental. For example, in the case of an early patient known as Emmy von N., Freud determined that anorexia and gastric pains symbolically represented all of the following: (1) a fear of catching her older brother's tuberculosis from inadvertently using his silverware; (2) disgust at the spittoon on the table, which he had used; (3) a case of dysentery contracted by drinking contaminated water; and (4) childhood battles with her mother about eating meat (Breuer & Freud, 1893–1895, pp. 81–83).

In a broader sense, however, somaticization also includes normal as well as pathological expression of psychological forces in symbolic form, through bodily activity; for example, in dance, sports, exercise, and even saunas and hot tubs! As Martha Graham, the famous modern dancer, put it in her autobiography (1991):

> Many times I hear the phrase, "the dance of life." It is an expression that touches me deeply, for the instrument through which the dance speaks is also the instrument through which life is lived—the human body. It is the instrument by which all the primaries of life are made manifest. It holds in its memory all matters of life and death and love. (p. 4)

A vivid example of nonpathological somaticization can be found in the novel *Zorba the Greek,* by Nikos Kazantzakis (1953). First, the hero Zorba was unable to prevent the brutal murder of a woman in his village. Then his cable railway project collapsed, leaving his dreams in ruins. Finally, Zorba responds as follows:

> "I've hundreds of things to say, but my tongue just can't manage them. So I'll dance them for you! Here goes!"
>   He leaped into the air and his feet and arms seemed to sprout wings. As he threw himself straight in the air against that background of sea and sky, he looked like an old archangel in rebellion . . . shouting to the sky: "What can you do to me, Almighty? . . . I've vented my spleen, I've said all I want to say; I've had time to dance . . . and I don't need you any more!" (pp. 290–291)

Somatic conversion might begin with a temporary organic condition such as a cold or minor injury. Drawing the attention of the ego, this illness becomes a foundation upon which symptoms are constructed to express the repressed motive or thought. Sometimes the symptom or body state expresses three things: the prohibition itself, the forbidden element, and the anxiety that would have resulted from its expression.

Regression

Regression is an alternative to repression. Here the anxiety-arousing wish is actually given up, and its place taken by an earlier wish that does not arouse anxiety. This mechanism is especially prominent during children's development from one psychosexual stage to the next. As a newly emerging motive encounters new punishments, the ego "retreats" to the well-established and safer motives of an earlier stage. For example, a child who experiences problems and worries in school may regress to thumb sucking and other gratifications of an earlier stage of development. And many people find that taking a nap, eating a snack, or watching adventure television shows are convenient (if temporary) forms of regression.

Denial

Repression bars from consciousness certain motives, memories, and feelings internal to the person. The barring of perceptions of the external world from consciousness is called *denial*, a term first suggested by Anna Freud

(1937/1946). (Sometimes, however, denial is used synonymously with repression.) Denial can take different forms: for example, fantasy, pretending, and daydreaming about a reality that is more pleasant and less threatening. Denial is a principal mechanism in many children's fairy tales, and is also the basis of such grown-up fantasies as James Thurber's "The Secret Life of Walter Mitty."

Denial is made easy by the magical words "no" and "not." When added to any statement about an anxiety-arousing wish, feeling, or perception, these words permit us to express the wish, yet evade the consequences of anxiety: because we did *not* have the wish, we do *not* feel that way, and the perception is *not* true. This *negation* involves a partial lifting of the denial or repression, so that we achieve "a kind of intellectual acceptance of the repressed, while at the same time what is essential to the repression persists" (Freud, 1925b, XIX, p. 236).

Denial has a cost. Since the main purpose of the ego is to perceive, recognize, and then critically evaluate reality, denying that reality jeopardizes normal functioning. If the denial process leads to renunciation of contact with reality, then the ego has started down the path to psychosis.

Reaction Formation

Because they attempt to abolish anxiety-arousing material, repression and denial are simple, elementary defenses. If successful, they leave no traces. Other defenses transform the anxiety-arousing material in more complex ways. Typically the original wish, thought, or feeling remains available to consciousness but is disguised so that it no longer arouses anxiety. In the case of *reaction formation*, the wish is changed into its opposite. For example, a desire to be very messy becomes the desire to be completely neat; voyeurism becomes a crusade against sex in books and television; hatred appears as love.

Reaction formation embodies an idea that is very important in psychoanalysis: that opposites are actually the same, or very similar. We have already seen this principle in the mechanism of denial: that "I am not angry" is equivalent to "I am angry." Freud wrote about this principle in many different contexts. For example, in interpreting dreams he suggested that "every element of a dream can, for purposes of interpretation, stand for its opposite just as easily as for itself" (1900, V, p. 471). He was fascinated with the fact that in many ancient languages, the same word is sometimes used to describe contraries. For example, the Latin word *altus* means both "high" and "deep," and the English word "taboo" (borrowed from the Polynesian languages) means both "sacred" and "unclean." Many societies and cultures that revere and protect a tabooed totem animal as a symbol of their common ancestors *also* on ritual occasions kill and eat this animal (Freud, 1913b, XIII). Thus if love and hate are in some sense the same, or ambivalent, and if expressing hatred would arouse anxiety, then the hatred could be reversed to become the "safer" alternative of love. (It could work the other way, too. If expressing love would arouse anxiety, then reaction formation would change love to "safe hate.")

The concept of the unity of opposites is one of the most controversial aspects of Freudian theory. If any given act can express either a motive or a reaction formation against its opposite, then can't anything mean anything? Not exactly. Love and hate do share two things, an emotional intensity and a directed focus of concern. Neither emotion is indifferent to its object. Thus for both the SPCA and the person who kicks the family pet, animals are *emotionally important objects*. Both the voyeur and the antipornography crusader share an intense concern with looking at (or looking at other people looking at) sexually arousing stimuli. But even if reaction formation can change a motive into its opposite, this does not mean that anything can be changed into anything. A reaction formation cannot change a strong motive into indifference, the state of being able to "take it or leave it."

Turning against the Self and Related Mechanisms

Turning against the self preserves the essential nature of the motive but changes the object to the self. For example, aggression that might arouse anxiety if directed outward (as in the rage of a child toward a parent) is "safe" when directed against the self. Thus the desire to punish a parent is transformed into the need to be punished by the parent, which may lead the child to act in ways that elicit punishment from the parent. Superficially, this looks like a reaction formation against aggression; in fact, however, it is the object of aggression rather than the aggression motive itself that has been changed.

Turning inward is thus a special case of a more general mechanism of *displacement*, or change of object. Other possible displacements of the child's aggression toward a parent might include kicking the family dog, yelling at classmates in school, or attacking a familiar and "safe" toy. In terms of the psychology of learning, displacement involves "stimulus generalization": the more similar the displaced object is to the original, the greater the potential for motive satisfaction—but also the greater the potential for anxiety. As the displacement moves toward less similar objects, anxiety drops off sooner than motive satisfaction. Experimental studies of conflict (see Miller, 1959) predict that a motive will be displaced to an object in which satisfaction and anxiety are balanced, as shown in Figure 3.3.

Turning against the self also involves mechanisms of *introjection* and *identification*, in which one person "takes in" or becomes another person (or thing). Thus the child who has turned aggression back on herself may also, through identification, imagine herself to be the punishing parent at the same time that she is the punished child. This permits some gratification of the child's original aggressive motive, at the same time that it punishes (1) the self, for having that motive, and (2) the internalized parent, as the original object of the aggressive motive.

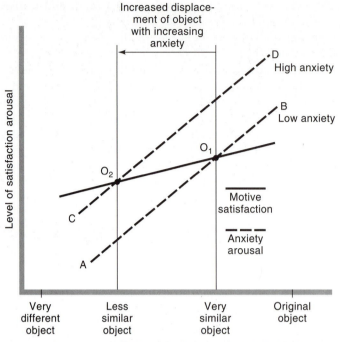

Note: Both motive satisfaction and anxiety increase as the object of the motive becomes more like the "real" original object, but anxiety increases more sharply. As similarity decreases, anxiety drops off more sharply. Thus the motive will be displaced to an object at that point where satisfaction balances anxiety.

Increases in anxiety (represented by changing from line *AB* to line *CD*) would increase motive displacement from O_1 to O_2—that is, to a less similar object. This will also decrease the level of motive satisfaction.

FIGURE 3.3
Resolution of conflicts between approach and avoidance motives (based on Miller, 1959, p. 207).

Projection

In *projection*, the nature of the motive or wish remains the same, but it is attributed to (or "projected onto") someone else. As a result, the wish enters consciousness as a perception of the external world rather than as an internal wish of the self. Projection is thus the opposite of introjection or identification. Both mechanisms involve an alteration in the sense of self and not-self, what is ego and what is world. Since this distinction is one of the earliest and most important things that we learn, the mechanisms of projection and identification may have roots in the child's earliest experiences. Object-relations theorists such as

Melanie Klein. A major theorist of the neo-Freudian object relations school. "Another stimulus for an increase of introjection is the phantasy that the loved object may be preserved in safety inside oneself. In this case the dangers of the inside are projected on to the external world" (Klein, 1948, p. 284).

Klein (1948) and Fairbairn (1952) suggest that the infant originally tries to include everything pleasant, "good," and powerful as part of the self (introjection), while expelling everything painful, anxiety-arousing, and "bad" out into the abyss of the not-self (projection).

Rationalization

Projection is often carried further by the mechanism of *rationalization*. If I project my anger at another person onto that person, then I am not angry at them, but rather they are angry at me. Now if they are angry at me, then my own angry feelings and wishes, in addition to being projected outward, can be retained and consciously acknowledged, as a reasonable and appropriate reaction to their anger. Since "they started it," I am justified in fighting back. This combination of projection and rationalization can be seen in children's explanations of playground fights. Unfortunately, it is also common among adults, especially political leaders. For example, when Adolf Hitler began World War II by ordering German troops to invade Poland on September 1, 1939, he justified his action as a "counterattack."

Isolation and Intellectualization

So far we have considered defenses that operate by altering the motive or the object in some way. *Isolation* disguises the anxiety-arousing motive by a kind of camouflage. One kind of isolation cuts the connections between the motive-related thoughts and actions and their context, so that the *meaning* is lost, along with the associated anxiety. Camouflaged in this way, thoughts and actions can be repeated over and over again, enabling the person to obtain gratification without arousing anxiety. These repetitions are called *obsessive thoughts* or *compulsive rituals.* As an example, consider a child in whom the desire to masturbate arouses anxiety. Associated with this desire are several different actions reflecting aspects of sexual gratification, such as rhythmic motion or tension rising to a peak and falling off (tumescence-detumescence). Through isolation, one of these actions, say any action that involves rhythmic repetition, is taken out of its original sexual context and instead put into some other nonsexual setting: rhythmically tapping a pencil, swinging a foot, or scratching an arm. Now the conscious meaning of the act has been camouflaged, and anxiety is avoided. The tapping, swinging, or scratching can be repeated over and over again, as a disguised and therefore "safe" source of masturbatory satisfaction.

Another kind of isolation involves cutting the connections between an action and the feelings or emotions normally associated with it. Once again, the action can be repeated over and over again; because it has no emotional significance, it does not arouse anxiety. The cut-off or "isolated" emotions, in turn, may become attached to some other action that originally had no emotional significance but now is laden with transferred emotions and energy. For example, a child may develop a fear of going to school, not because of anything about school but because the emotion of fear has been redirected from some other action.

When displacement is added to isolation, the possibilities for disguise become almost endless. Sometimes the isolated emotion is displaced onto an abstract idea so that the original motive is expressed through intellectual contemplation. This mechanism is called *intellectualization,* a kind of compulsive thinking or brooding that never seems to go anywhere but just circles around and around itself.

Undoing

Sometimes a repeated action represents a symbolic *undoing* of the original anxiety-arousing wish. This is different from reaction formation in that instead of reversing the original wish, it attempts to reverse or mitigate the consequences of that wish. Shakespeare's character Lady Macbeth is a classic example of attempted undoing. Having urged her husband to kill King Duncan, she recoils in horror from that murder. She does *not* renounce violence and protest her love for Duncan (which would be a reaction formation), but rather tries to wash her hands clean of the imaginary, symbolic blood:

> Out, damned spot! Out, I say! . . .
> What, will these hands ne'er be clean? . . .
> Here's the smell of blood still: all the perfumes of Arabia will not sweeten this little hand.

(Macbeth, act 5, scene 1)

COMBINATIONS OF DEFENSE MECHANISMS

Defense mechanisms often act in combination or in a series, leading to transformations of the original motive that are quite complex and difficult to unravel. We have already seen how turning against the self is a combination of displacement, introjection, and identification. There are two other such combinations.

Identification with the Aggressor

Here the person seems to abandon the original motive or wish, and instead takes on the characteristics of the feared external person (the aggressor or oppressor) whose threats or punishments arouse anxiety about the wish. Anna Freud gave the example of a little girl who had been afraid to cross the hall at home because she was scared of seeing ghosts. Suddenly, however, she hit on a way to overcome her fear: as she later triumphantly explained to her little brother, "There's no need to be afraid in the hall; you just have to pretend you're the ghost who might meet you" (1937/1946, pp. 118–119). Similarly, a child who is scared of lions might "become" a lion, complete with attacking gestures and a loud roar.

One of the most vivid and disturbing examples of identification with the aggressor comes from the observations of the psychoanalyst Bruno Bettelheim. Bettelheim, a Jew, was imprisoned in Dachau and Buchenwald concentration camps just before World War II. As a way to maintain a sense of integration and self-respect, he drew on his professional training to study the changes taking place in his fellow prisoners (Bettelheim, 1943/1958). He observed that most concentration camp inmates simply tried to endure the appalling and brutal conditions. With luck, skills, and above all mutual aid, a few survived. After a long time in the camps, however, many prisoners began to imitate the behavior of the Nazi guards, copying gestures, manner, verbal expressions, and tone of voice. They even tried to make their ragged prison garments look like the guards' uniforms. The camp officials used these kapos, or prisoner-guards, to enforce camp rules and punish their fellow inmates.

These prisoners had apparently sold out. Why? Under massive threat and anxiety, they introjected, or *identified with,* the source of the threat, in this case the guards. This identification made possible a *change from the passive role to an active role:* instead of being threatened prisoners, they became the concentration camp guards who made the threat.[7] Any "bad" wish (something the guards might punish) could be avoided; further, it could be *projected* on to someone else, typically another prisoner, and punished by the kapo. This complex sequence of defenses is one common (though by no means universal)

---

[7]This is another example of Freud's observation, discussed above, that motives tend to move from passive to active forms.

reaction to extreme oppression and cruelty: in concentration camps, in chattel slavery (Elkins, 1959), and in milder form among colonized peoples who become "more English than the English," or servants who imitate and identify with their masters. In fact, Freud believed that identification with the aggressor is a nearly universal phenomenon; the parent, perceived by the child as harsh and oppressive, becomes introjected as the first superego.

Altruistic Surrender

In the combination of defenses known as *altruistic surrender*, first discussed by Anna Freud, the original anxiety-arousing motive is *projected* onto someone else, with whom the person then *identifies*. Thus the original wish achieves vicarious or substitute gratification and no longer arouses anxiety because it only exists in the life of another person. In fact, people who have made an altruistic surrender often *insist* that the other person's motive (really, their own projected wish) be satisfied. What was unacceptable as something "inside" can demand satisfaction, without hindrance or anxiety, when it is felt to be safely "outside." To other people, it appears that such people have surrendered their own interests to act altruistically on behalf of someone else. Perhaps you know people who live vicariously through the lives of other people; for example, most parents are fiercely protective and fondly proud of their children. One source of this parental altruism may be that their own renounced wishes can thereby survive in their children's lives. Another common example is the older sibling whose jealousy becomes transformed, through altruistic surrender, into concern and caring for the younger brother or sister.

SUBLIMATION

Sublimation is quite different from the other defense mechanisms we have discussed. In fact, it may not even be a defense. Sublimation is the healthy alteration or displacement of a motive toward some productive and socially useful aim. Sometimes Freud wrote of sublimation as the redirection of motives away from sexual aims; at other times he referred to it as the *neutralization* or desexualization of libidinal energy (1923, XIX, pp. 44–45). In either case, Freud conceived of sublimation as the hallmark of mature functioning. To the individual, sublimation makes possible the growth of competence in ego functions and skills. To society, sublimation makes possible the development of culture and civilization, including works of art and literature, science and technology, religion, and all the other familiar features of any civilization. Sublimation therefore stands apart from the other defense mechanisms as something "higher," healthier, or at least socially more valuable. (The Latin *sublimare* means "to raise.")

Freud's fullest description of sublimation is in his study of the life and work of Leonardo da Vinci (1910a, XI). One example will illustrate how sublimation operates. Most people know at least two things about Leonardo: he painted the portrait of *Mona Lisa del Giocondo*, famous for the subject's enigmatic smile, and he had an insatiable scientific curiosity about everything from anatomy and nature to weapons of war and flying machines. So far as his childhood goes, we know very little more than that he was illegitimate, reared initially by his mother alone but then (by age 5) by his father and stepmother. To Freud, both the mysterious smile of the Mona Lisa and Leonardo's scientific curiosity were sublimations of libidinal instincts dating back to childhood. Leonardo's ordinary childhood curiosity about where babies come from and the role of the father, strengthened by his unusual family history, escaped the inhibitions that so often befall children's curiosity about sex. In later life it expanded into a wide variety of areas, many of them with symbolic links to their original sexual focus (for example, anatomy itself, and flying, which Freud viewed as symbolic of the erection of the penis). And in the smile of Signora del Giocondo, Freud wrote, Leonardo saw a combination of reserve and seduction—tenderness and menace—that reawakened the memory of his birth mother (1910a, XI):

> Influenced by this revived memory . . . [and] with the help of the oldest of all his erotic impulses he enjoyed the triumph of once more conquering the inhibition in his art. . . . Only a man who had had Leonardo's childhood experiences could have painted the Mona Lisa. (pp. 134, 136)

Thus Leonardo's artistic skill made possible a sublimation of the evoked memory of his mother, just as Leonardo's intelligence made possible a sublimation of sexual curiosity into scientific investigation.

SPECULATIONS ABOUT RICHARD NIXON'S DEFENSE MECHANISMS

We have discussed the defense mechanisms as separate processes. By taking another look at Richard Nixon's words, we can see all or most of them operating together in the life of a real person. Since we lack information about Richard Nixon's early anxieties, conflicts, and Oedipus complex, the best place to observe his defense mechanisms is during the heavily documented last two years of his presidency, from the Watergate break-in (June 17, 1972) to his resignation (August 9, 1974). The historical record shows that during this period, Nixon engaged in illegal actions to cover up the break-in. The possibility that these actions might be revealed increased with each passing day. The threats mounted: investigations by the FBI and investigative reporting by the press, grand jury indictments of the burglars and members of Nixon's own staff, Senate committee hearings, a special prosecutor, discovery and publication of Nixon's secret tapes, a House of Representatives judiciary committee vote for his impeachment, and finally the Supreme Court's demand that he release the "smoking

TABLE 3.2 STATEMENTS SUGGESTING RICHARD NIXON'S
DEFENSE MECHANISMS

Repression

"In the year 1972, I am afraid I was too busy . . . that I frankly paid too little attention to the campaign." (Press Conference, March 19, 1974; p. 292)*

Denial

"The White House has had no involvement whatever in this particular incident [Watergate]." (Press Conference, June 22, 1972; p. 691)

"I welcome this kind of examination, because people have got to know whether or not their president is a crook. Well, I am not a crook." (Press Conference, November 17, 1973; p. 956)

Somaticization

In June 1974, Nixon suffered an attack of phlebitis, a painful blood clot and inflammation, in his left leg. If the clot had broken loose, it could easily have been fatal. Nevertheless, Nixon continued with a trip to the Mideast and the Soviet Union. The condition twice recurred shortly after his resignation, in September and October 1974.

Reaction formation

"The action [Watergate] was wrong; the action was stupid. . . . It should not have been covered up, and I have done the very best that I can over the past year to see that it is uncovered." (Press Conference, March 19, 1974; p. 292)

Turning against the self

"Everybody wants to tell the president what to do, and boy, he needs to be told many times." (Speech, August 9, 1974; p. 630)

Projection

"We must reform our political process—ridding it not only of the violations of the law but also of the ugly mob violence and other inexcusable campaign tactics that have been too often practiced and too readily accepted in the past." (Speech, April 30, 1973; p. 332)

---

gun" tape that made his resignation or impeachment certain. Despite every attempt at concealment, the truth slowly emerged. During this period, therefore, we would expect that Nixon used many different defense mechanisms to handle increasing anxiety.

Table 3.2 illustrates some of the major defense mechanisms with Nixon quotations from this period, from official transcripts. Taken somewhat out of context, these brief quotations are no substitute for a clinician's intensive and deep study of defenses, but they will serve as illustrations of the ways in which defense mechanisms can transform motives and feelings.

The examples in the table suggest that Nixon showed most of the major defense mechanisms at least once in his public statements during this period. Some biographers claim that Nixon's most characteristic defense was denial. For example, Brodie (1981) quotes a 1978 Nixon statement on French television as typical: "I was not lying. I said things that later on seemed to be untrue"

TABLE 3.2 (*Continued*)

Rationalization

"I would say only that if some of my judgments were wrong—and some were wrong—
they were made in what I believed at the time to be the best interest of the nation."
(Speech, August 8, 1974; p. 628)

Isolation

"It is also essential that we not be so distracted by events such as this that we neglect
the vital work before us, before this nation . . . at a time of critical importance to
America and the world." (Speech, April 30, 1973; p. 331)

Intellectualization

"Now when we talk about a clean breast [of Watergate], let's look at what has
happened. The FBI assigned 133 agents to this investigation. It followed out 1,800
leads. It conducted 1,500 interviews. [The investigation of U.S. State Department
official Alger Hiss, accused of being a Communist agent, in which Nixon participated
as a member of Congress during the late 1940s] was basically a Sunday School exercise
compared to the amount of effort that was put into this." (Press Conference, October 5,
1972; p. 957)

Undoing

"I urge citizens, all of you, everywhere, to join in working toward a new set of
standards, new rules and procedures to ensure that future elections will be as nearly
free of such abuses as they possibly can be made." (Speech, April 30, 1973; p. 332)

*Page references are to the volume of *Public Papers of the Presidents of the United States:
Richard Nixon* (Washington, D.C.: Government Printing Office) for the year of the
quotation.

(p. 503). Other biographers emphasize Nixon's obsessiveness and suspiciousness (Ambrose, 1991, pp. 585–590), which imply that isolation and projection
are his most prominent defenses. As the examples in Table 3.2 suggest, however, even though people may prefer certain defenses, under extreme stress
they may deploy a broad range of mechanisms.

*A*RE DEFENSES INEVITABLE?

From Freud's perspective, defense mechanisms are inevitable, because our
motives, being selfish and limitless, are bound to conflict with those of other
people in the real world. This conflict between limitless desires and limited
resources is symbolized in Freud's theory of the Oedipus complex. King Oedipus, the tragic hero of Sophocles' play, unknowingly killed his father and married his mother, thereby gratifying every male child's wish for exclusive and
unrivaled possession of all physical and emotional resources (in the form of
the opposite-sex parent), along with the destruction of any rival (the same-sex
parent). For Freud, this play is a "drama of limits," for it is impossible for a

woman to love exclusively both her husband and son. Because they are limit-less and selfish, then, our motives are certain to cause punishment and anxi-ety; hence they are certain to be transformed by one or more mechanisms of defense.

On the other hand, if we do not assume that human motives are inher-ently either limitless or selfish, then conflict between motives and social reality is no longer inevitable, and nondefensive functioning is possible. We shall take up this possibility further in the next chapter, when we consider alternatives to Freudian theory.

DEFENSE MECHANISMS: NEUROTIC OR ADAPTIVE?

At first, the operations of all these defense mechanisms may seem quite patho-logical, since in one way or another they all distort reality, which is usually a sign of neurotic (that is, conflicted or disturbed) functioning. By employing defense mechanisms, the ego may purchase relief from anxiety, but at the cost of reduced effectiveness. For example, Richard Nixon's defenses may have helped him avoid anxiety during his final public crisis, but in the long run an early, honest, and full disclosure of the truth would have been more effective and less costly.

How Defense Mechanisms Are Neurotic

It is true that defense mechanisms can be roots of neuroses. In some of his ear-liest writings, Freud distinguished two groups of defense mechanisms accord-ing to the kind of neurosis that they often precipitated: *hysteria*, involving mainly repression, and *obsessive-compulsive neurosis*, involving mechanisms such as isolation and intellectualization (1894, III; 1896, III). Later clinical and research studies have elaborated the distinction between these two groups of defense mechanisms, as shown in Table 3.3. An alternative way of labeling this distinction is *repressing defenses* (hysteria) and *sensitizing defenses* (obsessive).[8] Repressing defenses are attempts to abolish whatever thoughts, perceptions, or memories cause anxiety. In their extreme form, they are at the root of hyste-ria and various psychosomatic illnesses. In a less extreme form, they are asso-ciated with slowness and inaccuracy at perceiving and remembering anything that is associated with anxiety. Even when they are not neurotic, such people can be said to have a hysterical *style*.

Sensitizing defenses, instead of abolishing threatening ideas and emo-tions, effectively remove any threat of anxiety by altering them through rever-sal (reaction formation, undoing), redirecting them (displacement, projection,

---

[8]David Shapiro (1965) gives an excellent discussion of how neurotic styles can show up in every-day behavior. Byrne and his colleagues (Byrne, 1961a; Bell & Byrne, 1978) describe how the repressing-sensitizing distinction can be measured, and how it is associated with individual differ-ences in the processing of anxiety-arousing stimuli and information.

TABLE 3.3 CLASSIFICATION OF DEFENSE MECHANISMS

Hysteria grouping	Obsessive grouping
Defense mechanisms	
Repression	Reaction formation
Somaticization	Projection
Denial	Turning against the self
	Isolation
	Intellectualization
	Undoing
Information-processing style	
Repressor: Motive-relevant material processed *less* effectively than is neutral material	Sensitizer: Motive-element material processed *more* effectively than is neutral material
Neurotic personal style (Shapiro, 1965)	
Cognitions: Diffuse and impressionistic; dominated by feelings; distractable	Cognitions: Rigid and accurate about details, but insensitive to emotional tone
Action: Vivid and colorful; sentimental fantasies; emotional outbursts	Action: Intense, concentrated activity; distrust of intuition and feelings
Control: Suggestible; cannot explain actions	Control: Emphasizes will power and autonomy; resists interference
Associated neurosis	
Conversion hysteria	Obsessive-compulsive neurosis

turning against the self), or taking them out of context (isolation, intellectual-ization). As a result, people who characteristically use these defenses are rela-tively quick and accurate at perception and memory of motive-related mater-ial because these do not arouse anxiety. In fact, such "vigilance" is often important to the successful operation of the defense. Thus someone who defended against the scopophilia motive with a reaction formation might organize a crusade to investigate the presumed "dangerous tide of erotic books," for the purpose of condemning them. In this case the defense mecha-nism *requires* the voyeuristic person to be on the lookout for sexual matters. In their extreme forms, these defenses are at the root of obsessive-compulsive neuroses and paranoia; but in normal people they would appear as a style of vigilance and mild compulsiveness. Thus the two categories of Table 3.3, whether we call them hysterical versus obsessive or repressing versus sensitiz-ing, are useful both for classifying the defense mechanisms and for describing ordinary behavior.

How Defense Mechanisms Are Adaptive

Although they may often be at the root of neuroses, defense mechanisms are not always maladaptive. Some personality psychologists have argued that the processes underlying defense mechanisms can actually help us cope effectively with the problems of day-to-day living. Kroeber (1963) suggests that in the presence of strong anxiety and unconscious inner conflicts, such mechanisms may indeed function defensively; but in dealing with real problems and conscious conflicts, they may be nondefensive and adaptive. In such cases, we might call them *coping mechanisms* instead of defense mechanisms. For example, the coping version of repression and denial is *concentration*—the ability to put aside disturbing feelings, thoughts, and impulses and shut out distracting stimuli until they can be dealt with at the proper time and place—so that we can stick to the task at hand. Similarly, the adaptive form of isolation may involve *objectivity*, the ability to separate ideas from feelings and contexts when objective judgments are necessary. This ability is important for doctors and therapists, who must be able to separate their emotions from their professional judgment when dealing with patients. The defense mechanism of rationalization has its coping counterpart in the capacity for *logical analysis*, the careful and systematic use of cause-and-effect thinking. Finally, the adaptive aspect of projection is *empathy*, the ability to put ourselves in other people's shoes and to understand and sympathize with how they think and feel. Consistent with this line of argument, Cramer (1991) suggests that defense mechanisms emerge in the course of normal growth and development to serve adaptive functions. In such cases, we could say that defense mechanisms can sometimes be adaptive sublimations.

Freud (1908b, VIII) believed that certain defenses, when turned in positive directions, made possible important social and cultural accomplishments. Creative writers, for example, make use of processes resembling reaction formation, denial, and projection as they rework and sublimate their private fantasies into fictional characters that capture our imagination. Through the work of creative artists, the audience's deepest wishes, defenses, and conflicts are aroused, transformed, and safely satisfied. Thus art (including music, literature, and drama) has important functions of expression and healing.[9]

Neurotic and Adaptive Defense Mechanisms in Everyday Life

Defense mechanisms play a major part in politics. Harold Lasswell, one of the first to apply psychoanalytic theory to political science, argued that most polit-

---

[9]The psychoanalytic study of the creative artist was explored much more fully in the early writings of Freud's one-time disciple, Otto Rank. Unfortunately, most of Rank's work on this topic is in untranslated German. Two relevant works translated into English are *The Don Juan Legend* (1924/1975) and *Art and Artist* (1932). By the time he wrote this latter book, however, Rank had modified and rejected a good deal of his earlier psychoanalytic theory as he broke with Freud. Holland (1968) and Kiehl (1963) also discuss psychoanalytic interpretations of art and literature.

ical leaders acted from "private motives, displaced on to public objects, ratio-
nalized in terms of the public interest" (1930, p. 75). George and George (1956)
applied Lasswell's analysis to interpret some puzzling aspects of the career of
President Woodrow Wilson. In many contexts and on many issues, Wilson
showed a blend of idealism, strength of purpose, and flexibility that was crucial to his many political successes. On some issues, though, Wilson seems to
have defeated himself. Thus, although he strongly supported U.S. membership in the new League of Nations after World War I, his rigidity and refusal to
compromise were largely responsible for the Senate's 1920 rejection of the proposal that the United States join the League. Ostensibly Wilson acted only in
the public interest, out of idealistic motives; in one speech, for example, he
claimed that "If I felt that I personally in any way stood in the way of this set-
tlement, I would be glad to die that it might be consummated." At the root of
Wilson's self-defeating stubbornness about the League, however, the Georges
discerned several private themes and motives: Wilson's identification with his
demanding and ridiculing father, a reaction formation to this identification,
and finally the displacement of aggression from the original target (his father)
onto his political opponents (see also Greenstein, 1969/1987, chap. 3; see also
Winter, 1992b, for a recent review of psychological studies of Wilson).

For many people, religious practices and other rituals and ceremonies
involve mechanisms of isolation and displacement (Freud, 1907b, IX). In these
cases, however, the rituals have become public ceremonies integrated into cultural institutions and customs at the center of human life. For our ancestors,
plowing and planting alternated with harvesting and hunting. Nowadays,
many rituals are driven by technology: the rhythm of the school year, the
repetitive routines of office and factory, the familiar cycle of television schedules, sports seasons, parties, and holidays. Displaced motives and isolated
actions are woven into a fabric and context of tradition that gives meaning to
our present by linking it to past and future.

From the broadest perspective, therefore, the Freudian concept of defense
means much more than pathological mechanisms that distort reality and cause
neurosis or psychosis. In less extreme form, directed toward real threats as
well as inner anxieties, defense mechanisms can be found throughout our
lives, in our individual styles of coping as well as our collective social institutions.

4

Beyond Freud: Evidence, Critique, and Alternatives

❖

This chapter extends the discussion of Freud's motivation theories in three different ways. First, we will consider how his theories could be scientifically tested, and if so, what evidence supports some of the more central aspects of psychoanalysis. Then we will take a critical look at Freud's theory of women's personality and development. This aspect of Freud's thinking has always been controversial, but with the resurgence of feminist thought in recent decades, it has come under strong attack. My own view is that Freud was quite wrong about women. However, I also think it is useful to understand *how* and *why* he went wrong, to consider whether his theory of women's development is essential to the rest of psychoanalytic theory, and then to suggest an alternative way of incorporating gender into psychoanalytic theory.

Finally, in the last part of this chapter, we will consider some of the major alternatives to Freud's views of motives. Modifications of Freudian theory involving other concepts will be considered at the appropriate place in later chapters—for example, narcissism and self-psychology in Chapter 9, and Erikson's psychosocial theory of personality development in Chapter 18.

TESTING FREUD: SOME RESEARCH EVIDENCE RELEVANT TO PSYCHOANALYTIC THEORY

As we have seen in the last chapter, Freud's psychoanalytic theory is a vast and formidable theoretical structure, consisting of many different concepts, forces, and mechanisms. For this reason it is difficult to do research on psychoanalytic concepts and impossible to prove or disprove such a theory with a few simple experiments. For example, many psychoanalytic concepts are so complicated and elusive that it is not easy to imagine how they might be defined and observed under rigorous research conditions. Further, psychoanalytic theory sometimes gives different future predictions for the same past conditions. For example, people with an anal character are said to be either very neat, or very messy, or even to alternate between very neat and very messy behavior. Finally, psychoanalytic reasoning is occasionally circular, as when we account for a symptom or a dream by hypothesizing an unconscious motive and then try to "prove" the existence of the motive by pointing to that same symptom or dream.

Still, the question of whether any of Freud's ideas can be experimentally demonstrated is important and deserves discussion. In this text there is not enough space to review the hundreds of studies carried out to test particular Freudian concepts (see Fisher & Greenberg, 1977; Kline, 1972; Masling, 1983–1990; and Sears, 1951, for general research reviews; see Cramer, 1991, and Eriksen & Pierce, 1969, for reviews of research on defenses). Instead we will focus on unconscious motives and defenses, citing a few key studies designed to illustrate their effects.

A preliminary warning. Trying to demonstrate the existence of unconscious processes can be tricky. If defense mechanisms are to work in avoiding anxiety, they must operate unconsciously. If we *knew* we were repressing, then the repression would not be successful! (I once had a professor who was unaware of this problem and earnestly claimed that he couldn't "remember ever having repressed anything."[1]) Thus asking people about their uncon-

---

[1]Interestingly enough, some of the early psychoanalysts did not seem to be aware of this point. At the same time they were insisting that patients could *not* give accurate accounts of their wishes and defenses, they were also trying to develop a "questionnaire" to measure people's sexual history, impulses, and feelings, or at least (in Freud's words) those aspects that "remained in the memory of the normal individual." Of course, the idea of a "psychoanalytic questionnaire" was a scientific dead-end because it was a contradiction in terms. (Nunberg & Federn, 1962, pp. 372–388, describe this interesting episode in the history of psychoanalysis.)

scious motives and defenses will not work. We must employ other, less direct means.

Rosenzweig's Study of Repression

One of the first systematic experimental investigations of psychoanalytic ideas was Saul Rosenzweig's series of studies of repression (1938, 1943). Rosenzweig tested college students individually, giving them a series of jigsaw puzzles to solve. Before starting each puzzle, the students were given a small picture of the completed puzzle (typically a boat, flag, house, etc.) to study. As they worked, the experimenter deliberately interrupted them on certain puzzles, so that they finished half the puzzles and did not finish the other half. Right after the last puzzle, the experimenter asked each student to write down the names of as many of the puzzles as possible.

So far, the experiment was a simple replication of Zeigarnik's classic experiment on the persistence of unsatisfied motives described in Chapter 2. According to the Zeigarnik effect, the students should have been able to recall more uncompleted than completed puzzles. When Rosenzweig tested students in an informal and relaxed setting, emphasizing that he wanted to know about the puzzles and implying that the interruptions did not reflect on their ability, this is just what happened, as shown in Table 4.1. However, Rosenzweig also tested some students in an intensely ego-involved atmosphere. Here the experimenter was formal and curt, held a conspicuous stopwatch, described the puzzles as an intelligence test, and emphasized that "your work will be interpreted as representing the full extent of your ability." In this setting an "interruption" meant "failure," which would presumably arouse anxiety among highly motivated college students. Judging from the comments of many students in the ego-involved group, the instructions worked. One student said that "My feeling was one of desperation. With each puzzle that I missed [I thought] that I wasn't getting on well, that I had no business being [in college]" (Rosenzweig, 1943, p. 66).

TABLE 4.1 RESULTS OF ROSENZWEIG'S EXPERIMENTS ON ANXIETY AND THE ZEIGARNIK EFFECT

	Pattern of recall of puzzles	
Condition	Remember more unfinished than finished (Zeigarnik effect)	Remember more finished than unfinished (reversed Zeigarnik effect)
Relaxed	19	7
Ego-involved	8	17
	Chi-square = 8.64	
	$p < .01$	

SOURCE: Adapted from Rosenzweig (1943).

Table 4.1 shows that the ego-involved group showed a significant reversal of the Zeigarnik effect, recalling more completed tasks than uncompleted ones. Why did this happen? If anything, their motivation to complete the unfinished tasks should have been stronger than that of the relaxed subjects, so they should have showed an even stronger Zeigarnik effect. Rosenzweig suggested that anxiety, aroused by the "failure" of not finishing a puzzle under the ego-involving conditions, caused memories of those puzzles associated with "failure" to be repressed. Yet the memories still exist, for in a related study Rosenzweig (1938) found that the ego-involved group was slightly *better* than the relaxed group at recognizing the puzzles from pictures. Both findings are consistent with Freud's theory. That is, while memories of failure are banished from consciousness (poor recall), they persist in the unconscious and are available when unavoidably aroused and made conscious (good recognition). Thus failure to recall an anxiety-arousing stimulus helps to avoid a little anxiety. When the stimulus is plainly put in front of you, however, it is difficult to avoid recognizing it unless you turn away your head or shut your eyes. During the recognition task, many students from the ego-involved group showed relatively great galvanic skin responses (GSR)[2] to pictures of the "failure" puzzles, suggesting that for them the *unavoidable* perception or memory of failure did indeed arouse anxiety.

Rosenzweig's results do not prove that repression exists, or that psychoanalytic theory is correct. Other explanations are possible, and modern researchers might question some of Rosenzweig's experimental procedures. However, because the overall results are consistent with Freud's ideas, they do increase our confidence in the concept of repression. In fact, what we call scientific proof is nothing more than increased confidence based on observations turning out as predicted.

Interestingly enough, Freud himself was not very impressed with these research studies. In 1934, Rosenzweig sent him copies of several early articles describing the results. In reply Freud wrote:

> I have examined your experimental studies for the verification of psychoanalytic assertions with interest. I cannot put much value on these confirmations because the wealth of reliable observations on which these assertions rest make them independent of experimental observation. Still, [experimental verification] can do no harm. (quoted in Weiner, 1980, pp. 23–24)

Such words may seem surprising in the light of Freud's early scientific training and his insistence that psychoanalysis was a science. How could Freud's own "reliable observations" be better than laboratory tests? But consider for a moment if Rosenzweig's studies had shown no differences between the two groups, or even the opposite results. I doubt that people who believed in the psychoanalytic concept of repression would reject it solely on the basis of

---

[2]The galvanic skin response, also called electrodermal activity (EDA), measures electrical conductivity of the skin due to perspiration. This reflects sympathetic nervous system arousal, which presumably results from anxiety.

these experiments. Rather, they would simply conclude that the studies were not an adequate test of Freud's ideas.

Silverman's Studies of Subliminal Psychodynamic Activation

A research technique called *subliminal psychodynamic activation*, begun by Lloyd Silverman and his colleagues at New York University and later taken up by many other investigators, has given some striking confirmations to Freud's ideas about the existence and operation of unconscious motives (Silverman, Lachman, & Milich, 1982; see also Silverman, 1976, and Silverman & Weinberger, 1985). While the conclusions drawn from this research are controversial (see Balay & Shevrin, 1988), most of the findings have been replicated by other independent experimenters (see Weinberger & Hardaway, 1990, and Weinberger & Silverman, 1990, for reviews of the research). There is no doubt that subliminal psychodynamic activation research is surprising, exciting, and of the greatest importance for personality and motivation theory.

Subliminal psychodynamic activation works as follows. Imagine that you are a subject in one of Silverman's studies. You enter the room, are seated at a table, and fill out some questionnaires. Perhaps someone observes your behavior. Then you look into the eyepiece of a tachistoscope (a machine that flashes a visual stimulus for a very brief time interval). You are aware of seeing only a brief flicker of light, lasting for no more than four thousandths of a second. This happens four times, 10 seconds apart. Then you fill out some more questionnaires, perform some simple tasks, or have the observer record more of your behavior. That's it.

In fact, though, the content of the message you have "seen" has a considerable effect on your behavior. If you were a schizophrenic, and the experimental message was DESTROY MOTHER, you would show short-term increases in such schizophrenic symptoms as thought disorder (unrealistic, illogical, or "loose" thinking) and pathological behavior (inappropriate emotions, severe speech blocks, and nervous gestures). If, however, the message was MOMMY AND I ARE ONE, then your thought disorder and pathological behavior would go down for a while. A neutral message, such as PEOPLE ARE WALKING, would have no effect.

This part of Silverman's research is based on a presumed "need for oneness" with the "good mother" of our infancy. According to psychoanalytic theorists of the object-relations school (see Ainsworth, 1969; Klein, 1948; and Mahler, Pine, & Bergman, 1975), this is one of our earliest and strongest motives, arising well before the time of the Oedipus complex. While most of us experience some satisfaction of this need in love, meditation, religious mysticism, and ecstatic or "peak" experiences (see Maslow, 1970), Silverman believed that this "symbiotic-like need" is intense and ungratified in many schizophrenic people. Satisfying this need, even by a very brief, subliminal verbal message, or frustrating it by an aggressive message suggesting disruption of oneness, therefore has observable and significant effects on schizo-

Lloyd Silverman, whose studies of subliminal psychic activation seem to confirm many of Freud's ideas. "Psychoanalytic theory, like any complex theory that claims to be scientific, must constantly seek new data, using a variety of methods, and then evolve accordingly" (Silverman, 1976, p. 634).

phrenic behavior. (Among women, however, the messages DADDY AND I ARE ONE and MY LOVER AND I ARE ONE also work, which suggests that sexual and early Oedipal motives may also be adding to or overlapping with the effects of oneness; see Tabin & Tabin, 1987.)

The method of subliminal psychodynamic activation has been applied to studying several other kinds of disturbed functioning. In each case the message presented in the experimental condition was relevant to the motive or conflict underlying the disturbance, according to psychoanalytic theory, while the control-condition message had neutral motivational content (typically, PEOPLE ARE WALKING). For example, the experimental message for people suffering from depression (which Freud believed was aggression directed toward a lost object that had become internalized) was therefore the same aggressive one (DESTROY MOTHER) that increased schizophrenic pathology. For stutterers, the experimental message was GO SHIT, which was presumed to arouse unconscious conflicts about autonomy and compliance. In their primitive forms of "holding on" versus "letting go," such conflicts originate during toilet training and other socialization at the anal stage of personality development; in the view of some theorists, such conflicts are a cause of stuttering (Glauber, 1958).

According to psychoanalytic theory, alcoholism involves an unconscious conflict about oral-dependency motives—initially, being touched and fed; later in life, being taken care of and being told what to do. Hines (1977) reasoned that presenting alcoholics with the subliminal message MOMMY FEEDS ME should arouse these conflicts. This message should increase difficulties in thinking and cognitive functioning, which for an alcoholic may be the first stage in "needing a drink."

The overall trend of results from all these studies can be summarized quite simply: in each case, subliminal presentation of the experimental message, derived from psychoanalytic hypotheses about unconscious motives, increased the relevant pathology. The depressive felt worse, the stutterers made more speech disturbances, and the alcoholics showed increased cognitive difficulties. What's more, these pathological behaviors were affected *only* by the "relevant" message. That is, GO SHIT had no effect on schizophrenic thought disorder or depression—only on stuttering. Thought disorder increased only after the aggressive anti-oneness message, and so forth (see Silverman, Bronstein, & Mendelsohn, 1976).

The messages *must* be subliminal to have any effect. Presenting any message long enough to be consciously perceived has almost no effect. Silverman's explanation is that when a message is consciously perceived, it becomes something that is "out there," a part of the external world and not the self. It might arouse a wish, but such arousal would be attributed to the external stimulus, and so dealt with effectively and adaptively. When the message is only perceived subliminally, however, the wish arousal is felt to be coming from within. In this form it takes us (and our defenses) unaware. Many messages in everyday life are complicated: they may be perceived in one way consciously, but they communicate another message subliminally. Much of what we consciously see, therefore, also has a latent or symbolic message, a subtext, in addition to its consciously perceived "real" message. In Silverman's view, these layers of messages may account for the evocative powers of art, literature, myth, advertising, and other forms of symbolic creation (Silverman, Lachman, & Milich, 1982, pp. 30–36).

If the need for oneness reflects a broad-based, universal motive, then gratifying it with the subliminal message MOMMY AND I ARE ONE should also have positive effects on ordinary people. Several studies by Silverman and others suggest the broad range of these beneficial effects, in comparison with those of a neutral message. For example, college students who subliminally "view" the MOMMY/DADDY message four days a week during a course showed increasingly better grades in the course (Parker, 1982). (You will be interested to know that the message MY PROF AND I ARE ONE also has some beneficial effect, but not as much.) The same positive effect on grades was observed in a study of Israeli high school students, for whom the messages were translated into Hebrew (Ariam & Siller, 1982).

The "oneness" message, when added to traditional behavior modification programs, also facilitates quitting smoking (Palmatier & Bornstein, 1980), losing weight (Martin, 1975), overcoming phobias (Silverman, Frank, & Dachinger, 1974), and learning to be assertive (Packer, 1983). When added to the usual Alcoholics Anonymous procedures, subliminal oneness messages also improve alcoholics' efforts to give up drinking (Schurtman, Palmatier, & Martin, 1982). From all these results, we can conclude that feelings of oneness or unity, *when subliminally or unconsciously stimulated* in certain ways, have widespread and powerful enhancing effects on performance and adjustment.

There is more. According to Freud (1916, XIV), people develop competitive motives in childhood as a part of their Oedipus complex (rivalry with same-sex parent for the affections of opposite-sex parent). Fearing punishment, children give up this rivalry. In later life, competitive ambitions are usually in conflict with anxiety and guilt. The battle may go first one way (boundless ambition, originally with the goal of surpassing the same-sex parent) and then the other (being racked by guilt following success). The balance between these two outcomes determines how adults perform in competitive situations. When guilt wins, we fear success, reduce our ambitions, and undercut our chances for doing well. In late-twentieth-century American culture, women may be especially vulnerable to this kind of conflict, because traditional sex-role pressures against ambition and competitive success are added to Oedipal guilt (see Hoffman, 1974, and Horner, 1972).

Starting from this Freudian hypothesis, Silverman, Ross, Adler, and Lustig (1978) found that the subliminal message DEFEATING DAD IS OKAY or WINNING MOM IS OKAY improved the competitive performance of college men in a game of dart throwing (!). Zuckerman (1980) found that the message SUCCESS IS OKAY improves the academic performance of high school women.

Table 4.2 draws together the major results from the entire body of subliminal psychodynamic activation research. As you might expect, these results have been controversial, with vigorous debates back and forth in the personality research literature (see Weinberger & Hardaway, 1990, and Weinberger & Sil-

TABLE 4.2 INTEGRATIVE SUMMARY OF RESEARCH ON SUBLIMINAL PSYCHODYNAMIC ACTIVATION

Condition or subject population	Hypothesized unconscious motive	Gratified (+) or made worse (−) by message	Short-term effects on behavior*
Depression	Aggression against internalized object	DESTROY MOTHER (−)	Higher depression scores on a mood checklist
Schizophrenia	Conflict over oral aggression	DESTROY MOTHER (−)	Increased pathology of thought and action
	Need for oneness	MOMMY AND I ARE ONE (+)	Reduced pathology of thought and action
Stuttering	Conflict between retention and expulsion	GO SHIT (−)	Increased stuttering
Alcoholism	Conflicts about oral dependency	MOMMY FEEDS ME (−)	Increased thought confusion
	Need for oneness	MOMMY AND I ARE ONE (+)	Improved results with Alcoholics Anonymous
People in behavior modification programs	Need for oneness	MOMMY AND I ARE ONE (+)	Greater success at stopping smoking, weight loss, curing phobias, or assertiveness training
Students	Need for oneness	MOMMY AND I ARE ONE (+)	Higher grades
College men	Conflict about Oedipal rivalry	BEATING DAD IS OKAY (+) WINNING MOM IS OKAY (+)	Improved scores in dart-throwing competition
		BEATING DAD IS WRONG (−)	Decline in dart-throwing scores
High school women	Fear of success	SUCCESS IS OKAY	Improved academic performance

*In comparison with neutral message (e.g., PEOPLE ARE WALKING)

SOURCE: Based on the following sources: Silverman (1976); Silverman, Bronstein, & Mendelsohn (1976); Silverman, Lachman, & Milich (1982); Silverman & Weinberger (1985); Weinberger & Hardaway (1990); and Weinberger & Silverman (1990).

verman, 1990, for the most recent reviews). Overall, I believe that the subliminal psychodynamic activation research offers strong support for the idea that motives operate unconsciously and that their unconscious arousal or blockage can have marked effects on behavior.

Mechanisms of Unconscious Perception

The concept of unconscious perception, of seeing without seeing, may seem strange. Yet it fits with modern experimental research on perception (Erdelyi, 1974, 1985; Kihlstrom, 1987). To understand how this can be, let us first review briefly the fairly well established sequence of hypothetical stages or mechanisms by which a stimulus is processed—that is, perceived and then stored in memory. Figure 4.1 shows the sequence as a visual model. A stimulus first strikes the *sensory receptor* (for example, the rods and cones in the retina of the eye). It is then immediately transmitted to a *sensory register,* which preserves a somewhat degraded version of the image for up to 200 to 300 milliseconds (visual) or 1 to 2 seconds (auditory), unless it is overwritten by new images from the receptors in the meantime. Thus as you read this book, the sensory

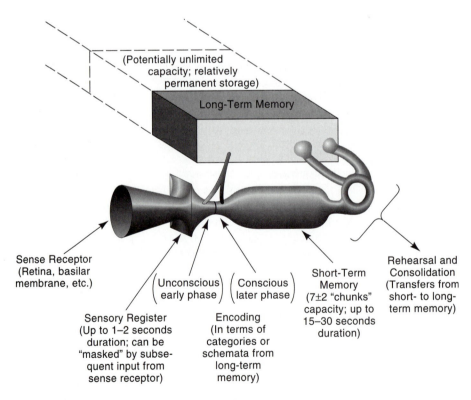

FIGURE 4.1
From sensation to storage in memory.

register of your visual system is constantly being overwritten by the changing input from your eyes. If you suddenly close your eyes, however, a quickly fading image of the last things you saw on this page will last for up to 300 milliseconds. This is, approximately, your visual sensory register. Its contents are often called an "icon" or "iconic storage"; your auditory sensory register is called "echoic storage."

At this first stage, the information is relatively unprocessed. From the sensory register, only a few things become *encoded* so as to enter *short-term memory*. In a classic paper, Miller (1956) estimated that only seven (plus or minus two) chunks or elements of information could be held in short-term memory at any one time. This is a serious limitation of capacity. Grouping information into larger chunks helps a little. Using more complex and abstract categories (drawn from long-term memory) also increases the amount of information that can be encoded. Even so, this stage of processing still remains a severe bottleneck. Once in short-term memory, information to be remembered is *rehearsed* and *consolidated* into long-term memory, where it has a reasonably stable and permanent existence, because capacity is almost unlimited.

Now consciousness—that which you are aware of at any given moment, as well as the sense of being aware of it—overlaps approximately with short-term memory. Therefore if a defense mechanism is going to prevent something from entering consciousness, it will have to operate on the processing sequence at some point before information enters short-term memory. Thus for the operation of defense mechanisms, the encoding stage is critical. Erdelyi suggested that encoding is not a simple all-or-nothing process, but rather takes place in several stages. First, there is a preliminary encoding that occurs before consciousness. On the basis of this preliminary coding, further encoding normally proceeds; but it *can* be disrupted, distorted, stopped altogether, or even accelerated (Erdelyi, 1974, 1985, chap. 5).

We can link these possibilities to the various defenses discussed in Chapter 3. Defenses such as repression or denial, in which the anxiety-arousing material is simply blocked from consciousness, would operate by disrupting further encoding after a preliminary encoding. In contrast, defenses such as isolation, projection, or reaction formation, which preserve and transform the anxiety-arousing material, might operate by accelerated and distorted encoding. Thus isolation might involve encoding part of the wish-related material but *not* the context, while projection involves faulty encoding of the source of the wish.

Before the advent of the cognitive revolution of the 1960s in psychology, many psychologists found concepts of defense and subliminal perception difficult to accept, because they seemed to imply that we could see but not see, that a little personlike creature (a kind of homunculus) somehow inhabited our brains and censored incoming messages. More modern conceptions of information processing, in contrast, show that perception involves many steps or stages, some under the control of others, and only a few accessible to consciousness (Erdelyi, 1985). Thus the early stages of encoding seem to involve multiple meanings of ambiguous words, symbolic as well as literal meanings, and contradictions. In his paper on "The Unconscious" (1915, XIV), Freud suggested that these three elements are important features of unconscious functioning.

For all of the complexities and ambiguities of Freud's psychoanalytic theories, and despite the difficulties of designing research to test major concepts of those theories, many of Freud's central ideas are supported (if not proved) by carefully designed research studies such as those discussed in this chapter. Increasingly these ideas are viewed as consistent with what we know about cognition, information processing, and the rest of psychology (see, for example, Bornstein, 1989, and Kihlstrom, 1987).

CRITICIZING FREUD: THE THEORY OF WOMEN'S DEVELOPMENT

While the preceding sections show that the psychoanalytic concepts of repression and the unconscious have some research support, you should not think that all of Freud's ideas are accepted as true. In Chapter 3, I indicated that his concept of the death instinct is not accepted by many psychoanalysts (though motives of mastery, aggression, and power are widely accepted). And Freud's ideas about women and women's development have been questioned and attacked by psychoanalysts such as Karen Horney, Melanie Klein, and Clara Thompson. In recent decades, the breakdown of traditional views about sex roles and the rise of feminist thinking and the women's movement led to further criticism (for example, Strouse, 1974). Theories often have political consequences; nowhere is this more true than in the case of Freud's views about women.

Let me be clear about my own view: I believe that on this topic Freud was wrong—not just wrong, but wrong in striking and strange ways. I say this not because his ideas are controversial and antifeminist but because they are incomplete, inconsistent with some basic psychoanalytic assumptions, and contradicted by several important kinds of evidence. Further, I believe Freud's mistakes have had unfortunate consequences for how women view themselves and how they are treated by psychologists. Nevertheless, I think we can learn from studying Freud's conclusions, when and how he arrived at them, and how they are contradicted by both logic and evidence. Perhaps it will then be possible to construct an alternative theory that is faithful both to the basic elements of psychoanalysis and also to the evidence, while at the same time contributing to our liberation from traditional roles.

The essential features of Freud's theory of women can be found in a 1925 paper that he wrote for the International Psychoanalytic Congress at Bad Homburg, Germany, titled "Some Psychical Consequences of the Anatomical Distinction between the Sexes" (Freud, 1925c, XIX, pp. 248–258). In order to understand this paper, which deals with women's psychosexual development, we must first sketch out Freud's earlier theory of men's development (Freud, 1923; 1924a, XIX).

The Oedipus Complex and Superego in Males

Desires at the phallic stage. Around age 2 to 5 (the so-called phallic stage, to use Freud's sexist term), boys experience arousal of libidinal motives involving specifically the genitals, as discussed in Chapter 3. The boy's mother becomes the focus for his associated feelings and desires. Perceiving his father as a rival, the boy develops feelings of aggressive hostility that complicate his existing love for his father. These two feelings—love for the mother and rivalrous hostility toward the father—make up the *Oedipus complex*, which Freud believed to be a universal and critical feature of male personality development. The two feelings lead an uneasy and conflicted coexistence in the little boy's mind. For one thing, the hostility is difficult to square with his prior love for his father. More important, however, he fears that both desires will lead to punishment from his father. Some of this fear may be a projection of the boy's hostility, but any actual parental punishment provides an easy rationalization for the fear. Eventually, these fears come to focus on a specific *fear of castration.* Typically, when the little boy is masturbating or touching his penis, a parent or baby-sitter may say that "it will fall off" (or worse, "I'll cut it off") if he doesn't stop. No matter whether the threat is serious or in jest; the boy takes it seriously.

Resolution of the male Oedipus complex. To avoid castration, the boy resolves, or gives up the two desires of, his Oedipus complex. He renounces his sexual love for his mother and transforms it into tender but nonsexual affection. He then *identifies* with his father and incorporates the feared threats and punishments into his newly formed superego. If the Oedipus complex is not resolved in this way, Freud believed, then one or more personality disturbances may result. If the boy feels no pressure to give up his Oedipus complex, then his superego will develop either weakly or else not at all. The result is an amoral, opportunistic, exploitative person who is charming but who lacks fear, cannot foresee consequences, and continually gets into trouble. In the language of contemporary abnormal psychology, he becomes a sociopath. The famous literary figure of Don Juan is one example of this type (see Rank, 1924/1975): he attempts to seduce an endless series of women (libidinal fixation on the mother) while taunting and then killing the father of one of his female victims (aggressive fixation on the father).

If the repression of the Oedipus complex is incomplete, then the two desires will "leak through," resulting in brooding, neurotic guilt, and self-defeating or self-punitive behavior. Shakespeare's Hamlet, who could never make up his mind whether "to be or not to be," illustrates this type (see Freud, 1900, IV, pp. 264–266; and Jones, 1949).

Finally, instead of giving up the erotic tie to his mother, the boy may transform it into an *identification* in his ego with her—"becoming" instead of "possessing" his mother. Freud suggested that this outcome leads to male homosexuality (1921, XVIII, p. 108), since for the boy one aspect of becoming his mother would be to have an erotic tie to his father (and by extension, to other men). While such a conclusion is highly debatable (see Fisher & Greenberg, 1977), this third outcome might result in the boy having a poorly defined sense of self, especially self-as-differentiated-from-mother. (Anthony Perkins portrayed just such a person in Alfred Hitchcock's chilling 1960 movie, *Psycho*.)

Amnesia. To finish off the resolution of the Oedipus complex, the little boy represses all memory of the Oedipal desires, the fear of castration, and the two renunciations. In fact, the boy loses almost all previous memories of any kind. Freud called this *infantile amnesia.*

The Oedipus Complex in Women

What happens to girls? Freud *might* have argued that their development was analogous to boys' development, that at the "phallic" stage, they would naturally develop love for their fathers and hatred for their mothers. This would result in an Electra complex[3] in girls, analogous to the Oedipus complex in boys. This was Freud's position early in his career, but later he came to reject the idea of an inherent Electra complex (1931a, XXI, pp. 226–227), insisting instead on the term "female Oedipus complex" to describe girls' development. As we shall see, though, by this term he meant something entirely different from the male Oedipus complex.

Freud's argument is most clearly laid out in the 1925 paper, "Some Psychical Consequences of the Anatomical Distinction between the Sexes" (1925c, XIX, pp. 248–258). In it Freud suggested that originally girls, like boys, love their mother and fear their father, since in both sexes libidinal motives are first directed toward the same person who satisfied self-preservation motives. Eventually, however, boys and girls discover that they are anatomically different—specifically, that boys have a penis and girls do not. (This is certainly not the only difference between men and women, but it is the only difference Freud mentioned! We will discuss this further below.) For boys, Freud believed, this discovery sharply increases fear of castration. The parental threat to "cut it off" suddenly becomes a real possibility. Thus the discovery of sex differences provides a motive for boys to resolve their Oedipus complex, first by renouncing their libidinal wishes for their mother and their hostile wishes toward their father and then by forming a superego and developing a sense of morality.

For girls, Freud postulated an entirely different reaction to the discovery of sex differences (1925c, XIX):

> They notice the penis of a brother or playmate, strikingly visible and of large proportions, at once recognize it as the superior counterpart of their own small and inconspicuous organ [i.e., the clitoris], and from that time forward fall a victim to

[3]Named after the heroine of Sophocles' play, *Elektra*, who loved her father ("the dearest mortal"); hated her mother Clytemnestra, who killed him and married Agamemnon ("tyrant I call you"); and encouraged her brother Orestes to kill both Clytemnestra and Agamemnon. Eugene O'Neill's dramatic trilogy *Mourning Becomes Electra* is a modern version.

envy for the penis. . . . She makes her judgment and her decision in a flash. She has seen it and knows that she is without it and wants to have it. (p. 252)

From this supposed *penis envy*, Freud derived several far-ranging consequences for women's personality development: (1) jealousy (because as girls they lacked something boys have); (2) hatred for their mother (because she had an "inadequate" body, which she gave to her daughter); (3) the wish to have a baby (that is, a symbolic penis) with the father, a wish that involves a "passive" attitude leading to (4) more general sexual and social passivity; and (5) attempts to compensate for the lack of a penis by way of denial (becoming like a man, the "masculine complex"), physical vanity, and narcissism. In one of his more breathtaking speculative leaps, Freud even went so far as to suggest that women also feel more (6) shame, which led them to (7) invent weaving as an imitation of pubic hair, in order to conceal their "genital deficiency" (Freud, 1933a, XXII, p. 132; see also 1931a, XXI). Further, since girls have no motive to give up the Oedipus complex, they have (8) less superego development (or a less "principled" moral sense) than do boys: "For women the level of what is ethically normal is different from what it is in men. Their superego is never so inexorable, so impersonal, so independent of its emotional origins as we require it to be in men" (Freud, 1925c, XIX, p. 257).

To summarize: according to Freud's theory, the discovery of female-male genital differences has two important consequences that distinguish the subsequent personality development of women and men. For boys, this discovery leads to abandoning the Oedipus complex out of fear of castration. In girls, however, the Oedipus complex is not given up but rather reversed: the originally loved mother is now hated, and the once-feared father is now loved. Because they never fully abandon their Oedipus complex and thus never fully develop a superego, girls should experience less guilt and shame (effects of the superego) and achieve a less complete moral development.

Critical Analysis of Freud's Theory of Women

Please understand my own view of Freud's theory: I think it is not only wrong but also bizarre: wrong because it does not even fit the facts (including many facts of Freud's own clinical experience), and bizarre because of its relation to his own life. I discuss it at such great length for two reasons. First, for all their absurdities and contradictions, Freudian notions of "penis envy" and "passive femininity" have had important and unfortunate social and political consequences. In psychiatry and clinical psychology, for example, they were used to support therapies that oppress women and then label their reaction to oppression as "madness" (Chesler, 1972). In the wider world of social thought, these two concepts were a cornerstone for the "feminine mystique"—that structure of post–World War II American attitudes and practices that restricted women's opportunities and crippled their self-esteem (Friedan, 1963). In everyday life, these terms are often used by men as put-downs for women who value themselves. To understand and combat these consequences, it is important to understand the theory upon which they are based. For this reason alone, it is important to understand Freud's theory of women and how it may be wrong.

There are also intellectual grounds for taking a close look at Freud's theory of women. If we reject this part of Freud's ideas, must we also reject the rest of psychoanalysis? Or are his theories of women an afterthought, a later addition that obscures rather than clarifies the rest of psychoanalytic thought? In any field of study, it is important to learn to distinguish aspects of a theoretical system that are useful from aspects that are not, preserving the former and discarding the latter.

Freud's theory and Freud's life. First of all, it is important to consider Freud's theory of women in relation to Freud's own life. In the long run, scientific theories may rise and fall according to their success in making sense of our experience. But science (especially psychological science) in the making is not a neutral activity sealed off from the ego, emotions and passions, cultural values, and politics of the scientist. To understand fully science as a human enterprise, we must examine scientists' lives in relation to their theories.

When we look at Freud's theory of women in the context of his life and career, we notice that he developed this theory quite late. Up to 1923, Freud had been seeing female patients for over thirty-five years, since 1886; he had worked out all the major elements of psychoanalytic theory—yet there is no hint of penis envy. As late as April 1923, Freud wrote that the Oedipus complex in girls was "precisely analogous" to that of boys (1923, XIX, p. 32): that is, that girls *originally* had a libidinal wish for their father and hostility toward their mother. Finally, in an early 1924 paper on "The Dissolution of the Oedipus Complex" (1924a, XIX, pp. 173–179), Freud made his first mention of penis envy, after making a famous remark (paraphrasing Napoleon) that "anatomy is destiny."

What happened to Freud between April 1923 and early 1924? First, in April 1923 his cancer of the upper palate (later spreading to the upper jaw and cheek) was diagnosed, and he underwent the first of many painful operations and radiation treatments. An ill-fitting prosthesis, which he nicknamed "the monster," made it possible to talk and eat, but for the remaining sixteen years of his life he endured distress and pain (Jones, 1953–1957, vol. 3, p. 100), and was embarrassed about speaking in public. In fact, Freud's 1925 paper on sex differences for the International Psychoanalytic Congress in Bad Homburg was actually read by his daughter Anna. She also served as Freud's own nurse, when necessary, for the remaining sixteen years of his life.

Second, in November 1923 Freud had a vasectomy, in the hope that its "rejuvenation" effects might delay any recurrence of the cancer (p. 104). Shortly after Freud's cancer operation, his favorite grandchild Heinerle died at age 4½, of complications following a tonsillectomy. His biographer Jones recorded that "he told me afterwards that this loss had . . . killed something in him for good . . . that he had never been able to get fond of anyone since that misfortune" (pp. 96–97).

Finally, Anna Freud, his youngest child, became a psychoanalyst. Earlier, she had trained to be a teacher and was analyzed by her father between 1918 and 1922. (At that time, it was not unusual for psychoanalysts to analyze members of their own family.) In order to establish herself as a member of the Vienna Psychoanalytic Society, Anna gave a lecture to the society in May 1922. After presiding over that meeting, her father rather curiously compared himself to Lucius Junius Brutus, a Roman judge who had to sentence his own son to death. At his suggestion, Anna then resumed her personal analysis with him in the spring of 1924. According to Young-Bruehl (1988, chap. 3), the themes that emerged from this later analysis are strikingly similar to those in Freud's 1924 and 1925 papers on women.

Thus at the time Freud was so radically revising his theory of women, he himself underwent the painful and embarrassing loss of a part of his body and the threat of death both to himself and to someone he loved. In psychoanalytic terms, these two "narcissistic injuries" both have symbolic overtones of castration. At the same time, his daughter Anna was his "patient" in analysis, became an analyst in her own right, and served both as Freud's "replacement" and his nurse. In these events we can detect some of the themes of his developing ideas about women: a concern with male genitals, castration, and death; a daughter who is at the same time the symbolic mother who nurses, the symbolic son who surpasses, and a real patient or partner who discloses intimate sexual secrets and fantasies. These connections help to explain why, in 1923–1924, Freud suddenly introduced dramatic changes in his theories of women and women's personality development.

Of course a theory is not necessarily wrong because it echos themes of the theorist's own life; in the end, any theory must be evaluated on its own terms, by the scientific standards of logical coherence, conformity to the evidence, and consistency with other findings. To these criteria we now turn.

Penis: appendage or symbol? Consider Freud's account of a young girl's discovery of the male genitals (1925c, XIX, p. 252): she "notice[s] the penis," which is supposedly "strikingly visible and of large proportions." Since according to Freud this discovery is usually made by seeing the penis "of a brother or playmate," we may ask whether Freud's characterization—"strikingly visible and of large proportions"—reflects what a girl might actually think or what he imagines (or wishes) she should think. After seeing a boy's penis, the girl supposedly "at once" recognizes it as "superior" and "wants to have it."

In terms of topology or shape, the penis is simply an anatomical appendage from the human body—something that "sticks out." For the girl's recognition and desire to arise "at once," Freud must assume that a body appendage—any body appendage—is inherently positive, desirable, and therefore enviable. Is it really true that anything sticking out of someone's body is "at once" so desirable? Think about your navel. Some of you have navels that go in and some of you have navels that stick out. Do those of you with protruding navels feel special? If your navel goes in, do you feel deprived? Have you developed "protruding-navel envy?" Or if you saw a person with six fingers, would you "at once" want the extra digit for yourself? Consider the 1980 movie, *The Elephant Man*, which told the tragic story of John Merrick, who suffered enormous skin growths from the disease neurofibromatosis. Far from envying Merrick, people reacted with horror, revulsion, and persecution.

From these examples, we might conclude that there is nothing inherently attractive about an appendage as such; some are enviable and some are not. What makes the difference is that if an appendage (or other body characteristic) is associated with superior social status, then it might well be envied by those who do not possess that status. Thus in a patriarchal culture, where men monopolize power and status and women are relegated to the inferior "separate spheres" of life, any anatomical feature or symbol associated with maleness is likely to be the focus of women's discontent, envy, and desire. In such cases it should be clear, however, that what is envied is the penis as symbol of male freedom and power, not the penis as anatomical appendage. Even little boys might "envy" grown men and wish for a larger penis. (Freud's characterization of the little boy's penis as "strikingly visible and of large proportions" may be a reaction formation to this wish.) In such a social and cultural context, penis envy is really status envy. This point has been made by Horney (1939, chap. 6; 1967), Thompson (1964), and many other female and male psychoana-

Karen Horney (1885–1952), who challenged Freud's concept of penis envy. "The wish to be a man . . . may be the expression of a wish for all those qualities or privileges which in our culture are regarded as masculine, such as strength, courage, independence, success, sexual freedom. . . ." (Horney, 1939, p. 108).

lytic "revisionists." Playwright Wendy Wasserstein weaves this analysis into her 1978 play, *Uncommon Women and Others*. The scene is a group of women college undergraduates who are discussing Freud and penis envy; one character, Holly Kaplan, speaks to her friend Katie and the others as follows (Wasserstein, 1978):

> I guess I envy men. I envy their confidence. I envy their options. But I never wanted a fleshy appendage. Especially a little boy's. Whenever I get fat I get nauseated because it looks like I have one in my pants. Katie, this is nonsense. The only people who have penis envy are other men. (p. 65)

Other anatomical distinctions. The title of Freud's 1925 paper describes the male penis as "*the* anatomical distinction between the sexes." Surely this ignores at least two other anatomical differences that are as prominent to young girls and boys: women have babies, and women have developed breasts. In fact, seventeen years before his 1925 paper, Freud acknowledged that even a very young boy can see the "connection between the increase in his mother's stoutness and the appearance of the baby" (1908c, X, p. 214). If anatomical differences are sources of envy, then we should also speak of "womb envy" or "breast envy" in little boys. In his book *Symbolic Wounds*, Bettelheim (1954) cited a wealth of clinical and cross-cultural evidence that men envy women's bodies and sexual functions. Such envy may be one root of male adolescent initiation ceremonies involving physical pain or injury.

I once overheard the following expression of womb envy from a 3-year-old boy, during a time when his nursery school teacher was visibly pregnant: "I'm getting fat because I'm going to have a baby. It's moving around inside. I'm going to lie down now and pat it." Clearly, each sex is capable of envy for whatever body parts and social functions are reserved to the other.

Women's superego and the "universal" castration threat. Freud thought that the threat of castration, once believed, was the motive for a boy's superego formation. Without this motive, Freud argued, girls would develop a less adequate superego. If this is true, then girls and women should be less vulnerable to anxiety, depression, and other traces of the superego's "cruel power" over the ego. Yet as a major prediction from Freud's theory, this hypothesis is completely contradicted by the evidence. Depression and depressive symptoms are consistently more frequent—perhaps twice as frequent—among women than men, both in the United States and in most other countries (Nolen-Hoeksema, 1987; see also Veroff, Douvan, & Kulka, 1981, pp. 349–352).

Even for men, Freud's hypothesis that the development of conscience and the superego depends on the threat of castration is suspect, on logical grounds. He believed that the superego was a human universal, an aspect of personality that developed in all people, in every culture. As a universal phenomenon, the superego would require a universal cause or causes. In other words, *every* male child, in *every* culture, would have to be threatened with castration during the critical time for superego development (say, before the age of 6). Perhaps joking threats to "cut it off" were common in nineteenth-century Vienna and even in the present-day United States, but this is a long way from always and everywhere for every male child. Thus the threat of castration seems a tenuous and weak foundation for a universal superego. If the only thing that makes men moral is a castration threat, then the world is in serious trouble![4]

Perhaps it is time to look for another motive to account for superego development. We need a motive that is (1) universal in human experience, while being if anything (2) slightly stronger for girls than for boys, in order to account for the consistent sex differences in anxiety and other superego traces.

A Revised Theory: Physical Threat and Superego Formation

What is the most obvious difference between adults and children? Everywhere, across all human cultures, adults are bigger and stronger. Surely all young children sometimes fear that they might be harmed or even killed by their parents—big, powerful, and sometimes angry. At the very least, children might worry that their parents would stop loving them. This does not mean that all parents actually abuse their children (although child abuse and even child murder occur far more often than we would like to admit) or even threaten not to love them. Rather, it means that during a critical period, all children develop such fears. Thus it follows that the threat or *fear* of physical harm or loss of love could be universal; from such a threat, therefore, a "universal" superego or conscience could develop.

Can such threats or fears also account for the observed sex differences? If girls are on average slightly smaller than, or not as strong as, boys, then on average they should have stronger fears of harm or loss of love. Thus they would develop slightly stronger superegos, which is what the evidence of Nolen-Hoeksema (1987) and Veroff, Douvan, and Kulka (1981) suggests. In American culture, we do not even need to assume sex differences in children's size and strength, since little boys are permitted or even encouraged to be "tough" and fight back, while little girls are encouraged to be "nice" instead. Thus girls should usually develop stronger superegos, even if they are the same size and strength as boys.

The role of parental elicitation. We still need to account for the girl's ultimate "Oedipal" attachment to her father, if her mother was her first libidinal object because she was her first caretaker. Cognitive-developmental theorists argue that gender identification (which includes identification with the same-sex parent and attraction toward the opposite-sex parent) is largely a matter of learning the meaning of the labels of "girl" or "boy" (Kohlberg, 1966). Parents teach these meanings, both through their explicit words and also by the way

---

[4]Of course, a truly committed Freudian might reply that the threat is truly universal, but only at the *symbolic* level. For example, a father might gaze out the window and say, "You know, we're going to have to cut down that tree limb [= penis?] before it falls on [= sexual desire?] the house [= mother?]."

they respond to girls and to boys. At an earlier point in his thinking, Freud acknowledged this: "[Parents] often exercise a determining influence on the awakening of a child's Oedipus attitude by themselves obeying the pull of sexual attraction . . . the father will give the plainest evidence of his greater affection for his little daughter and the mother for her son" (1916–1917, XVI, p. 333).

Oedipus in the Trobriand Islands: Malinowski's cross-cultural study. Some additional support for the revised theory of the Oedipus complex and superego formation comes from a classic study of Trobriand Island culture by the anthropologist Malinowski (1927). (The Trobriand Islands lie off the northeast coast of New Guinea and are now part of Papua New Guinea.) Trobriand family and kinship structure is matrilineal rather than patrilineal. This means that although parents live together with their children, kinship and social status are reckoned only through the mother's line. Fathers are nurturant. Affectionate and uncomplicated relationships develop between fathers and their children, *especially* between fathers and sons. In contrast, the mother's brother exercises stern authority and discipline over children. Marriage is sexually exclusive and permanent, and there is an extremely strong sexual taboo between sister and brother (that is, between a mother and her brother).

Thus among the Trobrianders, the roles of disciplinarian and exclusive sexual partner of mother—two roles that are combined in a Western "father"—are separated. Freudian theory would predict that a young Trobriand boy would direct his Oedipus complex toward his sexual rival (father); according to the revised theory outlined above, however, the boy's Oedipal target would be the bigger, more powerful adult who disciplines him but who is never a sexual rival (the mother's brother). On this point Malinowski's observations were clear-cut: the mother's brother was decidedly the target of the Trobriand male Oedipus complex (1927, pp. 79–81; Malinowski preferred the term "matrilineal complex" to describe the Trobriand version). This difference is echoed in Trobriand folklore, which is full of threatening evil *uncles* instead of fathers!

Death and castration. According to our revised theory of the Oedipus complex, then, castration is only a symbol for physical harm and death. It is only one form of physical harm; though as we have seen, it was a particularly salient one for Freud during the time when he revised his theory of women. From the fear of harm or loss of love, rather than from a fear of castration, almost all men and women develop superegos.

GOING BEYOND FREUD: ALTERNATIVE CONCEPTIONS OF MOTIVE

Freud's two groups of motives are one answer to the question of how many basic motives people have, but psychologists (and before them philosophers) have given a bewildering variety of other answers. For example, Carl Jung, who was at one time Freud's disciple and heir as head of the psychoanalytic movement, parted company with Freud over the issue of motives. Jung rejected Freud's dualisms and concept of the libido as a sexualized group of motives in favor of a more neutral single form of "psychic energy." Other psychologists have elaborated Freud's dualism of Eros and death instincts. Still others have added other motives on theoretical or research grounds. Finally, some psychologists have adopted a more empirical, open-ended approach. Instead of working downward from grand theories about human nature, they worked upward from actual observations of human behavior, asking how many different motives would be necessary to account for what they observed. We shall consider each of these positions in turn.

Other Dualisms of Love and Aggression Motives

Freud's theory that love and aggression are the two great human motives actually originated with the Greek philosopher Empedocles (active from 477 to 432 B.C.), who theorized that all things are composed of the four elements of earth, air, fire, and water. These elements, in turn, are acted upon by two powers or motive forces: *love,* which unifies or joins them, and *strife,* which separates them. Human society grows out of the antagonism between love and strife, each struggling for exclusive control of the four elements. Freud was pleased to discover how closely Empedocles' ancient ideas corresponded to his own motivational theory.

Some modern versions of psychoanalytic theory have elaborated one of Freud's motive groups. For example, object-relations theory and Silverman's need for oneness can be understood as elaborations of certain libidinal component motives (for example, the need for touching; see Silverman, Lachman, & Milich, 1982).

Otto Rank: Life-fear and death-fear. Many psychologists further developed Freud's dualism of love and aggression or death motives. Otto Rank (1884–1939), another loyal disciple of Freud who later broke with him, conceived of human life as driven by two conflicting fears (Rank, 1931/1936). On the one hand, we have a *fear of life.* We fear separation, growth, and individuation, those very experiences that establish us as living individuals in our own right. For Rank, this fear of life is most vividly symbolized by the moment of birth, the moment at which we enter life as a separate individual (Rank, 1924/1973). The shock of separation from mother, together with the sudden rush of new stimuli (what William James called a "blooming, buzzing confusion") constitutes the trauma of birth, which is later repeated every time we separate or move away from established family or friends and encounter new and strange experiences. Sometimes the fear of life, of being separate and living on our own, makes us run away from individuation and try to fuse or merge ourselves with other people. In extreme cases death may appear as a

Otto Rank (1884–1939). As one of Freud's most loyal disciples (until 1924), he used psychoanalytic theory to interpret myth, legend, and the artist. After his later break with Freud, he developed his own motivational concepts of fear of life (or desire for fusion) and fear of death (or desire for individuation).

desirable goal, since it frees us from the feared life (see Rank, 1924/1975, pp. 95–96).

On the other hand, Rank also believed that we have a *fear of death*, since death represents the extinction of individuality. This fear is often expressed in a desire for individuality and immortality. It leads us to flee from fusion with others (often symbolised by the prebirth fusion with mother), which are seen as symbolic forms of death. This tension between life-fear and death-fear can be traced in the literary figure of Don Juan.[5] Out of a fear of death and fusion, Don Juan drives himself to ever stronger assertions of his own individuality, by seducing and then abandoning an endless series of women. According to Rank, these many women stand for the one original woman from whom he is fleeing—his mother. At the same time, Don Juan actively seeks death by taking risks, and finally by murdering the father of one of the female victims and then mocking that father's memorial statue. The statue seizes Don Juan's hand in an invitation to dinner that is also the grip of death. To Rank, the statue's grip and the grave beckon to Don Juan as sym-

---

[5]The Don Juan legend is one of the most popular and durable themes in Western literature, with more than 1,700 different versions since the first one, *El Burlador de Sevilla* by the Spanish playwright Tirso de Molina in the early 1600s. The most famous versions are plays by Molière and Shaw *(Man and Superman)*, and of course Mozart's opera *Don Giovanni*. Interestingly enough, Rank's interpretation of the Don Juan legend was written just at the time he broke with Freud (Rank, 1924/1975). Some of the details of Rank's interpretation of Don Juan reflect the deterioration of the Freud-Rank relationship.

bols of fusion with mother—long sought-after but at the same time ambivalently feared.

Thus for Rank the fear of death drives us to life, growth, and assertion; while the fear of life drives us to fusion and finally death. We can still recognize Freud's two major classes of motives in Rank's duality, but with Rank they are reactions to fears rather than independent goals in themselves. As MacKinnon (1965, p. 276) put it, people move "through life from the trauma of birth to the trauma of death." In Rank's view, the conflict between these two forces has three possible outcomes. The adjusted or *average person* retreats from life into the protective "womb" of society. Such people are well-socialized and thoroughly integrated into their environment. In contrast, the conflicted or *neurotic person* struggles to escape from society by asserting individuality but founders on feelings of anxiety, guilt, and inferiority. Finally, the creative person or *artist* manages to integrate both forces through an act of will (in more familiar psychoanalytic terms, "ego strength"). The resulting harmony of abilities and ideals releases a creative energy that can be expressed in ordinary living as well as in artistic production.

In a study of highly creative and less creative architects, MacKinnon (1965) found striking confirmation of Rank's three types. Helson and her colleagues have also used Rank's typology to study creativity among mathematicians (Helson & Crutchfield, 1970), authors of fantasy (Helson, 1977), and college-educated women (Helson, 1987; see also York & John, 1991). Rank's ideas have also influenced psychologists who study the meaning of death and its implications for personality and motivation. Thus Becker (1973) applied Rank's theme of the human struggle against death to the analysis of heroism, narcissism, religion, and neurosis.

Angyal and Brown. Other theorists have developed Freud's duality in a more straightforward way. Angyal (1941), for example, wrote of the desires for autonomy (or independence) and homonomy (that is, surrender). In his book *Life Against Death*, Brown (1959) extended Freud's duality along cultural lines: life and death are seen as basic forces at work throughout human history and social institutions.

David Bakan: Agency and communion. David Bakan used the terms "agency" and "communion" for his motivational dualism (1966). By *agency* he meant the tendencies toward mastery and individual separateness, but as approach motives and not reactions to a fear of death or fusion. *Communion* means relatedness, a readiness to fuse or merge one's self with others, but as a positive motive and not out of a fear of individuation or life. Bakan went on to elaborate the concept of agency, which in his theory is equivalent to Freud's death instinct. Like Freud, Bakan viewed agency or agentic mastery as an expression of aggression and death motives. That is, the path of ambition and individual assertion ultimately leads to death (either death of self or death of others), for it cuts people off from life-sustaining contact and communion with other people. Bakan intended these words quite literally: he believed that cancer, for example, is an expression of *unmitigated agency*. (A study of cancer patients by Rivera, 1983, lent some support to Bakan's claim.)

While Bakan himself emphasized the dangers of agency and the benefits of communion, other personality psychologists believe that each motivational tendency has advantages and disadvantages. For example, people with total communion and no agency would have little curiosity, little desire for growth or enhancement, and no way to cope with separation and loss. Many studies suggest the importance of balance between agency and communion (see the research reported in Crosby, 1993). For example, Stewart and Salt (1981) studied 120 women college graduates who had reached early middle age. Among women who had careers but were not married and had no children (agency tendencies much stronger than communion tendencies), life changes and stress led to physical illness, just as they do among men, whose strivings are also more agentic than communal. Among married women with children but no career (communion much stronger than agency), life changes and stress led to depression. Among women with *both* career and marriage and children (strong agency and strong communion tendencies), however, life changes and stress did not affect either illness or depression. These results may seem surprising, because we might expect that combining career and family responsibilities would make for a hectic and demanding life. While such a life might be difficult, the combination of agentic and communal roles seems to protect people from the effects of stress and so promote health. With both a career and a family to care about, who has time to get sick or depressed!

Stewart and Malley (1987) studied a group of over 100 recently separated or divorced women who had custody of school-age children. They found that the best adjustment to divorce was made by women who somehow managed to express both agency and communion tendencies in their work and family lives. Usually the agentic tendency was expressed in a job and the communal tendency with family, but adjustment was just as good the other way around, so long as both tendencies were balanced.

Adding Other Major Motives: Competence and Self-Actualization

Many personality theorists have proposed other motives that in their view are as basic to human functioning as the love and death instincts were to Freud. Here we will mention three prominent additional motives: altruism, competence, and actualization.

Altruism. The Viennese physician Alfred Adler (1870–1937) was an early psychoanalytic disciple who broke with Freud in 1911 to found the movement known as individual psychology. Adler's disillusionment with Freud centered around the issue of motivation, for he rejected the overriding importance of the libido. In its place, Adler at first substituted a *drive for perfection*, the tendency to compensate for any perceived inferiority. The term "inferiority complex," which is related to this tendency, is an Adlerian term that has become a part of everyday language. Later, as a result of his medical experiences in World War I as well as his political commitment to socialism, Adler developed another motivational construct—altruism, or social-feeling motives. (Adler's German word, *Gemeinschaftsgefühl*, can be translated a little more awkwardly as "sense of fellowship with the human community.") For Freud, remember, all motives are completely selfish; only with difficulty (and never completely) can they be transformed into love for others. For Adler, however, social feeling was inherently an altruistic motive. From the very beginning of life it is centered on others (Adler, 1927):

> The first evidence of the inborn social feeling unfolds in [the child's] early search for tenderness, which leads him to seek the proximity of adults. The child's love life is always directed towards others, not, as Freud would say, upon his own body. (pp. 42–43)

For Adler, our inherent social feeling evolved as a necessary adaptation to humanity's weakness against nature. Adler eloquently expressed his conviction on this point (1927):

> Consider the difficulties of childbirth and the extraordinary precautions which are necessary for keeping a child alive during its first days. . . . Think of the number of sicknesses and infirmities to which the human flesh is heir, particularly in its infancy, and you have some comprehension of the universal amount of care which human life demands. (p. 29)

Social feeling is expressed in many ways: in sexual love, in neighborly love, and in cooperative work and helping. In some people, social feeling is inadequate (largely as the result of early experiences); in the seriously disturbed, it may even be absent altogether. Still, social feeling is an innate human aptitude, a basic motive that is not reducible to other motives such as transformed egoistic libido.

Competence. Robert W. White (b. 1904), a student of Henry Murray and for many years a professor at Harvard University, expanded the psychoanalytic theory of motives with the concept of *competence,* which he called "a different kind of motivational idea." In a landmark paper (1959), White argued from observations as diverse as the exploration and manipulation behaviors of animals, the play of contented human children, and the phenomena of boredom and novelty seeking in nearly all creatures. To White, these all suggest a major gap in the tension-reduction motivational concepts of psychoanalysis and the experimental psychology of the 1930s.

For example, consider the results of two classic experiments. Animals will cross an electrified grid (presumably this is unpleasant), for no reward other than the chance to explore new territory on the other side of the grid (Nissen, 1930). They will learn complex discriminations in order to open a window so that they can see what is happening outside, in the reception room of the psy-

The intense curiosity of these young macaques is analogous to human children's desires to explore and manipulate. Robert White suggested that such behaviors reflect a broader competence motivation.

chological laboratory (Butler & Harlow, 1957). Or consider the Swiss psychologist Jean Piaget's observations of his 3-month-old son Laurent, three days after Laurent first discovered that pulling a chain could make a noise from an attached rattle (Piaget, 1952):

> Laurent, by chance, strikes the chain while sucking his fingers. He grasps it and slowly displaces it while looking at the rattles. He then begins to swing it very gently, which produces a slight movement of the hanging rattles and an as yet faint sound inside them. Laurent then definitely increases by degrees his own movements. He shakes the chain more and more vigorously and laughs uproariously at the result obtained. (p. 185)

White argued that humans and most animals have an intrinsic need to interact effectively with the environment; a need, in short, to develop competence. (To clarify White's terms: effective interaction with the environment is called *competence;* the motivational force behind the development of this competence is called *effectance.* In fact, however, many psychologists have come to use the term "competence motivation" instead of "effectance.") White does not reject Freud's contributions to the psychology of motivation; indeed his popular textbook on abnormal psychology (White & Watt, 1981) is heavily influenced by psychoanalysis. Nevertheless, White is clear that his proposal of innate "effectance motives" is a sharp break from Freud. These motives are *not* libidinal or aggressive energy that has been transformed by defense mechanisms acting under the pressure of reality, but rather they are "there in the first place as part of the natural make-up of an adaptive organism" (White, 1959, p. 310).

Behavior motivated by effectance motives involves a continuous process as much as or even more than it involves a goal, in the ordinary sense. In White's words (1959):

> It [the goal of effectance motives] does not lie solely in sensory stimulation, in a bettering of the cognitive map, in coordinated action, in motor exercise, in a feeling of effort and of effects produced, or in the appreciation of change brought about in the sensory field. These are simply aspects of a process which at this stage has to

be conceived as a whole. . . . It is constantly circling from stimulus to perception to action to effect to stimulus to perception, and so on around; or, more precisely, these processes are all in continuous action and continuous change. (pp. 321–322)

Perhaps we can clarify the effectance motives by using the notion of a series of "components," just as with the libido. What starts out as a single perception-action-effect cycle of effectance motivation may in later life become differentiated into three separate motives, depending on which part of the cycle is emphasized. Thus there would be a *desire to cognize* or desire to "know," if the perceptual and cognitive aspects of the effectance sequence were emphasized. Emphasis on motor actions, in contrast, would lead to a later construction and *mastery motive*. Finally, a focus on the effects or results of interacting with the environment would lead to a *need for achievement* or achievement motive.

White suggested that effectance motives display two essential characteristics in everyday behavior. First, the person will show *focalization or sustained attention* toward some particular part of the external environment. In other words, random activity in which a person jumps around from object to object or activity to activity is not competence-motivated behavior. Second, the person will show *exploration or experimentation*—a kind of playfulness—instead of the single-track behavior characteristic of strongly aroused drives such as hunger. White summarized these two characteristics of effectance motivation in the phrase "variation within a focus."

Self-actualization. Beginning in the 1940s, several theorists proposed actualization or self-actualization as a major human motive. Their work marked the beginning of what was later to be called the "humanistic" tradition in personality psychology. Goldstein (1878–1965) first introduced the term "actualization." He rejected the idea that people had isolated separate drives and argued instead for the importance of a single, unified, "holistic" self-actualization tendency. "An organism," he wrote, "is governed by the tendency to actualize, as much as possible, its individual capacities, its 'nature,' in the world" (Goldstein, 1939, p. 196). His ideas were later developed by Carl Rogers (1902–1986) and Abraham Maslow (1908–1970), among others. Born in Chicago, educated originally for the protestant ministry, Rogers was professionally active at the universities of Chicago and Wisconsin. In later life he was identified with the human potential movement in California. His life, like his motivational theory, is thus in many respects a great contrast from that of Freud.

Self-actualization is the process of becoming (or actualizing) what one can become. To actualize yourself is to realize or live up to your potential in the broadest sense. Humanistic theorists maintain that we can best see the self-actualization motive by looking at the lives of people who have coped with difficulties and problems, instead of focusing (as did Freud) only on people who are disturbed, disordered, and destroyed by life. Consider some historical examples of people who, in spite of obvious signs of disturbance, were yet able to attain greatness. Humanistic theorists would emphasize their self-actualization motives rather than their pathologies. (1) An inconsiderate young man with a taste for bathroom humor had great musical potential but was mercilessly driven by his overambitious father. Still, he developed into the greatest musical genius of Western music—Wolfgang Amadeus Mozart. (2) A frightened and shy young wife, dominated by her mother-in-law and humiliated by her husband's infidelities, emerged as a courageous champion of human rights and human dignity—Eleanor Roosevelt. (3) An embarrassed and tongue-tied young lawyer named Mohandas Gandhi gave up his slavish imitation of English ways to lead 400 million Indian people, in pride and peace, to independence, thereby earning the name Mahatma, or "Great Soul."

It is often difficult to know whether a particular person has reached this goal of self-actualization or to tell whether any particular action is really the result of a self-actualization motive. Consider the extreme case of Adolf Hitler. Perhaps his potential was really demonic; so in becoming one of the most evil, feared, and hated persons in human history he was merely actualizing his potential. If you think this is a ridiculous question, then ask yourself what Hitler's "true potential" really *was*. Hitler might have had the potential to become another Gandhi, but how could we know? It is difficult to define potential in a way that is not circular. Simply judging people's potential by looking at what people do with their lives is circular. Yet we can scarcely say that all people have the same potential, that everyone could become Mozart, Eleanor Roosevelt, or Gandhi.

Humanistic personality theorists have struggled with this question. At one extreme is Rogers, who argued that each individual person's potential is unique and cannot therefore be specified in advance. In fact, however, Rogers did describe "fully functioning persons," those who have actualized their potential (1959): (1) They perceive reality, especially themselves, correctly. (2) They use their uniquely human abilities of imagination, understanding, and play. (3) Their work is productive. (4) Their social relationships are based on mutuality and warmth rather than exploitation and cynicism.

Maslow gave a more elaborate description of at least eighteen characteristics of self-actualizing people, based on a study of fourteen living people and thirty-seven historical figures such as Eleanor Roosevelt, Lincoln, Harriet Tubman, and George Washington Carver (Maslow, 1970, chap. 11). These characteristics are listed in Table 4.3. It is easy to imagine that self-actualizers are perfect, but Maslow stressed that "there are no perfect human beings!" and went on to suggest at least four imperfections of self-actualizers, which I have also included at the bottom of the table. Though Maslow went into much greater detail, his views are similar to those of Rogers and also Allport (1961) about the actualized or mature personality, namely an emphasis on humanist values of growth, optimism, conscious choice, and hope. A modern conception of psychological well-being (Ryff, 1995) emphasizes six dimensions: autonomy, environmental mastery, personal growth, positive relations with others, purpose in life, and self-acceptance. As Table 4.3 shows, these dimensions are related to Maslow's characteristics of self-actualizing people.

TABLE 4.3 CHARACTERISTICS OF SELF-ACTUALIZED PEOPLE (MASLOW) AND DIMENSIONS OF PSYCHOLOGICAL WELL-BEING (RYFF)

Characteristics of self-actualized people (Maslow)	Dimensions of psychological well-being (Ryff)
General characteristics	
1. More efficient perception of reality; can detect what is fake or dishonest; judge people correctly and efficiently; comfortable with unknown or ambiguous things	
2. Acceptance of self; good appetite, sleep well, enjoy sex; not defensive	Self-acceptance
3. Spontaneous; simple and natural	
4. Problem-centered rather than self-centered; a sense of mission in life; concerned with basic issues and question	Purpose in life
5. Need for privacy and solitude	
6. Autonomous; able to be independent of immediate environment and culture	Autonomy
7. Capacity for freshness of appreciation	
8. Mystic or "peak" experiences	
9. Sympathetic identification with others	
10. Deep and profound interpersonal relations; able to dissolve boundaries of own ego; deep ties with a small number of other people	Positive relations with others
11. "Democratic" character structure: differences of class, race, education, or political belief not important	
12. Able to distinguish means from ends, good from evil	
13. Philosophical, with a sense of humor	
14. Creative	Personal growth
15. Able to transcend the boundaries of own culture	Environmental mastery
Possible imperfections	
16. Sometimes so decisive as to appear ruthless	
17. Sometimes so unconventional as to appear shocking	
18. Sometimes absent-minded	
19. Not free from guilt, anxiety, sadness, or conflict	

SOURCE: Adapted from Maslow (1970, chap. 11) and Ryff (1995).

Many self-actualization theorists also admit the importance of the Freudian groups of motives, anxiety, unconscious conflicts, and defensive transformations of motives. To Rogers, however, defenses are not inevitable and universal. Rather, they are the result of *conditions of worth* imposed by parents on the young child. A child who believes that "I am good only when I do such-and-such" would have conditions of worth; that is, feeling self-*worth* or worthy only on *condition* of doing (or not doing) some particular act (see also Chapter 9). In contrast, when children are given warmth and love regardless of what they do (*unconditional positive regard,* in Rogers's terms), they grow up without conditions of worth. As adults, they have fewer defenses and barriers that block expression of self-actualization motives.

Empirically Based Classifications of Motives

So far we have considered some rather grand philosophical theories about human nature which try to collect all of our motives into a few broad groups. At the other extreme are theorists who postulate as many different motives or instincts as they need to account for human behavior. Lists of this kind were popular in the early decades of the twentieth century. Because of the prestige of biology, these were often called lists of instincts, but they were really patterns of action and thought with names generated by society (Bernard, 1924, pp. 163, 513–514): in other words, motives. Most of these lists were developed out of speculation rather than out of any systematic attempt to analyze and classify motivated behavior into basic underlying motives. As we might expect, the results of such armchair theorizing were many different lists of "basic" human motives, each made up by a different theorist.

In an early and influential textbook that ran to over twenty editions, McDougall (1908) developed a list of eleven such "innate propensities," or motives: gregariousness, sexuality, parental instinct, acquisition, construction, pugnacity, self-assertion (and its opposite, self-abasement), curiosity, repulsion, and flight. In 1924, the sociologist Bernard and his students tried to construct a master list by collecting all the different "instincts," or motives, that had been postulated by major writers in the social sciences and related fields. In all, they examined over 600 books, resulting in a list of over 300 pages— much too long even to publish! After eliminating instincts mentioned only once and grouping together related instincts, they still ended up with over 298 different motives, grouped into twenty-two broad categories.

Once we depart from a very small number of major motives (as in Freud's trio of self-preservation, libido, and death instincts, which are each groups of components), therefore, it seems that there is no easy or obvious place to stop. McDougall's list of innate propensities seems reasonable, but so does Bernard's list of categories, which is twice as long. Further, even these broad categories may group together motives that ought (or ought not) to be distinguished from each other. For example, under the classification "altruistic instincts," Bernard includes affection, good will, helping, humanitarianism, kindliness, love, peacefulness, pity, protection, sacrifice, sympathy, and tenderness. Some people would argue that some of these be put together, while others would insist that they be kept separate. Consider the many separate classes of "sex instincts" (including carnal, flirting, loving, and purity instincts, among others) or "social instincts" (including twenty-seven specific components): should they be combined or not? It is difficult to imagine how we might decide such questions.

MURRAY'S LIST OF MOTIVES FROM A STUDY OF COLLEGE MEN

As we have seen, then, the questions of how many basic motives we have and what they are may have no final empirically based answers. For many personality psychologists, however, the work of Henry Murray (1893–1988) and his associates at Harvard University provided answers that have lasted for over fifty years. Murray was originally trained as a surgeon, and then got a Ph.D. in biochemistry. Becoming interested in psychology, he was psychoanalyzed by Franz Alexander (a disciple of Freud's) and had a brief but intense visit with Jung. In the mid-1930s, with support from the Rockefeller Foundation, Murray gathered around him over two dozen associates (including a sociologist, an anthropologist, a physician, a poet, and psychologists of widely varying backgrounds and approaches) at the Harvard Psychological Clinic to carry out one of the first major systematic research studies of *normal* personality, published as *Explorations in Personality* (Murray, 1938; see also Robinson, 1992, for a biography of this extraordinary person, and White, 1981, for an account of what it was like to work with Murray). Murray's group intensively studied fifty-one people—thirty-nine male Harvard undergraduates and twelve unemployed young men. Of course this is scarcely a representative sample of humanity. Whether Murray's list of motives and model of personality will prove applicable to people of both genders—and all classes, cultures, and times—is still an open question.

To study personality, the Murray group used or invented methods that later became standard: autobiographies, interviews, experimental procedures, questionnaires, and the so-called projective tests (see Chapter 5). Their goal was to identify and catalog all important personality variables that were operating in their young male subjects: the motives necessary to account for important goals, the traits needed to describe how these goals were pursued, and so forth.

In developing his list of personality variables, Murray made a deliberate analogy to organic chemistry (1938, p. 142). That is, the list of motives and traits was seen as a limited number of *elements* capable of combining into an almost infinite number of complex and unique individual personality *compounds*. With this manageably short list of personality elements, Murray intended to reconstruct all important aspects of personality, avoiding both the oversimplified reductionism of the two or three "master motives" postulated by theorists such as Freud and also the endless proliferation of motives put forward by the instinct theorists.

Henry A. Murray (1893–1988), senior author of *Explorations in Personality*: "the first version of a reasonably comprehensive classification of aimed motive forces (needs, wants, drives) as a necessary revision and extension of Freud's irrational, sentimental, and inadequately differentiated division of instincts into Eros and Thanatos" (Murray, 1981, p. 72).

In the end, Murray and his colleagues decided on twenty basic motives (or "needs," in their terminology).[6] While each is usually directly expressed in behavior, six also occur in a repressed or inhibited form as *latent* motives, affecting thoughts and emotions directly but actions only indirectly. Table 4.4 gives the name and a brief description of each motive. The symbol "*n*" (for need) is conventionally used to refer to the Murray needs or motives. You can find a fuller description of these twenty motives in *Explorations in Personality* (Murray, 1938, chap. 3).

Since 1938, this list has been widely adopted by many personality psychologists as a useful working list of basic human motives. As Hall and Lindzey put it, Murray's list "is a classification of motives that is probably more widely useful than any other comparable classification" (1978, pp. 235–236). Several popular personality questionnaires, or inventories, are based on it: for example, the Adjective Check List, the Edwards Personal Preference Schedule, the Personality Research Form, and the Stern Activities Index (see Wiggins & Broughton, 1985, for further details of these instruments). Some researchers employ the whole list, while others concentrate on only a few motives. Entire books have been written about certain motives, for example, the achievement motive (McClelland, Atkinson, Clark, & Lowell, 1953).

[6]Seven additional motives were less systematically studied: *n* Acquisition, *n* Blamavoidance (blame avoidance), *n* Cognizance, *n* Construction, *n* Exposition, *n* Recognition, and *n* Retention.

TABLE 4.4 MURRAY'S LIST OF MOTIVES

Motive Name	Description
n Abasement	To accept or submit passively to fate, injury, blame, criticism, or punishment (often inhibited or latent)
n Achievement	To accomplish something difficult, attain a high standard, or surpass others
n Affiliation	To win affection, be near, and enjoyably interact with others
n Aggression	To oppose with force, fight, attack, injure, or kill another person (often inhibited or latent)
n Autonomy	To resist restraint, coercion, and restriction
n Counteraction	To overcome weakness, fear, and failure by striving again
n Deference	To admire, support, and yield eagerly to a (superior) other person
n Defendence	To defend against criticism and blame and vindicate one's self
n Dominance	To control, influence, or direct other people (often inhibited or latent)
n Exhibition	To excite, amaze, shock, entertain, or make an impression on other people (often inhibited or latent)
n Harmavoidance	To avoid or escape from pain, injury, illness, and death (harm avoidance)
n Infavoidance	To avoid humiliation, embarrassment, or scorn (inferiority avoidance)
n Nurturance	To nurse, support, protect, or take care of another person
n Order	To arrange, organize, balance, or put things in order
n Play	To act "for fun" or amusement, without further purpose
n Rejection	To exclude, abandon, or separate one's self from a disliked other person
n Sentience	To seek and enjoy sensuous impressions (visual, auditory, kinetic, tactile, or olfactory)
n Sex	To form an erotic, sexual relationship with another person (often inhibited or latent)
n Succorance	To be nursed, supported, protected, or taken care of by a sympathetic other person (often inhibited or latent)
n Understanding	To analyze and generalize events, to develop theories

SOURCE: Adapted from Murray (1938, pp. 144–226).

Organization of Murray's Twenty Motives

These twenty motives can be organized in various ways. If we consider the relationships among separate motives, Affiliation and Rejection seem to be opposites, while Dominance, Exhibition, and Aggression are closely associated with each other and opposed to Deference. Thus someone who wants to control and direct other people (Dominance) might go about it by trying to excite, amaze, or make an impression on them (Exhibition), by using force (Aggression), or even by moving back and forth among all three. Nurturance (taking

care of other people) seems to combine Affiliation and Dominance, while Suc-
corance (being taken care of by others) involves Affiliation and Deference.

Motives can also be arranged in *hierarchies of subsidiation* (a Murray term),
in which one motive is a step on the path toward gratifying another motive.
We can observe this subsidiation in Richard Nixon's description of his early
life: for example, achievement (success as a debater) in order to obtain affiliation (his father's approval), or aggression as a reaction to frustrated affiliation.

Motives also can be grouped in *hierarchies of generality,* in which specific
motives are grouped into a small number of broader classes—the number
depending on the level of generality. A study by Wicker, Lambert, Richardson,
and Kahler (1984) illustrates this point. Wicker and associates gave subjects a
list of fifty-six hypothetical goals, including most of the ones on the Murray
list. With a mathematical procedure called hierarchical cluster analysis, they
studied how people grouped these goals. At one level of generality, six or
seven clear clusters emerged: competitive ambition, success, personal growth,
material security, interpersonal security, orientation toward other people, and
playful exploration. At a higher level of abstraction, however, these six or
seven clusters reduced to two fundamental dimensions: individual assertive
striving and interpersonal harmony seeking. Figure 4.2 shows a two-dimensional arrangement suggested by the results of Wicker and associates, super-
imposed on most of the motives of Murray's list. (The locations of Autonomy
and Sex are tentative and debatable; perhaps they don't really fit into this two-
dimensional arrangement.)

We can also label the two fundamental dimensions of Figure 4.2 as *power*
and *affiliation*. (Murray used the term "dominance" instead of "power." Since
dominance suggests overbearing influence, I prefer the more neutral word
"power," which means simply "having an effect on some other person.")
Most of the rest of the motives on the Murray list—in fact all motives that are
interpersonal or involve interaction with others—can be fit into this two-
dimensional space. They can be thought of as points in a compass which is
defined by the two directions of power-versus-deference and affiliation-
versus-rejection. (Compare this to the idea of a motivational compass that
Freud borrowed from Lichtenberg, as described in Chapter 3.)

Some of Murray's motives do not fit into the figure. For example, defensive or avoidance motives such as Harmavoidance and Infavoidance may be
interpersonal but are really focused on the self, and so do not fit into these two
dimensions. (The interpersonal motives Defendence and Counteraction, which
do fit, also have overtones of avoidance.) There are also *impersonal motives*,
those involving physical sensations (Sentience, Play), mental processes (Order,
Understanding), or performance quality (Achievement, Counteraction) but
not necessarily interpersonal behavior.

We can conclude that the twenty motives of the Murray list fall into four
basic groups: two fundamental interpersonal dimensions (power and affiliation), a cluster of impersonal motives, and the avoidance or self-protective
motives. Further, we can link these four groups to Freud's categories. Thus
power includes the components of Freud's death instinct, while affiliation

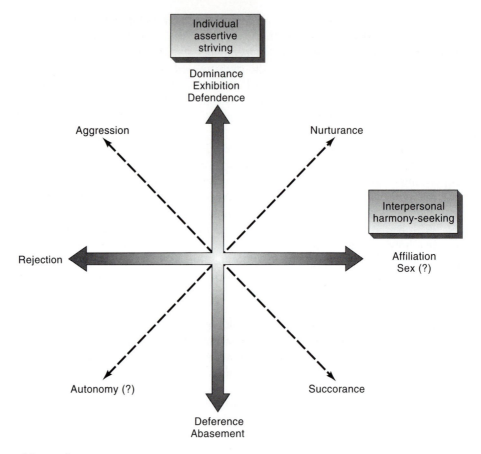

FIGURE 4.2
Two-dimensional arrangements of Murray's motives.

overlaps with most of the libidinal motives. Even the impersonal and avoid-ance motives can be linked to the positive (approach) and negative (avoid-ance) aspects, respectively, of Freud's self-preservation motives.

Under varying names, the two dimensions of power and affiliation emerge over and over, from many different kinds of studies, as the most important dimensions of interpersonal behavior. Thus the social psychologist Brown (1965, chap. 2) argued that the dimensions of status (power) and soli-darity (affiliation) emerge from our evolutionary inheritance as basic dimen-sions of social relations. They are also built into our language. For example, among friends we use first names and nicknames reciprocally to indicate solidarity or friendship. To each other, two friends are Jane and Dan; to strangers, they are Ms. Jones or Mr. Smith. (Languages such as Spanish, German, and French have alternative familiar and polite forms of the second-person pronoun "you" that are used in this way: familiar form among friends, polite form among strangers.) To indicate status and power, in contrast, these forms are used *nonreciprocally*. Thus a teacher might call a student John, but would expect to be addressed in response as Ms. Jones. And after inauguration, a president of the United States suddenly becomes Mr. President (someday it will be Ms. President) to even his closest associates, whom he continues to address by their first name. President Kennedy's close adviser Theodore Sorenson described the sudden change after Kennedy's inauguration (Sorenson, 1965, pp. 248, 262).

In studies of small groups, Bales (1958) found that leadership was usually divided between *task leaders,* who dominated and directed the discussion, and *social-emotional leaders,* who smoothed relationships among group members and released tension. Studies of the social behavior of individuals also suggest the importance of these two dimensions, often arranged in a compasslike or "circumplex" fashion (Conte & Plutchik, 1981; Freedman, Leary, Ossorio, & Coffey, 1951; Kiesler, 1983; Wiggins & Broughton, 1985).[7] Finally, studies in ethnopsychology (how ordinary people in other, non-Western cultures describe psychological processes and characteristics) suggest that these two dimensions are nearly universal ways of arranging goals (Kornadt, Eckensberger, & Emminghaus, 1980).

Motivation and Behavior

While there may be no fixed and final list of motives, many lines of evidence suggest that power and affiliation (or close synonyms to them) are the two most important classes of interpersonal human motives or dimensions of interpersonal motivated behavior. A third impersonal cluster involves seeking stimulation (sentience, play, curiosity, understanding) or evaluating the results of action (achievement). A final cluster involves self-protection and self-maintenance motives that are usually defensive or avoidant because they regulate our reactions to threat.

While each of these clusters can be divided into more specific motives as necessary, this risks confusion and proliferation of labels. Another approach, elaborated in the next chapter, uses the three broad motive classes to conceptualize the motivational aspects of personality. More specific motivated behavior can then be explained as the result of various combinations of these basic motives, along with other personality variables.

---

[7]Wiggins and Broughton (1985) reverse the positions of affiliation and nurturance in their discussion of the structure of Murray's list of motives. However, I believe that nurturance is a fusion of power and affiliation rather than that affiliation is a fusion of power and nurturance.

5

Scientific Measurement of Motives

---- ❖ ----

Motives are difficult to identify and measure. Asking people about their motives doesn't always work. For example, think of the examples at the beginning of Chapter 2. We would probably accept Jane's account of why she crossed the street, but we might not believe what Lee Harvey Oswald had to say about his motives. Sometimes we estimate people's motives by looking at the broad themes or outcomes of their lives, as we did in Chapter 2 with the opening chapter of Richard Nixon's autobiography. Yet this method has its problems. For one thing, we usually don't have a lifetime's worth of behavior to observe. Then too, different observers may detect different motives at work in the same sequence of behavior, as we saw in the case of Oswald. Finally, we must be careful to distinguish *goals* from *results:* people don't always get what they want, or want what they get. So for a science of personality psychology, we need a reliable and valid way of measuring motives.

*R*ELIABILITY AND VALIDITY

A measure is reliable if different observers get the same results, and if the measure gives the same results under the same conditions. Thus a good thermometer is reliable because it always gives the same reading, to all observers, when the temperature is the same. A measure is valid when the measurements it gives fit with our understanding of what is being measured. Thus a good thermometer is valid because when it reads –5°C, water will freeze and we feel cold without a warm coat; and when it reads 40°C, we perspire and want to turn on the air conditioner. In short, the readings of the thermometer fit with our conception of temperature and are a trustworthy way to anticipate future conditions. With these general guidelines, let us examine some of the ways that psychologists have tried to measure motives.

FREE ASSOCIATION AND THE INTERPRETATION OF FANTASY

Freud assessed people's motives by interpreting their dreams, fantasies, and other products of their imagination. This method, he argued, "is the royal road to a knowledge of the unconscious activities of the human mind" (1900, V, p. 608). Freud began by focusing on some surprising or unusual part of the dream or fantasy. He told the person to say whatever came to mind—no matter how irrelevant, farfetched, or embarrassing—without censoring and without any concern for coherence or logical connection. This is called *free association*. After some practice and further encouragement against blocking or editing, people usually produced longer and longer chains of free associations. As these chains grew, they seemed (in metaphorical terms) to circle and twist around each other, forming *networks* or *complexes*. These networks, Freud argued, reflect the person's underlying motives.

The term "complex," as a noun, was introduced in 1904 by Jung, to refer to a complex (used as an adjective) cluster of ideas or images bound together by a common (positive or negative) feeling. When the emotion is especially strong, the complex affects or motivates (Jung's term is "constellates") thought and behavior. The most familiar example of a complex is the Oedipus complex, discussed in Chapter 4, but Jung used the term to refer to any cluster of ideas or associations saturated by a strong emotion—for example, the family complex, mother complex, hero complex, or even "alcohol complex" (Jung, 1910/1973, 1913/1973).

The Technique of Interpretation

In analyzing associative chains or complexes back to their motive sources or complexes, Freud believed that he was decoding what the ego had put into code in order to escape the censorship of the superego. Thus when several different motives were *condensed* into a single dream element, Freud skillfully separated out each motive. If emotional emphasis had been shifted or *displaced* on to some trivial content, Freud sought to restore the original emphasis. Motives concealed in *symbolic disguises* were translated back to their original form. Since each person's symbols might have unique meanings, this translation backward had to be based on that person's free associations; they couldn't just be looked up in a fixed symbol dictionary of the kind you find in pop psychology books. Still, over time Freud concluded that certain symbols were very common, if not universal. (In successive editions of *The Interpretation of Dreams*, 1900, IV–V, the section on "representation by symbols" got longer and longer.) Finally, since the ego uses *secondary revision,* or secondary elaboration, to give a veneer of plausibility and sense to the dream, the work of interpretation has to break down this surface rationality.

These four coding processes—condensation, displacement, symbolic transformation, and secondary revision—are called the "dream work." They transform the *latent dream* (the dreamer's actual wishes or motives) into the *manifest dream* (what the dreamer experiences and remembers). To interpret the dream, one must reverse or undo the dream work. The best single example is Freud's interpretation of his own dream about his patient, Irma (1900, IV, pp. 106–121): beneath the confused manifest dream content Freud discovered two latent wishes: (1) to avoid responsibility for problems in Irma's treatment and (2) to take revenge on an annoying friend.

Freud believed these same four processes were also at work in other areas of mental life: in people's daydreams and fantasies, mistakes and symptoms, religious practices and interests—in short, in almost every aspect of thought and action. Thus the techniques of dream interpretation can be applied to analyzing any other kind of fantasy or work of imagination, such as works of literature, or even a nonverbal work of art such as a painting or statue. Here, for example, is Freud's interpretation of Shakespeare's *Hamlet* (1900, IV):

> The play is built up on Hamlet's hesitations over fulfilling the task of revenge [for his father's murder] that is assigned to him; but its text offers no reasons or motives for these hesitations and an immense variety of attempts at interpreting them have failed to produce a result. . . . What is it, then, that inhibits him in fulfilling the task set him by his father's ghost? The answer, once again, is that it is the peculiar nature of the task. Hamlet is able to do anything—except take vengeance on the man who did away with his father and took that father's place with his mother, the man who shows him the repressed wishes of his own childhood realized. Thus the loathing which should drive him on to revenge is replaced in him by self-reproaches, by scruples of conscience, which remind him that he is literally no better than the sinner whom he is to punish. . . . The distaste for sexuality expressed by Hamlet in his conversation with Ophelia fits in very well with this. (pp. 264–265)

Freud's methods of interpretation usually assume the presence of the person being analyzed, in order to give free associations. On occasion, however, he used them at a distance to analyze historical figures he had never met, by substituting his own knowledge and experience for the unavailable free associations. To support his *Hamlet* interpretation he added the following comment about Shakespeare (1900, IV):

> I observe in a book on Shakespeare by Georg Brandes a statement that *Hamlet* was written immediately after the death of Shakespeare's father (in 1601), that is, under the immediate impact of his bereavement and, as we may well assume, while his childhood feelings about his father had been freshly revived. It is known, too, that Shakespeare's own son who died at an early age bore the name of "Hamnet," which is identical with "Hamlet." (pp. 265–266)

Why Not Ask People about Their Motives?

Some psychologists argue that direct questions are the best way to get at what people want. As Gordon Allport, the best-known advocate of this position, put it: "To my mind [Freudian interpretation] seems to mark the culmination of a century-long era of irrationalism, and therefore of distrust. Has the subject no right to be believed?" (1953/1960, p. 97). For all of his different techniques of interpretation, however, Freud did *not* use this method. He believed that self-reported motives are often distorted by the ever-present operation of defense mechanisms, so we are not able to report on them accurately.

Of course, for much of everyday life, Freud did accept people's accounts of their motives; only in exceptional cases did he look for "deeper" interpretations. Using the example in Chapter 2, Jane *says* she is crossing the street because she wants to get a book from the library; under ordinary conditions, Freud would likely have accepted this as her motive. But now let us change the example a little. Jane *says* that she is crossing the street to go to the library. But what would we conclude about her motive if there were no library on the other side of the street? Or if she looked around anxiously and suspiciously as she walked? Or if she crossed the street, went into the library, and tore her notebook into little pieces while madly singing and dancing? For the ordinary behaviors of life, psychoanalysis is usually content with ordinary explanations, but when the behavior begins to show what Freud called "surprising or unusual connections," then the search for unconscious goals may be necessary for a full explanation.

Regardless of whether we believe that people may not know their own motives, there are other problems with self-reported motives. First, answers to questions about goals and motives are not given in a vacuum, but in social situations; thus they are affected by considerations of *social desirability*. For example, people usually try to manage the impressions they create, to appear in a good light to others, and to figure out the "right" answer. They tend to report what they believe they should report or what they believe the questioner wants to hear. All of these factors introduce bias and distortion into self-reports of motives, reducing their validity.

Also, people's beliefs about themselves and their motives are subjective *constructions* about their goals, rather than objective systematic observations about the goals they have sought. In metaphorical terms, they are portraits rather than photographs. When we are asked about our motives, we tend to examine our lives for a unified thread of purpose, rather than accurately recalling the actual day-to-day tangles of conflicting purposes, goals, pleasures, and fears. As a result, our motivational self-reports, like our memories, are *schemas*, or organized abstractions constructed around certain features that strike us as important, rather than complete records of actions and goals (see Chapter 9). Thus we are often in a poor position to estimate our own motives, as well as many other things about ourselves, as Nisbett and Wilson (1977) argue. As an analogy, we are like tourists viewing the ancient castles of France. We are impressed with what we can see (the magnificence of the visible remains), but we may not be aware of the whole story—for example, the blood and toil of thousands of people that went into their construction, the daily activities that went on inside them, or the revolutionary forces that changed them from royal residences into tourist sights.

Motives versus Cognitions about Motives

For all these reasons, we may conclude that interpreting or decoding motives from people's dreams or free associations will often give quite different results from what we would get by asking them directly. Depending on what we want to know and predict about personality, both kinds of measures may be interesting and useful. That is, both measures may have validity, but different kinds of validity: they would predict different behaviors and outcomes. Freud was mainly interested in unconscious motives, and so preferred his techniques of interpretation. Modern personality psychologists often find it useful to ask people direct questions about themselves and their goals, as well as using Freud's methods. To avoid confusion, I will use the term "motive" to refer to measures based on Freud's conceptions and techniques. In contrast, I will label people's conscious beliefs about their motives, as revealed by their responses to questions, as *cognitions* or self-schemas, to be considered in Part Two (especially Chapter 10).

SYSTEMATIC MEASUREMENT OF MOTIVES IN FANTASY

Freud's technique of interpreting and decoding dreams, free associations, and fantasies presents several practical problems. For one thing, it is slow and cumbersome. In therapy, a person might free-associate to a single dream or fantasy for several hours, with many false starts and a good deal of blank time, before a Freudian psychoanalyst would feel that the "real" underlying motives had been discovered. Even then, we might wonder whether this was a *representative* sample of the person's fantasy. Perhaps this particular fantasy was aroused, reawakened, or strengthened by some particular experience of that day. (Freud called such arousing experiences the "day residue.") Or perhaps it was elicited by something the analyst said. Would another analyst have elicited the same fantasy or arrived at the same interpretation? And while psychoanalytic interpretation may identify a motive, it does not tell us much about the strength of that motive—how strong it is in comparison to the person's other motives or to other people's motives. Even brilliant interpretations, for all their appeal when made by a clinician as gifted as Freud, are not of much help when we want to make more precise assessments and comparisons. For that we need methods that are *systematic*, in that they are carried out under standard conditions, and *objective*, in that they are based on defined criteria, as well as reliable and valid. The goal, therefore, is to refine and improve the scientific credentials of psychoanalytic assessment of motives, while at the same time preserving their capacity to detect complex unconscious motives.

Early Techniques for the Analysis of Fantasy

Jung and word association. Perhaps the first attempt to refine clinical methods of assessment was made by Jung (1910/1973), who drew on early experimental psychology research on word association to develop the Word Association Test as a way of identifying and measuring complexes or unconscious motives. People taking the test are read a series of words with instructions to reply to each word, "as quickly as possible with the first word that occurs to you." Sometimes people delay their answers, repeat the stimulus word, or respond with personal references, stereotyped answers, or a flood of words. In such cases, Jung argued, an emotionally charged complex is disturbing, or "constellating," their behavior. By considering the stimulus word and the contents of the person's answer, Jung would then make a judgment about which complex was involved. As he put it, "with practice and experience one may easily attain the faculty of collecting those stimulus-words which will most likely be accompanied by disturbances, then of combining their meanings and deducing therefrom the intimate affairs of the subject" (1913/1973, p. 599). Freud admired the scientific precision of the test (stopwatch, careful recording of responses, quantitative results) and declared that "this procedure offers the psychoanalyst what qualitative analysis offers the chemist." Still, he never used it himself, for "in the treatment of neurotic patients it can be dispensed with" (1909b, XI, 32).

Murray's "Explorations in Personality" group. With his colleagues at the Harvard Psychological Clinic in the 1930s, Murray used both the Word Association Test and Hermann Rorschach's famous inkblot test and developed several new methods of assessing fantasy (see Morgan & Murray, 1935; Murray, 1937, 1938, chap. 6). In the Dramatic Productions Test, for example, people are shown a table covered with small children's toys and then asked to construct a dramatic scene (as in a movie) and explain it. In "The Minister's Black Veil," people read the following paragraph (Murray, 1938):

> This story by Hawthorne is laid in the last century. The central idea is that a minister, after many years with his congregation, appears in the pulpit one Sunday morning wearing a black veil over his face, and thereafter for a long time is never without it. It would be interesting if you would take this idea as the nucleus for a story of your own. You may develop it in any way you please and make any modifications you desire. (p. 549)

Since the minister's action suggests shame or guilt, the ways in which people explain his action presumably reflect their own "guilty" unconscious motives.

The Thematic Apperception Test (TAT)

Undoubtedly, Murray's most important method of measuring motives—indeed, his most widely cited contribution to the study of personality—is the Thematic Apperception Test, or TAT (Morgan & Murray, 1935). (*Apperception* means the process of assigning meaning to a stimulus, in contrast to *perception*, which refers to the process of sensing and labeling of the stimulus.) People taking the test are shown a series of pictures and asked to make up a story about each picture. They are left completely on their own, with no suggestion that there is any one "correct" story. Sometimes questions like the following are used to help people cover the elements of a story plot: (1) What is happening in the picture? Who are the people? (2) What has led up to this situation; that is, what has happened in the past? (3) What is being thought? What is wanted? By whom? (4) What will happen? What will be done?

The pictures are vague, in that they could suggest a variety of different stories, themes, or motifs. The picture in Figure 5.1 is an example. (It is not one of Murray's original set of TAT pictures, but it is now widely used in motivation research; see Smith, 1992, p. 635). It shows two people, probably a woman and a man, sitting on a bench by a river, probably during cold weather. Before you read further about the TAT, you may want to take about five minutes and write out whatever story this picture suggests to you. You can then refer to your story as you read the rest of this chapter, in order to apply the concepts discussed to yourself and to get some sense of your own motives.

The TAT actually originated from the experience of Cecelia Roberts, an undergraduate student in Murray's abnormal psychology course. Anderson (1990) reconstructed the story from later interviews with Murray:

> But it was difficult to gather fantasies; merely asking someone for his or her fantasies did not work well. . . . [Cecelia Roberts] faced the same difficulty as . . .

Christiana Morgan (1897–1967), co-developer, with Henry Murray, of the Thematic Apperception Test. "Since the subject is led to believe that it is a test of creative imagination . . . he is unaware of the fact that he is revealing his innermost thoughts. . . . Of all the short procedures and tests which we have tried, the results of this one have given us the best understanding of the deeper layers of personality" (Morgan & Murray, 1935, p. 306).

FIGURE 5.1
Example of a picture from a modified TAT (from Smith, 1992, p. 635). What is happening? Who are the people? What has led up to this situation? What is being thought and wanted? What will happen?

she tried to get her son to tell her his fantasies. "He wasn't being productive; he thought it was silly to tell his mother what his fantasies were," Murray said. "She had a book and asked him to tell a story about one of the pictures." Her son responded by making up a rich, imaginative story. When Roberts told Murray about this experience, he capitalized on it and started working on the Thematic Apperception Test. (p. 321)

Together with Morgan and his other colleagues, Murray put together the first set of TAT pictures. Shortly afterward, Murray showed several of them to his recently widowed mother during a visit. Her stories were full of grief, although as Anderson (1990) reports from an interview with Murray:

> At the time she was putting on a facade of being over her mourning, and she had no idea that the stories were about herself. Murray felt "guilty" . . . but this experience—with his very own mother—convinced him of the power of the TAT. (pp. 321–322)

Murray believed that when people make up TAT stories, their apperceptions reflect their conscious and unconscious motives, just as a literary work reflects the personality of its author.[1] The TAT and other tests of this type are often called projective tests, because it is assumed that people project their unacceptable (unconscious) needs on to characters in the stories (see the discussion of projection in Chapter 3). This may be true sometimes for all of us, and most of the time for pathological cases, but it is certainly not the whole story of the TAT. Motives in TAT stories may be conscious and acknowledged, unconscious and denied, or both. A study by Combs (1947) compared people's TAT stories with their autobiographies. Some motives were equally likely to appear in both sources (for example, motives to belong, to be safe, to be attractive, or to be loved). Other motives were more likely to appear in "conscious" autobiographies (for example, to overcome a handicap, to be accepted, or to avoid blame). Finally, certain motives were likely to appear only in the TAT

---

[1]Murray published several literary and psychological papers on the nineteenth-century American novelist Herman Melville (see Murray, 1981).

(for example, to die, to atone, or to have sexual relations). Thus while TAT stories may contain deeper, less socially acceptable motives, at least some of the motives they express are also consciously acknowledged motives. In fact, we might conclude from Combs's study that Freud and Allport were both right: motives can be expressed both unconsciously and consciously.

Perhaps the best way to characterize the TAT is to say that it is a sample of imaginative verbal material, saturated with conscious and unconscious motives, wishes, and goals, but also containing conscious impressions, images, meanings, and associative traces (Murray, 1933, pp. 312–314, 323). It can be thought of as a "thought sample" or "imagination sample," analogous to the blood samples collected by physicians. In contrast to the wide variability of day residues that evoke dreams, the TAT uses a standard set of stimuli to elicit the imaginative material. The TAT administrator uses a few standardized instructions and probes, in contrast to the variable interventions and interpretations of a psychoanalyst. Finally, the TAT stories are either written or recorded, so an exact record is preserved. In contrast, patients' dreams are usually only summarized afterward in the analyst's notes.[2] For purposes of precise and objective measurement of motives, all of these characteristics represent a considerable scientific advance on Freud's methods. Yet the TAT does preserve the essential feature of Freud's technique—namely, measuring motives through the interpretation and analysis of fantasy. Thus Gordon (1954) collected dream reports and TAT stories from the same people and found that the two kinds of fantasy were similar in form and content.

Modifications of the TAT

Originally the TAT was used for individual testing. The clinician or test administrator held up a card with a TAT picture on it while the person being tested told a story about that picture. The standard questions were used as probes, but there was no standard rule for their use and no fixed time limit for telling a story.[3] (With small children and in large survey studies, some version of this procedure is still advisable; see Stewart, Sokol, Healy, & Chester, 1986; and Veroff, Atkinson, Feld, & Gurin, 1960; respectively.) Largely through the work of McClelland and his colleagues, however, several modifications were introduced in order to increase the objectivity of the TAT and adapt it to group testing situations (see Smith, 1992). For example, by using a slide projector instead of cards and asking people to write their stories, the TAT can be given to several people at once in a group. The pictures can be replaced by sen-

---

[2]Freud's complete works include only one example of this kind of case notes, what a patient said and did, that he typically made at the end of each day (1909c, X, pp. 259–318).
[3]With no time limit, TAT stories vary widely in length, which means that scores for any variable may then be correlated with the length of stories. In other words, the longer the story, the more likely it is to be scored for any variable, regardless of the person's "true" score. While the effects of such correlations can be removed statistically (see Winter, 1973, pp. 146), they still pose methodological problems. Standard time limits reduce this problem, though they do not eliminate it entirely.

tences. For example, the following sentence could be used in place of the picture shown in Figure 5.1: "A woman and a man are sitting on a bench by a river on a cold day."

One modification, however, changes the TAT completely. When people are given several different interpretations of the picture and asked to choose one (the Iowa Picture Interpretation Test, or IPIT; see Hurley, 1955; Johnston, 1955), the results are not at all comparable to the stories they make up on their own (Heckhausen, 1967, p. 15). In other words, the IPIT converts the TAT from an essay test into a multiple-choice test. As you probably have experienced with regular exams, these two are not the same.

SCORING THEMATIC APPERCEPTION

How can we measure a person's motives from a TAT? Consider the following story, which might be written in response to the picture in Figure 5.1:

> A husband and wife are sitting on the banks of the river on a cold winter day. The sun is dazzling on the snow and ice, and it feels just wonderful for a few minutes. They've been through a lot, some very rough times. She's talking about how discouraged she is. It is the 1950s. Discrimination against women is rampant, and the honors college degree in English wasn't as easy to turn into a successful management career as it would have been for a man. But he has encouraged her, as he is doing now, and tried his best to help. They'll decide both to take off the rest of the day and to have a fancy dinner that evening.

Does this story express an achievement motive? The woman did get an "honors degree" and is concerned about a "successful career." Or does it reflect concerns with affiliation? After all, the *main* theme of the story seems to be the close relationship between the two people. On the other hand, perhaps the husband's "help" is really a gentle kind of power. And shouldn't the "discrimination against women" also count as power? How are we to decide among these different interpretations? Are they all true?

Clinical Scoring Systems

Initially, Murray's group scored motives in the TAT on the basis of clinical judgment. Trained and experienced clinicians would immerse themselves in a person's whole series of TAT stories and then, on the basis of theory and intuition, list the person's predominant motives (see Murray, 1938, pp. 673–680 for an example). As you might expect, even expert clinical scorers sometimes disagree with each other, either because they work from different theories or because their intuitions are different. Such disagreements could be settled by a vote (as was sometimes done in the Murray group), but this does not seem like a sound way to establish a science of personality.

Besides Murray's original system, at least seven different systems for scoring motives in the TAT have been developed by clinicians (see Murstein, 1963, pp. 25–44). While these scoring systems are usually longer and more detailed than Morgan and Murray's original scoring outline, they also sprang largely from the minds and intuitions of their authors. That is, a particular motive is scored the way it is because the author of the scoring system believed that that was the way it should be scored. Such a procedure can create problems, for example, in constructing a scoring definition of the power motive (or *n* Power) in TAT stories. Certainly we should count stories where one character is trying to influence another, or stories where one character has some intentional impact on another. But this definition leaves many questions unanswered. Should we also score stories where the impact is not intended, but merely accidental, or where the impact is the result of some other goal such as achievement? What about stories about giving help? Is help—even help that is asked for or solicited—necessarily an aspect of power? What about pure aggression? Or stories where characters dream about power but do nothing to get it? Given the number of different theories, conceptions, and definitions of power, and making allowance for the effects of reaction formation and sublimation, different researchers could probably justify scoring almost anything in a TAT story as evidence of a "power motive." There is no easy way to decide these cases before doing research on the power motive, and yet some kind of scoring definition is needed in order to do that research.

Measuring Motives through Experimental Arousal

David McClelland and his colleagues at Wesleyan, and later at Harvard and Boston universities, developed a different approach to deciding how to score motives in the TAT (see Atkinson, 1958; Atkinson & McClelland, 1948; McClelland, Atkinson, Clark, & Lowell, 1953; and Smith, 1992). Instead of deciding in advance how to score a motive, they *first* aroused the motive experimentally and *then* observed its effects on TAT story content. For example, one group of people would be exposed to an experience arousing hunger, achievement, or power; a matched control group would have a neutral experience. Both the aroused and neutral groups then took TATs. If the two groups were equivalent before the arousal experience (which would be assured by assigning people randomly), then any differences between the stories written by the aroused group and those written by the neutral group would be due only to the effects of the aroused motive. These differences can then be developed into a measure of that motive. (Winter, 1973, chap. 3, provides a detailed example of the process of developing a motive scoring system.) People who score high in a particular motive can be thought of as being in a state of self-arousal: that is, they customarily react to the TAT picture cues in ways that most people do only under special, externally induced arousal.

Motive scoring systems developed by this technique are said to be *empirically derived*, because they are based on the actual effects of the motive on fantasy. McClelland and Koestner (1992) summarized the logic of this procedure as follows:

> No characteristics were included in the scoring scheme, regardless of how theoretically justified they might be, unless they appeared more often in the stories of sub-

David C. McClelland. "I had started out not believing what people said about their motives. . . . In contrast, the method of arousing a motive experimentally, detecting its effects in fantasy, and using those effects . . . to get an estimate of the strength of the motive proved to be an extremely useful way of predicting a variety of different things that people with a strong motive would in fact do" (McClelland, 1984b, p. 449). (Courtesy Boston University)

jects exposed to motive arousal than in stories written under neutral testing conditions. (p. 143)

Scoring systems developed in this way usually have several categories scored as present or absent in each TAT story. This is the *principle of simplified scoring*, in which complex motive concepts are broken down into simpler basic scoring elements. Such a principle is an important advantage over most of the clinical scoring systems, which often apply complex rating scales to the entire set of TAT stories. While it runs the risk of ignoring complex TAT story characteristics (see Arnold, 1962), breaking down complex and multidimensional judgments into a series of simpler decisions about presence-absence makes it easier to get agreement among scorers. Such agreement, or interscorer reliability, is an essential feature of any scientific system of measurement. For the TAT measures developed by the McClelland-Atkinson research strategy, the usual standard for interscorer agreement is at least 85 percent agreement, or correlation between scorers of .85 or better (see Smith, 1992).

Achievement, Affiliation-Intimacy, and Power Motives

Researchers have used the McClelland-Atkinson technique to develop measures of four important human motives: achievement, affiliation, intimacy, and power. Since affiliation and intimacy are closely related (see below), I prefer to think of them as a single complex motive with different facets (see McAdams, 1982, 1985), and I will sometimes refer to them together in the rest of this chapter. Although the motive scoring systems were developed to code TAT stories, they can be adapted to score almost any kind of imaginative verbal data, such as literature, song lyrics, speeches, or interviews (see Winter, 1991a). For each motive, Table 5.1 gives a brief outline of the scoring system and illustrates some of the arousal experiments that were used to develop it. Research on these motives has been summarized by Smith (1992), where you can also find detailed scoring definitions and instructions for measuring motives, learning to score, and using scores in personality research.

These three motives fit rather well with the major dimensions that emerge from Freud's groupings (see Figure 3.2), or Murray's empirical list (see Figure 4.3). Since the three motives are usually independent or uncorrelated with each other, we can think of them as defining a three-dimensional space, as illustrated in Figure 5.2. To make the figure easy to remember, power is the up-down

TABLE 5.1 BRIEF CHARACTERIZATION OF THE ACHIEVEMENT, AFFILIATION, AND POWER MOTIVES

	Motive		
Characteristic	*Achievement*	*Affiliation*	*Power*
Typical verbal images	Excellence, quality of performance, innovation	Warmth, friendship, unity	Having impact on the behavior or emotions of others, prestige
Associated actions	Moderate risks, seek and use information to modify performance, entrepreneurial success, dishonest when necessary to reach goal	Cooperative and friendly under "safe" conditions, defensive and even hostile under threat	Leadership and high morale of subordinates, if high in sense of responsibility. Profligate impulsivity, if low in sense of responsibility
Negotiating style	Cooperative and "rational"	Cooperative under "safe" conditions, defensive and hostile under threat	Exploitative, aggressive
Own view of partner in negotiations	Cooperative	Either "fellow worker" *or* "opportunist"	Yielder, gambler, competitor, resister
Seeks help from	Technical experts	Friends and similar others	Political "experts"
Political-psychological manifestations	Frustration	Peacemaking and arms limitation, but vulnerability to scandal	Charisma, war and aggression, independent foreign policy, rated greatness

SOURCE: Based on McClelland (1985), Winter (1991, 1992b), and Winter & Stewart (1977a, pp. 46–47).

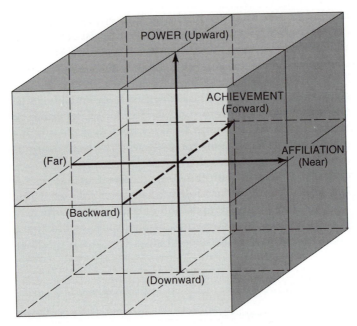

FIGURE 5.2
Three-dimensional arrangement of achievement, affiliation, and power motives.

dimension, achievement is the forward-backward dimension, and affiliation-intimacy is the sideways dimension of near-far. These three or four motives are not the only important human motives (for example, there is also curiosity), but by themselves and in combination, they do cover a good deal of important territory of human motivation. We shall examine them in detail, looking at their characteristic primary goals and substitute goals, their associated actions or ways of reaching those goals, and their typical expressive styles.

THE ACHIEVEMENT MOTIVE: A CONCERN FOR EXCELLENCE

In fantasy and imagination, the achievement motive is expressed as a concern for excellence, for doing a good job or a better job—a "personal best." When looking at the TAT picture in Figure 5.1, someone scoring high in achievement motivation might write a story such as the following:

The woman is a *brilliant* scientist at a well-known university. The man next to her is a colleague. *They have done excellent work,* slowly advancing toward their goal of curing cancer. Today they are in the middle of a crucial experiment. Within a few days they will have the results. Some *apparatus broke* unexpectedly, *making them impatient.* So they have taken a lunch break by the river to *figure out how to fix* things. In fact, both are excited, *anticipating a great discovery* yet trying to keep some composure. Each is *worried about making a mistake* at this point.

The images that score for achievement motivation are underlined. Notice the repeated mention of excellence or high standards along with obstacles, action to overcome obstacles, and positive and negative anticipations. People whose TAT stories are filled with imagery of this kind act in certain distinctive ways, although they do not always succeed at everything.

Economic Success

There is a good deal of evidence that the achievement motive leads to good performance and success in business (see reviews by McClelland, 1961, 1985, chaps. 7 and 11; McClelland & Koestner, 1992; McClelland & Winter, 1969, chap. 1; and Spangler, 1992.) More precisely, people scoring high in achievement motivation are good *entrepreneurs*—that is, people who by their own efforts organize labor, capital, and technology to produce and market some new product or service.

This evidence consists of three kinds of studies.

1. Small companies, especially companies of the high-tech or research-and-development type, grow faster when their owner-operators are high in achievement motivation: not only in the United States (Wainer & Rubin, 1969), but also in Australia (Morris & Fargher, 1974), Hungary (Varga, 1975), and India (Hundal, 1971; Nandy, 1973). Even in large American and Japanese corporations, the levels of achievement motive imagery in annual reports is correlated with subsequent sales (Chusmir & Azevedo, 1992; Diaz, 1982).

2. Farmers who score high in achievement motivation are more innovative and achieve higher crop yields per unit of land than do other farmers, as shown by studies in Australia (Chamala & Crouch, 1977), Colombia (Rogers & Svenning, 1969), and India (Singh, 1969, 1979; Singh & Gupta, 1977).

3. Finally, among managers in progressive companies, achievement motivation is associated with more rapid promotion and salary increases (Andrews, 1967; Cummin, 1967). Among individual men and women, achievement motivation measured at age 31 predicts earned income ten years later (McClelland & Franz, 1992).

What do all these high-achieving people with high achievement motivation have in common? They are all in situations where they can define their own achievement goals and then decide on their own how to reach them. Either they themselves are in charge (farmers, small business owners-operators), or the work climate of their company is "open" and not strongly bound by tradition. Thus they have the freedom, scope, and responsibility to plan and carry out plans in the ways they think best.

Thus the achievement motive is not a universal motive for success. It is only aroused in certain kinds of situations—where the probability of success is at least moderate and attractive incentives are available (McClelland & Winter, 1969, chap. 1; see also Atkinson, 1982, and Atkinson & Feather, 1966, for a more formal model of the conditions for achievement motive arousal).

Other Kinds of Success

In other kinds of situations, though, high achievement motivation does not necessarily lead to greater success and accomplishment. For example, many studies have shown that high school and college students who score high in achievement motivation do not get better grades. The reason is probably that in academic settings, both the goals and methods of procedure are usually defined by the teacher. This leaves less scope for students' personal responsibility. Moreover, students may strive for good grades in order to satisfy many other motives, such as pleasing family, impressing others, or responding to a teacher's warmth. McKeachie (1961), for example, found that the affiliation motive predicted grades in those college courses where the instructor took a personal interest in students and called on them by name. Still, achievement motivation is not completely irrelevant in academic settings. Andrews (1966) found that college students who score high in achievement motivation do act in achievement-oriented, entrepreneurial ways even if they don't get higher grades. For example, they try out more courses, they check with professors more often to understand their grades, and they start more businesses of their own on the side.

Successful doctors, scientists, lawyers, and professors are not particularly high in achievement motivation. In these professions, the rules of the game are more fixed than they are in starting up a business. Furthermore, other motives, such as the desire to help others or to have control or sheer curiosity may determine professional success.

The Entrepreneurial Style

How does achievement motivation lead to success in those situations where people are free to do things in their own way? First, achievement-motivated people have *high but realistic aspirations*. They carefully calculate both how pleasant success will feel and how difficult it will be to obtain. As a result, they usually choose tasks of middle-level difficulty. So long as the chances for success are at least moderate, they work with *energy* and *persistence*; thus they usually end up performing well. (Many early research studies on these topics are summarized in Atkinson & Feather, 1966; see also Biernat, 1989; French & Thomas, 1958; and Wendt, 1955.)

Second, achievement-motivated people are restless and travel around a lot. As a result, they learn and effectively *use new information to improve* their performance. For example, in a study of farmers in India by Sinha and Mehta (1972), forty-two farmers watched a television program about new kinds of inexpensive farm irrigation equipment. Later they discussed the program with fifty-four farmers who had not seen it. In later interviews, the more achievement-motivated farmers from both groups remembered more of the new information from the telecast than did those with lower scores. In addition, those farmers who had not watched the program also remembered more information if the farmer they discussed it with had high achievement motivation! In other words, people high in achievement motivation pick up and remember more new information and communicate it better to others. No wonder they tend to do well in innovative business situations.

Personal Style

Achievement-motivated people show an interesting pattern of personal styles and expressive behavior. On the one hand, they can control themselves and delay gratification (Mischel, 1961), patiently waiting for a bigger reward tomorrow (or next year), rather than settling for less today. This greater ability to delay gratification may be the result of a sense of time as moving faster and stretching farther into the future (Agarwal & Tripathi, 1980; McClelland, 1961, pp. 237–238, 327–328). They like subdued, somber colors such as blue and green (for example, the Black Watch tartan pattern) and dislike bright, vibrant colors such as red and yellow (Knapp, 1958).

On the other hand, achievement-motivated people are not necessarily tightly controlled law-and-order citizens. Sometimes they cheat and use illegal means when necessary (Cortes & Gatti, 1972; Mischel & Gilligan, 1964), and in extreme circumstances they may even turn to radical or revolutionary tactics (Winter & Wiecking, 1971).

Perhaps this curious combination of characteristics helps to explain two common but conflicting stereotypes of successful people in business: first, that they are cautious and conservative; and second, that they will do anything, legal or not, to get what they want.

Achievement Motivation and "Rationality"

Overall, achievement-motivated people approach life as a series of rational calculations. They are adept at figuring odds and maximizing outcomes, especially in situations that they themselves can affect. In negotiations, they are rational and cooperative, working toward solutions that maximize the benefits to all parties (Terhune, 1968).

You may think that the achievement motive is simply a pursuit of rational self-interest, the motivation that capitalist economic and political systems assume to be a basic fact of human nature. While achievement motivation *does* seem to be an important psychological factor in the rise of technologically advanced and capitalist industrial civilizations (see McClelland, 1961), it is only one aspect of our total motivational endowment. As we shall see, there are other important motives.

THE AFFILIATION AND INTIMACY MOTIVES: A CONCERN FOR CLOSE RELATIONS WITH OTHERS

A person scoring high in affiliation or intimacy motivation might respond to the TAT picture in Figure 5.1 with a story like the following:

> They were young and *in love*. Time seemed to stop. Hours would they *sit together, taking in the shining beauty* of the snow and ice, talking softly. Anyone could tell they were totally in love by the *contentment* that shone from their faces. They smiled secret smiles, exchanged understanding glances, and *planned for a future together*. Yet their future was not the security they would have wished. The air was full of the tensions of war. They didn't know if they would even see the beginning of another winter. So *they retreated into their world,* where no one could come, where they could dream and plan, *feel safe and protected*, and hope.

Images scoring for affiliation-intimacy motivation are underlined. Notice the emphasis on being "in love," which is a close interpersonal relationship. This relationship is described in terms of unity, harmony, and shared time and space (a "future together"). Casual conversation and informal interaction are signs of that relationship. Happy, positive feelings ("contentment"), a close connection to nature ("taking in the shining beauty"), and escape from outside threats result from the relationship. Finally, there is action to continue the relationship.

Notice how different this story is from the last one. It is fairly saturated with imagery of the affiliation-intimacy motive, and there is no achievement imagery. People motivated by the goal of affiliation and intimacy have their own distinctive style and ways of acting that are quite different from achievement-motivated people.

Orientation toward Other People

First of all, affiliation- and intimacy-motivated people are oriented toward other people. At any given moment, they are more likely to be found interacting with others or at least thinking about others, and these interactions give them more pleasure. McAdams and Constantian (1983) demonstrated these effects in a very imaginative study. For a week they sampled the experiences of fifty college students (who had previously taken TATs), by having them carry electronic pagers of the kind used by many doctors. Students were beeped seven times a day, at randomly selected times between 9 A.M. and 11 P.M. Right after each beeping, they wrote down what they were thinking about and doing and filled out a brief mood questionnaire. The higher the students' affiliation or intimacy motivation, the more often they were talking with or writing a letter to another person (correlation coefficients, or r's, = .41 for affiliation and .40 for intimacy). For intimacy motivation, the relationship between motivation and thinking about other people was even stronger ($r = .52$), presumably because it is possible to think about other people at any time and in any place, while actual inter-action depends on things like the time of day and location. Among those people who were interacting with others when beeped, the higher the intimacy motiva-tion score, the happier their reported mood.

An earlier study by Lansing and Heyns (1959) showed that affiliation-motivated people made more social telephone calls, wrote more letters, and visited other people more often. (Perhaps the telephone company's advertis-ing campaign to "reach out and touch someone" used these findings in order to increase long-distance profits!) French (1956) found that they prefer work-ing with friends rather than experts.

The Affiliation Cycle

For a long time, research on the affiliation motive produced paradoxical results (see the review by Boyatzis, 1973). Sometimes people scoring high in affiliation motivation were found to be *less* sociable, less interested in being with other people, and less popular than low-scorers. To explain these findings, let us consider an experimental study by Fishman (1966), who tested college women and then had them interact in prearranged small groups. He found that women with high affiliation motivation scores were more likely to be friendly and sociable in small groups with other women *so long as* they knew the people in their group. When placed in a group of people they did not know, however, affiliation-motivated women were actually less likely to be friendly and sociable. Thus the Fishman study suggests that the affiliation motive seems to require a sense of security and reciprocity for its fullest expression in behavior.

To put this explanation in a more formal manner, let us consider the con-cepts of *liking, interaction,* and *similarity,* as shown in Figure 5.3. For most peo-ple, these three concepts go together, at least moderately. That is, we usually tend to interact with the people that we like, and we usually like other people more after spending a lot of time with them. Similarly, we generally like and interact with other people who are similar to ourselves in beliefs, attitudes, and lifestyle. And people who like and spend time with each other tend to become more similar in attitudes, and even superficial characteristics such as dress and language. As a rough generalization, then, liking, interaction, and similarity are all reciprocally related. (These reciprocal relationships have been repeatedly demonstrated in social-psychology research; see, for example, Homans, 1961.)

Many studies suggest that the affiliation motive makes these relationships even stronger and tighter. Thus, for example, while most people interact with others whom they like, people scoring high in the affiliation motive are even *more likely to interact with others whom they like.* This latter qualification is very important; thus Fishman found that they are not more likely to interact with just anybody. Presumably the people studied by Lansing and Heyns were

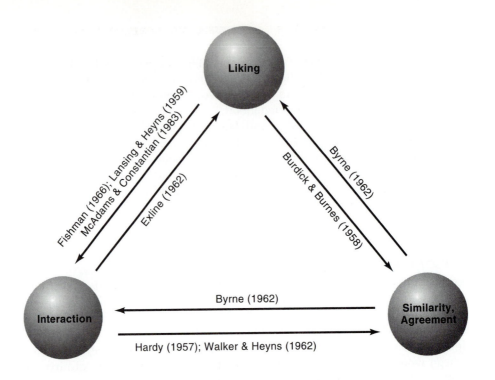

Representative studies showing how the relationships of the positive affiliation cycle are stronger for people high in affiliation motivation:

Fishman (1966): People high in affiliation motivation interact more warmly with others whom they expect to be friendly.

Lansing and Heyns (1959): People high in affiliation motivation make more telephone calls, write more letters, pay more visits.

McAdams and Constantian (1983): People high in intimacy motivation (related to affiliation motivation) are more likely at any given moment of the day either to be with other people or to be thinking about others.

Exline (1962): People high in affiliation motivation prefer getting to know coworkers to completing a task.

Byrne (1962): People high in affiliation motivation have relatively greater liking for another person who expresses opinions similar to their own.

Burdick and Byrne (1958): People high in affiliation motivation change their opinions toward those of someone they like, relatively more.

Byrne (1962): People high in affiliation motivation are more likely to want someone with similar opinions as a coworker.

Hardy (1977): People high in affiliation motivation are more likely to conform in an Asch-type experiment.

Walker and Heyns (1962): People high in affiliation motivation are more likely to cooperate with a request to "please slow down" from an unacquainted coworker.

FIGURE 5.3
The positive affiliation cycle.

writing, calling, and visiting people whom they liked, and the college students paged by McAdams and Constantian were mostly thinking about or talking with their friends (see also French, 1956, and de Charms, 1957).

Similarly, for most people there is a reciprocal relationship between liking or interaction, on the one hand, and similarity, on the other; but for affiliation-motivated people, this relationship is much stronger. Thus they are more likely to cooperate or go along with other people's requests, at least as long as they feel safe and in a friendly setting (Burdick & Burnes, 1958; Hardy, 1957; Walker & Heyns, 1962).

To make the final connection, Byrne (1962) found that the stronger people's affiliation motives, the more they like others who express beliefs and values similar to their own.

The negative affiliation cycle. Given the links of the affiliation cycle, you may wonder why affiliation-motivated people are sometimes unfriendly, uncooperative, and unpopular, instead of drifting through life on a warm ocean of friendship. Consider again the affiliation cycle in Figure 5.3. In a large and heterogeneous world, the more time we spend with some people, the less time we have to spend with others. The closer (and more similar) we are to some people, the farther away from (and less similar) we are to other people. In fact, the affiliation cycle of Figure 5.3 only tells half the story because it describes only the relationships among positive concepts. There is also a negative affiliation cycle, as shown in Figure 5.4. It consists of reciprocal relationships between *distance, dislike, and dissimilarity.*

Many of the early, paradoxical studies of the affiliation motive can be summarized by the statement that this negative cycle is also stronger among people high in the affiliation motive. Thus Byrne (1961) also found that affiliation-motivated people expressed more dislike for people whose views were dissimilar to their own. Burdick and Burnes (1958) also found that affiliation-motivated people were relatively less likely to change their attitude or go along with others who were not like themselves. Perhaps this negative cycle can also explain a puzzling finding by Atkinson, Heyns, and Veroff (1954), that among members of a college fraternity affiliation motivation was *negatively* related to popularity. If affiliation-motivated people go off to interact with a small circle of people like themselves, then they will spend less time with those who are outside their immediate circle. As a result, they would be less well known and less liked by the larger group, and so score lower in overall average popularity.

Dependence of behavior on the interpersonal situation. We can summarize both sets of results by saying that the affiliation motive makes people especially sensitive to their interpersonal environment. They are more aware of and respond more strongly to their friends as friends *and* to their "enemies" as enemies. They respond more strongly to others who are similar to themselves *and* (in the opposite direction) to others who are different. They react more to people with whom they spend a lot of time *and* to strangers. In other

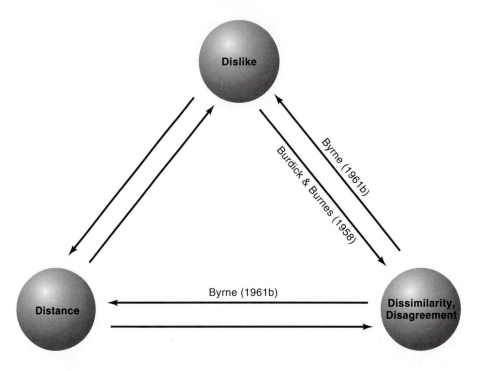

Representative studies showing how the relationships of the negative affiliation cycle are stronger for people high in affiliation motivation:

Bryne (1961b): People high in affiliation motivation show relatively greater dislike for another person who expresses disagreeing opinions.

Burdick and Burnes (1958): People high in affiliation motivation change their opinions away from someone they dislike, relatively more.

Byrne (1961b): People high in affiliation motivation are less likely to want a person expressing dissimilar opinions as a work partner.

FIGURE 5.4
The negative affiliation cycle.

words, the friendliness and agreeableness of other people makes more of a difference for people high in the affiliation motive than it does for most people. Being more aware of others and more sensitive to rejection, their performance often deteriorates in competitive situations (see Koestner & McClelland, 1992). Overall, they may seem warm and friendly to intimate friends, but to an outsider, they appear "prickly" and defensive.

Their dependence on the interpersonal situation affects their performance even in less personal situations and organizations. As negotiators, affiliation-motivated people are erratic and unstable (Terhune, 1968). In safe and cooperative settings they are sometimes cooperative in return, but when they think they are being exploited, they become obstinate and defensive. Given their great sensitivity to the cues of other people's friendship, you might expect that

"Those who hate you don't win unless you hate them. And then you destroy yourself."
With these farewell words, Richard Nixon, who as president kept an "enemies list,"
returned to California after becoming the only U.S. president to resign. Under threat,
the affiliation motive often has a prickly, defensive, and hostile edge. (AP/Wide World)

they would make poor managers, since managers have to work with and get
along with total strangers and people they do not like. This is just what Kock
(1965) and Wainer and Rubin (1969) found.

The Intimacy Motive

So far, the emerging picture of the affiliation motive is mixed, suggesting
almost as much fear of rejection as positive goals of affiliation: warmth and
closeness under some conditions and closeness, defensiveness, and anxiety
under others. To distinguish the positive aspects of the motive more clearly,
McAdams (1982, 1985, 1992b) developed a separate measure of the *intimacy*
motive (or the intimacy facet of the affiliation motive).[4] The distinction
between affiliation and intimacy can be expressed as follows. In TAT stories,

---

[4]Weinberger and McLeod (1989) have used the subliminal psychodynamic activation methodol-
ogy (see Chapter 4) to develop yet another affiliation-related motive, called the "need to belong."
One group was exposed subliminally to the cue MOMMY AND I ARE ONE, which is presumed to activate a symbiotic-like need for fusion or oneness, while the other group was exposed subliminally
to a neutral cue.

intimacy motivation involves themes of warm, close, and communicative interaction among people that are expressed in terms of the *joint perspective* of people interacting with each other. The affiliation motive, in contrast, involves more the perspective of a single individual—that person's concerns, desires, worries, and instrumental actions related to relationships. Thus someone worrying about having friends or being popular would score for affiliation but not intimacy.

Communion and adaptation to life. Longitudinal studies show that people scoring high in intimacy motivation have more enjoyable marriages and are better adapted to life. For example, McAdams and Vaillant (1982) studied fifty-seven men who had taken TATs in 1950–1952, when they were about 30 years old. They found that the higher a man's intimacy motivation, the better his life over the next seventeen years in terms of income, occupational advancement, marital happiness, job enjoyment, and freedom from drug, alcohol, or psychiatric problems. In a national sample of 500 men and 683 women, McAdams and Bryant (1987) reported significant positive relations between intimacy motivation and subjective well-being, though the results were slightly different for women and men. For women, the intimacy motive predicts happiness and satisfaction; for men, it predicts absence of worries and psychophysical symptoms. Finally, a study of male and female medical students by Zeldow, Daugherty, and McAdams (1988) also found that intimacy motivation scores predicted well-being.

One reason intimacy motivation is associated with well-being is that people who are motivated to seek warm, close relationships with others will usually have more such relationships. These relationships are likely to give social support and so buffer the effects of bad events, stress, and problems. Intimacy-motivated people also smile and laugh more and maintain more eye contact in conversations (McAdams, Jackson, & Kirshnit, 1984), which suggests that they are happier, more optimistic, and better able to maintain relationships. There may also be links between the intimacy motive and physiological functioning, as discussed below in connection with the topic of power motivation and health.

Affiliation versus intimacy. The similarities and differences between affiliation and intimacy have been summarized by McAdams (1982, pp. 159–163), who suggests that intimacy involves a "being" orientation, a focus on the mutual pleasures of relationships. Affiliation, in contrast, involves a sense of "doing" or "getting there." The fundamental concern of the affiliation motive is "What can I do to gain friends and avoid rejection?" For the intimacy motive, the concern is not to gain or avoid something, but rather to enjoy—here and now, and above all *together.*

Another important difference can be expressed in terms of Bakan's two master motives of agency and communion (see Chapter 4). The intimacy motive is almost pure communion. Intimacy-motivated people have *surrendered control (agency) in the process of relating to others.* For them, the state of communion with another person sweeps away thoughts of who is controlling whom. Affiliation-motivated people, however, seek communion and agency; more precisely, they seek communion through agency. To grasp friendship from the world and avoid rejection, they may desperately try to control others (see also McClelland, 1986).

*T*HE POWER MOTIVE: A CONCERN FOR IMPACT

Even though the cues for love and friendship are so strong in Figure 5.1, a person high in power motivation might write a story such as the following:

> The man is an agent of the *notorious* secret police, pretending to be a potential member of a revolutionary group. The woman is an active member of the group. She originally joined in anger, after her mother (a *famous* leader) was *framed by the government and imprisoned.* Now she *wants to carry on the campaign.* The police have been *checking up* on her. The agent is pretending to be a man who wants to join the group. Actually he is *eagerly waiting for the chance* to plant a listening device on her.

Notice how the italicized themes reflect positive and negative prestige ("famous" and "notorious"), different kinds of impact on others ("imprisoned," "campaign," and "checking up"), and explicit wants and anticipations connected with that impact. This story, then, comes from the mind of someone dominated by the power motive.

Formal Social Power

The notion of a power motive (or "will to power," in the vivid phrase of the nineteenth-century philosopher Friedrich Nietzsche) may stir up images of Hitler, Napoleon, Franklin D. Roosevelt, or even Mahatma Gandhi—in different ways, each a powerful national leader who seemed to enjoy influencing millions of people. But power is also a goal for many people, and the research evidence suggests several different channels for power motivation in everyday life (see Jenkins, 1994; McClelland, 1975; Veroff, 1992; Winter, 1973, 1988, 1992c; Winter & Stewart, 1978).

Power-motivated people are drawn to power-related careers—occupations such as business executive, teacher, psychologist or mental health worker, journalist, and the clergy. They are likely to succeed as managers and executives in a large corporation, especially if their power is also tempered by a sense of responsibility or self-control (McClelland & Boyatzis, 1982; Winter, 1991b; see also the section on "taming power" below, and Chapter 10). What makes these occupations attractive to power-motivated people is that they give an *opportunity (even a duty) to direct the behavior of individual other persons in accordance with some preconceived plan, and to use positive and negative sanctions on others' behavior,* all within a "legitimate" institutional structure. Thus a business executive directs and controls the behavior of subordinate workers, teachers direct and sanction the learning behavior of students, the clergy exhort and sanction the behavior of believers, and psychologists and other mental health workers direct and sanction the behavior of their clients. (Physicians, who are not especially high in power motivation, also exert a good deal of control over people, but at least until recently they have been concerned about their patients' body systems rather than their behavior.)

The kind of power that is important to power-motivated people, then, is direct and legitimate *interpersonal* power. Careers such as science and the law, and even some positions in politics, which involve more indirect and abstract kinds of power, are not necessarily associated with power motivation. (A zero correlation between power motivation and being a scientist or lawyer means that there is no relationship, not that all scientists and lawyers score low.) Thus by inventing the transistor, a scientist may revolutionize the lives of millions of people, but that scientist's power is not nearly as direct and interpersonal as the power of executives in a transistor manufacturing company. And although some lawyers are deeply involved in the mechanics of power, their role seems to be that of the hired expert rather than the direct power seeker. Thus we might expect that people high in power motivation are likely to *use* lawyers rather than to be lawyers. Even politicians may be driven by many motives: some seek power, some are looking for love and acceptance, and still others are trying to achieve excellence. One study of local political leaders found that those who sought positions with high power potential *and* who initiated their own candidacy scored higher in power motivation than other political leaders and a matched control group (Winter, 1973, pp. 102–105).

Organizational activity.   Notice that these power-related occupations are all middle-class. Among working-class people and college students, where opportunities for "real" social power are rarer, power motivation is often expressed through organization membership and office holding.

The strategies of power.   The strategies and tactics that power-motivated people use to get power are similar to the advice and recommendations of writers such as Machiavelli (1469–1527), who studied the tactics of Rennaissance princes in Italy; Haley (1969), who analyzed the career of Jesus in power terms; and Martin and Sims (1956), who studied how successful executives operate.

The first tactic is to become *visible* and well-known. For example, in gambling situations they take the kind of extreme risks that draw other people's attention (McClelland & Teague, 1975; McClelland & Watson, 1973). Even in less public situations, they take risks. For example, Wormley (1976) studied mutual fund managers and found that the portfolios managed by those with high power motivation showed relatively more volatility over a five-year period. In other words, their portfolios swing both much higher and much lower than the market trend.

College students high in power motivation become visible in many ways, such as by writing letters to the campus newspaper or even simply putting their names on their dormitory room door. Acquiring and using *prestige*—self-display—also enhances visibility. Power-motivated students are likely to spend their money on prestige possessions (among college students in the 1960s, such items as TV sets, wine glasses, and framed pictures) and to have more credit cards. A study of graduating seniors at one college in the early 1970s gives a more vivid illustration (Winter & Stewart, 1978). This was a time of social unrest on American college campuses, when many students were challenging traditional commencement rituals such as wearing caps and gowns. At this college, some students chose to wear ordinary suits, dresses, or shirts and pants instead. Several seniors who had scored high in power motivation, however, graduated in what can best be described as "costumes": walking up to get their degrees while being tied to a cross, or dressed in "jail-bird" clothing dragging a ball and chain. They were certainly visible!

The concern with visibility suggests an essential difference between the power and achievement motives: In the words of the old proverb, people high in achievement motivation might "build a better mousetrap so that the world would beat a path to their door." In contrast, power-motivated people would try to get the world to come to their door without having to build the better mousetrap first.

The second tactic of getting power is to build *alliances* with other people, especially with lower-status or less well known people who may feel they are outsiders and have nothing to lose. In studies of small groups, power-motivated people emerge as the ones who define the situation, encourage others to participate, and influence others. They are not especially well-liked, however, and they are not seen as working hard or offering the best solutions to the problem (see Jones, 1969, cited in Winter, 1973). Whether they are personally liked or not, power-motivated leaders create high morale among their subordinates (McClelland & Burnham, 1976).

Does Power Corrupt?

The famous remark by Lord Acton (1949), "Power tends to corrupt and absolute power corrupts absolutely," suggests that while the power motive may be an important source of leadership, it also has some negative features.

Groupthink and the response to negative information. In an ingenious series of studies at Clarkson University, Fodor compared how groups function differently with leaders that are high and low in power motivation (Fodor, 1990; Fodor & Farrow, 1979; Fodor & Smith, 1982). Power-motivated leaders are especially vulnerable to flattery and ingratiation by subordinates. If a member of their work group tells them, "Personally, I think you're doin' a great job," they tend to give that person a better performance evaluation and higher pay increases. Groups run by power-motivated leaders, while more cohesive and higher in morale, are less effective in gathering and using information and less able to deal with moral concerns. Finally, while power-motivated leaders show high activation and energy arousal in stressful situations when their power is at stake, they show high creativity only after they succeed and not after their failures. (Contrast this with achievement-motivated people, who use knowledge of negative results to modify their behavior and improve performance.)

Taken together, these effects are similar to what Janis (1983) called "group-think"—the tendency for groups to make defective decisions and perform much less intelligently than their members would as individuals. Janis cited several historical examples of the groupthink phenomenon that ended in miscalculation and disaster, including President Kennedy's ill-fated decision to attempt the 1961 Bay of Pigs invasion of Cuba. Perhaps these results help to explain why power so often involves a fatal flaw, or as the ancient Greeks called it, *hubris* (excessive pride). Power-motivated leaders listen mostly to followers who tell them what they want to hear, with the result that they do not pay attention to important but unpleasant information.

Aggression and the "profligate impulse". When they have the upper hand in negotiation or bargaining situations, people scoring high in power motivation are likely to break agreements and demand better terms (Schnackers & Kleinbeck, 1975; Terhune, 1968). Under some circumstances, power-motivated men and women are involved in fights, arguments, and other kinds of exploitative aggression. Sometimes they also drink and use drugs, gamble, and exploit members of the opposite sex—behaviors that can all be labeled "profligate impulsivity" (see Winter & Stewart, 1978, pp. 408–412; Winter & Barenbaum, 1985). College-educated men high in power motivation are relatively less likely to have wives with a career outside the home (Winter, Stewart, & McClelland, 1977). If they are in relationships, such men also tend to inflict physical abuse on their partners (Dutton & Strachan, 1987; Mason & Blankenship, 1987). Not surprisingly in view of these findings, power motivation is associated with the break-up of relationships, marital conflict, and divorce (Dutton & Strachan, 1987; Stewart & Rubin, 1976). These profligate behaviors are not an inevitable feature of the power motive, however. Winter and Barenbaum (1985) found that people's sense of responsibility has a big effect on the way their power motivation is expressed, as discussed below in the section on taming power.

Stress and Illness

Research by McClelland and his colleagues illustrates another cost of power motivation to the individual (summarized in Jemmott & Locke, 1984; McClelland, 1979, 1982, 1984, 1989). People scoring high in power motivation tend to show greater sympathetic nervous system arousal in response to threat and stress (see also Fodor, 1985). That is, they are more primed for the body's natural fight-or-flight responses to threat. Chronic high levels of sympathetic nervous system activity, in turn, are associated with many different health problems: lowered efficiency of the immune system, which leads to more infectious diseases; higher blood pressure; a variety of cardiovascular problems, including heart attacks; and generally lower levels of health. McClelland's research also shows direct links from power motivation to each of these negative health outcomes, as shown in Figure 5.5. These results suggest an ironic conclusion: our bodies' sympathetic nervous system mechanisms, designed to protect us from threat, are the physiological and evolutionary foundation of power motivation; yet when the power motive is aroused to excess, these same mechanisms may cut short our lives. Perhaps this is what Freud meant by the concept of a death instinct.

Taming Power

While the power motive can corrupt, as Lord Acton suggested, perhaps the corruptions of groupthink, aggression, profligate impulsivity, and illness are not inevitable. Several studies have focused on identifying some way to

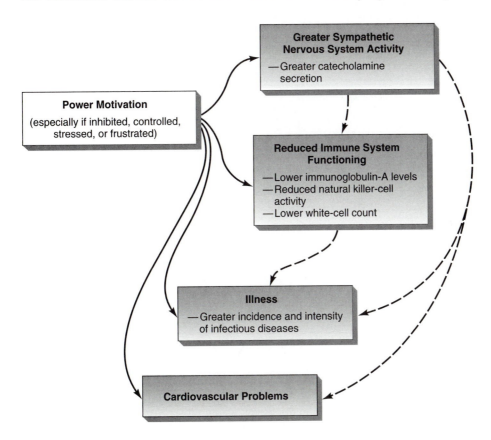

The relationships indicated by solid-line arrows have been established by McClelland and his colleagues (McClelland, 1982; 1984; 1989). Relationships indicated by dashed-line arrows have been established in other biological, immunological, and medical research studies.

FIGURE 5.5
Power motivation, sympathetic nervous system arousal, immune system functioning, and illness.

temper or tame the power motive by means of altruism (regard for others), self-control, or some similar variable (for example, see McClelland, 1975, chap. 7; McClelland & Boyatzis, 1982; McClelland, Davis, Kalin, & Wanner, 1972). In this way we could benefit from the good features of power motivation, such as leadership, while avoiding its perils. Winter and Barenbaum (1985) showed that the expression of people's power motivation is strongly affected by their sense of responsibility. The responsibility measure, scored from TAT stories, includes themes such as moral standards, feelings of obligation, caring about other people, and anticipating the effects of actions (see the discussion at the end of Chapter 10 below). Winter and Barenbaum found that among women and men high in responsibility, power motivation predicts many kinds of responsible social power, such as having a power-related career, holding office in organizations, and effective

TABLE 5.2 EFFECTS OF RESPONSIBILITY ON THE EXPRESSION OF POWER MOTIVATION IN ADULT WOMEN AND MEN

| | Correlations among women | | | Correlations among men | | |
| | | Power motivation, with | | | Power motivation, with | |
Variable	Power motivation	high responsibility	low responsibility	Power motivation	high responsibility	low responsibility
Responsible social power[a]	−.05	.12	−.14	.03	.52 (b)	−.38
Profligacy[b]	.17	−.10	.30	.11	−.11 (a)	.51*
Effective functioning[c]	−.08	.27 (a)	−.29*	.05	.52 (a)	−.24
Openness to experience[d]	.04	.57 (b)	−.40	.30	.58*	.26
Overall responsible power[e]	−.09	.49* (b)	−.46*	.12	.64* (c)	−.49*

*p < .05
(a) *p* of difference between adjacent correlations < .05
(b) *p* of difference between adjacent correlations < .01
(c) *p* of difference between adjacent correlations < .001
SOURCE : Adapted from Winter and Barenbaum (1985, p. 350).
[a]Having a power-related job; being a member of voluntary organizations; and finding work "a source of enjoyment" rather than "boring" or "a distraction from things you would rather be doing"; each standardized and combined.
[b]Drinking a lot of liquor often; drinking "to forget everything"; reading erotic magazines; and preferring nonmonogamous relationships; each standardized and combined.
[c]Maturity of adaptation to the environment (Stewart, 1982; Stewart & Healy, 1992); few physical symptoms; and being perceived as "a responsible person"; each standardized and combined.
[d]Enjoying travel; enjoying new foods; and great self-disclosure; each standardized and combined.
[e]Scores on responsible social power; effective functioning; and openness to experience; minus score on profligacy; each standardized and combined.

functioning. In a longitudinal study of AT&T executives, men with the high power motive and high responsibility pattern advanced to higher levels in the corporation (Winter, 1991b). Among people high in responsibility, power motivation does *not* predict the profligate drinking, aggression, or sexual exploitation variables. For men and women low in responsibility, however, power motivation predicts only profligate impulsivity and not responsible social power. Table 5.2 summarizes these results. These studies give promise that the power motive can indeed be tempered or tamed for the benefit of both individuals and society.

POWER, AFFILIATION-INTIMACY, AND MOTIVATIONAL THEORY

Earlier I suggested that the achievement, affiliation-intimacy, and power motives can define a space in which many of our most important goals and strivings can be located (see Figure 5.2). This three-dimensional space fits well with the dimensions of Freud's duality and Murray's empirical list, as shown in Figure 5.6.

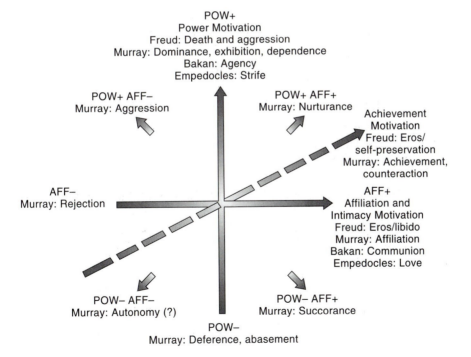

FIGURE 5.6
Integration of different categories of motives.

The power and affiliation-intimacy motive clearly correspond to the Murray dimensions of power and affiliation, since they were developed in the Murray tradition. Several studies suggest that power and affiliation combine as the diagram says they should. For example, McClelland's studies (1975, chaps. 8–9) show that people scoring high in power and low in affiliation act aggressively toward others, as they should if they are really located in the upper-left part of the diagram (Pow+/Aff–). People high in both motives are more helpful to others, just as location in the upper-right space (Pow+/Aff+) would suggest. McAdams (1985, chap. 6) found that such people see themselves as *powerful figures who promote relationships and the welfare of others*, much as in the classical Greek images of Apollo (the god of light), Athena (goddess of peace, wisdom, and prudence), and Prometheus (the "revolutionary" god who brought the gift of fire to humanity).

McClelland's studies of power motivation, stress, and illness cited in the previous section suggest that the power motive does indeed act like a death instinct. When turned inward, it works against the body's defenses against infection and disease and so brings us nearer death. When less controlled and directed outward, the power motive leads to aggression and violence—in extreme cases, homicide or the death of others.

The affiliation-intimacy motives can also be linked to the libido or life instincts, Freud's other motive group. They lead to warm and loving relationships with other people, which are one form of libidinal tie. Other research by McClelland and his colleagues (McClelland, 1989) also shows that high scores on the affiliation-intimacy motives are associated with *better* immune system functioning and *greater* resistance to infection and disease. In other words, these motives are truly a form of life instincts.

The achievement motive is an impersonal concern, having little to do with interpersonal power or love. It can be represented as a third independent dimension, as shown in Figure 5.6. In terms of Freud's motivational theory, achievement motivation might be analogous to the self-preservation motives, especially in Freud's sense of muscular and sensory activities for their own sake (see the discussion at the beginning of Chapter 3; also Freud, 1913a, XIII, p. 181).

MEASUREMENT CREDENTIALS OF THE TAT

The research reviewed in the last few sections suggests that the TAT measures of achievement, affiliation-intimacy, and power motives have considerable validity. That is, they predict behaviors and outcomes that would be expected on the basis of theory, and they add to our previous conceptions of these motives.

Ever since the TAT measures were first introduced in the 1940s, however, methodological questions and problems have been raised about them. Having discussed what these measures predict, we must now consider these questions.

TAT versus Questionnaire Measures

Many standard personality questionnaires include scales intended to measure achievement, affiliation, and power or dominance—whether they are called motives or not. Personality psychologists have also tried to develop questionnaire measures of particular motives; for example, Mehrabian (1969) and Hermans (1970) have developed questionnaires that are supposed to measure achievement motivation. While it would certainly be simpler to use these questionnaire measures, they do not in fact correlate with the TAT measures and they do not predict the same behaviors as the TAT measures do (see, among many such comparative studies, the first by de Charms, Morrison, Reitman, and McClelland, 1955, and the most recent comprehensive analysis by Spangler, 1992).

Interpreting these results, McClelland and his colleagues have suggested that the TAT- and questionnaire-based measures reflect two fundamentally different kinds of personality characteristics. Over the years, various pairs of terms have been used to label the difference: motives versus values (de Charms et al., 1955), operant versus respondent motives (McClelland, 1980), implicit versus self-attributed motives (McClelland, Koestner, & Weinberger, 1989), and finally traditional versus cognitive motives (Weinberger & McClelland, 1990).

Let us consider what this distinction means. Consider a typical questionnaire item that was part of Murray's (1938) original questionnaire measure of n Achievement and later used by de Charms and associates (1955):

"I set difficult goals for myself which I try to reach." (True or False)

Presumably, people who are high in achievement motivation set such goals, and so they would answer True. Of course, if their achievement motivation was partly repressed or conflicted, they might deny it and answer False. Also, in American culture, this statement sounds like a good thing to agree with, and so many people with low achievement motivation might also answer True in order to appear virtuous.

Once a question like this is asked, it has to be answered somehow, whether or not "setting difficult tasks" is part of the way people spontaneously think about themselves. For example, let us imagine what might go through a college student's mind in responding to a direct question like this one:

Is this true of me or not? Well, I chose some hard courses this year. Still, I didn't always study very hard last year; perhaps, though, that was because I spent so much time trying to write for the college newspaper and playing with my computer. Well, I do set myself difficult computer programming tasks—but that's more like fun than work. I guess overall, it's probably true of me, sort of, at least sometimes.

As you can see, responding to questionnaire items like this one involves consulting your memory and calling up cognitions about yourself. For these reasons, Weinberger and McClelland (1990) suggest that such questionnaire items actually measure cognitions (in this case, cognitions about the self), rather than spontaneously expressed motives. If this is true, then many questionnaires that say they measure "motives" actually belong in Part Two, as cognitive elements of personality.

Reliability and Consistency

Many personality researchers have expressed doubts about the reliability of the TAT, since interstory correlations are usually low, and typical test-retest correlations are around +.30 (see, for example, Entwisle, 1972, and Fineman, 1977). If the TAT is not reliable, they argue, then it cannot be used to measure anything. After all, a thermometer that doesn't give the same reading each time you use it is not useful for measuring temperature.

Actually, the issue of TAT reliability is more complex than the numbers, and these criticisms, would suggest. Most psychological tests contain several questions that ask about the same general topic. This encourages high interitem correlations, or internal consistency, which is one kind of reliability. Also, most questionnaire items are phrased in terms of what is "usually" true or how the person "typically" feels. This wording encourages people to give the same answers over time. This creates high test-retest correlations, which constitute another kind of reliability.

The usual TAT instructions, however, are quite different. People are told to be creative and make up an imaginative story. Thus, after telling one kind of story, they are likely to tell a quite different story to the next picture. This gives low interstory correlations. If at some later time they are again asked to make up stories to the same pictures, the instructions to "be creative" may lead them to tell a different story to the same picture. This would give low test-retest correlations and apparent low reliability. However, when the effects of such implicit instructions are removed, by telling people to tell whatever stories they like without worrying about whether these new stories are the same or different, TAT test-retest correlations rise to .60 or higher (see Lundy, 1985; Winter & Stewart, 1977b). This suggests that for TAT-based motive measures, the usual interstory and test-retest correlations, which are apparently low, are not fair estimates of reliability.

Agreement among scorers is a different kind of reliability. As noted in the discussion of the McClelland-Atkinson research strategy at the beginning of this chapter, the TAT measures typically have interscorer reliability or agreement of 85 percent or better (see Smith, 1992).

Gender Differences

The question of gender differences is another issue with TAT motive measures. On the basis of a few early studies, many researchers believed that the achievement motive arousal experiments and measures somehow "didn't work" with women. Such a conclusion also crept into many textbooks; for example, Heckhausen, Schmalt, and Schneider concluded that "female subjects have been exceptions to the rule since the beginning of achievement motivation research" (1985, p. 36). However, a more comprehensive review of the evidence should dispel these concerns. Reviewing *every* known study (published and unpublished) of the achievement, affiliation, and power motives in which women and men were tested together or in comparable situations, Stewart and Chester (1982) concluded that there were essentially *no* gender differences in the ways in which these three motives are aroused, the structure of the three motive scoring systems, the average motive levels,[5] or the behaviors related to each motive. For example, there initially seemed to be differences in how women and men expressed power motivation, especially the expressions involving profligate impulsivity (see McClelland, 1975, chap. 2). Further research, however, showed that these apparent gender differences were actually due to differences in early socialization (Winter, 1988) and sense of responsibility (Winter & Barenbaum, 1985).

MEASURING MOTIVES AT A DISTANCE

In laboratory research studies of personality, motives are usually measured by some version of the TAT. However, researchers have adapted the TAT motive scoring systems for other material such as children's readers (McClelland, 1961), literary material (Berlew, 1956; Bradburn & Berlew, 1961), folktales (Child, Storm, & Veroff, 1958), political speeches and interviews (Donley & Winter, 1970; Hermann, 1980a, 1980b; Winter, 1980), testimony of Supreme Court justices at their confirmation hearings (Aliotta, 1988), reports of dreams (Le Vine, 1966), and even television programs (Winter & Healy, 1984). Winter (1991a) codified these modifications into a single integrated manual for scoring motives in any kind of imaginative verbal material. This makes it possible to measure motivation at a distance, without direct access to the people being measured.

As an example of such studies, Table 5.3 shows the motive scores of American presidents from George Washington through Bill Clinton, based on their first inaugural addresses, and Table 5.4 shows presidential actions and outcomes correlated with these motive scores (adapted from Winter, 1987, 1991a; see also Winter, 1994). Notice that the presidents who score high in power motivation are those whom historians rate as "great" or "charismatic" presidents (see also House, Spangler, & Woycke, 1991). This would be pre-

---

[5]The intimacy variant of the affiliation motive may be one exception to this conclusion, however, since McAdams (1992b) has found that women usually score higher than men.

TABLE 5.3 MOTIVE SCORES OF AMERICAN PRESIDENTS BASED ON THEIR FIRST INAUGURAL ADDRESSES

| President | Standardized score* | | |
	Achievement motive	Affiliation motive	Power motive
Washington	39	52	41
Adams, John	39	48	41
Jefferson	48	49	51
Madison	54	50	56
Monroe	56	45	50
Adams, John Quincy	47	50	36
Jackson	42	47	45
Van Buren	42	47	40
Harrison, William	32	41	39
Polk	33	41	49
Taylor	52	51	40
Pierce	48	44	49
Buchanan	45	46	41
Lincoln	36	45	52
Grant	55	46	35
Hayes	50	47	48
Garfield	45	36	48
Cleveland	52	45	62
Harrison, Benjamin	37	44	45
McKinley	46	41	45
Roosevelt, Theodore	61	39	38

dicted from the results of research on leaders and managers, discussed above. Unfortunately, the United States also tends to become involved in wars during their administrations, and they are victims of assassination attempts. Perhaps this is consistent with the results on power motivation and aggression.

Affiliation-motivated presidents seem to be especially concerned with arms limitation and control, which fits with a concern for warm, positive relationships with others. Power leads to aggression (war), while affiliation brings love (peace). On the other hand, affiliation-motivated presidents tend to be drawn into political scandals, probably because they are easily influenced by close associates and find it difficult to say no. Among presidents, then, we see the same pattern as among ordinary people, only in more dramatic form.

TABLE 5.3   *(Continued)*

President	Standardized score*		
	Achievement motive	*Affiliation motive*	*Power motive*
Taft	44	39	57
Wilson	64	48	53
Harding	47	55	42
Coolidge	43	46	45
Hoover	66	44	47
Roosevelt, Franklin	52	44	60
Truman	54	61	77
Eisenhower	42	55	48
Kennedy	49	78	77
Johnson, Lyndon	54	56	48
Nixon	65	70	53
Carter	73	56	58
Reagan	59	49	63
Bush	57	83	54
Clinton	71	60	65

*Each motive standardized separately on scores of the first inaugural address of presidents Washington through Clinton. Overall mean = 50 and standard deviation = 10 for each motive.

SOURCE: Adapted and updated from Winter (1987). Tyler, Fillmore, Andrew Johnson, Arthur, and Ford are excluded because they never delivered an inaugural address after being elected in their own right.

Since achievement motivation predicts success in business, you may be surprised to find that it is not related to any dimension of presidential greatness. Why not? Achievement-motivated presidents are full of aspirations and are rated as idealistic by historians. Yet in the give-and-take of politics they often become bogged down and impatient, ending up frustrated and even defeating themselves, as in the cases of Wilson, Hoover, Lyndon Johnson, Nixon, and Carter (all high in achievement motivation). Their frustration may result from a lack of interest or pleasure in the political process, which is the necessary *means* for getting things done in politics. In contrast, power-motivated presidents (such as Franklin D. Roosevelt, Truman, Kennedy, and Reagan) seemed to relish the political game for its own sake. Reviews of research on the motives of other political leaders can be found in Winter (1991a, 1992a, 1992b, 1993c).

TABLE 5.4 OUTCOMES CORRELATED WITH PRESIDENTIAL MOTIVE SCORES

Outcome variable	Standardized regression coefficients[a]		
	Ach	Aff-Int	Pow
War[b]	−.13	−.03	.58**
Arms limitation treaty[c]	.07	.69+	−.51
White House staff or cabinet resignations in scandal[d]	−.03	.40+	−.28
Assassination attempt[e]	−.09	−.19	.52*
Barber (1977) classification:			
Active-positive	−.03	.02	.86*
Active-negative	.85**	.14	−.46

+p < .10   *p < .05   **p < .01

[a]Standardized regression coefficients for each motive (also called beta weights) are similar to correlation coefficients with the effect of the other two motives removed.
[b]Entry of the United States into war, as defined by Richardson (1960) and Wilkinson (1980).
[c]Agreeing with one or more major powers for the abolition or limitation of one or more specific weapons systems.
[d]Based on information in Woodward (1974).
[e]Based on information in Clarke (1982).
SOURCE: This analysis is based on all presidents up to Nixon (George Washington through Lyndon Johnson) for whom information is available.

MEASURING RICHARD NIXON'S MOTIVES

Richard Nixon's scores for achievement, affiliation, and power motivation, based on both his 1969 and 1973 inaugural addresses, are shown in Table 5.5. These are *standardized* scores, calculated in terms of the overall mean (50) and standard deviation (SD = 10) for the first inaugural addresses of all American presidents from Washington through Clinton. Although Nixon's two sets of

TABLE 5.5 MOTIVE PROFILE OF RICHARD NIXON BASED ON HIS INAUGURAL ADDRESSES

	Raw scores (Images/1000 words)			Standardized scores*		
Year	Achievement	Affiliation	Power	Achievement	Affiliation	Power
1969	8.94	8.00	7.06	65	70	53
1973	7.75	4.43	6.64	59	54	51

*Standardization based on scores of the first inaugural address of presidents Washington through Clinton, including Nixon (see Table 5.3). Overall mean = 50 and SD = 10 for each motive.

John F. Kennedy and Richard Nixon shaking hands before one of their televised debates during the 1960 presidential campaign. Nixon's recollection of their relationship reflected his very high affiliation motive: "Kennedy and I were too different in background, outlook, and temperament to become close friends, but we were thrown together throughout our early careers, and we never had less than an amicable relationship"(Nixon, 1978, p. 43).

scores are slightly different, the basic motive profiles are very similar: high achievement (his 1969 score of 65 is one and a half standard deviations above average), very high affiliation (two standard deviations above average in 1969), and average power motivation.

Since presidents rarely have time to write their own speeches, do these scores reflect the motives of Nixon or his speech writers? Like most political leaders, Nixon picked his speech writers because they could write what he wanted; further, there is evidence that he was closely involved in preparing his speeches and often wrote much of the speech himself (see Price, 1977, pp. 42–50 about the 1969 inaugural). Thus we can assume that these inaugural scores do reflect Nixon's own motives.

Forecasting Nixon's Presidency

One way to establish the validity of the scores in Table 5.5 is to compare them with the clinical analysis of Nixon's motives presented in Chapter 2. In general, the two assessments fit together well. A second way to establish their validity is to determine whether the 1969 scores would have led to accurate predictions about Nixon's presidency at the time of his first inauguration. (Since we are talking about predicting past events, the proper term is "retrodiction.") Based on the research of Winter (1987, 1991a), we could have made several predictions in January 1969: for example, (1) that the United States would not enter a war, (2) that the United States would conclude a major-power treaty for limiting or abolishing a major weapons system, (3) that there would be a big political scandal, and (4) that Nixon would become frustrated and rigidly self-defeating in office. All of these predictions are confirmed by the events of Nixon's presidency, suggesting that he did act like a president high in achievement and affiliation-intimacy motivation and only average in power motivation.

On the other hand, on the basis of Nixon's inaugural motive scores, we would have predicted (5) that there would be no assassination attempts during his presidency. Clarke (1982, pp. 128–142) recounts the curious story of Samuel Byck, who was shot and killed in February 1974 trying to hijack an airliner which, according to a tape recording that he left behind, he planned to crash into the White House. Even though Byck never got close, a conservative reckoning would count this prediction as not confirmed. Overall, then, four out of five predictions (80 percent) would have been correct.

Validating Nixon's Motive Profile through His Associates' Descriptions

Winter and Carlson (1988) further validated Nixon's motive profile by comparing Nixon's actual behaviors with the behaviors that would be expected on the basis of the known behavior correlates of the three motives. After searching Nixon's autobiographies and the memoirs of six former close aides who

TABLE 5.6 CONFIRMATION OF NIXON'S MOTIVE SCORES IN THE ACCOUNTS OF HIS ASSOCIATES

	Behavior correlates of the motive				
Motive	Confirmed	Not confirmed	Inconclusive	Percent confirmed	Hypothesized percent of correlates Nixon would show, based on his percentile score on that motive*
Achievement	23	3	2	88	93
Affiliation	13	0	1	100	99
Power	8	10	3	44	62

*Nixon's standard scores from his 1969 inaugural address (Table 5.5) translated into percentile scores of 93 (achievement), 99 (affiliation), and 62 (power).
SOURCE: Adapted from Winter and Carlson (1988).

worked directly with Nixon during his presidency and who continued to have positive or at least neutral feelings about him, Winter and Carlson constructed a box score of confirmations, disconfirmations, and inconclusive results, as shown in Table 5.6.

Compared to other U.S. presidents, Nixon scored at about the 95th percentile on achievement, the 99th percentile on affiliation, and the 62nd percentile on power. From these scores we could therefore expect that he would display 95 percent of the known achievement motive behavior correlates, 99 percent of the affiliation correlates, but only around 62 percent of the power correlates. In fact, the actual percent of behavior correlates confirmed for each motive (based on the autobiography and memoirs) are fairly close to these expectations, as shown in Table 5.6.

Nixon Paradoxes Reconsidered

These motive scores can also help us understand the five paradoxes of Richard Nixon's behavior that I mentioned back in Chapter 2. Let us examine each paradox in turn.

The "honest lawyer" and Watergate. Nixon's announcement to his mother that he would like to be an "honest lawyer, who can't be bought by crooks" expressed a long-range future career goal that is typical of achievement-motivated young people (see McClelland, Atkinson, Clark, & Lowell, 1953, pp. 118–119). At the same time, it probably also reflected a strong affiliation-based desire for his mother's approval. Nixon's later involvement in the crimes of Watergate and the other illegal wiretaps and break-ins can be viewed as a typical instance of the tendency of achievement-motivated people to use illegal means to reach a valued goal.

Changing political beliefs. In 1950, Nixon's electoral tricks and changing political beliefs earned him the nickname "Tricky Dick" (from his defeated rival Helen Gahagan Douglas). The nickname stuck, partly because of Nixon's reputation for campaign tricks and partly because of his many apparent changes of political belief. Such changes of belief are easily explained in terms of the tendency for achievement-motivated people to change their actions and tactics on the basis of results. While this may lead to success in business, in politics it can arouse suspicion and distrust, as suggested by the "Tricky" nickname.

The campaigner. Nixon's persistence and ultimate success in the 1968 election is yet another reflection of his high achievement motivation. He used feedback to modify performance; thus, in 1968 journalists wrote about a "new Nixon" with a different political style. (Actually, the "new Nixon" theme first surfaced eight years earlier in the 1960 campaign.) However, Nixon's 1968 campaign was not just the result of blind persistence, but was related to his careful calculations of the chances of success. Even before President Kennedy's assassination in 1963, Nixon had decided to stay out of the 1964 contest because Kennedy "was almost certainly going to be re-elected" (Nixon, 1978, p. 250). By 1968, however, "the chances for a Republican to be elected President . . . looked better all the time. My chances of being that Republican had also improved" (p. 290).

Cambodia and the night at the Lincoln Memorial. The April 1970 invasion of Cambodia was undeniably an aggressive widening of the Vietnam war, but this does not necessarily mean that Nixon was high in power motivation. Nixon's behavior was erratic and ambivalent during the invasion, suggesting that he was not really comfortable about using such military force. This conclusion is confirmed by Nixon's Secretary of State, Henry Kissinger (1979, p. 482). In one memo, for example, Nixon endorsed the Cambodia invasion in *affiliative* terms: "We are going to *find out who our friends are*" (Hersh, 1983, p. 189*n*; emphasis added). His ambivalence about power and overriding concern with affiliation is even more clearly expressed in his sudden decision to talk with protesting college students at 4:35 A.M. at the Lincoln Memorial. Yet the actual conversations reflected Nixon's interests rather than the students' interests, which is typical of the problems affiliation-motivated people have when they try to connect with people of different backgrounds and concerns.

The Watergate tapes. Making the tapes was in part an achievement-motivated act. In Nixon's own words, "From the very beginning I had decided that my administration would be the *best* chronicled in history" (Nixon, 1978, p. 500, emphasis added). At the time there seemed to be little risk, for "I had believed that the existence of the White House taping system would never be revealed" (p. 900). But by 1973, it became clear that if he "were to to survive, [the tapes] would clearly have to be destroyed" (p. 902). Yet Nixon did not destroy them, apparently for two reasons. The first is consistent with the tendency of affiliation-motivated people to be influenced by trusted others: he was "persuaded" by presidential assistant Alexander Haig that their destruction would create an "indelible impression of guilt . . . [worse than] anything I had actually done." The second nicely reflects both his achievement and affiliation motives (the latter in its defensive mode): "the tapes were my *best insurance* against the unforeseeable future. I was prepared to believe that *others, even people close to me, would turn against me* . . . and in that case the tapes would give me at least some protection" (pp. 902–903; emphases added).

Another, more complicated explanation for Nixon's refusal to destroy the tapes could even be derived from a peculiarity of his high affiliation motivation. As we saw in Chapter 2, Nixon often connected love from other people with death and failure. Perhaps Watergate and his refusal to destroy the tapes, then, were also manifestations of a Nixon "wish to fail," or death wish, that had reunion with a loving mother as its ultimate goal. Farfetched as this may seem, in his final, tearful farewell speech to the White House staff on August 9, 1974 (shown live on national television)—at the moment of his own political "death"—Nixon talked of his "saintly" mother, of the boys she nursed who died of tuberculosis, and of the death of Theodore Roosevelt's young wife (see the quotations in Chapter 2).

Thus the Nixon case shows that the concept of motive is not limited to laboratory research studies of personality but can also help us understand real-life situations and historical events. Motives can be defined and measured in ways that remain faithful to the sensitive insights of Freud, while meeting the standards of objectivity, reliability, and validity that are characteristics of rigorous scientific research.

Our cognitions—beliefs, values, sense of self—are the enduring structures of our mental life and personality. They make it possible for us to learn by instruction, as in Henry Ossawa Tanner's painting *The Banjo Lesson*, instead of only by trial and error. As the foundation of abstract thinking, cognition is also the basis of art, music, and the highest attainments of human culture.

Henry Ossawa Tanner (1859–1937), The Banjo Lesson, 1893, oil on canvas, 49" x 35 1/2", Hampton University Museum, Hampton, Virginia

PART TWO

———— ❖ ————

Self-Theory and Cognitions: Kelly and Rogers

6

Cognitions, Constructs, and Personality

❖

In this chapter we begin the study of cognitions, the upper-left box in Figure 6.1. Our enormous capacity for cognitive activity is the most obvious difference between human beings and other animals. Our cognitions make it possible for us to remember and understand the world, other people, and ourselves. Cognitions are the foundation of thinking and planning. They guide action, as we pursue goals and learn from experience in a constantly changing world (Cantor, 1990). At any moment, we experience fleeting, momentary images; over time, however, these images are organized into stable cognitive structures.

Personality psychologists use a variety of terms to describe different kinds of mental structures—*categories, schemas* (Hastie, 1981), *prototypes* (Cantor & Mischel, 1979a, 1979b; Rosch, 1978), *beliefs, attributions, scripts* (Abelson, 1981; Tomkins, 1979, 1987), *attitudes,* and *values*—but all these structures share several characteristics. First, they differ across people, and so they are a part of personality. Second, they are *internal* structures, like motives. That is, we experience our own cognitions directly, but they are known to others

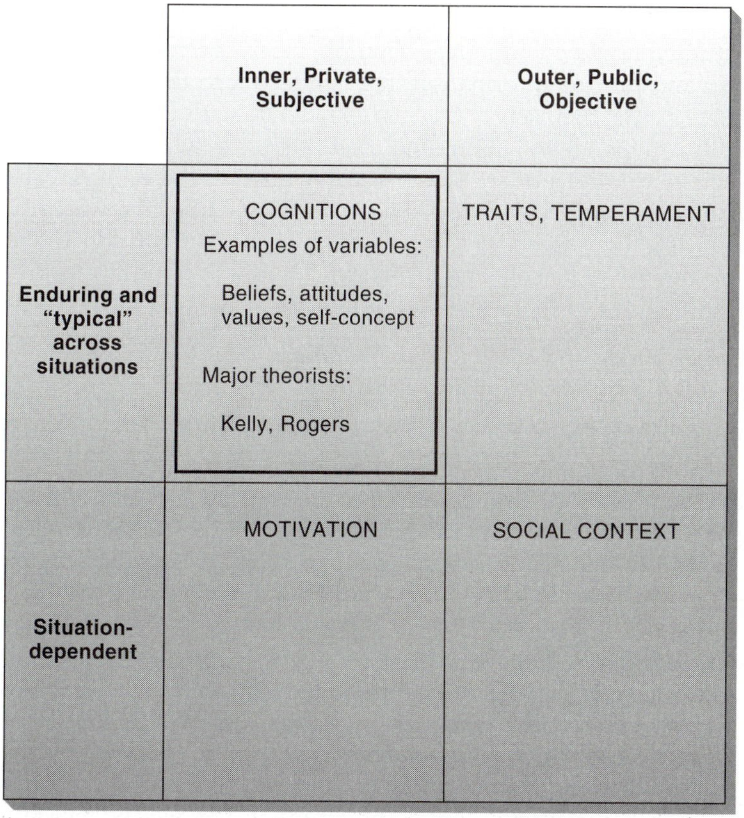

	Inner, Private, Subjective	Outer, Public, Objective
Enduring and "typical" across situations	COGNITIONS Examples of variables: Beliefs, attitudes, values, self-concept Major theorists: Kelly, Rogers	TRAITS, TEMPERAMENT
Situation-dependent	MOTIVATION	SOCIAL CONTEXT

FIGURE 6.1
Cognition and the elements of personality.

only indirectly, through our reports. Third, they are relatively stable across situations, or *trans-situational*. Of course they change over time and are affected by situations, but they do not wax and wane, and fluctuate moment by moment in response to changing situations, as motives usually do. (If your cognitions *did* change suddenly and radically, as for example when entering college, other people would probably describe it as a change in your personality.)

PSYCHOLOGICAL STUDIES OF THE EFFECTS OF COGNITIONS ON BEHAVIOR

While we don't always live up to our beliefs and values, our cognitions do affect our behavior. Some research findings from *social cognition* (a topic shared by personality and social psychology) illustrate these effects.

Self-Schemas and Processing Information about the Self

Markus (1977) studied how people's ideas about themselves affect the ways in which they select and process information that is relevant to themselves. She compared women rating themselves as "independent" with women rating themselves highly "dependent," assuming that people's adjective ratings reflected their self-conceptions or *self-schemas*. After making the ratings, each woman was then shown a series of adjectives. After each adjective was projected on a screen for two seconds, she was to push a "Me" button if she thought the word described herself, and a "Not Me" button if it didn't. As predicted, those who thought of themselves as independent pressed the Me button more often for adjectives which suggested independence, such as "assertive," "outspoken," and "unconventional"; they also selected fewer adjectives suggesting dependence, such as "conforming," "conventional," and "timid." For women with dependent self-schemas, the results were reversed: they selected more dependent and fewer independent adjectives.

Markus also found that all women took less time to push the button for words consistent with their self-schemas and more time to decide about adjectives inconsistent with them. Then in a second part of the study, the women were asked to give concrete evidence illustrating how the adjectives they had originally rated described them. They were better able to give such evidence for the consistent adjectives. Finally, they were asked to predict how likely they would be to engage in a series of actions, some of which reflected independence and some dependence. Each woman's predictions were consistent with her self-schema; for example, independent women were likely to predict that they would "speak up as soon as you have some comments on the issue being discussed," while dependent women thought that they would "hesitate before commenting, only to hear someone else make the point you had in mind."

We can conclude from the Markus study that people's self-schemas affect how they deal with personally relevant information—the speed and depth of information processing and making predictions. The final part of the study illustrates yet another important function of schemas. Markus tried to modify self-schemas by providing fake feedback on the basis of a fictitious Suggestibility Test and GSR apparatus. For example, women with independent self-schemas were told that the test showed them to be "generally quite susceptible to social influence," while dependent self-schematic women were told the opposite. Compared to a third group of "aschematic" women (self-schemas neither independent nor dependent), both groups of women were relatively less likely to accept the fake feedback as true, sticking to their original choices in a subsequent test. In other words, schemas can make us resistant to inconsistent or contradictory new information. Interestingly, both the independent and dependent groups took longer deciding which button to push the second time around (after the contradictory information), while the aschematic women showed no such difference. This relative delay suggests that whereas schema-consistent information is processed relatively quickly, schema-inconsistent information slows down processing.

Overall, the differences in reaction time and other effects observed by Markus are important not so much in themselves, but because they demonstrate the existence of internal cognitive structures or schemas by their effects on the speed, facility, and accuracy of information processing.

Attributing Causes and Assigning Blame

People's *causal attributions,* or their beliefs about the causes of an event, affect many other judgments, feelings, and decisions. Carroll and Payne (1977) studied how causal attributions affect people's judgments of crimes and criminals. They first prepared descriptions of different hypothetical crimes, ranging from murder to larceny and drug dealing. Here is their "murder" sketch:

> Mr. Green is a 25-year-old male convicted of second-degree murder. He was in a bar having a drink and talking to the victim when they began to argue, push, and punch each other. He pulled out a gun and shot the victim several times; the victim was pronounced dead on arrival at the hospital. Mr. Green surrendered himself to police called by the bartender. He has no previous record of convictions. (pp. 200–201)

In order to control causal attributions, Carroll and Payne also prepared a set of alternative endings to the sketches, manipulating whether the cause was internal or external to the perpetrator, and stable or unstable (temporary). Here are two examples:

> Interviews indicated that he had thought about this situation for some time and had developed several plans. (*internal stable* cause)
> Interviews indicated that he had been temporarily laid off work due to economic situations. At the time of the act, circumstances seemed to come together to make it happen. (*external temporary* cause) (p. 201)

Carroll and Payne systematically combined various crimes and causes into eight different descriptions of crimes that "actually occurred last year." A group of college students was asked to read descriptions that combined different crimes and causes, rate each on several scales, and then decide on a length of prison term for its perpetrator.

Across all crimes, students who were led to attribute the cause to internal and stable factors gave the harshest judgments about the severity of the crime and the risk that the perpetrator would repeat the crime and meted out the longest prison sentences. In the case of murder, their average recommended sentence was 9.1 years, as compared to the 3.6 years recommended by students who were led to attribute the cause to external and unstable factors.

Carroll and Payne then repeated this study with actual members of the Pennsylvania State Board of Probation and Parole—that is, people who make decisions about the fate of real convicted criminals. The results were in the same direction, although the differences were not as great, probably because the parole board members took other factors into account. Even so, they were affected by the experimental manipulation of causal attributions. Overall, these results demonstrate the power of cognitions about why things happen to affect judgment, feelings, and action.

Availability Heuristics and Prediction

Life is so complex that we rarely have the time or ability to perceive and process all relevant information in order to make perfect decisions. Usually we rely on *heuristics* (operating rules or cognitive shortcuts) to reduce the information load. For example, in estimating the likelihood that some event will occur, our judgments are heavily influenced by single particularly vivid past occurrences. Their vividness enhances their "availability" in memory. Thus instead of counting past frequencies and calculating future probabilities, we rely on an *availability heuristic,* "estimat [ing] frequency or probability by the ease with which instances or associations could be brought to mind" (Tversky & Kahneman, 1973, p. 182; see also Kahneman, Slovic, and Tversky, 1982). In our minds, the most vivid or memorable event becomes the most likely event. Such availability heuristics are often efficient and useful, but they can also mislead us—sometimes with unpleasant or even disastrous results.

Availability heuristics and television watching. People who watch a lot of television provide a good example of how availability heuristics can distort judgment. Studies of television program content suggest that the frequency of crime on television is at least ten times as great as it is in the real world. For people who watch a lot of television, therefore, "crime" is a highly available heuristic, or prediction, since they can easily recall so many vivid instances of television crime. Thus it is not surprising that heavy television viewers overestimate their chances of being the victim of a violent crime and are more likely than light viewers to feel that the world is a dangerous place where people cannot be trusted. They also tend to overestimate the proportion of people employed in law enforcement (Gerbner & Gross, 1976; Gerbner, Gross, Morgan, & Signorelli, 1980; Morgan, 1983).

Because it is vivid and repetitive, television provides viewers with images of reality that are so easy to retrieve that they override more systematic and careful estimates based on our actual experience. Gerbner and his colleagues label these heuristic effects "enculturation" or "mainstreaming" to emphasize how television-based heuristics can communicate subtle political and cultural messages.

Availability heuristics in history. History provides many vivid examples of the availability heuristic gone astray. For example, consider the deep U.S. involvement in the Vietnam conflict during the 1960s. One powerful reason for this tragedy was that Presidents Kennedy and Johnson, as well as most other American policymakers of the time, had been young adults when the British and French tried to "appease" (or give in to) the demands of Hitler and Nazi Germany at a famous 1938 summit conference in Munich. That policy failed, and in the minds of many people it was an important cause of World War II. Thus the vivid heuristics "no appeasement" and "not another Munich" were etched in the minds of the young men who, as adults, were to decide American policy twenty-five years later. But the Vietnamese leaders were not Hitler, and Vietnam was not Munich. Over 50,000 Americans and many more Vietnamese were killed and the United States experienced a decade of bitter social disruption—quite a price for relying on a vivid but misleading heuristic! In fact, many so-called lessons of history are really little more than a collection of contradictory, misleading availability heuristics, as Neustadt and May (1986) illustrate.

A CASE STUDY: COGNITIONS IN THE EARLY LIFE OF HELEN KELLER

In Part Two of this book, we will consider the different kinds of cognitions that are important for personality, how they are arranged, how they develop, and how they are related to motivation. Most of the cognitions of adults are quite complex, and originate far back in the inaccessible mists of early childhood. To illustrate the role of cognition in personality, therefore, I have chosen Helen Keller as an illustrative case. She was born in 1880, in Tuscumbia, Alabama. At the age of 18 months, an illness made her blind, deaf, and thus for many years also mute. (The exact diagnosis is still not clear.) Unable to see, hear, and understand language for five years, Helen existed as a "wild, destructive little animal" (her own words), until Annie Sullivan came to be her Teacher[1] and life companion (Keller, 1908):

---

[1] I will follow Keller's own usage and refer to Sullivan as Teacher when I want to emphasize her relationship to Helen.

Before my teacher came to me . . . I lived in a world that was a no-world . . . that unconscious, yet conscious time of nothingness. I did not know that I knew aught, or that I lived or acted or desired. I had neither will nor intellect. I was carried along to objects and acts by a certain blind natural impetus. (p. 113)

With Teacher at her side, teaching words by spelling them into her hand, Helen went on to attain the highest levels of cognitive functioning: graduating from Radcliffe College with honors, writing many articles and books, and becoming a world-renowned advocate for blind and handicapped people.

Since illness had plunged Helen into the "unconsciousness of a new-born baby" (Keller, 1903b, p. 7),[2] most of the cognitive elements of her personality developed only after age 7, when she learned language and could remember and later record them in her eloquent autobiography written as a college junior (the sequel, *Midstream: My Later Life*, 1929, was written at age 49). Most of us can't remember our childhood cognitive development, but we can grasp these processes in Helen Keller's account—from learning the simplest concepts such as "water" (the first word that she understood as a word) to understanding more abstract ideas such as "love" and "self," and finally to the complexities of her Platonic philosophy, socialist politics, and Swedenborgian[3] religious ideas.

Keller was aware that her personal experiences were important material for the newly developing psychological science of her day—though she once expressed some impatience with "modern philosophers who apparently think I was intended as an experimental case for their special instruction" (1903a, p. 27). In a fascinating series of articles later published in book form as *The World I Live In* (1908), she described how her sensory and cognitive processes functioned and how the senses of smell, touch, and taste made it possible for her to infer the world of sight and hearing. Two plays by William Gibson, both later made into movies, have perpetuated Helen Keller's story: *The Miracle Worker* and *Monday after the Miracle*. Lash's biography, *Helen and Teacher* (1980) gives a detailed account of her entire life.

Helen Keller's Cognitive Structures

A love of cognition. The most striking thing about Helen Keller's account of her cognitions, learning of language, and coming to understanding is how much pleasure these processes gave her. On April 5, 1887, Helen finally came to understand the secret of language when Annie Sullivan spelled "w-a-t-e-r" into her hand while at the same time pumping cold water over it. In a letter written that same day, Sullivan described Helen as "highly

[2]This and all subsequent page citations are from the original 1903 edition of *The Story of My Life* (Keller, 1903b), unless otherwise specified.
[3]Emmanuel Swedenborg (1688–1772), a Swedish scientist, tried to harmonize science and religion. His followers believe that people attain salvation by a combination of faith, work, love, and obedience.

excited" and "like a radiant fairy. . . . She has flitted from object to object, asking the name of everything and kissing me for very gladness" (Sullivan, 1903, p. 317). Later, Helen described "an intense longing to touch the mighty sea and feel it roar" (p. 47). After a toboggan ride: "What joy! What exhilarating madness! For one wild, glad moment we snapped the chains that bind us to earth, and joining hands with the winds we felt ourselves divine!" (p. 57). At the 1892 Chicago World's Fair: "With an eagerness as insatiable as that with which Pizarro seized the treasures of Peru, I took in the glories of the Fair with my fingers" (p. 76).

Internal freedom and control. Contrasting the years before she understood language with the time after Teacher's arrival, Helen used metaphors of bondage and freedom: "I came up out of Egypt and stood before Sinai, and a power divine touched my spirit and gave it sight, so that I beheld many wonders" (p. 20). A few years later, when she had learned to speak instead of relying only on the manual alphabet, "my soul, conscious of new strength, came out of bondage" (p. 60). In college she was an eager student because "in the wonderland of Mind I should be as free as another" (p. 96).

Helen Keller (right), with Eleanor Roosevelt. "My friends have been the story of my life. . . . They have turned my limitations into beautiful privileges, and enabled me to walk serene and happy in the shadow cast by my deprivation" (1903b, p. 140).
(Courtesy of the American Foundation of the Blind)

Cognition and emotion. Thinking back to the time before she learned language, Helen could not recall feeling real emotion. "Never in a start of the body or a heart-beat did I feel that I loved or cared for anything. My inner life, then, was a blank without past, present, or future, without hope or anticipation, without wonder or joy or faith" (1908, p. 114). She recalled her feelings after a moment of impatience when she smashed a new doll: "Neither sorrow nor regret followed my passionate outburst. . . . In the still, dark world in which I lived there was no strong sentiment or tenderness" (p. 23). "[Only] thought made me conscious of love, joy, and all the emotions" (1908, p. 117).

Self and others. Before she learned language, Helen had little sense of herself as a person. (In recalling that time, she would often describe herself in the third person, with the name Phantom.) Further, she had only the most primitive sense of other people and relationships with them (1908):

> Before my teacher came to me, I did not know that I am. . . . Since I had no power of thought, I did not compare one mental state with another. So I was not conscious of any change or process going on in my brain. . . . When I learned the meaning of "I" and "me" and found that I was something, I began to think. (pp. 113, 116–117)

Once, while Helen was concentrating on how to string some beads:

> Miss Sullivan touched my forehead and spelled with decided emphasis, "Think." In a flash I knew that the word was the name of the process that was going on in my head. This was my first conscious perception of an abstract idea. (pp. 30–31)

Keller's experience further suggests that our capacity to have deep relationships with other people depends on abstract ideas and this sense of self. Thus after recalling an incident before the coming of Teacher, when she overturned the cradle and nearly killed her baby sister, Helen wrote that "when we walk in the valley of twofold solitude [blindness and deafness] we know little of the tender affections that grow out of endearing words and actions and companionship" (p. 16). Later Helen asked, "What is love?" Teacher first responded in terms of analogies from nature, then suddenly "the beautiful truth burst upon my mind—I felt that there were invisible lines stretched between my spirit and the spirits of others" (p. 31).

A Crisis of Identity and First Self-Definition

As children, we gradually develop a sense of ourselves as distinct and separate from other people. During adolescence and young adulthood, we usually have developed some kind of identity that is symbolized by a sense of career or vocation. For Helen Keller, this process started later, was slower, and involved special problems. Much of her experience of the world came, literally, through Teacher's hands. This left Helen vulnerable to confusion about the exact boundaries between herself and others: "My teacher is so near to me that I scarcely think of myself apart from her. . . . I feel that her being is inseparable from my own, and that the footsteps of my life are in hers" (pp. 39–40).

Even at age 22, as a junior in college, the boundary of self was not always clear. For example, whenever she wrote something, "it is certain that I cannot always distinguish my own thoughts from those I read, because what I read becomes the very substance and texture of my mind" (p. 70). As one long-time friend later wrote (Lash, 1980):

> As long as Annie Sullivan lived, and she died in 1936, a question remained as to how much of what was called Helen Keller was in reality Annie Sullivan. The answer is not simple. During the creative years neither could have done without the other. (p. 3; see also pp. 319–320 and 576–582)

Confusion of identity. When Helen was 11, the confusion of self and others led to a major crisis. She had written a short story called "The Frost King," about Jack Frost. She sent it as a birthday present to Michael Anagnos, president of Boston's Perkins School for the Blind, where she had been a student for three years. Anagnos published the story in the Perkins alumni magazine. Within a few weeks, it was discovered that "The Frost King" very closely resembled "The Frost Fairies," a story by Margaret Canby that had been published in a book of children's stories seventeen years before. Helen was accused of unwitting plagiarism and Annie Sullivan was charged with deliberate deception. Anagnos convened a special court of investigation, which heard witnesses and concluded after deliberations that Helen's reproduction of the story was unconscious and innocent, probably resulting from a friend's reading the Canby book to her during a visit to Cape Cod three years before.

Helen was dismayed and distressed by the affair. "Even now [in college] I cannot be quite sure of the boundary line between my ideas and those I find in books . . . because so many of my impressions come to me through the medium of others' eyes and ears" (p. 64). In fact, the Frost King episode marked the end of Helen's childhood and the beginning of her adolescence. Up to then she had been surrounded by unconditional affection; everyone she met was "kind" or "a dear friend," and Boston was a "City of Kind Hearts." Strangers on train trips had given her toys. She had met President Grover Cleveland, Alexander Graham Bell, and Mark Twain and had been adored by the public. But now for Helen, as for most people during adolescence, this easy indulgence was at an end. Helen felt the change when she was summoned to testify at the court of investigation, in the very office "where Mr. Anagnos had so often held me on his knee and . . . had shared in my frolics" (p. 71). Before the investigating committee, and without Teacher:

> I felt that there was something very hostile and menacing in the very atmosphere. . . . Joy deserted my heart, and for a long, long time I lived in doubt, anxiety and fear. . . . No child ever drank deeper of the cup of bitterness than I did. I had disgraced myself; I had brought suspicion upon those I loved best. (pp. 71, 63, 65)

Meeting standards. Beginning with the Frost King affair, Helen first became conscious, as do most people sooner or later, that she had to meet standards, prove herself worthy of love, and justify herself. As all people must, she began to encounter the world on its own harsh, demanding terms. At first she was swamped with self-doubts and focused on the plagiarism issue and the boundary between self and other:

> I have ever since been tortured by a fear that what I write is not my own. . . . In the midst of a paragraph I was writing, I said to myself, "Suppose it should be found that all this was written by some one long ago!" An impish fear clutched my hand, so that I could not write any more that day. (pp. 68, 73)

She became exceptionally conscientious, and tried to match her behavior to the self she thought she ought to be. For example, when she wrote to her mother, she started carefully going over the sentences, "to make sure that I had not read them in a book" (p. 68).

Definition of self. Soon after the Frost King episode, Helen left Perkins and returned to Alabama. The Youth's Companion (a Boston magazine) had solicited a sketch of her life, and she now began to write an article entitled "My Story" (Keller, 1894). She described her childhood, concluding with an account of how she raised money to bring an orphaned, blind, and deaf boy to Perkins. Writing this article gave her an opportunity for self-definition, and so resolved the crisis of self that began over "The Frost King." "My Story" was a clear statement of personal identity, but it was also her first step toward a life-long career as a writer and advocate for the blind.

As a case study on the role of cognition in personality, then, Helen Keller's autobiography demonstrates the importance of cognition in general and certain specific cognitions, such as the sense of internal control and the definition of self, in particular.

KELLY'S THEORY OF PERSONAL CONSTRUCTS

While many personality theories involve cognition, the personal construct theory of George Kelly (1905–1967) is based almost exclusively on cognitions, or in Kelly's terms, *constructs*. A construct is an organized verbal structure for grouping and anticipating events. Constructs develop from the process of construing or construal. ("Category" is an approximate synonym.) For Kelly, our personalities *are* our constructs. Describing someone's personality means describing the nature and arrangement of that person's construct system. Successful therapy involves modification or rearrangement of the client's construct system.

Kelly's image of human beings is that they are scientists, "ever seeking to predict and control the course of events" (Kelly, 1955, p. 5). They have theories, test hypotheses, and weigh the evidence of their experience in the process of construing. All other psychological processes (emotion, choice, and

George Kelly. "Each individual [person] formulates . . . constructs through which he views the world of events.
. . . We take the stand that there are always some alternative constructions available to choose among in dealing with the world" (1955, pp. 12, 15). (Ohio State University Photo Archives)

action) are derived from the ways in which people construe or construct events (p. 46).

For Kelly, reality is really something that we construct or represent in our minds. Alternative constructions are always possible. In philosophical language, this point of view is called *constructive alternativism*. Different people construct reality in different ways, and our own constructions change with time, experience, and major life changes. For example, college students who suddenly have to make decisions on their own come to view the world in new ways. Students who have spent a semester in another country return with a new perspective on their own nation. New parents, suddenly responsible for a young child, often reconstrue their own parents' behavior and values. And with the passage of time, historians revise earlier constructions about the past. In all these instances, we are engaging in constructive alternativism.

Motivation

If our system of constructs determines our personality, what is the role of motivation? Kelly claimed that he did not need a motivation concept, arguing (from physics) that motivation or energy is only necessary to explain changes or movement in something originally at rest. By contrast, personal-construct theory assumes that people are active from the start: the organism is "delivered fresh into the psychological world alive and struggling" (1955, p. 37). In fact, however, I do not think that Kelly can so easily do away with all concepts of motivation. Personal-construct theory certainly does assume that all people have a basic "need for cognition," a motive to make and expand constructions of the world. (Such a motive is similar to White's concept of competence or effectance motivation, particularly those components of effectance having to do with perception, or cognizance, as discussed in Chapter 4.) A second motivation concept, involving the principle of elaborative choice, will be discussed later in this chapter.

Constructs

A construct is "a way in which some things are construed as being alike and yet different from others" (Kelly, 1955, p. 105). In other words, constructs are like adjectives that describe the nouns (persons, places, things) of our experience. Constructs are arranged as *bipolar* pairs: black versus white, cheerful versus sad, sincere versus insincere, and so forth. We have constructs for things, events, other people, ourselves—in short, for any important aspect of our experience. Our construct system is the entire structure of different constructs that we use to arrange and describe our experience.

Constructs and concepts. While constructs are cognitions, they are not always expressed in words; that is, not all constructs are verbal concepts. For example, infants clearly make distinctions among their experiences, and all of us have spontaneous preferences and aversions that we are not able to put in words. These, too, are constructs. Constructs can even be unconscious. Because our earliest constructs are nonverbal (or preverbal), they may not be available to our later adult consciousness, though they give rise to symbolic connections (Kelly, 1955, p. 462). This is similar to Freud's notion of transference, in which our early thoughts and feelings shape our later conscious thoughts, feelings, and actions.

For most of us, these early preverbal constructs are buried in the dimly remembered past; but this was not true of Helen Keller. Because she learned language at such a late age, her preverbal constructs persisted much longer; and because she learned language so rapidly, she was able to "capture" these early constructs and express them in words. For example, recalling the time of her blinding illness:

> I especially remember the tenderness with which my mother tried to soothe me in my waking hours of fret and pain, and the agony and bewilderment with which I awoke after a tossing half sleep, and turned my eyes, so dry and hot, to the wall, away from the once-loved light, which came to me dim and yet more dim every day. (p. 7)

Helen Keller's constructs. Helen Keller's account of the process by which she learned language illustrates several of her most important bipolar constructs. In the following passages, emphasis has been added to words that suggest a pole of an important construct. Before she learned language:

> Sometimes I stood between two persons who were conversing and touched their lips. I could not understand, and was *vexed*. I moved my lips and gesticulated *frantically* without result. This made me so *angry* at times that I kicked and screamed until I was *exhausted*. (p. 10)
>
> Many incidents of those early years are fixed in my memory, isolated, but clear and distinct, making the sense of that *silent, aimless dayless* life all the more intense. (p. 13)
>
> I felt as if *invisible hands were holding me,* and I made *frantic* efforts to free myself. . . . If my mother happened to be near I crept into her arms, too *miserable* even to remember the cause of the tempest. (p. 17)

To this experience she contrasted the sense of understanding brought about by learning "w-a-t-e-r":

> Suddenly I felt a misty consciousness as of something forgotten—a *thrill* of returning thought; and somehow the mystery of language was revealed to me. . . . That living word *awakened* my soul, gave it *light, hope, joy, set it free!* There were barriers still, it is true, but *barriers that could in time be swept away.* . . . It would have been difficult to find a *happier* child than I was as I lay in my crib at the close of that *eventful* day and lived over the *joys* it brought me, and for the first time *longed for a new day* to come. (pp. 23–24)

The emphasized words suggest labels for the poles of this set of related constructs. First, there is the simple perceptual contrast of "dayless" and "silent" versus "light." Closely related to this is the emotional contrast of "vexed," "angry," and "miserable" with "joy" and "happy." This leads on to a motivational polarity of "exhausted" and "aimless" (perhaps also "frantic") versus "awakened" and "longed for." Finally, these three constructs are brought together by an overarching contrast between bondage and freedom—"hands holding me" versus "set free" and "barriers swept away."

Submerged constructs. Not all constructs appear to have opposite poles. For example, consider the concluding sentence from Helen Keller's first autobiography, "My Story" (Keller, 1894):

> I am spending the winter at my home in the *lovely* south, the land of *sunshine and flowers,* surrounded by all that makes life *sweet and natural; loving* parents, a *precious* baby brother, a *tender* little sister, and the *dearest* teacher in the world. (p. 4, emphasis added)

What are the opposite poles to "lovely," "sunshine and flowers," or "precious" and "dearest?" Nowhere in the article did Keller give even a hint. We could suggest words such as "disgusting," "cloudy and gray," "bitter and unnatural," "hateful," "cheap," "tough," and "meanest," because these are logical opposites to the words Helen used. For personal-construct theory, however, this is not correct, because it is not based on Helen Keller's own consciousness. In more technical terms, it ignores her *phenomenology*. Because Kelly defined people's constructs in terms of their phenomenology, his theory is often called a *phenomenological* theory.[4]

You may think that these constructs of Helen Keller are not bipolar, but this cannot be, because in personal-construct theory all constructs are bipolar. Whenever people use only one pole of a construct, as Helen did in this case, the opposite pole is said to be *submerged*. For example, we may say that someone is "gentle," without ever mentioning the opposite pole. In such a case, that opposite pole (perhaps "rough" or "brutal") is submerged. Kelly believed that poles of a construct are likely to be submerged when they arouse anxiety, an idea that is similar to Freud's concepts of repression and the unconscious. Thus Kelly believed that submerged constructs often appear in dreams, and that psychotherapy works by helping people to verbalize "submerged" (unconscious) poles of constructs and in other ways to clarify their constructs.

In the Helen Keller example, personal-construct theory might suggest that Helen's constructs of "loving," "tender," and "sunshine and flowers" were really bipolar, but that the opposite poles, involving coldness, hostility, and darkness were submerged because they aroused memories of the pain and confusion of her earlier existence before Teacher's arrival. Thoughts of these submerged poles might arouse anxiety about her relationship to Teacher and thereby jeopardize her entire world. It is easy to understand why these poles would remain mostly submerged.[5] Eventually, these submerged poles broke through to consciousness, at the time of the Frost King episode when she was accused of plagiarism.

Dimensions of Individual Difference

People's construct systems vary, not only in their content but also in their structure; that is, how constructs fit together. Kelly identified three dimensions of individual difference, which are the main personality variables of personal

---

[4]Phenomenology or phenomenalism is a philosophical position that focuses on how the world appears from the perspective of some person, rather than from the objective nature of the world. It is related to two other philosophical movements that have also been influential in psychology: (1) The method of *hermeneutics* seeks to understand something by interpreting its meanings and implications, rather than by explaining its sources or consequences. (2) *Existentialism* rejects the idea that people are part of a world with an integrated, rational, orderly structure of essences. Instead, people create their own "essences" through their choices and actions. Kelly's theory of personality has a good deal in common with all three movements, and partly through Kelly's theory, all three have influenced psychology.

[5]Actually, the profusion of unipolar constructs is a stylistic feature that Helen Keller's autobiography shares with most writing of her time (the early 1900s). This was a time of great optimism and widespread belief in progress and goodness, with the opposite poles of decline and evil often submerged (in Freudian terms, a time of broad and deep repressions). Nowadays, after the disillusionment of two world wars and other major social upheavals, these particular repressions have been shattered. As a result, such a unipolar writing style strikes us as childlike, naive, and Pollyannaish.

construct theory: *permeable-impermeable, consistent-inconsistent,* and *preemptive-constellatory-propositional.* These terms may be hard to understand at first, and Kelly's own discussion (1955, pp. 151–157) is sometimes obscure. After defining each dimension, therefore, I will give illustrations from Helen Keller's autobiography.

Permeability. Life never fits our system of constructs exactly, because we are continually encountering new things and new experiences. Constructs that can easily incorporate new experience (perhaps with some modification) are said to be permeable, or "open." In contrast, constructs that cannot incorporate new experiences are rigid and impermeable. Permeability of constructs is thus an important dimension of difference among people: some people's construct systems are more permeable than others'. Even within the same person, some constructs are more permeable than others.

Kelly suggested that constructs may be rigid and impermeable for several reasons. In some cases we lack the opportunity to try out our constructs, like a scientist without a laboratory. In other cases our constructs become rigid because we feel threatened: change in even one construct might put some construct essential to our well-being into jeopardy. Thus to protect ourselves, we may avoid change by making our constructs impermeable, or closed to new experiences. However, impermeability carries a risk: because rigid constructs do not change, they may collapse in the face of new experience. In contrast, permeable constructs are more flexible: they change, they grow, they bend—but they do not break.

Construct permeability is especially important during major life changes or milestones such as going to college, getting married, becoming a parent, or retiring from a career. At these times we are especially likely to have experiences that do not fit our previous constructs. If those constructs are permeable, they may be able to change and accommodate the new experiences. If they are rigid, they may collapse, thus setting off a personal crisis. For this reason, Kelly thought that highly permeable constructs were more adaptive. On the other hand, the collapse of old construct systems and the development of new and more adequate constructs in response to new experience may be an important mechanism of cognitive growth (see Stewart & Healy, 1985, 1992, pp. 446–447). Think back to the transition from high school to college, for example. If you came to college with highly permeable constructs that were readily able to incorporate your new experiences, the transition may have been easy; but if you had to develop completely new constructs to replace your old inadequate ones, you may have been forced to pay more attention to your surroundings and thus have experienced more cognitive growth.[6] Perhaps some middle level of construct permeability—constructs that are open to moderately new experience but that can be torn down and rebuilt in the face of wholly new experience—is the most adaptive.

---

[6]This is similar to the distinction in developmental psychology between *assimilation* (of new information) and *accommodation* (of the self to new information), respectively (see Block, 1982).

Consistency, hierarchy, comprehensiveness. These dimensions refer to how constructs fit together. If different constructs fit with each other, they are consistent. A system in which constructs are arranged from the specific to the general is a hierarchy. For example, the constructs of "square" and "trapezoid" are specific, narrow constructs that are subordinate to the more general construct of four-sided figures or "quadrilaterals." At this next level of the hierarchy, the construct of quadrilaterals, along with "triangles" and "circles," is subordinate to the more general and abstract construct of "geometric figures" at the top of the hierarchy. A construct system that covers every aspect of a person's experience is more comprehensive than a system in which much experience is unconstrued and left out.

Preemptive-constellatory-propositional. These three terms actually define a single dimension of individual differences. A *preemptive* construct is one that, when applied, permits no other construct to be applied. In other words, if something fits that construct, then it cannot fit any other construct. A *constellatory* construct is one that, when applied, requires the application of certain other constructs. Finally, a *propositional* construct is one that neither requires nor excludes any other construct.

The differences between these terms can be illustrated with the construct of "terrorist," as it might exist in different people's construct systems. For some people, "terrorist" is a *preemptive* construct. In their minds, anyone who is a terrorist is *only* a terrorist and cannot be anything but a terrorist—that is all you need to know. For them, height, weight, religion, personal background, family situation—everything else is irrelevant once a person is labeled "terrorist." For people with a *constellatory* construct of "terrorist," anyone who is a terrorist is necessarily certain other things as well—for example, wild-eyed, excitable, a loner who has no close relationships with other people, and quite likely "crazy." You may think the constellatory construct of terrorist is like a stereotype; in fact, stereotypes are good examples of constellatory constructs. (Not all constellatory constructs are stereotypes, however. For example, once we apply the construct "square" to a geometrical figure, we necessarily also apply the construct "rectangle" and "quadrilateral.")

Finally, a *propositional* construct implies few if any other constructs. For people with a propositional construct of "terrorist," a terrorist could be of any size, shape, sex, background, and family situation. Terrorists could be calculating and sane, devoutly religious, and family-loving—*or* they could be intemperate and wild-eyed, religiously skeptical, and loners. In other words, the relationship between any two constructs is a proposition—something that might or might not be true—rather than something that is given or assumed. Obviously, propositional constructs are important for flexible thinking and intelligent action, though in emergency situations preemptive or constellatory constructs may lead to quicker, automatic, and more decisive action. If you hear the cry "Fire! Get Out!" it's probably best not to treat the danger as propositional.

Dimensions of Helen Keller's Constructs

We can place Helen Keller's construct system on each of these dimensions. The permeability of her major constructs, or their ability to incorporate new experience, can be seen in her response to the Frost King episode. Accusations of plagiarism threatened her major construct of *other-people-as-loving*. For the first time since Teacher's arrival, she experienced the submerged opposite pole of people-as-suspicious-and-hostile, which tested the permeability of the construct. Helen's first response recalled the time of her illness: she could not follow the names and details of the investigation and was "dazed and did not notice my teacher's caresses, or the tender words of my friends" (p. 66). "I could scarcely think what I was saying, or what was being said to me" (p. 72).

In the long run, however, she was able to broaden this construct so as to construe or represent the experience. She retained the positive pole of other-people-as-loving: "I received many messages of love and sympathy. All the friends I loved best, except one, have remained my own to the present time" (p. 68). The previously submerged other pole was linked to her early preverbal constructs, now put into words. Just as Teacher's love had earlier swept away "unreal" and "fleeting memories," now "the angel of forgetfulness has gathered up and carried away much of the misery and all the bitterness of those sad days" (p. 67). Hostility and hatred became part of a "dark" world of anger and blindness, at the opposite pole from a "loving" world of sunshine and flowers.

This broadened bipolar construct of *bright-seeing-love* versus *dark-unhappy-hatred*, with both poles now explicitly verbalized, was to prove extraordinarily permeable when applied to Helen Keller's later adult experience. For example, after college, she ventured out from a protected and sheltered life into the harsh social and economic realities of the early twentieth century. In her own words (Lash, 1980):

> As I journey on, I leave behind thoughts that once looked like reason. I gain new thoughts which serve me better because they are more equal to the rushing, swirling and sometimes inclement atmosphere of the world. (p. 368)

As her experience and knowledge increased, her advocacy for the blind focused on social conditions that were responsible for blindness. At that time, for example, about one-third of all blindness was due to opthalmia neonatorum—the blindness of infants that occurs at birth if the mother has gonorrhea. Opthalmia neonatorum can easily be prevented by putting silver nitrate drops into the eyes of each newborn child (as is now required by law in all states). In the 1900s, however, Helen had to struggle against sexual prudery to advocate this simple practice of preventive medicine.

With the concept of "social blindness" (Lash, 1980, p. 382), Helen expanded the construct of *sighted-love* versus *blind-hatred-anger* to represent her broadening political and economic concerns (Lash, 1980):

"What surgery of politics," she wrote, "what antiseptic of common sense and right thinking shall be applied to cure the blindness of our judges and to prevent the blindness of the people who are the court of last resort?" (p. 369)

She advocated women's right to vote, supported striking women mill workers, and spoke out against American involvement in World War I. She praised the Communist revolution in Russia, hung a large red flag in her study, and preached socialism. All of these social and political views seem to have been built on the original but highly permeable *seeing-blind* construct that dated back to the arrival of Teacher (Lash, 1980):

Something in me waked when I read the radical literature. . . . The very sweetness and light that have gladdened me [and] have lifted me up in revolt against the powers of darkness [have challenged] the night of ignorance, oppression and poverty. (pp. 387, 474)

She concluded that "people turn to revolution only when every other dream has faded into the dimness of sorrow" (Keller, 1929, p. 334).

Helen Keller's constructs of self and friends were also permeable. She concluded her first autobiography with the words, "my friends have made the story of my life" (p. 140). That is, her construct of self was closely bound up with her construct of other people—indeed, so close as to cause continuing anxiety after the Frost King episode. As she developed her social and political concerns, the permeability of these constructs allowed her to link this sense of personal "closeness" to a sense of solidarity and comradeship with others. At the same time, her personal struggles to be self-reliant developed into a broader concern for all people, expanding her sense of self to include the community as well as the individual (Lash, 1980):

I have always looked upon the blind as a part of the whole of society, and my desire had been to help them regain their human rights so as to enable them to keep a place of usefulness and dignity in the world economy. What I say of the blind applies equally to all hindered people—the deaf, the lame, the impoverished, the mentally disturbed. (pp. 688–689)

Of course this brief survey does not do justice to the full range of Helen Keller's construct system as it was reflected in her extraordinary range of knowledge and opinions. She knew classic and modern literature. She was able to read several languages, and could write in German. She believed that Shakespeare's plays were actually written by Francis Bacon.[7] She spent time in Hollywood and played herself in *Deliverance*, a 1918 movie about her life, and for years she and Annie Sullivan performed on the vaudeville circuit.

Helen Keller's constructs were resilient, permeable to new experience, and also consistent with each other. They were largely propositional rather than

---

[7]Freud, incidentally, believed they were written by Edward de Vere, the Earl of Oxford.

preemptory or constellatory. Thus even when she fundamentally disagreed with someone, she was able to distinguish areas of agreement.

Construing and Acting: The Principle of Elaborative Choice

At this point, you may feel that Kelly's personal-construct theory leaves the person lost in thought. How do our constructs get converted into action? For Kelly, the answer involves the *principle of elaborative choice*, which really functions as a kind of motivational concept. All action involves making choices among alternatives—to act or not act, to carry out one action instead of another. According to Kelly, we choose so as to maximize (or "elaborate") our anticipations of events to follow. This is called *elaborative choice* (1955, pp. 64–68).

At first it is difficult to see how such a principle actually determines our choices. Consider an everyday example: I want to buy some coffee. What kind should I buy? Not only are there many different brands of coffee, but there are many different features or characteristics on which I could base my choice. Focusing on price, I could buy the cheapest coffee. Focusing on taste, I could buy the best-tasting coffee. But coffee "taste," in turn, is not simple. There are many different dimensions of taste. There are many different kinds of beans, different countries of origin, different methods of roasting, and finally, different blends or combinations of all of the above. Or I could focus on prestige, choosing whatever kind of coffee is currently most fashionable or buying at the most trendy coffee shop.

Let us try to explain how the principle of elaborative choice can explain my concrete decision about buying coffee. Kelly suggested that in elaborating our constructs to anticipate the future, we always face a trade-off between *extension* and *definition*. That is, when we make any given choice, we can gain either greater extension or greater definition of that part of our construct systems. A more *extended* construct system has a greater range of convenience or applicability. It leads to broader understanding and anticipation of a wider range of future events, but at the cost of less certainty in any specific situation. A more sharply *defined* construct system, on the other hand, gives a greater sense of certainty and more confident prediction, but of a smaller range of future events. According to Kelly, my final choice in the coffee example will be the one that gives me the best trade-off between the broad understanding of extended constructs and the certainty of sharply defined constructs—that is, the choice that maximizes anticipation of future events. Of course, different people will make different trade-offs, depending on their relative preferences for extension (range of applicability) versus definition (clarity). Thus the principle of elaborative choice cannot explain or predict any person's actual choice until we add in the person's preference for extension versus definition.

With coffee, if I prefer definition over extension, I will pick one dimension and make my choice solely on that dimension. For example, if I choose by the single dimension of price, my choice is simple: buy the cheapest coffee. It may not taste very good, I may lose prestige with my coffee-drinking friends, and I may not enjoy drinking it, but I *have* made a quick, clear-cut, and simple decision. In Kelly's terms, I anticipate future events with greater definition and clarity. If, on the other hand, I prefer extension over definition, I will try to take account of several different dimensions: taste, prestige, price, even self-concept as a certain kind of coffee drinker. My decision may not be easy or quick, but I will have learned a lot about the broad topic of coffee and so extended my coffee construct system (greater range of convenience). In Kelly's terms, I anticipate future events with greater extension.

Thus while all people are motivated to make elaborative choices, different people choose in different ways, depending on their characteristic preference for extension versus definition. This preference is an important aspect of cognitive style.

SOME LIMITS OF PERSONAL CONSTRUCT THEORY

"We are our constructs," wrote an early reviewer of Kelly's theory (Bruner, 1956). You may wonder whether that is all, whether we can cover all aspects of personality with a purely cognitive theory. At this point I want to suggest three limits or problems for personal-construct theory, and perhaps for all cognitive-personality theories: the problem of cognition and emotion, the problem of cognition and oppression, and the issue of cognition and illusion.

Cognitions and Emotion

When we think of the whole range of our experience, personal-construct theory may seem too dry and cerebral. Of course we have constructs, but we also have intense feelings and emotions. Helen Keller, for example, suffered from anxiety and guilt during the Frost King episode, and in her early years before the coming of Teacher she certainly felt anger and rage. Kelly's interpretation of the emotions (1955, chap. 10) is both ingenious and complex. It can best be illustrated by applying it to Helen Keller's emotional experience.

Anxiety. According to personal-construct theory, we feel anxiety when our construct system no longer works: we have new experiences, an old construct is no longer valid, and there is nothing to replace it. We are caught unprepared; our constructs have been overrun by events. As a result, we feel anxiety. This analysis does explain one common feature of anxiety, namely that we usually cannot pin down a specific cause for it. (Fears, in contrast, are usually focused on a specific object.) Kelly's theory suggests that anxiety is vague or free-floating precisely because it arises from experiences that cannot be adequately dealt with by existing cognitive resources or constructs.

During the Frost King episode, Helen Keller wrote that "for a long, long time I lived in doubt, anxiety and fear" (p. 63). Her description illustrates the connections between inadequate constructs or cognitive confusion ("doubt") and anxiety. First, someone asked Helen whether she had read the story in a book. "The question surprised me very much; for I had not the faintest recollection of having it read to me" (p. 64). Then it became clear that her story had been heavily influenced by Margaret Canby's book. "It was difficult to make me understand this; but when I did understand I was astonished and grieved. . . . I was dazed" (p. 65). "I was too excited to notice anything, too frightened to ask questions" (p. 72). Finally, Helen struggled to overcome this anxiety *by elaborating new constructs:*

> It seems to me that the great difficulty of writing is to make the language of the educated mind express our confused ideas, half feelings, half thoughts, when we are little more than bundles of instinctive tendencies. Trying to write is very much like trying to put a Chinese puzzle together. We have a pattern in mind which we wish to work out in words; but the words will not fit the spaces or, if they do, they will not match the design. (p. 70)

Guilt. Kelly believed that we feel guilt when constructs about our "core role" (that is, who we are in relation to other people) are challenged and overturned. For example, we may take pride in the belief or construct of ourself as a responsible student, dutiful son or daughter, or courageous citizen. If events prove us something else, however, then our core construct of self is invalidated and we feel guilt.

In personal-construct theory, guilt is closely related to anxiety. When any construct is challenged by experience, the result is anxiety; when the challenged construct involves the self, however, then we also feel guilt. For Helen Keller, the charges of plagiarism in the Frost King episode clearly aroused guilt: "No child ever drank deeper of the cup of bitterness than I did. I had disgraced myself; I had brought suspicion upon those I loved best" (p. 65).

Hostility. Usually we deal with anxiety by changing and developing our construct system. Sometimes, however, we keep our constructs unchanged and instead try to force reality to fit them. According to Kelly, this is hostility; "the continued effort to extort validational evidence" in favor of failed constructs (1955, p. 510). This seems like a very unusual conception of hostility; yet Helen Keller's account of her early years before Teacher's arrival gives striking support to Kelly's position. Her meager construct system, hampered as it was by the lack of sight and hearing, had become less and less adequate to her experience. Her efforts to force her constructs to work produced hostile rage:

> I had noticed that my mother and my friends did not use signs as I did when they wanted anything done, but talked with their mouths. Sometimes I stood between two persons who were conversing and touched their lips. I could not understand, and was vexed. I moved my lips and gesticulated frantically without result. This made me so angry at times that I kicked and screamed until I was exhausted. (p. 10)

By hostility, we ordinarily mean feelings of anger or actions intended to hurt other people. Kelly's conception can be connected to this ordinary meaning as follows. In a social world, each person's constructs are related to the constructs of other people. Thus if some people try to force experience and reality to fit their own failing constructs, they are likely to threaten the constructs of other people.

At first you may think this an artificial interpretation of hostility: Why should I care if someone else threatens my constructs? On the other hand, most of us have a core construct of self as alive and free. If this is jeopardized, as it might be through the aggressive action of a tyrant, then we would become aggressive, in turn, to protect it by forcing experience to fit. This would lead to a vicious circle of aggression, quickly escalating from constructs to blows and swords. Of course for some people, another *principle* (construct of the self) might be more important (closer to the core) than life itself. Their core constructs of self would not be threatened by the tyrant's aggression; they would not respond with aggression; and so the escalating cycle might come to a stop. Such people often become martyrs and heroes of nonviolent resistance.

Any analysis of aggression can be evaluated by how well it helps us understand the life of Adolf Hitler, whose actions led to incalculable aggression, suffering, and death. Kelly might suggest that Hitler tried to make central Europe fit his construct of a domain in which inferior peoples were ruled by a racially pure and ruthless Aryan "master race" (see Jaeckel, 1972). As events resisted or contradicted this construct, Hitler tried to force them to fit. Inevitably, however, these hostile actions collided with the core constructs of millions of other Europeans. From a personal construct-theory perspective, then, World War II can be seen as a battle of two sets of inconsistent core personal constructs, each threatening to the other.

If you find Kelly's interpretation of the Hitler example unconvincing, I think the reason is that personal-construct theory—unlike that of Freud and many other motivation theorists—assumes no inherent aggressive instinct or love of hurting others. For Kelly, aggression itself is never a primary goal, but is always derived from the primary goal of preserving one's constructs. For Hitler as for any other aggressive and hostile person, "the injury he may imagine that he would like to inflict upon another person, [is not] a primary goal in itself, but . . . an incidental outcome of something more vital that he is trying to accomplish" (Kelly, 1955, p. 510). Perhaps so. But many people, reflecting on World War II and the Holocaust, might agree with Freud that we should give motives for aggression and destruction "due place in our interpretation of life" (Freud, 1930, XXI, p. 120).

Then Are Emotions Nothing but Cognitions?

The Hitler example illustrates an aspect of Kelly's theory that has bothered many personality psychologists. We may agree with Kelly that there is often a close relationship between constructs and emotions: when our constructs are threatened or inadequate, we do feel anxiety; and our attempts to force reality to fit our constructs may be acts of hostility. Still, Kelly's discussion of emotion seems incomplete. Personal-construct theory only focuses on a few familiar negative emotions and has little to say about positive feelings such as pleasure and excitement. (Perhaps they result from successful prediction, when our constructs "work.") It has nothing at all to say about love. In other words, personal-construct theory seems to offer a limited theory of only a few emotions.

Kelly also seems to leave out the *affective* aspects of emotion, the familiar subjective juices that we actually feel: the ecstatic pleasure of intimate friendship, the butterflies of anxiety in the pit of our stomach, the red curtain that descends across our vision in moments of blinding rage. If emotions have a cognitive component, they also involve physiological processes. Psychologists have debated about which causes which. Overall, the evidence suggests a relationship of complex reciprocity, in which each can cause the other and can be caused by the other (see Plutchik & Kellerman, 1980, as well as the debate between Lazarus, 1982, 1985, and Zajonc, 1980, 1984). By focusing only on those instances when confirmation or disconfirmation of constructs causes emotions, then, personal-construct theory may neglect some of the most dramatic and compelling aspects of human experience. Over thirty years ago, Jerome Bruner, himself a cognitive theorist, pointed out this limitation in his review (1956) of Kelly's book:

> When some people get angry or inspired or in love, they couldn't care less about their "[construct] system as a whole." One gets the impression that the author is . . . overreacting against a generation of irrationalism. . . . The book fails signally, I think, in dealing convincingly with the human passions. . . . If it is true that Freud was too often the victim of the dramatic instance, it is also true that with the same coin he paid his way to an understanding of the depths and heights of *la condition humaine.* By comparison, the young men and women of Professor Kelly's clinical examples are worried about their dates, their studies, and their conformity. If Freud's clinical world is a grotesque of *fin de siècle* Vienna, Kelly's is a gloss of the post-adolescent peer group of Columbus, Ohio, who are indeed in the process of constructing their worlds. Which is more "real"? I have no idea. I wish Professor Kelly would treat more "most religious men in their most religious moments"[a phrase of William James]. (p. 356)

To be fair, many followers of Kelly tried to extend the personal-construct theory coverage of emotion, even extreme emotions. Stefan and Linder (1985) interpret suicidal emotions and behavior as the result of either a sense of chaos ("my entire view of self and events are in need of change") or fatalism ("I can no longer control events or validate my constructs"). The former sounds like an intensification of anxiety and guilt, while the latter would be a consequence of failed aggression.

More recent cognitive theory and research on personality by Markus, Weiner, Higgins, and others have expanded the analysis of positive and negative emotions. This work will be discussed in Chapters 8, 9, and 10.

Constructs and Oppression

"To the living creature, then, the universe is real, but it is not inexorable unless he chooses to construe it that way" (Kelly, 1955, p. 8). With these words, Kelly emphasizes that we can construe our world however we like, and that we are always free to change our constructions. Such an optimistic emphasis on human freedom and individuality puts personal-construct theory in the mainstream of American humanism: if you aren't happy with the way your life is going, you can change it by thinking differently about it (Lemann, 1994). Taking a closer look, however, we may find that this view is not only wrong but also terribly unfair. Social structure is real, and it can sharply constrain the range of alternative constructions we can make. Some people are *not* free to make any alternative constructions they like because they are oppressed by powerful people and institutions. The belief that people can always be free, merely by construing their situation differently is a form of blaming the victim (Ryan, 1971) rather than blaming the true oppressor. The reality of oppression is especially clear in the case of the Holocaust, where no amount of simple reconstruing could free people from the concentration camps. It is also apparent in more subtle and pervasive forms of institutional racism or sexism.

Perhaps it is possible to reconcile the reality of social power with Kelly's "freedom" to construe reality. Organized power can certainly compel obedience, on pain of death or imprisonment. On the other hand, oppressed peoples are always free to accept or reject their oppressors' *definition* of the situation, as the French philosopher Jean-Paul Sartre pointed out in his discussion of the Jewish response to anti-Semitism (1946): Jews can accept the anti-Semite's construction of "Jew" (and some did), or they can ignore it and define themselves. Stewart and Winter (1974) elaborated these two alternatives into a more general measure of *self-definition* (defining ourselves independently of how others define us) versus *social definition* (accepting the definition of others, especially more powerful others). At that time, they found that self-defining women were more likely to plan careers in fields typically dominated by men. Later studies have shown that self-defining people are also more effective at managing life crises and personal stress (Stewart, 1978, 1992b).

Institutions can certainly oppress individuals. People cannot escape oppression merely by reconstruing it, but they always have *some* freedom to define and construe the situation in their own terms. This is what great religious and political leaders, such as Gandhi, Franklin D. Roosevelt, or Martin Luther King, Jr., are able to do for large numbers of people (see Erikson, 1969).

Cognitions or Illusions?

Surely facts are sometimes facts, and attempts to reconstrue them are illusions. Consider the following example from act 1, scene 3, of Shakespeare's play *King Richard II*. King Richard had banished Bolingbroke from England. Before Bolingbroke departs, however, his father, John of Gaunt, tries to ease the pain by suggesting alternative ways to construe banishment. Their dialogue raises the question of whether it is better to believe painful truths or reconstrue them as comfortable illusions.

John of Gaunt begins by suggesting another construction for the banishment:

> Call it a travel that thou tak'st for pleasure.

But Bolingbroke finds this a distortion:

> My heart will sigh when I miscall it so,
> Which finds it an enforced pilgrimage.

Gaunt then suggests that Bolingbroke focus on the pleasure of return rather than the pain of banishment:

> The sullen passage of thy weary steps
> Esteem as foil wherein thou art to set
> The precious jewel of thy home return.

Bolingbroke sees through this cognitive trick:

> Nay, rather every tedious stride I make
> Will but remember me what a deal of world
> I wander from the jewels that I love.

Gaunt then suggests a whole series of clever alternative constructions that would do credit to any therapist working with personal construct theory:

> Think not the king did banish thee,
> But thou the king. . . .
> Go, say I sent thee forth to purchase honor,
> And not, the king exiled thee; or suppose
> Devouring pestilence hangs in our air
> And thou art flying to a fresher clime.
> Look what thy soul holds dear, imagine it
> To lie that way thou goest, not whence thou com'st.

But Bolingbroke will have no illusions:

> O! who can hold a fire in his hand
> By thinking on the frosty Caucasus?
> Or cloy the hungry edge of appetite
> By bare imagination of a feast?
> Or wallow naked in December snow
> By thinking on fantastic summer's heat?

Bolingbroke was a realist who preferred to face uncomfortable truths about the way things really are, rather than surround himself with comfortable illusions. Probably that is why he was able to wrest the crown away from Richard during the course of Shakespeare's play. The question of whether the illusion of reconstrual is better than the bitter truth of realism is a lively one in personality psychology, as we shall see in Chapter 8.

CONSTRUCTS AND PERSONALITY

Kelly's fundamental principle, that people's individual constructs are important for understanding the rest of their functioning, has been widely cited and very influential. This principle could be viewed as part of the cognitive revolution of the 1950s and 1960s in psychology—that part of a wave that washed over the shores of personality psychology. On the other hand, the explicit influence of the comprehensive personal-construct theory has been concentrated on clinical psychology and consumer psychology rather than personality, and more in the British Commonwealth and the Netherlands than in the United States (see Jankowicz, 1987, and Neimeyer, 1985). Within personality psychology, Kelly's influence has been more diffuse, indirect, and subtle. Many personality psychologists accept Kelly's general principles. From that perspective, they have gone on to study a bewildering array of "cognitive" variables—cognitive styles, schemas, attitudes, beliefs, and values—that are loosely related to personal-construct theory. The rest of this chapter is devoted to several variables reflecting people's *cognitive style*, because these are most closely derived from Kelly's theory. In the rest of Part Two, we will consider other kinds of cognitive personality variables.

Measuring Personal Constructs

To understand cognitive style, it is first necessary to know how Kelly measured people's constructs. He preferred to have them write a character sketch of themselves in the third person, as if writing about someone they knew well. "For example, start out by saying, 'Harry Brown is . . .' " (Kelly, 1955, p. 323). From these *self-characterizations* and other personal documents, Kelly extracted people's principal constructs. He paid special attention to images, sequences, repetitions, and contexts, and looked for similarities and contrasts (1955, pp. 329–340). This is reminiscent of the way Freud interpreted his patients' words and dreams and has been formalized by Leitner (1985) for use with interviews.

Since it is difficult to elicit and compare peoples' self-characterizations, Kelly also developed another technique, the Role Construct Repertory Test, or rep test. Under the name "repertory grid technique," the rep test has been used in almost all published studies of personal constructs (see Adams-Webber & Mancuso, 1983, and Bonarius, Holland, & Rosenberg, 1981). Kelly described the rep test as follows (quoted in Bannister & Mair, 1968):

> Suppose I were to give one of you a card and ask you to write on it the name of your mother. Then I would give you another and ask you to write the name of your father. On a third you might write the name of your wife. . . . We could continue until you had as many as twenty or thirty cards, each showing the name of a person important in your life.
>
> Then suppose I should select three of these cards, perhaps the ones of your father, your mother, and your boss or supervisor. Suppose I should ask you to think of some important way in which any two of them seem to be alike and in contrast to the third. What will you say? Perhaps you will say that your mother and your boss have always seemed to know the answers to the questions you asked [*emergent pole* of the construct] but that your father hesitated or told you to seek out your own answers [*implicit pole* of the construct].
>
> Now if this is a distinction you can apply to your father, your mother, and your boss, can you extend it also to the other persons you have named? You probably can. The important fact is that as you can apply it to person after person you are not only characterizing those persons but you are also providing an operational definition of what you have in mind. (p. 45)

Notice how the compare-and-contrast procedure of the rep test is closely related to Kelly's key concept of bipolar constructs.

In the repertory grid technique, each construct elicited from a particular selection of three cards (called a sort) is then applied to all the different people (or role titles), resulting in a checkerboard grid of constructs (rows) and persons or role titles (columns),[8] as shown in Figure 6.2. Such a grid can be analyzed in many different ways: for example, to determine the degree of similarity between two persons or the degree of overlap among constructs.

Content and Structure

When we examine people's repertory grid, we can look at either the *content* or the *structure* of their constructs. The analysis of content asks about the particular constructs people employ: How do they construe the world? Do their constructs reflect authority? Love? Emotionality? In contrast, the analysis of structure asks how these dimensions are arranged, regardless of their contents: Are they complex or simple? Permeable or impermeable? Broad and comprehensive or narrow and specific? Most researchers focus on the structural aspects of the rep test because they can more easily be measured and compared across persons.

---

[8]While the role constructs (columns) are usually defined in terms of significant other *people*, almost anything could be used: important experiences, personal catastrophes, films, paintings, emotions. One market research investigator even used different types of bread (Bannister & Mair, 1968, p. 72)!

Initials of person in role-title number:										Construct from sort number:	
										Emergent pole	Implicit pole
1	2	3	4	5	6	7	8	9	10		
										1.	
										2.	
										3.	
										4.	
										5.	
										6.	
										7.	
										8.	
										9.	

FIGURE 6.2
Example of a role repertory (rep) test grid.

COGNITIVE COMPLEXITY: DIFFERENTIATION

Cognitive complexity is the most widely studied single variable of cognitive structure. While important in many theories (see Streufert & Streufert, 1978), it is especially important in personal-construct theory because it brings together several dimensions along which construct systems differ. The more complex a person's constructs, the more likely that they are *hierarchical, comprehensive,* and *permeable,* and the less likely they are to be *constellatory* or *preemptive;* the more likely that the person will make elaborative choices with a *preference for extension* instead of definition.

Bieri (1955) carried out the first experimental study of cognitive complexity based on personal-construct theory. He measured complexity from a repertory grid like that in Figure 6.2 by calculating the degree of overlap across constructs. Two constructs are said to overlap if they are applied in the same way to a group of persons or role titles. The greater the overlap, the lower the complexity score. In an initial study, Bieri found that more cognitively complex college students were able to make better predictions about other students' responses, especially when those responses were different from their own. In other words, they were able to see differences between themselves and others instead of projecting their own wishes onto others (see Chapter 3).

Other studies have found that cognitively more complex people attend to a wider range of information, especially information that doesn't fit preconceived notions or that violates familiar rules and schemas (Delia & Crockett, 1973). They are less swayed by striking or obvious events; that is, they are less affected by availability heuristics. In contrast, people scoring low in cognitive complexity are more suggestible and more vulnerable to manipulation by brainwashing (Suedfeld, 1964; Suedfeld & Vernon, 1966).

Hermann (1980a, 1980b) measured cognitive complexity in verbal text by the ratio of high-complexity words (for example, "may," "possible," "sometimes") to low-complexity words ("always," "without a doubt," "absolutely," and so forth). She found that world leaders scoring high interact more cooperatively with other nations, whereas low-complexity leaders tend to advocate their own foreign policy goals. Complex thinking, in other words, seems to be an important ingredient of international cooperation.

COGNITIVE COMPLEXITY: INTEGRATION

Bieri's measure of cognitive complexity involves mainly differentiation, that is, making distinctions when processing information. However, Bieri argued that the complexity also includes hierarchical organization, or the integration of differentiated elements. Harvey, Hunt, and Schroder (1961) and later Schroder, Driver, and Streufert (1967) developed this idea into a measure of *integrative complexity*. People functioning at the low end of the integrative-complexity scale view events from only a single perspective. Higher scores reflect some differentiation of perspectives. People at the top of the scale are able to integrate or combine alternatives into higher-order, more abstract unities. They can deal with multiple possibilities, hypothetical situations, and new interpretations. Thus differentiation and integration can be understood as two related but separate aspects of cognitive complexity.

To measure integrative complexity, Schroder and his colleagues score responses to a paragraph completion test, in which people write paragraph-length responses (three or four sentences) to a series of incomplete sentences, such as "When I am criticized. . . ." More recently, Suedfeld and his colleagues have revised the scoring manual so that it can be applied to almost any verbal material, such as letters, interviews, or political speeches (see Suedfeld, Tetlock, & Streufert, 1992).

Integrative Complexity and Performance

Stress, life, and death. In a variety of studies, integrative complexity is positively associated with effective performance and negatively associated with stress. For example, Suedfeld (1980, 1985) and Porter and Suedfeld (1981)

Peter Suedfeld, who has adapted the measures of integrative complexity to the study of political leaders, authors, and historical persons. "[Our research] concentrates on changes in integrative complexity as a function of environmental characteristics, as well as on how such changes are related to the outcomes of particular problem-solving or conflict resolution dilemmas" (1980, p. 117). (Courtesy Peter Suedfeld)

found that integrative complexity in literary writings and editorials is lower in times of war, international tension, and personal illness. Particularly striking is Suedfeld and Piedrahita's (1984) analysis of the correspondence of eighteen famous people of the past three centuries. Among those who died after a protracted illness (for example, cancer, tuberculosis, or simple old age), integrative complexity declined markedly over the last five years of life. Among those who died suddenly (for example, heart attack or typhoid fever), there was a sharp decline only during the final year of life. These results are shown in Table 6.1 and Figure 6.3. They suggest that there may be a connection between cognition and life itself, though we do not know which causes which. Integrative complexity may act as a cognitive control on the effects of stress (perhaps by decreasing sympathetic nervous system arousal); alternatively, stress may simply lower integrative complexity.

War and peace. Tetlock (1979) measured integrative complexity at a distance by scoring political speeches and found higher levels of integrative

TABLE 6.1 FAMOUS PERSONS USED IN STUDY OF INTEGRATIVE COMPLEXITY
AND APPROACHING DEATH

Name	Sex	Nationality	Major occupation	Year of death	Age at death	Cause of death*
Lewis Carroll	M	British	Clergyman, author, mathematician	1898	66	Pneumonia (P)
D. H. Lawrence	M	British	Author	1930	45	Long illness (P)
Sigmund Freud	M	Austrian	Physician, psychologist	1939	83	Cancer (P)
Franz Liszt	M	Hungarian	Composer, musician	1885	74	Sudden death (S)
Aldous Huxley	M	British	Author	1963	69	Cancer (P)
Napoleon I	M	French	Ruler, soldier	1821	52	Cancer or slow poison (P)
Franz Kafka	M	Czech	Author	1924	41	Tuberculosis (P)
Louis Brandeis	M	American	Jurist	1941	85	Heart attack (S)
Gustave Flaubert	M	French	Author	1880	59	Sudden death (S)
Robert Browning	M	British	Poet	1889	77	Heart failure (S)
Marcel Proust	M	French	Author	1922	51	Pneumonia (P)
Walter Raleigh	M	British	Professor of literature	1922	61	Typhoid fever (S)
Ruth Draper	F	American	Actress	1956	72	Old age (P)
Queen Victoria	F	British	Ruler	1901	82	Old age (P)
Mary Russell Mitford	F	British	Novelist, dramatist	1855	68	Accidental death (S)
Gertrude Bell	F	British	Author, traveler	1926	58	Sudden death (S)
Mary Gilmore	F	Australian	Author, teacher	1962	97	Old age (P)
Mary Wollstonecraft Shelley	F	British	Author	1851	54	Gradual paralysis (P)

*As indicated in biographies; (S) Sudden or (P) Protracted.
SOURCE: Adapted from Suedfeld and Piedrahita (1984, p. 850).

complexity during international crises that were effectively managed (the Marshall Plan, the 1962 Cuban missile crisis) than during crises that were bungled (the 1950 U.S. invasion of North Korea during the Korean War, the 1961 Bay of Pigs invasion of Cuba, and the military escalation in Vietnam during the late 1960s). Reflecting on these results, Tetlock suggests that low integrative complexity may be one cause of the phenomenon of groupthink (Janis, 1983; see also Chapter 5), in which "intense social pressures toward uniformity and in-group loyalty . . . seriously interfere with both cognitive efficiency and moral judgment" (Tetlock, 1979, p. 1314). Other at-a-distance studies show that the integrative complexity of government-to-government statements is higher during crises that are peacefully resolved than during

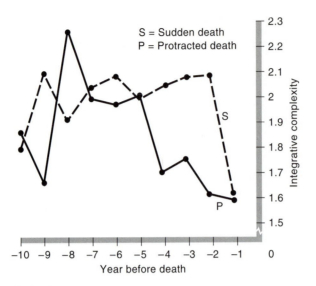

FIGURE 6.3
Declines of integrative complexity prior to lingering and sudden death.

crises that escalate to war (Suedfeld & Tetlock, 1977; Suedfeld, Tetlock, & Ramirez, 1977).

Integrative complexity in the American Civil War. A study of Confederate General Robert E. Lee during the American Civil War, by Suedfeld, Corteen, and McCormick (1986), vividly illustrates how integratively complex people function effectively by efficient and organized use of information and other resources. Lee had the reputation of being a military genius who was repeatedly able to defeat numerically stronger Union forces. Suedfeld and his colleagues identified six Civil War battles where Lee was engaged against larger enemy forces: three victories (Antietam, Fredericksburg, and Chancellorsville) and three defeats (Gettysburg, the Wilderness, and Spotsylvania). They scored levels of integrative complexity in the dispatches and orders of both Lee and the opposing Union generals for the week before each battle. Figure 6.4 presents the results. Initially, Lee scored high in integrative complexity, a good deal higher than the three Union generals whom he defeated, but not much higher than Meade, who defeated Lee at Gettysburg in 1863. Lee's integrative complexity then dropped off markedly, falling below that of Union General Ulysses Grant, who repeatedly defeated him toward the end of the war. After his surrender to Grant at Appomattox, Lee's integrative complexity then rose and remained stable at a high level. While these results do not prove that integrative complexity wins battles, they do suggest that Lee's generally high scores may reflect some aspects of his capacity to marshal and deploy people and resources in a complex and ever-changing situation.

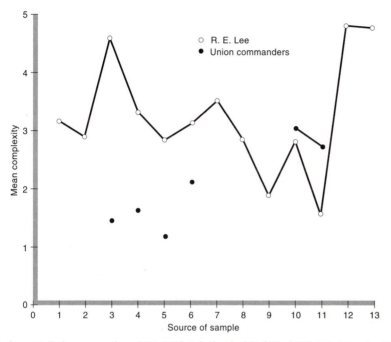

Sources: 1. Early correspondence (1839–1854); 2. Outbreak of Civil War (1860); 3. Antietam (vs. McClellan); 4. Fredericksburg (vs. Burnside); 5. Chancellorsville (vs. Hooker); 6. Gettysburg (vs. Meade); 7. July–Oct. 1863; 8. Nov. 1863–Jan. 1864; 9. Feb.–Apr. 1864; 10. The Wilderness (vs. Grant); 11. Spotsylvania (vs. Grant); 12. Appomattox (Apr. 1865); 13. Postwar correspondence (Aug. 1865–1867).

FIGURE 6.4
Integrative complexity scores of Robert E. Lee and various opposing Union generals.

Is Integrative Complexity Always a Good Thing?

Tetlock, Peterson, and Berry (1993) have summarized many different studies of integrative complexity. High scorers are cognitively self-directed; they seek out information, listen well, and are tolerant of and open to new information. They hold balanced and moderate opinions. Surely these are virtues! On the other hand, Tetlock and colleagues caution that high integrative complexity can also get in the way of making clear-cut decisions and standing fast on important moral principles. It can inhibit taking decisive action. Thus, for example, during the debate on slavery before the American Civil War, moderate leaders occupying positions in the middle scored high, but those at the extremes (abolitionists and advocates of slavery) were quite low (see Tetlock, Armor, and Peterson, 1994). Tetlock, Peterson, and Berry also report results from an intensive study of business management graduate students suggesting that integrative complexity is associated with observer ratings of creativity (as expected) but also with ratings of disagreeableness, lack of conscientiousness, and narcissism! At the other end of the scale, integratively "simple" people were seen as acquiescent and conforming (as expected), but also as warm, giving, and self-controlled. Perhaps, then, integrative complexity confers both benefits and vulnerabilities.

A study by Suedfeld and Rank (1976) adds yet another dimension to integrative complexity. They studied revolutionary leaders who were successful (such as Oliver Cromwell in sixteenth-century England, George Washington, or Lenin in 1917 Russia) and revolutionary leaders who started out well but in the end failed (Alexander Hamilton, Trotsky in 1917 Russia, and Lin Biao in the 1949 Chinese Communist revolution). Both kinds of leaders showed low levels of integrative complexity during the takeover phase of the revolution. This is the time when popular support must be rallied by simple rhetoric, portraying the enemy as wholly evil and the revolution as completely good. Among successful leaders, however, integrative complexity went back up after the revolution, during the phase of consolidation and later. Suedfeld and Rank concluded that while simple-minded fanaticism may be needed to start a revolution, running a postrevolutionary government requires more complex integrative abilities:

> Various factions must be reconciled and conciliated, policies must be based on diverse considerations in complex interactions, and both ideology and practice must be flexible and adaptable to dynamic events. Leaders who remain too fanatic in this phase are unable to cope with the new set of requirements. (p. 172)

EGO DEVELOPMENT

Most people show increased cognitive complexity with age, at least up to early adulthood. To many developmental theorists (for example, Werner, 1957), the movement from simplicity to complexity *is* development. This perspective led Loevinger (1966, 1976) to combine cognitive-developmental and psychoanalytic perspectives into a general theory of ego development that is related to (but distinct from) integrative complexity.

Drawing on Freud's work, Loevinger suggested that the essential task of the ego is *synthesis and integration*—synthesis of motives, internal standards, perceptions, memories, and the demands of the external world. As it carries out this task, the ego develops in a series of separate and distinct *stages*. Table 6.2 describes the five most important stages and illustrates their characteristic thoughts and feelings with quotations from Keller's autobiography (see Loevinger, 1976, pp. 24–25, for a full summary chart). Each stage has its own characteristic cognitive style, or way in which the ego transforms, modifies, processes, and integrates motives, perceptions, and demands.

Loevinger's ego-development stages clearly represent a sequence of increasing cognitive complexity, involving first differentiation and then integration. For example, at the first *impulsive stage*, when children have barely learned the basics of language, their cognitive and emotional experiences are organized into two broad and simple categories: "good" (whatever or whoever is nice to me right now; also clean, happy, etc.) and "bad" (whatever or whoever is mean to me now; also dirty, sad, sick, etc.). The growth of anticipa-

Jane Loevinger, who developed measures of the stages of ego development. "The child's way of construing the world goes through stages that differ qualitatively, not just quantitatively; indeed, the qualitative difference is so great that adults can hardly understand the child's way of looking at things. . . . The sequence is hierarchical; . . . each stage incorporates and transmutes the insights and accomplishments of the previous stage and prepares for the next stage" (1987, p. 240). (Courtesy Jane Loevinger)

tion, at the *self-protective stage*, makes it possible to distinguish what is happening now from what will be later. This increase in complexity makes it possible for children to delay gratification. The further development of language brings the *conformist stage*, with its vast increase in the number of available categories and labels to be learned. This stage is called "conformity" because it involves making sure that everything—including the self—has the right name and is in its correct place. This is the stage at which stereotypes develop.

Gradually the child acquires the sense of an inner self, with its own thoughts and wishes, which may not correspond to what the outer world requires or expects. Discrepencies between inner and outer can give rise to shame, guilt, and self-criticism. Children come to understand "psychological" concepts (motives, feelings, and attitudes) as characteristics of persons rather than situations. At this stage they begin to understand what is meant by personality. It is called the *conscientious stage* because children try to match their inner behavior to their conception of the external world, as contrasted with the earlier conformist stage, in which they simply take their sense of self uncritically from the world.

TABLE 6.2 HELEN KELLER'S STAGES OF EGO DEVELOPMENT

Stage name and code	Characteristic features of cognitive style	Examples from Keller's autobiography
Impulsive (I-2)	Present-oriented Need-based Conceptual confusion	[After meeting Alexander Graham Bell] He understood my signs, and I knew it and loved him at once. (p. 19) I became impatient at her repeated attempts and, seizing the new doll, I dashed it upon the floor. I was keenly delighted when I felt the fragments of the broken doll at my feet. . . . I felt my teacher sweep the fragments to one side of the hearth, and I had a sense of satisfaction that the cause of my discomfort was removed. (p. 21)
Self-protective (Delta)	Anticipation Wariness Opportunism	[On Christmas Eve] I knew the gifts I already had were not those of which my friends had thrown out such tantalizing hints, and my teacher said the presents I was to have would be even nicer than these. . . . That night, after I had hung my stocking, I lay awake a long time, pretending to be asleep and keeping alert to see what Santa Claus would do when he came. (p. 30)

Loevinger's final two stages are labeled *autonomous* and *integrated*. After the self has been differentiated from the world, the ego must learn to reconcile these two differentiated opposites. This final task requires tolerance for ambiguity, cognitive complexity, and the capacity for "dialectical thinking," in which opposites continue to exist while at the same time being merged into a higher synthesis or whole.

Loevinger measures the stages of ego development with a sentence-completion test, in which people write completions to a series of sentence fragments such as the following:

"Raising a family. . . ."
"When a child won't join in group activities. . . ."
"When they talked about sex, I. . . ."

Studies using Loevinger's stages of ego development are reviewed by Hauser (1976) and Loevinger (1979, 1987, pp. 222–233).

TABLE 6.2 (Continued)

Stage name and code	Characteristic features of cognitive style	Examples from Keller's autobiography
Conformist (I-3)	Categories Stereotypes External rules	I left the house eager to learn. Everything had a name, and each name gave birth to a new thought. (p. 21) This habit of assimilating what pleased me and giving it out again as my own appears in much of my early correspondance and my first attempts at writing. (p. 44)
Conscientious (I-4)	Internalization Self-criticism Guilt Long-term goals	Indeed, I have ever been tortured by the fear that what I write is not my own. For a long time, when I wrote a letter, even to my mother, I was seized by a sudden feeling of terror and I would spell the sentences over and over, to make sure that I had not read them in a book. (p. 44)
Autonomous (I-5)	Tolerance of ambiguity Reconciliation of opposites Complexity	While my days at Radcliffe were still in the future, they were encircled with a halo of romance, which they have lost; but in the transition from romantic to actual I have learned many things I should never have known had I not tried the experiment. (p. 62)

COGNITIVE COMPLEXITY AS A DIMENSION OF PERSONALITY

In the last few sections of this chapter, we have seen that theorists starting from Kelly's cognitive theory, from psychoanalysis and ego psychology, and from cognition all agree that that *simplicity versus complexity is a fundamental dimension of individual difference.* Further, there is broad agreement that complexity involves a combination of *differentiation* (distinguishing among different thoughts, attitudes, feelings, goals, plans, outcomes, and objects) and *integration* (combining these differentiated thoughts and feelings in multiple, often hierarchical ways).

Using a variety of different methods and measures, the research studies of cognitive complexity also show considerable agreement. "Complex" people usually function better than "simple" people, especially in complex, changing situations. A study of ego development and political reasoning among college students by Candee (1974) illustrates this convergence. Candee found that students' stage of ego development was not related to the *content* of their political beliefs or attitudes but did predict the ways in which they justified and reasoned about politics. Students at the lower stages saw issues in global, simplistic terms that were usually related to how they themselves would be affected. Students at the highest stages, however, saw politics as a complex process that involved abstract values such as human development and justice. Ego development, Candee concluded, "is marked by a *more differentiated perception of one's self, of the social world, and of the relationship of one's feelings and thoughts to those of others*" (1974, p. 622, emphasis added).

7

Authoritarianism and Other Beliefs about the Social Order

———————— ❖ ————————

In order to discuss the contents of cognition, it is first necessary to distinguish several different terms that psychologists use to refer to different kinds of cognitive structures. As discussed in Chapter 6, a *construct* refers to a (bipolar) descriptive attribute or adjective that we apply to persons, places, and things. A *schema* (plural schemas or schemata) is an internal model or representation in memory; for example, the defining attributes or constructs applying to the person, place, or thing. Our self-schema includes those adjectives that attach to our internal sense of self or self-concept.

A *belief* is a representation of what "is"—what we think the world is like, how it appears to us, or what it might be like under certain circumstances. In terms of Kelly's theory, a belief results from the application of a construct to a particular object. Beliefs can range from trivial details of everyday life ("I believe the writing paper in front of me is yellow") to matters of profound philosophical importance ("I believe human life is meaningful").

A *value* is a belief about the way the world "ought to be," sometimes expressed as an evaluation about the way things are (for example, good or bad, worthwhile or worthless). Values are different from motives: motives involve the things people actually want (the goals they try to reach), while values involve the things people believe they ought to want. While motives and values often overlap, people do not always want to do what they feel they should do. In fact, the conflict between motives (want) and values (ought) is a major theme of philosophy, law, and religion. As we saw in Chapter 5, people are not always consciously aware of their motives; but they are aware of their values and usually will express them quite freely to others. Thus values can be measured by direct questions, whereas indirect techniques may be necessary to get at motives, as discussed in Chapter 5.

When a broad and general value is applied to some particular object, action, person, or group, the result is an *attitude*—a favorable or unfavorable emotion toward that object or person. The relationship between values and attitudes can be illustrated in the writings of Helen Keller. In a 1924 letter to Robert La Follette (the Progressive Party candidate for president), she mentioned several important positive and negative values (quoted in Foner, 1967):

All human beings should have leisure and comfort, the decencies and refinements of life. . . . The people should rule. . . . labor should participate in public affairs. . . . Curtailment and limitation of wealth and special privilege [that is, a *negative value* on wealth and privilege]. . . . International cooperation and amity. (pp. 113–115)

Because she believed that La Follette shared these values, Keller had a positive *attitude* toward his candidacy: "My heart rejoiced when I heard of your nomination" (Ibid). Because she believed that socialism promoted these values, Keller also had a positive attitude toward the symbols of socialism: "I love the red flag and what it symbolizes to me and other Socialists. I have a red flag hanging in my study, and if I could I should gladly march with it past the office of the [New York] *Times* and let all the reporters and photographers make the most of the spectacle" (Foner, 1967, p. 25).

When conflicting positive and negative values apply to the same object or action, the result is a conflicted attitude. In recent years, for example, the values of "preserving life" and "individual choice" have come into conflict in many arenas; for example, abortion, euthanasia, physician-assisted suicide, and laws requiring the use of seat belts or motorcycle helmets.

In this book, we will give special attention to two broad kinds of beliefs and values. They involve such fundamental questions as how society should be organized (this chapter) and why things happen the way they do (Chapter 8). We begin with authoritarianism, which is a cluster of beliefs and values that represents one answer to the question of organizing society. It is probably the single most studied variable in all of personality and social psychology research.

*T*HE AUTHORITARIAN PERSONALITY: A CLASSIC CLUSTER OF VALUES AND BELIEFS

Explaining Prejudice

As the victorious Allied armies swept over the ruins of Hitler's Germany in the spring of 1945, they liberated extermination camps in which more than 6 million Jews had been systematically murdered, along with millions of Polish citizens, Soviet prisoners of war, Sinti and Roma (Gypsies), political dissidents, homosexuals, and other groups hated by the Nazi regime. A horrified world, no longer able to turn away from the results of Hitler's "final solution," asked Why? How could such racial and religious hatred, such eager willingness to exterminate one's fellow human beings, have occurred in a "modern" country celebrated for its civilized attainments in philosophy, science, and music? And so began the search for the psychological and social roots of such unreason.

Prejudice and discrimination had been a sadly familiar part of human history long before the Holocaust. For example, in the same year that the Spanish monarchs Ferdinand and Isabella bankrolled Columbus's first voyage to the New World, they also expelled all Jews and Muslims from Spain. Forty-eight years earlier, in 1444, the Portuguese began the practice of the enslavement of Africans by Europeans, a practice that was to last until the late nineteenth century. For centuries, Hindus and Muslims on the Indian subcontinent have slaughtered each other. In our own time, parts of former Yugoslavia have been subjected to "ethnic cleansing." Finally, the oppression of women by men is a continuing feature of many societies and eras (see, for example, Brownmiller, 1975; Ortner, 1974; Stewart & Winter, 1977). Clearly, historical, economic, and social forces are involved in such oppression, but personality factors may also lead some people to hate, torment, and murder others of their fellow human beings.

Beginning in 1944, the American Jewish Committee launched a major social science research effort to explain anti-Semitism. The result was *The Authoritarian Personality* (Adorno, Frenkel-Brunswik, Levinson, & Sanford, 1950), a massive 990-page landmark book. It introduced the F scale ("F" is an abbreviation for fascism), which has become the single most widely used questionnaire measure in personality research. Although the original book generated many methodological disputes, and although the F scale has been replaced by better measures, the concept of authoritarianism introduced by Adorno and his colleagues continues to be a lively topic of personality research and theory (Altemeyer, 1988; Stone, Lederer, & Christie, 1992).[1]

Constructing Scales to Measure Authoritarian Beliefs and Values

Adorno and his colleagues (often called the Berkeley group, because their research was carried out at the University of California at Berkeley) studied a variety of Americans: college students, members of Rotary and Kiwanis clubs, parent-teacher organization members, labor union members, office workers, prison inmates, merchant marine officers, and church groups. They began by developing a series of questionnaire items that reliably measured anti-Semitic beliefs (the Anti-Semitism, or A-S, scale). People answering the questionnaires were asked to mark each statement according to how much they agreed or disagreed with it, using the following choices (called Likert-scaling):

+1: slight agreement   −1: slight disagreement
+2: moderate agreement   −2: moderate disagreement
+3: strong agreement   −3: strong disagreement

---

[1]Early reviews of the authoritarianism literature can be found in Brown (1965), Cherry and Byrne (1977), and Dillehay (1978), along with the theoretical analysis and discussion of Forbes (1985). Altemeyer (1981, 1988) introduced a major new measure and conceptualization of this variable as *right-wing authoritarianism*. Samelson (1986) has reviewed the entire history of authoritarianism research, while Sanford (1986), one of the original authors of *The Authoritarian Personality,* gives a fascinating inside account of that enterprise.

Typical anti-Semitic items included the following:

> Jews seem to prefer the most luxurious, extravagant, and sensual way of living.
> One trouble with Jewish businessmen is that they stick together and connive, so that a Gentile doesn't have a fair chance in competition.
> It is wrong for Jews and Gentiles to intermarry.

Notice how all these items, which involve stereotyped negative opinions about Jews, also reflect a sense of threat. People who feel this way about Jews also have negative stereotypes about other groups. That is, A-S scale responses correlated quite highly with responses to items such as the following, from a broader Ethnocentrism (E) scale:

> Negroes have their rights, but it is best to keep them in their own districts and schools and to prevent too much contact with whites.
> The worst danger to real Americanism in the last 50 years has come from foreign ideas and agitators.
> Zoot-suiters[2] prove that when people of their type have too much money and freedom, they just take advantage and cause trouble.

The high intercorrelation of the A-S and E scales suggests that these negative attitudes may have more to do with internal forces than with the actual characteristics of the particular groups. On the other hand, these correlations do not tell us much about the origins of these prejudices and the underlying personality processes that maintain them. Moreover, the A-S and E scales so obviously measure prejudices that they would be of little use if people wanted to conceal their true thoughts about other groups. To get around this problem and to understand the deeper forces behind prejudice, the Berkeley group constructed a new scale that would correlate highly with the A-S and E scales, without mentioning minority groups. The result was a measure of "implicit antidemocratic trends"—in simpler language, the Fascism or F scale. In developing F scale items, the researchers drew on many sources, such as the writings of American and foreign anti-Semitic agitators, and interviews and Thematic Apperception Test stories of people who scored high on the A-S and E scales. Overall, the items reflected several different themes, each illustrated in Table 7.1 by a few items.

The final version of the F scale correlated quite highly with the E scale ($r = .77$), indicating that anti-Semitism and ethnocentrism do cluster with the broader themes illustrated in the table.

To the Berkeley group, the major common thread running through the F scale items was "a general disposition to glorify, to be subservient to and

---

[2]Who are zoot-suiters? In the California of the 1940s, they were young men, often of Chicano background, who wore a style of baggy clothing, called zoot suits, that was even more extreme than today's baggy style.

TABLE 7.1 F SCALE THEMES AND TYPICAL ITEMS

Conventionalism, and *Authoritarian submission:*	Obedience and respect for authority are the most important virtues children should learn.
Authoritarian aggression:	Most of our social problems would be solved if we could somehow get rid of the immoral, crooked, and feeble-minded people.
	Homosexuals are hardly better than criminals and ought to be severely punished.
Anti-intraception (opposition to inner thoughts and feelings):	When a person has a problem or worry, it is best for him not to think about it, but to keep busy with more cheerful things.
Superstition and stereotypy:	Some day it will probably be shown that astrology can explain a lot of things.
Power and "toughness":	People can be divided into two distinct classes: the weak and the strong.
Destructiveness and cynicism:	Human nature being what it is, there will always be war and conflict.
Projectivity (projection of unconscious impulses), and *Sex* (exaggerated concern with sexual "goings-on"):	The wild sex life of the old Greeks and Romans was tame compared to some of the goings-on in this country, even in places where people might least expect it.

remain uncritical toward *authority* figures of the ingroup and to take an attitude of punishing outgroup figures in the name of some moral *authority*" (Adorno et al., 1950, p. 228, emphasis added). To emphasize this role of "authority," they gave the name *authoritarianism* to the personality characteristic measured by the F scale. Although the conclusions of the Berkeley group were based only on studies of prejudiced West-Coast Americans, their concept of authoritarianism fit closely with the results of other researchers who had studied fascists and Nazi leaders (e.g., Dicks, 1950; Stagner, 1936). In fact, Fromm had introduced the term "authoritarianism" in his book *Escape from Freedom* (1941), which first analyzed the historical and social forces in Germany that underlay the appeal of the Nazi movement. According to Fromm, the increased freedom brought about by urbanization and capitalist industrialization in nineteenth-century Germany also brought with it a greater sense of isolation and fear, especially among people of the lower middle class. The economic and political stresses of the 1920s and 1930s (defeat in World War I, staggering inflation, the worldwide depression) made matters worse. Fearing freedom, many Germans sought refuge in Hitler as an idealized authority.

They gave fanatical allegiance to him, while exploiting and aggressing against those who were seen as "different" or "inferior."

You can see that the themes of the F scale touch on important and profound beliefs and values about other people and social organization. The beliefs of an authoritarian can be summarized in the following three statements: (1) Hierarchy is the lens through which all social life is focused. (2) Moralism saturates all judgments, evaluations, and social relationships. (3) Thus there is no general, broad-based humanitarian perspective toward other people; rather, people are viewed with either moral suspicion or solidarity, depending on their group membership.

MEASURING PERSONALITY WITH QUESTIONNAIRES

Before taking a closer look at the authoritarian personality, we will pause to consider some of the methodological implications of the Berkeley group's research. Like many other researchers, they chose to measure personality variables through questionnaires in which people respond to a series of individual items or statements with agreement or disagreement. This is a cheap and efficient way to collect data, but it raises several problems.

Social Desirability

When they fill out a questionnaire, many people try to appear in the best possible light or at least control the impression they are creating. As a result, their response to any particular item is affected by the perceived social desirability of the different choices given. In a classic study, Edwards (1953) found that the more socially desirable a particular response, the higher the proportion of people who give that response. We can, of course, consider people's tendency to give socially desirable responses as a personality variable in its own right (as did Crowne & Marlowe, 1964), but usually personality psychologists view social desirability as a contaminant, something to get rid of when designing a questionnaire. This can be done by matching alternative choices for social desirability or using people's social desirability scores to adjust their scores on other variables (Edwards, 1970).

Acquiescence

When they fill out a questionnaire, some people have a strong preference for answering Yes (True, Agree, etc.) to *any* item, regardless of its content. Technical names for this preference are *acquiescence, agreeing response set,* or simply *yea-saying.* (An extreme yea-sayer might even "agree" with an item and with its opposite.) Other response sets include tendencies to answer No or Disagree (nay-saying), to avoid extreme responses in either direction, to alternate choices, or to answer items randomly.

Recall that the F scale items of Table 7.1 are all scored in the Agree direction—that is, the Agree choice is the authoritarian response. In fact, this is true of every item in the original F scale. In taking the test, therefore, yea-sayers will tend to have high scores regardless of their actual level of authoritarianism—in other words, the original F scale may be confusing acquiescense with authoritarianism. This problem was identified by Hyman and Sheatsley (1954) soon after the publication of *The Authoritarian Personality* (see also Cherry & Byrne, 1977, pp. 114–116). To get around it, many researchers have developed "balanced" versions of the F scale, with some items scored in each direction. The most recent balanced version by Altemeyer (1981, 1988) is called *right-wing authoritarianism* (RWA). Since this balanced measure correlates quite highly with the original F scale and predicts the same kinds of behaviors (Altemeyer, 1988, pp. 8–11; Meloen, 1990), I will use it along with the original measures interchangably in the rest of this chapter. (In a later section of this chapter I will discuss right-wing and left-wing authoritarianism.)

UNDERSTANDING THE AUTHORITARIAN

How do the themes of authoritarian beliefs and values function within the person to produce prejudice? Since the research literature is enormous, I will only cite some of the most interesting and vivid studies.

Intolerance of Ambiguity

Perhaps the key component of authoritarianism is actually a cognitive style—intolerance of ambiguity or rigidity. One of the original Berkeley group, Else Frenkel-Brunswik (1949), demonstrated the connection between intolerance of ambiguity and prejudice in an experiment carried out with children. They were shown first a picture of a dog, then a further series of pictures representing a gradual transformation of the dog into a cat (see Figure 7.1). After looking at each picture, the children were asked to identify the animal pictured. Compared to the unprejudiced children, the more prejudiced children held on longer to their original answer ("dog") and responded more slowly to changes in the series. They seemed to be reluctant or fearful to "see" things that didn't fit with their original judgment, avoiding any intermediate categories between the extremes of cat and dog.

Pettigrew, Allport, and Barnett (1958) demonstrated the relationship between prejudice and intolerance of ambiguity in an unusual and intriguing perception experiment. Participants from each of the major racial groups of South Africa (Afrikaans-speaking whites or Afrikaners, English-speaking whites, Indians, Coloured, and Blacks) looked through a binocular viewing apparatus in which they saw very brief exposures of a series of ordinary portrait-style pictures. For each picture, they were asked to identify the person's racial group. Unknown to the subjects, however, pictures of people of *different*

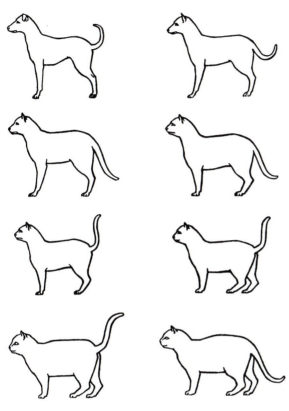

How well can you tolerate ambiguity? Starting with the dog (in the upper-left corner), when does the picture "turn into" a cat? In a study of prejudiced children (presumably higher in authoritarianism and therefore less able to tolerate ambiguity), Frenkel-Brunswik found that "the prejudiced group tended to hold on longer to the first object and to respond more slowly to the changing stimuli." They showed "greater reluctance to give up the original object about which one had felt relatively certain and a tendency not to see what did not harmonize with the first set" (1949, p. 128).
(Drawings reproduced from Eysenck, 1954, p. 223)

FIGURE 7.1
Drawing series used to study intolerance of ambiguity: A dog changes into a cat.

races (e.g., black and white) were sometimes projected separately to each eye. Given only a moment's glance at the "combination" of a white person and a black person, most participants labeled the person as Asian or Coloured (inter-mediate between black and white). The Afrikaners, however, tended to label these combinations as *either* black or white. Their either-or responses suggest an intolerance for ambiguity that extends even to the perceptual level. While Pettigrew and colleagues did not directly measure authoritarianism, other evi-dence suggests that the Afrikaners would have scored high on the F scale. From 1948 until 1994, they were the group that ruled South Africa on the basis of apartheid, an ideology of extreme racial separation and discrimination. Consistent with this history, Orpen (1970) found that students at the Univer-sity of Stellenbosch (often described as the Oxford of apartheid) had among the highest F scale scores ever reported.

Studies of American college students by Block and Block (1951) and Brown (1953) also showed relationships between prejudice and perceptual rigidity (or intolerance of ambiguity) on laboratory problem-solving tasks, especially under stress.

Anti-Intraception

In a complex and confusing world, many things are ambiguous, especially aspects of one's self. We have feelings of love *and* hate, pleasure *and* pain, kindness *and* hurtfulness, good *and* bad. As children, we all experienced reward *and* punishment from our parents. Whenever we look inward to our feelings, wishes, fears, and fantasies (a process called "intraception" by Murray, 1938, pp. 210–218), therefore, we confront an ambiguous inner world. People who cannot tolerate ambiguity should avoid focusing on their inner mental processes; that is, they should be *anti-intraceptive.* Instead of looking inward, they should direct their gaze to the less ambiguous "hard realities" of the external world ("extraception," in Murray's terms).

As a part of the original Berkeley group study, M. H. Levinson (1950) explored the connection between ethnocentrism and intraception in a sample of fifty-nine patients in a California state psychiatric hospital. (Ethnocentrism was measured with the E scale; but since the E scale correlates highly with the F scale, we can take her results as true of authoritarians in general.) Levinson was not interested in whether the patients as a group scored high in authoritarianism. In fact, their F scale scores were on the low side, and many subsequent studies have shown little relationship between authoritarianism and maladjustment or psychopathology (see Dillehay, 1978, p. 124). Rather, she was interested in whether prejudice affected how patients *viewed* or understood their psychiatric problems. Almost by definition, psychiatric patients have problems that involve "inner" impulses, feelings, fears, or conflicts. Patients who are intraceptive should be able to focus on these internal matters, experiencing their symptoms as part of themselves and their history. On the other hand, patients who are anti-intraceptive should turn away from internal problems and describe their complaints as originating from outside, the result of wholly external causes.

Levinson examined the records of each patient's first psychiatric interview (in clinical jargon, the intake interview). These contained the patients' initial discussion of their problems, condition, and symptoms. Independent coders, who did not know the patients' E scale scores, coded each intake interview for four different measures: (1) an overall category of intraception—how in touch the patients were with their inner world of feelings, wishes, and conflicts; (2) physical versus psychological complaints; (3) internal versus external cause of symptoms; and (4) "ego-alienness" or the feeling that one's problems and symptoms are not part of the self.

Levinson's results, summarized in Table 7.2, are clear-cut and statistically significant for three of the four measures. Prejudiced patients scored lower than nonprejudiced patients on overall intraception. They scored higher on physical (versus psychological) complaints and external symptom causes. Differences in the ego-alienness category, while in the right direction, were not significant.

You can get a clear sense of Levinson's results by looking at the following excerpts from two interview summaries, one scoring high and one scoring low

TABLE 7.2 INTERVIEW DIFFERENCES IN INTRACEPTION AMONG PREJUDICED AND UNPREJUDICED PSYCHIATRIC PATIENTS ($N = 59$)

Intake interview characteristic	Patients with high E scale scores (%)	Patients with low E scale scores (%)	Statistical significance
Intraception: Patient appreciates the psychological content of problems (e.g., mentions a specific fear, conflict, or interpersonal problem) vs. seeing the problem as purely physical or emphasizes malfunctioning (e.g., "I can't work")	43	71	$p < .05$
Somatic symptoms vs. psychological disturbance as main complaint	54	26	$p < .05$
"External" cause and onset: Patient denies all precipitating factors ("it just happened"), or relates symptom to some specific external event vs. acknowledgement that problem has existed "for a long time"	75	23	$p < .01$
Ego alienness: Patient describes impulses, problems, or even symptoms as completely "foreign" to the self ("I cannot understand what makes me do that") vs. acknowledgement that they are part of self and life experience	32	19	$p = $ n.s.

SOURCE: Adapted from Levinson (1950, p. 934).

on the E scale. (I have italicized phrases that suggest intraception or anti-intraception.) First the highly prejudiced patient, who was committed to the hospital because he had exposed himself sexually to a small girl (Levinson, 1950):

> The patient *doesn't know why he does it.* . . . . Three years ago he noticed that his *ability to concentrate and to think fast was somewhat impaired.* His job as an oil driller necessitated keen coordination and he was responsible for several injuries to the ground crew for which he subsequently blamed himself and felt that he could have prevented them if he had been more on his toes. Decided to give up oil drilling, became a welder. The patient confessed and stated that he was guilty of sexual exposure on one occasion but vigorously denied the others. The incident occurred when he was driving to work early in the morning, *and the next thing he remembers was sometime in the afternoon.* He recalls having exposed himself to a young girl on the corner, offering her a nickel to play with his penis. He became violently upset over this, *felt he had been working too hard,* and took a week's vacation. (p. 946, emphasis added)

Notice how this man saw his behavior as something apart from his experience of self: he "doesn't know why he does it," and he didn't even remember the actual incident itself. He looked for an external cause ("working too hard") and described his original problem (couldn't concentrate or think fast) in words that could suggest the breakdown of a machine.

In contrast, here is the interview summary of a man scoring low in prejudice:

> The patient says that *since childhood he has been somewhat withdrawn,* making very few social contacts, remaining in his room for days at a time. *Never has had any particular interests,* heroes, or ideals other than the vague feeling that he should somehow get a good job and become a respectable member of society. But he "loses interest and becomes bored with a job as soon as he finds out that he can handle it." He has had a variety of positions from laborer to personnel interviewer. When the job becomes intolerable, *feelings of anxiety and frustration* are at their height. He will feel very dissatisfied with himself as with the job and then try to change jobs. He shot off the middle finger of one hand "in a *hysterical effort* to escape the [World War II military] draft." He feels that psychotherapy is his "last chance" to *straighten out* and settle down permanently. (p. 954, emphasis added)

This patient openly acknowledged his problems as psychological. He admitted to specific feelings and inner problems and traced the origins of his problem to longstanding internal factors.

Clearly both patients have profound psychological problems and both need help. Their prejudice or authoritarianism did not predict degree of distress experienced and psychopathology, but rather how they viewed themselves and their problems. Authoritarians do not readily acknowledge feelings, impulses, and conflicts; they have little sense of the psychological nature of their problems; and they look to causes external to themselves. In short, they are anti-intraceptive. People who are not authoritarians (often called "egalitarians") are more inclined to look for the internal or "psychological" roots of their problems.

Projection and Idealization

When ambiguous inner feelings and desires cannot be acknowledged and experienced directly, they are often split into separate "good" and "bad" sets. The bad thoughts and impulses can then be projected outward on to other people (see the discussion of projection as a defense mechanism in Chapter 3). Several research findings document the existence of projection in authoritarians. When authoritarians look at paintings involving nudity or read sexually explicit books, for example, they tend to judge that the material is pornographic and should be legally restricted. Eliasberg and Stuart (1961) showed slides of thirteen museum paintings to a large sample of adult extension college students. (Some of these paintings are shown in Figure 7.2.) There was a highly significant correlation ($r = .46$) between people's F scale scores and the proportion of paintings they judged as pornographic. Using erotic reading materials, Byrne, Cherry, Lamberth, and Mitchell (1973) confirmed the relationship between authoritarianism and judgments of pornography. Authoritarians also reported experiencing greater sexual arousal and perceived more erotic themes in the pictures and verbal passages, and they advocated stronger censorship of such materials.

Do you feel that these works of art are pornographic? If so, why? Using paintings such as these, Eliasburg and Stuart (1961) found a correlation between people's authoritarianism scores and the number of such works of art they judged to be "pornographic." This suggests that authoritarians are made anxious by their own "evil" sexual impulses. To deal with this anxiety, they project sexual drives onto other people and things in their environment, then condemn these as "pornography."

In the decades since the Eliasburg and Stuart study, the influence of the women's movement may have changed our thinking about sex and pornography. If this study were repeated today, do you think the results would be the same or different? LEFT: Pablo Picasso, *Woman Dressing Her Hair* (Royan, June 1940. Oil on canvas, 51¼" x 38¼". Collection of Mrs. Bertram Smith, New York. The Museum of Modern Art, New York © 1995 The Museum of Modern Art). BOTTOM LEFT: Edouard Manet, *Luncheon on the Grass* (Musée D'Orsay, Paris. Scala/Art Resource, New York). BOTTOM RIGHT: Jean Fouquet, *Virgin and Child* (Koninklijk Museum voor Schone Kunst, Antwerp, Belgium).

FIGURE 7.2
Examples of paintings used in a study of authoritarianism and art judgments.

We can fit these findings together by assuming that authoritarians experience sexual impulses as bad (probably because they were punished in childhood). This labeling and (presumed) prior punishment does not block sexual arousal; in fact, authoritarians feel *greater* sexual arousal in response to the visual and verbal stimuli. Rather, the bad arousal is attributed, by projection, to the pictures or the words themselves, rather than to the self and its desires. Once projected in this way, sexual arousal can be controlled and condemned through censorship. To summarize: the authoritarian seems to be saying "these pictures and stories aroused me sexually, so they are pornographic and should be censored"; rather than "I became sexually aroused by these pictures and stories."

Obedience

Since everything bad has been projected outside the person, what remains inside is uncomplicated and good: ideals, conscience, and above all, the voice of parental authority. These are good, and because they are good, they are to be *obeyed*. Thus authoritarians are likely to subscribe to conventional political and social beliefs (Altemeyer, 1988; Cherry & Byrne, 1977, p. 120).

The clearest demonstration of authoritarian obedience comes from a study by Elms and Milgram (1966) that used the procedures of Milgram's (1963, 1975) famous obedience experiment, in which people are instructed by an experimenter to administer what they believe are increasingly severe electric shocks to a "learner," whom they believe to be a fellow volunteer. As the shocks apparently reach higher and higher levels, the learner protests, refuses to continue, and cries out in pain; at the same time the experimenter uses a series of prods to bring about obedience (e.g., "The experiment requires that you continue," or "You have no other choice, you *must* go on"). In fact, the experiment is about obedience and not learning: the learner is actually a paid confederate of the experimenter, and no shocks are actually given. Nearly all subjects feel conflict. Some defy the authority of the experimenter and refuse to continue. About 65 percent of the subjects, however, obey the authority and carry the series of shocks through to the end—a much higher percentage than Milgram or anyone else had expected before the experiments were carried out. Even when they personally had to force the learner's hand down onto a shock plate (Milgram's touch condition), 30 percent of the subjects still obeyed.

Most of the research reported by Milgram (1975) involved the effects of different conditions on levels of obedience. Elms and Milgram, however, studied the relationship of people's authoritarianism to their obedience. They found that the most obedient participants—those who obeyed even in the touch condition—scored significantly higher on the F scale than did the least obedient participants—those who rebelled when the victim learner was in another room and not visible. The difference held up even when complicating factors such as level of education were taken into account. Given what we know about authoritarianism, these results are not surprising, but they serve as a chilling demonstration of the connection between authoritarian beliefs and actual obedience. Even though Milgram's procedure is only a psychological experiment, it is an uncomfortable reminder of the real-life horrors of obedience.

Aggression

Milgram designed his experiment as a way to measure obedience, but the act of (apparently) giving lethal shocks also illustrates the connection of authoritarianism to aggression. Further evidence comes from Epstein's (1966) variant on the Milgram procedure, in which the participants themselves select the level of shock to be applied to the learner. People with higher F scale scores chose higher levels of shock. In their aggressive desire to punish or hurt others, then, authoritarians go beyond what is required for mere obedience. In a more conventional laboratory experiment by Dustin and Davis (1967), using monetary rewards or penalties and written evaluations, authoritarians preferred giving out punishments (taking away money, negative comments) to rewards (giving money, positive comments). Thus authoritarianism involves a punitive and aggressive style of controlling other people.[3]

Punitiveness. Authoritarians are also more aggressive and punitive in real-life situations. Narby, Cutler, and Moran (1993) reviewed a number of studies of authoritarianism and jury verdicts, concluding that people scoring high in authoritarianism tend to vote for a guilty verdict. (This tendency was stronger in studies of actual jury members in live trials than in studies of college students reading trial transcripts.) In a study of over 1,000 American state legislators, Altemeyer (1993) found a highly significant correlation ($r = .47$, $p < .001$) between legislators' levels of authoritarianism and the number of crimes for which they advocated the death penalty.

Mean-spiritedness. Authoritarians seem to enjoy the misfortunes of others. For example, in high school you may have known students who got into trouble for taking drugs, drinking, shoplifting, breaking rules, disobeying parents, running around with the "wrong sort of kids," getting pregnant, and so forth. If you were high in authoritarianism, you probably thought they "got what they deserved" and took a little secret pleasure from their misfortunes. Altemeyer (1988, pp. 154–157) found that college students high in authoritarianism did express these two responses to the troubles of other people.

Support for aggressive war. Authoritarianism is also related to taking aggressive positions on public issues, as for example support of U.S. involvement in the Vietnam war (Izzett, 1971). Doty, Peterson, and Winter (1992)

---

[3]In experimental psychology, there is an ongoing debate about whether punishment is actually an effective way to control behavior and facilitate learning, as compared to reward. The behaviorist B. F. Skinner, for example, argued strongly against using punishment. We may speculate from these results that the propunishment and antipunishment experimental psychologists would line up as more and less authoritarian, respectively.

studied students' attitudes and reactions during the 1990-1991 Iraq-Kuwait crisis and Gulf War. During the crisis but before the war, students scoring high in authoritarianism advocated stronger U.S. responses, including even the use of nuclear weapons. And after the quick victory of the U.S.-led coalition forces, these students were more likely to gloat and less likely to express regret.

Constructs of the Authoritarian

Because they are intolerant of ambiguity, authoritarians are likely to be low in cognitive complexity. They make relatively few distinctions and differentiations, for their cognitive world is simple, orderly, and rigid; it does not change in response to new experience. In Kelly's terms, their constructs are not permeable and are likely to be constellatory (perhaps also preemptive) rather than propositional (see Chapter 6). For an authoritarian, in other words, once a person or group has been construed in a particular way, then many other constructs will definitely apply or definitely not apply. For example, if a person is construed as belonging to some minority ethnic, political, or social group, then for the authoritarian that person *will certainly* have certain qualities and *definitely cannot* have certain other qualities.

The authoritarian cognitive style lacks propositional constructs—constructs whose relationships to other constructs is not fixed but rather open to experience, doubt, and revision. The reason is that when we use propositional constructs, the world becomes complex, uncertain, and ambiguous; that is just what is so uncomfortable for the authoritarian.

The constructs of the authoritarian also have a characteristic content. Strong versus weak, good versus bad, and obey versus rebel all come together into one large overriding cluster. Concepts such as "sexuality," "feelings," and "Them" (members of any other group, especially a low-status or minority group) usually fall at the bad/weak pole of this cluster; in contrast, concepts such as "leader," "aggression toward the bad," and "Us" are at the good/strong pole. From the perspective of Kelly's cognitive theory, therefore, authoritarianism is a cognitively simple combination of these particular three correlated constructs.

Authoritarianism and Prejudice

The strong relationship between authoritarianism and prejudice, which was the reason why the concept was developed in the first place, continues to hold up over time and across many countries (see Altemeyer, 1988; Meloen, Hagendoorn, Raaijmakers, & Visser, 1988; also the review in Forbes, 1985, chap. 3). For example, among several large samples of Dutch students, correlations between authoritarianism and ethnocentric prejudice averaged an extremely

Bob Altemeyer, who refined the original F scale into a measure of Right-Wing Authoritarianism (RWA). "Rules about being 'well-mannered' and respectable are chains from the past which we should question very thoroughly before accepting" [an item endorsed by people scoring *low* in RWA] (Altemeyer, 1988, p. 22). (Courtesy Bob Altemeyer)

high +.59. And supporters of an explicitly fascist Dutch political party, which advocated expelling immigrant workers from the West Indies, scored almost half a standard deviation higher than supporters of the next most extreme party.

Authoritarianism and "freedom." Among U.S. state legislators, Altemeyer (1993) found an extraordinarily high correlation of +.71 between authoritarianism and a measure of ethnocentric prejudice. And even though legislators high in authoritarianism list freedom as a major value, they are prepared to support laws that would restrict freedom, such as the following:

- A law requiring Christian religious instruction in public schools
- A law that would prohibit television broadcasts (such as CNN's from Baghdad [during the 1991 Gulf War]) from a foreign country when the United States is at war with that country
- A bill giving police much wider, much less restrictive wiretap, search-and-seizure, and interrogation rules

Among U.S. college students, Altemeyer also found that authoritarians tend to support pro-Christian religious instruction in public schools, but would be against Muslim religious instruction in the schools of a Muslim country, suggesting that any value of freedom is restricted to "correct" channels. Thus it seems that in the authoritarian mind, freedom is a kind of verbal formula rather than a value reflected in actual laws. (Presumably authoritarian students in a predominantly Muslim country would oppose Christian religious instruction even in a Christian country, but so far as I know, no one has tested this presumption.)

Unconventional groups. Authoritarian prejudice can apply to almost *any* group that is in some way different from conventional norms. Thus Duncan, Peterson, and Winter (1994) found that authoritarian women and men espouse traditional sex-role attitudes and are hostile toward feminism and the women's movement (see also Worrell & Worrell, 1977). Peterson, Doty, and Winter (1993) found that authoritarians hold hostile and punitive attitudes toward people with AIDS, drug users, and the homeless, as illustrated in Table 7.3. Regarding the environment, however, their punitiveness is directed toward environmentalists rather than polluters, probably because the environmental movement is viewed as "deviant," while polluting corporations, in contrast, are seen as part of the conventional order. Crandall and Biernat (1990) found that authoritarians even hold prejudices about obese people, while Cowan, Underberg, and Verillo (1958) found that they tend to see blind people as all alike, helpless, and limited in capacity. In India, authoritarianism is associated with support for the caste system, in which society is organized into a hierarchy of four major castes (or *varnas*) based on birth (Hassan & Sarkar, 1975).

Explaining prejudice. Figure 7.3 illustrates a model of how all the components of authoritarianism are related to each other and, finally, to prejudice and aggression toward groups perceived to be different. Intolerance of ambiguity is the prime mover, in the sense that all of the other authoritarian characteristics can be derived from it. Avoidance of intraception, projection, idealization, and obedience are more or less direct effects of intolerance of ambiguity. The resulting residue of aggression, denied normal direct expression, then follows the lines of projection. What better target for aggression than people who are already perceived as different? By being "different" and "bad," they easily become perceived as a threat. Such perceptions, exaggerated by intolerance for ambiguity, serve as rationalizations for aggression. The whole sequence is fur-

TABLE 7.3 AUTHORITARIANISM AND ATTITUDES ON MODERN SOCIAL ISSUES

Social issues item	Correlation with RWA measure of authoritarianism
AIDS	
They should quarantine everyone with AIDS, just like they would do with the plague or chicken pox.	.46***
AIDS is a plague that homosexuals pass on to the decent people.	.52***
Children with AIDS shouldn't be allowed to attend school, because they put other children at risk; and anyway they probably only have a few years to live.	.34***
The real tragedy of AIDS is that it reveals our distrust and lack of compassion for suffering fellow human beings.	−.28***
In dealing with AIDS, it is essential to control our unreasonable fears and to remember that AIDS victims are people, with human feelings and civil rights.	−.43***
Drugs	
We need a Rambo-like crusade against drug smugglers and pushers.	.37***
We really need to have comprehensive drug testing of all teenagers in high school.	.48***
There are no safe "recreational drugs": it's just as important to stop occasional marijuana use as it is to stop crack addiction.	.42***
In the end, it's really impossible to prevent people from using drugs; we're better off making them legal so that they can at least be regulated.	−.30***
Drug education, rather than punishment, is the best way to keep our schools drug-free.	−.19**
Most people who take drugs do so to escape from painful everyday lives; to solve the drug problem, we must try to improve their lives.	−.29***
If we really want to win the so-called war on drugs, we should spend more money on providing treatment programs for those who want to give up the habit, rather than sending soldiers abroad to destroy drug crops.	−.32***
Environment	
Fines aren't enough. It's time we told every polluter, "If you poison our water, you will go to jail and your money will be spent to clean up the mess."	−.01
We should never forget that human beings were given dominion over nature; the environment is ours to use as we see fit.	.21***
Environmental issues are being exaggerated by overzealous special interest groups that don't really care about the jobs and lives of average working people.	.32***
If it succeeds, the environmental movement will reduce this country to a second-rate power.	.32***

(Table continues on next page.)

TABLE 7.3 AUTHORITARIANISM AND ATTITUDES ON MODERN SOCIAL ISSUES *(Continued)*

Social issues item	Correlation with RWA measure of authoritarianism
So-called threats to the environment are blown way out of proportion by sentimental people who are overly concerned about obscure and useless species of plants or insects.	.33***
If our economy is going to survive, we have to punish some of the so-called environmentalists who unreasonably disrupt legitimate business.	.32**
Abortion	
Abortion is not only a matter of individual conscience; it is also a legitimate concern of many institutions of our society.	.38***
No matter how strongly a person may oppose abortion, there can be no justification for violent demonstrations at health clinics.	−.21**
Child abuse	
Preventing child abuse nowadays may interfere with family life and parents' legitimate duty to discipline their children as they see fit.	.29***
The homeless	
The homeless are basically lazy; they simply don't take advantage of opportunities and social programs that are already in place.	.56***
The homeless are usually decent American citizens who have suffered from bad luck and the problems of our economic system.	−.38**
Colleges and universities	
We need to return to a core curriculum—where all students learn a common body of knowledge about our heritage.	.21**
The university should be a center of openness and diversity—diversity of students, values, courses, and opportunities.	−.33***

** $p < .01$ *** $p < .001$

SOURCE: Adapted from Peterson, Doty, and Winter (1993).

ther strengthened if prejudice and aggression are encouraged by a strong leader.[4]

A note of caution: prejudice, racism, sexism, and other forms of aggressive discrimination have complex roots. Personality characteristics of the prejudiced person are one important cause, but institutional and cultural factors are also important; indeed, they are often more important (see Allport, 1954, chap. 13; Pettigrew, 1958).

[4]This raises the intriguing possibility of whether a genuinely unprejudiced leader could steer authoritarian and obedient followers *away* from prejudice, as Forbes (1985) speculates.

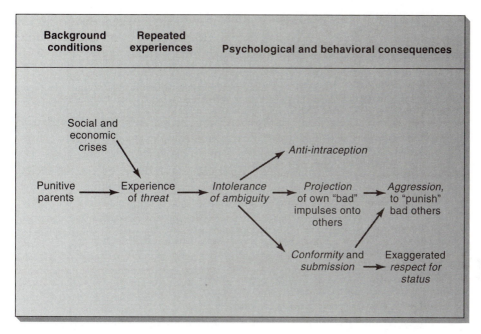

FIGURE 7.3
Relationships of the components of authoritarianism to each other and to prejudice.

DEVELOPMENT OF AUTHORITARIANISM

Family

Authoritarianism, this extraordinary set of beliefs and style, has many roots. Let us begin with the family. Most of the early research evidence (reviewed by Cherry & Byrne, 1977, pp. 116–120) suggested that authoritarians come from autocratic families in which parents (especially fathers) are restrictive and use punishment rather than love-oriented discipline. Baumrind (1972) further argued that a parental style involving low emotional expressiveness and independence training was even more important than family structure or parents' beliefs.

Growing up in such a family atmosphere, children would surely receive many confusing and ambiguous emotional messages, which could lead to a low tolerance for ambiguity. Further, heavy doses of parental punishment would increase a child's anxiety about having a bad inner self, and consequent desire to get rid of this badness through projection. Finally, by arousing the child's anger and hostility, excessive punishment would increase the child's emotional ambivalence toward the punishing parent.

Later research has emphasized the importance of learning mechanisms such as imitation and modeling (see Chapter 15) in the development of authoritarianism (Altemeyer, 1988). Thus strong demands for obedience are likely to increase children's obedient behavior, while at the same time being a model or example of high-status people (parents) acting aggressively toward lower-status or weaker people (children). Further, parents who are emotionally inhibited are modeling anti-intraception for their children.

Social Class Background

Before we blame all authoritarianism on punitive parents, it is important to look at the role of social background. Authoritarianism usually shows consistent and strong negative correlations with social class (Brown, 1965, pp. 518–523, and Dillehay, 1978, pp. 105–110). In line with these results, the sociologist Lipset (1960/1963) has argued that prejudice and most other authoritarian behaviors are relatively more frequent among working-class people. However, others have argued in opposition that the concept of authoritarianism is simply a negative prejudice about working-class people that is held by (middle-class) psychologists.

Threat

The notion of *threat* may be the key to explaining the relationship between social class and authoritarianism. Almost by definition, working-class people have fewer material resources, and so they are likely to confront more crises, feel greater threat, and experience more stress than middle-class people. At the same time, threat is also a good characterization of the parental behavior and family atmosphere that produces children with high F scale scores in any social class.

Altemeyer's study of parental teachings (1988, pp. 145–147) lends support to this explanation. He asked college students how much their parents had tried to teach them that people such as communists, atheists, kidnappers, motorcycle gangs, homosexuals, and reckless drivers were dangerous. Students' authoritarianism scores correlated significantly ($r = .38$) with the sum of their perceptions of such parental danger teaching. Altemeyer also tested the parents of these students and found an even higher correlation ($r = .48$) with parental authoritarianism and parents' recollections of their own danger teaching. Authoritarians, it seems, have been *taught* to feel threat, to see the world as a dangerous place, to agree with statements such as the following: "Any day now, chaos and anarchy could erupt around us. All the signs are pointing to it" (p. 168–169).

An integrated social-psychological explanation of the origins of authoritarianism would therefore run as follows: Working-class family life usually (but not always) involves a greater sense of threat. Therefore many (but not all) working-class parents raise their children in more punitive and less expressive ways, which results in higher levels of authoritarianism in the children. On the other hand, under certain conditions (for example, an economic depression) many middle-class parents might feel very great threat—even greater than most working-class parents. Finally, some parents probably feel threatened regardless of conditions. In all these cases, threatened parents will transmit a sense of threat to their children by direct teaching and imitation. If they are also more punitive toward their children, their punishment will add further to the child's sense of threat. Thus the sense of threat, whether from objective social-economic conditions of life or from parents' subjective feelings and fears, becomes the critical final pathway to the development of the authoritarian personality.

This key role of threat can be demonstrated in several ways. Sales and Friend (1973) showed that even in a laboratory study, when participants were made to fail on a task (thereby creating a sense of threat), their scores on the F scale increased.

Societal Threat

Sales also demonstrated this same connection between threat and authoritarianism at the societal level, in a series of imaginative analyses of archival data (Sales, 1972, 1973). First, he identified periods in twentieth-century American history high and low in social and economic threat. For example, the 1930s, which spanned the years of the Great Depression and the build-up to World War II, were clearly a time of high threat. In contrast, the 1920s were a time of relative prosperity, social calm, and therefore low threat. Similarly, the 1967–1970 period, with the Vietnam war and antiwar protests, economic inflation, sharply increased drug use, the assassinations of Martin Luther King, Jr. and Robert Kennedy, and widespread urban violence, were another high-threat period. And the years 1959–1964, though not without their troubles, were a relatively less threatening time.

Sales reasoned that if threat is an important cause of authoritarianism, then authoritarian thoughts and actions should be higher during high-threat times than during low-threat times. Testing this prediction, however, raises a problem: we must somehow measure past authoritarianism levels in American society, since we cannot go back in time to test individual people. Sales's solution to this problem was imaginative and ingenious: for each aspect of the authoritarian syndrome, he identified variables that could be measured from statistical and archival records, as shown in Table 7.4. Because these variables are based on society-level aggregates rather than the questionnaire scores of particular individuals, they are called social-indicator variables or social indicators. (See Webb, Campbell, Schwartz, & Sechrest, 1966, for a discussion of how to use social indicators and other archival measures in psychological research.) Table 7.4 also includes social indicator variables used by Doty, Peterson, and Winter (1991) in a replication of Sales's results.

For example, Sales measured the "power and toughness" component of authoritarianism at the societal level by looking at the characters in popular comic strips. He reasoned that if authoritarianism had increased from the 1920s to the 1930s, then "powerful" comic strip characters (such as *Superman* or *Dick Tracy*) should be more popular during that later period. From a stan-

TABLE 7.4 DIFFERENCES IN SOCIAL INDICATORS OF AUTHORITARIAN BEHAVIOR DURING TIMES OF HIGH AND LOW THREAT

Component of authoritarian syndrome	1920s (low threat) vs. 1930s (high threat)		1959–1964 (low threat) vs. 1967–1970 (high threat)	
	Measure used	Confirmed during high threat?	Measure used	Confirmed during high threat?
Power and toughness	More "powerful" comic strip characters	Yes	Greater popularity of "attack dog" breeds*	Yes
	More interest in boxing	Partial	Same	Partial
Cynicism	More cynicism in magazine articles	Yes	Higher reported cynicism among college students	Yes
Superstition	More books and articles on astrology published	Yes	Same	Yes
Authoritarian submission	More state laws requiring teacher loyalty oaths	Yes	Increased circulation of a popular conservative religious magazine	Yes
Anti-intraception	Fewer articles in popular magazines about psychotherapy and psychoanalysis	Yes	Same	Mixed
			Fewer college psychology majors	No
Authoritarisn aggression	Greater city budget shares for police (vs. fire) departments	Yes	Same	Yes
			Increased public support for the death penalty	Yes
Sex	Longer prison sentences for people convicted of rape (vs. voluntary manslaughter)	Yes	Same	Yes
Convention-alism	N/A		N/A	
Prejudice	N/A		N/A	

dard reference book on the history of comic strips (Becker, 1959), Sales identified twenty strips that began in the 1920s and twenty-one that began in the 1930s. He asked an independent judge (who was unaware of his hypothesis) to decide whether the main character of each strip was "physically powerful or controlled great power." The results were striking: while only two of the new comic strips of the 1920s had powerful protagonists, twelve of the twenty-one new strips from the 1930s emphasized the power of the main character. The difference is highly significant statistically.

Due to the increasing popularity of television, there were not very many new comic strips during the second pair of time periods. Sales therefore

TABLE 7.4 *(Continued)*

Component of authoritarian syndrome	Measure used	Confirmed during high threat?
	1978–1982 (high threat) vs. 1983–1987 (low threat) comparison	
Power and toughness	More "powerful" television characters	Partial
	Greater popularity of "attack dog" breeds*	Yes
	Greater interest in boxing	No
Cynicism	Higher cynicism in polls of college students and the general public	Yes
Superstition	More books and articles on astrology	No
	Higher superstition in polls of general public	Yes
Authoritarian submission	More library censorship incidents	Yes
Anti-intraception	Fewer articles in popular magazines about psychotherapy and psychoanalysis	Yes
	Fewer books about psychotherapy and psychoanalysis	Yes
	Greater growth in non-intraceptive vs. intraceptive divisions of the American Psychological Association[†]	Yes
Authoritarian aggression	Greater city budget shares for police	No
	Increased public support for the death penalty	No
Sex	Longer prison sentences for people convicted of rape (vs. voluntary manslaughter)	No
	Increased violent video pornography	Yes
Conventionalism	Greater vote for conservative (vs. liberal) Congressional candidates	Yes
Prejudice	More anti-Semitic incidents	Yes
	More Ku Klux Klan activity	Yes
	Higher prejudice in public opinion polls	Yes

*German shepherds, Doberman pinschers, and Great Danes
[†]Intraceptive divisions include clinical psychology, counseling psychology, psychotherapy, and humanistic psychology; nonintraceptive divisions include experimental psychology, physiological and comparative psychology, experimental analysis of behavior, and applied experimental and engineering psychology.

turned to other measures to see whether concerns with power and toughness were greater in 1967–1970 than in 1959–1964. In his own words (Sales, 1973):

> If individuals are attracted to strength and power in times of stress, then perhaps they might be more inclined to purchase strong and powerful dogs during these periods. The American Kennel Clubs annually reports registrations in each of 166 different breeds. Thus, it was an easy matter to compute the number of registrations each year of dogs which might be termed (whether justifiably or not) "attack dogs": German Shepherds, Doberman Pinschers, and Great Danes. (p. 52)

The results were as expected: the "attack dog" share of all registrations went up from 9.8 percent to 13.5 percent between 1959–1964 and 1967–1970 (a highly significant increase), while registrations of low-power "lap dogs" such as Boston Terriers and Chihuahuas went down. Sales also measured interest in boxing as a reflection of power and toughness concerns for both time-period comparisons, with mixed results. There were slightly more championship fights during the high-threat periods, but overall attendance and public interest in boxing were greater in the 1920s than the 1930s. On the other hand, both the number of people making a living as professional boxers and the total gate receipts from boxing were higher during 1967–1970 than 1959–1964. Overall, two measures of power and toughness concerns (comics and dog registrations) clearly support Sales's hypothesis of higher authoritarianism during times of threat; for the boxing measures, the results are mixed.

Sales used a variety of other social-indicator measures to assess the cynicism, superstition, authoritarian submission, anti-intraception, authoritarian aggression, and concern-with-sex components of authoritarianism. In replicating Sales's findings for the period 1978–1982 (high economic threat) and 1983–1987 (low threat), Doty, Peterson, and Winter (1991) introduced still more social indicator measures. These are all described in Table 7.4. For example, Doty and colleagues measured intraception and anti-intraception by examining changes in the interests and professional orientations of psychologists as reflected in membership rates of different divisions of the American Psychological Association (APA). For this purpose, divisions 12 (clinical psychology), 17 (counseling psychology), 29 (psychotherapy), and 32 (humanistic psychology) were counted as introspective, while divisions 3 (experimental psychology), 6 (physiological and comparative psychology), 25 (experimental analysis of behavior), and 21 (applied experimental and engineering psychology) were counted as nonintraceptive. As reported in Table 7.4, growth in the nonintraceptive APA divisions as compared to growth in the intraceptive divisions was higher during times of high threat than during times of low threat.

Sales (1972) also studied the relation between threat and authoritarianism by examining the rates of joining or conversion to different Christian religious denominations. First, he classified denominations as authoritarian and nonauthoritarian on the basis of their organizational structure and beliefs. From archival data, he then calculated conversion rates for each year from 1920–1939, and correlated these rates with levels of per capita income over the two decades. The results, shown in Table 7.5, confirmed Sales's predictions that (1) during times of high economic threat (that is, relatively low per capita income), conversions to the authoritarian denominations would be high; while (2) during times of low threat, people would join nonauthoritarian religious groups.

Of course there are problems and limitations in using archival data in personality research. For example, the social indicators used by Sales and Doty and colleagues may not be valid measures of the psychological characteristics they represent. For example, we might quarrel with Sales's definition of "tough" dogs. Our family's first poodle certainly thought of himself as fierce,

TABLE 7.5 ESTIMATED CONVERSION RATES TO AUTHORITARIAN AND NONAUTHORITARIAN DENOMINATIONS IN RELATION TO ECONOMIC CONDITIONS

Denomination	High per capita income	Moderate per capita income	Low per capita income	Correlation of conversion rate with per capita income, by year:
Authoritarian				
Church of Jesus Christ of Latter-Day Saints (Mormon)	55	59	62	−.46*
Roman Catholic	314	376	378	−.46*
Seventh-Day Adventist	59	71	99	−.87**
Southern Baptist	1720	1874	1820	−.19
Nonauthoritarian				
Congregational-Christian	351	324	282	.50*
Northern Baptist	568	512	480	.41*
Presbyterian Church in the U.S.A.	305	273	213	.53**
Episcopal	100	101	92	.31†

Estimated yearly conversions (per million nonmembers) during years of

†p <.10   *p <.05   **p < .01
SOURCE: Based on Sales (1972).

and most people who rang our doorbell agreed, though Sales would not have considered him an attack dog. And in any case, dog registration figures only reflect the power concerns of the minority of dog owners who purchase pure-bred dogs *and* register them with the American Kennel Club. What about cat lovers, dog haters, or people living in small apartments where large dogs are not allowed? Or you may question whether interest and divisional membership patterns among professional psychologists has anything to do with intraception and anti-intraception in the general public. Or perhaps Sales wrongly classified certain religious denominations.

Problems such as these always arise in indirect research where social indicators are used to infer psychological characteristics. On the other hand, variables based on "artificial" behavior in laboratory settings or checkmarks on questionnaires may have validity problems also. Thus while questions can be raised about each of these measures, the overall pattern of consistent results across different studies and methods strongly supports the conclusion that social and economic threat is an important cause of authoritarianism. As Webb and associates (1966) put it:

Once a proposition has been confirmed by two or more independent measurement processes, the uncertainty of its interpretation is greatly reduced. The most persuasive evidence comes through a triangulation of measurement processes. If a proposition can survive the onslaught of a series of imperfect measures, with all their irrelevant error, confidence should be placed in it. (p. 3)

Social and Family Origins of Authoritarianism

We conclude, then, that *threat* from any source—personal failure on an important task, income decline, or widespread social disruption—leads to intolerance of ambiguity and thus the other authoritarian characteristics. Perhaps this is another illustration of the Yerkes-Dodson Law (Chapter 2 and Figure 2.2). Threat may activate people's sympathetic nervous system and increase their arousal; but when arousal rises above the optimal point, their perception narrows (intolerance of ambiguity), and so their performance deteriorates.

Under ordinary conditions, working-class people might feel more threatened than middle-class people, because they are exposed to more environmental dangers and because they have access to fewer resources. Thus the "working-class authoritarianism" documented in surveys and discussed by Lipset (1960/1963) would be a kind of personality adaptation to chronically high levels of threat. In a social and economic catastrophe such as the Great Depression of the 1930s, however, middle-class people may suddenly face an even more severe threat from unfamiliar dangers, both because they may have more to lose and because they have less experience coping with poverty. This was certainly the experience of many middle-class Germans in the years after World War I, when first a war was suddenly and surprisingly lost, then revolution threatened, and finally economic crises, hyperinflation, and widespread unemployment swept over the nation. The upper classes survived because their wealth was mostly protected in various ways. The poor survived, because they had a good deal of experience with difficult conditions. Thus it was the threatened middle classes who were especially responsive to the authoritarian appeal of Hitler's message of simple answers, clearly designated scapegoats, and a "final solution" for the complexities and ambiguities of Germany's experience. And so it was precisely these groups who were all too ready, in Fromm's (1941) words, to "escape from [the threat of] freedom."

Not just in Germany. While most Americans like to think of themselves as skeptical and critical of authority and their country as "the home of the free," there is a thread of authoritarianism or paranoid tradition running through American history from early colonial times down to the present day (Hofstadter, 1967; Wilkinson, 1972), usually connected with a heightened sense of threat. Thus in seventeenth-century Boston Anne Hutchinson was persecuted and exiled for her unconventional religious views and advocacy of religious liberty during a particularly stressful time. And the 1692 Salem trials and hanging of nineteen people (mostly women) as suspected witches coincided with a difficult harvest and increased anxiety about attack from Native Americans. The nineteenth-century anti-Mason, anti-Catholic, and anti-immigrant movements flourished when rapid social and industrial change threatened the established order. Long past the legal end of slavery, racism has persisted as a kind of societal virus that flares up especially during times of economic threat. For example, during the years 1882–1930, Hovland and Sears (1940) found a significant negative correlation between the price of cotton and the number of lynchings of African Americans in the U.S. South. And in the 1950s, at the height of the Cold War, some people became concerned that fluoridation of water supplies was a communist plot. Whenever there are threats to familiar ways, it seems, Americans tend to narrow their perceptions and their tolerance for ambiguity goes down, leading to the search for scapegoats and all the other features of the authoritarian syndrome.

Reducing authoritarianism. While threat increases authoritarianism, higher education, especially liberal arts education, appears to reduce people's F scale or RWA scores (Altemeyer, 1988, pp. 92–93; Meloen, Farnen, & German, 1993; Winter, McClelland, and Stewart, 1981, pp. 13, 79). Probably this is because exposure to the liberal arts leads students to confront and explore that which is threatening, while forging the intellectual tools (constructs) to overcome their fears with knowledge.

THE PROBLEM OF LEFT-WING AUTHORITARIANISM

The original F scale research clearly delineated an authoritarianism that had politically conservative or right-wing overtones. One of the early scales correlated with the F scale was actually called *political and economic conservatism.* This emphasis was only natural, since this research was carried out in the shadow of the right-wing anti-Semitism of Hitler's Germany. By the time *The Authoritarian Personality* was published in 1950, however, many Americans had come to view communism and Stalin's Soviet Union as the enemy. Reflecting this new point of view, the social theorist Edward Shils (1954) criticized the Berkeley group for a bias that led them to ignore authoritarianism of the left:

> Fascism and Bolshevism, only a few decades ago thought of as worlds apart, have now been recognized increasingly as sharing many important features. Their common hostility towards civil liberties, political democracy, their common antipathy for parliamentary institutions, individualism, private enterprise, their image of the political world as a struggle . . . their belief that all their opponents are secretly leagued against them and . . . their own aspirations for concentrated and total power—all these showed that the two extremes had much in common. (pp. 27–28)

Shils's analysis of the similarities of fascism and Soviet communism led many psychologists to assert that there was another kind of authoritarian, an "authoritarian of the left," in addition to the type identified by the Berkeley group. Others have questioned the existence of left-wing authoritarianism. For decades, the debate has seemed to generate as much heat as light. In the 1990s, new research from countries of the former Soviet Union may at last resolve the debate. As we shall see, the story is long and complicated. It is worth telling, however, because it raises many issues of theory, method, and the wider social and political context of personality psychology. Brown (1965, pp. 526–544) and Stone (1980) summarize the early decades of the debate.

Left-Wing Extremists and the F Scale

At first, psychologists tried a quick test of Shils's critique. If both political extremes *are* authoritarian in the sense used by the Berkeley group, then we should find that communists or others with extreme left-wing political views score high on the F scale. But even this simple hypothesis turned out to be complicated. On the basis of small and perhaps unusual samples of different English groups, Eysenck (1954) argued that communists do indeed score high on the F scale, but Christie (1956) challenged Eysenck's data and conclusions.

A later study by Knutson (1974) is particularly important. Rather than testing college students or ordinary adults, she gave questionnaires to seriously committed political leaders from a truly broad range of the political spectrum: the Democratic and Republican parties, of course, but also George Wallace's American Independent Party and the American Nazi Party on the extreme right, and the Peace and Freedom Party and the Communist Party U.S.A. on the extreme left. (All questionnaires were actually given out by party leaders and returned to Knutson by mail, to ensure anonymity.) Knutson's results, presented in Table 7.6, show that the right-wing leaders score higher than the moderates, both on the F scale itself and on separate measures of intolerance for ambiguity and threat orientation. Left-wing leaders, in contrast, score *lower*

TABLE 7.6 AUTHORITARIANISM AND DOGMATISM SCORES OF LOS ANGELES POLITICAL ACTIVISTS, BY PARTY

	Average scores		
*Personality variable**	*Left-wing parties: Communist (N = 11); Peace and Freedom Party (N = 40)*	*Center or moderate parties: Democratic (N = 21); Republican (N = 11)*	*Right-wing parties: American Independent (N = 11); American Nazi (N = 13)*
Authoritarianism			
Overall F scale	1.59	2.42	4.55
Intolerance for ambiguity	2.83	2.95	3.66
Threat orientation	2.74	3.28	4.87
Faith in people	2.45	2.37	3.76
Dogmatism	3.50	3.27	4.59

*On each variable, left-wing and center-moderate activists scored significantly *lower* than right-wing activists.

SOURCE: Adapted from Knutson (1974).

than moderates and significantly lower than right-wing leaders, on all three measures. These results directly contradict both Shils's critique and Eysenck's claim.

The Eysenck and Knutson studies involve only people from advanced industrial democratic countries, but two studies using the F scale in India give similar results. Bushan (1969) found that Communist Party members scored significantly lower in authoritarianism than (right-wing) Jana Sangh members and (moderate) Congress Party members, while Raina (1974) found the same among Indian college students.

Dogmatism: An Ideologically Neutral Measure?

Instead of trying to find left-wing groups that scored high on the F scale, Rokeach (1960) developed a new measure of *dogmatism*, the tendency to be close-minded (have impermeable constructs) and dogmatic. He hoped to capture the presumed personality characteristics shared by right-wing and left-wing political extremists (in Shils's view, authoritarianism), without picking up conservative right-wing ideology. As you can see from the following examples, many of the dogmatism items do resemble F scale items:

> In the history of mankind there have probably been just a handful of really great thinkers.
> There are a number of people I have come to hate because of the things they stand for.
> Even though freedom of speech for all groups is a worthwhile goal, it is unfortunately necessary at times to restrict the freedom of certain political groups.

In fact, the overall dogmatism scale correlates quite highly with authoritarianism (r's range between .54 and .77; see Kerlinger & Rokeach, 1966).

Dogmatism in action. Highly dogmatic people also act in ways that suggest the authoritarian syndrome (Rokeach, 1960; see also Ehrlich, 1978, and Vacchiano, 1977). For example, they are sure of themselves and ready to assert their opinions without bothering to check whether they are correct, which suggests intolerance of ambiguity and preemptive or constellatory constructs. Their minds are closed to new information and new beliefs. They accept information on the basis of authority, reject negative things about themselves, and see the world as fundamentally hostile.

Many studies illustrate this rigidity of highly dogmatic people. Pyron and Kafer (1967) found that they were less able to learn nonsensical sentences such as "From his whiskers, John Brown combed friendly historians," or "The climax invents itself through goat-hair brushes." These sentences present familiar elements in strange combinations, which makes them harder to learn for a dogmatic person with a rigid mental organization. Costin (1968) studied how students modified their beliefs as a result of taking an introductory psychology course. He created a list of sixty-six common misconceptions about psychology that are contradicted by the available research evidence: for example, "cats can see in complete darkness" (not true) or "a person who won't look you in the eye is probably untrustworthy" (not true). In the course itself, Costin carefully discussed the evidence disproving these beliefs. After the conclusion of the course, he found that students scoring high in dogmatism were *least* likely to give up their misconceptions about psychology during the term. (Since dogmatism was not related to mastery of psychological knowledge, these results cannot be explained away as the result of dogmatic students paying less attention or learning less.)

Dogmatism and political ideology. In terms of its item content and its behavior correlates, then, dogmatism does resemble authoritarianism. *If* the dogmatism measure were uncorrelated with conservative political ideology—that is, if left-wing and right-wing extremists both scored higher than people in the middle—then the existence of left-wing authoritarianism could be demonstrated. But this is precisely the problem: the accumulated evidence suggests that people with extreme left-wing beliefs do *not* score high in dogmatism, just as they do not score higher in authoritarianism. Across several studies, communists and others of left-wing political orientation score lower than right-wingers, and no higher than people in the middle (Stone, 1980; see also Vacchiano, 1977, pp. 291–292.)

One of the most convincing studies, by DiRenzo (1967), involved giving the dogmatism questionnaire to 129 professional politicians—members of the Italian Chamber of Deputies (parliament)—representing several different parties across the political spectrum, as well as 436 "nonpolitical" university students in Rome from the same parties. The results, shown in Figure 7.4, are clear. Among both deputies and students, dogmatism scores were high for the right wing, average for the middle-of-the-road, and *low* for the left wing. The politicians usually scored significantly higher than students of the same political orientation, which suggests that politicians in general may be more dogmatic.

Knutson (1974) also included Rokeach's measure of dogmatism in her study of Los Angeles political party activists that was described above. Consistent with DiRenzo's results, she found that activists from right-wing parties scored highest and activists from left-wing parties scored almost as low as the moderates, as shown at the bottom of Table 7.6.

The dogmatism results, then, leave us with the same conclusion as the F scale research: there is no evidence for the existence of "left-wing authoritarianism" (dogmatism). Yet it is difficult to dismiss Shils's argument completely. Up to the collapse of the Communist regimes in Eastern Europe and the Soviet Union, many (if not all) Communists seemed to have minds closed to new information. Often (if not always) the Communist Party required strict obedience to its "party line." Finally, throughout much (if not all) of its existence, the Soviet Union maintained an active secret police, punished political dissidents with prison, carried out brutal purges, and even officially encouraged

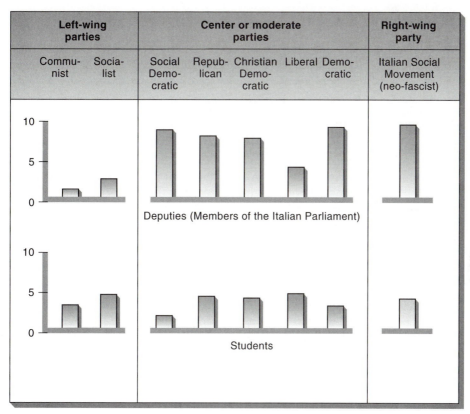

FIGURE 7.4
Average dogmatism scores of Italian deputies and nonpolitical students, by party.
SOURCE: Adapted from DiRenzo (1967, p. 124).

anti-Semitism. Surely these practices—acknowledged and condemned by some Soviet leaders since 1956—are "authoritarian," if the word has any meaning at all.

On the other hand, Stone and Smith (1988) cautioned against equating the behavior of political systems with the personality characteristics of individuals:

> The existence of regimes that proclaim leftist ideology while engaging in authoritarian governance may indeed be "obvious from even the most casual observation," but it is neither correct nor obvious to . . . translate this observation into evidence that authoritarian personality traits are as common among leftists as among rightists. (p. 12)

In the absence of a range of options and free choice of political affiliations, we cannot assume that individual people in an authoritarian system are themselves authoritarian. To answer the question of left-wing authoritarianism, studies of actual individual people from the Soviet Union were really needed.

Until recently, of course, this was impossible because Marxist-Leninist doctrine held that authoritarianism was inapplicable to Soviet socialist reality. With *glasnost* and the break-up of the Soviet Union, however, several studies have been carried out with the RWA or F scale measures.

Authoritarianism in Russia

In one of the first studies, McFarland, Ageyev, and Abalakina (1992a) administered a Russian translation of the RWA measure to a carefully selected sample of 340 adults in Moscow and Tallinn (now the capital of Estonia) during 1989, before the 1991 attempted coup and the break-up of the Soviet Union. Their major findings are presented in Table 7.7, with correlations adjusted for background factors such as age, education, and occupational status. The first thing to notice is that among Russians, authoritarianism predicted prejudice against Jews, women, people of other nationalities (that is, non-Russians living in the former Soviet Union), and dissidents, just as it does in the West! If anything, the correlations are considerably higher than in Western samples. Second, authoritarians in Russia were against youth, democracy, and a free press. Since these were forces on the side of change from the established Soviet political system, the results are certainly consistent with Western findings of *authoritarian resistance to change when the established order is threatened*. Finally, Russian authoritarians were against capitalism, just as American authoritarians were against communism! Overall, this initial study suggests that with just a few changes in the label of the "enemy," authoritarianism is the same among Russians and Americans.

Two later studies clarify the picture still further. In June 1991 (before the attempted coup), McFarland, Ageyev, and Abalakina-Paap (1992b) found that Russian authoritarians supported hard-line Communist leaders against such "liberals" as Eduard Shevardnadze and Boris Yeltsin, approved a Soviet army crackdown against the breakaway Baltic republics, and wanted to preserve the Soviet Union. They also favored equality and were against laissez faire individualism (which is the reverse of findings among American authoritarians). In June 1993 (before the autumn 1993 coup attempt when Yeltsin's government fired upon the parliament building in Moscow), McFarland, Ageyev, and Djintcharadze (1996) found that Russian authoritarians were nostalgic for communism, supported various national-front organizations such as the quasi-fascist *Pamyat*, regretted the break-up of the Soviet Union, and rejected "freedom," as shown in the bottom part of Table 7.7. In addition, their attitudes about AIDS and the environment were similar to those of the American authoritarians studied by Peterson, Doty, and Winter (1993). Finally, among those low in communist beliefs, authoritarianism is significantly correlated with religious faith ($r = .24$, $p < .001$), suggesting that over time religion may replace communism in Russia as the "authority" to which authoritarians feel they owe obedience, just as it is in the West (see Altemeyer, 1988).

Samuel McFarland (above left), Vladimir Ageyev (above right), and Marina Abalakina-Paap (left), who pioneered research on authoritarianism in the former Soviet Union. "We believed that understanding Soviet authoritarianism could help in gauging the readiness of the Russian population for . . . democratic institutions . . . and for democratic rather than power-oriented solutions to . . . ethnic and nationalist issues" (McFarland, Ageyev, and Abalakina, 1992, p. 200). (Courtesy Samuel McFarland)

TABLE 7.7 CORRELATES OF RIGHT-WING AUTHORITARIANISM (RWA) IN RUSSIA AND THE FORMER SOVIET UNION

Attitude variables	Correlation with RWA measure of authoritarianism
Research carried out in 1989: Scales measuring prejudice against:	
Jews (15 items)	.55***
Non-Russian nationalities (13 items)	.63***
Women (5 items)	.39***
Capitalists (9 items)	.71***
Dissidents in Soviet society (6 items)	.71***
Youth (8 items)	.72***
Democracy (10 items)	.74***
A free press (4 items)	.65***
Research carried out in 1993: Agreement with questionnaire items	
"I very much regret the breakup of the Soviet Union."	.29**
"I very much regret that Russia is going the way of capitalism and the market economy."	.32**
"I support the views of the front of national salvation and such patriotic organizations."	.34**
"The concern to preserve the environment is greatly exaggerated by those who are too concerned about unknown and useless plants and animals."	.18*
"AIDS is a plague that homosexuals pass on to decent people."	.41**
"Despite the fact that Russia is going through a very hard time, I still prefer economic, political, and intellectual freedom."	−.32**

*$p <.05$ ** $p <.01$ *** $p <.001$

SOURCES: McFarland, Ageyev, and Abalakina (1992a); McFarland, Ageyev, and Djintcharadze (1996).

Overall, McFarland, Ageyev, Abalakina-Paap, and Djintcharadze (1993) observe that when similar samples of Russians and Americans are compared, Russian authoritarianism scores are on the average significantly lower than American scores.

Unraveling Left and Right Authoritarianism

Taken together, all of the Russian and Western results finally suggest how the debate about left-wing authoritarianism might be resolved. In the West, "communist" and left-wing people score, if anything, low in authoritarianism. In Russia, at least during the period of transition away from communism, authoritarianism scores are slightly lower than in the West. In both countries, people scoring high in authoritarianism are prejudiced against any group that is seen as "different" or a threat to the established system. Russian authoritarians support communism and specific communist beliefs against capitalism and a market economy, which is the reverse of findings among American authoritarians; but they also support Russian ultranationalist groups. Are these Russian authoritarians left-wing or right-wing? Perhaps these two terms are no longer clear or useful to describe political life in the former Soviet

Union. What *is* clear from all of these results is that *in Russia as in the West, authoritarians do support—and are prepared to use aggressive force on behalf of—the existing structures of power.*

Back to Joseph Stalin, the Soviet Communist dictator who purged and imprisoned his enemies. He was almost certainly an authoritarian. On the other hand, Nikita Khrushchev, who after Stalin's death began a new era of openness in the USSR and in relations with the West, was probably not authoritarian. As for Lenin, the leader of the 1917 Russian Revolution, or Trotsky, who opposed the postrevolutionary policies of Lenin and Stalin, it is difficult to say without a way of measuring authoritarianism at a distance.

*M*EASURING AUTHORITARIANISM AT A DISTANCE

Hermann (1980a, 1980b) developed at-a-distance measures of two components of authoritarianism. Ethnocentrism, or nationalism, the tendency to see one's own group as better than others, is measured by how often people describe their own group with favorable or strong adjectives and describe other groups with weak or hostile adjectives. Suspiciousness, or distrust of others, is measured by phrases suggesting doubts and misgivings about others or fear that others will harm oneself or the group.

In her analysis of President Ronald Reagan's responses to press conferences, Hermann (1983) found that Reagan scored higher than most world leaders in nationalism but about the same in distrust. Further, Reagan's nationalism score dropped significantly after his first election in 1980. With knowledge of this drop, perhaps we could have predicted that Reagan's initial concerns about the Soviet Union as the Evil Empire would, by the end of his administration, give way to friendly approaches to Soviet leaders and the signing of a major arms limitation treaty.

To resolve the question of who (if anyone) was really a left-wing authoritarian, and when, researchers could apply the Hermann measures to the speeches, writings, and interviews of Lenin, Trotsky, Stalin, and other revolutionary communists, as well as to similar material from noncommunist contemporaries.

*H*ELEN KELLER'S BELIEFS ABOUT PEOPLE AND THE SOCIAL ORDER

To my knowledge, Helen Keller never filled out an F scale questionnaire, but she seems to have been one of the least authoritarian people I can imagine. Her writings often read like reversed F scale items. A few examples, arranged according to the themes of the authoritarian personality described above, will illustrate what I mean. Regarding *authoritarian submission,* she wrote (Foner, 1967):

No one has ever given me a good reason why we should obey unjust laws. But the reason why we should resist them is obvious. Our resistance proves our manhood and our womanhood. The dignity of human nature compels us to resist what we believe to be a stumbling block to our fellow men. When [a government] depends for "law and order" upon the militia and the police, its mission in the world is nearly finished. (p. 61)

You may be pleased to know that college professors were part of the hierarchical authority that she opposed. She wrote in her autobiography that after taking an exam in college, "with a feeling of intense disgust you . . . go home, your head full of revolutionary schemes to abolish the divine right of professors to ask questions without the consent of the questioned" (p. 103).

Helen Keller was against any kind of *aggression*. In 1915, before the United States entered World War I, she spoke against war, armaments, and military "preparedness" (Foner, 1967):

I look on the whole world as my fatherland, and every war has to me a horror of a family feud. I look upon true patriotism as the brotherhood of man and the service of all to all. The only fighting that saves is the one that helps the world toward liberty, justice, and an abundant life for all. (p. 73)

In place of *power and toughness*, she advocated cooperation and friendship (Foner, 1967):

A new will has come into the world, not a will to power, but a will to service. Everywhere I feel there is a growing desire to restore, to rehabilitate, to reclaim and promote better living for all men. It seems to me we Americans are foreordained to lead in humanitarian enterprises. (p. 117)

Cynicism was so alien to her belief structure that she did not even accept it in others. She was a friend of Mark Twain, who was considered by most people as one of the most ironic and cynical American authors of the nineteenth century. Here is how Helen Keller described him in her autobiography:

I love Mark Twain—who does not? The gods, too, loved him and put into his heart all manner of wisdom; then, fearing lest he should become a pessimist, they spanned his mind with a rainbow of love and faith. (p. 117)
I feel the twinkle of his eye in his handshake. Even while he utters his cynical wisdom in an indescribably droll voice, he makes you feel that his heart is a tender *Iliad* of human sympathy.[5] (p. 139)

Helen Keller was relatively free from *prejudice*, especially so for a white woman growing up in Alabama during the last decades of the nineteenth century. When she sent a contribution to the National Association for the

---

[5]Mark Twain apparently returned Helen Keller's affection. Anne Sullivan's husband John Macy, who edited Keller's autobiography, quoted Mark Twain that "the two most interesting characters of the nineteenth century are Napoleon and Helen Keller" (Macy, 1903, p. 286); while according to Van Wyck Brooks, Twain described Keller as "the most marvellous person of her sex who had existed on the earth since Joan of Arc" (Brooks, 1956, p. 3).

Advancement of Colored People in 1916, she declared her position in an accompanying letter (Lash, 1980):

> It should bring a blush of shame to the face of every true American to know that ten million of his countrymen are denied the equal protection of the laws. . . . Ashamed in my very soul I behold in my own beloved south-land the tears of those who are oppressed, those who must bring up their sons and daughters in bondage to be servants, because others have their fields and vineyards, and on the side of the oppressor is power. (p. 454)

You can imagine the stir these words caused among her Alabama friends and family. Out of deference to her family, Lash suggested, she muffled her views somewhat but did not change them fundamentally. In later years she made special appeals on behalf of blind people of color, and in a visit to South Africa strongly criticized apartheid (Lash, 1980, pp. 683, 724–725).

OTHER IMPORTANT BELIEFS ABOUT PEOPLE AND THE SOCIAL ORDER

While authoritarianism and dogmatism are two of the best-known and most widely studied cognitive elements of personality, several other beliefs and values deserve mention as important features of the cognitive element of personality.

Left and Right: Tomkins's Polarity Scale

While Shils (1954) initiated debate about the similarities of left-wing and right-wing politics, Tomkins (1963) explored further the psychological differences between left and right. To Tomkins, the left-right contrast reflects a much broader divergence, between humanistic ideology (accepting people's feelings, desires, and sensitivities on their own terms) and normative ideology (judging people against some predetermined standard or norm), respectively. Stone and Schaffner (1988, chap. 4 and pp. 289–298) review studies using the Tomkins polarity measure.

Machiavellianism

Christie and Geis (1970) developed a new personality variable based on the writings of Niccolo Machiavelli, the sixteenth-century Italian political theorist. You may have read *The Prince*, Machiavelli's classic guide for power seekers, which he wrote on the basis of his observations of intrigue, corruption, and power competition in Renaissance Italy. Machiavelli advised would-be princes to maintain the appearance of virtue, while at the same time taking whatever actions were necessary to achieve goals and consolidate power. Over the years, Machiavellianism has come to mean *manipulation* in a negative sense.

Elms (1976, pp. 136–148; 1986) used the concept to analyze Henry Kissinger, who between 1960 and 1976 managed the extraordinary feat of being a major foreign policy adviser to both Democratic presidents Kennedy and Johnson and also Republican presidents Nixon and Ford. In a book on the history of diplomacy, Kissinger expressed an appropriately Machiavellian sentiment about foreign policy leadership: "There is inevitably in every great leader an element of guile. . ." (1994, p. 382).

Christie and Geis measured Machiavellianism by converting Machiavelli's precepts into personality questionnaire items that suggest a cynical view of other people as mere objects to be manipulated:

> The best way to handle people is to tell them what they want to hear.
> It is wise to flatter important people.
> Most people forget more easily the death of their parents than the loss of their property.

As described by Geis (1978), the Machiavellian (who agrees with such statements) *believes* that people can be manipulated, *wants* to manipulate them, is *skilled* at manipulation, and feels *no remorse* at success. It should come as no surprise that Machiavellians usually have only superficial relationships with other people. In contrast to the power motive, or *wanting* power, Machiavellianism is a set of beliefs, skills, and lack of moral restraints about having and using power. Some—but not all—power-motivated people are Machiavellians. It is no accident that psychologists began to describe and study the Machiavellian style during the 1970s, a time when the highest U.S. government officials practiced deception and manipulation, both in Vietnam and in the Watergate scandal.

Interpersonal Trust

In many respects, trust in other people is the opposite of Machiavellianism. According to Stark (1978), people who score high on interpersonal trust tend to believe the government and are more trusting in a variety of everyday situations (including psychological experiments). They are also more trustworthy. For example, given the chance to look surreptitiously at folders containing personal and private information, they resist. In bargaining experiments, they are more likely to be cooperative, at least as long as others reciprocate.

Approval Motivation

In discussing the problems of measuring authoritarianism, I mentioned the social desirability of questionnaire items was a methodological problem. Crowne and Marlowe (1964) studied the tendency to choose socially desirable alternatives as a personality variable in its own right. The following three items suggest the flavor of their social desirability scale. Each mentions a behavior that is highly desirable but (according to Crowne and Marlowe) not *really* true of most people:

> Before voting I thoroughly investigate the qualifications of all the candidates.
> I have never intensely disliked anyone.
> My table manners at home are as good as when I eat out in restaurants.

While Crowne and Marlowe call their scale a measure of the "approval motive," it really seems to measure a more cognitive style of *evaluative dependence* on others. People scoring high on this scale either do not have strongly formed opinions of their own or else hold back on expressing these opinions until they sense the drift of other people's views (see Millham & Jacobson, 1978; Strickland, 1977a).

Evaluative dependence closely resembles *other direction,* a concept introduced by the sociologist Riesman (Riesman, Glazer, & Denny, 1950) in his landmark study of American society in the middle of the twentieth century. In place of the guiding forces of tradition or individual conscience, Riesman argued, Americans had developed sensitive antennae for picking up cues from other people. When they sense these cues, they adjust their own thoughts, actions, and feelings accordingly so as to fit in.

Social-Psychological Attitudes

While the study of specific attitudes is more the province of social psychology than personality, some attitudes typically measured in survey research reflect important individual differences in personality: for example, alienation, misanthropy, acceptance of others, and religious beliefs and practices (see the reviews by Robinson & Shaver, 1973; Robinson, Shaver, & Wrightsman, 1991; and the discussion by Dawes & Smith, 1985).

8

Beliefs about the Causes and Control of Events

❖

In this chapter, we consider people's beliefs about the world itself. In their theory and research, personality psychologists have focused mostly on people's beliefs about the causes of events, whether they can be controlled, by whom, and how. Most of the chapter will be devoted to these issues, but at the end we will consider some other kinds of beliefs and values that are emerging as important.

CONTROLLING EVENTS AND OUTCOMES

At the beginning of Shakespeare's play *Julius Caesar*, Cassius recalled the many humiliations he had suffered at the whim of Caesar, who:

> Doth bestride the narrow world
> Like a Colossus, and we petty men
> Walk under his huge legs and peep about
> To find ourselves dishonorable graves.

So far, this could have been the complaint of any jealous follower of a political leader, but then Cassius uttered the famous sentence that aroused Brutus to join the assassination conspiracy:

> Men at some time are masters of their fates:
> The fault, dear Brutus, is not in our stars,
> But in ourselves, that we are underlings.
> > I, ii, 135–141

These lines express a question that has perplexed human beings probably ever since they began to reflect on the world: Are we at the mercy of external forces, or are the results of our actions under our own control? Most of the great religions take a position on this question (for example, the doctrines of predestination in Christianity, or karma in Hinduism). Philosophers have debated the issue of free will versus determinism for centuries. And ordinary people often wonder whether they are in control of their lives.

Most Americans would argue that people are indeed masters of their fate. Certainly this is the message that we get from school, the mass media, and our political leaders. President John F. Kennedy (1963) eloquently expressed this viewpoint in a famous speech:

> Our problems are manmade—therefore, they can be solved by man. And man can be as big as he wants. No problem of human destiny is beyond human beings. Man's reason and spirit have often solved the seemingly unsolvable—and we believe they can do it again. (pp. 460–461)

Yet even in the United States we may find quite a different answer if we ask people who are poor, oppressed, or homeless—that people are not so much in control of their destinies. We also find this alternative answer in our literature and drama. The valiant and hopeless struggle of characters against fate is what makes plays such as Arthur Miller's *Death of a Salesman* or Eugene O'Neill's *Long Day's Journey into Night* so compelling.

In worldwide terms, the belief that fate is stronger than individual effort is probably the majority view. For example, the *Mahabharata*, a sacred text of Hinduism, the world's oldest religion, holds that

> It is not man who is the doer of good and evil words, for man is not independent. He is made to act like a wooden puppet. Some are motivated by God, others by chance, and yet others by the works they have performed in former [lives]. (quoted by Zaehner, 1962, pp. 139–140)

Five times daily, the orthodox Muslim (the word itself means "surrender") bows and prays to Allah, "almighty, omnipotent . . . the Creator of life and death in whose hand is dominion and irresistible power" (Smith, 1958, p. 231). Even American psychologists have debated the question, with the behaviorist B. F. Skinner arguing for strict determinism and the humanist Carl Rogers, though acknowledging the possibility of control, emphasizing individual free will and choice. Excerpts from their remarks at a symposium on the control of human behavior (Rogers & Skinner, 1956) are given in Table 8.1.

Given the importance of the question, you may be surprised that personality psychologists are mostly not concerned with determining the "correct" answer. Rather, they study the *consequences* of a person's belief in fate or individual mastery. And in fact these consequences are often critically important, both in the psychological laboratory and in life. In Shakespeare's play, for example, the words of Cassius influenced Brutus to join the conspiracy to assassinate Julius Caesar. At a more mundane level, changing people's beliefs about whether results are due to their own efforts (free will) or to chance (fate) can have important effects on their cognitive and emotional state. Under free will conditions, people generalize better from their prior experience and learn

TABLE 8.1 REMARKS ON THE CONTROL OF HUMAN BEHAVIOR BY CARL ROGERS AND B. F. SKINNER

Skinner: Science is steadily increasing our power to influence, change, mold—in a word, control—human behavior. . . . Until only recently it was customary to deny the possibility of a rigorous science of human behavior by arguing . . . [that] man was a free agent. . . . What is needed is a new conception of human behavior which is compatible with the implications of a scientific analysis. All men control and are controlled.

Rogers: Science has its meaning as the objective pursuit of a purpose which has been subjectively chosen by a person. . . . Consequently, any discussion of the control of human beings by the behavioral sciences must first and most deeply concern itself with the subjectively chosen purposes which such an application of science is intended to implement. . . . In client-centered therapy, we are deeply engaged in the prediction and influencing of behavior, or even the control of behavior. . . . that the client will become self-directing. . . . Behavior, when it is examined scientifically, is surely best understood as determined by prior causation. This is one great fact of science. But responsible personal choice, which is the most essential element in being a person . . . is an equally prominent fact in our lives.

Skinner: What evidence is there that any client ever becomes truly *self*-directing? What evidence is there that he ever makes a truly *inner* choice of ideal or goal? Even though the therapist does not do the choosing . . . he is not out of control. . . . [And] what about all the other forces acting upon the client? Is the self-chosen goal independent of his early ethical and religious training? Of the folk wisdom of his group? Of the opinions and attitudes of others who are important to him? Surely not.

SOURCE: Excerpted from Rogers and Skinner (1956)

more; but where conditions are determined by "fate," they feel anxious and stressed (Phares, 1978, pp. 267–269; these experimental differences even hold for animals). In laboratory studies of instrumental conditioning, successful learning requires that organisms perceive some contingency or causal connection between their own actions and the reinforcement consequences.

*F*ROM FATE TO CONTROL OF REINFORCEMENT

Following the lead of Julian Rotter (1966), personality psychologists have posed the question of fate versus individual control in the following terms: Does the person believe that reinforcements (or outcomes) are under internal control (within the self) or under external control (outside the self)? Rotter developed a twenty-three-item questionnaire to measure *internal versus external locus of control of reinforcement*, usually abbreviated as locus of control or I-E. He assumed that this was a generalized construct; in other words, that people who are internal about one outcome will be internal about other outcomes. Each item consists of a pair of statements, asking people to choose the one they "personally believe to be more true."[1] The following items are typical of the I-E questionnaire:

1. a. What happens to me is my own doing. (internal)
   b. Sometimes I feel that I don't have enough control over the direction my life is taking. (external)

2. a. In the case of the well-prepared student there is rarely if ever such a thing as an unfair test. (internal)
   b. Many times exam questions tend to be so unrelated to course work that studying is really useless. (external)

3. a. As far as world affairs are concerned, most of us are the victims of forces we can neither understand nor control. (external)
   b. By taking an active part in political and social affairs the people can control world events. (internal)

As you can see, these items are fairly obvious. Over the years, personality researchers have used other items and formats and developed special questionnaire versions on particular topics (e.g., academic achievement or health), or for special groups (e.g., young children or older persons). Some researchers believe that there are at least two different kinds of external beliefs—control by "chance" and control by "powerful others" (Strickland, 1977b).

Responses to the Rotter measure are scored in the external direction; that is, a high score means a belief in external control. In presenting the characteristics of people who score at one or the other extreme on the internal-external measure,[2] I will use the word "external" or "externals" to refer to high scorers, people who choose the external or "fate" alternatives. By "internal" or "internals," I mean people who choose the internal alternatives more often and so score low.

Internal Control in Everyday Life

Assigning responsibility. Internals are more likely to hold other people responsible for events and outcomes such as automobile accidents (Phares & Wilson, 1972; Sosis, 1974). Probably they generalize from their own beliefs: "If I am in control of what happens to me, then they must have been in control of what happened to them." Other studies have demonstrated this same "personal responsibility" effect for major public events. For example, in 1968 during the Vietnam war, American soldiers deliberately murdered at least 175 and probably more than 400 civilians (mostly old men, women, and children) in the village of My Lai. Initially, the story was suppressed by higher-level army

---

[1]This is called a forced-choice format and is often used to increase the discriminating power of socially desirable statements by pairing them with equally desirable alternatives. Whether it works has been disputed (see Scott, 1969, pp. 212, 241).

[2]See Lefcourt (1976, 1981–1984); Phares (1976, 1978); and Strickland (1977b).

officers, but when the facts finally became known, several soldiers were court-martialed and convicted (see Hersh, 1970). Shortly after the verdicts were announced, Hochreich (1972) asked a sample of college students about who or what was to blame. She found that among men (but not women), internals were more likely to hold the soldiers who actually did the killing responsible, while externals felt that other people such as higher-up officers shared the guilt. Consistent with this result, Hamsher, Geller, and Rotter (1968) found that internal men (but not women) were more likely to believe the Warren Commission report's conclusion that Lee Harvey Oswald acted alone in assassinating President Kennedy. That is, externals were more likely to believe in conspiracy theories.[3] These results all suggest that in their everyday judgments of responsibility, internal men agree with Shakespeare's Cassius, that people "are masters of their fates." In contrast, externals would reply that "the fault *is* in our stars, not in ourselves."

Conformity and strategies of social influence. Early laboratory studies suggested that internals are less likely to conform and more likely to resist. Sometimes they even try to figure out the experimenter's purpose and work against it (Strickland, 1977b, pp. 230–231)! More generally, internals respond to the *content* of a persuasive message (especially if they are permitted to draw some of the conclusions themselves, so that they feel it is "their" message), while externals respond to the prestige of the *source* or to peer pressure (see Ritchie & Phares, 1969). Thus if you want to persuade an internal, use logic; if you want to convince an external, cite "experts" and refer to "public opinion."

A similar pattern emerged when people are asked to influence others. Among students acting the part of a supervisor dealing with a "problem worker," internals used personal persuasion (encouragement, praise, admonishment, or setting new standards), while externals leaned toward the use of coercive force (Goodstadt & Hjelle, 1973). In other words, internals and externals try to influence others in the ways they themselves are most effectively influenced. In organizational terms, these two results suggest that leaders might be more effective if they have the same locus-of-control beliefs as their followers.

Academic Performance

As we have seen, internals pay more attention to the content of information than to the prestige of the source. They also play more quiz and skill games and spend more time looking through science books. They have a longer future-time perspective; they can delay gratification and persist longer on tasks, especially tasks of skill. Given all these characteristics, internals ought to do better in school, and this is exactly what many studies have found, at least in elementary and high school grades (Strickland, 1977b, pp. 236–240). Even

---

[3]In both of these studies, there were no differences between internal and external women. One explanation, at least for Hochreich's differential results, is that at the time of her study, only men faced the possibility of being drafted into the army and forced to fight.

when social class (Harrison, 1968) and intelligence (Lessing, 1969) are controlled, internality still predicts getting good grades. In the mid-1960s, one landmark study of almost 500,000 minority children from all parts of the United States found that internal control beliefs strongly predicted school performance, even after social class and intelligence were taken into account. In fact, students' internality was a better predictor of academic performance than were variables such as quality of teacher or quality of school.

Locus of control is not as successful in predicting college grades, probably because college students are high on both ability and internal control. (When the ranges of variables are restricted, correlations between them drop.)

Knowledge and Health

Across a wide variety of situations, internals seek information and pay attention to relevant cues (Phares, 1978, pp. 278–279). Among prisoners, internals know more about institutional procedures, policies, and parole regulations than do external prisoners. Among hospitalized tuberculosis patients, they ask more questions of the medical staff and know more about their disease or condition (Seeman, 1963; Seeman & Evans, 1962).

Internals also act on their knowledge. After learning about the health dangers of smoking, they are more likely to quit. They benefit more from weight-control programs. They have more frequent dental checkups, use seat belts, and practice more effective contraception. As patients, they follow medical instructions more carefully. They are even better at learning biofeedback (voluntary control of autonomic nervous system functions such as heart rate, galvanic skin response, or alpha-rhythm brain waves). Literally, then, internals are more in control of their bodies and their health (Strickland, 1978). A careful year-long study of over 1,000 randomly selected adults in the Los Angeles area by Seeman and Seeman (1983) illustrates the connection between locus of control and health directly. After the effects of age, sex, social class, race, education, and health status at the *beginning* of the year are taken into account, external control predicted more frequent illness during the year and poorer health at the end of the year.

What about AIDS? While there is at present no cure, there are guidelines about sexual activity (safer sex) and other behaviors that reduce the danger of contracting the disease. Although the relationships are sometimes of small magnitude, many studies suggest that internals do know more about AIDS (Aruffo, Coverdale, Pavlik, and Vallbona, 1993), are more likely to practice safer sex (Dardeau, 1992; St. Lawrence, 1993; Vanwesenbeeck, deGraaf, Van Zessen, & Straver, 1993; Willis, 1990), and, if HIV-positive, progress more slowly through the spectrum of HIV-related illnesses (Spalding, 1992).

In the case of psychological health, externals show more signs of certain psychological disturbances, such as anxiety or mood swings. (One particular psychological problem, depression, has drawn the most research, but these studies fit better under the topic of attribution and so will be considered in the next section.) Locus of control is also related to the effectiveness of particular kinds of psychotherapy. Internals like (and do better with) nondirective counseling, a form of therapy that leaves a good deal of freedom (or the impression of freedom) to the patient, whereas externals do better with a more directive therapeutic regimen, such as behavior therapy (Phares, 1978, p. 294). Notice how these differences are consistent with the different ways that internals and externals are influenced and persuaded, as discussed above.

Results about alcohol and substance abuse treatments are inconsistent (see Strickland, 1978, p. 1282), perhaps because some treatments manage to appeal to both groups. Alcoholics Anonymous, for example, asserts that chronic drinkers are under the "higher power" of alcohol (external control), which they can overcome by their own efforts (internal control), but only if they have support from other people and/or some other higher power (external control, again).

Social Action

Two landmark studies in the early 1960s found that internal African American college students were more likely to participate in civil rights activities such as community organization and freedom rides (Gore & Rotter, 1963; Strickland, 1965). Many personality psychologists concluded that internals were more likely to take social action. Later on, however, as the civil rights movement grew and protests against the Vietnam war spread, the role of locus of control also changed. Thus Ransford (1968) found that externals were more likely both to approve of urban riots and also to participate in them. Perhaps internals and externals can both be socially active, but in different ways: internals through calculated and controlled action to seek redress and improve conditions, and externals through more spontaneous expressions of frustration and rage against conditions felt to be intolerable. Both kinds of social action are rational, depending on one's beliefs about who controls outcomes. If you yourself are in control, then you can change things by your own planned action. But if events are beyond your control, then you may be reduced to striking out blindly, to control by destroying. Both kinds of action can bring about change.

Development and Change of Locus-of-Control Beliefs

People's beliefs about the causes of events develop out of their actual experience with events. Thus white middle-class people are more likely to be internal; while working-class, poor, African American, and physically handicapped people are more likely to be external. This is easy to understand, even obvious. The more "internal" groups generally have more *real* control over their lives;

not surprisingly, therefore, they also *believe* they have more control. You may wonder, therefore, whether locus of control as a "personality" variable tells us anything about people that we don't already know from their social position. Some critics argue that speaking of "belief in internal control" rather than "middle-class" or "moderate income" is psychologizing—that is, inappropriately giving psychological labels to what are really social and material realities.[4]

While it is true that race, social class, income, and education affect locus-of-control beliefs, the correlations are far from perfect. People's locus-of-control beliefs, in other words, are more than the superstructure of their social position. When background factors are held constant, moreover, locus of control beliefs *still* show significant relations to school achievement, health, and so forth (see Strickland, 1977b). For example, after controlling for seven different background factors, Seeman and Seeman (1983) still found internals to be healthier than externals. Thus it seems that beliefs can predict behavior over and above the influence of social factors that underlie those beliefs.

Further, although our beliefs may be rooted in our social backgrounds, they are certainly not fixed and unchanging over the rest of our lives. Internal beliefs can be increased by psychotherapy and self-improvement groups (Strickland, 1978, pp. 1202–1203). DeCharms (1976) actually designed special courses and teacher-training programs to increase underachieving students' sense of being "origins" (internals), rather than "pawns."

The above discussion suggests that beliefs are important in their own right, whatever their sources. To understand people, we need to know their backgrounds (the distal, or far-away, part of their personalities), but we also need to know their current (proximal, or close-at-hand) characteristics. Will someone do well in school, be healthy, or act instrumentally for a social cause? It helps to know that person's age, race, and social class, but it is also important to know the person's locus-of-control beliefs.[5] And although we cannot change background factors, we can change locus-of-control beliefs, with a resulting change in the associated behaviors.

The Bright Side of Externality

Internal control seems to be the key to so many good things—health, good grades, and instrumental social action. However, I don't think it is *always* a good thing. There are many outcomes that we really cannot control. Here is a personal experience from my travel diary:

---

[4]This criticism raises the fundamental issue of the extent to which personality is more than a projection of social and economic backgrounds. This issue will be more fully discussed in Part Four.

[5]*Path analysis* is a statistical technique often used to estimate the independent contributions of a series of different kinds or levels of variables. For example, Stewart, Lykes, and LaFrance (1982) used path analysis to estimate the independent effects of women's social background, their current situation, and their beliefs and values on their career level and achievements.

I write these words while sitting in the Dallas–Ft. Worth airport, making connections on the first day of the July 4 weekend to get to San Francisco for a convention. Local thunderstorms and air traffic delays have snarled airline schedules to and from both coasts. Plane after plane, running at least an hour and a half late, is oversold. Standby passengers are being "rolled over" to the flight after the next flight after the next flight. Hungry babies are crying, parents are trying to amuse active young children, tape recorders are blaring, no smoking signs are freely violated, and the air-conditioning cannot cope. There is a twenty-minute line at the snack bar. Stretching the limits of belief, my airline has just announced that the flight, already two hours late, is waiting for a flight crew to appear. Some say the crew is in the building; others say they are "trapped" in a plane that has landed but has no available gate space at which to park.

During those hours at the airport, I had no control over outcomes and reinforcements. What conceivable good would it have done to believe that I had such control? Surely it was healthier to resign myself to the situation and go on writing. Eventually, I did get to my destination, so my problems were over. But if I had been poor, uneducated, or a member of a minority, these would have been the daily conditions of my life. So which beliefs would be "accurate" and "healthy" then?

Assuming personal responsibility for outcomes that are in fact uncontrollable can be highly frustrating (see Strickland, 1978, p. 1205). As Janoff-Bulman and Brickman (1982) put it:

> Mathematicians burn out by staking their careers on finding solutions to extremely difficult, perhaps insoluble problems. Ordinary people ruin their lives by persisting in efforts to maintain relationships with spouses, parents, or children in ways that may once have worked, but cannot work any longer. (p. 207)

Holding people responsible for outcomes that are really uncontrollable is a form of blaming the victim (Ryan, 1971). In situations that we really cannot control, therefore, it may be healthier to admit the facts and resign ourselves to whatever will be. As the nineteenth-century American poet James Russell Lowell put it, "There is no good in arguing with the inevitable. The only good argument available with the east wind is to put on your overcoat."

More systematic evidence for a possible bright side to externality comes from a nationwide survey of over 2,000 adult Americans by Veroff, Douvan, and Kulka (1981, pp. 522–524). They found that people who prayed when they were unhappy had higher levels of "subjective mental health" (that is, they were happier and felt more zest). While prayer can be seen as a kind of last-resort way of controlling things, to most believers it is really a religiously sanctioned way of giving up control over things that cannot be controlled: "Not my will, but Thine be done." For reasons I do not understand, this kind of "resignation" is often called "defensive externality" (Phares, 1978, pp. 288–290; Strickland, 1977b, pp. 245–247). Surely it does not always involve the distortion and pathology implied by the word "defensive."

PATTERNS OF CAUSAL ATTRIBUTION

For Shakespeare's Cassius, there were only two choices: events were controlled by ourselves (internal) or by our stars (external). Many psychologists, however, make finer distinctions. For example, when we say an outcome depends on internal factors, we might mean that it has to do with either ability or effort. Both factors are internal, but they are very different explanations. Effort can easily be increased or reduced, but ability is more fixed: it makes sense to tell a friend to study harder before an important exam, but it would not be helpful to say "be smarter." Similarly, external factors could mean the structure of the task or situation, the actions of other people, or sheer luck.

Kinds of Attributions: Ability, Effort, Task, and Luck

In technical terms, asking people about reasons or causes of outcomes elicits their *causal attributions*. Drawing on the locus-of-control research and the work of Heider (1958) and Kelley (1973), Weiner (1980) and his colleagues at the University of California at Los Angeles combined the dimension stable-unstable with internal-external, resulting in four kinds of attribution: *ability, effort, task difficulty,* and *luck.*[6] These are illustrated, with examples from both Shakespeare's *Julius Caesar* and college experiences, in Table 8.2.

[6]Weiner also suggested *intentionality* or controllability as an additional third dimension (1980, pp. 346–350; 1985, p. 554). For example, *effort* is internal and unstable, and intentional or controllable; but *mood* is internal, unstable, and unintentional or uncontrollable. Alternatively, Abramson, Seligman, and Teasdale (1978) have suggested globality versus specificity as a third dimension.

TABLE 8.2 KINDS OF CAUSAL ATTRIBUTIONS

	Internal locus of control	
Weiner's label	*College example*	*Shakespeare example*

Ability	"Jane got a good grade on the calculus exam because she is exceptionally good at mathematics." (stable)	Mark Anthony (ironically), on Brutus's oratorical ability:
		    But were I Brutus,
		    And Brutus Anthony, there were an Anthony
		    Would ruffle up your spirits and put a tongue
		    In every wound of Caesar that should move
		    The stones of Rome to rise and mutiny.
		               Julius Caesar, III, ii, 230–234

Effort (or Desire, Want)	"John got a good grade on the calculus exam because he studied very hard." (unstable)	Caesar, agreeing to his wife's request to stay home from the Senate:
		    Bear my greeting to the senators
		    And tell them that I will not come today:
		    Cannot, is false, and that I dare not, falser:
		    I will not come today; tell them so, Decius.
		               Julius Caesar, II, ii, 61–64

Explaining outcomes in everyday life. The college examples of Table 8.2 were easy to classify, since Weiner and his associates began by studying achievement tasks among college students, but these four categories may not work so well in other situations. Since the speech of Brutus in Shakespeare's *Julius Caesar* was a good illustration of internal versus external control, I tried to select other passages from the play to illustrate each of Weiner's four attribution categories. This was much harder; the plot of the play is much more complex than a series of laboratory achievement tasks. My choices are shown in Table 8.2.

I decided to try the four categories out with my younger son, then 7 years old and in the second grade. I asked about spelling, an achievement situation to which it should be easy to apply the four categories:

DGW: You did quite well in spelling this year. When you do well in spelling, is it because you are a good speller, because you tried hard, because the words were easy, or because of luck?

SON: Partly luck, and partly because when I was little I was interested in spelling and so I learned a lot.

This answer combines at least three of Weiner's alternatives: luck ("partly luck"), effort ("I was interested"), and perhaps ability ("learned a lot"). Then I turned to a less successful outcome:

DGW: You didn't seem to like gym this year. Why not?

SON: I didn't do well in gym.

DGW: Why not?

TABLE 8.2 *(Continued)*

	External locus of control	
Weiner's label	*College example*	*Shakespeare example*
Task Difficulty	"John got a good grade on the calculus exam because the problems were quite easy." (stable)	Caesar, on death and the gods: What can be avoided Whose end is purposed by the mighty gods? Yet Caesar shall go forth. . . . It seems to me most strange that men should fear; Seeing that death, a necessary end, Will come when it will come. *Julius Caesar*, II, ii, 26–27, 35–37
Luck	"Jane got a good grade on the calculus exam because she was lucky." (unstable)	Brutus, on whether to fight: There is a tide in the affairs of men, Which, taken at the flood, leads on to fortune; Omitted, all the voyage of their life Is bound in shallows and in miseries. *Julius Caesar*, IV, iii, 218–220

SON: I'm not very good at sports.

DGW: Why not?

SON: I haven't had much practice . . . because I'm not interested in them.

Here we find ability ("not very good") and effort ("not interested") linked together. Which comes first: is "not very good" the result of "not interested," or is "not interested" a rationalization for "not very good?" In everyday life people often give multiple explanations that involve two or three different categories. Establishing which is the primary explanation may be difficult.

The problems I encountered in coding my son's analysis of his school performance and the musings of Shakespeare's characters suggest that the categories used to study causal attribution in the laboratory may not always fit the more complicated and somewhat messy attributions people actually make in everyday life. For example, they may give causes that cut across or combine the four categories, as my son did. Or they may give causes that cannot be classified at all. This is especially true in other cultures (see Miller, 1984). Among Hindus, outcomes are often explained as the result of one's karma (that is, the effect of something one did in a former life). This could be seen as an internal cause (in the previous life) or an external cause (in the present life). What about "habit" or "health," two causal explanations that are common in China (Bond, 1991, p. 44)? Or "a bad relationship between self and family"?

Finally, people may not spontaneously mention *any* causes, even for severe and unanticipated bad events. For example, Taylor, Lichtman, and Wood (1984) studied women with breast cancer and found that only 64 percent made spontaneous attributions about the cause of their illness. Along these same lines, Downey, Silver and Wortman (1990) interviewed parents of infants who had recently died of sudden infant death syndrome (SIDS), a devastating tragedy that is unforeseen, unpreventable, and not fully understood by doctors. If any real-life event should engage a parent's search for causes, surely SIDS should. Within three weeks after the child's death, Downey and her colleagues asked parents the following:

> Even though no one knows why babies die of SIDS, most SIDS parents have some hunch or theory about what caused *their* baby to die. Would you please share with us any thoughts or theories you have about why *your* baby may have died? (p. 940)

Even with such a strong prime for giving causal attributions, fully one-quarter of the parents did not give any theory or cause. When the parents were directly asked, "This past week, how important was it for you to figure out who or what was responsible for your baby's death?" almost half chose the alternatives "not at all" or "just a little." (However, when the parents were given a list of eight possible causes, such as "something I did," "God," or "chance," almost all reported having earlier considered at least one of the alternatives at some point.)

Even in more conventional studies asking school children and college students to explain their successes and failures at various activities, the proportion of their spontaneous answers that can be classified into the four categories has ranged from only one-fourth (Falbo & Beck, 1979) to three-fourths (Frieze, 1976; Frieze & Snyder, 1980).

Explaining important social events. On October 16–21, 1987, the stock exchanges of the world recorded one of the most extreme sequences of price changes in their history. In New York, for example, the Dow-Jones industrial average dropped over 500 points on October 16, and dropped further on October 19, the next trading day. Then on each of the next two days, it rose by more than 100 points. How did business people, stockbrokers, and economists explain these wild fluctuations? Table 8.3 contains a representative sample of explanations, drawn from newspaper accounts. Do you find these easy to classify into the four categories? Can you detect any differences between the attributions for the fall and attributions for the recovery?

Development of Causal Attributions

We develop attributions about causes from observing the relationships between features and outcomes. "An effect is attributed to [that] one of its possible causes with which, over time, it covaries" (Kelley, 1973, p. 109). For example, if you are one of the few people in the class who did well on an exam (low *consensus* of outcome across persons), and if you do well on exams in general (low *distinctiveness* or high *consistency* between this and other outcomes within the person), then you are likely to attribute the result to a stable internal factor such as ability or enduring effort (McArthur, 1972). But if everyone did well (high consensus), then an external factor such as low task difficulty would be a more likely attribution. And if your performance this time was much better than usual, you are likely to choose a variable factor (effort or luck).

Causal attributions are also affected by certain general tendencies. For example, Ross argued that people tend "to underestimate the impact of situational factors and to overestimate the role of dispositional factors in controlling behavior" (1977, p. 183). This is called the *fundamental attribution error,* though I have never understood why it is necessarily an "error." Surely dispositional attributions must be correct sometimes, as Harvey, Town, and Yarkin (1981) suggest.

Further, Jones and Nisbett (1972) suggested that people view their own behavior as caused by the situation but judge the same behavior in other people to be the result of inner intentions or other dispositional factors. In other

TABLE 8.3 EXPLANATIONS FOR STOCK MARKET PERFORMANCE, OCTOBER 16–21, 1987

Reasons for the decline of over 600 points in 2 days (October 16 and 19):

- The federal budget and trade deficits (Chrysler chairman Lee Iacocca)
- Lack of confidence in political leaders (stock exchange executive)
- "Maybe some people saw a chance to grab a profit." (President Reagan)
- Statements made by the Treasury Secretary (presidential candidate Jack Kemp)
- "The fault, dear fellow investors, is not in our system but in ourselves, that we are forgetful." (columnist William Safire)
- "Something's going on in the world that we don't know about. Otherwise this couldn't be happening." (a Florida investor)
- Events in the Persian Gulf (IBM Corporation)
- Herd behavior: "Like a theater where someone yells 'Fire!' " (high-technology executive)
- Falling out of the United States, West Germany, and Japan (a bank economist)
- Divine retribution, computer-programmed trading, despair (various experts)
- "The events of the last few months have been trying to tell this country something about its mindless excesses." (columnist James Reston)
- "I just don't know." (consumers, in a survey)
- Removing tax benefits for takeovers (a speculator)
- A correction (a banker)
- An inevitable consequence of the "casino economy" in the United States (a Chinese economic official)
- "Our hegemonic role in the last couple of decades has been slowly declining." (a Stanford University political scientist)
- The capitalist system is in a constant state of crisis. (Marxist-Leninist theory)

Reasons for advances of over 200 points in 2 days (October 20 and 21):

- "The steps taken by the Federal Reserve" (President Reagan)
- The decline in interest rates; smaller investors looking for bargains; talks in Washington between White House officials and Congressional leaders (market analysts)
- Foreign investors (investment bankers)

words, we acted out of sheer necessity, but others had a choice. This is usually called the *actor-observer difference*. It can be readily observed in everyday life, but it is especially clear in cases of escalating conflict. Consider the Japanese attack on Pearl Harbor on December 7, 1941. Speaking to Congress the next day, President Roosevelt attributed the attack to dispositional factors on the part of the Japanese: it was a "premeditated invasion," and the word "deliberate" was used three times. The Japanese leaders, however, saw things quite differently. To them, a deliberate American policy (dispositional attribution) had forced Japan's hand (situational attribution), as illustrated in the words of Prime Minister Tojo at the meeting where the final decision for the attack was made (Ike, 1967):

The United States not only refused to make even one concession with respect to the position she had maintained in the past, but also stipulated new conditions. . . . This not only belittled the dignity of our Empire and made it impossible for us to harvest the fruits of the China Incident, but also threatened the very existence of our Empire. (p. 263)

Who was right, Roosevelt or Tojo? In 1945, the United States won the war and hanged Tojo. This resolved the attribution question for a few decades, but later on, revisionist historians reopened the debate about the origins of the Pacific war.

Attributional Style

While causal attributions are affected by features of the situation and other factors such as the actor-observer difference, many people develop a consistent *characteristic attributional style*. That is, they make the same kinds of attributions across different situations. For example, some people consistently attribute successful outcomes to stable internal factors such as ability, while explaining failure as the result either of lack of effort or else external causes such as task difficulty or luck. "When I do well on an exam," they might say, "it's because I'm smart; but when I mess up, it's bad luck." People with this attributional style are likely to take great pleasure and pride in success and are more likely to persist after failure (see Weiner, 1980, chaps. 7–8). In fact, we can call this a *facilitating attributional style*, because it facilitates persistence and performance.[7]

This attributional style facilitates persistence because if my success is due to enduring internal factors, then I am likely to succeed again the next time I try. Moreover, I will feel pride and self-esteem from a sense of competence and ability (see Weiner, Russell, & Lerman, 1978). On the other hand, if my failures are only due to external (especially temporary) causes, then I may succeed on another attempt because of greater effort or because my luck may change. I will not feel too bad about externally caused failures. In short, if I succeed, I win and feel good; if I fail, at least I do not lose, and I do not feel so bad. Thus I will persist.

Now consider the opposite *debilitating attributional style*. If my failure is due to a stable internal factor such as lack of ability, then I am likely to feel incompetence, guilt, and shame. Moreover, there is no point in trying again, because the result will likely be the same. And if my success is the result of luck, there is no reason to think I would succeed next time. In short, if I succeed I do not really win and do not feel particularly good; and if I fail I lose and feel bad. Thus I will not persist. The contrast between these two patterns, summarized in Table 8.4, illustrates the powerful motivational consequences of attributional styles.

[7]Some social psychologists call it the "self-serving attributional bias" or the "hedonic [pleasure] bias" (Harvey & Weary, 1981).

TABLE 8.4 EMOTIONAL EFFECTS OF CAUSAL ATTRIBUTIONS

	Outcome	
Attribution dimension	*Success, positive*	*Failure, negative*
Internal	Pride, self-esteem	Low self-esteem, depression Guilt (if temporary and/or controllable Shame (if enduring and/or controllable)
External	Gratitude (especially if controllable)	Resignation
Temporary	Surprise, delight, relief	Surprise, guilt (if internal and controllable
Enduring	Pride, self-esteem (if internal)	Hopelessness
Controllable	Gratitude (if external)	Anger (especially if external and enduring), guilt (if internal)
Uncontrollable	—	Pity (especially if stable)

Facilitating attributional pattern: ———
Debilitating attributional pattern: - - - - -
SOURCE: Based on the work of Abramson, Seligman, & Teasdale (1978) and Weiner (1982, 1985, 1986)

HELEN KELLER'S ATTRIBUTIONS AND EXPLANATORY STYLE

Helen Keller's (1903b) account of her college entrance exams clearly reflects her optimistic or facilitating attributional style.

> If I passed with higher credit in the preliminaries than in the finals, there are two reasons. In the finals, no one read my work over to me [external cause of relative failure], and in the preliminaries I offered subjects with some of which I was in a measure familiar [internal cause of relative success]. (p. 88)

Her internal attributions for this success brought pleasure, pride, and persistence, just as Weiner's theory predicts: "Professor Schilling came in and informed me I had passed satisfactorily in German. This encouraged me greatly, and I sped on to the end of the ordeal with a light heart and a steady hand" (p. 89). In contrast, she attributed her difficulties with mathematics to a variety of external factors (quite properly, I think):

> The college authorities did not allow Miss Sullivan to read the examination papers to me. . . . I was familiar with all literary braille in common use in this country—English, American, and New York Point; but the various signs and symbols in geometry and algebra in the three systems are very different, and I had used only the English braille in my algebra. . . . Mr. Keith had relied too much on my abil-

ity to solve problems mentally, and had not trained me to write examination papers. . . . The administrative board of Radcliffe did not realize how difficult they were making my examinations. (pp. 93–95)

In the end, Helen passed, though "I did not do so well as I should have done" (p. 257), and again her pride is evident: "If they unintentionally placed obstacles in my way, I have the consolation of knowing I overcame them all" (p. 95).

*A*PPLICATIONS OF ATTRIBUTIONAL STYLE

Depression

The debilitating attributional style resembles the clinical portrait of depression: feelings of guilt and self-blame, lack of a sense of control over life, and low activity level. Depressed persons make internal, stable, and global attributions for negative events and outcomes, while attributing positive events to external, unstable, and specific causes. This pattern is also called the *pessimistic explanatory style.* The global-specific dimension reflects their tendency to overgeneralize failures: if one thing goes wrong, everything else will follow in its wake. Nondepressed persons, in contrast, tend to have an *optimistic explanatory style,* which reverses each element of the pattern: failure is attributed to external, unstable, and specific causes, and success to internal, stable, global causes. They, in contrast, may overgeneralize success and positive outcomes.

While studies of explanatory style and depression give some empirical support to this model (see the reviews by Peterson & Seligman, 1984a, and Sweeney, Anderson, and Bailey, 1986), it is not clear whether explanatory style is a cause or consequence of depression. Longitudinal studies of children suggest that explanatory style can cause depression (Nolen-Hoeksema, Girgus, & Seligman, 1992), but longitudinal studies of adults (e.g., Lewinsohn, Steinmetz, Larson, & Franklin, 1981) suggest only correlation, not causation, between the two variables.

Everyday Consequences

People's explanatory or attributional styles are also related to many other aspects of their lives.

School achievement. Nolen-Hoeksema, Girgus, and Seligman (1986) found that children who used the pessimistic style (internal, stable, and global explanations for bad outcomes) were rated by teachers as showing more helpless behaviors and fewer mastery behaviors at school. They also scored lower on standardized achievement tests and showed more depressive symptoms.

Loneliness. Peplau and her associates (Peplau & Perlman, 1982; Peplau, Russell, & Heim, 1979) studied loneliness among college students. Those who

Susan Nolen-Hoeksema, who has studied the relationship between explanatory style and depression. "Children who [tend] to explain bad events by internal, stable, and global causes and good events by external, unstable, and specific causes [report] more depression and [show] more achievement-related problems" (Nolen-Hoeksema, Girgus, & Seligman, 1986, p. 440). (Stanford News Service)

believed that their loneliness was the result of stable internal causes more often felt "helpless," "hopeless," "despair," and "shut out" when they were lonely. In contrast, students who attributed their loneliness to unstable causes engaged in more coping behaviors such as "trying harder" and "looking for activities where I could meet new people" (see also Anderson, Horowitz, & French, 1983).

Performance. Seligman and Schulman (1986) studied 101 newly hired life insurance sales agents, measuring explanatory style at the beginning of training and following the agents through their first year of selling insurance. Their results are shown in Figure 8.1. Agents with the most optimistic explanatory style at the beginning of training sold more insurance (measured by commissions on new policies) during their first year than did agents with more pessimistic styles. At the end of that first year, they were more likely to stay with the company, while agents with pessimistic style were more likely to quit. Thus in the highly competitive world of life insurance sales, explanatory style seems to make a difference in performance. The Seligman and Schulman study is especially noteworthy because explanatory style was mea-

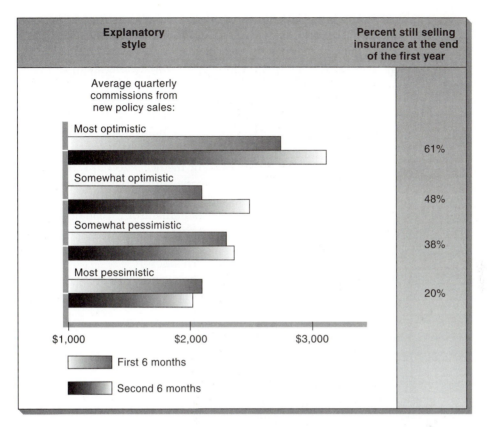

FIGURE 8.1
Explanatory style and performance among life-insurance salespeople.

sured *before* sales performance and survival-quitting, which rules out the alternative explanation that sales success causes optimistic explanatory style, rather than the other way around. (Of course, the optimists' style may have developed from *past* success at selling something, like life insurance, that people often resist buying.)

Seligman, Nolen-Hoeksema, Thornton, and Thornton (1990) used a similar technique in a study of women's and men's college swimming teams. They found that pessimistic explanatory style, measured at the beginning of the season, predicted relatively poor swimming performance during the season. In a second study, Seligman and his colleagues asked swimmers to perform their best event and then gave false feedback (reporting their times as several seconds slower than their actual times). When the swimmers swam the event again, the performance of those with pessimistic explanatory style deteriorated, while the performance of the optimistic swimmers remained stable.

Long-term health. If longitudinal studies are important to establish the direction of causality between cognitions and life outcomes, then a thirty-five-year longitudinal study by Peterson, Seligman, and Vaillant (1988) is especially notable. Starting over fifty years ago, the Study of Adult Development intensively studied over 200 male Harvard students who entered college between 1938 and 1940. These men were later followed up with questionnaires, interviews, and periodic medical exams (see Vaillant, 1977). In 1946, when they were in their late twenties, 99 of the men who had served in World War II answered open-ended questionnaires about their difficult wartime experiences. Several decades later, Peterson and his colleagues scored these 1946 questionnaire responses for explanatory style and then related the scores to the men's subsequent physical health, as assessed by the periodic medical checkups. As shown in Figure 8.2, the more pessimistic the men's explanatory style in 1946 (at age 25), the poorer their health in later life. In fact, the correlations are at their highest for the time period twenty years after measurement of explanatory style, when the men were at midlife! (In carrying out this analysis, Peterson and his colleagues controlled for the effects of level of the men's prior physical health, at age 25, by the statistical technique of partial correlation.)

Two mechanisms may mediate the relation between explanatory style and health. First, people with a pessimistic explanatory style may take poorer care

Christopher Peterson, who has related explanatory style to health and performance outcomes. "When people face uncontrollable events, they ask why. Their answer affects how they react to the events. . . . The depressive explanatory style tends to produce depression when bad events are encountered" (Peterson and Seligman, 1984a, pp. 348, 364). (Courtesy Christopher Peterson)

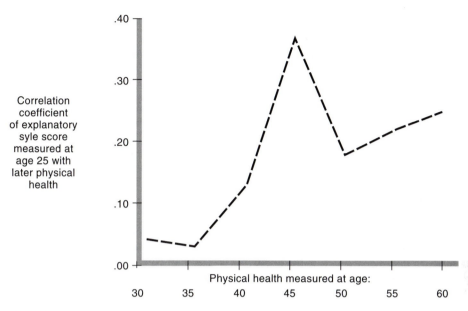

FIGURE 8.2
Explanatory style at age 25 and later physical health among male college graduates.

of themselves and seek medical attention less often. They may also be worse at problem solving, so they may also have more problems and accidents. Second, in line with the work of Peplau and others on loneliness, pessimistic style may affect interpersonal relations. People who feel helpless and avoid others when lonely are not likely to build up a very strong network of social support, a factor known to be an important buffer or protection against illness.

Employment and unemployment. Explanatory style is a useful concept for understanding other problems as well. For example, women who return to the labor market in middle adulthood, after raising children, are likely to encounter difficulties and failures because they lack recent work experience. They may attribute their failures to stable internal factors ("I don't have the ability," "I'm too old," "I have no work experience"). As a result, they may become discouraged and give up trying.

Similarly, the effects of major social forces such as unemployment also depend on people's attributions. Those who believe that they have been laid off because of temporary, external causes look for work more persistently and with more hope than do people who believe their unemployment is their own fault (Prussia, Kinicki, & Bracker, 1993; Winefield, Tiggeman, and Winefield, 1992).

"Pocketbook economics" and voting. Attribution theory can help to explain a curious set of findings that have emerged from public opinion research. One of the most basic rules of American political wisdom is that "people vote their pocketbook." That is, people's personal economic circumstances (becoming unemployed, decreased family income, personal economic

worries) are believed to affect how they vote, how much confidence they have in government, and how well they think elected officials are doing. Kinder and Mebane (1983), however, dispute this conventional wisdom. They assemble evidence showing that people's political opinions and choices are affected by their judgment about the economic condition of the nation as a whole, but *not* by their own personal economic circumstances. In simplest terms, most people do *not* vote their pocketbook.

Why not? Kinder and Mebane explained this surprising conclusion with the concept of causal attribution. Even during hard times, people tend to attribute the causes of their own economic fortunes either to *internal* factors ("I lost my job because I'm too old") or else to highly specific, proximal (nearby) external factors (e.g., "because the plant closed," or "because business was slow"), *without* making a further causal connection to government (" . . . and business is slow because of the president's economic policy"). Only among the rather small proportion of people who do attribute the causes of their own economic situation to remote external factors such as the government (about one-fifth of most samples) do we find any significant correlation between personal economic experience and evaluation of political leaders.

A 1979 public opinion study, for example, showed a significant relationship between having experienced unemployment in one's own family and negative evaluations of President Jimmy Carter *only* among people in the "collective" or external attribution group, as shown in Table 8.5. And even in this group, people's judgments of *national* economic conditions predicted their evaluation of Carter much more powerfully than did their *personal* or family unemployment experiences. Thus while most people do not see their personal economic fate in terms of government action, they do see government as a prominent cause of the country's economic situation, and that does affect their vote (Kinder & Mebane, 1983, p. 149).

Controversial as these conclusions are, they are supported by polling results. In April 1986, for example, the Gallup Poll asked a sample of Ameri-

TABLE 8.5 EFFECTS OF FAMILY UNEMPLOYMENT AND RATING OF NATIONAL ECONOMIC CONDITIONS ON EVALUATIONS OF PRESIDENT CARTER IN MARCH 1979

	Relationship[a] to evaluation of Carter among those whose attributions for their family's economic predicament were		
	Privatistic (internal) N=329)	Mixed (internal-external) (N=201)	Collective (external) (N=146)
Family unemployment	−.01	−.05	.25*
Judgment of national economic conditions	.33[+]	.30[+]	.88*

[a]Unstandardized regression coefficients.
[+]$p < .10$ *$p < .05$
SOURCE: Adapted from Kinder & Mebane (1983, p. 164)

cans, "How do people get rich?" The first-choice answers are shown in Figure 8.3. Most Americans adopt internal explanations for wealth; even when they do mention external factors, they rarely (16 percent) mention things that could be affected by government action ("advantages" or perhaps "luck"). Thus in their everyday economic life, the great majority of Americans seem to make internal attributions for their personal economic success. If their explanations of personal economic failure are also internal, then they would be inclined to work harder rather than blame the government, just as Kinder and Mebane suggest.

Changing Attributions

If an optimistic explanatory style promotes adjustment, then altering people's explanations (especially their explanations of failure) should help them to overcome depression and cope more effectively with life problems. There is some evidence that people can be taught to attribute failures to unstable or

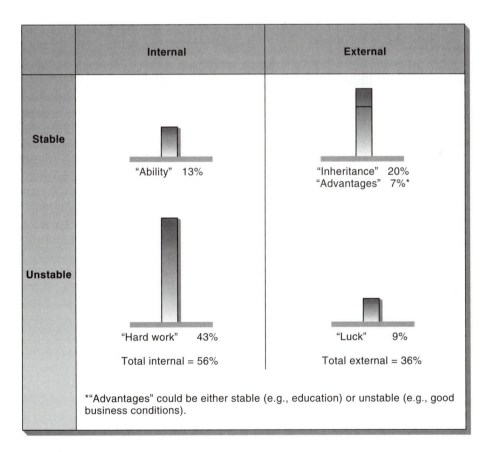

FIGURE 8.3
Americans' causal explanations for "Why people get rich."
SOURCE: "How do Americans" (1986)

external causes and to take credit for their successes. Effective attributional retraining programs have been carried out with a wide variety of groups: school children (e.g., Dweck, 1975), especially underachieving or learning-disabled students; juvenile delinquents; bureaucrats caught in situations of role conflict; and people suffering from depression (e.g., Rehm & O'Hara, 1979).

MEASURING EXPLANATORY STYLE AT A DISTANCE

Peterson and his associates have developed a technique called content analysis of verbatim explanations (CAVE), to measure explanatory styles at a distance, instead of relying on questionnaires (Peterson, 1992). The first step in this procedure is to extract causal statements about specific bad events (usually identified by phrases such as "because," "since," or "this led to"). Then each statement is rated on 7-point scales for the dimensions of externality-internality, stability-instability, and globality-specificity. Finally, the overall measure of pessimistic explanatory style is calculated as the average of internality, stability, and globality scores across all causal statements.

The CAVE technique has been applied to many different kinds of materials: psychotherapy transcripts, young adults' accounts of how and why their romantic relationships broke up, professional baseball and basketball players' explanations for defeats, cancer patients' accounts of their illness, and President Lyndon Johnson's press conferences (Peterson, 1992; Zullow, Oettingen, Peterson, & Seligman, 1988). Results using the CAVE at-a-distance measure are very similar to those obtained in the laboratory with direct questionnaires, suggesting that the two measures can be used interchangeably. Table 8.6 gives examples of some of these statements and their scores. For example, among women cancer patients with pessimistic explanatory styles, cancer is more likely to recur after surgery or chemotherapy treatment than among matched-control women cancer patients who have optimistic explanatory styles. Professional basketball teams with an optimistic explanatory style tend to rebound from defeats and beat the point spread in subsequent games.

Aggression

Zullow and his associates (1988) found that President Johnson's explanatory style changed during the Vietnam war along with American military fortunes. Johnson was highly optimistic just before the summer 1964 Gulf of Tonkin Resolution (an early landmark of the American military involvement), but he became very pessimistic after the February 1968 Tet offensive and his decision the next month to withdraw from the 1968 presidential campaign.

Similarly, Satterfield and Seligman (1994) measured explanatory style in press conferences and speeches of George Bush (between 1989 and 1991) and Saddam Hussein (between 1979 and 1991). Relating the scores to subsequent actions by each leader, they found that optimistic explanations were followed

TABLE 8.6 EXAMPLES OF EXPLANATORY STYLE MEASURED AT A DISTANCE

Extracted causal statement	Average of judges' ratings (1 = low; 7 = high)			Overall pessimism score
	Internality	Stability	Globality	
I didn't buy the [car because] it looked good from the outside but didn't have extras and didn't sound very good.	1.0	3.5	1.0	5.5
We have recently moved in together and have been experiencing the usual difficulties in adjustment [because] we both have difficulty in expressing our anger with each other.	3.5	5.0	1.0	9.0
When you come out and get beat the way we did, it's embarrassing [because] maybe there is something wrong with us.	6.0	5.0	5.0	16.0
[We lost because] nothing but the breaks beat me in that first game, but I never complain about that for I feel that things square themselves, and I'll get my share next time.	1.0	1.0	1.0	3.0
Well, we were having quite a few financial problems too during the year [because] my husband's in construction and everything's gone way down.	1.0	3.0	3.0	7.0
[I developed cancer because] I was tearing myself apart. I was feeling miserable, and I feel as though that had a lot to do with having the illness.	6.7	3.3	6.3	16.3

SOURCE: Adapted from Peterson & Seligman (1984b)

by risky, aggressive acts (such as Bush's 1989 invasion of Panama or Hussein's invasions of Iran in 1980 and Kuwait in 1990).

Electoral Success

Zullow and Seligman (1990) measured explanatory style in the nomination acceptance speeches of Democratic and Republican presidential candidates from 1900 through 1984. For eighteen of these twenty-two elections, the candidate with the higher score on "pessimistic rumination" (pessimistic explanatory style plus rumination or the tendency to dwell on problems) lost the election. Taking into account factors such as incumbency and initial differences in popular support as reflected in polls, differences in pessimistic rumination were quite highly correlated ($r = .89$) with differences in the margin of votes between winner and loser.

OPTIMISM AND ADAPTATION

Pollyannaism

You may wonder whether it is a good thing for people to be as optimistic as possible. In the discussion of locus of control, I suggested that an excessive sense of internal control, especially in the absence of opportunity or when contradicted by events, could lead to excessive and needless distress. Similarly, excessive explanatory optimism may have its drawbacks as well.

Pollyanna was the heroine of Eleanor Porter's 1913 novel of the same name, later made into a movie. Pollyanna was a classic optimist: whenever difficulty, disappointment, or punishment threatened, she played the "glad game" (Porter, 1913):

> "Is it far? I hope 'tis—I love to ride," sighed Pollyanna, as the wheels began to turn. "Of course, if 'tisn't far, I sha'n't mind, though, 'cause I'll be glad to get there all the sooner, you know." (p. 20)
>
> "You get so used to it—looking for something to be glad about, you know. And most generally there *is* something about everything that you can be glad about, if you keep hunting long enough to find it." (pp. 65–66)

Popular as *Pollyanna* was (twenty-five printings in two years), people soon started using the word "Pollyanna" as a criticism. Today when we call someone a Pollyanna, we do not mean that they are cheerful, but rather that they are too cheerful—unreasonably, even annoyingly cheerful.

The optimistic explanatory style may seem to be a form of Pollyanna thinking—cheery happiness purchased at the price of distorting reality and self-delusion. After all, Rogers and Maslow argued that accurate perception of reality is a hallmark of psychological adjustment and self-actualization (see Chapter 4). Surely successful people who ignore the influence of help, luck, and the situation are insensitive. And not many people would want to work with someone who denied all personal responsibility for failure. Yet seventy-five years after the publication of *Pollyanna*, an influential paper by Taylor and Brown (1988) suggested that illusions of control and unrealistic optimism are indeed associated with positive mental health and adjustment, and that "realism" may be a sign of depression and psychopathology. You may wonder whether Pollyanna was right.

Reality versus Illusion

Recently, Colvin and Block (1994) have challenged the evidence cited and conclusions drawn by Taylor and Brown. Colvin and Block distinguish the optimistic *views* of well-adjusted people (particularly in situations that are new, unfamiliar, and vague) from *illusions*. Moreover, as reality intervenes (the situation becomes familiar, relations between responses and outcomes are learned or appreciated), even this well-adjusted optimism changes into realistic appraisal. Related to this line of argument, moreover, John and Robins (1994) have shown that self-enhancement is highly correlated with narcissism ($r = .46$), rather than with optimal adjustment or mental health.

Thus we can distinguish healthy optimistic explanatory styles from Pollyannaism as follows. When the causes of events are clear, there is little room for individual differences in explanatory style. Accuracy is adaptive. Often, however, events are complex and their causes are fuzzy. In these circumstances—when the true proportions of internal-external, stable-unstable, and global-specific causation are unknown or ambiguous—then an optimistic explanatory style, and attribution retraining, may lead to more successful and satisfying outcomes.

I want to illustrate this conclusion with a personal example. At one point in my life I very much wanted a particular job, but obstacles and delays created the real possibility of a disappointing outcome. I felt responsible and began to be upset, but then I decided to analyze the situation in terms of attributional principles. Using a four-fold table like that illustrated in Table 8.2, I listed causal explanations from each category for the outcome of not getting the job. Given my mood at the time, I had no trouble thinking of many internal, stable, and global explanations! Still, I forced myself to put down *something* in each box. As I looked at all the explanations, I realized that many (though not all) of the internal explanations were rather unlikely and even preposterous, while many of the external causes were quite likely. I am happy to report that I felt better after this exercise. (In the end I also got the job.)

I don't think that I had simply talked myself into self-serving but unrealistic causal explanations. Initially, I was upset because I was focusing only on those particular attributions (internal causes for a bad outcome) that aroused negative emotions such as guilt, shame, and depression. When I systematically tried to think of causes for *all* of the boxes, I became aware of other kinds of attributions and began to focus on them. These explanations aroused other, less negative emotions (for example, resignation instead of guilt). Looking at the four categories of possible explanations, I was then able to revise my judgments about the relative influence of internal and external factors if I didn't get the job. Rather than hiding the truth and creating illusions, then, my attribution exercise pointed me toward a more balanced and accurate conception of reality. Had I been Pollyanna, I might simply have ignored the uncomfortable attributions.

Defensive Pessimism

In addition to anticipations of *simple optimism* ("I will succeed, or else it isn't my fault") or *simple pessimism* ("I will fail, because it's my fault") Norem and Cantor (1986) have suggested that some people have anticipations of *defensive pessimism*. That is, they tell themselves that they expect to fail (pessimism); but these expectations actually drive them to work harder (defensive functioning), so they ultimately succeed—sometimes very well. (You probably know students who announce before an exam, to anyone who will listen, that they will surely fail but who then get among the highest grades in the class.) Defensive pessimists deliberately set their expectations low, even well below what they have done in the past. Then they use these negative anticipations to motivate themselves to work harder, just so they don't fail. Trying to convince defensive pessimists that they won't fail actually interferes with their performance! Defensive pessimism is a truly paradoxical set of anticipations, anticipations almost deliberately designed to be proven wrong. To a defensive pessimist, though, the very act of verbalizing failure is a way to put to rest the anxiety associated with actual failure.

VALUES

So far we have concentrated on a few broad clusters of beliefs and values that involve major aspects of human experience. We all have many more specific beliefs about the way things are and values about the way things ought to be. "Values" are a concern of scholars from many different disciplines. Philosophers, and anthropologists, for example, have elaborated frameworks for classifying and understanding values. I will introduce two such systems before moving on to more psychological conceptions of values.

From Anthropology: Variations in Value Orientations

Within our own culture, people have many different conceptions of the good life, but if we turn to other cultures, the variety increases even more. Kluckhohn and Strodtbeck (1961), drawing on anthropology and sociology, have developed a system for describing values within and across cultures. What Kluckhohn and Strodtbeck refer to as "value orientations" actually include people's beliefs about what is as well as what ought to be; so the Kluckhohn-Strodtbeck framework really consists of value-belief orientations. In a critical review of cross-cultural psychological research, Triandis (1972, pp. 76–78) suggests that this framework offers the most complete and cross-culturally applicable conception of human values.

Kluckhohn and Strodtbeck began with certain universal questions. All cultures, they suggested, must deal with at least five basic issues or problems. Each problem has only a few different solutions, as shown below:

1. What is the character of human nature? (Is it *good, evil, mixed* good-and-evil, or *neutral?* Is it *fixed*, or can it *change?*)

2. What is the relationship of people to nature? (Are they *subjugated* to nature, *dominant* over nature, or in *harmony* with nature?)

3. What is the time focus of human life? (*past, present,* or *future?*)

Florence Kluckhohn, who identified fundamental dimensions of variation in human values. "Value orientations are complex but definitely patterned . . . principles . . . which give order and direction to the solution of 'common human' problems" (Kluckhohn & Stodtbeck, 1961, pp. 1, 4). (Courtesy Lucy Kluckhohn)

4. What is the modality of human activity? (*being,* the spontaneous expression of impulses and desires; *doing,* "getting things done"; or *being-in-becoming,* the development of the self?)

5. What is the modality of people's relationship to other people? (*lineal,* based on a hierarchy with hereditary roots; *collateral,* based on peer groups; or *individual*?)

Probably each answer has merit, but most people and most cultures have only one favored or dominant answer to each question. According to Kluckhohn and Strodtbeck, the typical American middle-class white male "answers" or values, as of 1961, were as follows: (1) *Human nature is evil but perfectable,* reflecting the nation's Puritan heritage. In recent decades, Kluckhohn and Strodtbeck suggest, this may be changing to a mixed good-and-evil conception. (2) We can (and should) *master or control nature.* (3) Primary emphasis should be given to the *future,* (4) *doing,* and (5) *individualism* (with a secondary emphasis on collateral or peer-group relations). Among different ethnic groups, social classes, and even geographic regions of the United States, however, there are very different value orientations. For example, Kluckhohn and Strodtbeck suggested that Italian American culture emphasizes human beings as subjugated to nature, being as a mode of activity, and collateral organization. And among the upper-class Eastern establishment, in contrast, the past and lineal social organization are dominant orientations. Within these broad social groups, however, individuals have their own unique blend of core cultural value orientations.

Since 1961, the core American values may have changed as a result of the civil rights movement, changes in women's roles, and the economic problems of the last few decades. Recent concerns for protecting the environment suggest more emphasis on human beings in harmony with nature, while economic and environmental problems may have altered our confident domination of nature (issue 2). Perhaps the human potential and self-development movements that began in the late 1960s reflected both a sense of humanity as good (issue 1) and a stronger being-in-becoming orientation (issue 4). Finally, there are signs that classic American individualism is becoming more tempered with a sense of community or collateral orientation (issue 5). By illuminating the ways in which American values have changed, the Kluckhohn-Strodtbeck framework may provide a way to understand the cultural values conflicts that have dominated American political life in the 1990s.

From Philosophy: The Study of Values

One of the most widely used direct questionnaires for measuring people's values is the *Study of Values*, originally developed in 1931 by Allport and Vernon (see Allport, Vernon, & Lindzey, 1960). It is based on a theoretical classification of values developed by the German philosopher Spranger (1928), who argued that all human values could be classified into six fundamental categories: *theoretical* (valuing truth), *economic* (valuing usefulness), *aesthetic* (harmony), *social* (altruistic love), *political* (power), and *religious* (unity). Each person's actual values are a mixture of these six ideal types. The *Study of Values* consists of a series of choices that pit two or more fundamental values against each other. The resulting scores give a profile showing the *relative* importance of each type for that person.

Figure 8.4 shows an example of research done with the *Study of Values* (Allport, 1966b). Value profiles of three groups of women—Peace Corps teachers, graduate students of business administration, and graduate nurses training to be teachers—are compared with each other and with the average scores of over 2,000 women college students. As we might expect, the two groups of teachers score higher in theoretical values and lower in economic values than the business school students. Not surprisingly, the business group scores high on political values and low on social values. Less easy to explain are the very high aesthetic scores for the Peace Corps teachers and moderately high aesthetic scores for the business students, as well as the high religious scores for the nursing teacher-trainees.

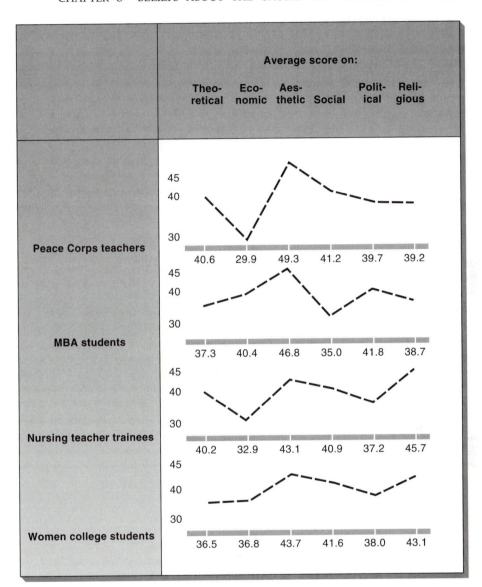

	Average score on:					
	Theo-retical	Eco-nomic	Aes-thetic	Social	Polit-ical	Reli-gious
Peace Corps teachers	40.6	29.9	49.3	41.2	39.7	39.2
MBA students	37.3	40.4	46.8	35.0	41.8	38.7
Nursing teacher trainees	40.2	32.9	43.1	40.9	37.2	45.7
Women college students	36.5	36.8	43.7	41.6	38.0	43.1

FIGURE 8.4
Study of values scores for selected groups of women.

There are important limits to the *Study of Values*. The six ideal types are all positive, reflecting only the best of human nature and values. In addition, they are only broad categories, which may conceal important individual differences. For example, many religious people would endorse a *general* "religious" or unity value, yet the values of their *particular* religions might be very different from each other.

TABLE 8.7 COMPARISON OF KLUCKHOHN AND STRODTBECK'S
VALUE ORIENTATIONS WITH ROKEACH'S INSTRUMENTAL
AND TERMINAL VALUES

Kluckhohn-Strodtbeck (1961) value issue and alternatives*	Related Rokeach (1973) values
1. Human nature:	
good	
evil	national security (T), salvation (T)
mixed good-and-evil	broadminded (I), forgiving (I)
neutral	
fixed	
can change	clean (I), honest (I), self-controlled (I)
2. Relationship of people to nature:	
subjugated to nature	family security (T)
dominant over nature	sense of accomplishment (T)
harmony with nature	a world of beauty (T), a world at peace (T)
3. Time focus:	
past	
present	
future	a sense of accomplishment (T)
4. Human activity:	
being	a comfortable life (T), an exciting life (T), pleasure (T), cheerful (I)
doing	a sense of accomplishment (T), ambitious (I), capable (I), logical (I)
being-in-becoming	happiness (T), inner harmony (T), wisdom (T), intellectual (I), imaginative (I)
5. People's relationship to others:	
lineal	social recognition (T), obedient (I), polite (I), responsible (I)
collateral	equality (T), mature love (T), true friendship (T), helpful (I), loving (I)
individual	freedom (T), self-respect (T), courageous (I), independent (I)

*Typical middle-class American value orientations (as of 1961), according to Kluckhohn and Strodtbeck, are italicized. (T) = Rokeach terminal value (desirable end state); (I) = Rokeach instrumental value (desirable way of reaching end states)

Rokeach's List of Values

Both the Kluckhohn and Strodtbeck and Allport-Vernon-Lindzey *Study of Values* are based on theoretical or philosophical analyses of value. In contrast, Rokeach (1973) developed a more empirical list of values, based on his observations of people's actual words and deeds. He identified eighteen *terminal values* (desirable states of affairs) and eighteen *instrumental values* (ways to attain terminal values). To measure values, Rokeach simply asked people to arrange the groups of value words in order of their preference. (To facilitate easy ranking, the Rokeach questionnaire has slightly sticky labels for each value. These can be moved around until the person is satisfied with the final ranking.)

Table 8.7 lists the thirty-six Rokeach terminal and instrumental values, showing how they might be compared with the Kluckhohn-Strodtbeck value orientations. As you can see, the two systems cover much of the same ground, although Rokeach's list concentrates more on typical middle-class American value orientations and a few orientations such as "being-in-becoming" and "harmony-with-nature" that are prominent in college and university communities. It also neglects the "human nature" and "time" issues.

Of the thirty-six values, freedom and equality are of fundamental importance in Rokeach's view, at least in societies influenced by Western thought

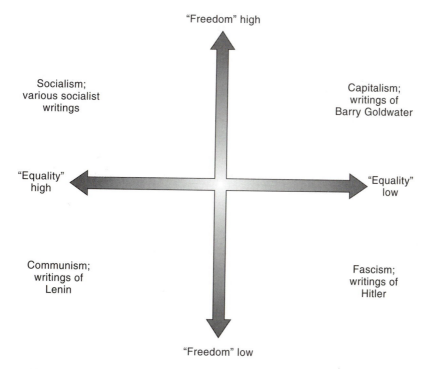

FIGURE 8.5
Rokeach's conception of freedom and equality values.

and institutions (1973, pp. 165–211). *Freedom* means "independence, free choice," while *equality* refers to "brotherhood, equal opportunity for all." While most Americans would endorse both values, Rokeach argued that they are in fact independent. Some people value equality more than freedom (for example, the revolutionary Soviet leader Lenin), while others value freedom more than equality (conservative capitalists). Some reject both (fascists). Figure 8.5 on page 285 illustrates how freedom and equality might be arranged in a four-fold table, with each quadrant defined as being high or low in valuing freedom and equality. Rokeach placed different political ideologies and leaders in each quadrant. He then analyzed the writings of Lenin, Barry Goldwater (the conservative 1964 Republican presidential candidate), Hitler, and various socialist writers by counting the number of references to each value. Lenin did appear to value equality more than freedom, while the conservative capitalist Goldwater valued freedom over equality. Socialists valued both, and Hitler valued neither. Direct testing of ordinary people from each of these political orientations further supported Rokeach's two-dimensional arrangement of fundamental values.

MEASURING VALUES AT A DISTANCE: THE METHOD OF VALUE ANALYSIS

Defining a value as "any goal or standard of judgment which in a given culture is ordinarily referred to as if it were self-evidently desirable (or undesirable)," White (1947, 1951) developed a system for measuring values at a distance in written material. The complete system includes definitions for scoring fifty values and several other psychological characteristics. This technique deserves to be better known and more widely used. For example, in his original study White analyzed *Black Boy*, the autobiography of the African American writer Richard Wright. Systematic counting of values mentioned by Wright both confirmed and extended White's initial impressionistic analysis. For example, Wright emphasized physical safety more than any other value (18 percent of all value-mentions). His second most prominent value, aggression (8 percent), usually occurred in contexts that suggested it was a means to obtaining physical safety rather than a free-standing value in its own right.

Using White's method, Eckhardt (1965) compared scores from political and moral writings from a variety of sources: political speeches by Franklin Roosevelt and Adolf Hitler, *The Communist Manifesto* by Marx and Engels, the *New Testament* gospels of Matthew, Mark, and Luke, and twelve case histories of recovering alcoholics published by Alcoholics Anonymous. Eckhardt compared scores for the following four clusters of twenty-five separate values:

> *Strength values:* freedom, achievement, recognition, dominance, aggression, strength, patriotism, determination, sovereignty, obedience, (denunciation of) democracy
>
> *Moral values:* morality, truth, justice, religion, democracy, nonaggression, nondominance, friendship, tolerance, generosity, carefulness

Economic values: economic welfare, ownership, work

Welfare values: any value wanted for someone else or any legitimate desire attributed to someone else

The five sets of writings show major value differences. Hitler and Marx and Engels scored highest on strength, while Franklin D. Roosevelt emphasized welfare. The three gospels scored highest on morality, though Hitler also scored surprisingly high. The values profile of recovering alcoholics is similar to that of the New Testament gospels, except for a greater emphasis on welfare.

In a detailed analysis of speeches by Nikita Khrushchev and John F. Kennedy, the respective heads of government of the Soviet Union and the United States during the early 1960s, Eckhardt and White (1967) showed that both leaders had similar value profiles. Perhaps this similarity was one reason why Khrushchev and Kennedy were able to communicate with each other so as to avoid war and peacefully resolve the 1962 Cuban Missile Crisis.

*T*HE OPERATIONAL CODE TECHNIQUE

When they study the beliefs and values of political leaders at a distance, political psychologists often use a systematic inventory of beliefs and values called an *operational code.* In elaborating this concept, George (1969) suggested that in order to process information, make decisions, and act, political leaders must simplify their perceptions of political reality through the prisms of certain fundamental beliefs:

Philosophical beliefs

1. What is the nature of political life: harmony or conflict? What is the character of our opponents?

2. What are the prospects for realizing our political aspirations: optimistic or pessimistic?

3. Is the political future predictable?

4. How much control or mastery can we have over history?

5. What is the role of chance in human affairs?

Instrumental beliefs

6. What is the best way to select goals: to maximize or to satisfy?

7. How can we pursue goals most effectively?

8. How can we calculate and control political risks?

9. What are the best means to advance our interests?

A particular leader's operational code is usually measured by examining the leader's writings, extracting and summarizing, in abstract form, all statements and passages relevant to these nine questions. For example, Walker (1984) analyzed the writings of former U.S. Secretary of State Henry Kissinger and constructed his operational code along the following lines:

> While people seek peace, deep national differences in philosophy and history, as well as miscalculations, often lead to conflict (question 1).
> Progress toward peace is possible, especially because of the present delicate balance of forces within the leadership of the other side (questions 3 and 5), but it is not inevitable (question 2), and cannot be taken for granted.
> We can move forward on a wide range of issues (question 7), but we must not let what is desirable jeopardize what is attainable (question 6).
> We should oppose aggression and irresponsible behavior, but we must not seek confrontations lightly (question 8).
> This means we must maintain a strong military defense (question 9).

Lists of operational-code studies of individual leaders can be found in Hermann (1977, pp. 81–82) and Walker and Falkowski (1984).

While the operational-code questions were designed for describing the beliefs and values of political leaders about political topics, we can discern some of the underlying value dimensions of Kluckhohn and Strodtbeck in the nine questions. For example, the issue of people's relation to nature (dominant, subordinate, or within nature) is reflected in almost every question. Most of Rokeach's instrumental values (see Table 8.7) are reflected in the instrumental beliefs of the operational code. More broadly, question 1 reflects the ethnocentrism and suspicion aspects of authoritarianism (Chapter 7), while questions 3 to 5 involve the locus-of-control and explanatory-style concepts of this chapter.

WHAT IS MISSING?

In the last two chapters, we have considered some widely studied clusters of beliefs and values about nature, human nature, society, and the causes of events. We have examined broader frameworks from anthropology, philosophy, psychology, and political science. Before leaving the topics of values and beliefs, we need to ask whether the different schemas and frameworks presented in these chapters leave out any important values and beliefs.

The Sociology of Personality Theory

First, it is important to realize that most belief frameworks reflect their social, cultural, and historical origins. For example, Rokeach's list emphasizes traditional American middle-class concerns. The dimension of authoritarianism versus egalitarianism reflects a conflict that has dominated Anglo-Saxon political thought for over 350 years, ever since John Locke advocated the consent of the governed as an alternative to Thomas Hobbes's absolute ruler. While many Americans are suspicious of authority, in parts of Asia, leaders are often viewed as all-powerful *and* benevolent (Pye, 1985, 1986). The concept of locus of control of reinforcement recalls the twentieth-century psychology laboratory, in which experimenters control the "reinforcement" of animal and human behavior. Kelly's view of the person as scientist is deliberately based on Western scientific culture. Finally, the concept of cognitive complexity betrays the influence of modern information-processing technology.

Some Alternative Values

Since so many of the most widely studied and familiar cognitive beliefs and values are drawn from certain realms of Western experience, they may not fully cover the whole range of human experience (see also Part Four and especially Chapter 17). I suggest that to be a truly transcultural discipline, personality psychology needs to pay more attention to at least three concepts that are important in many cultures and groups in human history. While each has been explored by some personality psychologists, none as yet exists as a well-defined and carefully measured personality variable.

Mystical consciousness and peak experiences. Many people experience and value a special state of experience or consciousness that can best be described as mystical. Words can hardly do justice; still, Freud's (1930, XXI) classic description of an "oceanic feeling" will give some sense of what I mean: "A sensation of 'eternity,' a feeling as of something limitless, unbounded . . . a feeling of an indissoluble bond, of being one with the external world as a whole" (pp. 64–65).

Freud thought that this feeling is the emotional basis of religious mysticism, adding that "I cannot discover this 'oceanic feeling' in myself. . . . This gives me no right to deny that it does in fact occur in other people" (p. 65). He went on to analyze such oceanic feelings as survivals of the infant's early sense of blissful fusion, before the ego or "self" and the "world" (i.e., mother) were differentiated. Later, "at the height of being in love the boundary between ego and objects threatens to melt away" (p. 66).

Maslow (1968) referred to such moments of mystical consciousness as "peak experiences": "Happiest moments, ecstatic moments, moments of rapture, perhaps from being in love, or from listening to music or suddenly 'being hit' by a book or a painting, or from some great creative moment" (p. 71). Peak experiences are felt to be rich, good, and ego-transcending. During them, we become detached from ordinary human concerns and may even become disoriented in time and space as we attend fully and completely to experience as a whole (Maslow, 1968, chaps. 6–7).

Environmental values. Throughout much of their history, Americans have viewed the environment as a wilderness to be "conquered" and "tamed," a "resource base" to be "exploited" to enhance human "domination." Recent years, however, have seen the growth of an alternative view, that people are immersed *in* nature rather than dominant *over* nature. For such people, "the environment has a semi-religious mystical quality; it is an object of wonder and beauty, a thing to be loved and cherished for its own sake" (Milbrath, 1986, p. 97). Kluckhohn and Strodtbeck (1961) did suggest that this view is common in many other cultures, but through the writings of Thoreau and John Muir, it has also been a part of American thought. Sometimes, people holding environmental values have become active politically, as for example in the Green political parties in many countries.

Environmental values do not occur in a vacuum, but usually go along with a "sense of compassion which springs from a highly developed sense of empathy, [and] extends not only to those near and dear but also to people in other countries, to other species, and to future generations" (Milbrath, 1986, p. 98). Thus environmentalism may be part of a broader new "postindustrial" ideology that has turned away from consumption, waste, hazards, and the institutions perceived to create them (Inglehart, 1990).

Consciousness of community. Personality psychology is usually focused on the individual. Indeed, as I suggested in Chapter 1, the very word "personality" suggests individual difference and distinctiveness. Variables such as internal attribution and internal control certainly reflect this individualist perspective. In recent years, however, many psychologists and other social theorists have emphasized the importance of community (Bellah, Madsen, Sullivan, Swidler, and Tipton, 1985), collectivity (Lykes, 1985), groups (Gurin, Miller, & Gurin, 1980), and an orientation toward communion as well as agency (see Chapter 4). While the United States is traditionally thought of as the home of individualism, the consciousness of community has repeatedly surfaced in American thought and social history: from the Shakers, the Oneida community, and other utopian movements of the nineteenth century down to the countercultures that sprouted up in the 1960s (Yinger, 1982).

Alternative Values in the Thought of Helen Keller

These three alternative values of mysticism, environmental concerns, and community were also prominent in Helen Keller's (1903b) thinking. She was devoted to the spiritual teachings of Emanuel Swedenborg (as mentioned in a footnote of Chapter 6, an eighteenth century Swedish scientist who suddenly became a religious mystic) and took intense pleasure in nature:

> It seems to me that there is in each of us a capacity to comprehend the impressions and emotions which have been experienced by mankind from the beginning. Each individual has a subconscious memory of the green earth and murmuring waters . . . a sort of sixth sense—a soul-sense which sees, hears, feels, all in one. . . .

What a joy it is to feel the soft, springy earth under my feet once more, to follow grassy roads that can lead to ferny brooks where I can bathe my fingers in a cataract of rippling notes. . . . It is splendid to feel the wind blowing in my face. . . . The rapid rush through the air gives me a delicious sense of strength and buoyancy, and the exercise makes my pulses dance and my heart sing. (pp. 122, 125)

Perhaps the most prominent alternative value in Keller's autobiography is that of community—friends and other people. She began the final chapter of her autobiography with this wish: "Would that I could enrich this sketch with the names of all those who have ministered to my happiness!" (p. 132). She then went on to mention an array of specific helpers that reads like a *Who's Who* of the late-nineteenth-century United States: Bishop Phillips Brooks, Oliver Wendell Holmes, the poet John Greenleaf Whittier, Edward Everett Hale, Alexander Graham Bell, William Dean Howells, Mark Twain, and many lesser figures. Her autobiography concludes:

Thus it is that my friends have made the story of my life. In a thousand ways they have turned my limitations into beautiful privileges, and enabled me to walk serene and happy in the shadow cast by my deprivation. (p. 140)

For Keller, any success was a collective success; any pleasure and pride had to be shared. On account of her blindness and deafness, the line between internal and external, between self and other does not seem to have been a simple boundary, but rather a complex, confusing, ambiguous, and shifting border territory. But Helen Keller's experience was not unique. Rather, her special experiences only serve to bring out certain aspects of cognition and personality, to highlight some truths of our common experience of being human. Nowhere is this more vivid than in her description of the relation of self to others.

9

Conceptions of the Self

❖

I, me, mine—that most vivid sense of self! It is a series of bodily sensations: at every waking moment since birth, I (and only I) have been receiving messages from my sense receptors, muscles, and internal organs. Yet, while this sense of body is the foundation of my sense of self, it is by no means the whole story. For example, people sometimes cope with extreme pain by telling themselves, "This is only happening to my body, not to *me*."

All the rest of personality—motives, beliefs and values, temperament, and social contexts—is bound together by the conception of self. The elements of my personality are in a special sense *mine*, experienced by me in a very special and personal way. No matter how much I try to describe them to you, you cannot get into my skin and experience me the way I experience me. Equally, I can never experience you the way you experience you. As the British political leader and novelist Benjamin Disraeli is said to have written, "Self is the only person whom we know anything about." As you read these words, what could be more real to you (yet at the same time completely unavailable to me or anybody else) than your own sense of yourself?

Yet the very privacy of our sense of self immediately leads to a paradox: though our self-experiences are private in a special sense, they are mostly social constructions—that is, they are built up out of other people's reactions to us. To reverse a sentence of the last paragraph, I can never experience me the way *you* experience me. We are what we are to ourselves *because* other people (family, friends, people at large) have told us so and interacted with us as if it were so. This is true even for our body experience, which is the foundation of the sense of self. For example, at 6 feet 8 inches, I think of myself as tall. But why do I think of myself in this way? First, because I *have been told so* repeatedly—by my parents, by friends of my parents, and by total strangers in supermarket lines. (I was once introduced to the Queen Mother of England; her first words were, "My, you're tall!") Second, because I can *compare* my height to that of other people. Third, because I am often uncomfortable with the *structures of social life*, such as furniture, doorways, and airplane and theater seats. Our sense of self, then, bridges the gap between body and social, private and public, subjective and objective (or "intersubjective"—that is, subjective matters that people can agree upon).

SELF AS THE CRITICAL CORE OF PERSONALITY

Of all the cognitive structures of our personality, the conception of self is one of the earliest formed, the most complex and elaborately developed, and the most significant for our overall functioning and well-being. In the psychology of personality, the self is so important that we shall discuss it in two chapters: the nature, content, and structure of self in this chapter, and the motivational effects of self in Chapter 10.

Development of a Sense of Self

By the age of 1 year, children recognize that their mirror image is themself and not another person. A rudimentary sense of self is usually established by a few months after that.

In Helen Keller's case, however, this normal development was delayed. "Before my teacher came to me, I did not know that I am. . . . My inner life, then, was a blank without past, present, or future" (1908, pp. 113–114). Her account of the period before she knew her name illustrates the importance of self as a foundation for the rest of cognition and personality. Writing of that time, Keller (1955) avoided personal pronouns and instead used the name Phantom to describe herself as a "little being governed only by animal impulses":

> I remember her as plump, strong, reckless, and unafraid. She refused to be led, and had to be carried upstairs when she received her first lesson. Another time her table manners required correction. Phantom was in the habit of picking food out of her own plate and the plates of others with her fingers. Annie Sullivan would not put up with such behavior, and a fight followed during which the family left the room. Phantom acted like a demon, kicking, screaming, pinching her would-be deliverer and almost throwing her out of her chair, but Annie succeeded in compelling her to eat with a spoon and keep her hands out of the plate. Then Phantom threw her napkin on the floor, and after an hour's battle Annie made her pick it up and fold it. One morning Phantom would not sit down to learn words which meant nothing to her, and kicked over the table. When Annie put the table back in its place and insisted on continuing the lesson, Phantom's fist flew like lightning and knocked out two of Annie's teeth. (p. 38)

Propriate Striving

Our conception of self is the focus for our most intense feelings and our most important strivings. Recall Rosenzweig's experiments from Chapter 4. When presented with a series of puzzles to solve, college students went about the task in a matter-of-fact way; when these same puzzles were presented as a test of their "overall intelligence," however, they felt anxious, and they repressed memories of failure. The difference between the two sets of instructions can be thought of as *ego involvement,* the feeling that "I am on the line." Allport (1961) used the term *propriate striving* to refer to this extra burst of motivation we feel when our innermost sense of self (the "proprium," in Allport's terms) is engaged in whatever we are doing. We shall consider propriate striving later in this chapter.

Possessions

Strictly speaking, the self stops at the boundaries of our physical body, but in fact we readily develop special relationships to other people and things. These are possessions or *self-extensions:* in an important sense, we are what we own. For example, power-motivated people surround themselves with possessions that reflect their sense of prestige (Winter & Stewart, 1978). Anything that happens to these self-extensions is experienced as happening (at least vicariously) to the self. Thus parents sometimes view their children's successes and defeats as if they were their own. After a victory, sports fans say, "We won!" even if they don't share any characteristics with the players. Adolescent gangs and adult nationalists often fight over "their" turf. And when you return the family car with some extra dents, don't expect to escape parental anger by saying, "It's only metal!"

Self and Psychopathology

Our conception of self not only affects our striving but also is essential to our psychological well-being. First of all, effective and mature functioning is often defined in terms of the strength and condition of the self-concept, using terms such as "extension of self" and "self-objectification" (Allport, 1961, pp. 283, 290), "identity" (Erikson, 1959/1980), "acceptance of self" (Maslow, 1954), and even Freud's often-quoted remark that "where id was, there shall ego be" (1933b, XXII, p. 80).

At the same time, any problem, confusion, or breakdown in the conception of self is often a sign of pathology. For example, in schizophrenia one common feature is the loss or dramatic alteration of the boundary between self and not-self—when internal feelings and perceptions are experienced as being outside the self, and vice versa. In multiple personality disorder, the self cannot hold together as a single unity and splits or fragments into plural selves. One important sign of depression is chronically lowered self-esteem. Thus anything that jeopardizes the conception of self may have serious consequences. For Helen Keller, the Frost King crisis (see Chapter 6) aroused strong emotions and distress precisely because it threatened her sense of self: years later, she still believed that "it is certain that I cannot always distinguish my own thoughts from those I read" (1903b, p. 70).

Origins of Self in Change and Difference

For all of its importance in modern personality research, though, self in the sense of the enduring, individual essence of a person is a relatively recent word. (The *Oxford English Dictionary* gives 1674 as the first citation for this usage.) Before that time, people's sense of self was so closely tied to their group (family, tribe, village) that a separate word was not necessary. Sometime between the Renaissance and the Industrial Revolution, then, Western society became more complex and differentiated. No longer was one person like everyone else. Literature, philosophy, and social thought began to focus on individuals: in literature, the novel recorded the story of individual people; in philosophy, Descartes, Locke, and Hume examined the world from the point of view of the individual knower; and in political thought, Hobbes, Locke, and Rousseau contrasted the individual with the state. In this setting developed the word and the idea of self as they came to be used in personality psychology. This gives us a clue to how the concept of self functions in personality. When external conditions are in flux and each person is no longer like everyone else, the concept of self preserves a sense of continuity in the midst of change, and identity in the midst of diversity.

WILLIAM JAMES: SUBJECTIVE I AND EMPIRICAL ME

In psychology, the appearance of William James's landmark text, *Principles of Psychology* (1890), marked a turning away from philosophical speculation about the self toward the distinctive perspectives and research methods of psychology. In recent years, "self" terms have proliferated: in addition to "self" and "ego," psychology now has a whole series of compound words, such as self-conception, self-concept, self-esteem, and (recently) self-schema.

Let us begin with a fundamental distinction, first introduced by William James (1892/1962):

> Whatever I may be thinking of, I am always at the same time more or less aware of *myself*, of my *personal existence*. At the same time it is *I* who am aware; so that the total self of me, being as it were duplex, partly known and partly knower, partly object and partly subject, must have two aspects discriminated in it, of which for shortness we may call one the *Me* and the other the *I*. I call these "discriminated aspects," and not separate things, because the identity of the *I* with *me*, even in the very act of their discrimination, is perhaps the most ineradicable dictum of common-sense. (p. 189)

While different authors use different terms, almost everyone writing about the self after James has maintained this distinction in one form or another. For convenience, we can call it the distinction between *self as subject* and *self as object*. Table 9.1 lists some other terms commonly used to describe these two fundamental aspects of the self.

Having made this fundamental distinction, James focused his efforts on the psychological analysis of the objective self, the self-as-known. The self-as-knower (or pure ego) was much more difficult to study; in fact, James argued that in a truly scientific psychology, "the hypothesis of such a substantial principle of unity is superfluous" (1892/1962, p. 214). Perhaps, he thought, the self-as-knower consists of nothing more than a series of overlapping states of consciousness, rather than some "thing" that actually exists. With the I unknowable, James was concerned as a psychologist only with the empirical me. In this, too, he was followed by almost all later psychologists, who were anxious to avoid postulating a homunculus, or miniature "person within the person." Thus Allport concluded that "the nature of 'the knower'—the process of knowing that we know—is elusive, and is not itself an object of knowledge" (1966a, p. 25; see also 1961, pp. 128–130). In recent years, however, some psychologists have taken issue with this James-Allport position and have argued that it *is* possible to study the knower or self-as-subject (see Blasi, 1991).

TABLE 9.1 WAYS OF DESCRIBING WILLIAM JAMES'S DISTINCTION BETWEEN THE SELF AS SUBJECT AND THE SELF AS OBJECT

Self as subject	*Self as object*
I	Me
"That which at any given moment is conscious" (James)	"One of the things which it is conscious *of*" (James)
Self-as-knower	Self-as-known
Ego, pure ego	Self, ego as seen by superego
	Self-concept, self-image, including: material (physical) me social me spiritual me
	Self-esteem
	Sense of personal identity ("I am the same as I was")
	Soul, a medium for combining together the things which are known (James)

William James. "The total self of me . . . partly known and partly knower, partly object and partly subject, must have two aspects discriminated in it, of which for shortness we may call one the *ME* and the other the *I*" (1892/1962, p. 189). (Harvard University Archive)

*T*HE BODILY SELF

In the beginning, infants probably have little sense of self as separate from other people and the world. The first notion of a differentiated self arises from bodily sensations, as suggested in the following passage from Freud (1930, XXI):

> An infant at the breast does not as yet distinguish his ego from the external world as the source of sensations flowing in upon him. He gradually learns to do so, in response to various promptings. He must be very strongly impressed by the fact that some sources of excitation, which he will later recognize as his own bodily organs, can provide him with sensations at any moment, whereas other sources evade him from time to time. (pp. 66–67)

Over 200 years earlier, in 1690, the English philosopher John Locke stressed the contribution of bodily experiences to our earliest ideas of power and will: "observing in ourselves that we can at pleasure move several parts of our bodies which were at rest."[1]

Bodily Self and Psychological Self

The physical or *bodily self*, then, is the original basis for the *psychological self;* for the rest of our lives, there are complex connections between these two selves. For example, psychological disorders and problems involving the self-concept often manifest themselves as physical symptoms or psychosomatic illness. The connection also works the other way, when our bodily self affects our psychological self. Many studies suggest that satisfaction with one's body is positively related to satisfaction with self (Polivy, Herman, & Pliner, 1990; Thompson, Penner, & Altabe, 1990.) One study has even tried to zero in on which parts of the body are most critical in this respect: the results were that, for both men and women, satisfaction with teeth and the shape of the legs has the highest and most consistent relation to self-satisfaction (Fisher, 1986, pp. 127–130). We often judge ourselves by the state of our bodies: any potential physical problem or injury might set off a series of defensive psychological reactions (see Fisher, 1986, pp. 315–327). For example, the midlife crisis, now identified by Levinson (1978) as a predictable stage of adult development for middle-class American males, often announces itself with a noticeable decrease in *physical* vigor: "several small changes often bring about a major, qualitative drop in body function by the early forties" (p. 25). Perhaps this is the reason middle-aged men often write to their college alumni magazines with proud claims such as, "Skiing and a great deal of tennis help me to fight back the encroachment of middle-age stomach," or "I stay in shape for my family via a combination of weights, Nautilus, racquetball, plus occasional softball and bowling."

[1]*An Essay Concerning Human Understanding,* Chapter 7, paragraph 8.

The psychological effects of body image played an important role in the early theories of Alfred Adler (1929), one of Freud's early disciples. Any perceived problem with a body part ("organ inferiority," in Adler's terms) gives rise to a broader inferiority complex, which the person then tries to overcome through a "will to power" (later called a "striving for superiority").

Manipulating the Body to Improve the Self

Many studies suggest that people who are satisfied with their bodies, and people whose bodies are considered attractive in the sense of fitting whatever happens to be the current ideal of fashion, score higher in self-esteem and lower in depression. This is especially true for women past the age of puberty (Thompson, Penner, & Altabe, 1990; see also Polivy, Herman, & Pliner, 1990). To fit current fashions, people are willing—even driven—to do the most extraordinary things to their bodies in order to "feel good" about themselves. Concerns about weight and dieting, for example, are a staple topic of supermarket tabloids. They are also the basis of a multimillion dollar business.

Americans have always been concerned about weight, weight loss, and dieting, according to Schwartz's (1986) historical study. One early example was the nineteenth-century reformer, Sylvester Graham, who believed that gluttony and obesity led to lust, sexual excess, and degeneration. To ward off these evils, Graham developed a "restorative diet" of unleavened bran bread, rice, unadorned fruits and vegetables, and pure cold water. Some descendents of Graham's ideas are the Graham cracker you learned to love at nursery school, the corn flakes popularized by Will Kellogg, and a baked-cereal substance originally called "granula" but later renamed granola. Oberlin College, when it was founded in 1836, was originally dedicated to Grahamism. Soon, however, it "had to abandon the Graham diet in 1841 after rumors of mass starvation at the college aroused the townspeople" (see Schwartz, 1986, pp. 45, 184).

Eating disorders. For many people (especially young women), control of the body is taken so seriously that what starts out as dieting escalates to the fasting or even starvation of anorexia, or the related binge-and-purge disorder of bulimia (see Brumberg, 1988, for a historical account of these disorders). Most clinicians conclude that anorexics are trying to exercise control over life, other people, and social conditions. For a variety of reasons, such as gender role stereotypes, this control cannot be directly expressed and so has become *displaced* onto the body, especially its weight and food intake. (Recall the discussion of displacement in Chapter 4.) In support of this interpretation, Zullow (1983) found that women suffering from anorexia scored higher than a matched control group of women in power motivation and concerns for control.

Fashion and fitness. Often our concerns with body image are expressed in the ways we cover, clothe, and display it. The fashion industry is built upon people's vulnerability to the belief that the body—hence the self—is only acceptable if it is concealed and modified by whatever appliances and garments are currently decreed to be fashionable. There are also changing fashions in ideal body size and shape (Fallon, 1990). In recent years, Americans have also developed an obsession with physical fitness, treating the bodily self as a "thing" or product that can be managed and improved, perhaps in a competition with others, thus transforming recreation from its original meaning of fun and relaxation into a grim quest.

Gandhi's mind control through body control. The tendency to link body and self goes well beyond American concerns about diet. A striking example can be found in the career of Mahatma Gandhi, the nonviolent spiritual and political leader who developed fasting as a political weapon against the British colonial occupation of India. When India achieved its independence in 1946–1948, Hindu-Muslim violence and massacres threatened to undo all of his life's work. Gandhi, now in his seventies, traveled to the worst centers of rioting. At night, when he was often subject to attacks of shivering, he would ask some of his women followers to lie in bed with him, naked, to cradle him and give him warmth. In discussing this with his friends and followers, he explained that he was proving to himself his ability to resist sexual arousal, "to ascertain if even the least trace of sensual feeling had been evoked in himself or his companion" (Bose, 1953, p. 174). According to Erikson's interpretation (1969, pp. 403–406), this behavior, like fasting, was a classically Gandhian attempt to *master not only the self but also the wider social and political situation by controlling one's own body*, specifically the most basic physical drives of hunger and sexuality.

SOCIAL SELF AND THE LOOKING GLASS

While our sense of self may originate with our experience of body, social factors quickly become even more important. As I argued in Chapter 4 in connection with Freud's concept of penis envy, our body size, shape, and contours mean little as such; rather they are embroidered with meanings, evaluations, and significance by social forces. In the words of sociologist Charles Horton Cooley (1922/1964):

> It is true that when we philosophize a little about "I" and look around for a tangible object to which to attach it, we soon fix upon the material body . . . [but] in ordinary speech, it is not very common to think of the body in connection with it. . . . Ordinarily it will be found that in not more than ten cases in a hundred does "I" have reference to the body of the person speaking. It refers chiefly to opinions, purposes, desires, claims, and the like, concerning matters that involve no thought of the body. (p. 176)

Part Four of this book focuses on the general significance of society and culture for the formation of personality. Here we are concerned with the social contribution to the sense of self—to use a recent term, the self as a *social construction*. To introduce this topic, let us consider the views of two early twentieth-century American social theorists: George Herbert Mead (1863–1931), a student of William James who later taught at the University of Chicago, and Cooley (1864–1929), who was a professor at the University of Michigan. In slightly different language, each made essentially the same argument.

Generalized Other and Looking Glass

Mead observed that we develop our concept of other people by looking at what they do and listening to what they say—in short, by taking them as the *object* of our perception and judgment. He went on to argue that we develop our concept of self in the same way, by taking on the role or attitude of the other—not any particular other, but rather other people in general, the so-called generalized other. In other words, we look at ourselves—our actions, motives, and feelings—from the standpoint of the other, or as if we were someone else. Thus we become the object of our own perception and judgment (Mead, 1925/1968):

> We are in possession of selves just insofar as we can and do take the attitudes of others toward ourselves and respond to those attitudes. We approve of ourselves and condemn ourselves. We pat ourselves upon the back and in blind fury attack ourselves. We assume the generalized attitude of the group. (p. 273)

Cooley described a similar process. First we imagine how we appear to other people, then we imagine how others will judge that appearance, and finally we experience emotions such as pride or shame in reaction to that judgment. Thus our sense of self is built up from our beliefs about how other people will react to us, just as our sense of body is constructed from what the looking glass or mirror reflects back to us. (Nowadays we would probably use the computer metaphor of "feedback" to describe the reflected appraisals of other people.) Cooley's famous term for this process is the *looking-glass self* (1922/1964):

> As we see our face, figure, and dress in the glass, and are interested in them because they are ours, and pleased or otherwise with them according as they do or do not answer to what we should like them to be; so in imagination we perceive in another's mind some thought of our appearance, manners, aims, deeds, character, friends, and so on, and are variously affected by it. (p. 184)

Notice how Cooley ties together cognition and emotion: we feel emotions as the consequence of our judgments of how other people will react to us.

Cooley's image of the looking-glass or mirror self may seem particularly American, but it also occurs in Chinese thought (Cummings, 1991):

> The wise person has three mirrors: a mirror of bronze in which to see their physical appearance, a mirror of the people by which to examine inner character and

conduct, and a mirror of the past by which to learn to emulate successes and avoid the mistakes of earlier times. (p. 58)

Intellectual and Research Heirs of Cooley and Mead

The views of Mead and Cooley gave rise to a movement in social psychology and sociology called *symbolic interactionism,* which emphasized the importance of social interaction as it was expressed in shared concepts or symbols (see Gergen & Gordon, 1968). At the theoretical level, the symbolic-interactionist perspective has moved toward the analysis of how concepts such as the self are the result of *social construction.* Social constructivists are especially concerned with identifying how the process of constructing important concepts and ideas works for the benefit of powerful groups and classes in society (Shotter & Gergen, 1989), and with "deconstructing" the concepts so as to reveal those benefits.

At the empirical level, symbolic interactionism has given rise to a variety of variables expressing the way in which the concept of self arises from social interaction and reflection.

Self-monitoring. Self-monitoring (Snyder, 1987) is based on the principle that while most people's self-concepts are affected by the generalized other, this is more true of some people than others. In other words, self-monitoring is a dimension of individual difference rather than a universal human characteristic. High self-monitoring people are more likely to view themselves from the perspective of the generalized other. Therefore, they control their "presentations" of self, adapting them to particular situations as appropriate. As a result, they have a pragmatic identity. They try to appear or become whatever works in the situation of the moment. Low self-monitoring people, in contrast, do not consult the looking glass to find out who they are. They are said to have a principled identity, because they act more in accord with their inner principles (attitudes and feelings). Self-monitoring is also called expressive control.

To measure self-monitoring, Snyder has developed a questionnaire that has been widely used in research studies. Typical items include the following:

> In different situations and with different people, I often act like very different persons. (scored True)
> I would not change my opinions (or the way I do things) in order to please people or win their favor. (scored False)
> I'm not always the person I appear to be. (scored True)

People who score high on the self-monitoring scale are adept at communicating (or is it pretending?) emotions on demand. They are good at deceiving and seeing through the deceptions of others. (Not surprisingly, professional actors score high.) If asked for their opinion, they first try to check out what everybody else thinks. Their choices and judgments are determined by the situations in which they find themselves, whereas the choices and judgments of low-scorers are more a function of their attitudes.

A study by Sampson (1978) pinpoints how people's self-monitoring is related to their construction of self. Sampson gave a sample of college students a list of twenty-two identity characteristics, asking them to rate how important each characteristic was to "my sense of who I am." Students scoring low in self-monitoring rated characteristics such as the following as most important:

> My emotions and feelings
> My thoughts and ideas, the way my mind works
> The ways I cope with my fears and anxieties, with the stresses and strains
>   of living
> The ways I deal with my good and loving feelings
> My dreams and imagination

These characteristics all refer to internal states; in Sampson's terms, if you were to draw a circle around "me," most of these characteristics would definitely be inside the circle. In contrast, high self-monitoring students constructed their sense of self on the basis of external characteristics such as the following:

> Memberships that I have in various groups
> My work or job
> Things I own, my possessions
> Places where I live or where I was raised
> My race or ethnic background

People high in self-monitoring also have a more segmented or partitioned social world. That is, they have different groups of friends for different activities: for example, work or study friends, dancing friends, concert friends, and hometown friends. Keeping these different groups of friends separate from each other makes it easier for them to maintain a repertoire of different self-presentations for different people. Their romantic relationships tend to be based on partners' external appearances and involve more casual sex (Snyder, Simpson, & Gangestad, 1986). Overall, then, the friendships of high self-monitoring people are based on the principle of utility.

In contrast, low self-monitoring people tend to have a single undifferentiated group of "people I like," with whom they engage in a variety of different activities. Their romantic relationships tend to involve commitment and sex only in the context of emotional closeness. Overall, their friendships are based on the principle of emotional connection or likability (Snyder, 1987, pp. 60–70).

High and low self-monitoring people even respond differently to advertising and persuasive messages. Highs are drawn to the images of products, while lows consider more objective qualities. Thus in buying a car, highs would be swayed by glossy images and a few slick advertising phrases, while lows would carefully compare performance evaluations and frequency-of-repair records in *Consumer Reports* and go for a series of comparative test drives.

The two poles of the self-monitoring scale define two different ways in which people form, maintain, and express the sense of self. At first you might think that only the high end fits Cooley's conception of the looking-glass self. A more careful analysis might suggest, however, that the two poles reflect two different *kinds* of looking-glass self. The high pole defines a present-tense self continually changing in response to feedback from the looking glass. In contrast, the low pole defines a past-tense self, formed originally from a looking glass but then internalized and stabilized.

Self-awareness. Two related concepts, *self-awareness* and *self-focusing,* reflect various specific ways in which self-monitoring and the looking-glass self affect behavior. Carver and Scheier (1981) used a variety of techniques to increase people's self-awareness, in the Mead-Cooley sense of the generalized other, for example, by putting people in a room with a mirror or a television camera (a looking-glass self in the literal sense). The result was an intensification of whatever emotions and actions people had: anxious people became more anxious; proud people became prouder. People who ordinarily persisted now persisted still longer; those low in persistence quit even earlier. In other words, increasing people's self-awareness by making the looking-glass self more prominent tends to bring their behavior more closely into line with whatever standards are already operating. Thus if a sign says No Smoking, putting a large mirror on the wall will increase people's compliance—but only among people who already accept the standard of not smoking. Among a group of smokers, who reject the standard, adding a mirror increases their *violation* of the No Smoking standard.

In these experiments, self-awareness is experimentally manipulated; but it is also a dimension of individual difference that can be measured by a questionnaire. Persons scoring high on the self-awareness measure characteristically feel and act like people in whom self-awareness has been experimentally increased: that is, as if they were in front of a mirror or television camera.

The research on self-monitoring and self-awareness demonstrates the fundamental claim of Cooley and Mead, that social influences and taking the perspective of other people contribute to the development and expression of the self. On the other hand, this research also suggests that the "looking glass" is only one component of self. Some people have an internalized sense of self that is not so easily altered by their immediate social surroundings. The sociologist Riesman and his associates (Riesman, Glazer, & Denny, 1950) described these people as "inner-directed"—people who act as if their behavior and emotions were directed by an internal gyroscope, in contrast to other-directed types who take their cues from the people around them.

Self-awareness and the validity of personality questionnaires. The research on self-awareness has implications for how we measure personality. Asking people to describe themselves, as in the typical questionnaire or interview, presumably increases their self-awareness. This should bend their answers toward whatever internal or external standards they accept. More-over, high self-monitoring people, especially, will try to figure out the prag-matic thing to say so that they can slant their answers in that direction. Thus, arousing self-awareness, which is inevitable when you ask people about themselves, will tend to distort their answers. In contrast, people's more spontaneous speech and writing that is not in response to direct questioning should yield less pragmatic and more accurate information about their per-sonalities and sense of self. Thus the differences between indirect (or projec-tive) and direct questionnaire measures of motives, discussed in Chapter 5, may be due in part to the effects of arousing self-awareness and heightening self-monitoring.

*M*IRRORING AND THE NARCISSISTIC SELF

The image of the self-as-mirror also appears in Kohut's (1985) theory of narcis-sism. Ordinarily, when we call someone a narcissist we are being critical. We mean that the person is selfish, self-centered, and inconsiderate of others. This is also true of Freud's thinking, where narcissism refers to an immature stage of development when libidinal motives are focused on the self instead of on someone else. (In psychoanalytic terminology, narcissism is contrasted to "object choice" or "object cathexis.") For Kohut, however, narcissism is an important part of the adult self, a potentially "good" force. His theory, often called *self-psychology*, has had an important influence on modern psychoana-lytic thinking.

The Role of Narcissism in Personality Development

Kohut assumes, as does Freud, that infants originally do not differentiate between themselves, their significant parent-caretakers, and the rest of the world. All are fused together into the original and omnipotent object of love and admiration. With further cognitive development, however, this original object becomes differentiated into "self" and "other." Correspondingly, the original cathexis is also differentiated into the *narcissistic self* and object love. Rather than narcissism developing into object love, as Freud suggested, Kohut believed that both object love and narcissism continue into adulthood as sepa-rate tracks or courses of libidinal development. At the core of narcissism is what Kohut called a "grandiose fantasy"—an infantile vision of being looked at and admired (exhibitionism), while at the same time being all-powerful, favored, and an effortless conqueror (narcissistic grandeur). This grandiose fantasy is the successor to the original omnipotent fusion of self-other-world.

In their original form, of course, the grandiose fantasies of the narcissistic self are bound to encounter disappointment and disillusion, because they are wildly unrealistic. For Kohut, the critical issue for development is how this disillusionment is handled. For example, if the narcissistic self meets with

Heinz Kohut, whose self-psychology elaborated the concept of narcissism. "The most important point to be stressed about narcissism . . . [is] its independent line of development, from the primitive to the most mature, adaptive, and culturally valuable . . . an integrated, self-contained set of psychic functions" (1985, pp. 126–127).

traumatic disappointment and rejection, it becomes a repressed "narcissistic wound." Being repressed, this wound is inaccessible to any later modifications by reality during development; hence it is likely to emerge in adult life as one or more *narcissistic disorders*. A typical narcissistic disorder might involve periods of wild, unrealistic grandiosity (typically in response to some small cue of success), alternating with hopeless feelings of mortification and despair. The result is similar to manic depression (bipolar affective disorder). According to Kohut, what has happened is that the most repressed and primitive form of the grandiose fantasy has broken through to consciousness, is quickly contradicted and humiliated by reality, and so turns to mortification and self-hatred. These two primitive emotions of grandiosity and despair rage with each other for possession of the self. In the process, the struggle can weaken the unifying powers of the ego and break down the cohesion of the self.

Another such disorder is *narcissistic rage*. Some ordinary, everyday event has aroused memories of the early narcissistic wound. What follows is not at all like ordinary aggressive behavior (Kohut, 1985), but rather:

> The need for revenge, for righting a wrong, for undoing a hurt by whatever means, and a deeply anchored, unrelenting compulsion in the pursuit of all these aims, which gives no rest to those who have suffered a narcissistic injury—these are the characteristic features of narcissistic rage in all its forms and which set it apart from other kinds of aggression. . . . In its typical form there is utter disregard for reasonable limitations and a boundless wish to redress an injury and to obtain revenge. (pp. 143, 145)

As an alternative to the development of a narcissistic wound, Kohut believed that loving parental support could mute or prevent these effects. The conflict between reality and the narcissistic self is inevitable, but if the self were gradually and lovingly let down instead of being completely frustrated, then it could be harnessed and incorporated into a healthy adult personality. Grandiosity and mortification would be "tamed" into appropriate and useful emotional reactions to success and failure. (The facilitating attributional pattern discussed in Chapter 8 is an example of such tamed narcissistic emotions.) A narrow concern with the self could be transmuted into a "higher" narcissism involving creativity, humor, and wisdom. In its most cosmic form, healthy narcissism enables us to endure and even in some ways to prevail against the inevitabilities of human limits that end in death.

Kohut's technical term for the kind of loving support that creates healthy narcissism is *mirroring*. It means giving the child attention and approval; more broadly, it means acknowledging the child's existence and presence by "reflecting" the child's own inner sense of worthiness back to the child, without judgment or criticism. Notice the difference between the ways in which Cooley and Kohut use the mirror as a symbol for the self. For Cooley, we gaze at the looking glass in order to gain distance and objectivity, to see ourselves as others see us. For Kohut, the mirror reflects back to us our own private sense of perfection. To illustrate the difference, consider the Queen in the story of "Snow White," looking into the mirror and asking the question:

Mirror, mirror on the wall,
Who's the fairest of them all?

Cooley's looking-glass would reflect back the opinions of other people—probably replying that Snow White was the fairest. Kohut's mirroring, however, would give the answer the fairy-tale Queen insisted upon:

You, O Queen!

Research Studies of Narcissism

While narcissism has always been an important topic in psychoanalytic theory, personality psychologists paid relatively little attention to it until the "me" decades of the 1970s and 1980s, when social analysts and cultural critics focused on the role of narcissism in American society (Lasch, 1979). New measures of narcissism, through self-report questionnaires (Emmons, 1987) and observers' ratings (Wink, 1992), have led to an outpouring of research studies. For example, Raskin and Hall (1979) drew upon the psychiatric diagnostic criteria for narcissistic personality disorder to construct the Narcissistic Personality Inventory (NPI), in which people choose among fifty-four pairs of items. Themes of grandiosity, self-display, and entitlement are clearly illustrated in the following examples of the narcissistic choices:

I really like to be the center of attention.
I like to look at my body.

I can make anybody believe anything.

I insist upon getting the respect that is due me.

Narcissism and performance. Confirming the portrait of narcissism suggested by Kohut's theory, Raskin, Novacek, and Hogan (1991) showed that scores on the NPI were related to an interpersonal style of grandiosity, hostility, and dominance. In everyday language, narcissists are people who think and talk mostly about themselves and have an inflated opinion of themselves. The first element was confirmed by Raskin and Shaw (1988). They asked forty-eight women and men college students to talk for five minutes about any topic and recorded what they said. Students' narcissism scores were positively correlated ($r = .27$, $p < .05$) with how often they used first-person singular pronouns (I, me, my, mine, and myself) and negatively correlated ($r = -.31$, $p < .01$) with their use of first-person plural pronouns (we, us, our, ours, and ourselves).

John and Robins (1994) demonstrated that narcissists have an inflated opinion of themselves. They recruited business school students to participate in a six-person group discussion about a management problem. Afterward, all participants ranked themselves and the five other participants on the "extent to which each of them had contributed to the overall effectiveness of the group" (p. 210). Those students scoring high on several measures of narcissism tended to rank themselves higher in contribution than they were ranked by their peer-participants, and also higher than they were ranked by a group of trained staff observers. In a follow-up to this study (though it actually appeared earlier than the study itself), Robins and John (1993) brought the participants back six weeks later, had them view a videotape of their group's discussion, and asked them to rerank their performance. Most people are a little embarrassed when they watch themselves on videotape, so it is not surprising that most of the participants lowered their self-rankings after viewing the videotape. The narcissists, however, actually ranked themselves *higher* than before! For them, the experience of watching themselves was enjoyable and led to even greater self-enhancement. Another study of business school students, by John, Robins, and O'Reilly (1994), suggests that the self-enhancing tendencies of the narcissists may actually interfere with performance. They found that narcissism scores at the time of assessment predicted relatively slower job advancement and lower earnings five years later.

Two kinds of narcissism. Several studies using the different questionnaire and observer measures of narcissism give support to Kohut's argument that there is a good or healthy kind of narcissism as well as the more familiar bad or unhealthy kind. Emmons (1987), for example, showed that the items on the NPI group themselves into four clusters: leadership and authority, self-admiration and self-absorption, superiority and arrogance, and exploitativeness-entitlement.[2] The latter three clusters certainly sound unpleasant or even pathological, but the first cluster is consistent with the creativity and wisdom of Kohut's healthy narcissism.

---

[2]Emmons used the statistical technique of factor analysis, which is described in Chapter 13.

Wink (1992) divided observer measures of narcissism into components of willfulness, hypersensitivity, and autonomy. In a longitudinal study of college-educated women, he found that women who (as college students) had scored high on the first two components showed deterioration in psychological health as they entered middle age. In contrast, women who had scored high in autonomy showed gains in such "healthy" and adaptive qualities as dominance, independence, and psychological-mindedness. Wink's findings about the childhood antecedents of the three components of narcissism are also consistent with Kohut's theory. Women scoring high in willfulness and hypersensitivity, the two "unhealthy" components, described their parents as cold and distant, and their mothers especially as critical. Women who scored high in autonomy, in contrast, reported participation in lots of imaginative or artistic activities.

To summarize and integrate the Emmons and Wink findings: cold and distant parents who simply reject their children's narcissistic selves may produce children who grow up as willful, hypersensitive, entitled, self-absorbed, and exploitative adult narcissists. In contrast, children who are encouraged by loving parents to translate their grandiose fantasies into imaginative and artistic play will tend to grow up with the healthy narcissism of autonomous, wise, and authoritative leaders.

SELF-CONCEPT

So far we have used the term "sense of self" as a general term to describe cognitive structures that develop out of the interaction of body experience and the reflections of the social mirror. The rest of this chapter surveys some of the more precise ways in which personality psychologists have described and studied the different senses of self. We will focus on three variables: (1) *self-concept*, which includes newer terms such as "self-schema" and "self-space"; (2) *self-esteem*, or the evaluation of the self-concept; and (3) *identity*, or the extent to which the self-concept successfully bridges the inner (body) self and the adult social self.

By whatever name we give it, our self-concept is our internal representation or picture of ourself—in William James's words, our "empirical self" (see Table 9.1). Personality psychologists have developed many different ways to describe and measure this internal picture. They may ask people to "tell me about yourself" (McGuire & Padawer-Singer, 1976). They may give an open-ended questionnaire with the phrase "Who am I?" at the top, followed by a series of blank lines (Gordon, 1968; Kuhn & McPartland, 1954). They may ask people to pick, from a list of adjectives, those words which most accurately describe themselves (Markus, 1977). The Adjective Check List (Gough & Heilbrun, 1965) is a widely used formal version of this last procedure. Finally, they might give people a pile of cards, each with a statement or phrase, and tell them to sort the statements into a series of piles ranging from "most descriptive" to "least descriptive" of themselves. This procedure is called a Q-sort (see Block, 1978) and can be done by the person being described, by peers or friends of that person, or by trained and expert observers.

Content and Development of the Self-Concept

We can describe ourselves in many ways, along many dimensions. To judge from the work of personality psychologists, the self-concept consists mostly of evaluation—whether we feel good or bad about ourselves. For example, over 90 percent of the thousand-plus self-concept studies reviewed by Wylie (1974–1979) involve *self-esteem*. Yet self-esteem and evaluation make up only a small part of the spontaneous self-descriptions obtained in a study of sixth-grade children (McGuire & Padawer-Singer, 1976). In this study, fewer than 10 percent of all self-concept elements spontaneously mentioned by the children involved evaluation of any kind, and less than one-third of the total sample used even one evaluative element. The same was true of the high school and college students studied by Gordon (1968). Table 9.2 brings together some results of these two studies, to illustrate the contents of people's self-concepts and how they change over time. For each age group, the table shows the percent giving at least one response in each of several categories.

TABLE 9.2 MAJOR DIMENSIONS OF SPONTANEOUS SELF-DESCRIPTION USED BY THREE SAMPLES OF STUDENTS

Category definitions, as used by:		*Percent giving one or more responses for category, among students in:*		
McGuire & Padawer-Singer (1976)	*Gordon (1968)*	*Sixth grade*	*High school*	*College*
Categories not closely related to age:				
Name	Name	19	17	30
Age	Age	25	82	60
Hobbies, amusements	Other activities	48	27	45
Family	Kinship role	38	17	43
School	Student role	71	80	82
Categories decreasing with age:				
Pets	Possessions	22	5	10
Categories increasing with age:				
Likes and dislikes	Likes, judgments, tastes	52	27	82
—	Interpersonal style	0	59	63
—	Psychic style ("how I typically think and feel")	0	52	82
Moral evaluation	Moral worth	20	22	31
Intellectual evaluation	Competence	10	36	40

SOURCE: Adapted from McGuire and Padawer-Singer (1976), for sixth-graders, and from Gordon (1968), for high-school and college students.

Comparing sixth-graders and college students, we see that activities, family role, and student role are aspects of self-concept that remain fairly important over time. Mention of possessions, in contrast, goes down over time. Several categories go up with age. Preferences and judgments, for example, increase sharply to become, along with mention of the student role, the *single most widely used category of self-description.* Close behind are mentions of interpersonal or psychic style, categories not used at all by sixth-graders. Finally, mentions of competence and moral worth, which may involve self-esteem, do go up over time, but even among college students these categories are mentioned by only about one-third of the sample.[3]

Summarizing these two studies, we can say that our self-concepts are originally based on *what we do*—our activities and roles; but that as we grow up they broaden out to include much more *what we are*—our styles and preferences. Using the terms of William James (see Table 9.1), we conclude that as we get older, the physical self diminishes slightly, the social self is constant, and the spiritual (or psychological) self develops markedly.

Distinctiveness and the Self-Concept

Using the "tell me about yourself" procedure described above, McGuire and his colleagues studied how the content of the self-concept differs among different groups. From this research they have developed the *principle of distinctiveness:* our self-concept is likely to include whatever is distinctive or unusual about ourself, as compared to our reference group (that is, the group of people around us with whom we compare ourselves). Thus tall or short people are more likely than average-height people to mention height in their self-concepts, left-handed people (about 12 percent of the population) are more likely to include handedness, those in an ethnic minority more likely to refer to ethnicity, and so on.

Using the principle of distinctiveness, we can understand how the self-concept can change from situation to situation and over time. For example, I am a U.S. citizen. When I am at home in the United States, I am surrounded by other Americans. Since my citizenship is not distinctive, it is not a salient or important part of my self-concept. Put me down in Paris or a village in India, however, and my American citizenship is suddenly distinctive. It becomes a more salient part of my self-concept.

According to the principle of distinctiveness, race should be less salient as a component of the self-concept for African American students attending historically black colleges than for African American students attending predomi-

[3]In comparing the responses of the sixth-graders and the older students, keep in mind a few methodological details. All groups were given a blank paper with the heading "Tell me about yourself" (sixth-graders) or "Who am I?" (high school and college students), and then a series of numbered lines. The sixth-graders averaged about eleven responses; the older students about sixteen. Conceivably these slight differences, as well as differences in the overall testing situation and the precise definition of categories, could have created some spurious differences between the groups.

nantly white colleges. Now *if* race involves painful experiences of racial oppression and discrimination, then reducing the salience of race should improve students' self-concepts and morale. This principle seems to explain the results of a study by Fleming (1984), who found that African American students attending historically black colleges tended to have better self-concepts and attain higher levels of cognitive and social-emotional growth than African American students attending predominantly white colleges. The same considerations could explain the role of gender in the self-concept of women at women's versus coeducational schools and colleges, since Lee and her colleagues (Lee & Bryk, 1986; Lee & Marks, 1990) have observed similar beneficial effects, for women, of single-sex schools.

The distinctiveness principle suggests a slight reformulation of the conclusion drawn from Table 9.2: the mature self-concept is made up of *what we are, on the basis of style and preferences, that makes us different from other people around us.*

ORGANIZATION OF THE SELF-CONCEPT

Models of Self-Organization

Somehow the different elements of the self concept are arranged into a coherent and unified whole. Almost every personality theorist with a concept of self or ego has emphasized its function of giving unity to the diverse aspects of personality. Freud, for example, included among the most important characteristics of the ego "a tendency to synthesis in its contents, to a combination and unification in its mental processes which are totally lacking in the id" (1933b, XXII, p. 76). Murray described the "unity thema" as "the most fundamental and characteristic determinant of a personality" (1938, pp. 604–605). Beyond such in-principle acknowledgments, however, few theorists have much to say about the actual nature and details of self-concept organization.

Figure 9.1 illustrates three ways in which the self-concept might be organized, using "Jane" and her honors thesis (Chapter 2) as an example. First, Markus and Sentis (1982) suggest that different elements of the self-concept are organized like links in a chain, where each link is a past experience or personal characteristic, as shown in diagram *A* at the top of Figure 9.1. In this particular self-concept, "self" consists of linked concepts such as "thesis," "college," and "friends," with looser links to "research" and "party." Other concepts, such as "television," are not part of the self at all. Markus and Sentis refer to the entire chain of self-linked elements as the "self-schema."

Many theorists have suggested that the self-concept is organized as a hierarchy (Kihlstrom & Cantor, 1984). Thus diagram *B* in the middle of Figure 9.1 shows how the same elements of diagram *A*, plus a few others, might be organized hierarchically. Each of the lowest-level elements represents the self in a different specific context. As we move up the hierarchy, we find increasingly broad and general representations of the self. Finally, at the top we reach the broadest and most general representation of the self, a construction that integrates all of the subordinate elements.

A. Jane's self-concept as links in a chain of memory

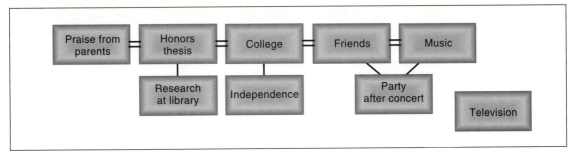

B. Jane's self-concept as a hierarchy

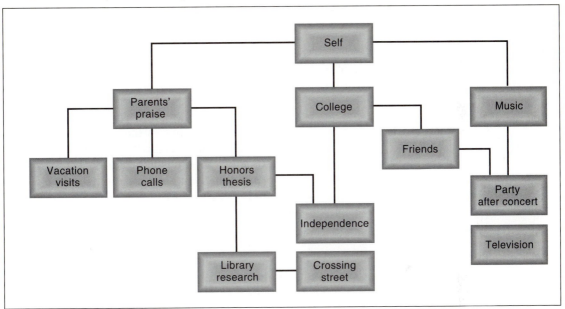

C. Jane's self-concept as proprium and periphery

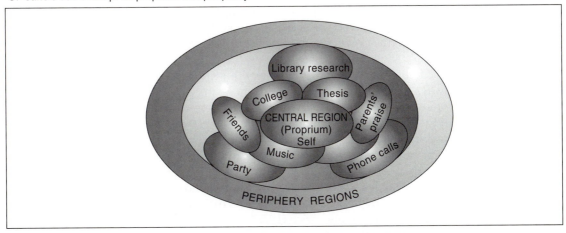

Note: Diagram *A* is based on principles discussed by Markus and Sentis (1982).
Diagram *B* is based on principles discussed by Kihlstrom and Cantor (1984). Diagram *C*
is adapted from Allport (1966, p. 141).
FIGURE 9.1
Three models for the organization of the self concept.

The hierarchical model suggests that some elements of the self-concept are more important than others. In the third model, shown in diagram *C* at the bottom of Figure 9.1, the self-concept is represented as a region or space, with the most important elements at the center (Allport, 1961). Allport used the word "proprium" to stand for this center region, as pointed out at the beginning of this chapter. (*Proprium* is a Latin-based word meaning "essential nature" or "selfhood.") Whatever is a part of (or touches) our proprium is thus of great importance and interest to us. "Propriate striving" refers to those actions we take to protect, maintain, express, or enhance the proprium or central region of the self-space.

The Nature of Self-Concept Organization

Organization and reorganization. However we choose to represent it in a model, the organization of the self-concept is often quite delicate. Changing just one element may bring about a major change in the whole configuration (see Rogers, 1959, p. 201). For example, most of us can recall experiences when some seemingly minor thing—a small accomplishment, a chance comment (praise or criticism) by someone else, or even a beautiful sunny day—seemed to transform our whole sense of self. If such transformations are possible, then the self-concept may be organized along the lines of gestalt principles of perception, in which a small change may lead to a major reorganization of what is perceived.

This reorganization process can be demonstrated with a classic gestalt psychology example shown in Figure 9.2 (see Boring, 1930, and Leeper, 1935). Version *A* is ambiguous: Is it a young woman turning away or an old woman staring to the left? If you look at *A* long enough, you will probably experience it as changing back and forth between the two. In version *B,* however, some small alternations fix the figure as a young woman. In contrast, different minor alterations in version *C* fix the figure as the older woman. In an analogous way, Rogers suggests that a few small changes can bring about massive changes in the organization of the self-concept.

Many selves. No matter how the self-concept is organized, it may not always be possible to fit every element into a single model. Extreme cases, where it seems as though two or more different selves are inhabiting the same body, are labeled multiple personality. Such cases usually arise from some powerful and traumatic early experience (for example, sexual abuse) that could not be acknowledged or assimilated into the ordinary self-concept. Instead, it became the nucleus of a separate, cutoff cluster of self-experiences. We all know less extreme cases of people whose self-concept seems to swing back and forth between two or more different organizations. For example, speechwriter Raymond Price (1977) spoke of Richard Nixon's "light side" and "dark side," while William Safire, another Nixon speechwriter, described

FIGURE 9.2
How minor changes of detail can have major effects on perceptual organization.

Nixon's personality as "layers of a cake" (1975). During most of Nixon's political career, journalists speculated about a "new Nixon" and sought to discover "the real Nixon." (As a commentary on this search, Safire once wrote, "to the real Nixon, the real Nixon is not the real Nixon"; 1975, p. 600.)

In fact, for most people the self-concept varies as a function of many factors, including the situations in which we find ourselves—just as a polished diamond has different facets that sparkle in different ways in different sources and kinds of light. We would do well, therefore, to think of the self-concept not as a single unity, but rather as a *bundle of self-concepts,* rearranged according to the situation and subject to sudden and dramatic change. Often these différent selves, and the relations among them, have powerful motivating properties, as we shall discuss in Chapter 10.

SELF-ESTEEM

To many personality psychologists, the most important part of the self-concept is evaluation (good-bad), or *self-esteem.* As you might expect, people's self-esteem is highly associated with their happiness and satisfaction with life. Low self-esteem, in contrast, is an important symptom of depression (see Rosenberg, 1979, p. 55; Beck, 1967). Many theorists have argued that the drive to maintain or enhance self-esteem is one of the most important human motives.

Self-esteem is also a prominent theme in the wider culture. The phrase "feel good about yourself" is a cliché of pop psychology. Personal-development magazines at the supermarket checkout lines are filled with the latest tips and techniques for raising self-esteem. And in California, the state legislature

Doonesbury/ Commentary by GARRY TRUDEAU

FIGURE 9.3
"Doonesbury" view of the California Task Force on Self-Esteem and Personal and
Social Responsibility. (*Doonesbury* © 1987 G.B. Trudeau. Reprinted with permission of
UNIVERSAL PRESS SYNDICATE. All rights reserved.)

even got into the business of promoting self-esteem. In 1986, Assemblyman
John Vasconcellos secured passage of legislation establishing the "California
Task Force to Promote Self-Esteem and Personal and Social Responsibility,"
which was to "make legislative findings and declarations as to the causal
relationship between a sense of low self-esteem and many of the state's social
problems"—problems such as alcohol and drug abuse, chronic criminal
behavior, welfare dependency, teenage pregnancy, and failure to learn in
school.[4] Cartoonist Garry Trudeau promptly satirized the commission in
Doonesbury, as shown in Figure 9.3.

The task force's definition of self-esteem shows traces of the heavy hand of
politics: "appreciating my own worth and importance and having the character to be accountable for myself and to act responsibly toward others" (California Task Force, 1990, p. 18; several members' dissents from this definition are
included on pp. 139–143). Unfortunately, a review of self-esteem research commissioned by the task force failed to support the central assumption of the
whole enterprise (Smelser, 1989):

[4]California Assembly Bill No. 3659, filed with the Secretary of State September 24, 1986, p. 1.

The associations between self-esteem and its expected consequences are mixed, insignificant, or absent. This nonrelationship holds between self-esteem and teenage pregnancy, self-esteem and child abuse, self-esteem and most cases of alcohol and drug abuse. (p. 15)

Still, in its final report the task force pressed on to the conclusion with which it began, nestled among inspirational quotations, pictures, and lists of self-help books (California Task Force, 1990):

Self-esteem . . . empowers us to live responsibly and that inoculates us against the lures of crime, violence, substance abuse, teen pregnancy, child abuse, chronic welfare dependency, and educational failure. The lack of self-esteem is central to most personal and social ills plaguing our state and nation. (p. 4)

For all of its easily satirized New Age trendiness, self-esteem does remain a powerful private experience. Psychologists have developed many different scales and other procedures to measure self-esteem, both as a single, overall dimension and also as a series of more specific components (see Robinson, Shaver, & Wrightsman, 1991, chap. 4; and Wylie, 1974–1979, for detailed reviews of the different measures).

Rosenberg's Four Principles of Self-Esteem

Summarizing several large-scale studies, Rosenberg (1979, chap. 2) suggests four broad principles that determine self-esteem: (1) *reflected appraisals*—what we think of ourselves is a reflection of what others think of us; (2) *social comparisons*—we evaluate ourselves by comparing ourself to other people; and (3) *self-attributions* about our ability, based on observing our behavior. (4) Finally, cross-cutting these first three principles is the concept *psychological centrality*, which is similar to Allport's concept of proprium, discussed above. By this principle, we only consider appraisals reflected from people whose opinion we care about, we only compare ourselves to certain other people (our "reference group"), and we only care about the outcomes of tasks that are important or central to us. In other words, we *select* the particular domains in which we are willing to risk our self-esteem. As William James put it (1890):

I, who for the time have staked my all on being a psychologist, am mortified if others know much more psychology than I. But I am contented to wallow in the grossest ignorance of Greek. My deficiencies there give me no sense of personal humiliation at all. (vol. 1, p. 310)

The principle of psychological centrality further suggests that what is important is not the outcome itself, but rather the outcome in relation to our expectations. To quote James again:

So our self-feeling [self-esteem] . . . is determined by the ratio of our actualities to our supposed potentialities; a fraction of which our pretensions are the denominator and the numerator of our success: thus, Self-esteem = Success/Pretensions. Such a fraction may be increased as well by diminishing the denominator as by increasing the numerator. To give up pretensions is as blessed a relief as to get them gratified. (vol. 1, pp. 310–311)

Empirical Studies of Self-Esteem

In addition to reviewing the literature, Rosenberg also surveyed self-esteem among almost 2,000 Baltimore school children. Some typical results, shown in Table 9.3, illustrate the joint effects of the principles of reflected appraisal and psychological centrality.

Influence of specific others. Consider your mother: what she thinks of you should affect your self-esteem. And indeed, as shown in the left-hand column of the top row of Table 9.3, this is true. Among children who say that their mother's opinion is important to them, there is a significant correlation between their perception of how their mother evaluates them and their own self-esteem. Now most children (over 95 percent in this sample) do care about their mother's opinion. But among those who do *not*, there is no relationship between mother's perceived evaluation and child's self-esteem. Even in the case of mothers, then, the influence of reflected appraisal (that is, mother's opinion) on self-esteem only holds among people for whom "mother" is a psychologically central person. As shown in the table, this is also true for fathers and siblings. The effects are significant but not very strong, probably because

TABLE 9.3 RELATIONSHIP BETWEEN CHILDREN'S SELF-ESTEEM AND OTHERS' PERCEIVED EVALUATION

Significant other person	Dependence[†] of own self-esteem on the perceived evaluation by other	
	Children who care what this other person thinks of them	Children who do not care what this other person thinks of them
Family members		
Mother	.18* (N = 1,722)	−.05 (N = 89)
Father	.14* (N = 1,410)	−.02 (N = 118)
Siblings	.17* (N = 1,358)	.06 (N = 232)
People outside of the family		
Teacher	.26* (N = 1,606)	.20* (N = 179)
Other kids in class	.22* (N = 1,274)	.14* (N = 513)

* $p < .05$

[†]Relationship estimated by gamma statistic, which is a measure of relationship among categories, similar in meaning to a correlation coefficient.

SOURCE: Adapted from Rosenberg (1979).

the reflected appraisal of any specific person (no matter how central they are) is only one influence on self-esteem.

The evaluations of teachers and school peers, however, affect self-esteem even if they are not central to the child. That is, the values of *gamma* (a measure of correlation) in the right-hand column are still significant, even though they are smaller than those in the left-hand column. Perhaps other school factors such as comparison groups or one's own performance override psychological centrality. Or perhaps children who say they don't care what their teacher or school classmates think of them are kidding themselves.

Performance outcomes. How well we do (for example, being a good student, being elected to office in an organization, being likable, honest, or hardworking) can affect our self-esteem, but *only if we value that performance.* Usually we value the things at which we excel, which is a convenient way to maintain and enhance self-esteem.

Social surroundings. Any kind of difference or dissonance between ourselves and our school or neighborhood surroundings tends to lower self-esteem. Whatever our religion, race, social class, or even grade-point average, if it is different from those around us, we feel worse about ourselves. The reason is that people in our immediate surroundings are almost always an important comparison group, so any difference easily becomes a focus for teasing and negative evaluations by others. (This principle may also explain Fleming's [1984] findings about African American students at historically black colleges versus predominantly white colleges, or Lee and Bryk's [1986] findings about girls in single-sex versus coeducational schools.)

Social stratification. Social class is an important determinant of self-esteem, but this is more true for adults than for children (Rosenberg & Pearlin, 1978). This is because children's groups are relatively homogeneous in terms of class, whereas adults live in a more heterogeneous world where they constantly make comparisons with people from different classes. It is interesting that the most important aspect of social class for self-esteem is whether a person has *opportunities for self-direction on the job.* In other words, if you can make your own decisions and exercise your own judgment about how to do what you do, and if you are not closely supervised, then the other aspects of social class (level of education, occupational prestige, and income) are likely to have very little effect on your self-esteem.

Attributional style. The facilitating attributional style (stable internal attributions for success and unstable or external attributions for failure; see Chapter 8) is related to high self-esteem. In other words, we select both the performances and the attributions that support our self-esteem. The relationship between attributions and self-esteem is probably reciprocal: people with high self-esteem tend to make facilitating attributions; but simply making such attributions can also raise self-esteem.

Race and ethnicity. Now for some surprising results. Obviously members of oppressed minority groups should feel low self-esteem, right? Wrong. Despite the widespread acceptance of the view that self-esteem is lower among disadvantaged groups, Rosenberg found little evidence of lowered levels of self-esteem among African Americans, Latinos/as, Jews, Native Americans, or any other minority group that has been subjected to discrimination and negative evaluation by the dominant culture. In a comprehensive review of the literature, Crocker and Major (1989) found essentially the same results for any stigmatized group.

How can this be? Recall the principle of psychological centrality, which steers us toward particular domains of performance and selects particular comparison groups and other-appraisals for reflection back to us. According to this principle, if I can't feel good about myself in a particular situation, I may attribute the negative reflection or feedback to prejudice. Or I may "disidentify"; that is, I will withdraw or reduce my effort in that situation. In other words, people avoid buying into an activity, an institution, a social system, or even a culture if it jeopardizes their self-esteem. Hare (1977) documented how African American children maintain self-esteem in the face of academic difficulties by deemphasizing school achievement and shifting to peer rela-

Claude Steele, a social psychologist who has studied how people maintain self-esteem. "Doing well in school requires a belief that school achievement can be a promising basis of self-esteem. . . . Tragically . . . black Americans are still haunted by a specter [of devaluation] that threatens this belief and the identification that derives from it. . . ." (1992, p. 72). (Courtesy Claude Steele)

tions as the basis of self-esteem. Steele (1992) described this general phenomenon as it applied to one minority student whom he mentored:

> She can sense that in [college] her skin color places her under suspicion of inferiority . . . a judgment that can feel as close at hand as a mispronounced word or an ungrammatical sentence. In reaction, usually to some modest setback, she withdraws, hiding her troubles from instructors, counselors, even other students. . . . She *disidentifies* with achievement; she changes her self-conception, her outlook and values, so that achievement is no longer so important to her self-esteem. (p. 74)

Yet there are limits and costs to disidentification, as Crocker and Major (1989) suggest. If the activity or institution that lowers self-esteem is viewed as essential to a valued long-term goal, or if it is inextricably linked with other activities and institutions that are sources of positive self-esteem or are otherwise valued, then disidentification may not be easy, or even possible. Sometimes one cannot bail out.

Measuring Self-Esteem at a Distance

Hermann (1983) measured self-esteem or self-confidence at a distance in speeches and interviews by examining the percent of all references to self (I, me, my, and myself) in which the self is seen as the instigator of activity, a figure of authority, or the recipient of positive feedback from others. With this measure, she found that President Reagan actually scored *low* in comparison to other world leaders, and that his self-confidence declined significantly after being elected president in 1980. Perhaps this self-effacing style contributed to Reagan's unthreatening image of geniality that helped him evade criticism—what political analysts called Reagan's "Teflon presidency."

HELEN KELLER'S SELF-CONCEPT AND SELF-ESTEEM

To illustrate Helen Keller's self-concept, Table 9.4 draws together a few sentences from her 1894 "My Story" (written when she was a little older than McGuire and Padawer-Singer's [1976] sixth-graders) and some self-descriptions from her 1903 autobiography (written when she was a little older than the college students in Gordon's [1968] study). Several self-related concepts from this chapter are indicated by the headings in the left-hand column of the table.

In both of her autobiographical accounts, Helen receives positive mirroring: first by a loving God and a tender mother, and later through the sympathy and loving touch of Annie Sullivan. With this patient and loving support from significant caretakers, Helen's early narcissism ("always had my way") developed and matured into adult creativity and wisdom.

Notice the change in the contents of Keller's self-concept: from family and activity at age 13 to psychological states and interpersonal style at age 21,

TABLE 9.4 HELEN KELLER'S SELF-CONCEPT

Category	Example from Keller's autobiographical writings
	At the age of 12 (from Keller, 1894)
Age	*I was born twelve years ago,* one bright June morning, in Tuscumbia, a pleasant little town in the northern part of Alabama. The beginning of my life was very simple, and very much like the beginning of every other little life; for I could see and hear when I first came into this beautiful world. But *I did*
Activity	*not notice anything* in my new home for several days.
Family	*Content in my mother's tender arms* I lay, and smiled as if my
Mirroring	little heart were filled with sweetest memories of the world I just had left.
Mirroring	I like to think I lived with God in the beautiful Somewhere before I came here, and that is why I always knew *God loved me,* even when I had forgotten His name. (p. 3)
Activity	*I am spending the winter at my home* in the lovely south, the land of sunshine and flowers, surrounded by all that makes life
Family	sweet and natural; *loving parents, a precious baby brother, a tender little sister* and the dearest teacher in the world. (p. 4)
	At the age of 21 (from Keller, 1903b)
Psychic and interpersonal style	I was strong, active, *indifferent to consequences. I knew my own mind well enough* and *always had my own way,* even if I had to fight tooth and nail for it. (p. 11)
Looking-glass, Psychic style	I felt that there were *invisible lines stretched between my spirit and the spirits of others.* (p. 31)
Mirroring	I cannot explain the *peculiar sympathy Miss Sullivan has with my pleasures and desires.* . . . At the beginning I was only a little mass of possibilities. It was my teacher who unfolded and developed them. *When she came, everything about me*
Mirroring	*breathed of love* and joy and was full of meaning. . . . My teacher
Mirroring	is so near to me that *I scarcely think of myself apart from her.* How much of my delight in all beautiful things is innate, and how much is due to her influence, I can never tell. I feel that her being is inseparable from my own, and that the footsteps of my life are in hers. All the best of me belongs to
Mirroring	her —*there is not a talent, or an inspiration or a joy in me that has not been awakened by her loving touch.* (pp. 34, 38–39, 40)
Generalized other	So I try to *make the light in others' eyes my sun,* the music in others' ears my symphony, the smile on others' lips my happiness. (p. 131)

which is consistent with the self-concept developmental studies of Gordon (1968) and McGuire and Padawer-Singer (1976).

Despite her obvious handicaps, Helen Keller managed to preserve a very high level of self-esteem that reflected several of the principles of self-esteem maintenance discussed above:

> Is it not true, then, that my life with all its limitations touches at many points the life of the World Beautiful? Everything has its wonders, even darkness and silence, and I learn, whatever state I may be in, therein to be content.
>
> Sometimes, it is true, a sense of isolation enfolds me like a cold mist as I sit alone and wait at life's shut gate. Beyond there is light, and music, and sweet companionship; but I may not enter. . . . Then comes hope with a smile and whispers, "There is joy in self-forgetfulness." So I try to make the light in others' eyes my sun, the music in others' ears my symphony, the smile on others' lips my happiness. (pp. 130–131)

*I*DENTITY: THE PSYCHOSOCIAL SELF

Our sense of self begins with awareness of our bodily self, to which are added the reflections and mirrorings of society. Most of the time, these two sources are consistent and in balance, but the equilibrium becomes precarious when major life transitions change either source of self. For example, during adolescence the bodily self changes dramatically as physical growth speeds up and hormonal changes radically alter the internal body environment. At the same time, the reflected social self is altered, as adolescents move out into wider circles from their familiar family homes—greater involvement in school activities, perhaps summer camps, and finally off to college and/or work and a wholly separate life. During adolescence and young adulthood, then, people are likely to experience confusions, crises, and changes in their self-concepts. (Retirement and the physical infirmities of old age probably present a similar challenge, but by that time people have learned how to master such crises.)

Erikson (1950/1963, chap. 8; 1959/1980) introduced the concepts of *identity* and *identity crisis* to describe what happens to the self-concept during such periods of change. For Erikson, the stage of identity development (typically during adolescence) is one of eight stages of personality development. At each stage, inner feelings, impulses, and wishes have to be brought into alignment with outer social expectations and influences. Because of his emphasis on this interaction of psychological and social forces, Erikson is called a *psychosocial* personality theorist. Erikson uses the term "identity" almost in its mathematical sense of a match or congruence between the two elements of bodily and social selves (1959/1980):

> The emerging ego identity, then, bridges the early childhood stages, when the body and the parent images were given their specific meanings, and the later stages, when a variety of social roles becomes available and increasingly coercive. (p. 96)

If the body and social selves are congruent or *identical,* Erikson suggested, then we have a stable *ego identity;* if not, then we will experience an *identity crisis.* For example, on the social side, we may be confused about the seemingly limitless number of roles; on the bodily side, we may experience confused feelings about sexuality or sexual identity associated with hormonal changes and altered body awareness. Erikson illustrated the feelings of identity diffusion by quoting the character Biff in Arthur Miller's play, *Death of a Salesman:* "I just can't take hold, Mom, I can't take hold of some kind of a life" (Erikson, 1959/1980, p. 97).

Themes of Identity Formation

How do we go about forging an identity that unifies our inner feelings with our outer social roles? Drawing on Erikson's scattered writings about identity formation, Stewart, Franz, and Layton (1988) developed a systematic measure of identity concerns and applied it to Vera Brittain (1893–1970), a prominent British feminist and pacifist writer. For identity, the key question is "Who am I?" People's earliest answers involve awareness of personal characteristics or *traits:* for example, "I am curious and perhaps lazy." Then come *tastes and preferences:* "I like music, prefer Bach to Stravinsky, and enjoy traveling." As preferences become abstract and codified, we speak of *values:* "I value peace and freedom." Many preferences and values are acquired from admired other people, as *identifications* or even *idealizations.* Looking to the future, I want to play a meaningful part in society, which usually means having an *occupational role.* In looking back over my earlier years, I usually feel a sense of *sameness and continuity* over time. And for my present sense of who I am, I receive *confirmation from intimate others* and *confirmation by society.*

Identity Crisis: Patterns of Resolution

Marcia and his colleagues (Marcia, 1966; Marcia, Waterman, Matteson, Archer, & Orlofsky, 1993) provide another perspective on the identity crisis by focusing on how it is resolved. During an identity crisis, society often provides for a period of moratorium or time out from the full demands of adult living. In different ways, institutions and customs such as college, the military, world travel, "bumming around," and service in the Peace Corps can all be thought of as giving young people a time-out experience to work on identity formation. This "work" involves exploring or trying out new aspects of identity to see how well they feel to our inner self and how well they fit with our changing social selves. A successful identity formation requires that we become committed to an identity—to a particular internal sense of who we are and to a particular set of social roles. We feel like a stable somebody to ourselves, and we have become a dependable somebody to other people.

These two processes of *exploration* and *commitment* define four ways of resolving an identity crisis, or "ego identity statuses," in Marcia's terminology.

If we avoid both processes, then we really have never ventured out of our childhood world and our identities remain in a *diffuse,* undeveloped state. If, on the other hand, we avoid the crisis and commit ourselves to the particular adult identity that is conferred by our family and immediate surroundings, as often happens in traditional societies, then we have *foreclosed* the process of identity formation. We have an adult identity, but without exploration, we have lost a major opportunity to grow and develop. If we become "stuck," exploring but never making a commitment, then we are in a *moratorium* status. Finally, if we weather the crisis and can, after exploration, make a mature commitment, then we have *achieved* a positive, stable adult identity.

Identity Formation in Helen Keller

Helen Keller's autobiography gives us a chance to see the process and problems of identity formation in detail. When Helen was 12 years old, just about the time when identity concerns might begin, the Frost King incident led people to claim that she had plagiarized the work of someone else. To Helen, this charge (and the interrogation that followed) raised deep problems of identity—problems greater than most people experience. In a literal sense, she not only had doubts about who she was, she was also not even sure about the boundary between self and not-self. The "eager" and "delighted" self, once reflected by Teacher's loving hands, was now thrown into jeopardy:

> Even now, I cannot be quite sure of the boundary line between my ideas and those I find in books. . . . It is certain that I cannot always distinguish my own thoughts from those I read. (pp. 64, 70)

Recalling this unhappy time, Helen described some responses common to many adolescent identity crises: "doubt and suspicion," then tears ("I wept as I hope few children have wept" [p. 66]).

As Helen Keller resolved this identity crisis, her actions and feelings were also similar to the actions of many other adolescents. First, she explored her world—literally, through visits to Washington, Niagara Falls, and the Chicago World's Fair. These took her mind off the crisis and greatly expanded her sense of possibility:

> I liked to visit the Midway Plaisance [site of the World's Fair]. It seemed like the "Arabian Nights," it was crammed so full of novelty and interest. . . . With an eagerness as insatiable as that with which Pizarro seized the treasures of Peru, I took in the glories of the Fair with my fingers. (pp. 75, 76)

Then, she began the process of commitment to an adult identity: "I took a long leap from the little child's interest in fairy tales and toys to the appreciation of the real and the earnest in the workaday world" (p. 77). In this process she displayed the kind of scrupulous moral energy that is often associated with identity commitment: "I was still excessively scrupulous about everything I wrote. The thought that what I wrote might not be absolutely my own tormented me" (p. 73). Finally, her identity achievement was appropriately symbolized by writing (at age 13) the first version of her autobiography, "My Story," for the magazine *Youth's Companion* (Keller, 1894). This article not only established her identity in the sense of who she was; it also set her on the path of her adult career identity in writing and journalism.

THE SELF AS STORY AND NARRATIVE

In the last paragraph, I wrote that Keller's writing the first version of her life story "symbolized" her achievement of identity. Several personality psychologists, including McAdams (1985, 1990b, 1993) and Spence (1983), have suggested that the "life story" not only is a symbol for identity but actually *is* identity.[5] In developing a narrative or biographical theory of the self, McAdams drew inspiration from one of Murray's fundamental propositions: "The history of the organism *is* the organism. This proposition calls for biographical studies" (1938, p. 39). As Spence put it, "part of the sense of self comes from being able to go backward and forward in time and to weave a story about who one is" (p. 457). These claims are similar to fundamental elements of existentialist philosophy (Charme, 1984; see also footnote 4 of Chapter 6 above):

> The nature of the self is not that of an object with fixed attributes determined by the past which can simply be discovered or analyzed into component parts. Rather, the essential form of the self is that of a retrospective story that creates order out of the chaos of experience. . . . [It] links together a person's past, present, and future into a coherent whole. (p. 2)

McAdams points out that good stories have certain characteristics: plot, characters, key events or turning points, and recurring themes. They have an ideological setting and a framework of values and beliefs that give meaning to the overall narrative. Finally, they have a "point" or conclusion. Most stories can be classified into different types or genres; for example, stories with happy endings and stories with sad endings. Frye's (1957) classification of story forms builds on this simple distinction: happy-ending stories can be either *comedy*, in which characters overcome obstacles to find happiness, or *romance*, in which they set out on a quest or journey. Sad-ending stories include both *tragedy*, in which characters are overcome by inescapable dangers or absurdities, and *irony*, in which they are caught up in the mysteries, ambiguities, and contradictions of life.

McAdams has developed the narrative approach to identity by translating these elements of real stories into a series of personality variables related to people's self-stories. Table 9.5 presents some of these translations, along with some others that are consistent with McAdams's work. For example, key

---

[5]In a similar fashion at the group level, nationalism and national identity are largely built upon a shared historical experience, or "national story."

TABLE 9.5 THE SELF-STORY AND CORRESPONDING
PERSONALITY VARIABLES

Story characteristic	Corresponding personality variable
Form or genre	
Happy ending	Optimistic explanatory style
Comedy	(facilitating attributional style; Chapter 8)
Romance	
Sad ending	Pessimism
Tragedy	(debilitating attributional style; Chapter 8)
Irony	
Narrative complexity	Integrative complexity (Chapter 6)
	Level of ego development (Chapter 6)
Key or "nuclear" episodes	Scripts (Carlson, 1981; Tomkins, 1979, 1987)
	Power and affiliation motives (Chapter 5)
Characters ("imagoes")	Power and affiliation motives (Chapter 5)
Zeus (ruler)	High power
Athena (wise counselor)	High power, high affiliation-intimacy
Hera (loyal friend)	High affiliation-intimacy
Hephaestus (worker)	Low power and affiliation-intimacy
Ideological setting	Beliefs and values (Chapters 6–8)
	Authoritarianism
	Values
	"Alternative values" of mysticism,
	environmental concern, community
Conclusion or "point" of the story	
Generativity script	Generativity (McAdams and de St. Aubin, 1992;
	Peterson & Stewart, 1990, 1993)

SOURCE: Adapted from McAdams (1985, 1990b, 1993).

events or nuclear episodes are the basic building blocks of the life story. They constitute the repeated intentions, the recurring goals, and repeated themes of the story. McAdams (1985, chap. 5) finds similarities between people's motives, as assessed on the TAT (see Chapter 5) and the nuclear episodes of their life stories (as measured, for example, by earliest memories, peak experiences, worst times, and so forth). Thus people with a high power motive on the TAT construct their life stories from many episodes involving impact and status, whereas people concerned with intimacy see their lives in terms of sharing, sympathy, and closeness to others.

People's life stories are also stocked with characters or "imagoes"[6] that also reflect their TAT-based motives. To describe these imagoes, McAdams drew upon the gods and goddesses of ancient Greece (1985, chap. 6). Thus power-motivated people describe themselves in Zeus-like terms, as omnipo-

[6]*Imago* derives from the Latin word for "image." McAdams (1985) adapted this term from Jung to mean an archetype that is personified or represented in human (or mythic) form (pp. 182–183). In psychoanalytic theory an imago is the idealized representation of the object of a motive.

tent rulers. People high in power and affiliation-intimacy are likely to see themselves as Athena, the wise counselor who used power in benevolent ways (for example, helping the wandering Odysseus during his ten-year-long homeward journey from the Trojan War). People high only in the latter motive appear in their own life stories as Hera, the companion and friend of Zeus, sometimes subordinate but usually loyal. Finally, people low in both motives are likely to present themselves in the image of Hephaestus, the unspectacular but steady worker.

People's explanatory or attributional styles are likely to be reflected in the overall feeling-tone or form of their self-story. People high in integrative complexity and ego development are likely to have complex narratives, with many different key episodes and turning points. Almost any of the specific beliefs and values discussed in the last few chapters could be the basis for the ideological setting of a person's life story. Finally, most stories have some point, a larger purpose or significance. McAdams calls this the "generativity script," because it involves people's generativity or efforts to create a legacy that can be passed on to the next generation. People begin to think seriously about such a legacy as they approach middle age, so generativity as a concept is particularly useful in studying the adulthood and old age chapters of people's life stories (see McAdams & de St. Aubin, 1992; Peterson & Stewart, 1990, 1993).

By taking seriously the idea that people's identities have the form of stories or narratives, we can borrow still other concepts of writing to expand our understanding of the self. For example, authors usually make revisions in what they write, and reporters revise their stories when new information becomes available. By applying the metaphor of revision, we can study how people change their life stories as a result of life changes—for example, during college, or after marriage, a new career, divorce, unemployment, loss of a loved one, or retirement. Sometimes they may rework earlier material, changing an emphasis here and highlighting new events there; other times, they may throw away the whole draft and start over from scratch. For some people, a personal disaster can transform a comedy into a tragedy; but for others, the original form is preserved. Finally, as every author knows, there must be a final draft that is handed over when the writing is complete. Thus, at the last stages of life, McAdams suggests, people review their life stories in order to get them into final form (1990b, pp. 187–190).

THE SELF AS STRUCTURE AND AS MOTIVATION

The self is a major, complex cognitive structure, but at the same time, many aspects of the self also have motivational power. For example, propriate striving, manipulating the body to improve the self, narcissism, maintenance of self-esteem through identification and disidentification, and revising the life story are all processes that may direct and energize certain actions. In the next chapter, we explore these and other linkages between motivation and cognition.

10

Cognitions as Motivating Forces

❖

While cognition and motivation are separate elements of personality, they are obviously related. Motives, as we saw in Chapter 5, have cognitive representations. Cognitive structures guide the flow of action as we try to reach goals and avoid dangers in a constantly changing world (Cantor, 1990). In addition, some cognitions may have motivational force in and of themselves. For example, people who attribute their successes to stable internal factors and their failures to unstable or external factors (the facilitating attributional style), are more motivated; that is, they pursue their goals with greater energy and persistence, as discussed in Chapter 8. Further, the phenomena of ego involvement (Chapter 4), propriate striving, and disidentification (Chapter 9) illustrate the motivational force of the engaged self-concept. This chapter discusses in a more systematic way how and when cognitions motivate action .

A BASIC MODEL OF MOTIVATION AND COGNITIVE BALANCE

Heider's (1958) theory of cognitive balance offers a simple model that will help us to understand how the relation between cognitions can have motivating effects (see also Brown, 1965, chap. 11; Cartwright & Harary, 1956; and Fiske & Taylor, 1984, chap. 12). This model involves two simple assumptions. The first assumption is that our internal cognitive world can be divided up into separate "cognitions" or elements. (An element might be any person or thing that we can discriminate from anything else.) And second, the relationship or bond between any two cognitions can be expressed by either a positive (+) or a negative (−) sign. Positive bonds might mean that the two cognitions occur together, are related as cause and effect, or have positive feelings toward each other. Negative bonds mean that the two cognitions do not occur together, or that they have negative feelings toward each other. (For the moment, ignore neutral bonds and assume that every relation is either positive or negative.) The following statements illustrate positive bonds in Heider's sense:

> Dianne likes Molly.
> Tennis players use racquets and balls.
> Studying improves grades.

Negative bonds include the following:

> Margaret dislikes Jill.
> We don't eat salt with ice cream.
> Freon harms the ozone layer.

For Heider's theory, the critical issue is whether the bonds among cognitions are balanced or unbalanced. The theory asserts that *if we consider at the same time any group of three cognitions, then the group will be balanced if either one bond or three bonds are positive. It will be unbalanced if no bonds or two bonds are positive.* Alternatively, a group with zero or two negative bonds is balanced, and one with one or three negative bonds is unbalanced.[1]

Here is the motivational part of Heider's theory: *whenever a group of cognitions is unbalanced (or in a state of imbalance), we will be motivated to change beliefs or action so as to achieve balance.* In other words, Heider assumes that we have a motive to achieve cognitive balance.

The model based on Heider's theory can be illustrated with the example shown in Figure 10.1, page 332. Let us consider the following group of three cognitions: self (*S* in the figure), air-conditioning (*AC*), and the ozone layer of the earth's atmosphere (*OL*). For myself, I like and use air-conditioning during the hot and humid Michigan summer weather. I also like the ozone layer, since it protects me from the sun's ultraviolet rays, which can cause skin cancer. Thus the bonds between *S* and *AC* and between *S* and *OL* are both positive. However, there is now a good deal of evidence that the freon in air conditioners damages the ozone layer, which means that the *AC-OL* bond would be negative. For the group of three cognitions in Figure 10.1, then, there is one negative bond. According to Heider's theory, it is unbalanced, and this unbalanced state should motivate me to change my behavior or attitudes so as to restore a state of balance.

I could restore cognitive balance in a number of different ways. By swearing off air-conditioning, I could change the *S-AC* bond from positive to negative. This would achieve balance, but the discomfort of making such a big change in summer living habits would tempt me to make other changes instead. I could disbelieve the link between freon and damage to the ozone layer. (At least I could argue that we don't know enough about the link, and that more research is needed.) If I could actually convince myself of this, then the *AC-OL* bond would be changed from negative to at least zero, thereby restoring a balance of sorts. Another way to achieve the same result would be to buy an air conditioner that did not use freon. Or I could try to deny that the ozone layer is important. With a gallows sense of humor, I might even joke that "skin cancer is good for you"—just as some smokers used to joke that "lung cancer is good for you." Probably this would not convert the *S-OL* bond from positive to negative, but the humor might enable me to deny or avoid the positive bond. Probably you can think of other ways to achieve cognitive balance without giving up air-conditioning. Most of these would involve denial or rationalization (for example, "My air conditioner helps my work, which is for the good of humanity," or "It only leaks a little bit of freon").

Any one of these changes would restore balance within this particular group of cognitions, though they would have very different effects. Probably I would choose the one that makes the fewest overall demands for cognitive and behavioral change, but that may not be easy to know in advance. Thus

---

[1]You may wonder why either one or three positive bonds are balanced and one or three negative bonds are unbalanced. Arkes and Garske (1982, p. 292) suggest that for balanced groups, the multiplicative product of the three signs is positive and for unbalanced groups, it is negative. This is a good way to remember which conditions are balanced, but I am not sure if it is an explanation.

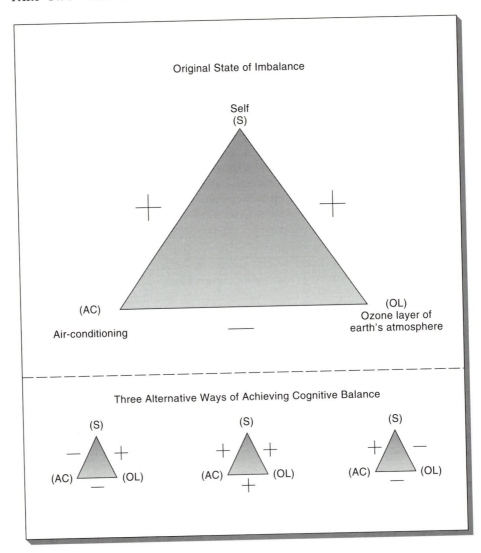

FIGURE 10.1
Heider's theory of cognitive balance illustrated.

while Heider's theory predicts that cognitive imbalance will motivate change
of behavior or attitude, it does not tell us *which* change will occur. Moreover,
even the very existence of an unbalanced state, which is so critical to the theory, depends on my considering all three cognitions together at the same time.
The simplest way to avoid cognitive imbalance would be to avoid ever considering the unbalanced cognitions as a group. (This would be similar to the
defense mechanism of isolation, as discussed in Chapter 3.) In Heider's terms,
such avoidance could be represented as a zero or neutral bond between various pairs. In terms of the example of Figure 10.1, I would simply avoid thinking about the ozone layer while the air-conditioner is running.

Finally, Heider's theory makes no provision for individual differences in tolerance for imbalance or inconsistency. Thus to make full use of Heider's theory to understand individual persons, we would need to know several additional things: the strength of their motivation for cognitive consistency, their preferred modes of reducing cognitive imbalance (changing behavior to fit attitudes, changing attitudes to fit behavior, or isolation of cognitive elements). Still, we can use the model illustrated in Figure 10.1 as a framework for understanding many motivating effects of cognitive structures and the relations between them.

DEVELOPMENT AND OPERATION OF THE IDEAL SELF

As was suggested in Chapter 9, the self is not a single cognitive element. Rather, we have many selves; each can have positive or negative bonds with the others, and with other objects of cognition. There is the self that we are (itself a bundle of different selves in different contexts), the self that we ought to be, the self that we used to be, and the self that we are striving to become. There are negative selves that we *don't* want to become. Often there is a "bad self," the self our parents warned us about becoming.

The most important distinction among these selves is that between the *real self* (RS, that which we are at the moment) and the *ideal self* (IS, that which we want to be or should be). Sometimes we experience our ideal self as an aspiration of what we might become, while at other times we experience it as a critic and judge. In the next few pages we shall consider how this ideal self develops and how it relates to the real self.

Freud: Ego Ideal and Superego

In Freud's theory, the *ideal self* ("ego ideal," in Freud's terms), along with the conscience or "censor," is an aspect of the *superego,* which was discussed in Chapter 3. The superego is an internal model of our parents' teachings, exhortations, and prohibitions. Actually it is not modeled after what our parents really were, but rather on how we experienced them when we were small children. Thus at its core, the superego is primitive and exaggerated, just like children's other concepts. Even with later additions derived from the influence of teachers, peers, admired leaders, and public opinion, the superego retains a childlike, primitive quality.

Voices of conscience. Since it originates from things that are heard, such as parental commands and prohibitions (see Freud, 1923, XIX, p. 52), the superego is often experienced as a "voice" that originates outside ourselves and directs and admonishes us. Joan of Arc, the Maid of Orleans who in 1429 rallied French armies to defeat the English and secure the crowning of the Dauphin as King of France, is a vivid example of the superego as voice. Bernard Shaw portrayed her as follows in the first scene of *Saint Joan* (1924/1956):

CAPTAIN ROBERT DE BAUDRICOURT: What did you mean when you said that St. Catherine and St. Margaret talked to you every day?

JOAN: They do.

ROBERT: What are they like?

JOAN: I hear voices telling me what to do. They come from God.

ROBERT: They come from your imagination.

JOAN: Of course. That is how the messages of God come to us.

ROBERT: So God says you are to raise the siege of Orleans?

JOAN: And to crown the Dauphin in Rheims Cathedral.

Superego and charisma. Sometimes the superego is dramatically altered in adult life. For example, Freud explained the extraordinary influence of charismatic religious or political leaders, who arouse waves of popular devotion among their followers as the result of their having replaced the followers' original superegos (1921, XVIII):

> A primary group of this kind is a number of individuals who have put one and the same object in the place of their ego ideal and have consequently identified themselves with one another in their ego. (p. 116)

When this happens, every word of the leader strikes the followers with the force of a superego command. Old moralities are swept away, and new ideal selves spring up in their place. These effects of charismatic leaders can be illustrated with quotations from their followers. For example, Jawaharlal Nehru (1948), the first prime minister of an independent India, wrote of Gandhi:

> And then Gandhi came. He was like a powerful current of fresh air that made us stretch ourselves and take deep breaths, like a beam of light that pierced the darkness and removed the scales from our eyes, like a whirlwind that upset many things but most of all the working of people's minds. (p. 14)

And Joseph Goebbels (1948), the Nazi minister of propaganda, wrote of Hitler during the difficult days of World War II:

> My work meets with the Führer's [Hitler's] highest approval and gives him great satisfaction. It is wonderful for me to be able to chat at length with the Führer about all sorts of personal things. He has the effect of a dynamo. After spending an afternoon with him, one feels like a storage battery that has just been charged anew. (p. 137)

Balance theory and the operation of the superego. The operation of the superego can be described in terms of Heider's balance theory, as shown in Figure 10.2. The three elements would be the self or ego (S), the superego (SE), and any particular action or attribute (A) that might be linked to the self. We assume a positive bond between self and superego, a positive A-SE bond for

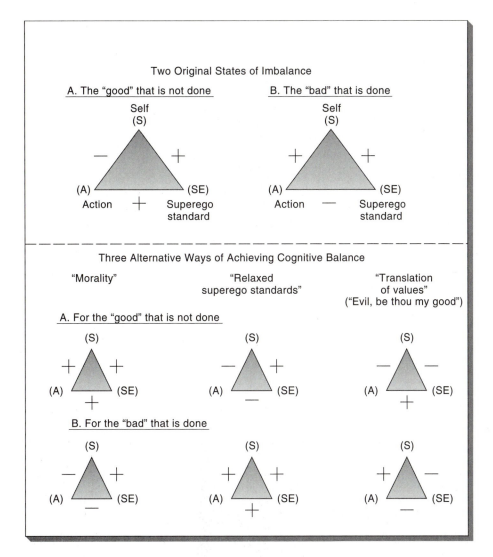

FIGURE 10.2
Cognitive balance theory and superego functioning.

every act consistent with or approved by the superego, and a negative A-SE bond for every act inconsistent with or disapproved by the superego. Since cognitive balance requires either zero or two negative bonds, the self will tend to construct negative bonds with those acts negatively bonded to the superego, and positive bonds with those acts positively bonded to the superego. These positive S-A bonds might take the form of endorsing the act, thinking about it, or actually doing it. Examples of negative bonds between self and an act would include moral disapproval, mental resistance, or actual avoidance and flight from the act.

As shown at the left-bottom of Figure 10.2, balance theory can explain why we endorse and carry out actions approved by our superego and reject or avoid actions disapproved by our superego. However, remember that there are other ways of achieving cognitive balance, as shown at the center- and right-bottom. For example, we could relax superego standards by changing the bond between *SE* and *A* rather than the bond between *S* and *A*. If an act is no longer positively or negatively bonded to the superego, then it can have any bond with the self. In other words, cognitive balance can be achieved by changing the aspirations and demands of the superego rather than by changing the self.

Even more extreme is the case where the positive bond between the self and superego is dissolved, or even changed to a negative bond. In this case, the self avoids imbalance by rejecting the claims of the superego entirely—in other words, by denying good and embracing evil. Many Western philosophers and writers have been fascinated by this possibility. Friedrich Nietzsche, the nineteenth-century German philosopher, called it the "transvaluation of values." Many writers have embellished the legend of Faust, who sold his soul to the devil. And in *Paradise Lost,* the English poet John Milton dramatized this transvaluation in his portrayal of Satan, who was exiled to hell for rebellion against God:

> Is there no place
> Left for repentance, none for pardon left?
> So farewell hope, and with hope, farewell fear,
> Farewell remorse: all good to me is lost;
> Evil, be thou my good.
> (Book IV, lines 79–80, 108–110)

From the perspective of morality, the alternatives of relaxing superego standards or overthrowing the superego are not morality but rather corruptions of morality. Still, since they bring about cognitive balance, they must be included as possible motivational effects of cognitions. Thus we can conclude that while any difference between the self and the superego will have motivational force, we cannot always predict the exact way in which this force will expressed.

Rogers: Real Self and Ideal Self

Although they used different terms to describe the process and results, Rogers and Freud both believed that the conversion of parental practices and values into internal cognitive structures that had motivating force was crucial to personality formation.

Conditions of worth. Like Freud, Rogers believed that children need to be socialized into appropriate behavior. In the socialization process, parents could discipline children by focusing on the child's act: for example, "Saying 'please' and 'thank you' is good," or "Tormenting your little brother is bad."

All too often, however, parents discipline by focusing on the child's self rather than the act: for example, "I love you when you say 'please' and 'thank you,' " or "You are bad because you tormented your little brother." This latter kind of discipline creates conditions of worth in the child. That is, the child feels good or loved or worthy only under certain conditions—when certain acts are done or certain acts avoided. Over time, the ideal self develops as the embodiment of all of these conditions of worth. Because the ideal self is the self that says please and thank you and does not torment little brother, it is the self that is loved and not punished. In contrast stands the real self, the self that is not inclined toward polite language and wants to torment little brother. It is the self that is punished and not loved.

Self-denial and defensiveness. Conditions of worth create an ideal self that is quite discrepant from the real self. To be loved, the child learns to deny the real self—to deny desires, feelings, and beliefs that are actually experienced, in favor of more "worthy" desires, feelings, and beliefs. Perhaps you remember being told as a child, "You don't want that!" or "You don't want to do that!" when actually you very much did want to do it. Now imagine that it is you yourself that is telling yourself, "I don't want to do that!" when all the time you really do. That is what Rogers (1959) meant by denial of experience:

Carl Rogers, who suggested that conditions of worth affect the self-actualization. "When a self-experience is avoided (or sought) solely because it is less (or more) worthy of self-regard, the individual is said to have acquired a condition of worth. . . . Experiences which run contrary to conditions of worth are perceived selectively and distortedly . . . or are in part or whole, denied to awareness" (1959, pp. 224, 226). (Carl Rogers Memorial Library)

> Experiences which were incongruent with the individual's concept of himself tended to be denied awareness, whatever their social character. . . . [The self is] a criterion by which the organism screened out experiences which could not comfortably be permitted in consciousness. . . .
>
> [The person] has not been true to himself, to his own natural organismic valuing of experience, but for the sake of preserving the positive regard of others has now come to falsify some of the values he experiences and to perceive them only in terms based on their value to others. (pp. 202, 226)

Denied awareness, these desires and feelings assume an unconscious existence, pushing toward expression and yet distorted by defensive transformations. With inner experience disconnected or dissociated from the sense of self, perceptions and memories also undergo distortion in order to maintain the dissociation. In describing this process Rogers used many of the traditional psychoanalytic defense mechanisms described in Chapter 3.

The dissociation of self and experience also jeopardizes our sense of *organismic trust*. Rogers believed human beings are originally born with a "trust in the direction of inner organismic processes," which leads them forward through life in a "total, unified, integrated, adaptive, and changing encounter" (1963, p. 21). "I have myself stressed the idea that man is wiser than his intellect," said Rogers, "and well-functioning persons accept the realization that the meanings implicit in their experiencing of a situation constitute the wisest and most satisfying indication of appropriate behavior" (p. 18).

Probably you have had the experience of naturally and effortlessly being able to do the right thing without thinking about it, a kind of "natural wisdom" or sense of flow. This is organismic trust. When our experience is subject to conditions of worth, however, it becomes edited or even denied. As a result, we no longer trust our experience; every action has to be thought through to make sure that it does not conflict with the conditions of worth that make up our ideal self. This editing and denial tend to block the actualizing tendency (Rogers's main motivational construct, discussed in Chapter 4).

Rogers and Freud Compared

For both Rogers and Freud, cognitive discrepancies between the real self (or ego) and the ideal self (or superego) have motivational force. Further, for both theorists, these discrepancies originate in a broader *conflict between the individual* (real self) *and society* (internalized ideal self). Both suggest that the conflict leads to defensive distortion, anxiety, and impaired functioning. Still, there are important differences between Freud and Rogers, differences that go beyond mere terminology.

Freud believed that the conflict between the individual and society is inevitable, because in his view the price individuals pay for living together in society, building a civilization, and enjoying the highest and best accomplishments of humanity is a considerable renunciation of their "natural" instincts (see Freud, 1930, XXI). Anxiety, defensive functioning, and guilt are therefore an inescapable consequence of living in society. While psychoanalysis was developed as a way to ameliorate the worst of these problems, at best it can only create a resigned understanding and acceptance of this inevitable conflict, along with some reduction in anxiety and guilt.

For Rogers, things don't have to turn out that way at all. What the real-ideal discrepancies motivate is only a neurotic and maladaptive striving, in contrast to the healthy striving of the unconflicted actualization motivational force (see Chapter 4). However, if parents give their children *unconditional positive regard*—that is, if they love them regardless of what they do—then children will not develop conditions of worth. As a result, they will have little discrepancy between real self and ideal self. Their perception and judgment will not be distorted, experience will not be dissociated from self, and they will feel organismic trust. In short, the children will be *fully functioning people,* able to achieve actualization and self-actualization. In *client-centered therapy* (Rogers, 1951), the therapist tries to provide whatever unconditional positive regard the patient ("client," in Rogers's terminology) missed in childhood.

Thus the most important difference between Freud and Rogers is whether socialization—by a superego or conditions of worth—is a necessary consequence of living in society. While Rogers paid little attention to what a society (in contrast to an individual) might need in order to function, he did imply that children could be adequately socialized without imposing on them conditions of worth. In fact, he even suggested that society would be better off with group-centered leaders who (like client-centered therapists) communicated unconditional positive regard to the rest of us (1959, pp. 242–243; see also Rogers, 1948).

While you may think it would be nice if we all gave each other unconditional positive regard, you may also be wondering whether Rogers's position is realistic. Surely children have to be disciplined sometimes. While he was an optimist, Rogers recognized the need for discipline. He argued, however, that discipline should focus on the act rather than the self: "Molly, I love you but I do not want you to torment your little brother." Phrased in this way, parental discipline would presumably not require Molly to deny her tormenting impulses, but only to inhibit them. According to Rogers, Molly would learn that her act may not be acceptable but that she will always be accepted in spite of her act.

But unconditional positive regard may assume a world of infinite abundance and resources. Molly's parents may lack the time or resources to give her nothing but unconditional positive regard. Or giving Molly unconditional positive regard may mean that they must cut back on the unconditional positive regard given to her little brother. Or both children may have insatiable needs for unconditional positive regard. It is easy to see how Rogers could have developed his optimistic theory among prosperous and untroubled white middle-class American clients in the late 1940s and 1950s, when energy was cheap, natural resources plentiful, pollution of little concern, and the economy rapidly expanding. In times of scarcity and conflict, though, societies may have to set limits. Freud sensed this problem and remained pessimistic (1933c, XXII):

We are told that in certain happy regions of the earth, where nature provides in abundance everything that man requires, there are races whose life is passed in tranquillity and who know neither coercion nor aggression. I can scarcely believe it and I should be glad to hear more of these fortunate beings. (p. 211)

Research Studies of Discrepancy between Real and Ideal Self

Measuring the various "selves." To do research on the discrepancy between real self and ideal self, personality psychologists typically take one of the self-concept measures and ask people to fill it out twice—once "as you actually are" and a second time "as the person you would like to be." Differences between the two responses are then combined to yield an overall measure of discrepancy between the two selves. Following Higgins's (1987) terminology, we can call this overall measure the "self-discrepancy." Table 10.1 illustrates how one measure of self-concept, the "semantic differential" (Osgood, Suci, & Tannenbaum, 1957), can be used to generate self-discrepancy scores.

Another widely used procedure involves the Q-sort technique (Block, 1978; see also Chapter 9). People are given a list of 100 statements or descriptive phrases, such as "Is a genuinely dependable and responsible person," "Is critical, skeptical, not easily impressed," or "Behaves in a giving way toward others." Having first sorted these phrases into nine piles, ranging from "extremely characteristic of me" to "extremely uncharacteristic of me," study participants then repeat the sort for "the person I would like to be." If the two selves are quite similar, most of the 100 phrases will end up in the same piles for the two sorts. To generate a self-discrepancy score, the discrepancies on all items are summed. Alternatively, the correlation (across all items) can be computed between the two sorts. If the two selves are similar, this correlation will be high, whereas a large self-discrepancy will produce a low or even negative correlation.

Adjustment and psychotherapy. Two classic studies of self-discrepancy illustrate Rogers's theory. Among college students, Turner and Vanderlippe (1958) found that self-ideal congruence (that is, low self-discrepancy) was related to such positive outcomes as participating in extracurricular activities, being viewed by others as being a fair and wise companion, and organizing group activities. Self-ideal congruence was also related to college grades, though not to intelligence test scores. Turner and Vanderlippe concluded that self-ideal congruence is associated with better overall adjustment. In terms of Rogers's theory, students with low self-discrepancies were better able to actualize their inherent abilities. In another study, Butler and Haigh (1954) found that people's self-ideal congruence went up after client-centered counseling, just as Rogers's theory would predict.

Subsequent research has usually supported the conclusion that high self-discrepancy scores have negative or neurotic motivational effects (see the

TABLE 10.1 SEMANTIC DIFFERENTIAL MEASURE OF REAL SELF
AND IDEAL SELF

Instructions: For each pair of adjectives, place an X in the appropriate column to express how closely those adjectives are related to the concept being measured.

To calculate the discrepancy between real self and ideal self: Subtract the value for ideal self from the value for real self (using the numbers in brackets) for each of the nine pairs of adjectives. In this example, the discrepancy is 12. (To facilitate calculation, the "good" or socially desirable adjectives are all on the left side in this example. In a real study, the left-right sequence should be randomized.)

Concept being measured:
Myself

	[7]	[6]	[5]	[4]	[3]	[2]	[1]	
pleasant	—	—	X	—	—	—	—	unpleasant
hard	—	—	—	—	X	—	—	soft
useful	—	X	—	—	—	—	—	useless
fast	—	—	—	—	—	X	—	slow
large	—	X	—	—	—	—	—	small
active	—	—	—	X	—	—	—	passive
bright	—	X	—	—	—	—	—	dull
deep	—	—	X	—	—	—	—	shallow
good	—	X	—	—	—	—	—	bad

Concept being measured:
The person I would like to be

	[7]	[6]	[5]	[4]	[3]	[2]	[1]	
pleasant	—	X	—	—	—	—	—	unpleasant
hard	—	—	X	—	—	—	—	soft
useful	X	—	—	—	—	—	—	useless
fast	—	—	X	—	—	—	—	slow
large	—	X	—	—	—	—	—	small
active	—	X	—	—	—	—	—	passive
bright	X	—	—	—	—	—	—	dull
deep	—	—	—	X	—	—	—	shallow
good	X	—	—	—	—	—	—	bad

SOURCE: Concepts and scales from McClelland and Winter (1969, p. 268). See Osgood, Suci, and Tannenbaum (1957) for the overall principles of semantic differential measurement.

review by Higgins, 1987). For example, a study by Higgins, Klein, and Strauman (1985) distinguished two kinds of ideal selves: an ideal self representing aspirations and an "ought" self representing duty and obligations. (Notice how this distinction is parallel to the ego ideal and critical conscience aspects of the superego.) These "ideal" and "ought" selves were measured both from people's own perspective and from what they thought was the perspective of some significant other person (spouse, friend, or parent).

To summarize, college students filled out a Selves Questionnaire asking for the attributes of six different selves: (1) their *real self*, the attributes they actually possess; (2) their *ideal self*, the attributes they would ideally like to possess; and (3) their *ought self*, the attributes they should or ought to possess. These three selves are the "own selves," because they are selves as viewed from the person's own perspective. In addition, the questionnaire asked for the attributes of the same three selves (real, ideal, and ought) as perceived by the person who was most significant to them. These are the "other selves," because they are selves viewed from the perspective of another.

Higgins and associates calculated four measures of discrepancy from own real self: (1) for own ideal self, (2) for own ought self, (3) for other ideal self, and (4) for other ought self. These discrepancy scores were then correlated with measures of people's emotional state. The results, shown in Table 10.2,

TABLE 10.2 FEELINGS ASSOCIATED WITH DISCREPANCY BETWEEN OWN REAL SELF, IDEAL SELF, AND OUGHT SELF

Ideal self	*Ought self*
Discrepancies between own real self and own view of own ideal/ought self	
Disappointment, dissatisfaction, frustration	*Agitation, guilt*
Disappointed	Feelings of worthlessness
Dissatisfied	Feeling irritated all the time
Blameworthy	No interest in things
Feel no interest in things	Everything is an effort
	Feeling low in energy or slowed down
Discrepancies between own real self and others' view of own ideal/ought self	
Shame, embarrassment, feeling downcast	*Agitation, fear, and threat*
Lonely	Shame
Blue	Suddenly scared for no reason
Not sure of self	So concerned with how or what I
No pride	feel that it's hard to think of anything else

SOURCE: Based on an analysis by Higgins (1987) of data originally collected by Higgins, Klein, and Strauman (1985). The italicized emotional states represent conclusions from the literature reviewed by Higgins (1987), while the phrases in roman type represent results of Higgins, Klein, and Strauman (1985) as reanalyzed.

show that different self-discrepancies have different effects on people's emotional state. These differences, in turn, imply different motivational effects. All
discrepancies are negative; in other words, all differences between one's real
self and any ideal or ought self are unpleasant. However, discrepancies from
ideal selves tend to involve depression, while discrepancies from ought selves
have a more agitated and restless quality that suggests future action to correct
them. In a follow-up study, Strauman and Higgins (1987) found that experimentally manipulating different kinds of self-discrepancy had similar effects
on short-term emotional states.

These results suggest that if you want to help depressed friends who have
failed to live up to some standard, you should *avoid* talking about how they
have fallen short of their own ideals. Instead, focus on their duty or obligation.
They may still be unhappy, but at least they will be more likely to act on their
unhappiness. Of course Rogers would argue that giving unconditional positive regard to reduce the discrepancy is the best help of all.

Discrepancy and change. Consistent with Rogers's theory, these results
stress the negative effects of real and ideal self-discrepancy. Surely there is
another side to the story. In the short run, failure to live up to standards may
make us unhappy, but it can also be the motivation for renewed efforts and thus
effect change. A study by McClelland and Winter (1969) illustrates this positive
aspect of self-discrepancy. They designed and carried out a program of intense,
short-term entrepreneurship training courses in India for owners and managers
of small businesses. While the courses had significant overall effects on the economic performance of the participants, McClelland and Winter were particularly
interested in understanding who changed as a result of the training and why. In
fact, those participants with relatively larger pretraining discrepancies between
"myself" and "the person I would like to be" were the ones who became more
active economically after the courses. In contrast, a matched group of participants who were satisfied with themselves before the training (smaller self-
discrepancies) were less likely to change. In other words, while self-discrepancy
may be uncomfortable in the present, it can promote change over the long run by
motivating dissatisfied people to try new ways and new selves. Stewart (1995)
found the same effects in a longitudinal study of middle-aged women.

Erikson: Positive and Negative Identities

In Chapter 9 we discussed Erikson's concept of identity as a bridge between
inner and outer selves. Identity begins to develop from early identifications,
that is, from the identities of admired others, which through imitation we "try
on" as a part of constructing our own identity. Such identities can be positive
and negative. Someone with desirable attributes, a hero or a person we would
like to become, is a *positive identity* motivating our approach or imitation.
Entertainment and sports celebrities are positive identities for many people.
Many professors have taken their graduate school mentors as positive identi-

ties, as models for their own lecture style, dress, jokes, and so forth. For many people, a grandparent is a positive identity.

A *negative identity* is a role that is available but rejected, a person we do *not* want to be, or perhaps a person we are frightened that we will become (Erikson, 1959/1980, pp. 139–143). Negative identities motivate avoidance behavior. Sometimes we are taught to avoid a negative identity, as when a parent says, "Don't be like Uncle Bill" (the legendary family ne'er-do-well who came to no good end). Other times parents or the community urge an identity on us, but in rebellion we take it as a negative identity, something to be avoided, instead.

Negative identities often become important during major life transitions and cultural changes. During the transition to college, many students view their former high school friends as negative identities, to be avoided and forgotten. And to a second-generation child, an immigrant parent or grandparent often becomes a negative identity—a reminder of the Old World ways that must be rejected in order to become a "real American." (This is sad, but by the third or fourth generation it often reverses: assimilated parents are rejected as negative identities by children in search of their cultural roots.)

*P*OSSIBLE SELVES

In this chapter and the previous one, I suggested that we do not have a single, unified self, but rather many different selves: positive and negative identities, real and ideal selves, continually revised self-stories, and so forth. These different selves may generate a variety of different motivational forces, both alone and in combination with each other. For example, the Higgins, Klein, and Strauman (1985) study described above and illustrated in Table 10.2 showed the different emotional and motivational effects of various discrepancies between own selves and others' real, ideal, and ought selves. Even this array of possible selves does not take account of partial selves or self fragments—that is, cognitive structures containing a few self-relevant features rather than complete alternative self-concepts.

It is now time to consider how and when these selves and self fragments fit together. At any one time we may experience both a diversity of selves and a unity of self. Markus and her colleagues have proposed the concept of "possible selves" to indicate how sets of selves and self fragments come together, motivate behavior, and then drift apart (Markus & Nurius, 1986; Markus & Ruvolo, 1989). They propose that our self-concept is really a pool of possible selves—fragments or elements—from which, at any given moment, certain possible selves are assembled or "recruited" into a working self-concept. Such a conception accounts for both the apparent diversity and the apparent unity and endurance of the self. It explains how the self-concept can undergo sudden and striking changes of direction and apparent motivation.

Hazel Markus, who developed the concept of possible self as a bridge between the self-concept and motivation. "An individual's repertoire of possible selves can be viewed as the cognitive manifestation of enduring goals, aspirations, motives, fears, and threats. . . . [They] provide the specific self-relevant form, meaning, organization, and direction" (Markus & Nurius, 1986, p. 954). (Courtesy Hazel Markus)

Possible Selves and the Working Self-Concept

A *possible self* is anything that you have ever considered as possible for your-self. It could be a general description (creative, selfish), a physical description (athletic, handicapped), a style of life (socially outgoing, alcoholic), a skill (a good cook, unable to ice-skate), an occupation (executive, taxidriver, criminal, unemployed), or something based on the others' opinions (appreciated, unpopular). Possible selves can be positive, negative, or neutral. They can be present-day selves, but they can also be future possibilities or even past selves that could be revived.

Our possible selves represent the cognitive aspect of our goals, hopes, ideals, fears, threats, and oughts. In other words, *motives and goals are often experienced most directly and intimately as possible selves.* Thus if I have a high affiliation motivation (Chapter 5), I would experience it as a characteristic series of possible selves: me-taking-a-quiet-walk-with-my-family or me-sur-rounded-by-friends (positive); alternatively, me-friendless-and-lonely or me-laughed-at-by-others (negative).

Some possible selves appear so often in our consciousness that we think of them as part of our core self (Chapter 6) or our enduring self-concept (Chapter 9). Others only come to mind occasionally, perhaps as a result of particular events. In the language of cognitive psychology, they are said to be *primed* by these events. Among premedical students, for example, the hoped-for possible self of "doctor" is probably part of the core self, while the feared possible self of "unsuccessful medical school applicant" might be primed by a low grade on an organic chemistry exam. Ruvolo and Markus (1987) manipulated the priming of possible selves directly, in the laboratory. Using a guided-imagery technique, they asked people to imagine pleasant or unpleasant future states. People who were told to imagine that "everything has gone as well as it possible could have; you have worked hard and succeeded in achieving your goals" subsequently showed more persistence on a task than those told to imagine failure. These results show that it is possible to prime "successful" possible selves,[2] and that possible selves, when primed, exert motivational force.

The working self-concept. A person's set of possible selves varies over time. At any particular moment it includes a few core selves and some other possible selves primed by features of the situation. Markus and Nurius call this fluctuating set of possible selves the *current working self-concept,* the "right now" self. It is a subset or selection of the total population of all the person's possible selves. Table 10.3, based on research by Markus and Nurius (1986),

[2]More precisely, the possible self of "me-as-successful-due-to-hard-work" was primed.

TABLE 10.3 WORKING SELF-CONCEPTS AND POSSIBLE SELVES OF COLLEGE STUDENTS

	Percent of students including item in their:	
Item	*current working self-concept ("Does this describe you now?")*	*total set of possible selves ("Have you ever considered this a possible self?")*
Make own decisions	93	99
Happy	88	100
Confident	84	100
In good shape	67	97
Depressed	40	50
Travel widely	44	94
Others think you powerful	33	75
Be owner of a business	1	80
Have nervous breakdown	11	43
Paralyzed	3	45
Be destitute	5	20
Be a janitor	3	7
Cheat on taxes	9	18

SOURCE: Data taken from Markus and Nurius (1986, p. 959).

illustrates the difference between the working self-concepts and the total population of possible selves among college students. As you can see, most of these working self-concepts included the following possible selves: "make own decisions," "happy," "confident," and "in good shape." Fewer than half included the "depressed" possible self. Other possible selves that were quite common but not so often part of the current working self-concept of most students were "traveling widely" or "being seen as powerful." In the future, circumstances might prime these possible selves and make them part of the working self-concept or even core selves. Possible selves such as "owning a business," "having a nervous breakdown," or "being paralyzed" were possible selves for almost half the sample but part of the working self-concept for only a small proportion. Finally, for the vast majority of students, "cheating on taxes," "being a janitor," or "being destitute" were not even possible selves.

Working self-concept and self-esteem. Some possible selves (usually the positive ones) are associated with positive emotions, while others (usually the negative ones) involve negative emotions. According to Markus and Nurius, our level of self-esteem at any given moment is the sum of the emotions associated with all core and primed possible selves in the current working self-concept. In other words, self-esteem is determined by the balance of positive and negative possible selves. Over time, the working self-concept changes as different possible selves are primed by events. If these newly primed selves are negative, self-esteem will tend to be lowered. In such a case, Markus and Nurius suggest that we maintain or restore self-esteem by reshuffling the contents of the current working self-concept, discarding some negative possible selves and recruiting other possible selves that bring with them more positive emotions (1986, p. 958).

Delinquency. A study of male and female delinquents and matched nondelinquents by Oyserman and Markus (1990) illustrates the importance of the balance between possible and negative possible selves. Among the nondelinquents, positive and negative possible selves are balanced; for example, they hope to get along in school and they fear not getting along in school. According to Oyserman and Markus, this balance between both possible selves reinforces the motivating effect of each, keeping the person focused on the goal. Thus if the positive self of "getting along in school" loses its motivating power or is withdrawn from the working self-concept, then the matched negative self ("not getting along in school") is still available to keep the person motivated to get along in school. Among the delinquents, in contrast, positive and negative possible selves (hopes and fears) lead in different directions, resulting in a scattered and diffuse motivational pattern. Thus if "getting along in school" drops out of the working self-concept and there is no parallel negative possible self, other positive and negative possible selves, such as "enjoying fancy possessions" or "being ridiculed by my gang," are likely to come into play and redirect the person's motivation.

Possible selves and personality "change." We have seen how the concept of a pool of various possible selves that can be primed or recruited into the working self-concept can explain sudden shifts of self-esteem. This concept can also help to explain inconsistencies and dramatic changes in behavior, as illustrated by the historical examples of Woodrow Wilson, president of the United States from 1913 to 1921, and Benito Mussolini, the fascist dictator of Italy from 1922 to 1943. On the one hand, Wilson was a highly moral, rigid, and inflexible political leader. Both as president of Princeton University and president of the United States, he often defeated his own programs by a stubborn refusal to compromise. For example, because he refused to compromise on the provisions of the Versailles Treaty and the League of Nations at the end of World War I, the U.S. Senate refused to ratify the treaty and Wilson failed to realize his vision. On the other hand, in his political career Wilson many times displayed extraordinary flexibility and skill as a leader. For example, in 1912 he ran for governor of New Jersey as a reform candidate while securing the support of the state political bosses.

These contrasting and inconsistent behaviors have been interpreted by George (1971/1987) as the result of Wilson's flexibility in *seeking* power and stubbornness in *exercising* power against opposition (see also Greenstein, 1969/1987, pp. 75–80). From the Markus and Nurius theory, we could construct a slightly different analysis: that situations of seeking power primed Wilson's "flexible" possible self (the idealist who could nevertheless work with political bosses), whereas situations in which he encountered opposition while exercising power primed the "stubborn" possible self, the Wilson who refused to compromise even at the cost of his policy and goal. Woodrow Wilson's population of possible selves contained some that were inconsistent and incompatible—in his case, flexible and stubborn—but this is not unusual, because most people's pool of possible selves includes inconsistencies and incompatibilities. From a psychological perspective, Wilson is interesting because two incompatible possible selves were primed by only slightly different aspects or features of the political process.

Up to 1937, Mussolini "recorded an impressive string of accomplishments, including creating an empire and improving Italy economically" (N. Winter, 1992, p. 2). In September of that year, however, after meeting for four days with Adolf Hitler, the Nazi dictator of Germany, he returned to Italy a changed man. Suddenly he adopted Nazi policies, going against his prior leadership skills, alienating his supporters, and ruining Italy economically and militarily. Winter found that after the Hitler meeting, Mussolini's speeches showed sharp and significant increases in power motivation and decreases in achievement motivation. Rephrased in terms of the theory of possible selves, this finding suggests that meeting Hitler primed Mussolini's possible self of "powerful and grandiose leader," while removing the possible selves of "achiever" and "leader who improves things." As Markus and Nurius suggest, our possible selves function as cognitive representations of our aroused motives.

In these two cases, the behavior of Wilson and Mussolini changed dramatically—in Wilson's case, several times. According to the theory of possible selves, these changes did not represent alterations of personality so much as priming of different possible selves by different cues in the situation. In theatrical terms, there were alternative Wilson and Mussolini selves, wholly formed and waiting backstage to make an appearance. At the appropriate cue or prime, these alternative selves did not emerge slowly and gradually, but rather stepped forward into the ongoing role of the working self-concept. For Wilson, the relevant cue was any hint of opposition to a program linked to his aspirations and ideals (George, 1971/1987, p. 150). For Mussolini, the cue for the entry of the grandiose self was Hitler's carefully arranged and dramatic welcome to Berlin, with over 1 million people crowding the streets (N. Winter, 1992; see also Kirkpatrick, 1964, p. 351). By viewing these "changes" as the priming of alternative possible selves rather than as a fundamental alteration of personality, we can understand them as expressions of variation or alternatives within an enduring personality.

Development of Possible Selves

While parents, peers, and teachers are an important source of possible selves, the broader influences of cultural and historical images are also important. For example, Mussolini's "grandiose" possible self undoubtedly had roots in the grandiosity of the Roman Empire and its first emperor, Julius Caesar. And the personality portrait of Egyptian President Anwar Sadat prepared for President Carter's use in the Camp David negotiations (Chapter 1) suggests that the pharaohs of ancient Egypt were possible selves for Sadat.

Important social events are another source of possible selves. For example, the Great Depression of the 1930s made "being poor" a possible self for many people who had never imagined themselves in poverty before. A longitudinal study of children whose families experienced a great drop in income during those years found that the effects of this possible self persisted into adulthood, long after economic conditions had improved during the prosperous years after World War II (Elder, 1974). For many people of my generation (the "politically silent" generation who went to college during the 1950s), the presidency of John F. Kennedy created a new "politically active" possible self. And as a result of Geraldine Ferarro's vice-presidential nomination in 1984, "being vice president" (perhaps also "being president") has become a possible self for many American women.

Ordinary experiences can also be a source of possible selves. When I became friends with a person who is confined to a wheelchair, "being handicapped" changed from a mere theoretical possibility to a vivid possible self. As a result, I now pay more attention to the issue of wheelchair access to public places, and I never park in spaces reserved for the handicapped. Perhaps people would be more sympathetic with the plight of homeless people if "homeless" were, for them, a possible self.

The Undesired Self

Ogilvie (1987) has studied the undesired self (defined as "how I hope never to be"), which is closely related to Erikson's concept of negative identity and can also be understood as a vivid and well-developed negative possible self. While positive ideal selves are often described in global and abstract terms (for example, peaceful, artistic, creative), undesired selves are more specific and concrete (for example, fat, bad-tempered, impatient). The reason for the difference, Ogilvie suggests, is that the desired self develops from broad and general exhortations of parents and others, while the undesired self grows out of specific aversive experiences and contains "memories of dreaded experiences, embarrassing situations, fearsome events, and unwanted emotions that actually occurred sometime in the individual's past" (Ogilvie, 1987, p. 380). Because undesired selves are rooted in people's concrete negative experiences, Ogilvie predicted that people's sense of life satisfaction should have more to do with avoiding undesired selves than with achieving ideal selves. He confirmed this prediction in a study of the relationship of undesired self, ideal self, and real self ("how I am most of the time") among college students. The negative correlation between overall life satisfaction and how close the real self was to the undesired self ($r = -.72$, $p < .0001$) was much greater than the positive correlation between life satisfaction and how close the real self was to the ideal self ($r = .37$, $p < .01$). In other words, for these students life satisfaction was much more a matter of avoiding what they did not want to be than of achieving their ideal self.

A COGNITIVE MOTIVATIONAL SYSTEM: POSSIBLE SELVES PERSONAL STRIVINGS, AND LIFE TASKS

Self-related cognitive structures are motivational. That is, when we try to follow the promptings of our superego, or try to realize our ideal selves, these positive possible selves affect our behaviors and choices. Alternatively, negative identities, negative possible selves, and undesired selves give rise to avoidance behavior. These motivational effects of self structures are usually experienced as conscious, specific, concrete goals, each with its own associated intentions and plans. Thus, for example, during the transition to college many students find that "me-as-independent" becomes an important new positive (sometimes also negative) possible self. Realizing this new self involves a variety of specific tasks such as learning to manage a bank account, learning to cook and do laundry, dealing with feelings of loneliness, and so forth.

In recent years, personality researchers have developed several concepts to study these conscious goals and tasks: *life tasks* (Cantor, 1990; Cantor, Norem, Niedenthal, Langston, & Brower, 1987), *personal strivings* (Emmons, 1986, 1989), *current concerns* (Klinger, 1987), and *personal projects* (Little, 1989). Although there are differences among these concepts, I will treat them as essentially equivalent and use the terms interchangeably (see also the reviews in Cantor, 1990, and Cantor & Zirkel, 1990). Perhaps the most inclusive term for all these concepts is "conscious goals"; more simply, "goals." Although they are motivational, they are more conscious and specific than the broad, long-term motives of Freudian theory (Chapter 3) and the thematic apperception measures (Chapter 5; see also Weinberger & McClelland, 1990).

Typical conscious goals. In personal strivings or life tasks research, people are asked questions such as the following:

What objectives are you trying to accomplish or attain?
What are your current life tasks—the goals toward which you direct your energy?
What are the personal projects on which are you currently engaged?
I typically try to . . .

They generally respond by listing between ten and fifteen different self-described goals or strivings. Since most of the research on personal strivings has been carried out with college students, these responses might include the following:

Finish my history paper
Making friends and getting along with others
Succeeding academically
Do as many nice things for people as I can
Lose 15 pounds
Set time aside for spiritual life
Figure out Mom and Dad
Show that I am superior to others
Being on my own
Trying to stay in shape physically
Do well on the GRE exam
Trying to avoid maliciously gossiping about others

Notice that while these goals are quite heterogeneous, they are all something between a broad, general motive and "something that could be scheduled into a 15-minute time slot" (Little, 1989, p. 21).

Goals and life transitions. Cantor's research on life tasks has focused on the new goals or strivings that emerge as people move through normal life transitions. For example, entering college presented most of you with such new opportunities and requirements as being on your own, managing time, and establishing an identity. These tasks are common and normative in the college setting; that is, most college students are working on them, and students, parents, and faculty feel that students *ought* to be working on them. Yet

Nancy Cantor—"Individuals set *tasks* for themselves, distilling from the many culturally prescribed and biologically based demands of social life and survival a set of personal life task goals for which to strive. . . . The full creativity of personality emerges in the *strategies* that individuals embrace as they attempt to . . . make progress on their significant tasks" (1990, pp. 736–737). (Courtesy Nancy Cantor)

different students construe these overall tasks in different ways. Consider the life task of independence or being on your own in college. Almost all students rate this task as important, but they vary in how broadly defined and how difficult, stressful, and time-consuming it is (Zirkel & Cantor, 1990).

Goals and Strategies

Cantor's research also focuses on the different *strategies* that people employ in their life tasks. Some people approach life tasks with *optimism* and zest, believing they will do well and mobilizing their energies in a straightforward way. Yet as we saw in Chapter 8, for other people a strategy of *defensive pessimism* works quite well. Forcing them to be optimistic only makes things worse (Norem & Cantor, 1986).

Still others engage in *self-handicapping:* faced with a difficult problem, they do something that makes their success less likely—for example, partying before an exam, not practicing before a concert, getting a slight injury before a game. I will illustrate self-handicapping with a personal example. Once, in a course I found particularly difficult to teach, I discovered to my horror that I had put off having students fill out course evaluations until there was only one possible day left—right after the lecture on the most difficult and obscure concept in the entire syllabus! If I was worried about getting low ratings, this might seem like a terrible mistake, a real handicap to my lecture performance and my ratings in the course. From the self-handicapping perspective, however, my "mistake" made it possible to attribute low ratings to the lecture topic rather than to my teaching ability. In attributional terms (Chapter 8), this is an external attribution for failure, which is part of the facilitating attributional pattern. Perhaps it worked for me that day. Freed from anxiety about failure and threats to self-esteem, I gave at least an adequate lecture on the dismal topic, and my ratings for the course were satisfactory.

This is a common pattern among self-handicappers: fortified by a non-threatening explanation for failure, they are then able to put forth their best efforts, often with success. Of course this is a risky strategy, because the handicap increases the objective probability of failure! Baumeister and Scher (1988, especially pp. 8–9) review research on self-handicapping and other behavior patterns that seem at first to be self-defeating.

Finally, can I put in a good word for *avoidance,* another strategy with a bad press? Often we are told that the worst thing to do with a problem is to avoid it. If the problem can be solved, this may be true; but some problems do not yield to a head-on encounter and do not have an easy solution. In such cases, evasion or avoidance may be a protective strategy, buying time until conditions might change.

The research of Cantor and her associates (Cantor, 1990; Cantor & Zirkel, 1990) suggests that there is no single best strategy for all people on all life tasks; rather, different strategies are best for different people under different circumstances.

Goals and Emotions

Emmons (1987, 1989) has studied how people's personal strivings are related to their emotional life and sense of well-being. He found that people who are happy tend to focus on strivings at which they have previously succeeded, that engage their emotions, and that they view as important. Unhappy people, in contrast, tend to feel ambivalent about their strivings, and their strivings conflict with each other.

Little (1989) obtained similar results in his study of personal projects. However, he speculates about what is cause and what is effect. Is our emotional state the result of the characteristics of our projects, or do our emotions affect our perception and construal of those projects? Perhaps emotions and project-construals are both the result of a broader personality trait such as anxiety (see Part Three of this book).

Little has also explored the *social ecology* of people's personal projects, that is, their connection with the physical and social world. For example, the personal projects of two different people may support or conflict with each other. This is a common experience of couples trying to make two sets of career choices that will facilitate both careers and a shared life together. Certain locations (a neighborhood, city, region, or even country) may help or hinder a project. Living in New York City is essential if you have the project of acting on

Broadway; but if you want to become a world-class skier, Colorado would be a more helpful place to live.

Finally, Klinger (1987) has explored the ways in which people's conscious goals become represented in the flow of their thoughts, images, daydreams, and fantasies—the microprocessing of conscious goal striving. He has found that we tend to allocate our mental time to goals that are important and close at hand (in space and time), but that have somehow become blocked or are in some other way frustrating.

Two Motivation Systems

While these conscious goals, derived from possible selves and the other cognitive structures, are somewhat related to the less conscious, more long-term and diffuse motives of Freudian theory (Chapter 3) or as measured in thematic apperception (Chapter 5), they are not at all the same. Our motives may be expressed in certain conscious life tasks or personal projects, but such connections are not likely to be very close, because a broad motive such as achievement, affiliation, or power can be expressed and satisfied in a variety of quite different actions or projects (see Chapter 2). For example, many people pursue power by becoming officers or leaders of organizations, but other people satisfy this same motive through their career, through competitive sports, through impulsive activities such as drinking, risk taking, or aggression, or even vicariously through escapist reading and fantasy. Moreover, even life tasks such as "getting good grades" or "learning to live on my own," which might seem to be linked to the achievement motive, can be reconstrued by people high in the affiliation motive as ways of satisfying that motive (see Fleeson, 1992).

Weinberger and McClelland (1990) have tried to formalize the distinctions between these two motivational systems. They suggest that the motives measured by the TAT develop early and are based on innate emotional-motivational mechanisms related to survival requirements for individual human beings and society (see also Buss, 1991b; MacDonald, 1991). For this reason, they can be called an "emotion-driven" motivation system, exerting powerful effects on long-run behavior in unstructured or unconstrained situations. In Freud's terms, this motivation system is built upon the original motive reservoir of the id; for Rogers, it is part of our organism. In any case, as a part of our biological heritage, this emotion-driven system is sluggish and difficult to change.[3] (The origin and development of this system is further discussed in Chapter 18.)

Consciously formulated goals, on the other hand, develop with the mastery of the words and language required for conceptualizing and expressing them, as seen in the case of Helen Keller. These goals exert powerful effects on short-term behavior in highly structured situations. Because they are based on language, conscious goals can be readily organized, arranged, rearranged, adapted, and modified. As a generalized cognitive human capability, the conscious motivation system can be nimbly and flexibly applied to a wide variety

---

[3]Though not impossible to change (see McClelland & Winter, 1969).

of new and changing situations. In Freud's and Jung's terms, this motivation system resides in the ego; for Rogers, it is in the self.

Motivation systems in conflict and in harmony. Emmons and McAdams (1991) found that among college students, personal strivings measured as described above show only moderate correlations with motives measured by the TAT (*r*'s range from .37 to .42 for achievement, affiliation, and power). This suggests that in ordinary life, the two motivation systems are only moderately correlated. Normally, Weinberger and McClelland (1990) suggest, the cognitive motivation system (strivings) is able to control and even override the more primitive emotion-driven system (TAT). However, when the two motivation systems are not consistent or are in conflict, there will be "leaks" (when the TAT emotion-driven system pushes aside cognitive goals) and "failures" (when cognitive goals are not supported by the emotion-driven system). These will be experienced by the person as discrepancies between ideal self (cognitive system) and real self (emotion-driven system). These will be felt either as "leaving undone those things we ought to have done" (cognitive system motives not supported by emotion-driven system), or else as "doing those things we ought not to have done" (emotion-driven system not supported by cognitive system), in the phrases of the Episcopalian General Confession.

Sometimes, however, the two motivational systems act in harmony. This would be experienced as ecstasy, a peak experience (Maslow), or the sense of "flow" (Csikszentmihalyi & Csikszentmihalyi, 1988). In Freudian terms, it would represent the mutual coordination (rather than mutual opposition) of the ego, id, and superego. From Rogers's perspective, it would be the experience of self-actualization that comes from the fusion of self and organism.

JUSTICE AND RELATIVE DEPRIVATION

People's concern with justice also involves a motivation based on cognition. While there are many different kinds of justice, the essential feature of the sense of justice is a cognitive comparison of a real state of affairs (for example, what I have) with some other state of affairs (what I might have had, what I deserve, what others have). Without making some comparison of this sort, people do not feel either justice or injustice, no matter what their present actual situation. Making such comparisons, however, can arouse powerful motivational forces. The cry for justice has probably been on the lips of more revolutionaries than even the cry for bread.

Types of Justice

Let us begin with the distinction between procedures and results. *Procedural justice* means that the procedures employed are accepted by everyone as just, that a decision was made in the "correct" way by "following the book." Procedural justice is especially important in elections, games, contests, and lotteries. No one would want to buy a state lottery ticket if the winner were chosen by the governor rather than by a random drawing. Even if the governor chose someone who needed the money and "deserved" to win, from the perspective of procedural justice it would be an unjust lottery.

Distributive justice, on the other hand, refers to the distribution of results rather than process. It is especially important in exchanges, contracts, and legal claims. There are two principles of distributive justice: *equality,* where everyone gets exactly the same result; and *equity,* where people get what they "deserve." Both principles are accepted as just in certain domains of American society. For example, every eligible citizen has the right to vote, and no one person's vote counts more than anybody else's. All children who live in a public school district have an equal right to attend school, but their grades depend on their performance. Sometimes the principles of equality and equity are in conflict, for example, in domains such as access to health care, merit pay for teachers, or corporate wage and salary structures.

When the principle of equity is applied, people's perceptions of a "just" outcome depend not on the absolute amount they receive (for example, their wages), but rather what they receive *in relation to* something else—what they expect, what they deserve, or what they see other people like themselves getting. Thus my satisfaction with my salary or rate of advancement depends on more than how much I make or how fast I am getting promoted. This principle explains several paradoxical research findings. For example, in a study of morale among soldiers, for example, Stouffer, Suchman, DeVinney, Star, and Williams (1949) found that military policemen, who were promoted only very slowly, were *more* satisfied with their rate of promotion than were pilots, who were promoted faster. At the society level, revolutions and violent protest often occur just when things are beginning to get better. The principle of equity also explains the following joke that citizens of the former Soviet Union used to tell about their system: "They pretend to pay us and we pretend to work."

Psychologists have developed two theories—equity theory and relative deprivation theory—to explain people's perceptions of justice and how they motivate action. *Equity theory* defines justice in terms of the relationship between the ratio of one's own inputs and outputs, on the one hand, and the ratio of others' inputs and outputs on the other (Adams, 1965, p. 281). That is, *a situation will be experienced as "just" if the ratio of one's own outputs to inputs equals the ratio of others' outputs to inputs.* If your own side of the equation is less than the others' side, then you may feel injustice. For example, if you have ever had the experience of putting in more work on a paper than your roommate or friend did but getting a lower grade, then you will probably understand equity theory. If your own side is larger than the others' side, then you may feel embarrassment (and the other may feel injustice). Did you ever work less on a paper than a friend but get a higher grade?

Relative Deprivation

Equity theory suggests that the perception of justice depends on making a comparison. The theory of relative deprivation (that is, feeling deprived *rela-*

tive to others) or resentment specifies some additional factors that need to be considered. According to Crosby (1976, 1982), relative deprivation depends on five separate preconditions. These preconditions can be illustrated with a simple everyday example. Let us assume that you do not have a high-quality stereo system. In order to feel relative deprivation or resentment about this, five things must also be true:

1. You must *want* the stereo. This may seem obvious, but it is true: you can't miss what you don't want.

2. You must see that *others have* stereos of this quality. If nobody has one, your own lack of a stereo is not likely to be felt as resentment. (Sometimes having had a stereo in the past can fulfill this precondition.)

3. You must feel you *deserve* or are *entitled* to a stereo. If you don't deserve something that you don't have, you might be disappointed but you wouldn't feel resentment or injustice. (Knocking out this precondition is a favorite strategy, on the part of people who have a lot, to prevent discontent among those who have less.)

4. Closely related to deserving, you must feel that it is *not your fault you don't have* a stereo. If you had given away or accidentally thrown away your stereo, you might be angry at yourself or even envious of others, but you probably wouldn't feel injustice.

5. Finally, you must feel that it is *feasible to get* a stereo. If stereos were no longer manufactured, or if you were in the wilderness without transportation and the nearest stereo was thousands of miles away, you might feel dissatisfaction instead of resentment.

Sometimes the emotions of resentment arising out of historical events can apply to a whole generation. As President Kennedy (1962) put it in a news conference, "There is always inequity in life. Some men are killed in a war . . . and some men never leave the country, and some men are stationed in the Antarctic and some are stationed in San Francisco. . . . Life is unfair" (p. 259).

Kennedy's point can be illustrated by the experience of the generation of young people that came of age during World War I. Millions of them were killed, millions more were injured, relatives and friends were lost, and dreams were deferred or forever abandoned. When they compared themselves to others who had actually gained from the war, this generation felt they had been unfairly robbed of their youth. Vera Brittain, an English feminist and later a staunch pacifist who lost her fiancé, her brother, and most of her male friends in the war, expressed the bitter resentment and sense of injustice of her generation. In the chapter of her autobiography (1933/1979), under the title "Survivors not Wanted," Brittain described how the attempt to return to "normal life" after the war was disturbed by the suspicion that "my generation had been deceived, its young courage cynically exploited, its idealism betrayed" (p. 470). Later, after spending several months as a university student again she concluded that:

Obviously it wasn't a popular thing to have been close to the War. . . . No doubt the post-war generation was wise in its assumption that . . . we pre-war lot were just poor boobs for letting ourselves be kidded. . . . The smashing-up of one's youth seemed rather a heavy price to pay for making the mistake, but fools always did come in for a worse punishment than knaves; we knew that now. (p. 490)

In the last sentence, Brittain seems to be wondering whether her generation may somehow be at fault for its resentment. Such a feeling would remove the fourth precondition of relative deprivation, and so convert the emotion of resentment into anger at self or envy of others.

In some situations, all five preconditions may be equally necessary, while at other times one or two may be particularly important for the sense of justice or injustice. Often the most critical precondition is the nature of the group to which one compares one's self. Thus in a survey of working women, Crosby (1982, p. 168) found that only those women who compared themselves with men who worked at similar jobs felt a sense of injustice about their own lower pay; women who compared themselves to other women actually felt better off.

From Resentment to Action

In Crosby's full model (1976), the emotion of resentment is only the beginning. It can be channeled into a variety of different actions, depending on several other factors, such as whether the person expresses resentment inwardly or

Faye Crosby, who has studied how people's outcomes and expectations contribute to their sense of justice and emotions of resentment. "Deprivation is relative, not absolute. . . . Because deprivation is relative, it is often true that those who are the most deprived in an objective sense are not the ones most likely to experience deprivation" (1976, p. 85). (Courtesy Faye Crosby. Photo by Jim Gipe)

outwardly, whether the person has high or low control (see Chapter 8), and whether opportunities are blocked or open. Figure 10.3 shows how these additional factors combine to create a series of alternative paths for the expression in action of the emotions of relative deprivation and resentment.

Two contrasting reactions to the World War I experience will illustrate the importance of these additional channeling factors. Vera Brittain externalized her resentment, felt a high sense of personal control, and found opportunities

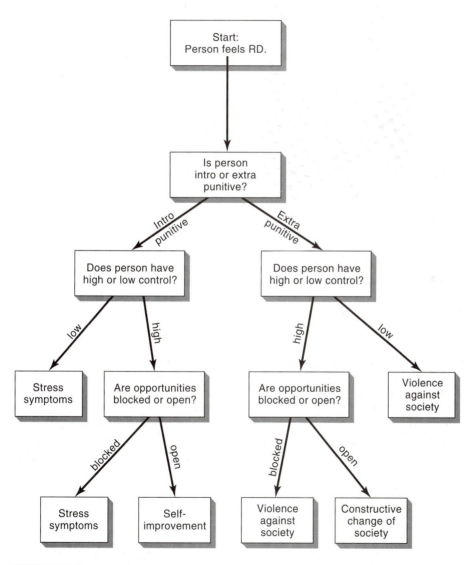

FIGURE 10.3
The behavioral effects of relative deprivation (RD or resentment) in combination with other factors.

open, so her resentment expressed itself in constructive work to change society through journalism and a commitment to peace and women's rights (see Stewart & Healy, 1986). In contrast, Adolf Hitler, another veteran of World War I, externalized his resentment at the outcome and felt a sense of control, but perceived Germany's opportunities to be blocked. Thus he followed the path of violence against society. So while relative deprivation or the sense of injustice, experienced as the emotion of resentment, can be a potent motivational force, its final direction and specific effect depend on many other aspects of the situation.

Power Motivation and Relative Deprivation

While resentment and the sense of injustice may seem purely cognitive, depending only on cognitions of the situation, they may also be influenced by motives and other personality variables. In a study of Connecticut state employees, Grupp (1975) found that people's power motivation predicted their level of discontent with the rate of promotion. Power motivation might increase relative deprivation by multiplying the effect of its preconditions (see Chapter 5). For example, power-motivated people might want more things (recall their interest in prestige possessions). They may be biased toward making "upward" comparisons, that is, choosing to compare themselves with others who have more than they do. Finally, power motivation may be linked to narcissism (Chapter 9) and a sense of entitlement, so they feel more deserving.

MORAL REASONING AND MORALITY

Justice is one important aspect of morality, which is a complex set of cognitive structures for evaluating and guiding behavior in terms of standards and principles. Originally, our moral sense is derived from cognitions such as the superego, positive and negative identities, and ideal or ought selves. That which we ought to do is "good"; that which we ought not to do is "bad." By adulthood, however, our sense of morality has developed into a more abstract code or set of principles, with an autonomous motivational force of its own. This means that labeling an act as "morally good" is often enough in and of itself for us to do it. Although it is easy to be cynical about how much people are actually motivated by morality, it does seem undeniable that some people—often our culture's heroes—have followed their moral principles regardless of rewards, sometimes even at the cost of their lives. For example, Edith Cavell, an English nurse in Belgium during World War I, helped Allied prisoners to escape until she was shot by the Germans as a spy. Raoul Wallenberg, a Swedish financier, saved thousands of Hungarian Jews during World War II. Rosa Parks risked jail or worse to challenge centuries of race discrimination. Mother Theresa gave up material comforts to care for orphans in India.

While some personality psychologists studying morality are concerned with the performance of "right" or "wrong" acts, most researchers are more interested in how people think and reason about moral issues. Blasi (1980) explains the reason for this preference:

> An action beneficial to the welfare of society . . . would not be considered moral if it were performed under hypnosis or under physical constraints but only if it were performed willingly, in response to values that are understood and accepted by the agent. (p. 4)

Thus psychologists studying moral reasoning ask people questions such as the following: *Why* should we do the things we ought to do? What makes an action right or wrong? Authority? Consequences? Or can a thing be right or wrong on principle? People differ in how they think about moral issues and problems; the study of these differences and their development is called *moral reasoning* or *moral development*.

Kohlberg's Stages of Moral Development

The most well-known and widely used theory of moral development was put forward by Lawrence Kohlberg, who suggested that moral reasoning develops in a series of six stages. These stages are related to Piaget's stages of moral judgment (1932/1966), which in turn are related to his more general stages of cognitive development. Table 10.4 illustrates the Kohlberg stages along with the approximate equivalent cognitive development stages.

Explaining moral dilemmas. According to Kohlberg, a stage of moral reasoning is not a particular kind of behavior, but rather a particular way or style in which people think about moral topics and issues. To assess people's stage of moral development, therefore, Kohlberg does not look at people's behavior or choices in a particular situation, but rather examines their thinking or reasoning about their choice. Kohlberg (1963) originally developed his sequence of stages by comparing the responses of boys aged 10, 13, and 16 to a series of moral dilemmas. Since this original study, he and others have studied a wide range of people, male and female, of different ages and backgrounds (see Kohlberg, 1981–1984). A typical Kohlberg dilemma involves a person in conflict between two different possible actions, each with valid claims to be a "moral" or "good" action, but inconsistent with each other. The conflict might be intense: for example, a man who cannot afford the medicine needed by his sick wife, and a druggist who is unwilling to lower the price. Should the man help his wife, or should he avoid stealing? Why? Or the conflict might involve an everyday matter: Should a girl who knows that her younger sister told a lie reveal this to their mother? The essential feature of a good moral dilemma is that two different "goods" are in conflict.[4]

In Table 10.4, each of the six stages is illustrated with sample responses to the dilemma of Nancy (the girl with the younger sister who lied). At the earli-

---

[4]Rest (1976, 1986) has developed an objective test of Kohlberg's stages that seems to correlate well with the moral-dilemmas interview method (see Blasi, 1980).

TABLE 10.4 RELATION OF KOHLBERG'S STAGES OF MORAL REASONING TO PIAGETIAN STAGES OF COGNITIVE DEVELOPMENT

Piagetian stage of cognitive development	Kohlberg's stage of moral reasoning and examples
Sensory-motor	[Moral reasoning not present until language develops]
Preoperational	*Level 1: Premoral or preconventional*
	1. Morality is avoiding punishment.
	"Nancy should not tell her mother about her sister's lie, because then her sister will hit her and break her toys."
	2. Morality is maximizing pleasure.
	"Nancy should tell her mother, because her mother will give her a treat."
Concrete operations	*Level 2: Conventional morality*
	3. Morality is maintaining approval of others.
	"Nancy should not tell her mother, because her sister will get very upset and angry at her."
	4. Morality is maintaining law and order.
	"Nancy should tell her mother, because telling lies is wrong and will create problems in the family."
Formal operations	*Level 3: Principled morality*
	5. Morality is reciprocity, acting in accordance with the "social contract."
	"Nancy should not tell her mother, because when Nancy last told a lie, her sister kept quiet."
	6. Morality is following principles of conscience.
	"Nancy should tell her mother, even though it will be difficult to do so. The sister's lying is a sign of a deeper problem, and if she keeps on lying, she will get into serious trouble."

SOURCE: Based on Kohlberg (1963).

est stage 1, the person's response indicates only a concern to avoid punishment. Whatever gets you punished is "bad"; whatever avoids punishment is "good." Notice that the reason given is independent from the act chosen; that is, avoiding punishment could justify either action—telling or not telling. Stage 2 expands the basis of morality to include getting rewards and serving one's own interests. Kohlberg labeled these first two stages *preconventional* or *premoral*, because they involve only self-related interests. There is no real consideration of other people.

In the *conventional stages,* there are signs of considering other people: particular feelings of particular others in stage 3, and abstract concerns ("rules"

Lawrence Kohlberg, who studied how people learn to think about morality. "We know that individuals pass through the moral stages one at a time. . . . To act in a morally high way requires a high stage of moral reasoning. One cannot follow moral principles (stages 5 and 6) if one does not understand or believe in them" (1981–1984, vol. 2, pp. 170, 172). (Harvard University News)

and "laws") of abstract others ("society") in stage 4. For people to function smoothly in any kind of social unit or organization, Kohlberg believed, their moral reasoning had to reach at least the conventional stages. The final two stages are *postconventional*, in that morality is based on principle rather than social convention. In stage 5, the principle is reciprocity ("Do unto others as you would have them do unto you"), while in stage 6 many different higher principles are brought to bear.[5]

Kohlberg considered these six stages to be a *developmental sequence*; that is, every person starts at 1 and moves toward 6. In support of this, he cited evidence of the kind shown in Figure 10.4, page 364. Notice how the percentage of lower-stage responses drops off and the percentage of higher-stage responses increases as we move from younger to older boys. Notice, too, that even among the oldest boys, the most common responses are at stages 3 and 4, the conventional level, with only a few signs of stage 5 and stage 6 moral reasoning. In a twenty-year longitudinal study, Colby, Kohlberg, Gibbs, and Lieberman (1983) found that people do progress through the stages in a regular sequence, neither skipping stages nor regressing to prior stages. On the other hand, research by Eisenberg (1986), using different measures of moral reasoning, shows that people do shift back to lower-level moral reasoning when the costs of carrying out a "good" act increase.

[5]Colby and Kohlberg (1987, p. 40) discuss doubts about stage 6.

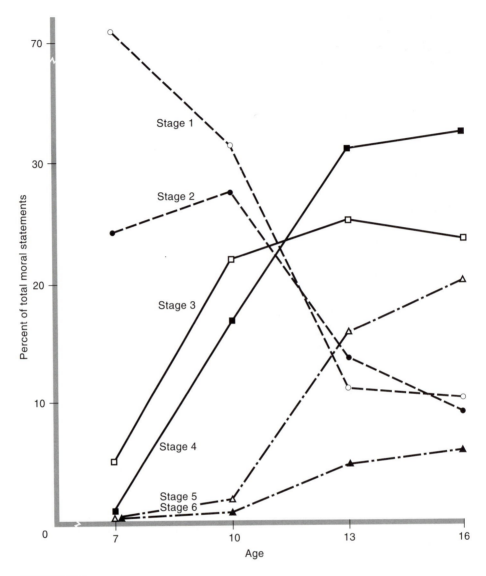

FIGURE 10.4
Development of moral reasoning: average stage levels of 7-, 10-, 13-, and 16-year-old boys. SOURCE: Adapted from Kohlberg (1963).

Moral Reasoning and Moral Behavior: Are Higher-Stage People More "Moral"?

Granted that people scoring at the higher Kohlberg stages may *think* about morality in higher ways (or at least more abstract and complex ways). But do they also *act* more morally? If you think about this question a bit, it may seem circular because it presupposes that we could agree on some particular moral behavior as the ultimate criterion against which to validate the measure of moral reasoning. Even if we could agree that the criterion behavior is in fact "moral," this might only be a sign of stage 4 reasoning about morality.

In more commonsense terms, however, the question is a valid one. Thus professional philosophers usually score in Kohlberg's highest stages (Nails, 1983, pp. 661–662), but this may only mean that they have learned an abstract language for talking about morality, rather than that they are actually more moral in their actions. Or imagine that some Nazi leaders were able to produce abstract and "principled" arguments for the Holocaust and other brutalities of the Nazi regime; we would certainly not want to say on that account that their actions were moral.[6]

Blasi (1980) and Rest (1986) review the evidence linking the Kohlberg measure to behavior. For example, studies comparing juvenile delinquents with matched nondelinquent control groups show that the nondelinquents score at significantly higher stages. (You can imagine how difficult it is, yet how essential, to be sure that the control group "nondelinquents" are truly nondelinquent, and not merely delinquents who evaded detection!) Further, laboratory studies of such presumably moral behaviors as honesty (resistance to temptation or cheating), resistance to conformity, and altruism or helping all tend to show positive relationships to stage of moral reasoning. Thus there is some evidence that moral reasoning is related to moral action.

Gilligan's Critique

In 1982, Gilligan leveled a major critique at Kohlberg's conception and measure of moral development, making three major claims. Studies using Kohlberg's stages, which tended to show that women ended up at a lower stage than men, give a seriously distorted picture of women's moral development. This is because Kohlberg's highest stages, which involve principles, rights, and rules, neglect the roles of *responsibility* and *caring* in morality. Further, these neglected themes are women's distinctive ways of thinking about morality—in Gilligan's terms, they are the distinctive moral "voice" of women. Gilligan concluded that Kohlberg's conception and measure are biased because, like so many other male theorists, he began by taking "male" as the norm for "human." Gilligan (1982) described her approach as an alternative:

> When one begins with the study of women and derives developmental constructs from their lives, the outline of a moral conception different from that described by Freud, Piaget, and Kohlberg begins to emerge and informs a different description of development. In this conception, the moral problem arises from conflicting

[6]As an informal exploration of this possibility, I took a passage from the diary of Nazi leader Joseph Goebbels in which he discussed whether he should obey Hitler's order to leave Berlin in 1945 or disobey and remain in Berlin to die with Hitler. I removed all identifying details and asked two experts in the use of the Kohlberg scoring system to score it. One replied that it was stage 4, the other that it was at least stage 4 and probably stage 5. On at least one issue, then, at least one Nazi leader reasoned at a high stage, suggesting that moral reasoning is not the same as moral behavior. On the other hand, Goebbels was unusually educated and intellectually sophisticated; perhaps most Nazi leaders would have reasoned at much lower stages.

responsibilities rather than from competing rights and requires for its resolution a mode of thinking that is contextual and narrative rather than formal and abstract. (p. 19)

Gender differences? If Gilligan is correct, these three points constitute quite a criticism. Let us evaluate each point in turn. First, do men typically score higher than women on the Kohlberg interview measure? Two widely cited early studies of activist student leaders (Fishkin, Keniston, & MacKinnon, 1973; Haan, Smith, & Block, 1968) suggested that men's scores clustered around stage 4, while women were usually at stage 3. However, several later and more systematic reviews of the moral development literature find little or no evidence of consistent sex differences on either the Kohlberg interview measure or the Rest objective measure (Broughton, 1983, pp. 616–622; Galotti, 1989; Rest, 1986, pp. 111–118; Walker, 1991).

A morality of caring and responsibility. Gilligan suggested an alternative conception of morality on the basis of a study by Belenky (1978; see also Gilligan & Belenky, 1980), who carried out intensive interviews with twenty-nine pregnant women who were considering having an abortion. Examining how these women constructed and resolved decisions about abortion, Gilligan concluded that they framed the moral issues not in terms of rights and rules, but in terms of care and responsibilities: caring for the self, responsibility for others, and a concern with relationships and interdependence (Gilligan, 1982, p. 74).

Carol Gilligan—"When one begins with the study of women and derives developmental constructs from their lives, the outline of a moral conception different from that described by Freud, Piaget, or Kohlberg begins to emerge . . . [arising] from conflicting responsibilities rather than from competing rights. . . . [For its resolution this requires] thinking that is contextual and narrative rather than formal and abstract" (1982, p. 19). (Harvard University. Photo by Julian Kemp)

Gilligan argues that these concerns with relationships, with care and responsibility, are characteristic of how women think about morality, and that they stand in sharp contrast to the male concern with rules, rights, and principles.

In discussing these results, Gilligan is actually making two different points: (1) caring and responsibility are neglected in Kohlberg's stages, and (2) caring and responsibility are (for reasons of biology, learning, or status) more characteristic of women than of men. Now it is certainly true that the language in which women discuss abortion decisions is different from the terms in which Kohlberg's original group of adolescent boys discussed hypothetical moral dilemmas. Further, these differences may well involve issues of caring and responsibility instead of abstract principles (although this is disputed by Broughton, 1983; Colby & Damon, 1983; and Nails, 1983).

Gender or method? Even granting these differences, however, this does not prove that they are due to gender. Recall that the women were discussing an urgent personal moral issue, an issue saturated with emotions, values, and conflicts that inescapably affected themselves and others in direct and very personal ways. In contrast, the boys (and anyone else responding to the Kohlberg interviews) were discussing a series of hypothetical verbal stories about hypothetical people. Gilligan and Kohlberg have clearly used very different methods to elicit people's moral reasoning. Thus the differences in responses may be due to gender, but they may also be due to differences in method. Belenky and Gilligan did not interview men, because men do not get pregnant and never have to face the moral issue of abortion in the same way that women do. We do not even know how the partners of the pregnant women would have discussed abortion. However, reviews of the available evidence suggest that there are few if any gender differences in concerns for caring or responsibility (Brayback, 1983; Colby & Damon, 1983, pp. 475–476; Galotti, 1989; Rest, 1986, p. 6).

Responsibility

Although Gilligan's gender-based critique of Kohlberg's conception and measure may be wrong, and although her own results may depend upon method rather than gender, her emphasis on caring and responsibility is a valuable addition to our understanding of moral reasoning and morality (see Kohlberg, Levine, & Hewer, 1983). Influenced in part by Gilligan's perspective, other psychologists have tried to conceptualize and measure responsibility (for example, Blasi, 1983; Winter & Barenbaum, 1985).

Table 10.5 shows some of the themes in people's writing or talking that are scored for responsibility according to the system developed by Winter and Barenbaum (1985). Notice how the first two themes, *moral-legal standards* and *internal obligation*, involve aspects of Kohlberg's higher stages, while the third theme, *concern for others*, is closely connected to Gilligan's conception of morality. In both systems, *self-judgment* would be a higher-stage concern and *concern*

TABLE 10.5 CATEGORIES FOR SCORING RESPONSIBILITY IN VERBAL TEXT

1. *Moral-legal standards of conduct:* Actions, people, or things described in terms of some abstract standard or principle involving legality, morality, or virtuous conduct.

2. *Internal obligation:* A person (or group) described as obliged to act because of internal or impersonal forces, versus in response to the act of another person or group. The feeling that one "has to" or "must" act (as an end in itself and not part of a means-end relationship).

3. *Concern for others:* A person (or group) described as helping or sympathetically concerned about someone else.

4. *Concern about negative consequences:* People (or a group) described as having some inner concern about possible negative consequences of their own actions.

5. *Self-judgment:* People (or a group) described as critically evaluating their own character (e.g., feeling shame or guilt), as the result of some action they have taken.

SOURCE: Adapted from Winter and Barenbaum (1985); see also Winter (1992d).

about consequences a lower-stage concern. In addition to channeling or moderating power motivation (as we saw in Chapter 5), this responsibility measure also predicts "responsible" behavior in its own right. For example, in a sample of upper-middle-class male college graduates, Winter (1992d) reported that men who scored high showed better long-term adaptation to aspects of adult life that involve other people but did not necessarily show better adaptation on aspects involving self-protection or self-enhancement. In other words, these responsible men act in accord with Gilligan's highest phase of moral reasoning.

While the new responsibility measure shows few male-female differences, there is some evidence that boys and girls develop a sense of responsibility in slightly different ways: for girls, verbal exhortation by parents is enough, while boys profit more by specific training in responsibility chores such as child care and food preparation. (Perhaps most parents assume that girls will carry out these chores naturally, without specific training!)

Although her work suggests (and has often been interpreted as supporting) gender differences in the structure of morality, Gilligan (1982) in the end conceded that the two "voices" of morality are not necessarily segregated by gender, at least in adulthood:

> Thus, starting from very different points, from the different ideologies of justice and care, the men and women in the study come, in the course of becoming adult, to a greater understanding of both points of view and thus to a greater convergence in judgment. (p. 167)

These two Dutch paintings—*Merry Company on a Terrace*, by Jan Steen, and *Girl Reading a Letter Near a Window*, by Jan Vermeer—illustrate one of the most fundamental dimensions of individual difference in temperament or traits. Some people ("extraverts") like lots of excitement and stimulation from other people and action. Other people ("introverts") prefer a quieter, solitary existence so that they can focus on inner thoughts.

Top: Jan Steen (1626–1679), Merry Company on a Terrace, *oil on canvas, 55 1/2" x 51 3/4", The Metropolitan Museum of Art, Fletcher Fund, 1958. (58.89)*

Bottom: Jan Vermeer, Girl Reading a Letter Near a Window. *Gemaeldgalerie, Staatliche Kunstsammlungen, Dresden.*

PART THREE

❖

Trait Theory and Temperament: Allport, Jung, and Eysenck

11

Introduction to Traits and Temperament

❖

We now turn to the study of traits and temperament, the upper-right box in Figure 11.1, page 374. In ordinary language, a trait is simply a distinguishing characteristic of something, a characteristic that varies from one person to another. The word comes from the French word *trait*, meaning "stroke" or "line," as in a drawing. A drawing of a person is made up of many strokes or lines (traits); you would recognize the person from the collection of "traits" or brush strokes that make up the drawing. In this original sense of the word, people have traits, but so do animals and even inanimate objects such as houses and cars.

As used in psychology, the word "trait" has three closely related meanings: (1) an aspect of personality that is directly or indirectly displayed in a person's behavior, (2) an aspect of a person's personality that is directly or indirectly visible to other people, or (3) a word that other people might use to describe an aspect of that person's personality. All three meanings involve aspects of personality that are *enduring and typical* or consistent across situations (top row of Figure 11.1) and *public* (right-hand column of Figure 11.1). Our motives may be secret (sometimes even from ourselves, as Freud argued) and our beliefs private, but the outward appearances or surfaces we present to the world are public (see Hogan, 1987, pp. 85–86). Even when we are rating our own traits, we do this by taking the perspective of an external observer on our behavior (McAdams, 1992a, p. 351). And while their expression may vary across contexts, traits are conceptualized as consistent and enduring (McCrae & John, 1992, p. 199). These enduring and public characteristics, along with internal structures and processes giving rise to them and other people's impressions of them, are all included in the personality domain of traits and temperament.[1]

WHAT IS A TRAIT OF PERSONALITY?

In a classic paper with the above question as its title, Gordon Allport (1931) introduced the concept of "trait" into the study of personality psychology. He suggested guidelines for its use and raised issues that are still being explored today.

First, Allport suggested that *traits are generalized characteristics that reflect individual distinctiveness.* Trait names, then, are broad and general labels for clusters of more specific acts or responses. Thus the generalized trait of "friendliness" might be reflected in a variety of more specific friendly behaviors: for example, spending time with other people rather than alone, being ready to "break the ice" by conversing with strangers, making lots of telephone calls, and being concerned about other people's happiness and well-being.

Of course, not even the most friendly person is friendly to everyone all the time and in all situations. Other traits (for example, cautiousness or domi-

---

[1]Many psychologists use *temperament* to refer to those traits that are presumed to have a strong biological or constitutional basis; others use trait and temperament interchangeably.

	Inner, Private, Subjective	Outer, Public, Objective
Enduring and "typical" across situations	COGNITIONS	TRAITS, TEMPERAMENT Examples of variables: Extraversion, Energy level Major theorists: Allport, Jung, Eysenck
Situation-dependent	MOTIVATION	SOCIAL CONTEXT

FIGURE 11.1
The major elements of personality.

nance) might get in the way, or the demands of the situation (for example, the desire for sleep, a plane to catch, or an exam the next day) might override the influence of even the strongest trait of friendliness. Thus *traits are not always expressed with perfect consistency in behavior.*

Finally, *we can study any trait in two ways—idiographically or nomothetically.*[2] As pointed out in Chapter 1, the word "idiographic" comes from *idioma*, a Latin and Greek word meaning "peculiarity" or "individuality," as in "idio-syncrasy," and *graph*, which means to write down or record. Thus *idiographic* can be defined as having to do with the record of a person's individuality. *Nomothetic*, derived from the Greek word *nomos*, or law, means the search for laws or lawfulness; in this case, the laws or regularities of traits. Any personality variable—motive, cognitive structure or style, belief or attitude, and trait—can be studied in idiographic or nomothetic ways.

[2]Allport (1937) is largely responsible for introducing and emphasizing the distinction between idiographic and nomothetic approaches to study of traits. Later, Allport (1962) rephrased the distinction as "morphogenic" (giving shape and structure) versus "dimensional," respectively, but personality psychologists continue to use the original names.

Gordon Allport, who emphasized idiographic (or morphogenic) methods in the study of personality. "Already we know that personality (in general) is an interesting topic for study. But only when morphogenic methods are more highly developed shall we be able to do justice to the fascinating individuality that marks the personalities of Bill, John, and Betty" (1962, p. 419). (UPI/Bettmann)

Using the skills of the clinician or the artist, idiographic studies explore the role of traits in the personalities of individual persons. Consider a person, Rachel, who is both "friendly" and "suspicious." Having determined that she possesses these two traits, we can ask how they are integrated in her behavior. For example, if Rachel is often suspicious of her friends, then her suspiciousness might get in the way of her friendships. (In this example I purposely chose two traits that conflict, which makes for a more interesting integration.) On the other hand, Rachel's friendliness and suspicion could be integrated in other, less conflicted ways: for example, she and her friends might be suspicious of other people.

However, we can also make a nomothetic study of friendliness or suspiciousness. We could develop scales to measure them in order to determine how they are distributed in the population. We could compare average levels of friendliness and suspiciousness in different groups—for example, students majoring in sociology versus physics, New Yorkers versus Californians, successful versus unsuccessful executives, and so on. Based on the case of Rachel, we could try to determine whether friendliness and suspiciousness go together or don't go together in the population as a whole.

DESCRIBING OTHER PEOPLE

Since traits are the element of personality we encounter most directly in every-day life, it is not surprising that many of the technical terms and scientific concepts of trait psychology are closely related to our everyday language for describing people. Thus in answering the question, "What kind of a person is Stephanie?" or the request "Tell me a little bit about Al," we usually begin by listing trait adjectives. If you have been (or know) a Boy Scout, you may remember the Boy Scout Law, which says that a scout should be trustworthy, loyal, helpful, friendly, courteous, kind, obedient, cheerful, thrifty, brave, clean, and reverent. Because everyday language is so saturated with trait words, therefore, we can learn a lot about traits by studying ordinary language. And because people in all cultures have been describing other people for thousands of years, we can also learn from studying a few examples taken from literature, philosophy, anthropologists' observations of other cultures, and even contemporary slang.

Trait Descriptions in Ancient Times

Jacob and Esau in the Book of Genesis. One of the first trait descriptions in the Bible contrasts the twins Esau and Jacob. Even within their mother's womb, we are told, they struggled as if they were two different nations. "Esau was a skillful hunter, a man of the field, while Jacob was a quiet man, dwelling in tents" (Genesis 25:27). Esau was the favorite of his father Isaac, while Jacob was preferred by his mother Rebekah. In the course of tricking Esau out of their father's blessing (with his mother's help), Jacob contrasted himself and his brother: "Behold, my brother Esau is a hairy man, and I am a smooth man" (Genesis 27:11). "Hairy" and "smooth" refer to physical characteristics, but they also suggest contrasting clusters of traits: "hairy" Esau, physically active in rough, outdoor pursuits, versus "smooth" Jacob, drawn more to indoor activities. (The Jacob-Esau contrast is illustrated in Figure 11.2, in connection with the discussion of Galen's four types.)

The "characters" of Theophrastus. Writing in the fourth century B.C., the Greek philosopher Theophrastus systematically described how people differed among themselves in their everyday behavior. "Greece has the same sky above it everywhere, and its people are all given a similar kind of upbring-ing," he observed. "How in the world, then, does it happen that we Greeks do not [all] have the same pattern of behavior?" (Anderson, 1970, p. 3). Since Theophrastus was a botanist, used to classifying plants, he described human variation by constructing a systematic description of different "characters" or types of people. He classified people according to "the type of behavior actu-ally exhibited and the mode of domestic life," which is what we would now call trait classification. The resulting series of witty character sketches is summarized in Table 11.1 with the name of each character and an example of behavior typical of that character. Theophrastus appears to have concentrated on undesirable character types, probably because he wrote for children, to "help them to choose the best people to know and be with" (Anderson, 1970, p. 3). (Some authorities believe that Theophrastus also wrote a companion book of "good" characters that was later lost.)

In the sixteenth through nineteenth centuries, many English and French authors wrote character sketches in imitation of Theophrastus, portraying such types as the "plodding student," the "younger brother," and the "fanatic" (compiled by Aldington, 1924).

Galen's typology of humors. About 500 years after Theophrastus, the Greek physician Galen (A.D. c. 130–c. 200), who is considered to be one of the founders of medicine, developed a theory of how physiological differences— specifically, the balance among four internal body fluids, or humors—determined people's major traits. The four humors were blood, phlegm, yellow bile, and black bile. If your *blood* predominated, you would be "sanguine" or warm, lively, and confident. (Sanguine comes from *sanguis,* the Latin word for "blood." "Hearty" and "cordial," which are synonyms for sanguine, come from the English and Latin words for "heart" and so are associated with blood.) If your *yellow bile* predominated, you would be "choleric" or angry. (*Chole* is Greek for "bile.") If your *black bile* was dominant, you were said to be "melancholic" or sad (*melan,* from the Greek word for "black," plus *chole*). A predominance of *phlegm* (slow-flowing mucus) would make you "phlegmatic"—sluggish, apathetic, and cold; not particularly responsive to social stimuli. Finally, if all four humors were in balance, you would be "good-humored." While modern personality psychologists do not accept Galen's humoral *theory,* his four-fold *classification* is still used in personality research, as we shall see later in Chapters 13 and 14. Further, the trait words inspired by his classification are still used to describe other people. Figure 11.2, page 379, shows how these four traits can be arranged in a two-dimensional table. As an illustration of how the classification works, I have placed Esau and Jacob in their appropriate locations in the figure.

Fashions in Trait Descriptions

The words we use to describe other people come from many different sources, and fashions in trait description are always changing. Thus an examination of our vocabulary of traits reveals historical layers showing the influence of different ideas and popular concerns (see Allport & Odbert, 1936, pp. 2–3). From astrology we have inherited words such as "lunatic" (someone under the influence of Luna, the moon), "jovial" (influenced by the planet Jupiter or Jove), or "mercurial" (affected by the planet Mercury). With the rise of the Christian church, qualities such as "pity" and "patience" assumed their present meaning as trait descriptions. From the time of the Protestant Reforma-

TABLE 11.1 THE "CHARACTERS" OF THEOPHRASTUS

Character name	Typical behavior (after Anderson, 1970)
Discrepancy between appearance and reality	
Insincerity	Praises you to your face after attacking you behind your back
Flattery	Will do anything to curry favor
Good impression maker	Changes underwear while it is still clean and uses scented lotions
Slander	Speaks ill things even of friends
Interpersonally active	
Garrulousness	Never stops talking
Talkativeness	Cannot control the impulse to talk
Officiousness	Takes on too much; would even try to settle an argument among strangers
Surliness	Gives a rude reply to a polite greeting
Complaining	When kissing lover, would stop to ask, "Do you *really* love me?"
Petty pride	Puts a monument on a pet puppy's grave
Pretentiousness	Claims to be shopping for expensive clothes but "forgets" to bring money
Arrogance	Says "See that you do this!" instead of "Would you please do this?"
Cowardice	"Pretends" to lose sword during battle
Love of rule	Pontificates about every public and political issue
Keeping bad company	Associates with rascals in order to seem "tough"
Uncouthness	
Boorishness	Wears shoes too large and talks too loud
Lack of moral feeling	Wouldn't support own mother in her old age
Rumor-mongering	Makes up and spreads stories, using "sources" no one could check
Offensiveness	Belches; sits around explaining intention to get drunk
Tactlessness	Invites you for a walk just when you're exhausted
Repulsiveness	Goes to bed without washing; has black and rotted teeth
Ill breeding	Talks about intimate bodily functions at the dinner table
Relation to money and possessions	
Greed	"Scalps" tickets and then sneaks in anyway and takes the seats
Pennypinching	Slices the meat very thin when guests come to dinner
Suspiciousness	Wants to ask for a deposit when a friend borrows something
Stinginess	Would cross the street to avoid a friend soliciting contributions
Avarice	Only visits museums when admission is free
Miscellaneous	
Absentmindedness	Wanders into the wrong room while going to the bathroom at night
Superstitiousness	Wants to build a shrine after coming across a sacred snake in the house
Immaturity	Plays children's games at adult festivals

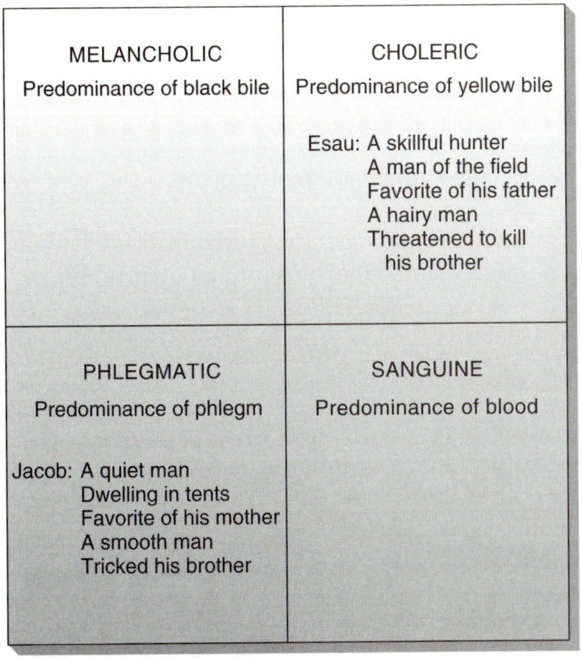

MELANCHOLIC
Predominance of black bile
	CHOLERIC
	Predominance of yellow bile
	
	Esau: A skillful hunter
	        A man of the field
	        Favorite of his father
	        A hairy man
	        Threatened to kill
	            his brother

PHLEGMATIC
Predominance of phlegm
 	
Jacob: A quiet man
        Dwelling in tents
        Favorite of his mother
        A smooth man
        Tricked his brother
	SANGUINE
	Predominance of blood

FIGURE 11.2
Placement of Esau and Jacob in Galen's typology of
temperament.

tion we have many individualist words, such as "self-esteem" or "self-confidence." Scots Presbyterians invented the word "selfish" in 1640. Perhaps people were less selfish before that year; or perhaps they were just as selfish, only their religion had not labeled their selfishness a vice. From the sixteenth-century Italian author of a manual on political power, we have the adjective "Machiavellian" to describe someone who deliberately and cynically manipulates others. (One of my students reported using "Malkovich," the name of one of the stars in the movie *Dangerous Liaisons,* as a new synonym for "manipulative.")

The influence of psychology. In modern times, the influence of psychology has turned technical terms such as "extraverted," "neurotic," "schizy," and "paranoid" into familiar trait words for describing other people.

Slang. The rich and constantly changing vocabulary of slang reflects the latest trends in trait language. The rise of psychedelic drug use in the 1960s gave us "flipped out," "laid back," "spacey," "unreal," and "uptight." Munro (1989) compiled a dictionary of student slang at UCLA, including some words that were up-to-the-minute in 1989. Are these words still in use when you are reading this book? Judging from past experience, at least some of the following words will find a permanent place in the English language as ways of describing people:

airhead: someone who is unintelligent, gullible, lacking in common sense, or ditzy

ditzy: flighty, airheaded

dweeb: a nerd, wimpy

nerd: someone who studies a lot

wimp: physically, emotionally, or socially inadequate person

At the beginning of a personality course, I ask my students at the University of Michigan to report on the latest slang. Here are some of their replies:

narly: gross, repulsive

wigged out: neurotic, unable to relax

sweet, key-sweet: good, cool

tool: person who doesn't realize things, and so gets used by others

buster: a dummy, complete dufus, idiot maximus

rad: really cool

slipper: comfortable to be with

oatmealish: plain, without substance

knob, door knob: dumb, boring

paper bag: [no definition given]

Notice how many of these terms are defined in terms of each other. For example, a "nerd" is also likely to be a "dweeb" or a "wimp"; in contrast to someone who is "rad," who is also likely to be "key-sweet" or "awesome." These two contrasting clusters seem to define people who don't and do fit some ideal of mainstream American college culture. Given the number of slang words devoted to these two clusters, college students must find this an important distinction to make. I'm not sure whether "wigged out" belongs with either cluster: some (but not all) nerds might be wigged out; but could someone who is rad also be wigged out?

TRAIT DESCRIPTION IN POETRY AND PHILOSOPHY

In the next few sections of this chapter, I will present examples of trait description from poetry, philosophy, a non-Western culture, police investigators, and a professional diplomat.

John Milton's L'Allegro *and* Il Penseroso

John Milton (1608–1674) was one of the leading authors of Puritan England, best known for several hard-to-read poetic epics such as *Paradise Lost,* and *Aeropagitica,* a vigorous defense of intellectual freedom. (He also served as secretary of state to Oliver Cromwell, the lord protector—that is, dictator—of England during the time of the Puritan Revolution. Cromwell had decided to corre-

spond with foreign governments in Latin instead of either English or the other
country's language, and so Milton's classical education made him useful.)

Shortly after finishing college, Milton wrote a famous pair of poems contrasting two types of person: *L'Allegro,* a celebration of mirth, and *Il Penseroso,*
a study of melancholy. To highlight the contrast between these two types, I
have collected some of the most vivid images from each poem in Table 11.2.
(Take a look at the full poems sometime; they appear in many anthologies of
English poetry.)

TABLE 11.2 COMPARATIVE TRAITS IN JOHN MILTON'S *L'ALLEGRO* AND *IL PENSEROSO*

Il Penseroso *These pleasures, Melancholy, give,* *And I with thee will choose to live.*	L'Allegro *These delights, if thou canst give,* *Mirth, with thee I mean to live.*
Movement	
Come, but keep thy wonted state With even step, and musing gait.	Come, and trip it as you go On the light fantastic toe.
Social behavior	
Come, pensive nun, devout and pure. Sober, steadfast, and demure, All in a robe of darkest grain. And may at last my weary age Find out the peaceful hermitage . . . Where I may sit and rightly spell Of every star that Heaven doth shew.	Jest and youthful jollity, Quips, and cranks, and wanton wiles . . . Sport that wrinkled care derides And laughter holding both his sides.
Aesthetic preferences	
And join with thee calm Peace, and Quiet. Sweet bird that shunn'st the noise of folly. There in close covert by some brook, Where no profaner eye may look. Hide me from day's garish eye.	Oft listening how the hounds and horn Cheerly rouse the slumbering morn . . . Through the high wood echoing shrill . . . Where the great sun begins his state, Robed in flames and amber light. . . . Straight my eye hath caught new pleasures. . . .
Literary preferences	
Sometime let gorgeous tragedy In sceptred pall come sweeping by . . . Or the tale of Troy divine.	Then to the spicy nut-brown ale, With stories told of many a feat. . . . Thus done the tales, to bed they creep.
Preferred environment	
But let my due feet never fail To walk the studious cloister's pale.	Towered cities please us then. And the busy hum of men.

Movement is the central contrast between the two poems. *L'Allegro* summons us to the rapid and lively movement of the dance . . .

> Come, and trip it as you go
> On the light fantastic toe.

. . . while *Il Penseroso* calls for the slow and deliberate movement of a procession.

> Come, but keep thy wonted state
> With even step, and musing gait.

As shown in the table, other contrasts involve *physical versus mental activity;* jesting, trickery, and *playfulness versus sobriety; preference versus aversion for strong stimuli* (loud sounds, vivid colors, spicy food); liking of *heroic adventure stories versus tragedy;* and *enjoyment of bustling cities versus quiet contemplation* of inner visions.

Nighttime brings out a more subtle contrast. For *L'Allegro,* nighttime means the excitement of staying up all night:

> To hear the lark begin his flight,
> And singing startle the dull night . . .
> Till the dappled dawn doth rise.

For *Il Penseroso,* however, night is a time for solitude and quiet contemplation:

> Or let my lamp at midnight hour,
> Be seen in some high lonely tower.

In modern terms, Milton here contrasts the student who stays up all night to party with the student who stays up to do the required reading or perhaps to think and "behold the wandering moon." No doubt you can recognize these two types among the people you know.

The differences in musical preference are at first a little surprising. As you might expect, the *L'Allegro* type enjoys music, and in today's world would be the kind of person who keeps the stereo turned up to the maximum:

> When the merry bells ring round
> And the jocund rebecks [stringed instruments] sound

But the *Il Penseroso* type also enjoys music:

> There let the pealing organ blow,
> To the full-voiced quire [choir] below,
> In service high, and anthems clear.

Two engravings representing Milton's poems, *L'Allegro* and *Il Penseroso*, by W. E. Frost and W. C. Thomas, respectively. (*From* L'Allegro *and* Il Penseroso, *by John Milton, with Thirty Illustrations Designed Expressly for the Art-Union of London, London, 1848; reproduced by permission of the Special Collections department, University of Michigan Library*)

Why should a quiet, contemplative person like loud and stirring organ music and full-voiced choirs? Perhaps because with this kind of music, there is little to see; all you are supposed to do is sit still and listen. Richard Nixon once expressed this same musical preference (1978):

> I have always had two great—and still unfulfilled—ambitions: to direct a symphony orchestra *and to play an organ in a cathedral*. I think that to create music is one of the highest aspirations man can set for himself. (p. 9, emphasis added)

Was Nixon, then, an *Il Penseroso* type? His public image certainly involved restraint and melancholy rather than mirth. In law school, he had the nickname "Gloomy Gus." As one fellow student recalled, "I can see him sitting in the law library hunched over a book, seldom even looking up. He never smiled. . . . Even on Saturday nights, he was in the library, studying" (Ambrose, 1987, pp. 75–76). As president, he typically made important decisions only after periods of solitary contemplation. In the discussion of measuring traits at a distance (at the end of Chapter 13), we will find further confirmation of Nixon as a true *Il Penseroso* type.

Schopenhauer's Good-Spirited and Intelligent Types

In his essay on "Personality, or What a Man Is," the German philosopher Arthur Schopenhauer (1788–1860) described two types of persons that are remarkably similar to Milton's paired poems (Schopenhauer, 1851/1901). For Schopenhauer, the type of person you are depends on the relation between two "master traits" that are part of your temperament: (1) your muscular and vital energy, representing the forces of life asserting themselves, which you experience consciously as "will," and (2) your sensitiveness or capacity for feeling pain.

According to Schopenhauer, if energy predominates over sensitiveness, then you are a *good-spirited* type of person—prone to boredom and constantly seeking the pleasures of energy or motion. Schopenhauer thought of this type as dull (1851/1901):

> A dull mind is, as a rule, associated with dull sensibilities, nerves which no stimulus can affect, a temperament, in short, which does not feel pain or anxiety very much, however great or terrible it may be. Now, intellectual dullness . . . betrays itself by a constant and lively attention to all the trivial circumstances in the external world. This is the true source of boredom—a continual panting after excitement. (p. 18)

In the beginning of human society, Schopenhauer admitted, the energetic and good-spirited person was well adapted to dealing with the challenges and problems of everyday life. With the advance of industrial civilization, however, the demand for muscular energy was reduced and so the energetic type began to be bored:

> But if this struggle comes to an end, his unemployed forces become a burden to him; and he has to set to work and play with them, use them, I mean, for no purpose at all, beyond avoiding the other source of human suffering, boredom. (p. 24)

On the other hand, if sensitiveness is greater than energies, then you would be an *intelligent* type of person, running the risk of melancholy:

> This high degree of intelligence is rooted in a high degree of susceptibility . . . [resulting in] an increased capacity for emotion, an enhanced sensibility to all mental and even bodily pain, greater impatience of obstacles, greater resentment of interruption . . . augmented by the power of the imagination, the vivid character of the whole range of thought, including what is disagreeable. (p. 19)

While sensitive people are thus vulnerable to a variety of painful emotions, Schopenhauer believed that their greater self-sufficiency actually made them more likely to find true happiness, especially in old age:

For all other sources of happiness are in their nature most uncertain, precarious, fleeting, the sport of chance; and so even under the most favorable circumstances they can easily be exhausted. . . . And in old age these sources of happiness most necessarily dry up: love leaves us then, and wit, desire to travel, delight in horses, aptitude for social intercourse; friends and relations, too, are taken from us by death. (p. 22)

Schopenhauer's typology of persons is summarized in Table 11.3. Comparing this table with Table 11.2 based on Milton's two poems, you can see that both authors have used essentially the same dimensions to describe and distinguish people. Of course each author had a bias: Schopenhauer, who was himself moody and irritable, intensely disliked good-spirited people, whereas Milton was more even-handed between *L'Allegro* and *Il Penseroso*.

Other Binary Distinctions in Western Thought

Milton's poems and Schopenhauer's typology are both *binary:* that is, they consist of two opposite, mutually exclusive types. Among Western thinkers, such binary typologies have been very popular for classifying people. Nietzsche (1871/1967), for example, contrasted *Dionysian* and *Apollonian* types.

TABLE 11.3 SCHOPENHAUER'S TYPOLOGY OF PERSONS

Trait or characteristic	The intelligent, melancholy type (Sensitiveness greater than muscular energy)	The good-spirited, dull type (Muscular energy greater than sensitiveness)
Reaction to impressions	Susceptible to unpleasant impressions	Susceptible to pleasant impressions
Intelligence	"High degree of intelligence" and vivid, powerful imagination	"A dull mind," "intellectually poor and generally vulgar"
Vulnerability	Vulnerable to pain and intense emotions; also to estrangement from other people	Vulnerable to boredom, "avoiding nothing so much as [one's] self"
Lifestyle	"Tranquil, modest life; solitude;" moderating desire and harboring one's resources	"Panting after excitement"
Typical goals	Wisdom	"Splendor, rank, pomp, titles and power"
Typical pastimes and pleasures	"Pleasures of sensibility:" reading and thinking, literature, music, meditation	Food and drink; sport and physical activity; violence and warfare; card games, gambling; travel
Source of life happiness	Inner things	Things external: property, people, society

SOURCE: Based on Schopenhauer (1851/1901).

The nature of this contrast should be clear once you realize that Dionysus was the ancient Greek god of wine, whereas Apollo was the god of wisdom! Along these same lines, many writers have contrasted *romantic* and *classic* styles of art, music, and behavior (Babbitt, 1919/1977; Barzun, 1961; Winter, Alpert, & McClelland, 1963). William James (1907/1955) distinguished between *tough-minded* people, who are pessimistic materialists, guided by facts; and *tender-minded* people, who are optimistic idealists, guided by principles (see also Jung, 1923/1971, especially chaps. 1–3 and 5–9, on other binary person typologies in Western thought).

TRAIT DESCRIPTION IN OTHER CULTURES

Ethnopsychology

For all their differences, John Milton and Arthur Schopenhauer were both white, wealthy European males. How do people from non-Western cultures describe persons? This topic is known as ethnopsychology or *ethnnopersonality* (Smith & Bond, 1993).

Almost halfway around the world from Western Europe, just below the equator, on the north shore of the island of New Britain (formerly a German and then a British colony, now part of the independent country of Papua New Guinea) is the culture of the Lakalei, consisting of about 3,000 people spread out among twenty-three villages (see the map in Figure 11.3). In culture and language, the Lakalei are similar to many other societies in the New Guinea–Melanesia area. According to Valentine (1963), the Lakalei are agriculturalists, supplementing the usual range of tropical crops with pig raising, hunting, and fishing. Since 1900 they have also become more and more involved in plantation work for Westerners or labor in the cash economy. While men hold most of the leadership positions, the Lakalei are matrilineal and reckon descent only through the mother.

In almost every respect, therefore, the Lakalei contrast with the ancient Greece of Theophrastus and Galen, the Europe of Milton and Schopenhauer, and our own contemporary society and culture. From an ethnopersonality perspective, the critical question is how the Lakalei describe other Lakalei. If their language of trait description converges with those of Galen, Milton, and modern psychology, it would suggest that there are at least some universal trait dimensions. If, on the other hand, the Lakalei descriptions are quite different, then we may conclude that different cultures have their own unique ways of organizing traits. This specific question is part of the broader issue of *psychic universalism versus localism*. That is, is personality more or less the same among all human beings, or are there important differences among different cultures in the elements of personality? And if so, how are they organized? In this chapter we shall consider only one aspect of this issue, namely whether there are cultural differences in trait description. We will return to the broader question in Part Four.

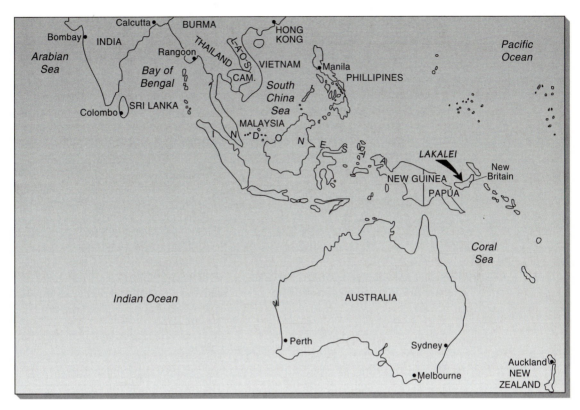

FIGURE 11.3
The Lakalei: A Melanesian preindustrial culture of New Britain Island.

How the Lakalei Describe People

According to Valentine (1963),[3] the Lakalei describe individual persons by placing them in one of two categories, each consisting of groups of trait words, as shown in Table 11.4: people of *anger* (which also includes play, movement, scattered attention, and sexuality) and people of *shame* (which includes silence, good conduct, knowledge, and art). These two categories contrast sharply with each other. That is, if the Lakalei describe someone with any adjective from one group, they are also likely to use other adjectives from the same group, and *un*likely to use adjectives from the other group. Thus Lakalei trait organization is binary: individual persons are usually described with the words of only one of the two groups.

People of anger are restless and impulsive, distractable, emotionally volatile, and fond of play and sexual activity. They would seem to fit Milton's

[3]A caution: Valentine's account is that of a Western anthropologist, trained to record and analyze other cultures in their own terms, but inevitably perceiving Lakalei "reality" through the filters of Western culture and the discipline of anthropology. Thus his account is not actually a Lakalei account of how Lakalei trait words are used and organized, but rather the observations of a trained and sensitive (but non-Lakalei) observer. Bias—that is, constructing the Lakalei in our own (Western) image—is still possible.

TABLE 11.4 COMPARATIVE TRAITS DESCRIBED BY LAKALEI

Person of shame	Person of anger
Primary trait phrase	
Person of shame: easily and often shamed; responds with embarrassed withdrawal	Person of anger: becomes angry frequently, easily, and without cause
Related trait phrases	
Person of silence: conducts self quietly; unresponsive	Person of play: fond of joking, teasing, impersonations, games
Person of good conduct: literally, "with a good way of sitting down"	Person of movement: restless; can't remain in one place for long
Person of knowledge: mastery of crafts, magical skills, and mythological knowledge	Person of diffuse attention: impulsive shifts of attention; does not work steadily in the gardens
Person of art: good at decorative carving, mask making, and feather work	Person of sexuality: becomes worn out by spending so much time in sexual activity
Role in Lakalei culture	
Industriousness, dependability; obedience and willingness to follow instructions; specialists, especially in sorcery	Leadership: originally in warfare and hunting; now in forceful and aggressive organizational ability
Relation to colonialism	
Emphasized as desirable (yet also exploited and, simultaneously, condemned) by colonial authorities and missionaries	Believed to be best able to deal with European colonial society

SOURCE: Based on Valentine (1963).

L'Allegro and Schopenhauer's good-spirited type. In contrast, people of shame are quiet, well-behaved, and able to persevere at demanding and delicate tasks such as carving masks. They seem like the *Il Penseroso* type, with one important difference: people of shame are not necessarily sad or melancholic. Perhaps the words "shame" and "silence" do suggest tendencies in that direction. On the other hand, we in the West may only *believe* that quiet people are sad because we place greater social value on the active *L'Allegro* type.

The Lakalei value both types of people. While people of anger tend to become leaders (especially in dealings with Westerners), people of shame fill the ranks of experts and specialists, thereby playing an honored part in Lakalei society. Trait description is somewhat related to gender and age. For example, women are more likely than men to be people of shame. Shame traits are believed to develop during childhood and to become especially prominent with maturity and old age, while anger traits are seen as important during midlife.

TRAIT DESCRIPTION BY EXPERT PRACTITIONERS

In our own society, describing other people is an important part of many careers. As examples, I have chosen two quite different jobs: police officers, who in the course of their work encounter all kinds of people; and former U.S. Secretary of State Henry Kissinger, who personally dealt with almost every important world leader in the course of his diplomatic career. In different ways, both police investigators and professional diplomats have to "size up" other people quickly, on the basis of small cues and minimal information.

Personality Judgments in Police Work

"Dangerousness." Police decisions often have life-or-death consequences: Is this person dangerous? Should I draw my gun? How much force will be necessary to subdue this person? In a study of how members of the Houston police force make such judgments, Rozelle and Baxter (1975) found that *hostility, cooperativeness, nervousness,* and *intelligence* were the four most common trait categories used by individual police officers to describe crime suspects or perpetrators. Holzworth and Pipping (1985) were particularly interested in the factors that lead individual police officers to draw their weapons as they approach a crime scene. They asked officers to respond to a series of hypothetical police radio calls, and found that the decision to draw a weapon depended on three kinds of "cues" about the hypothetical person to be encountered: their appearance (neat versus disheveled), their attitude (cooperative versus belligerent), and their behavior (submissive versus threatening). In fact, these three characteristics were more important than the person's race, sex, age, or size.

Criminal personality profiling. When a major crime, especially murder, has been discovered and the perpetrator is unknown, police psychologists are often called upon to provide a "personality profile" of the offender on the basis of the crime scene. In classic detective fiction, Sherlock Holmes would briefly examine a few clues and then pronounce a judgment (Conan Doyle, 1893/1938):

> He was a man of untidy habits—very untidy and careless. He was left with good prospects, but he threw away his chances, lived for some time in poverty with occasional short intervals of prosperity, and finally, taking to drink, he died. That is all I can gather. (p. 95)

Even today, criminal profiling is as much art as science, but in recent years one typology of murderers, based on observed characteristics of the murder scene, has become widely used (Holmes, 1989).

Many murders (hence also murderers) can be classified as either *disorganized* or *organized*. Table 11.5 describes the murder-scene characteristics and personality characteristics of each type. The disorganized person murders suddenly and spontaneously, without advance planning, and with no particular thought for avoiding detection. To avoid being overpowered or having the victim escape, the murderer acts quickly, often using whatever weapon happens to be at hand. As a result, the investigation usually begins with many clues and a lot of evidence.

Organized murderers, in contrast, plan their crime and work out details in advance: the weapon to be used, disposal of the body, how to cover their own tracks. Their organized control extends to the victim, who is often restrained with rope, tape, or a blindfold. The killing itself is likely to be slow and deliberate. Sometimes the murderer enacts compulsive rituals at the scene of the crime; the murder becomes a symbolic drama in which the perpetrator plays a star role. Many famous serial killers fit this pattern. With fewer obvious clues, detection is more difficult and often depends upon interpreting the ritual aspects of the crime.

While the disorganized and organized types are specialized categories used by the police to evaluate murders and murderers, they do overlap with

TABLE 11.5 PERSONALITY TYPES COMMONLY USED IN PROFILING MURDERERS

Organized nonsocial	Disorganized asocial
Typical crime scene details	
Crime scene reflects overall control	Crime scene random and sloppy
Restraints used on victim	Few restraints used on victim
Victim forced to submit	Sudden violence to victim
Body hidden	Body left in view
Weapon and other evidence absent	Weapon and other evidence often present
Body left at death scene	Body transported from death scene
Overall, a planned offense	Overall, a spontaneous offense
Personal characteristics of perpetrator	
Socially competent, manipulative	Socially inadequate
Controlled mood during crime	Anxious mood during crime
Likely to have used alcohol during the crime	Not likely to have used alcohol during the crime
Crime likely precipitated by situational stress	Crime not precipitated by situational stress
Living with a partner	Living alone
Follows crime in news media	Not interested in news media

SOURCE: Adapted from Holmes (1989, chap. 5) and Ressler and Burgess (1985).

many other sets of categories mentioned above. Thus the disorganized murderer resembles the *L'Allegro,* Dionysian, or person of anger types, while the organized murderer shares many characteristics of the *Il Penseroso,* Apollonian, or person of shame types.

Henry Kissinger's Gallery of World Leaders

As national security adviser and later secretary of state, Henry Kissinger played a major role in several United States foreign policy initiatives between 1969 and 1977. For example, his secret visits laid the groundwork for Richard Nixon's historic 1972 visit to the People's Republic of China. His personal negotiations finally ended U.S. involvement in the Vietnam war in 1973. Later that year, his so-called shuttle diplomacy almost single-handedly brought about a cease-fire in the 1973 war between Israel and its Arab neighbors. How did Kissinger do it? Among his many other skills and personal characteristics, Kissinger's legendary ability to understand and negotiate with a variety of world leaders played an important part (see Rubin, 1981). Kissinger left a detailed written record of his observations and judgments of these leaders in his two volumes of memoirs, *Years of Upheaval* (Kissinger, 1982) and *White House Years* (Kissinger, 1979).

Swede and Tetlock (1986) studied the way in which Kissinger organized his perceptions of other people's traits. First, they carefully searched both volumes of Kissinger memoirs, noting any passage that described the personal characteristics of some leader. Kissinger had described thirty-eight leaders with at least fifteen paragraphs, which produced a total of 3,759 instances of trait descriptions. Swede and Tetlock were able to group about half of these descriptions into 106 trait categories (trait words with their various suffixes, prefixes, and negations). They then went back and noted, for each of the thirty-eight leaders, whether Kissinger used or did not use each of the 106 categories. Finally, they applied a statistical procedure called factor analysis (see Chapter 13) to determine how these 106 trait categories clustered across the descriptions of thirty-eight leaders. In other words, when Kissinger employed one of the 106 trait categories to describe a leader, what other categories did he also use? The resulting factors or clusters are the major trait dimensions that Henry Kissinger used to describe the significant other people whom he encountered in his professional role of diplomat.

With their clustering procedure, Swede and Tetlock identified five trait clusters in Kissinger's descriptions of people: *professional anguish, ambitious patriotism, revolutionary greatness, intellectual sophistication,* and *realistic friendship.* Table 11.6 illustrates some of the adjectives that make up each cluster and identifies one or two world leaders scoring high in that cluster. For example, Kissinger described revolutionary leaders such as Mao Zedong and Anwar Sadat as "self-assured" and "ruthless," but also as "great." They can be contrasted to Richard Nixon, a different kind of active leader, who is seen as "ambitious" and "patriotic" but also "suspicious" and "ungenerous."

TABLE 11.6 HENRY KISSINGER'S IMPLICIT THEORY OF PERSONALITY

	Trait cluster[a]				
	1 *Professional* *anguish*	2 *Ambitious* *patriotism*	3 *Revolutionary* *greatness*	4 *Intellectual* *sophistication*	5 *Realistic* *friendship*
Associated adjectives	Insecure Lonely Tough Proud	Patriotic Suspicious Ambitious Ungenerous	Great Revolutionary Self-assured Ruthless	Humorous Knowledgeable Skilled Subtle	Ambivalent Decisive Friendly Close
Examples of high scorers	Indira Gandhi[b] Henry Kissinger	Richard Nixon Nguyen Van Thieu[f]	Mao Zedong[c] Anwar Sadat[g]	Le Duc Tho[d] Zhou Enlai[h]	Nelson Rockefeller[e] Georges Pompidou[i]

[a]Label as used by Swede and Tetlock.
[b]Prime Minister of India, 1966–1977 and 1980–1984.
[c]Chinese revolutionary hero and Communist Party chairman.
[d]North Vietnamese diplomat with whom Kissinger negotiated an end to U.S. participation in the Vietnam war.
[e]Governor of New York (1959–1973) and U.S. vice president (1974–1977).
[f]President of South Vietnam during the latter years of U.S. involvement in the Vietnam war.
[g]President of Egypt, 1970–1981.
[h]Premier of China, 1949–1976.
[i]President of France, 1969–1974.
SOURCE: Adapted from Swede and Tetlock (1986).

At first glance, the trait structure employed by Henry Kissinger seems much more complicated than the simple binary typologies we have been considering so far: five trait clusters and nine leader types based on combinations of clusters. Yet even this analysis underestimates the actual complexity of Kissinger's descriptions. The five clusters account for only 70 percent of the variation in the 106 trait categories; the categories only include 43 percent of the total number of trait descriptions of the thirty-eight leaders; and the material on these thirty-eight leaders is only 87 percent of the total number of passages in which Kissinger described other people. Multiplying these three percentages together gives 26 percent, which means that these five dimensions capture about one-quarter of the "subtle, highly differentiated quality of Kissinger's perceptions of others" (Swede & Tetlock, 1986, p. 641).

Nevertheless, a close examination of Table 11.6 reveals some similarities to the Milton and Schopenhauer types. Clusters 3 (revolutionary greatness) and 5 (realistic friendship), for example, both suggest features of the good-spirited *L'Allegro* type. In Kissinger's mind, this type occurs in separate "forceful" and "friendly" versions. Clusters 2 (ambitious patriotism) and 1 (professional anguish) have elements of the *Il Penseroso* type, but they are both tinged with negative terms, such as "insecure" and "suspicious," that do not appear in Milton. (Recall, though, that Schopenhauer's intelligent type was also "melancholic.") In Kissinger's view, both *Il Penseroso* clusters involve insecurity—what might be termed a "Woody Allen" dimension. Finally, Kissinger's cluster 4 (intellectual sophistication) bears some resemblence to both *Il Penseroso* and Schopenhauer's intelligent type. Overall, then, Henry Kissinger's trait descriptions involve elements of many other typologies reviewed above, but elaborated and combined in complex ways.

CONVERGENCES IN TRAIT DESCRIPTION

Table 11.7 draws together the many different patterns of trait description that we have considered so far in this chapter. It includes many different time periods, cultures, and purposes. Yet these different patterns converge in some important ways. For example, consider the contrast between Esau and Jacob. To the Lakalei, they would be a person of anger and a person of shame, respectively; to Milton they would be *L'Allegro* and *Il Penseroso*; to Schopenhauer, a good-feeling type and an intelligent type. As murderers, Esau would likely be disorganized and Jacob organized. Had he known them, Henry Kissinger would probably have described Esau as a "great revolutionary" or "realistic friend," whereas Jacob might have been seen as an "anguished professional" or "sophisticated intellectual."

TABLE 11.7 INTEGRATION OF DIFFERENT PATTERNS OF TRAIT DESCRIPTION

Writer or theorist	Categories	
Book of Genesis	Jacob: a quiet man	Esau: a skillful hunter
Characters of Theophrastus		Interpersonally active characters
Galen's types	Phlegmatic and melancholic	Sanguine and choleric
Milton's poems	*Il Penseroso*	*L'Allegro*
Schopenhauer's personality types	Intelligent type (sensitiveness greater than energy)	Good-spirited type (muscular and vital energy greater than sensitiveness)
Nietzsche's types	Apollonian (god of light, music, poetry, and prophecy)	Dionysian (god of fertility, wine, and drama)
Literary and artistic styles	Classic	Romantic
Lakalei terms	People of shame	People of anger
Types of murderers	Organized nonsocial	Disorganized asocial
Henry Kissinger's types	Sophisticated intellectual, anguished professional	Great revolutionary, realistic friend

Describing Albert Einstein

At this point, it is useful to turn away from discussing abstract types and trait dimensions and focus on the concrete task of describing a particular person. As an example, I have chosen the physicist Albert Einstein, arguably the most famous and influential scientist of the last several hundred years and one of the most extraordinary people of the twentieth century. Though Einstein has been dead for more than forty years, his face, wreathed with an unforgettable shock of hair, is still a familiar sight in surprising places, such as on T-shirts and in the 1994 movie *I.Q.* To many people Einstein is the personification of the word genius. Even today, bright young children, (especially if they are socially awkward) are taunted (or is it envied?) with the nickname "Einstein" by their elementary school classmates. Why is Einstein's name still magic? He was not a political leader, a war hero, a sports champion, or an entertainment star. Unless you have taken physics, I doubt that you could name any other physicist of his era. Einstein transformed our understanding of physical reality with the concept of relativity and the famous formula, $E = mc^2$, but few people can actually explain his general and special theories of relativity. Perhaps we can understand what keeps Einstein's name and image alive by considering his traits, or in everyday language, the kind of person he was.

Einstein's Traits

The outer world and the inner life. Einstein never wrote a full autobiography, but he did leave autobiographical notes and several collections of his views on the world, human nature, and society. Let us examine the first sentences of his autobiographical notes (Einstein, 1949/1979):

> Here I sit in order to write, at the age of sixty-seven, something like my own obituary. I am doing this . . . because I do, in fact, *believe* that it is a good thing to show those who are striving alongside of us how our own striving and searching *appears* in retrospect. After some *reflection,* I *felt* how imperfect any such attempt is bound to be. (p. 3, emphasis added)

Thus Einstein began his life story not with an account of his earliest memory or family history, but rather with a description of his internal mental processes while writing. (In fact, in the entire autobiographical notes, he mentions only one relative—his father.) From Einstein, then, we can expect not a narrative of events but rather a recording and analysis of inner states. Einstein continued with a discussion of subjectivity itself:

> Every reminiscence is colored by one's present state, hence by a deceptive point of view. This consideration could easily deter one. Nevertheless much can be gathered out of one's own experience that is not open to another consciousness. (p. 3)

At this point, I can imagine that you might ask, "Is this an autobiography?" Einstein anticipated that question and answered, "Essentially yes. For the essential in the being of a man of my type lies precisely in *what* he thinks and *how* he thinks, not in what he does or suffers" (p. 31, emphasis in original).

For contrast, we can examine the opening words of the autobiography of Benjamin Franklin—also a scientist, but a very different kind of person. They reflect an intense awareness of other people and interest in the world of action (Franklin, 1788/1990):

> I have ever had a Pleasure in obtaining any little *Anecdotes of my Ancestors.* . . . Hereby, too, I shall indulge the Inclination so natural in old Men, to be talking of themselves and *their own past Actions,* and I shall indulge it, without being troublesome to others who thro' respect to Age might think themselves oblig'd to give me a Hearing. . . . And lastly, (I may as well confess it, since my Denial of it will be believ'd by no Body) perhaps I shall a good deal gratify my own *Vanity.* (pp. 3–4; first two emphases added)

To return to Einstein: his first reference to a personal past comes in the second paragraph. As you might expect by now, though, it is not the memory of an event, but rather a discussion of his early worldview and philosophy of life, which involved preference for the inner life over the external social world of desire and hypocrisy (Einstein, 1949/1979):

> When I was a fairly precocious young man I became thoroughly impressed with the futility of the hopes and strivings that chase most men restlessly through life. Moreover, I soon discovered the cruelty of that chase, which in those years was much more carefully covered up by hypocrisy and glittering words than is the case today. By the mere existence of his stomach everyone was condemned to participate in that chase. The stomach might well be satisfied by such participation, but not man insofar as he is a thinking and feeling being. (p. 3)

From the perspective of old age, Einstein saw his life as an effort to free himself from this "chase" of human society, first by religion but finally through science:

> Out yonder there was this huge world, which exists independently of us human beings and which stands before us like a great, eternal riddle, at least partially accessible to our inspection and thinking. *The contemplation of this world beckoned as a liberation,* and I soon noticed that many a man whom I had learned to esteem and to admire had found *inner freedom* and security in its pursuit. The mental grasp of this extra-personal world within the frame of our capabilities presented itself to my mind, half consciously, half unconsciously, as a supreme goal. (p. 5; emphasis added)

Thus at the very beginning of his life story, Einstein makes clear that whereas direct *physical* contact with the external world is unpleasant and frustrating, *mental* comprehension of that world, through intuition and thought, can be the highest form of satisfaction. The external world is mainly important as a "hook" upon which to hang our concepts and theories, rather than as a "thing" in its own right. It is not fixed and definite, but rather always changing even as our ideas about it change, for "we now know that [our concepts] will have to be replaced by others farther removed from the sphere of immediate experience" (p. 31). Notice how similar Einstein's views are to Kelly's principle of "constructive alternativism," discussed in Chapter 6.

As we shall see, Einstein's *focus on contemplation and the internal world* is a psychological thread that runs throughout the course of his life and work, unifying his scientific interests and accomplishments, his philosophical writings (Einstein, 1950, 1954a), and his more specific traits (Clark, 1971/1984), to which we now turn.

Early focus on the internal. Einstein recalled two early experiences of intense satisfaction through contemplation. First, when he was 4 or 5, he was shown a compass by his father. "That this needle behaved in such a determined way . . . made a deep and lasting impression upon me. Something deeply hidden had to be behind things" (1949/1979, p. 9). Then at age 12 he received a book about geometry:

> I experienced a second wonder of a totally different nature. . . . Here were assertions . . . that—though by no means evident—could nevertheless be proved with such certainty that any doubt appeared to be out of the question. This lucidity and certainty made an indescribable impression upon me. (p. 9)

From this point on, Einstein's brief autobiographical fragment focuses exclusively on his intellectual life: his discovery of physics as his life's work, his criticisms of Newton's theories, and a modest account of his own ideas—ideas that were in fact a scientific revolution:

> My intuition was not strong enough in the field of mathematics to differentiate clearly the fundamentally important, that which is really basic, from the rest. . . . [but in physics] I soon learned to scent out that which might lead to fundamentals and to turn aside from everything else. (p. 15)

Aloofness from the external world of things. For Einstein, "the trite objects of human efforts—possessions, outward success, luxury—have always seemed to me contemptible" (1954a, p. 9). His strongest and most enduring ties were not to things, institutions, or even other people, but rather to the world of thought. To Einstein, the great thinkers of the past and present were "friends who could not be lost" (1949/1979, p. 5). Einstein was a legend in his own lifetime. He endured publicity and the intrusions of the external world, but he did not enjoy them. For example, when he was besieged by companies to endorse their products (like an athlete or rock star would be today), he did not understand ("Einstein puzzled," 1930):

> Why popular fancy should seize me, a scientist dealing in abstract things and happy if left alone, is one of those manifestations of mass psychology that are

Albert Einstein, whose theories of relativity revolutionized physics, and whose name has become a synonym for "genius." "I'm not much with people, and I'm not a family man. I want my peace. I want to know how God created this world. . . . I want to know His thoughts, the rest are details" (quoted in Salaman, 1955, p. 371). (United States Postal Service)

beyond me. I think it is terrible that this should be so and I suffer more than anybody can imagine. (p. 13)

Though a staunch supporter of Israel, in late life he refused an offer to be president of Israel (a largely honorary position), telling the Israeli ambassador, "I know a little about nature and hardly anything about men" (Clark, 1971/1984, p. 749). Expanding on this theme, he declared that "all my life I have dealt with objective matters, hence I lack both the natural aptitude and the experience to deal properly with people and to exercise official functions" (Nathan & Norden, 1960, p. 572).

In everyday life, Einstein's aloofness often took the form of absentminded forgetfulness, at least forgetfulness about things that didn't matter to him. He often misplaced keys (even doing so on his wedding day!) and abandoned suitcases at the homes of friends. He was quite indifferent to his physical appearance and dress, preferring sandals to shoes and a sweatshirt to a tweed jacket. When forced to wear a dress suit, he often didn't bother to put on socks (Clark, 1971/1984, pp. 387–389). According to his physician, "Einstein never took any exercise beyond a short walk when he felt like it (which wasn't often, because he has no sense of direction, and therefore would seldom venture very far afield)" (Plesch, 1949, p. 216). Even close personal relationships were of secondary importance to Einstein, as he once admitted to another physicist (Salaman, 1955):

I'm not much with people, and I'm not a family man. I want my peace. I want to know how God created this world. . . . I want to know His thoughts, the rest are details. (p. 371).

Though it was not part of the usual Einstein legend, his aloofness had its negative side. During his adolescence, some of Einstein's fellow students described him as sarcastic, insolent, and contemptuous. "Sure of himself," one later wrote, "he strode energetically up and down in a rapid . . . almost crazy tempo of a restless spirit which carries a whole world in itself" (Seelig, 1956, p. 14). Like many an intelligent, inward child lacking smooth social skills, he was a behavior problem in school. At age 15 he was expelled because "your presence in the class destroys the respect of the students" (Frank, 1947, p. 17).

Doing one's best work alone. Some scientists work in groups and make discoveries through discussion and collaboration (as, for example, did Watson, Crick, and others when they worked out the structure of the DNA molecule). Einstein, however, strongly preferred to work alone (1954a):

> It can easily be seen that all the valuable achievements, material, spiritual, and moral, which we receive from society have been brought about in the course of countless generations by creative individuals. . . . Only the individual can think. (pp. 13–14)

Einstein's 1905 paper on the special theory of relativity, arguably the most important scientific paper of the twentieth century, contained no supporting evidence, no footnotes, and no references to the work of any other physicist (Clark, 1971/1984, pp. 42–43, 116). His characteristic method was not a laboratory research team but rather the solitary "thought experiment." Actually, these were not experiments at all in the usual sense, but rather reflections about certain paradoxical observations that a hypothetical observer would make under unusual conditions. For example, the theory of relativity grew out of Einstein's consideration of what would be seen by an observer who followed a beam of light at the speed of light.

Even the small details of Einstein's work habits reflect this desire for solitude. After settling in Berlin in 1924, he worked in his study, a corner turret room reached by a small stairway. Neither the cleaner nor his wife was ever allowed to enter (Clark, 1971/1984, pp. 380–381).

Resistance to outside influence. Throughout his life, Einstein resisted intrusions by the external world. In college, he skipped lectures and relied on the notes of a conscientious friend. He found cramming for exams such a "coercion" that afterward he was unable to think about science for a whole year. His adult philosophy of education reflected this resistance.

> It is, in fact, nothing short of a miracle that the modern methods of instruction have not yet entirely strangled the holy curiosity of inquiry; for this delicate little plant, aside from stimulation, stands mainly in need of freedom. (1949/1979, p. 17)

> An autocratic system of coercion, in my view, soon degenerates. For force always attracts men of low morality, and I believe it to be an invariable rule that tyrants of genius are succeeded by scoundrels. (1954a, p. 10)

As you might expect from this latter quotation, Einstein took a dim view of government. In a letter published after his death, he railed against "those ignoramuses who use their public positions of power to tyrannize" (Einstein, 1955, p. 6). He was especially critical of compulsory military service (1954a):

> Heroism on command, senseless violence, and all the loathsome nonsense that goes by the name of patriotism—how passionately I hate them! (p. 10)

> Compulsory military service seems to me the most disgraceful symptom of that deficiency in personal dignity from which civilized mankind is suffering today. (p. 15)

Finally, at the end of his life Einstein expressed his distress at how, during the Cold War era, the widespread public fear of communism and the Soviet Union led U.S. science to become entangled in matters of secrecy, loyalty oaths, and political control (Einstein, 1954b):

> If I would be a young man again and had to decide how to make my living, I would not try to become a scientist or scholar or teacher. I would rather choose to be a plumber or a peddler in the hope to find that modest degree of independence still available under present circumstances. (p. 8)

Einstein in love. While Einstein was independent, he was not a hermit. Some extracts from his love letters to Mileva Maric, a fellow student of physics who later became his first wife, display the passions, enthusiasms, longings, the mawkish and sentimental language—tinged with condescension toward women—that were common among young men in love at the turn of the twentieth century (Einstein, 1992):

> I long terribly for a letter from my beloved witch. I can hardly believe that we will be separated so much longer—only now do I see how madly in love with you I am! Indulge yourself completely so you will become a radiant little darling and as wild as a street urchin. (p. 21; August 1900)
>   I will be doubly happy when I can press you close to my heart once again and see those loving eyes which shine for me alone, and kiss your sweet mouth which trembles blissfully for me alone. (p. 30; September 1900)

Far from drawing him back into the rejected external world, though, Einstein's love for Mileva gave him a refuge, a place to which he could retreat from the world. Thus sheltered, he could pursue his work with intensified dedication:

> When I read [the physicist] Helmholz for the first time I could not—and still cannot—believe that I was doing so without you sitting next to me. I enjoy working together very much, and find it soothing and less boring. (p. 9; August 1899)
>   Without the thought of you I would no longer want to live among this sorry herd of humans. (p. 29; September 1900)
>   Soon I'll be with my sweetheart again and can kiss her, hug her, make coffee with her, scold her, study with her, laugh with her, walk with her, chat with her. . . .

Even my work seems pointless and unnecessary if not for the thought that you are happy with what I am and what I do. (p. 31; September 1900)

I'm so lucky to have found you, a creature who is my equal, and who is as strong and independent as I am! I feel alone with everyone except you. (p. 36; October 1900)

For a person of Einstein's temperament, then, relationships with others are important, but they are important in a special way. Einstein doled out energy for relationships sparingly and kept them subordinated to his work. Because he kept the rest of the world at a distance, however, this single intimate relationship was probably critical to his happiness and personality integration:

I kiss you then with all my heart and want you to know that your devotion makes me so happy that without it my life would be dismal beyond words. (p. 42; April 1901)

Was this, however, really love? *Could* Einstein love? Reviewing the love letters, Pais (1993) thought not:

It seems to me, they show Einstein as a "soul in ferment, the character undecided. . . ." I do not believe that Einstein was capable of love for either of his wives. As he himself wrote shortly before his death, he had twice "failed miserably" in marriage. (p. 74)

Activity on behalf of social causes. For all his rejection of the external world in favor of quiet contemplation in his study, Einstein *did* leave his study more and more in the years between World Wars I and II, becoming intensely involved (in his own way) in several social causes. Consistent with his pacifist temperament, he worked to establish world peace. At the urging of a League of Nations committee, he and Freud exchanged open letters on the topic *Why War?* Einstein put these questions to Freud (Einstein & Freud, 1933):

Is there any way of delivering mankind from the menace of war? . . . (pp. 11–12)
. . . The normal objective of my thought affords no insight into the dark places of human will and feeling. . . . (p. 12)
Is it possible to control man's mental evolution so as to make him proof against the psychoses of hate and destructiveness? . . . (pp. 18–19)
. . . It would be of the greatest service to us all were you to present the problem of world peace in the light of your most recent discoveries, for such a presentation well might blaze the trail for new and fruitful modes of action. (p. 20)[4]

As his awareness of anti-Semitism increased, Einstein undertook speaking tours and fund-raising activities in support of Zionism and the estab-

---

[4]Einstein's letter and Freud's reply are also published in the *Standard Edition* of Freud's complete works (1933c, XXII, pp. 203–215).

lishment of Israel, though his simultaneous desire for cooperation with the Arabs did not always find favor with Zionist leaders (Clark, 1971/1984, chap. 14).

Finally, of course, Einstein was involved in the development of the first atomic bomb. Actually, although the destructive power of a nuclear explosion does illustrate Einstein's equation of $E = mc^2$, nuclear weapons developed out of a completely different line of experimental research in physics. Einstein himself took no direct part in the United States bomb program. Still, he did write a famous letter in 1939 to President Roosevelt, in which he urged an all-out U.S. project to develop an atomic bomb before Nazi Germany could. Later he would call this letter the "one great mistake" of his life (Clark, 1971/1984, p. 672).

Einstein's pacifism, his support for Israel, and his advocacy of an atomic bomb program were all attempts to influence the world of public affairs and politics. At first they might seem difficult to reconcile with his aloofness from the external world. Einstein was certainly not a scientist-politician in the fashion of Edward Teller (the "father of the U.S. H-bomb") or Andrei Sakarov (the "father of the Soviet H-bomb," who later advocated disarmament and was sentenced to house arrest for many years). Einstein lacked the skills of political bargaining and compromise, and did not easily mingle with people of power (Clark, 1971/1984, p. 721). While he felt "a passionate sense of social justice and social responsibility," he also added that (Einstein, 1954a):

> [This] has always contrasted oddly with my pronounced lack of need for direct contact with other human beings and human communities. I am truly a "lone traveler" and have never belonged to my country, my home, my friends, or even my immediate family, with my whole heart; in the face of all these ties, I have never lost a sense of distance and a need for solitude. (p. 9)

Politically, then, Einstein was an idealist rather than a politician. While he was active in the "outside" world on behalf of his ideals, his style of activity was that of a person who remains focused on inner things.

Was Einstein "Adjusted"?

Most of Einstein's contemporaries thought he was strange. Does this mean he was actually unstable, or was he simply well-adjusted in his own unique way? I can find no signs of anxiety, guilt, dramatic mood alteration, depression, low self-esteem, or obsessive rituals, either in Einstein's own writings or in others' descriptions of him. It is clear that for Einstein, the inner life of the mind was a happy life. For example, he once described how he felt about attending formal academic dinners: "On occasions like this I retire to the back of my mind and there I am happy" (Clark, 1971/1984, p. 388). In later years, he was quite explicit about his sense of contentment with the inner life (1950):

> I live in that solitude which is painful in youth, but delicious in the years of maturity. . . . Arrows of hate have been shot at me too; but they never hit me, because somehow they belonged to another world, with which I have no connection whatsoever. (p. 5)

Erikson's evaluation of Einstein's adjustment. Reviewing Einstein's life and writings from a psychoanalytic perspective, ego psychologist Erik Erikson concluded that Einstein's unusual behaviors were not signs of pathology or neurosis, but rather signs that he "succeeded in saving the child in himself." According to Erikson, this preserved child—that is, the childlike qualities of curiosity and questioning, openness to experience, and not being socialized to complete acceptance of intellectual and social customs—was both the foundation of Einstein's unique creativity and also the reason for his extraordinary appeal to the public (Erikson, 1982, pp. 155–156).

Facing death. Perhaps the ultimate sign of people's psychological stability can be found in how they face death. Here Einstein (1954a) was clearly undisturbed and at peace with himself and the world:

> Neither can I nor would I want to conceive of an individual that survives his physical death; let feeble souls, from fear or absurd egoism, cherish such thoughts. I am satisfied with the mystery of the eternity of life and with the awareness and a glimpse of the marvelous structure of the existing world, together with the devoted striving to comprehend a portion. (p. 11)

In short, Einstein was happy with himself the way he was. He was drawn to contemplation and the world within, but he was not "maladjusted."

Placing Einstein in the Patterns of Trait Description

Einstein's personality traits can be described in terms of the different patterns discussed earlier in this chapter. Beginning with the book of Genesis, we would classify Einstein as a Jacob rather than an Esau—"a quiet man, dwelling in tents." (Einstein's hair flowed freely from his head, but that was his only resemblance to Esau!) In Galen's two-dimensional typology, Einstein would be phlegmatic, not melancholic (little evidence of negative emotions or poor adjustment), and certainly not sanguine or choleric. Einstein is a little harder to place in terms of Theophrastus's characters, since these are all negative. However, he was certainly absent-minded and perhaps "immature" or "uncouth." In Milton's typology, Einstein was clearly an *Il Penseroso* type. Schopenhauer's terms present a problem: Einstein was clearly an intelligent character, but—partly because he was protected by Mileva Maric and, later on, by many other people—he was not melancholic. Similarly, among the Lakalei Einstein would have been classified as a person of shame rather than a person of anger, though he rarely seems to have felt shame. Finally, Henry Kissinger would probably have described Einstein in terms of intellectual sophistication and (in terms of his ideas and perhaps also his politics) as a great revolutionary.

Albert Einstein, when asked to "smile" for the photographer on the occasion of his 72nd birthday. "The true value of a human being is determined primarily by the measure . . . in which he has attained liberation from the self. . . . Without creative personalities able to think and judge independently, the upward movement of society is unthinkable" (1954, pp. 12, 14). (UPI/Bettmann)

WHY DESCRIBE PEOPLE'S TRAITS?

As we have seen, people have developed many different words and patterns of words to describe persons. Why do we have these categories, types, and dimensions for classifying other people? Clearly, trait words and patterns make it possible to give a brief summary description of the most striking or important features of another person's enduring and public personality, just as an artist's "traits" (brush strokes) capture the important features of a person's physical appearance. Classifying people helps us to "locate" them in comparison to other persons that we have encountered in the past.

More specifically, *our classifications help us to understand or interpret their behavior.* As an example, if we learn that once Einstein not only stuck out his tongue to a news photographer (Sugimoto, 1989, p. 168) but then sent the photograph to friends as a greeting card, we might reflect that this was, indeed, not unexpected behavior from someone who possessed the following three traits: uninterested in worldly prestige and power, playful, and slightly uncouth: "Yes, that's Einstein!" Second, *our classifications also help us to anticipate their behavior in the future.* Knowing the kind of person Einstein was, you would have been better prepared for meeting and talking with him. Finally, *our classifications provide a quick and efficient way to communicate with other people.* You might ask, "Tell me, what kind of person was Einstein?" Instead of asking you to read Clark's (1971/1984) entire biography, I could instead simply reply,

"He was both intellectually sophisticated and phlegmatic, like Milton's poem *Il Penseroso.*" Of course this is not a complete description of Albert Einstein's personality, but it is useful as a quick first approximation to the kind of person most other people found him to be. If you want to know the complete and "real" Einstein, however, you would need to go beyond these simple trait words and types.

PSYCHOLOGICAL STUDY OF TRAITS: HOW MANY TRAITS ARE THERE?

As we have seen, our potential trait vocabulary is large and complex, for we have many different ways of describing other people. Fashions in trait description change over time, as new words constantly enrich our everyday trait language and others drop out. While some of these new words may simply be new names for old traits, the actual number of traits themselves may also be expanding. From a psychological perspective, the everyday language of traits raises several questions and problems: How many traits are there? Is something necessarily a trait if there is a word for it? How are traits organized? Which ones are fundamental? Such questions may not be important to most people, or even to poets and philosophers who construct typologies for describing other people. It probably does not matter whether Henry Kissinger and Arthur Schopenhauer used exactly the same dimensions for describing people. However, these questions do arise as soon as we move from everyday language to the precise description and careful analysis of traits and temperament that characterize a scientific psychology of personality.

The Lexical Strategy

For many personality psychologists, the starting point for answering such questions is a monumental study of trait usage by Allport and Odbert (1936), entitled *Trait-Names: A Psycho-Lexical Study.* Using the 1925 edition of *Webster's New International Dictionary,* Allport and Odbert compiled a list of every word in the English language that might describe personality or personal behavior. (Their approach is called the "lexical" strategy because it started with the dictionary, or "lexicon.") After discarding obsolete words, they were left with 17,953 potential trait words, which they grouped as follows:

> 4,504 real traits (that is, words referring to enduring, public aspects of personality)
>
> 4,541 state words (referring to temporary states or fluctuations of mood rather than enduring qualities)
>
> 5,226 words that were mainly evaluative rather than descriptive (that is, synonyms for "good" and "bad")

3,682 miscellaneous terms (metaphors, past participles, abilities, or descriptions of physical features)

There isn't space to list 17,953 words, so for illustrative purposes I will mention only words beginning with the letter *Q*. First, Allport and Odbert found twenty-five *Q* traits: quaesturary, Quaker, Quakerish, quaky, qualmish, quarrelsome, quavery-mavery, queasy, queme, queromonious (which means the same as "querulous"), querist, querulous, quick, quick-fire, quidditative (rare), quidnunc, quiet, quipsome, quirky, quitter, quiverish, quixotic, quizzical, quodlibetarian, and quotationist (rare). Then there were twenty-eight *Q* temporary states (such as quacking, quatted, or quetching) and twenty-seven evaluative *Q* words (for example, quack, quaggy, qualityless, quick-witted, questionable, and quenchless). Finally, there were five *Q* metaphors: quadrivious, Quakerized, quaquaversal ("facing all ways at once," a word borrowed from geology), queechy, and quiescent.

Problems with the Lexical Strategy

How many traits? There can be few (if any) English words for describing persons that Allport and Odbert did not capture. If we add in trait words that entered the language since 1936, we can be reasonably certain that we have the entire universe of terms for describing the enduring, public aspects of personality, that any given trait is somewhere on the Allport-Odbert list. Yet as it stands, this list and its underlying lexical strategy raise several problems. For example, do we *really* need all 4,504 different words (plus any post-1936 additions) to describe other people? Are there really that many separate traits? If there are, then the task of systematic trait description becomes so unwieldy and difficult that we may leave it to novelists and poets. On the other hand, if there aren't 4,504 separate traits, then how many are there? And how shall we boil down this list to get them? Which are the "basic" traits? In the next two chapters, we shall consider several different ways in which personality psychologists have answered these questions.

Does a word mean a trait? Meanwhile, the lexical strategy also raises a logical problem. The trait words people use may actually be descriptions of other people, but they may also be descriptions of the beliefs (expectations, categories, values, and prejudices) of the person who uses them. That is, do traits exist out in the world or in our minds? Because we have a word for some particular trait, that may mean that the trait actually exists, but it may also mean simply that someone invented a word that others have picked up. For example, the word "Quakerish" appears on the Allport-Odbert list. Does that mean there is an actual trait called "Quakerish"? Are quipsome, quidditative, and queromonious real traits or just names?

In answering these questions, we want on the one hand to avoid the logical fallacy known as hypostatization (assuming that anything that can be named must therefore exist); but on the other hand, trait words presumably evolved in order to describe qualities of persons that people found important. In pruning the Allport-Odbert list, we don't want to miss any important qualities of other people.

Consider the case of "quidditative." At least once upon a time, someone thought "quidditative" was the perfect word for describing something important about somebody else. (It means, literally, "pertaining to the quiddity or essence of something." By extension it means a "quirk"; hence, when applied to a person, it means someone who is "quirky.") Does the mere existence of the word mean that "quidditative" is a real, important, trait? (The *Oxford English Dictionary* cites 1611 as the date of its first use, but for all I know that may also be its last use as well!) Perhaps it is now obsolete because it has been replaced with "quirky"; but perhaps we could do a better job of describing other people if we used "quidditative" more often.

Traits as description or evaluation. Many Allport-Odbert trait words are saturated with evaluation; that is, they are used to applaud or put down other people as well as to describe them. Recall the twelve points of the Boy Scout Law described at the beginning of this chapter. These words (trustworthy, loyal, helpful, friendly, etc.) are not just neutral trait descriptions; they are *virtues*. Boy Scouts are *supposed to be* trustworthy, loyal, and so on. Yet in order to describe other people objectively, we need to strip away such evaluation and extract the actual behavior. Can this be done with trait words drawn from ordinary language?

*H*OW MANY TRAITS? IDIOGRAPHIC VERSUS NOMOTHETIC APPROACHES

For personality psychologists, the most important problem has been how to boil down the 4,504-plus Allport-Odbert trait words to some smaller number of basic traits or fundamental dimensions. For example, the Boy Scout Law lists twelve different traits, but several of these trait words are nearly synonyms (trustworthy and loyal, cheerful and friendly), so perhaps we could do with fewer than twelve words. Of course we would also need some additional words for not-so-nice traits such as mean, quarrelsome, or sulky, which are not mentioned in the Boy Scout Law.

Personality psychologists have answered the questions about the number and nature of fundamental traits in many different ways. *Idiographic* trait theorists such as Allport (1961, 1962), who are concerned mainly with the patterning and structure of traits in particular individuals, do not take a strong position about the number of basic traits or which traits are basic. We shall examine the idiographic approach in greater detail in Chapter 12. Other trait theorists have tried to reduce the large number of trait words to a few basic traits or dimensions—two, three, five, or even as many as sixteen. Because they attempt to measure individual differences along a few common or universal dimensions, they are called dimensional or *nomothetic* theorists. There are two fundamental kinds of dimensional approaches to traits. Some theorists define a structure of basic traits on *rational* or theoretical grounds. The typology of Galen, described earlier in this chapter, is a classic example, while the types of Jung, which will be discussed in Chapter 12, are a modern example. Other theorists proceed empirically, looking for which trait words actually go together, or co-occur. Nowadays they employ a complex mathematical procedure known as *factor analysis* to calculate patterns of co-occurring trait terms. We shall examine their work in Chapter 13.

12

How Many Traits? Idiographic and Typological Approaches

❖

In this chapter we shall examine the idiographic and typological approaches to determining the number and nature of fundamental traits. To personality psychologists who use the idiographic approach, these are not important questions. They believe that different traits will be "fundamental" for different people, so that it is not necessary (and may even be impossible or unwise) to reduce the number of trait terms to a few basic ones. Jung's typological approach, in contrast, lays out a structure of eight types, constructed from the various combinations of one basic trait (or attitude) with four functions (or stylistic traits).

WHAT IS THE IDIOGRAPHIC APPROACH?

As described at the beginning of Chapter 11, studying traits idiographically involves exploring how particular traits are expressed, structured, and combined in particular individual persons. From the idiographic perspective, aggregated data or average scores based on groups of people can never provide an adequate basis for understanding and predicting the behavior of individual persons. In Murray's (1938) words, "the objects of study [of personality psychology] are individual organisms, not aggregates of organisms" (p. 38). In its extreme form, such a position might sound as if it were a rejection of the possibility of doing personality as a science. In fact, however, idiographic theorists believe that their approach makes possible a *science (that is, systematic and orderly knowledge) of the individual person.*

Runyan (1983) suggests several possible forms that such a science might take: searching for individualized traits (traits particularly relevant to a particular person), identifying central themes in an individual life, describing the patterning or organization of variables within a single case, exploring causal relationships among variables within a single case, or making predictions about a single case on the basis of trends or patterns (p. 415; see also Allport, 1961, 1962, and Lamiell, 1981, for a further discussion of the idiographic perspective).

CREATING AN IDIOGRAPHIC TRAIT DESCRIPTION

In describing an individual, idiographic personality psychologists would *not* reduce the Allport-Odbert list of 4,504-plus trait words (see Chapter 11) to a smaller number of fundamental or underlying dimensions. Instead, they would preserve as much variety of trait vocabulary as possible, in order to do justice to individual uniqueness. Rather than trying to force the person into a few general pigeonholes, they would search for the "natural cleavages that mark an individual life" (Allport, 1966b, p. 7).

Consider the word "quidditative," one of the Allport-Odbert traits beginning with the letter Q (see Chapter 11; it means, approximately, "quirky"). It may not be a word that you have ever used, nor would you use it very often;

but for describing the traits of a truly quidditative person (if there is one), it would be exactly right. From the idiographic perspective, therefore, we should not try to force "quidditative" into some broader general dimension such as "unusual" or "unpredictable." Instead, we should retain the word in case we need to describe a truly quidditative person. As you can see, the idiographic approach emphasizes the richness of the English language, as reflected in its more than 4,504 trait words.

So far we have considered what idiographic personality psychologists would *not* do. Now we must ask what they *would* do in constructing an idiographic personality description of a person. What follows is a general discussion. Surveys of specific idiographic methods can be found in Allport (1962), Runyan (1983), and a special issue of the *Journal of Personality* (51(3), 1983) devoted to "Personality and Prediction: Nomothetic and Idiographic Approaches."

Allport (1958, pp. 253–257) suggested that most people can be adequately characterized by *the right five to ten trait words or phrases* if two cautions were observed. First, these five to ten phrases must be carefully chosen from a long list of trait terms, rather than being scores on a few general dimensions. Second, the unique structure or arrangement of these five to ten words must be appropriately represented. Thus to Allport, the art of personality description is the ability to "put together a phrase or sentence that will pinpoint individual structure [of traits]." In such a task, "the gifts of the novelist and biographer exceed those of the psychologist" (1958, p. 255).

As an example of idiographic description, Allport cited with approval the biography of William James by Ralph Barton Perry (1936). According to Perry, James had four positive, or benign, traits: sensibility (focus on here-and-now reality), vivacity (liveliness), humanity, and sociability. These were balanced by four neurotic, or morbid, traits: hypochondria, mood oscillations, "repugnance to exact processes of thought," and a "preoccupation with exceptional mental states."[1] Perry chose these particular eight phrases because they were especially appropriate for describing William James, not because they are fundamental or basic traits that apply to all people. Some are indeed applicable to many people (for example, sociability and mood oscillations); but others might apply to only a few people (for example, "preoccupation with exceptional mental states"). The idiographic approach emphasizes the precision and subtlety of trait phrases. Thus the phrase "repugnance to exact processes of thought" has a much more specific and narrow meaning than broader categories (such as "imprecise," "sloppy," or even "not careful"), which might be used by a personality psychologist concerned with identifying a few broad and general trait dimensions.

In James's life, the *structure* of the eight traits was important; that is, each morbid trait was balanced and blended with a positive trait. For example, his

[1]For example, James liked to inhale nitrous oxide, or laughing gas, a mild hallucinogen that dentists used to use. Perry's analysis of William James can be compared to Feinstein's (1984) psychologically oriented biography.

mood swings were kept in check by his sensibility, and his hypochondria was neutralized by his sociability. To a personality psychologist using the idiographic approach, these *particular* eight phrases, blended into an integrated, latticed network or structure, convey the essence of William James better than any set of scores or ratings on a standard list of personality traits.

THE CASE OF JENNY

Although he emphasized idiographic personality description throughout his career, Allport actually published only one example, *Letters from Jenny* (Allport, 1965). Allport found Jenny personally fascinating and professionally useful as a teaching device. The case is interesting both for what it shows about the idiographic method and also for what it discloses about Allport himself as a person and as a personality theorist (see Winter, 1993a).

Background: Jenny's Letters

In 1946, as editor of the *Journal of Abnormal and Social Psychology*, Allport published selections and abridgements from a series of 301 letters written during the years 1926–1937 from Jenny Masterson, who was at the beginning of the correspondence a 58-year-old widow, to Glenn, the college roommate of her son Ross, and his wife Isabel (Anonymous, 1946). (All names are pseudonyms.) In 1965, he republished the letters in a book version (Allport, 1965). In his words, these letters "tell the story of a mother-son relationship and trace the course of a life beset by frustration and defeat" (Allport, 1965, p. v). During the early years of the correspondence, Jenny's extreme possessiveness of her son erupted in periodic suspicions, recriminations, and hatred of any women in his life. Ross's unexpected death in 1929, from an infection and complications following surgery, was a turning point. Thereafter, according to Isabel's later account, "Jenny's hostility and suspicion turn into full-fledged paranoia, [while] the more benign qualities seem to diminish" (Allport, 1965, p. 156).

In fact, Gordon Allport and his wife Ada were Glenn and Isabel; Jenny was actually the mother of Allport's college roommate. Close examination of the letters suggests that the correspondence with Jenny may have reinforced several features of Allport's personality theory, such as the sharp distinction he made between "normal" and "abnormal" functioning (Winter, 1993a). Jenny was certainly someone Allport knew well—perhaps too well for his own comfort.

Allport's Everyday-Language Description of Jenny

Before presenting Allport's idiographical analysis of Jenny's personality, we shall begin with his description of her personality in everyday language. As it

Jenny Masterson (1868–1937), with her son Ross. During the years before and after Ross's death, Jenny corresponded with his college roommate, Gordon Allport. According to Allport, "the bitter dilemma of Ross and his mother often seems to echo . . . a Greek tragedy. . . . For eleven years [her letters] served as a projective screen upon which Jenny displayed the story of her hopes, jealousies, striving, and defeat" (1965, pp. vi, viii). (Courtesy Gordon Allport)

happened, in 1931 Jenny applied for admission to a church-sponsored home for elderly women in New York City. Allport wrote a supporting letter of recommendation that included what he called a "sketch [of] her personality and her unhappy history." The following extended excerpt will give you a sense of the kind of person Jenny was.[2] As you read it, before going on to the analysis, you might want to write down your own summary of Jenny's personality.

> She is a striking and remarkable woman . . . a fascinating and appealing personality. . . .
>
> Left a widow when her only son was a very small child, she devoted her entire life to the task of giving him the best possible education and opportunity. She worked as telegrapher, in offices, and for a great many years as librarian. She was entirely alone. She felt (perhaps unwisely) that by shutting herself off, by not marrying again, she could pursue better her single purpose of giving Ross the best education. Her self-denial almost defies description. Even in the time that I have known her she has lived in cramped quarters (once in a linen closet) and has gone hungry in order that her son might attend the best preparatory school, summer camps, and college. I have never known a person to live on less money than she, although she is a highly cultivated, intelligent, and aesthetic woman.
>
> Combined with her devotion and frugality there has always gone a commendable pride and utter integrity. I have never known her to accept charity or to incur

[2]These excerpts are reprinted by permission of the Harvard University Archives. The letter is part of the Gordon Allport papers in the archive (Miscellaneous correspondence 1930–1945, box 1:A-Bühler). Since Jenny died without heirs in 1937, quoting from the letter here does not violate any right of privacy or ethical standard.

debts that she did not, by additional self-denial, immediately commence to discharge. She has been a superb manager of her very slender income.

At the time of her son's death he was not yet securely established. The result was that he left nothing excepting about $1500 in the government insurance fund. [Ross had been a World War I veteran.] This slender legacy, even with her ability, naturally has dwindled until she is faced with the immediate necessity of pooling her remaining dollars to enter a home. She is, of course, unable to take employment any longer; but naturally she wishes to provide for her old age without at this late date becoming dependent.

Her character is unquestionable. In addition to the personal integrity I spoke of, I should mention her kindness to others during her difficult life. Although holding aloof from intimate contacts, she has always been helpful and generous. Even at present, though broken, grief-stricken, and in poverty, she is looking after a neighbor, older and, if possible, more alone than she. Mrs. Masterson is keenly appreciative of any genuine manifestations of human kindliness. She is critical of hypocrisy, and has an austere philosophy of life. But she regards kindliness as the fundamental virtue, and possesses it herself. She is also very appreciative of beauty in whatever form she finds it. I often think that it is this interest that has kept her so well-integrated throughout a sad life.

Her vivid personality is in part her Irish inheritance. She was born in Ireland of Protestant parentage. Her life of utter concentration upon one purpose, and the tragic sequel of her effort, has naturally called for great fortitude and courage. Both these qualities are strikingly developed in her. But also this mode of life has resulted in independence and solitude.

This observation leads to the subject of her adaptability to an institution. I believe that in any home where privacy is permitted and respected, where there is no meddlesomeness or undue pressure and restriction, Mrs. Masterson would be an asset. She is bright, kind, conversational, and appreciative. She does however require dignity and mutual respect in her associations. She is quick to resent patronage or injustice.

Do you feel you understand Jenny? As a first step toward a more systematic idiographic description, I have extracted most of the trait adjectives from Allport's letter and arranged them in the left-hand column of Table 12.1. Based on everyday language, but selected to be especially descriptive of Jenny as an individual, this "pool" of individualized trait words would be the foundation of an idiographic science of the single case of Jenny.

Constructing and Validating an Idiographic Portrait

Observers' trait judgments. Table 12.1 illustrates two different approaches to selecting the "right" set of five to ten trait adjectives or phrases—the core of an idiographic trait description, according to Allport. The first approach involves trait judgments made by observers. Allport asked thirty-six people to read the published letters between Jenny and Glenn and then list the essential characteristics of Jenny as they saw them (Allport, 1965, pp. 193–196; 1966b, pp. 7–8). These judges produced a combined list of 198 traits, averaging 5.5 traits per judge. Many words were overlapping or synonymous, so Allport grouped them into eight clusters, as shown in the middle column of Table 12.1. Because this grouping process involved only trait words

TABLE 12.1 TRAIT ADJECTIVES USED TO DESCRIBE JENNY IN A LETTER OF RECOMMENDATION, A PSYCHOLOGICAL RATING, AND A COMPUTER

Allport's letter of recommendation	Characterizations by observers who read the published letters	Factors from systematic computer-based content analysis
Critical of hypocrisy	Aggressive Quarrelsome-suspicious	} Aggression

Kind
Helpful and generous
Appreciative of
  genuine kindness
	Sentimental	Need for affiliation
		Need for familial
		  acceptance

Austere Self-denying Frugal	[Frugal]	
Independent Proud Aloof from intimate contacts Asocial (solitude) Resents being patronized Personal integrity	Independent-autonomous	Need for autonomy
	Cynical and morbid	
Striking and remarkable Vivid Fascinating and appealing	Dramatic-intense	[Overstatement]
Highly cultivated Intelligent, bright Aesthetic, appreciative of beauty	Aesthetic-artistic	Sentience
Devoted to son	Self-centered	Possessiveness Martyrdom Sexuality
Singleness of purpose Fortitude and courage		

SOURCE: Observers' ratings are based on Allport (1965, pp. 193–194); the computer-based factors are from Paige (1966).

already assigned to Jenny, it is different from the kind of grouping that nomothetic personality psychologists might use to reduce the 4,504 words from the Allport-Odbert list to a small number of traits basic to all persons.

Since only 13 of the 198 words could not be classified into one of the eight clusters, Allport believed that these clusters reflected a reasonable consensus on the part of the judges. Whether this is true depends on how well Allport grouped the 198 words. For example, he combined the following nine traits into a cluster called *self-centered:* selfish, jealous, possessive, egocentric, proud, snobbish, martyr complex, self-pitying, and oversacrificial. Probably you will agree that these nine words all go together, and that "self-centered" is the best label. However, in constructing Table 12.1, I moved the word "frugal" from the Allport's "independent-autonomous" cluster into a separate ninth cluster. In my view, frugality and independence are two quite different traits. Not every "independent" person is frugal; some are self-indulgent rather than self-deny-ing. Thus to say that Jenny was "frugal" (which she surely was) is to suggest something quite different from her being "independent" (which she also surely was).

The adjectives extracted from Allport's letter to the church home, in the left-hand column of the table, fit quite well into the clusters based on the observers' descriptions, though there are some differences. For example, in his letter Allport toned down Jenny's aggressiveness into "critical of hypocrisy," and he embroidered her fierce independence into "singleness of purpose" and "fortitude and courage." He said nothing about her being quarrelsome, suspi-cious, cynical, and morbid. These discrepancies are easy to understand; after all, Allport was writing a letter of recommendation to a church home! Allow-ing for these differences of purpose and audience, the two trait clusters (All-port's everyday-language letter of recommendation, and the observer-based impressions) match up rather well with each other. To an idiographic person-ality psychologist, this suggests that we may be close to identifying the right five to ten trait words that best describe Jenny.

At this point you may be wondering whether these traits are actually pat-terns of Jenny's public personality or the biases of the observers—including Allport himself. Jenny was certainly a difficult correspondent who demanded time and attention from Allport, while playing on his emotions and arousing guilt. He surely had a personal perspective about Jenny. Moreover, those who read Jenny's letters and then described her personality surely have their own experiences, needs, fears, and stereotypes about "possessive" mothers and older women. Such factors may well have affected their perceptions and judg-ments of her traits.

Analyzing traits by computer.   A computer-based analysis of Jenny's let-ters by Paige (1964, 1966) illustrates a second way of selecting the right five to ten phrases of an idiographic description of a person's traits. Because the com-puter proceeds without preconceptions, emotions, or biases concerning Jenny, it may give us a more objective description. Paige used a computer system called the General Inquirer (Stone, Dunphy, Smith, & Ogilvie, 1966), which first classifies most of the important words of Jenny's letters into one or more of eighty-three tags (broad categories) on the basis of a preexisting dictionary. For example, the General Inquirer tag POSSESS (meaning "to own or consume") includes thirty-seven words such as "belong," "occupy," and "lock." The tag ATTEMPT includes "aim," "effort," and thirty-three other words. After tagging was completed, the computer calculated patterns of tag co-occurrence across the entire set of letters. For example, when Jenny used a word in the POSSESS tag, what other tags was she likely to use in the same sentence (or the same paragraph, or the same letter)?

From the resulting pattern of relationships or correlations among tags, Paige used a mathematical procedure called factor analysis (see Chapter 13) to identify factors or clusters of tags that occurred together in Jenny's letters. For example, the three tags POSSESS, ATTEMPT, and ROSS (her son's name) often occurred together in the letters—along with the tags ECONOMIC (references to money) and MESSAGE-FORM (usually reference to financial agreements). Paige named this cluster "possessiveness" because it reflected Jenny's "attempts to bind Ross to her by legal and financial means" (1966, p. 444). Of course Paige's naming and interpreting the tag cluster as "possessiveness" reflects his own judgment and possible biases; but the actual co-occurrence of the five tags in Jenny's letters is a matter of objective fact.[3] He suggested that a factor of co-occurring tags represents a "personal trait expressed in a number of different situations" (p. 435).

Overall, Paige identified nine major factors or clusters of concepts that went together in Jenny's writing; these are shown in the right-hand column of Table 12.1. As you can see, there is a fairly high degree of correspondence among the three sources of personality description—Allport's letter of recommendation, the observer's characterizations, and Paige's study. The computer technique missed the clusters of "austere-frugal" and "cynical-morbid," but it did pick up a factor of "sexuality" that is missing from both Allport's letter and the observers' descriptions. This latter theme is an interesting example of the value of objective techniques for detecting themes that observers might miss. The computer tag of SEXUALITY includes three elements: Jenny's descriptions (often in highly "romantic" terms) of activities with Ross, her fixation on Ross's "immoral" relationship with women (including his wife), and her vicarious sharing of affection with the Allport family through the correspondence. Now if these themes are really erotic or sexual, they have been greatly modified by defense mechanisms and sublimations (see Chapter 3). As a result, most observers would be unlikely (and in Allport's case, perhaps also unwilling) to detect them.

Even with the use of something as apparently unbiased and objective as computer content analysis, Paige's study still has some sources of subjectivity and possible error. His factor labels involve subjective judgments about the meaning of patterns of co-occurring words. The analysis was based only on Jenny's letters to the Allports over eleven and a half years, letters that had been selected and edited by Allport. This is only a small sample of her personality, a sample obtained only during her late adulthood and old age. Neither the computer nor the observers could take account of the many constraints in Jenny's real situation: for example, she was a widow, without family or finan-

---

[3]The alert reader may have detected that the grouping of words into tags is another element of subjective judgment in the supposedly "objective" computer analysis. While this is true, Paige did use a social-psychological tag dictionary previously employed in several other studies (see Stone, Dunphy, Smith, & Ogilvie, 1966, pp. 170–186).

cial resources, at a time and in a place with few opportunities (for example, no Social Security, Medicare, or welfare). Thus there is always the danger that behaviors that are largely responses to her *situation* may be perceived as resulting only from her personality. (The relationship between personality and situation will be discussed in Part Four.) These considerations suggest that we proceed cautiously.

Nevertheless, the fact that three quite different sources of trait descriptions of Jenny fit together so well is an encouraging sign. Perhaps it *is* possible to construct an adequate idiographic description of someone's public personality by selecting the five to ten most appropriate traits.

In Search of Jenny's Personality Structure

In one sense, the eleven trait clusters of Table 12.1 represent Jenny's unique personality, at least at the trait level. By saying that she was sentimental, austere, quarrelsome, dramatic, courageous, and so forth, we are distinguishing her from most other people, who do not possess this set of traits. In mathematical terms, it is conceivable that this particular combination of traits describes only a very few other human beings—or even none at all. But Jenny's uniqueness also involves the *structure* of her personality traits. Table 12.1 consists of three lists, but a list is hardly a structure. Rather, personality structure involves the way in which traits are arranged or organized. The arrangement or organization of traits has at least three different aspects, as will be illustrated below in terms of the trait lists of Table 12.1.

Unique or unusual combinations of adjectives within a broad trait cluster. The first aspect of personality structure involves particular (often unusual) combinations of trait adjectives within each of the eight trait clusters. Most observers agree that Jenny is *self-centered* (Allport, 1965, p. 193). However, there are many ways of being self-centered: for example, some people are simply oblivious to others, while others feel a sense of entitlement (that is, that they deserve riches, attention, or gratification, without doing anything to earn them). Neither of these kinds of self-centeredness seems true of Jenny; rather, her self-centeredness appears in the form of a *martyr complex*. Thus, for example, she repeatedly claimed that although she had sacrificed herself for her son Ross, he behaved badly in return. Now true martyrs are rarely self-centered; they give up everything without conditions or demanding something in return. In Jenny, however, *self-sacrifice* was combined with continued *possessiveness* toward her son. This somewhat unusual combination of traits, making up a "martyr complex" instead of true martyrdom, is Jenny's own unique variety of self-centeredness, along with her other self-centered traits such as *proud* and *jealous*.

The first aspect of Jenny's personality structure, then, involves the internal structure (selection and arrangement of adjectives) within her broad trait of self-centeredness. Like many people, Jenny is self-centered; but she is self-centered in her own particular way.

Unique or unusual combinations of broad traits.   The second aspect of personality structure involves patterns among the eight broad trait clusters. For example, the observers who read *Letters from Jenny* characterized her as "aggressive" and "independent-autonomous." These two trait clusters seem to fit together easily. That is, someone who is independent can easily be *aggressive*, and vice versa. Furthermore, aggressive people are often *self-centered* or even *dramatic-intense*, as Jenny was also characterized. On the other hand, adding to this combination the trait clusters of *sentimental* or *aesthetic-artistic* seems surprising and incongruous. We don't usually think of aggressive, independent people as being artistic and sentimental. Yet an idiographic theorist would argue that it is precisely this unusual combination of traits that constitutes Jenny's individuality. That is, if she were not at the same time aggressive *and* artistic, independent *and* sentimental, she would not be Jenny!

If traits such as independent and sentimental are normally inconsistent or opposed to each other, how can they fit together in a single personality such as Jenny? One answer is that two or more opposed traits in the same person cause difficulty, conflict, and strain. Thus the tension between aggression and sentimentality is one obvious fault line in Jenny's personality. It is probably at the root of a repeated behavior pattern in which she attempted (1) to control Ross, and was angered by any obstacles to this control (aggression), in order (2) to recreate the lost world of Ross's infancy (sentimentality). Once Ross became an adult, these attempts were bound to fail, which only intensified her martyr complex.

On the other hand, traits that conflict with each other can also be a source of strength. For example, just when Jenny's aggression is about to consume her in bitterness, her aesthetic-artistic trait emerges as a source of consolation or counterbalance. Thus she once described her reaction to the sea in terms that suggest a muting of aggression (Allport, 1965):

> There's nothing, no place, like the sea. I've been out twice. Nothing else makes me feel their insignificance—the paltry troubles of living—the immensity of space—the grandeur of God—the strength and power of the Great Unknown. (p. 88)

In another letter she spoke of the deeply personal meaning of art as a consolation:[4]

> The only thing in the world that has lasting qualities—
> "All things pass—Art alone remains with us,
> The bust out-lives the throne,
> The coin, Tiberius." (p. 138)

Notice how in these two passages Jenny's cynical outlook, also listed in Table 12.1, combines with her artistic sensitivity to give a slight edge. The

[4]Slightly misquoted by Jenny from "Ars Victrix," by Henry Austin Dobson (1840–1921).

combination of aggression *and* artistic sensitivity, sharpened by a morbid cynicism, emerges even more clearly in one of her favorite passages of poetry:[5]

> I thank with deep thanksgiving
> Whatever gods may be,
> That no man lives forever,
> That dead men rise up never,
> And even the weariest river
> Flows somewhere safe to sea. (p. 223)

Perhaps for Jenny the "safety" image in the last line of this passage added the further exquisite complexity of sentimentality and affiliation to images of nature, aggression, and death.

These examples from Jenny suggest that *in analyzing the structure of an individual personality, those traits that are ordinarily mutually opposed or even contradictory may in fact be the most critical ones.* At the descriptive level, such combinations may best communicate the most individualized characteristics of the person. At the interpretive or explanatory level, moreover, these contradictory combinations suggest sources of both stress and compensating strength. Thus for Jenny, art was a means by which she sublimated her aggression so as to handle the conflict between aggression, on the one hand, and sentimentality and affiliation, on the other.

Master traits and unity thema.   A final aspect of personality structure involves the hierarchical arrangement of traits. Often one trait cluster predominates and organizes all the others, thus giving a unified thematic quality to the personality and life course. Allport described such a predominant trait as a "central trait" or a "cardinal trait" (1937, pp. 337–338; 1961, p. 365), while Murray (1938, pp. 604–605) called it a "unity thema." Various observers have described Jenny's cardinal trait as "the archetype of motherhood," "possessiveness toward Ross," or "self-vindication" (Allport, 1965, p. 195), but Allport's own final choices were *resentment* (pp. 196, 210) and *self-defeat* (p. 220). That is, all of Jenny's traits were subordinated and organized around self-defeating expressions of resentment.

*I*DIOGRAPHIC DESCRIPTION AND THE SCIENCE OF PERSONALITY

Many personality psychologists, while perhaps mentioning Jenny in a brief reference to Allport, rarely present the details of his idiographic method. Therefore I have illustrated the idiographic approach to personality description at some length, with the two examples of William James and "Jenny."

---

[5]A slight variant on "The Garden of Proserpine," by Algernon Charles Swinburne (1837–1909).

Still, you may be thinking that the idiographic approach is fine for writing a novel or a biography but wondering whether it has anything to do with scientific psychology. How can we have a science of personality if we preserve 4,504 or more different trait words and use different trait categories ("variables") for describing each case?

Scientific Credentials of the Idiographic Approach

Allport (1962) believed that the idiographic approach was accurate, reliable, economical, and therefore scientifically defensible. In support of this claim, he cited a classic study by Conrad (1932), who asked three teachers to rate thirty nursery school children on a list of 210 traits. The median correlation among the judges' ratings across the 210 traits was .50, a figure that does indicate some agreement among raters but also implies considerable divergence. This original task was strictly nomothetic, in that the raters were asked to apply the same standard list of 210 traits to each of the thirty children. However, each rater was also asked to put an asterisk by any rating for which the trait was "of central or dominating importance in the child's personality" (p. 673). This request to identify particular traits that were important for particular children was a much more idiographic task. Figure 12.1 shows that when we consider only the ratings on the asterisked traits, agreement between the judges goes up dramatically. For the traits identified as important by all three judges, the median interjudge correlation was an almost-perfect .95. Conrad's study supports the conclusion that raters were able to achieve much higher agreement on an "idiographic" task (rating children only on those traits judged to be important or central for the particular person being rated) than on a more "nomothetic" task (rating all children on universal dimensions).

Several modern studies that use Conrad's method (Bem & Allen, 1974; Cheek, 1982; Kenrick & Braver, 1982; and Kenrick & Stringfield, 1980) have confirmed and extended his results. In one sense, as Bem and Allen (1974) point out, these results only confirm the wisdom of common sense, as when we describe a friend.

> We do not invoke some a priori fixed set of dimensions which we apply to everyone. Rather we permit ourselves to select a small subset of traits which strike as pertinent and to discard as irrelevant the other [thousands of] trait terms in the lexicon. (p. 510)

In another sense, though, these results show that the idiographic approach can be carried out with acceptable interobserver agreement or reliability, which is one important requirement of any science.

Art History versus Organic Chemistry

One way of thinking about idiographic versus nomothetic approaches to personality description is to compare them to the academic disciplines of art his-

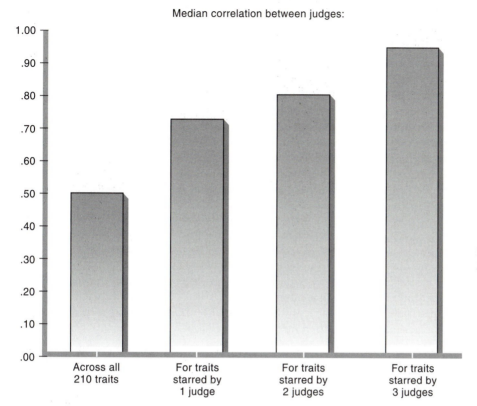

FIGURE 12.1

Interjudge agreement of trait ratings as a function of the "importance" of the traits rated. (Data adapted from Conrad, 1932)

tory (or literary history) and organic chemistry. Like idiographic personality psychologists, art historians customarily make analyses and draw scholarly conclusions about the stylistic development of individual artists in relation to their works of art, as in the following (hypothetical) statements that might be made by an art critic:

> In this painting, Picasso is moving away from cubism toward a style more influenced by Greek sculpture.
> This particular shade of red, along with the modeling of the hands, suggests that the artist was Judith Leyster rather than her mentor Frans Hals.
> The treatment of light is characteristic of Vermeer's interior scenes.

These statements are objective and scientific in the sense that they are carefully defined and supported by evidence; but they are also idiographic because they apply only to particular artists and works of art.

In contrast, organic chemists analyze all living matter into a few basic components or elements—carbon, hydrogen, oxygen, and nitrogen—plus traces of a few others. Similarly, nomothetic personality psychologists have sought to identify a relatively small number of basic elements of personality. Yet we should remember that, for all the simplicity of their constituent elements, organic compounds display an immensely complicated variety of structures, as many premed students learn to their dismay. Metaphorically, at least, organic compounds can be said to have considerable individuality.

It is interesting to note that both Allport (who so strenuously advocated idiographic methods) and Murray (who developed the first "periodic table" of the elements of personality) also framed the contrast between their approaches in terms of the art history versus organic chemistry comparison. Thus Allport (1938/1960) wrote that:

> It would be becoming for psychology to learn a few basic truths from literature. . . . [The problem of traits] has been handled more successfully through the assumptions of literature than through the assumptions of psychology. (pp. 6, 8)

In contrast, Murray (1938) asked, "Does not every elementary textbook of chemistry . . . [begin with an] account of the different entities that constitute its subject-matter?" He then indicated his vision:

> We believe that a primary task for psychology is the proper analysis of behavior into functions or phases, each of which . . . may be subsumed under a construct, a construct that defines a uniformity (a class of such entities). (p. 142)

Rather than asking whether art history is a science in the same way that chemistry is, we should recognize that art history and chemistry are both legitimate and systematic branches of scholarship. The psychological analysis and interpretation of personality, employing idiographic and nomothetic methods, can learn from both models.

THE TYPOLOGICAL APPROACH TO IDENTIFYING BASIC TRAITS

While the idiographic approach would preserve the rich variety of trait terms, a nomothetic perspective requires that we boil the Allport-Odbert list down to a manageably small number of fundamental trait dimensions. How shall we proceed with such a task?

The *typological approach* groups and arranges traits according to some formal typology or system of categories. The categories of Galen or Schopenhauer, discussed in Chapter 11, are examples of informal typologies, but in modern personality psychology, typologies are more formal and are based on explicit psychological theory. Freud described the anal character type, in which fixation of libidinal components at the anal stage of development led to traits of orderliness, stubbornness, and parsimony or stinginess (1908a, IX;

see also Chapter 3). Other psychoanalytic theorists elaborated oral, phallic, and genital types (Abraham, 1927; Fenichel, 1945, pp. 487–496). Freud also sketched out two other, less well-known sets of personality types. In 1916 he described the reactions to therapy of three different character types: people who feel themselves to be "exceptions," people who are "wrecked by success," and "criminals from a sense of guilt" (1916, XIV, pp. 309–333). Several years later, he described three "libidinal types"—erotic, narcissistic, and obsessional—based on the relative dominance of the person's id, ego, or superego, respectively, as well as several combinations or mixed types (1931b, XXI, pp. 215–220; see also Chapter 3). Spranger's (1928) sixfold classification of values (theoretical, economic, aesthetic, social, political, and religious), which was the basis of the Allport-Vernon-Lindzey Study of Values test (described in Chapter 8), could also be a typology of traits and temperament.

More recently, in a longitudinal study of personality development, Block (1971; see also Block & Block, 1980) developed a typology of persons based on their level of ego control (restraint of impulses and emotions) and ego resiliency (capacity to be calm under stress). This typology will be discussed further in Chapter 13. As discussed in Chapter 4, York and John (1992) have recently defined and measured four types—individuated, traditional, conflicted, and assured—on the basis of Rank's theories. Murray (1981) coined the term "Icarian"[6] (or Icarus-type) to describe people who had fantasies of flying, were fascinated by fire, and experienced urethral eroticism (sexual pleasure from urination). Wink (1992) developed a typology of different kinds of narcissism, as mentioned in Chapter 9.

The most famous rational classification of traits in personality psychology, however, is undoubtedly Jung's theory of psychological types, to which we now turn.

JUNG'S THEORY OF PERSONALITY

At one time, the Swiss psychiatrist Carl Gustav Jung (1975–1961) was Freud's closest disciple, colleague, and heir apparent—the crown prince of psychoanalysis and Freud's personal choice as president of the International Psychoanalytic Association. After less than a decade as Freud's colleague, however, Jung broke away in 1914. This rift was neither the first nor the last break between Freud and his disciples, but it was the most significant. On the surface, Freud and Jung disagreed over whether motivating forces were always and necessarily sexual, and whether there was such a thing as childhood sexuality: Freud said yes and Jung said no. After the break, Jung began to conceive of motivation as (asexual) *psychic energy* and began to develop his own theory called *analytical psychology*. As with any break between close colleagues, how-

---

[6]In ancient Greek mythology, Icarus flew too near the sun. His waxen wings melted, and he fell into the sea and drowned.

ever, the real story was not so simple. Intellectual, personal, interpersonal, and cultural differences all played a part.[7]

Personally, Jung was a great contrast to Freud: raised in a Swiss village instead of urban Vienna, the son of a Calvinist minister instead of a Jewish immigrant from the countryside, solitary and bookish instead of gregarious. Jung's mother was very disturbed, so as a young boy he used to seclude himself in the attic, inventing games and ritual ceremonies with carved manikins. Jung and Freud visited the United States together in 1909, when they each gave lectures at Clark University in Worcester, Massachusetts. Jung liked the United States and came back often, whereas Freud disliked the country and never returned. Jung traveled widely (for example in India and Africa) and always lived near water, while Freud (until he escaped from the Nazis in 1938) remained in central Europe and spent his vacations in the mountains. Both wrote extensively on religion, art, and culture; but Jung's interpretations, emphasizing intuition and mysticism, are quite different from Freud's more reductive psychological analyses. In Jungian terms (to be described below), Jung was an "intuitive introvert" in contrast to Freud, a "thinking extravert."

ATTITUDE, FUNCTIONS, AND TYPES

Jung's concept of psychological types (1923/1971) is a major part of his overall theory of personality. A person's *type* is made of two elements: the person's attitude—*extraversion*[8] or *introversion*—combined with the person's dominant psychological function—*thinking, feeling, sensing,* or *intuiting.* Later elaborations of Jung's typology (Myers, 1980) allowed for two dominant functions, one from the thinking-feeling pair and one from the sensing-intuiting pair, as well as a third dominant function from a pair called *judging-perceiving* (to be discussed below). Because of space limits, however, we shall consider only Jung's original eight types, beginning with the fundamental extraversion-introversion attitude and then exploring how that attitude is modified by the person's dominant function.

Extraversion-Introversion: Jung's Original Conception

Jung introduced the terms extraversion and introversion into modern psychology in 1913, just before he broke with Freud. He used the terms to designate two types of persons, based on "two opposite movements of the libido"—either toward the external world of objects and other people (extraversion) or toward the subjective world that lies within (introversion) (Jung, 1913/1971, p. 500). While Jung initially phrased the contrast between extraversion and intro-

---

[7]Details of the Freud-Jung relationship can be found in the letters they exchanged between 1906 and 1914 (McGuire, 1974), as well as Jung's autobiography (Jung, 1973), a biography by Brome (1978), and an excellent comparative analysis of Freud and Jung by Steele (1982).

[8]While the spellings "extraversion" and "extroversion" both occur in psychological writing, the English translators of Jung and most other personality psychologists have preferred the former.

Carl Gustav Jung, one-time disciple of Freud, who later developed a typology of personality traits. "Individuals can be distinguished not only according to the broad distinction between introversion and extraversion, but also according to their basic psychological functions . . . *thinking, feeling, sensation,* and *intuition.* If one of these functions habitually predominates, a corresponding type results" (1923/1971, p. 6). (The Bettmann Archive)

version in terms of the orientation of the libido, after the break with Freud he modified it to refer to the direction of a person's "psychic energy" or "motivation," but with the essential meaning unchanged.

A decade later, after the break with Freud, Jung expanded this initial formulation into the full-fledged theory of *Psychological Types* (1923/1971). In the Bollingen edition of Jung's collected works, this book contains 495 pages. The first 329 pages review typologies of persons in classical and medieval thought; in the philosophical theories of Schiller, Nietzsche, and William James; and in poetry, physiology, aesthetics, and biography. Only at this point, two-thirds of the way through the book, did Jung introduce his own description of the extraverted and introverted attitude as two alternative expressions of psychic energy. Because Jung worked out these two alternatives on a purely rational basis, drawing on many existing typologies in Western thought, his method can be described as *rational* or a priori rather than *empirical* (for example, examining what traits actually go together in ordinary people, which is the approach described in the next chapter).

Jung's own descriptions of extraversion and introversion make clear the contrast he had in mind (Jung, 1936/1971):

> Extraversion is characterized by . . . a ready acceptance of external happenings, a desire to influence and be influenced by events, a need to join in and get "with it," the capacity to endure bustle and noise of every kind, and actually find them

enjoyable . . . the cultivation of friends and acquaintances, none too carefully selected, and finally by the great importance attached to the figure one cuts, and hence by a strong tendency to make a show of oneself. . . .

The introvert holds aloof from external happenings, does not join in, has a distinct dislike of society as soon as he finds himself among too many people. In a large gathering he feels lonely and lost. . . . He is not in the least "with it," and has no love of enthusiastic get-togethers. . . . His own world is a safe harbour, a carefully tended and walled-in garden, closed to the public and hidden from prying eyes. . . . His best work is done with his own resources, on his own initiative, and in his own way. Crowds, majority views . . . popular enthusiasm never convince him of anything, but merely make him creep still deeper into his shell. (pp. 549–551)

Jung believed that these differences were quite visible in young children. Here is the extraverted young child (Jung, 1925/1971):

Fear of objects is minimal; he lives and moves among them with confidence. His apprehension is quick but imprecise. . . . He likes to carry his enterprises to the extreme and exposes himself to risks. Everything unknown is alluring. (p. 516)

In contrast, here is the introverted child:

A reflective, thoughtful manner, marked shyness and even fear of unknown objects. . . . Everything unknown is regarded with mistrust; outside influences are usually met with violent resistance. The child wants his own way, and under no circumstances will he submit to an alien rule he cannot understand. When he asks questions, it is not from curiosity or a desire to create a sensation, but because he wants names, meanings, explanations to give him subjective protection against the object. (p. 517)

Nowadays the words "extravert" and "introvert" have passed from technical psychological jargon into everyday language. We think of an extravert mainly as someone who is lively, sociable, and friendly; while introvert is quieter, perhaps withdrawn and shy. Notice, though, that Jung also contrasts the two types in terms of other characteristics not related to sociability: reflection versus action, attitude toward objects, preference for risk, and desire for autonomy.

You probably know some people who fit each type, though most people are some mixture of the two. Be careful, however. Jung believed that if one attitude dominated a person's conscious functioning (conscious motives and attitudes), then the other type would dominate unconscious functioning (1923/1971, pp. 521–522). Thus an extreme extravert might occasionally be overwhelmed by primitive inner fantasies erupting from the unconscious, fantasies that seem alien and unfamiliar because they are subjective. Similarly, the unconscious extraversion of an extreme introvert might burst out in social behavior that is awkward because it is unconscious, causing unintended offense to others.

Another reason for caution when you classify people as extraverts or introverts is that what you observe also depends on the situation (Jung, 1923/1971):

A tense attitude is in general characteristic of the introvert, while a relaxed, easy attitude distinguishes the extravert. [But] give an introvert a thoroughly congenial, harmonious milieu, and he relaxes into complete extraversion, so that one begins to wonder whether one may not be dealing with an extravert. . . . Put an extravert in a dark and silent room, where all his repressed complexes can gnaw at him, and he will get into such a state of tension that he will jump at the slightest stimulus. (p. 287)

By now you will probably recognize in Jung many elements from John Milton's poems, Schopenhauer's types, the Lakalei descriptions, and even Henry Kissinger's gallery of personality types. It certainly seems as though many other ways of describing people converge in the terms of Jung's distinction—partly, of course, because he took account of these earlier typologies.

While the distinction between extraversion and introversion is an important part of Jung's typology, it is not the end of the story. As Jung put it, "While people may be classed as introverts or extraverts, this does not account for the tremendous differences between individuals in either class" (1931/1971, p. 535). For Jung, there are many different ways of being extraverted or introverted, depending on which *psychological function*[9] predominates in the person. In Jungian terminology, this dominant psychological function is said to orient the person's basic attitude of extraversion or introversion.

Jung described four such functions, each representing a different aspect of mental activity: *thinking* and *feeling* (also called the "rational" functions because they involve rational processes that transform raw perceptual information), and *sensing* and *intuiting* (also called "irrational" functions because they involve simple reception of raw perceptual data rather than rational transformation of them). Jung's principle of compensation applies to the functions as well as to the extraversion-introversion attitude: if one function is especially prominent in your conscious experience and activity, then one or more of the others usually dominate your unconscious.

To describe people's traits fully, then, we need to know both their attitude and their dominant function. A "thinking extravert," for example, would be different from a "feeling extravert" or a "sensing extravert," even though all three would have the same fundamental attitude of extraversion. Similarly, the thinking function in a "thinking extravert" would be quite different from the thinking function in a "thinking introvert," even though both would share the same predominant function. We shall discuss the four functions in some detail, noting how they modify and are in turn modified by extraversion-introversion.

---

[9]In recent years, some Jungian theorists have preferred to use the term *process* instead of function. Myers (1980) suggests that the "dominant" function is simply the best developed and therefore the preferred process.

Thinking

Thinking involves making conceptual connections among the images and ideas that float through consciousness. In order to think, we need both external objects ("facts" or experiences of the external world) and internal processing resources.

Among extraverts, the thinking function is externally focused on facts and "objective data." As an example of this type, Charles Darwin wrote in the introduction to his *Origin of Species* (1859/1936):

> When on board the H.M.S. "Beagle," as naturalist, I was much struck with certain facts. . . . On my return home, it occurred to me . . . that something might perhaps be made out on this question [the origin of species] by patiently accumulating and reflecting on all sorts of facts which could possibly have any bearing on it. After five years' work I allowed myself to speculate on the subject. (p. 11)

Thinking extraverts see the world as a rational place, efficiently organized by natural laws and rational principles that can be discovered through the application of thought—the field of economics, for example. With this viewpoint, they may have difficulty understanding things (in their own behavior and in that of others) that do not fit into their orderly arrangements. As a careful collector of facts, Darwin was for Jung the prototypical thinking extravert.

Thinking extravert Charles Darwin, whose careful observations of "facts"— slight variations in animal characteristics—led him to develop the theory of evolution. (The Bettmann Archive)

Thinking introvert Immanuel Kant, who argued that "facts" are subordinate to the mind, which creates them by the act of knowing. (The Bettmann Archive)

Other examples would include many business people, technicians, engineers, and those scientists who do experiments.

Among introverts, the thinking function is quite different, even taking on a life of its own. To a thinking introvert, facts, if they are important at all, are only of interest as a starting point: pure thought is the real interest. The German philosopher Immanuel Kant displayed his introverted thinking style in the preface to his *Fundamental Principles of the Metaphysic of Morals* (1785/1948, p. 55): "Do we not think it a matter of the utmost necessity to work out for once a pure moral philosophy completely cleansed of everything that can only be empirical?" At their best, thinking introverts can create intellectual revolutions, because they are freed from the already organized facts of the everyday world. On the other hand, their freedom from the world of facts may also mean that they make no sense to their colleagues. Typically lacking social skills and neglectful of the external world, thinking introverts may easily become social and intellectual isolates—the stereotype of the absent-minded and reclusive professor, for example. Convinced of their own correctness, they may make little effort to communicate, teach, or win approval for their ideas. As Jung put it, they "never introduce [their ideas] like a mother solicitous for her children, but simply dump them there and get extremely annoyed if they fail to thrive" (1923/1971, p. 384).

Feeling

While thinking involves making conceptual or cognitive connections among objects or mental images, the feeling function involves immediate emotional reactions and valuing of these objects and images—liking or disliking them, accepting them with pleasure or rejecting them as a source of pain. Often the feeling function is detached from specific objects and appears simply as an overall mood.

In extraverts, a predominance of the feeling function leads to feelings that are synchronized with the external world, thus to enjoyment of popular culture. Feeling extraverts laugh when others laugh and cry with the crowd. In extreme cases they are prone to hysteria, which Jung viewed as being overwhelmed with feelings by an external object. Since their values, tastes, and reactions are often highly conventional, they are the target audience for soap operas and popular music, books, and movies. Sometimes the reactions of feeling extraverts appear put on or fake to other people.

The late Virginia Kelley, mother of President Clinton, is an example of the feeling extravert type. The prominence of the feeling function is suggested by the title of her autobiography, *Leading with My Heart* (Kelley, 1994), while her extraverted attitude is expressed in repeated statements such as the following:

> I make friends easily. I've always enjoyed talking with strangers—the more different they are, the better I like them. (p. 56)
> Ever since I was a girl, when I've showed up someplace, I've wanted people to know I'm there. (p. 157)

Feeling extravert Virginia Kelley, mother of President Clinton. "I've always liked bright colors and I like people to notice me. In fact, I hate for them *not* to notice me" (quoted in Oates, 1994, p. 14). (Reuters/Bettmann)

The comments of Joyce Carol Oates, in reviewing Kelley's autobiography, support Jung's idea that feeling extraverts readily fit in with conventional popular culture: Kelley's "experiences have sometimes resembled the sort of stories told in country-and-western music," and "in this zestful world, emotional peaks and crises are best expressed through popular song, as if, in her memory, Kelley's life were a romantic Technicolor film, complete with soundtrack" (Oates, 1994, pp. 14, 15).

Feeling introverts, on the other hand, are often difficult to figure out, emotionally a little out of reach. They are concerned with feelings, but those feelings are oriented around an inner life. In everyday encounters with feeling introverts, you would scarcely guess their inner emotional intensity—an intensity that, in extreme cases, becomes a mystical ecstasy.

Emily Dickinson (1830–1886) is a good example of a feeling introvert. After a year as a student at what is now Mount Holyoke College, she lived at home almost as a recluse for thirty-seven years, while writing a kind of intense, inward poetry that only began to be appreciated in the midtwentieth century. Some examples illustrate the predominance of feeling and inward focus:

> How dreary to be somebody!
> How public, like a frog
> To tell your name the livelong day
> To an admiring bog!
>   (from "I'm Nobody! Who Are You?" Dickinson, 1891, p. 21)

> I measure every grief I meet
>   With analytic eyes;
> I wonder if it weighs like mine,
>   Or has an easier size.
>   (from "Griefs," Dickinson, 1896, p. 47)

> The soul selects her own society,
> Then shuts the door;
> . . . .
> Unmoved, she notes the chariot's pausing
> At her low gate;
> Unmoved, an emperor is kneeling
> Upon her mat.
>   (from "The Soul Selects Her Own Society," Dickinson, 1892, p. 26)

Rational-irrational versus judging-perceiving functions. According to Jung, thinking and feeling are both *rational functions* because they involve active mental participation or effort (that is, reasoning or rationality). It is easy to see that thinking is rational, because it involves reasoning, but normally we think of feelings as irrational, in contrast to "rational thought." Jung used the word "rational" in a special sense: feeling, like thinking, involves judgments or calculations—not about the qualities of objects but rather *about the feelings of pleasure or pain* that are involved. As Emily Dickinson put it in lines quoted

Feeling introvert Emily Dickinson, whose life was secluded but whose poems reflect an inner intensity of feeling. (United States Postal Service)

above, "I measure every grief I meet / With analytic eyes." Thus the feeling function is rational in the special sense of involving calculation of feeling. Jung's terminology here is confusing: the thinking and feeling functions are "rational" because they involve voluntary active judgment, and the sensing and intuiting functions are "irrational" because they do not. To express more clearly the distinction between a person's relative dominance of thinking and feeling, on the one hand, versus sensing and intuiting, on the other, many of his followers have rephrased it as *judging* versus *perceiving* (see Myers, 1980, pp. 8–10; and Thorne and Gough, 1991, pp. 76–77). The judging function involves active processing, transforming, and organizing of mental life, while the perceiving function has more the sense of going with the flow of mental currents. I find this later terminology much clearer than Jung's distinction between rational and irrational.

Sensing

The sensing function includes the operation of our five senses: seeing, hearing, touching, tasting, and smelling. From a realist perspective, sensing involves apprehending the real qualities of real external objects. The apple I see in front of me really exists and really is red: the apple and redness do not result from my reasoning, feeling, or judgment; they simply *are*. Thus the sensing function is related to perceiving rather than judging (Thorne & Gough, 1991, pp. 26, 76–77). The only value is the *intensity* of the sensations produced.

Naturally, sensing extraverts are oriented toward sensations that arise from the external world: strong tastes, vivid colors, and loud sounds. Any mysterious internal sensation would immediately be related to external factors. Thus to a sensing extravert, a psychological symptom would be the result of "something I ate," and feelings of depression might be caused by the weather. Sensing extraverts love life for its surface textures: good food and drink, vivid sunsets, fast rollercoasters, pulsating rhythms. They are happiest in the middle of the fray, for example, in Times Square at midnight on New Year's Eve, because that is where the most vivid sensations can be found. Some sensing extraverts carry the craving for strong sensations to a crude or gross extent; others, who have developed subtle refinements of taste, are gourmet cooks and wine connoisseurs. To them, people *do* live by bread alone, as long as the bread tastes good.

Sensing introverts are focused on sensation, but their orientation is toward inner sensations—that is, their experience of sensations rather than an object that is the external source of those sensations. Such people are often difficult to understand and may appear remote, as if there were an invisible shield between themselves and the outer world. You might get the impression that to them, you did not quite exist but were rather just a "bundle of sensory impressions" in their minds. It is easier if sensing introverts have artistic ability, for then they can communicate their subjective perspectives.

To understand the difference between a sensing extravert and a sensing introvert, consider two paintings of river gorges, one by Claude Monet and one by Vincent Van Gogh, as reproduced in Figure 12.2. Each painting was done during the late 1880s and is related to the impressionist movement in French art. To Monet, impressionism was an attempt to *represent the reality of nature more effectively*, especially to capture the subtle, everchanging play of light. Canaday (1965) wrote of Monet:

> He wished he had been born blind and could have gained his sight so that he could paint without knowing what the objects before him were, since this would allow him to see them purely in terms of light. Never having seen a bush he would not know that the green blur in the distance was a bush, and would reproduce it in a matching green blur of paint without having to forget his detailed acquaintance with it as a form. (pp. 182–183)

Now look at the Van Gogh painting. The setting and subject are similar, but the result is completely different. The painting is vibrant and alive, but with the power of Van Gogh's imagination rather than the play of the light itself. Whereas for Monet, "impressionism was the ultimate imitative realism, where the eye becomes only a lens," the world of Van Gogh "is accessible to no such lens [for] it is an *inner world of his own*" (Canaday, 1965, p. 368, emphasis added). Today Van Gogh is considered one of the first expressionist painters. In contrast to Monet, who put on canvas that which is "out there," he painted his inner reactions to it.

Intuiting

While most of us have had intuitions, it is not easy to give a clear account of such elusive experiences. We say that an image or thought simply "comes to mind"; it does not arise from any sense perception, rational thought, or emo-

FIGURE 12.2
A painting by Claude Monet (top) and a painting by Vincent Van Gogh (bottom).
Although both paintings have similar subject matter, their contrasting styles reflect the
difference between the sensing extravert and the sensing introvert, respectively. [*Oscar
Claude Monet,* Valley of the Creuse. (Sunlight effect), *Julia Cheney Edwards Collection.
Courtesy, Museum of Fine Arts, Boston;Vincent van Gogh,* Ravine, *Bequest of Keith McLeod.
Courtesy, Museum of Fine Arts, Boston.*]

tional feeling that we can identify. Jung spoke of intuition as "perception by the unconscious." We can elaborate this definition by saying that intuition is perception that is heavily influenced by free associations, unconscious memories, and primary process (see Chapter 3). It involves rapid, nonconscious reception of small cues not noticed by ordinary perception; thus under the dominance of intuition we come to "see" possibilities that we could not describe or reason out with our other mental functions.

Focused toward the external world, intuiting extraverts are quick to grasp worldly possibilities even before they can put them into words: a basketball star "knows" just the right play that will work against a particular defensive alignment; a speculator has a "feel" for the way the stock market will rise and fall; a promoter "senses" what an audience can be persuaded to buy or believe and how to persuade them to do it. Each of these cases is an example of extraversion oriented by the intuiting function. (I put "know," "feel," and "sense" in quotation marks to indicate that this is not ordinary thinking, feeling, or sensing.) Intuiting extraverts were probably the first to realize that automobiles (electric lights, airplanes, television, CD players, personal computers, or fax machines) were here to stay. At their best, they may be visionary entrepreneurs who enrich our society by transforming their intuitions into economic, social, and cultural realities. At their worst, they are fly-by-nights, exploiters who, in Jung's (1923/1971) words:

> Seize on new objects or situations with great intensity, sometimes with extraordinary enthusiasm, only to abandon them cold-bloodedly, without any compunction and apparently without remembering them, as soon as their range is known and no further developments can be divined. (p. 368)

For such a person, today's intuition may be dropped before completion, in order to pursue tomorrow's new vision. Let other people pick up the pieces.

Joseph P. Kennedy, the father of president John F. Kennedy, was almost certainly an intuiting extravert. According to Goodwin (1987), he was a financial genius who could work out "in a flash" a radical strategy to save a company from a hostile takeover bid (pp. 387–391). In early 1929, Kennedy's intuition was to get out of the stock market, so he was actually able to profit from the October 1929 crash of the market (pp. 486–489). Later, in the summer of 1930, a brief success by the Pathé motion picture company enabled him to make good his personal losses on the company's stock and sell out at a profit, leaving many ordinary stockholders with only worthless shares (pp. 489–491). Recognizing the dangers that the Great Depression posed to his personal wealth, he became an early supporter of Franklin Roosevelt and the New Deal (pp. 495–497). (After the election, Roosevelt chose Kennedy to be the first chair of the new Securities and Exchange Commission, among whose tasks was the prevention of just those insider trading tactics he had earlier used so well!)

Intuiting extravert Joseph P. Kennedy, father of President Kennedy, whose practical intuitions about business and politics enabled him to amass a fortune and get his son elected president. (UPI/Bettmann)

Among introverts, the intuiting function leads to subjective, almost mystical dreams and prophecies. Jung believed that intuiting introverts were somehow able to comprehend directly the archetypes or symbolic residues of the accumulated human experience. Because of their inward orientation, however, they are often only able to communicate their intuitions in broken fragments and disjointed utterances. While such persons may become cranks who are totally unintelligible to the world, at their best they may be visionary artists or mystical gurus. Ludwig Wittgenstein, one of the most important twentieth-century philosophers (and one of the most difficult to comprehend), will serve as an example of both the difficulty and the vision of the intuiting introverted type. His major work (Wittgenstein, 1922) begins with a frank confession of unintelligibility: "This book will perhaps only be understood by those who have themselves already thought the thoughts which are expressed in it" (p. 27). It ends with visions and paradoxes:

> The solution of the problem of life is seen in the vanishing of this problem. . . . There is indeed the inexpressible. This *shows* itself; it is the mystical. . . . My propositions are elucidatory in this way: he who understands me finally recognizes them as senseless, when he has climbed out through them, on them, over them. . . . Whereof one cannot speak, thereof one must be silent. (pp. 187, 189)

Summarizing Jung's Typology

Table 12.2, page 438, which is based on Jung's original work as well as the elaboration by Myers (1980), summarizes the characteristics of each of Jung's

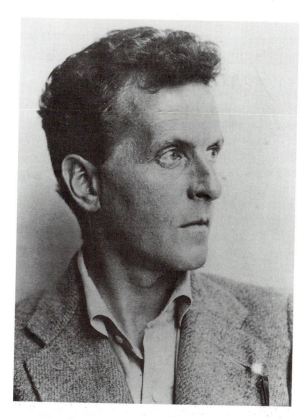

Intuiting introvert Ludwig Wittgenstein, a Viennese philosopher who maintained that philosophical problems and debates are really questions about how we use language. (Bildarchiv der Österreichischen Nationalbibliothek, Wien)

eight types. The four functions can be thought of as alternative channels for the expression of the fundamental attitude of extraversion-introversion. To put it another way: your extraverted or introverted attitude gives the direction in which you are headed (outer versus inner), while your dominant functions tell how you will be getting there (which mental functions you will use).

Other typologies. Jung's types can be compared to the other typologies discussed in Chapter 11. Each of those typologies has a dimension corresponding to extraversion-introversion, but none is as elaborate as Jung's eight-fold typology. Galen's sanguine and choleric types, for example, correspond to the extraverted attitude and his phlegmatic and melancholic types correspond to introversion. Further, his choleric and melancholic types have some similarity to the dominance of Jung's feeling function. Schopenhauer's good-spirited type is probably a sensing extravert, while his intelligent type is likely to be a either a thinking introvert or an intuiting introvert.

Types and life choices. Table 12.3, page 439, presents data accumulated by Myers (1980, p. 168–172) showing how the eight types related to subsequent choice of different medical specialties in a sample of over 4,000 medical students. Not surprisingly, the introverted types tend to go into specialties that

TABLE 12.2 OUTLINE OF JUNG'S EIGHT TYPES

Dominant orienting function	Primary attitude	
	Introversion	*Extraversion*
Thinking	Values truth as underlying principles	Values truth as facts
	Organizes concepts and ideas	Organizes institutions and technical matters
	Inwardly absorbed, outwardly reserved or even aloof	Social and emotional life are incidental
Feeling	Values harmonious inner life	Values harmonious human relationships
	Passionate convictions masked by independence and reserve	Friendly and tactful in dealing with people
	Uninterested in impressing or influencing others	Sensitive to praise and criticism
Sensing	Values own unique reactions to life	Values concrete pleasures and life experiences
	Hard-working and thorough	Good at details; learns from experience
	May have difficulty communicating	Adaptable, easy-going
Intuiting	Values inner vision	Values inspiration, initiative, and new possibilities
	Creative, ingenious; with insight into deeper meanings	Versatile; impulsive and energetic
	Discontent with routine	May lack concentrated will power, thus projects not completed

SOURCE: Adapted from Myers (1980, chap. 9).

do not require extensive contact with patients as people (medical research, pathology), specialities that focus on internal mental states (psychiatry, neurology), or both (anesthesiology). Among extraverted doctors, those with a thinking orientation tend to become all-around generalists concerned with the big picture or the total patient—the "Charles Darwins" of medicine. Intuiting extraverts become psychiatrists, a specialty that requires extensive personal contact and the ability to figure out people's problems from often fragmentary cues. Not surprisingly, pediatricians and medical faculty tend to be feeling extraverts: the cheerfulness and tact characteristic of this type are important skills, either for tending to the aches and pains of children or for dealing with the anxieties of medical students (neither group usually being very sick). For sensing types of either attitude, obstetrics involves childbirth, that most vivid medical event that also brings forth a tangible "product." Finally, sensing extraverts also tend to become surgeons. As members of a surgical "team," they treat body parts of (anesthetized) patients as objects—touching, prodding, cutting, and sewing.

TABLE 12.3 RELATIONSHIP OF JUNG'S EIGHT TYPES TO CHOICE OF MEDICAL SPECIALITY AMONG DOCTORS

Dominant orienting function	*Primary attitude*	
	Introversion	*Extraversion*
Thinking	Anesthesiology Neurology Research Psychiatry	General practice Internal medicine
Feeling	Psychiatry Anesthesiology	Pediatrics Medical faculty
Sensing	Obstetrics and gynecology	Obstetrics and gynecology Surgery
Intuiting	Neurology Medical research Pathology	Psychiatry

SOURCE: Adapted from Myers (1980, p. 171).

Stephens (1972, cited by Myers, 1980, p. 167) studied art majors and found that those who wanted to be artists were often intuiting introverts. Those planning to be art therapists, however, were feeling extraverts; and students aiming to teach art had dominant intuiting and feeling functions. Such studies show how people's trait types affect the course of their lives over time. Both doctors and art majors, as heterogeneous groups, may not have a distinctive trait or type profile; but within such broad areas of interest, people do appear to seek out particular situations or niches that fit their own preferred types.

Einstein.   In Jung's typology, Albert Einstein would clearly be an introvert, with both thinking and intuiting functions dominant. In fact, he was a brilliant abstract thinker, but his theories were constructed in his own mind on the basis of thought experiments rather than laboratory experiments. For example, Einstein's theories and ideas led scientists to predict that converting a small amount of mass to energy would produce an enormous, explosive amount of energy; but the experiments of the German physicists Hahn and Strassmann in 1938 and 1939 actually demonstrated that a uranium atom could be split and its nuclear energy thereby released.

Einstein's cheerful irreverence for social conventions, his absentmindedness, his two unsuccessful marriages, and many of his other idiosyncrasies can now be understood as manifestations of his less developed (even childish) functions of sensing and feeling. These were, in Erikson's (1982, pp. 155–156) terms, the "preserved child" within Einstein's personality.

MEASURING JUNG'S TYPES: THE MBTI

Although Jung's major typology work was completed by the early 1920s, personality psychologists did not develop a systematic way of measuring the types and functions until almost forty years later. During the early years of the twentieth century, Katharine Briggs developed—entirely on her own—a trait typology similar to Jung's. After World War II, Briggs and her daughter, Isabel Briggs Myers, and Myers's son Peter Myers, began to develop a pool of items to measure the Jungian dimensions. Lacking the usual establishment creden-

TABLE 12.4 CHARACTERISTICS OF HIGH AND LOW SCORERS ON THE MYERS-BRIGGS TYPE INDICATOR (MBTI) DIMENSIONS

Dimension and source of data	Characterization by trained staff observers*
Extraversion adjectives	Active, cheerful, energetic, enthusiastic, sociable
Q-sort statements	"Behaves in an assertive fashion"
	"Emphasizes being with others; gregarious"
Introversion adjectives	Aloof, inhibited, quiet, reserved, retiring, shy, silent, withdrawn
Q-sort statement	"Keeps people at a distance; avoids close interpersonal relationships"
Thinking adjectives	Ambitious, logical
Q-sort statement	"Prides self on being objective, rational"
Feeling adjectives	Affectionate, sentimental
Q-sort statements	"Has warmth; has the capacity for close relationships; compassionate"
	"Enjoys aesthetic impressions; is aesthetically responsive" (males only)
Sensing adjectives	Conservative, contented, conventional, interests narrow, practical
Q-sort statements	"Favors conservative values in a variety of areas"
	"Is uncomfortable with uncertainty and complexities"
Intuiting adjectives	Imaginative, ingenious, original
Q-sort statements	"Thinks and associates to ideas in unusual ways"
	"Is unpredictable and changeable in behavior, and attitudes"
	"Genuinely values intellectual and cognitive matters"
	"Tends to be rebellious and nonconforming"
Judging adjectives	Conservative, conventional, deliberate, industrious, methodical
Q-sort statements	"Is fastidious"
	"Favors conservative values in a variety of areas"
	"Is moralistic"
Perceiving adjectives	Careless, changeable, rebellious
Q-sort statements	"Is unpredictable and changeable in behavior and attitudes"
	"Enjoys sensuous experiences (including touch, taste, smell, physical contact, etc.)"
	"Tends to be rebellious and nonconforming"

*See Thorne and Gough (1991, pp. 4–7)
SOURCE: Based on Thorne and Gough (1991, pp. 49–57).

tials of an academic base, formal psychology and statistics training, and government or foundation grants, Myers taught herself what she needed to know and tested preliminary versions of the Myers-Briggs Type Indicator (MBTI) on thousands of subjects. In 1962 all three published the MBTI. Today, it is one of the most widely used measures for describing the traits of normal (that is, nonpathological) people. In 1990, for example, an estimated 2 million people took the MBTI (Thorne & Gough, 1991, p. 2)!

The MBTI is a forced-choice self-descriptive inventory, in which people are given a series of paired alternatives and asked to choose for each pair the alternative that best describes how they feel or act. For example:

> Are your interests:
>   (A) few and lasting
>   (B) varied

Another part of the test contains pairs of words, asking people to pick the word in each pair that appeals to them more. The results include four scales (extraversion-introversion, thinking-feeling, sensing-intuiting, and perceiving-judging). These scales are then combined in complex ways to estimate the person's type. Thorne and Gough (1991) present the results of an extensive program of research on the MBTI at the University of California at Berkleley, in which hundreds of people were tested and then observed and rated in a variety of situations and with a large number of measuring techniques. Table 12.4 presents some adjectives and Q-sort statements that trained observers used to characterize women and men who scored high on each pole of the four dimensions.

RESEARCH ON THE JUNGIAN TYPES

Everyday Conversation

In recent years, personality psychologists have carried out several research studies involving Jung's typological theory. Most of these are focused on the extraversion-introversion attitude. Thorne (1987), for example, identified groups of extraverted and introverted college women on the basis of MBTI scores. Each woman then participated in two 10-minute conversations with someone she did not know before, one with another woman of the same type and the other with another woman of the opposite type. Thorne recorded and analyzed the conversations as they occurred. After each conversation, each woman rated her partners' traits and her own level of comfort with the conversations.

Table 12.5 shows some of the results of Thorne's study. We shall consider mainly the comparisons between the introvert-introvert and extravert-extravert conversations, since the mixed extraversion-introversion conversations fell somewhere between the two. The extravert conversationalists were rated by their partners as more "cheerful," "enthusiastic," and "outgoing,"

TABLE 12.5 HOW INTROVERTS AND EXTRAVERTS CONVERSE

	Average score	
Rated variable or conversational category	*Introvert-introvert conversations*	*Extravert-extravert conversations*
Rating of partner [*]		
Cheerful	3.0	4.1
Enthusiastic	2.7	3.7
Outgoing	2.6	3.9
Serious	3.6	2.9
Reserved	3.6	2.7
Shy	3.1	2.0
Own rated comfort during conversation [*]	2.9	3.8
Topic [†]		
Extracurricular activities	.9	3.5
Family and hometown roots	.6	1.3
Miscellaneous people	.5	1.5
School	6.5	4.4
Speech acts (with example) [†]		
Things that give pleasure ("I like jogging.")	3.7	7.6
Agree ("I think so, too." "Yeah, me too.")	3.0	4.8
Reach for similarity ("You're from Los Angeles? I have an aunt who used to live there.")	1.0	1.7
Compliment ("I like your blouse.")	1.2	2.0
Hedge or qualification ("I sort of like her.")	3.5	1.9
Problem or dissatisfaction ("I've got to look for an apartment because my roommates are driving me nuts.")	9.2	5.8

[*]Rated on a 5-point scale.
[†]Number of occurrences during 10-minute conversation.
SOURCE: Adapted from Thorne (1987).

while the introverts were seen as "serious," "reserved," and "shy." These results confirm that people's own MBTI self-descriptions of type fit with how others describe them. Consistent with Jung's theory, extraverts were more comfortable during the conversations.

The actual conversations were also different. While both groups were equally talkative, they differed in what they talked about and how they talked about it. The cheerful and outgoing extraverts talked about extracurricular activities, family and home, and other people. Their conversations were focused on pleasure and were full of agreements, compliments, and attempts to establish similarity as a way of breaking the ice. The serious introverts, in contrast, talked mostly about school, especially their problems and dissatisfactions. Perhaps because they were reserved, they tended to hedge or qualify their statements, as if to avoid commitment or protect themselves against a challenge. No wonder the extraverts felt more comfortable during the conversations!

Some of the women who participated in the mixed extravert-introvert conversations had especially interesting comments (Thorne, 1987):

> Many of the introverts felt that the conversation with the extravert was a breath of fresh air. Some extraverts, on the other hand, said they did not feel so pressed to say nice things and to refrain from complaining about problems when talking with an introvert, as opposed to an extravert. (p. 724)

This latter remark suggests that, for all their impression of cheerfulness, extraverts often carry a burden (perhaps a self-imposed one) of keeping up a conversational front.

Memory and Perception

Carlson carried out a series of studies (Carlson, 1980; Carlson & Levy, 1973) illustrating differences in basic psychological processes among the Jungian types. From Jung's description of the types, Carlson and Levy reasoned that thinking introverts (such as the philosopher Kant; see above) would be better at remembering impersonal information, while feeling extraverts (such as Virginia Kelley) would be better at remembering personal information. This is just what they found. For example, when presented with a series of different geometric shapes, each of which had either a number (impersonal) or a person's first name (personal) and later asked to remember what was associated with which shape, thinking introverts did better at the first task and feeling extraverts did better at the second.

These same two types also have characteristically different emotional memories. For example, here are the responses of two women who were asked to recall their most vivid experience of joy (Carlson, 1980):

Thinking introvert

> I was 22. I awoke in the hospital after giving birth to my only son. It was Mother's Day. My first conscious move was to see if my stomach was flat, and the next to find out whether I had had a boy or girl. When the nurse told me that it was a healthy boy, I felt a wave of elation to know that we had both come through safely, and when my son was given to me to hold, I felt pride, protectiveness, and happiness. Physically, I felt calm and able to undertake anything. (pp. 803–804)

Notice that although two other people are involved (nurse and new baby), the memory is focused within the speaker herself (introversion). Also, notice how the memory is sequentially organized, and the specific emotions carefully analyzed and described (thinking function).

Feeling extravert

> One day we were visiting in our daughter's home. As I sat watching my husband playing with our granddaughter, I experienced a sense of tremendous joy. I had a lump in my throat and tears in my eyes, and I thought, "This is really living!" I didn't say anything to anyone. (p. 804)

This memory is more focused on the activity of other people (husband and granddaughter). The phrases indicating emotion ("joy," "lump in my throat," "tears," "This is really living!") are simpler, more direct, and less intellectualized.

Overall, Carlson found that extraverts had more interpersonally focused memories than introverts, and feeling types had more vivid memories than thinking types.

Carlson also found important differences in how sensing and intuiting types organize information about other people into personal constructs on the Kelly Rep test (see Chapter 6). Sensing types used personal constructs that involved concrete, observable characteristics (for example, "they're good cooks" or "both are students"). In contrast, intuiting types used constructs that went beyond easily observable facts and required some inference (for example, "little self-insight" or "both know how to be tactful"). Carlson also asked people to write a letter introducing themselves to an imaginary pen pal in a foreign country. Here again, sensing types made more references to their own physical appearance (for example, "I am quite tall"), while intuitives conveyed personal information in a way that involved the imaginary other person (for example, "You would find me quite tall").

Information Processing Styles and Literary Criticism

Helson (1982) viewed the Jungian types as reflecting three different aspects of how people process information. Extraversion-introversion refers to whether the person's attention is focused on objective or subjective information, sensing-intuiting tells whether the information gathered is literal or symbolic, and thinking-feeling indicates whether the information is evaluated by logical or emotional standards (pp. 407–408).

To explore these ideas, Helson examined the work of different literary critics. Literary criticism can be seen as a mixture of *appreciation* (expressing delight about the form, beauty, style, or insights of a literary work) and *elucidation* (explaining or analyzing the principles or structures of a literary work). Helson suggested that among particular critics, the balance between these two aspects of literary criticism will be related to their dominant function. Thus critics who emphasize elucidation over appreciation would have a dominant thinking function, while those who emphasize appreciation over elucidation would have a dominant feeling function. Those who emphasize both aspects should be intuiting types, and those who emphasize neither should be sensing types. From these hypotheses, Helson developed a typology of styles of literary criticism that relates each critical style type to the critic's dominant functions, as illustrated with examples in Table 12.6.

Jungian Functions Measured at a Distance

Helson's technique suggests how the Jungian functions could be measured indirectly, through analyzing the language people use in speaking and writing. Seegmiller and Epperson (1987) developed a simple indirect measure of

TABLE 12.6 JUNGIAN TYPES AND STYLES OF LITERARY CRITICISM

	Role of the literary critic			
Jungian function	*Appreciation*	*Elucidation*	*Style of literary criticism*	*Example*
Thinking	L*	H*	Philosopher-critic; "Language of distance"[†]	"'Intention,' as we shall use the term, corresponds to what [the author] intended in a formula which more or less explicitly has had wide acceptance. . . . We begin our discussion with a series of propositions summarized and abstracted to a degree where they seem to us axiomatic" (Wimsatt & Beardsley, 1953, p. 4).
Feeling	H	L	Humanitarian teacher; "Language of camaraderie"[†]	[The critic's] perceptions and judgments are his . . . [but] they are inevitably collaborative. Collaboration may take the form of disagreement, and one is grateful to the critic whom one has found worth disagreeing with" (Leavis, 1952, p. v).
Sensing	L	L	Text scholar, literary historian; "Language of clarity"[†]	"What is meant by the words 'prose,' 'verse,' and 'poetry' [is] a question which is sometimes debated but which never gets straightened out. Yet are not the obvious facts as follows? What we mean by the words 'prose' and 'verse' are simply two different techniques of literary expression" (Wilson, 1948, p. 15).
Intuiting	H	H	Poet	"I propose to use the word [ambiguity] in an extended sense, and shall think relevant to my subject any verbal nuance, however slight, which gives room for alternative reactions to the same piece of language. Sometimes . . . the word may be stretched absurdly far. . . ." (Empson, 1930/1947, p. 1).

*H = high; L = low
[†]Adapted from Lakoff (1979).
SOURCE: Adapted from Helson (1982).

the thinking-versus-feeling functions based on the specific words people use. People scoring high in the thinking function on the MBTI tend to use verbs such as "think," "analyze," "decide," "know," and "question" more frequently. In contrast, people scoring high on the feeling function more frequently use "feel," "love," "fear," "enjoy," "care," "hope," and similar verbs. This research strategy could be extended to develop at-a-distance measures of the other Jungian functions.

Orbovich (1985) measured the functions in a more complex way. Drawing on Nutt's (1979) theory of cognitive styles in management, she developed categories to score the four functions in material from the archives of U.S. presidents Harry Truman and Dwight Eisenhower: diaries, letters, memos, and even telephone transcripts and minutes of meetings. On the basis of their scores, she classified Truman as a sensing-feeling type, and Eisenhower as an intuiting-thinking type. Orbovich then showed how these type differences were related to the ways in which Truman and Eisenhower as presidents managed foreign policy decision making.

GOUGH'S "CUBOID" TYPOLOGY

Gough (1987) has developed a typology of traits based on the California Personality Inventory (CPI), another widely used self-report measure of personality. The CPI consists of 480 statements to which people respond by answering True or False, as in the following examples:

> Some of my family have quick tempers.
> I always follow the rule: business before pleasure.

Originally, the CPI consisted of some twenty scales measuring such everyday trait terms as dominance, self-acceptance, responsibility, well-being, tolerance, and flexibility. In 1987, however, Gough developed a revised structural model in which the scales were recombined to form three vectors or fundamental dimensions. The first vector, labeled v.1 or *internality*, is conceptually similar to Jung's introversion-extraversion attitude (high scores mean introverted, low scores extraverted). The second vector, v.2 or *norm-accepting*, represents the person's orientation toward social norms and rules (high scores mean accepting, low scores rejecting). Finally, v.3 or *realization* reflects the person's self-perception of fulfillment or actualization, similar to Rogers's concept of self-actualization discussed in Chapter 4 (high scores mean more actualized).

The three vector scores can be thought of as three independent dimensions, which together define a three-dimensional space or cube, as shown in Figure 12.3. Scores on each vector are classified as either high or low. Thus within the overall three-dimensional cube, there are eight smaller cubes that represent the eight possible combinations of high or low scores on three vectors. Gough's "cuboid" typology consists of these eight smaller cubes. People are classified into one of these eight types on the basis of their vector scores.

In Figure 12.3, the v.1 (internality) and v.2 (norm acceptance) vectors are represented by the horizontal and vertical dimensions, respectively. High or low scores on these two vectors define four cells or types, as labeled in the figure. In addition, each cell can have two different levels of realization or actualization (v.3 score), as represented in the figure by the forward-backward dimension. In the cuboid typology, a person's full type is described as (1) one

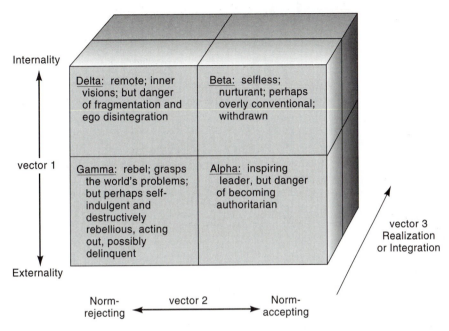

FIGURE 12.3
Gough's cuboid typology of traits based on the CPI. (Based on Gough, 1987, and Thorne and Gough, 1991)

of the four cells defined by the v.1 and v.2 scores, together with (2) the level of realization (high or low), defined by the v.3 score.

The following description of each cell is based on Thorne and Gough (1991). The *Alpha* cell (low internality, high norm acceptance) consists of active, decisive, prosocial people. At high levels of realization, Alphas may be inspiring leaders; at lower levels, they could be rigid paranoids. The *Beta* cell (high internality, high norm acceptance) contains selfless people who seek peace and take care of the needs of the world. At high levels of realization, Betas may be true saints, but at lower levels, they are subdued and inhibited. The *Gamma* cell (low internality, low norm acceptance) includes the rebels who grasp the world's problems and contradictions. If realized, Gammas are agents for change, but at low levels of realization they may be self-indulgent criminals. Finally, the *Delta* cell (high internality, low norm acceptance) consists of those who are "marching to a different (internal) drummer." At high levels of realization, they are the visionaries who can transform our ways of thinking and acting, but at low levels they are fragmented, prone to regression, and even psychotic.

Gough's model is essentially a rational model constructed on the basis of theory. However, in the process of construction he used a variety of mathematical clustering procedures to aggregate items and scales and construct the model. Hence the Gough cuboid model is a bridge to the more mathematically based procedures for clustering and aggregating traits that will be discussed in Chapter 13.

13

Searching for Basic Traits: Factor Analysis

❖

448

*F*ACTOR ANALYSIS

In the sixty-plus years since Allport and Odbert (1936) constructed their exhaustive list of English-language trait words, many nomothetically oriented personality psychologists have used a mathematical procedure known as *factor analysis* to reduce the Allport-Odbert list to a more manageable set of basic trait dimensions. While other mathematical methods have been used to analyze the structure of traits, factor analysis is the most common technique. In order to understand this work, it is first necessary to describe factor analysis briefly. Further details can be found in an advanced statistics text.

Factor analysis is a mathematical way to reduce a large number of different things (ratings, scores, or other variables) down to a few underlying dimensions. Think again about the twelve trait adjectives of the Boy Scout Law mentioned at the beginning of Chapter 11: trustworthy, loyal, helpful, friendly, courteous, kind, obedient, cheerful, thrifty, brave, clean, and reverent. These are twelve separate words, but they probably represent a smaller number of fundamental trait dimensions. For example, a scout who is trustworthy is probably also loyal—not always, but more often than not. Trustworthy and loyal are nearly synonymous. Scouts who are helpful are also likely to be kind, though they may not necessarily be trustworthy. Friendly and cheerful also seem to go together; courteous, obedient, and reverent seem to make up a different cluster. Clean and thrifty are still another group. Brave seems to stand off by itself, not part of any cluster. For example, some scouts who are brave—such as by striking out and doing things on their own—may be *less* obedient! In that case, we could construct a bipolar cluster, with brave at one pole and obedient-reverent-courteous at the other. Thus by using my hunches and some rational ideas about how these twelve traits go together, I have reduced the twelve to a smaller and simpler structure of six dimensions. You may disagree: perhaps this list can be simplified further, or perhaps I have already gone too far.

Factor analysis is a different way of reducing the list. It applies mathematical criteria for *simple structure* to the *scores* of a group of *subjects* (people) on a series of *variables* (the original list of trait words). The result is a series of clusters or *factors* representing groups of variables that covary.

An Illustration: Factor Analysis of the Boy Scout Law Traits

Factor analysis begins with the matrix of correlation coefficients among all variables. Suppose, for example, that we take scoutmasters' ratings of 100 scouts on the twelve traits of the Boy Scout Law and then calculate a correlation matrix of each trait with every other trait. These correlations can vary from +1.00 (a perfect relationship, where a scout high on one is high on the other) through .00 (no relationship at all) to −1.00 (a perfect negative relationship, where a scout high on one is low on the other). While factor analysis is a very complex procedure, the underlying principle is fairly simple: with the aid of a computer, underlying or latent factors (clusters, dimensions) are extracted from the correlation matrix according to some criterion of simple structure. In other words, factor analysis identifies variables that go together, and constructs underlying factors that can account for the observed mutual variation or correlations among the variables.

Table 13.1 shows a correlation matrix of the twelve traits of the Boy Scout Law. (For convenience, decimal points are omitted.) To construct this table, I used an existing set of data collected by McClelland and Franz (1992), which contained self-rating Adjective Check List (ACL) forms (see Gough & Heilbrun, 1965) filled out by seventy-six adult women and men.[1] (This was easier

[1] I am grateful to Carol Franz for making these data available to me.

TABLE 13.1 CORRELATION MATRIX AND FACTOR STRUCTURE OF TRAIT ADJECTIVES IN THE BOY SCOUT LAW

	Correlations							
	Trustworthy	Loyal	Helpful	Friendly	Courteous	Kind	Obedient	Cheerful
Trustworthy (reliable)	—							
Loyal	20	—						
Helpful	−05	15	—					
Friendly	13	23	*41*	—				
Courteous (mannerly)	*31*	16	13	13	—			
Kind	03	18	20	20	16	—		
Obedient (submissive)	18	15	−06	12	11	17	—	
Cheerful	15	15	33	15	09	15	00	—
Thrifty	21	10	12	−03	10	09	09	05
Brave (courageous)	05	09	−14	15	18	12	−02	−05
Clean (healthy)	*40*	−01	11	*41*	13	−03	−06	33
Reverent (idealistic)	20	14	−02	−02	16	05	10	−10

Note: All decimal points are omitted. Correlations above .23 and factor loadings above .40 are considered significant and are emphasized in the table.

than asking real scoutmasters to do ratings of 100 real scouts.) Because the ACL did not include all twelve adjectives of the Boy Scout Law, I had to make some substitutions: "reliable" for "trustworthy," "mannerly" for "courteous," "submissive" for "obedient," "courageous" for "brave," "healthy" for "clean," and "idealistic" for "reverent."

Table 13.1 also gives the results of a rotated factor analysis of that matrix. (Rotation is a process involving the use of particular mathematical criteria for simple structure. It will be discussed further below.) The extracted factors are the columns and the original traits are the rows. Each trait (row) is said to have a *loading* on each factor (column). This loading can be thought of as the correlation of that individual trait with that factor. When a factor has some traits with positive loadings and other traits with negative loadings, that factor is *bipolar*; if all loadings are in the same direction, it is *unipolar*.

Subjective Judgments in Factor Analysis

On the one hand, factor analysis is a strictly mathematical process, simply a matter of applying the appropriate formulas and writing the correct instruc-

Thrifty	Brave	Clean	Reverent	Elements of the Boy Scout Law	I Sociable virtues	II Impulse-control virtues	III Orderly virtues
					Loadings on factor		
				Trustworthy (reliable)	−03	34	75
				Loyal	43	39	11
				Helpful	76	−22	07
				Friendly	70	14	02
				Courteous (mannerly)	20	45	36
				Kind	55	29	08
				Obedient (submissive)	12	41	06
				Cheerful	50	−27	42
				Thrifty	01	08	49
—				Brave			
−07	—			(courageous)	01	58	08
19	00	—		Clean (healthy)	07	−21	79
				Reverent			
09	26	−09	—	(idealistic)	−11	67	06

tions for the computer. On the other hand, many aspects of factor analysis call for subjective judgments on the part of the researcher (see Block, 1995). The two most important judgments were my initial decisions regarding what variables to use (the twelve traits) and what subjects to use (the McClelland and Franz data set). Factor analysis is not magic. Its results are only as good as the initial data (variables and subjects) that we use and are necessarily true only for those particular variables and subjects. Any extension of the results is a matter of judgment. Further, while the computer *can* extract as many factors as there are variables (in this case, twelve), I decided to pay attention only to the first three, because each of the remaining factors involved only single variables (that is, only one trait had a high loading on these factors). Finally, the names of each factor were also a matter of judgment. I looked at those traits with high loadings (higher than +.40 or lower than −.40) and tried to pick an appropriate name to describe what they had in common.

Based on this factor analysis, I concluded that the twelve trait adjectives of the Boy Scout Law reflect three underlying factors: (1) sociable virtues such as friendliness, (2) impulse-control virtues such as courtesy or reverence, and (3) orderly virtues such as trustworthiness or reliability. Other people might interpret the results differently, and using different subjects or different rating procedures might give different results. With some assumptions and cautions, then, these results have reduced the list of twelve traits to three intelligible factors, based on an empirical criterion—that is, a real-world sample of what goes with what. This reduction of complexity, based (in part) on empirical procedures and mathematical criteria, makes factor analysis attractive to many personality researchers.

FACTOR-ANALYTIC STUDIES OF FUNDAMENTAL TRAITS

While many personality psychologists have used factor analysis to identify the fundamental dimensions of traits, in this chapter we shall focus on a few major trends. We begin with a brief comparison of two important and widely cited factor-analytic theorists, Raymond Cattell and Hans Eysenck. After a more detailed consideration of Eysenck's work, we move on to recent studies of the five-factor model (FFM), or "Big Five."

Cattell's Sixteen Factors

Cattell (1957) began with the Allport-Odbert list of 4,504 traits. On the basis of similarity of meaning, he first reduced the list to 171 elements or groups of adjectives. Then on the basis of the intercorrelations of element ratings, he further reduced these 171 elements to thirty-five adjectives. Factor analyses of rating scales for these adjectives yielded twelve factors; to these Cattell added four additional social-attitude factors from other questionnaires. The final result was the sixteen-factor model of the structure of traits shown in Table

13.2. Eleven factors are bipolar; five are unipolar. Among these sixteen factors are measures of intelligence (factor B) and social attitudes (factors Q_1 to Q_4), as well as the more familiar traits. This model is the basis for Cattell's widely used 16-Personality Factor (16PF) questionnaire measure of personality. Its construction is more fully described in Cattell (1957).

Perhaps the first thing you will notice about Cattell's factors is that some of them have strange names—for example, "parmia" or "premsia." Why didn't Cattell use more familiar words? This question illustrates a common dilemma in personality research. Using ordinary words to name precise concepts measured in particular ways means that people will understand the concepts more easily: for factor H, "shyness" or "timidity" are more familiar names than "threctia," a word you probably never saw before reading this page. On the other hand, because "shyness" is such a familiar word, we all have experiences and personal associations related to it. If Cattell had named factor H "shyness," our understanding of its meaning might be contaminated with those experiences and associations. Thus in an attempt to keep the meaning of factor H pure, to remind us that it means precisely and only what is measured by certain items on the 16PF questionnaire and nothing else, Cattell coined the word "threctia." For these same reasons, scientists in many fields coin new words for key concepts: they gain precision but risk obscurity. In

TABLE 13.2 THE SIXTEEN TRAIT FACTORS ACCORDING TO CATTELL

Factor name		Description
A	Sizothymia vs. affectothymia	Reserved, detached, stiff vs. outgoing, warmhearted, easygoing
B	Bright	Intelligence
C	Ego strength	Emotionally stable, mature, calm
E	Submissive vs. dominant	Humble, mild, accommodating vs. assertive, aggressive, stubborn
F	Desurgency vs. surgency	Sober, taciturn, serious vs. happy-go-lucky, enthusiastic
G	Superego strength	Conscientious, moralistic
H	Threctia vs. parmia	Shy, timid vs. venturesome, socially bold
I	Harria vs. premsia	Tough-minded, self-reliant vs. tender-minded, clinging
L	Alaxia vs. protension	Trusting vs. suspicious
M	Praxernia vs. autia	Practical, "down to earth" vs. imaginative, absent-minded
N	Artlessness vs. shrewdness	Forthright, genuine but socially clumsy vs. astute, polished
O	Untroubled adequacy vs. guilt-proneness	Self-assured, serene vs. apprehensive, insecure, troubled
Q_1	Conservative vs. radical	
Q_2	Group adherence vs. self-sufficiency	
Q_3	Strength of social sentiment	Controlled, will power, compulsive
Q4	Ergic tension	Tense, frustrated, overwrought

naming trait factors, most personality researchers have opted to use ordinary language, but at the cost of some confusion and looseness of meaning.

Eysenck's Two (and Three) Factors

Hans J. Eysenck (b. 1916) was born in Germany; he obtained his doctorate from the University of London and settled in England. While he began his career as a clinical psychologist, his broad interests in the nature and structure of personality have taken him into regions as diverse as psychiatric diagnosis, intelligence, questionnaire design, physiological and sensory processes, the effects of drugs, behavior genetics, parapsychology and astrology, the effectiveness of psychotherapy, political and social attitudes, national and cultural differences, and applied topics such as smoking, sex, crime, and cancer. His goal was to develop a single "tough-minded" conception of personality: focused on traits and temperament, based on factor analysis, grounded in genetics and physiology, and applicable to all of the above areas of interest. Eysenck is a prolific author and has been very influential in personality psychology, especially in Great Britain and the countries of the British Commonwealth, but his views have also aroused controversy and criticism. In this book I will sketch his conception of personality with broad strokes. His ideas on more specialized topics can be pursued through the references in Eysenck and Eysenck (1985).

At the beginning of his career during World War II, Eysenck (1944, 1947) applied factor analysis to ratings of psychiatric and psychosomatic symptoms (for example, hysterical attitude, depression, headache), as well as personal-history items (for example, wartime separation, narrow interests) from a

Hans J. Eysenck, who has used factor analysis to identify fundamental traits. "The best method for studying the association of individual . . . variables into traits and the association of traits into types is factor analysis. . . . It is usually possible to . . . emerge with a few meaningful factors that account for most of the variance" (Eysenck & Eysenck, 1985, p. 19). (Hulton Deutsch Collection)

group of over 1,000 British soldiers. Later he included questionnaire items, performance on laboratory tasks of perception and learning, and everyday normal and abnormal behaviors. While he has continually revised and expanded his views over the years (see Eysenck, 1957; Eysenck & Eysenck, 1969), the core conception remains the same: that *the domain of personality traits and temperament is best described by two (later three) broad dimensions, or superfactors.* The first two factors—*extraversion-introversion* and *neuroticism-stability*—are bipolar and date from his earliest research. The third factor, psychoticism, is unipolar and was added in the 1970s (see Eysenck & Eysenck, 1976). We shall consider these three factors in some detail below, after a brief discussion of differences between Cattell and Eysenck in the use of factor analysis.

Cattell versus Eysenck

How can it be that Cattell and Eysenck, both using factor analysis, arrived at such different answers about the number of fundamental trait factors—sixteen (or twelve) versus two or three? Actually, the differences are not as great as they seem, but an explanation of why this is so will require some more discussion of factor analysis.

When they carry out a factor analysis, some researchers, such as Eysenck, want the fewest number of completely independent factors that will best account for the covariation among the variables (questionnaire items, trait adjectives, etc.) being examined. Hence they require the computer factor analysis program to extract factors that have exactly zero correlation with each other. Such independent factors are said to be *orthogonal.* Other researchers, such as Cattell and (more recently) Cloninger, Przybeck, and Svrakic (1991), prefer factors that represent meaningful clusters; they are less concerned about whether these factors are completely independent or orthogonal, hence they permit the computer factor analysis program to allow some degree of correlation among the extracted factors. Such factors are called *oblique.*[2] For any given set of variables, there will usually be more oblique than orthogonal factors, since oblique factors are correlated with each other. (As an example, on a two-dimensional piece of paper you can draw only two orthogonal lines that pass through a single point, but you can draw any number of nonorthogonal lines passing through a single point.)

Apart from statistical independence or correlation of factors, what are the differences between orthogonal and oblique factors? What are the advantages of each, and why would researchers choose one kind instead of the other? Since factors are often represented geometrically, we can answer these questions by thinking about maps, directions, and locations in everyday life. Since you, the readers, live in many different places, I will use the White House in

---

[2]Strictly speaking, the contrast is between "orthogonally rotated" and "obliquely rotated" factors, because the difference between the two approaches or instructions to the factor analysis program enters only at the stage of factor rotation.

Washington, D.C., as an example. Figure 13.1 shows a map of downtown Washington that will illustrate our discussion.

Imagine you are the president, sitting at your desk in the Oval Office of the White House. (In factor analysis terms, this is called the zero point or *origin*.) How would you describe the location of other significant places in Washington—for example, the U.S. Capitol, the Pentagon, or the Vietnam Memorial? One way is to use the two independent (orthogonal) dimensions of north-south and east-west. Thus from the president's office, the Capitol is about 875 meters south and 2,433 meters east. The Pentagon is 2,894 meters south and 1,526 meters west. And the Vietnam Memorial is 731 meters south and 906 meters west. Notice that the exact location of any other place in Washington (or indeed, in the whole world) can be expressed in terms of distances along these two dimensions. (For the hilly parts of northern Washington, D.C., or for locations in space or below the surface of the earth, we would also need a third vertical dimension.) Thus north-south and east-west are the *smallest*

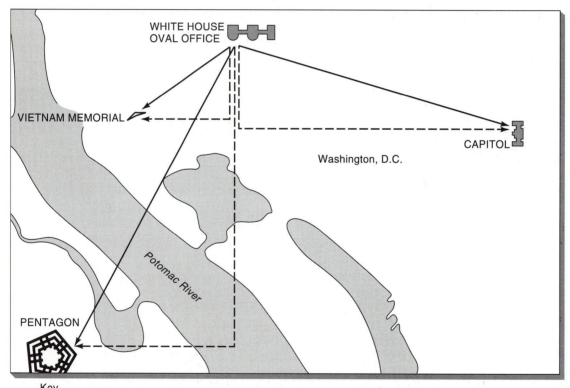

Key
————— Directions given in terms of many oblique (not independent) directions.
– – – – Directions given in terms of two orthogonal (independent) dimensions.

FIGURE 13.1

Illustration of factorial dimensions: giving directions from the White House.

number of completely independent dimensions (like the orthogonal factors) that will account for the location of all places (like the variables) in Washington, D.C. The street plan of Washington, laid out in a grid, usually makes it possible to move that way, too: "To get to the Capitol from your Oval Office, Ms. President, go sixteen blocks east and five and a half blocks south."

People sometimes give directions this way, particularly if they have had military, geographical, or scout training or if they are in a city laid out like Washington, D.C. In everyday life, though, most of us go about it differently. From the Oval Office to the Capitol is about 2,624 meters "down that way, toward the Capitol" (which happens to be the route of Pennsylvania Avenue). Going to the Vietnam Memorial from the White House, as the crow flies, would be about 1,161 meters in the "Vietnam Memorial direction," which also happens also to be "Lincoln Memorial direction." (Using the standard orthogonal direction terms, we could also describe it as "a little more south than southwest"). The Pentagon is 3,260 meters away "over there, toward the Pentagon." Notice how this second way of giving directions uses more than two directions, and that each direction is named according to the meaningful locations that lie in that direction. We could invent many other directions from the White House Oval Office: "Andrews Air Force Base direction," "Holocaust Museum direction," "toward the Rose Garden," and so forth. In fact there is no limit to the number of possible directions, because they are not independent of each other (that is, they are nonorthogonal). For example, "Vietnam Memorial direction" and "Pentagon direction" are quite similar in terms of their standard geographic coordinates (they are both approximately southwest), though their *meanings* are very different.

Neither directional system is better than the other; it all depends on our purposes. North-south and east-west are efficient but abstract; "Capitol direction" and the other named directions are less efficient but closer to our everyday meaningful experience. In terms of factor analysis, then, the choice of oblique versus orthogonal factors is largely a matter of the researcher's personal preference. Since Cattell's sixteen factors are correlated (sometimes highly correlated) with each other, we can always perform a further, orthogonal factor analysis on them to get *second-order factors*. (Similarly, it is possible to redescribe "Vietnam Memorial direction" in terms of north-south and east-west.) Second-order factors from the Cattell 16PF (sometimes called superfactors) resemble Eysenck's extraversion, neuroticism, and psychoticism. Similar results are usually obtained from second-order factoring of other oblique-factor questionnaires, such as the Guilford-Zimmerman Temperament Survey or the Costa-McCrae NEO Personality Inventory, as well as questionnaires such as the Minnesota Multiphasic Personality Inventory (MMPI) or the California Personality Inventory (CPI) (Eysenck & Eysenck, 1985, pp. 122–158), which were not originally constructed on the basis of factor analysis. Broadly speaking, then, the sixteen factors of Cattell and the three factors of Eysenck *are* compatible; their differences are due to orthogonality and level of abstraction.

EXTRAVERSION AND NEUROTICISM

At this point we will consider the first two of Eysenck's superfactors, reserving psychoticism for a later section. Borrowing Jung's two terms, which are now a part of everyday trait language, Eysenck named the first factor *extraversion-introversion*. The second factor, *neuroticism-stability* (sometimes labeled "emotionality" or "negative affectivity"), also appears in our everyday language. We use the word "neurotic" to characterize people who are anxious or upset, and perhaps unable to make up their minds. Eysenck's names for both factors, then, come from everyday language, but he uses them with more precise and specialized meanings. Let us consider each factor in turn.

Extraversion-Introversion

Eysenck versus Jung. Items from Eysenck's factor-analytic measure of extraversion-introversion include the following (adapted from Eysenck & Eysenck, 1985, p. 84):

1. Do you enjoy meeting new people?

2. Are you mostly quiet when you are with other people? (scored negatively)

3. Do you like mixing with people?

4. Do you like plenty of bustle and excitement about you?

5. Can you easily adapt to new and unusual situations?

Notice how closely these items fit with Jung's descriptions (see Chapter 12). Extraverts are lively and like excitement and new situations, while introverts are quiet and reflective. Extraverts say they are physically active and sociable, and make friends easily. Their emotions are easily aroused but are not very deep. Because they are changeable, they may be a little insensitive. You will always find them in the middle of the party, playing their stereo a little too loudly (too loudly for an introvert, anyway). They would enjoy being in New Orleans during the height of Mardi Gras.

Introverts, in contrast, direct their activity into mental rather than physical channels. They are sensitive and experience strong emotions, but they are not especially sociable. They would be uncomfortable in the middle of the party, preferring quiet music with a few close friends. They would enjoy living in a remote lighthouse. (A mathematician who knew Einstein once described him as "the only scientist who could be content as a lighthouse keeper" [Infeld, 1947, p. 340].)

Just how similar is Eysenck's variable of extraversion-introversion to Jung's original conception? In his first work, Eysenck (1947) drew extensively on Jung's ideas. But in later formulations (Eysenck & Eysenck, 1985), Jung's theory is abandoned and his ideas are described mainly in historical terms. However, since Steele and Kelly (1976) found that the MBTI measure of extraversion correlates highly with Eysenck's measure ($r = .74$), we can still consider the two concepts of extraversion as equivalent (see also McCrae & Costa, 1989).

Is extraversion the same as "normal"? Some of you may feel that extraversion is normal and healthy, and that introverts must have some kind of psychological problem. Since they don't enjoy being with other people, they must be shy or even withdrawn. In the United States, the definition of extraversion—being expressive and sociable—seems to overlap with the criteria for good adjustment and positive mental health that are used by kindergarten teachers, sorority and fraternity officers, Kiwanis Club speakers, and so forth. Since Lynn and his colleagues (Lynn, 1981; Lynn & Hampson, 1975) report that on average, Americans score higher in extraversion than do people from almost every other country, the American vision of "normal" may simply reflect American extraversion. (When I lectured on personality psychology to Chinese students in Beijing, they said that people in China have the opposite view: introversion is considered healthy, and extraverts are thought to be maladjusted!)

Freud (1916–1917, XV–XVI) also thought that introverts were more vulnerable to neurosis, because any libido that remained within the person simply became dammed up and would eventually seek unhealthy internal outlets: "An introvert is not yet a neurotic, but he is in an unstable situation: he is sure to develop symptoms at the next shifting of forces, unless he finds other outlets for his dammed-up libido" (p. 374).

Jung disagreed, in blunt language: "It is a mistake to believe that introversion is more or less the same as neurosis. As concepts the two have not the slightest connection with each other" (quoted by Eysenck & Eysenck, 1985, p. 49). More precisely, Jung suggested that the *potential for neurosis* is present in both extraverts and introverts, while only the *form of neurosis* is different for each type. For extraverts, the characteristic forms of neurosis were either classical hysteria or some other psychosomatic condition—the result of too great absorption in the external world and a consequent neglect of inner, subjective matters. Among introverts, in contrast, neurosis typically took the form of "psychasthenia" (an obsolete term that includes what we now call depression and obsessive-compulsive disorders) (Jung, 1923/1971, pp. 336, 379).

In two of his earliest papers, Freud (1894, III, pp. 41–61; 1896, III, pp. 157–186) also speculated that different kinds of people would be vulnerable to hysteria and obsessive-compulsive neurosis,[3] depending on their characteristic defense mechanisms. Thus hysterics use repression, denial, and somaticiza-

---

[3]In this connection, Freud and Jung both used the phrase "choice of neurosis," which is unfortunate in that it suggests that people consciously and deliberately "choose" the form of their disturbance. This is *not* what Freud and Jung meant.

tion, while obsessive-compulsives employ isolation, undoing, and intellectualization. (See the discussion of defense mechanisms in Chapter 3, and especially the grouping of these defense mechanisms shown in Table 3.3.) He also speculated that constitutional or physiological factors might play a role in determining the form that neurosis took.

Jung adapted this distinction to the extraversion-introversion dimension. Extraversion and introversion, he suggested, affect the specific *form* of neurosis, but neither involves any *general tendency* toward disturbance. We can express this conclusion in terms of Galen's humoral model of personality (see Chapter 11 and especially Figure 11.2): the sanguine and choleric types are both extraverted, while the phlegmatic and melancholic types are introverted. However, the choleric (angry and aggressive) and the melancholic (sad and depressed) types are both disturbed or neurotic, while the sanguine and phlegmatic types are stable, not disturbed.

Neuroticism

According to this line of reasoning, hysteria and obsessive-compulsive neurosis, while very different, must share some cluster of traits that are associated with neurotic disturbances but are independent of the extraversion-introversion dimension. Considering Galen's model and Jung's argument, Eysenck argued that this "disturbance" cluster was none other than the second superfactor that usually emerged from factor-analytic studies of traits. He therefore labeled this superfactor "neuroticism" and concluded that the two-dimensional trait-space defined by extraversion and neuroticism is identical to Galen's four-humor model. Figure 13.2 illustrates this overlap, with Freud's grouping of defense mechanisms for each type of neurosis added in.

In the figure, each quadrant defines a definite type. (In the real world, of course, there are many gradations of both extraversion and neuroticism.) Starting at the lower right corner is the happy, bouncy, stable extravert—sanguine, in Galen's terms. With increased neuroticism, we have the angry, acting-out, raging, and choleric neurotic extravert of the upper right corner. Changing extraversion to introversion yields the melancholic neurotic introvert in the upper left corner. Finally, with lowered neuroticism we have the phlegmatic stable introvert in the lower left corner. Theoretically, then, neuroticism can be thought of as the disposition to develop disturbances such as hysteria, depression, or obsessive-compulsive disorder.

Let us explore the nature of this disposition. Items such as the following make up Eysenck's neuroticism factor (adapted from Eysenck & Eysenck, 1985, p. 84):

1. Does your mood often go up and down?

2. Do you often feel fed-up?

3. Would you call yourself a nervous person?

4. Are you easily hurt when people find fault with you or your work?

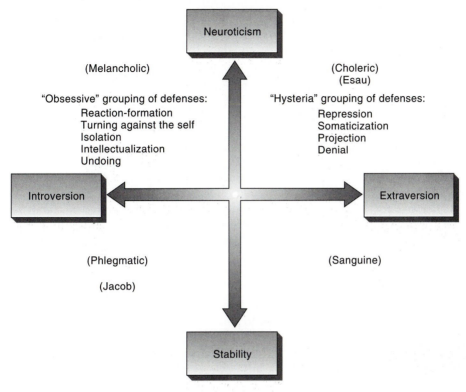

FIGURE 13.2
Eysenck's E and N dimensions; Galen's model, Esau-Jacob, and groupings of Freud's
defense mechanisms.

You can see that neuroticism involves feelings of nervousness and dissatisfaction, and alternating moods. Other aspects might include anxiety, depression, guilt feelings, low self-esteem, shyness, irrationality, feelings of tension
and self-consciousness, impulsiveness, and hostility. The review of studies by
Watson and Clark (1984) suggests that neuroticism involves experiences of a
variety of *negative mood states,* even in the absence of actual stress: for example,
distress, nervousness, tension, worry, anger, scorn, revulsion, guilt, self-dissat-
isfaction, a sense of rejection, and sadness. Perhaps we can draw all these different traits together into a dimension of *emotional instability versus uncomplicated easygoingness* (see Eysenck & Eysenck, 1985, pp. 15, 54–55, 138).
Depression, then, would be located in the high-introversion, high-neuroticism
("melancholic") quadrant of Figure 13.2, and hostility in the high-extraversion,
high-neuroticism ("choleric") quadrant.

Neuroticism and coping. Bolger's (1990) study of how premedical students cope with the Medical College Admission Test (MCAT), a grueling day-
long ordeal that weighs heavily in the medical school admission process, illus-

trates how neuroticism functions in normal people and gives some clues about its role in psychological disturbance. Bolger followed fifty premedical students during the three-week period before they took the MCAT. Some students focused on the MCAT itself and tried to "prepare"; others simply reassured themselves or sought support from friends. Students high in neuroticism, however, dealt with the MCAT stress by wishful thinking (fantasies of escaping or avoiding the situation) or self-blame. As a result, they showed much sharper increases in anxiety during the week before the exam. Interestingly enough, their high neuroticism did not affect their performance. Perhaps this is because they were a highly selected group to begin with, or maybe they have simply learned to live with their anxiety. In any case, Bolger's study suggests two important features of neuroticism in normal circumstances: (1) higher anxiety arousal in response to stress, and (2) less effective mechanisms for coping with anticipated stress. Each feature could be a cause of the other; for example, high anxiety reduces the likelihood of effective coping (remember the Yerkes-Dodson law in Chapter 2 and Figure 2.2), but ineffective coping can also arouse anxiety.

Neuroticism versus anxiety. In Figure 13.2, high versus low "anxiety" could be represented as a line close to neuroticism, but tilted a little toward the introversion pole. That is, *conscious* feelings of high anxiety seem to involve high neuroticism and some degree of introversion, while low anxiety is a fusion of low neuroticism and a little extraversion. (Hostile people may not feel anxiety consciously.) Feelings of shyness (see Zimbardo, 1977) probably are tilted even further toward introversion. Shyness, however, is a vague word that can mean many things. At the very least, it is important to distinguish negative shyness rooted in fear from a more positive shyness (or apparent shyness) that is based on discretion and self-control (see Gough & Thorne, 1986; also Eysenck & Eysenck, 1985, pp. 289, 316).

Why Does Extraversion Give the Impression of Psychological Health?

As we have seen, factor-analytic studies consistently show that introversion and neuroticism are independent or orthogonal. Yet many people (especially Americans) believe that they go together. In some way, then, extraversion must give off the impression of psychological health. Eysenck suggests that neurotic introverts and neurotic extraverts experience their neuroticism in different ways. In introverts, neuroticism appears in the form of cognitions (thoughts, feelings, and worries), whereas in extraverts it is reflected in physical signs such as a quickened heartbeat or sweating palms (Eysenck & Eysenck, 1985, p. 144). Since they are focused on their inner life, neurotic introverts are aware of their emotional instability. In contrast, neurotic extraverts may say they aren't nervous because (not being so aware of their inner life) they do not label the physical changes as anxiety.

In addition, the behaviors associated with extraverted neuroticism—impulsivity and hostility—seem quite different from anxiety. For example, Captain Ahab, in Melville's *Moby Dick,* was clearly a man possessed, driven by a frenzied rage in his hostile quest for vengeance on the white whale. It is difficult to imagine he shared any psychological trait (that is to say, neuroticism) with a neurotic introvert—say a Woody Allen character. These two considerations may explain why people sometimes think of extraversion as being healthy and introversion as disturbed, even though both trait factors come in healthy and disturbed forms.

A Note on Gray's Factors

In an attempt to develop a physiologically based theory of personality, Gray (1964, 1981) has suggested an alternative two-factor structure, consisting of anxiety and impulsivity. Gray's anxiety is a combination of Eysenck's high introversion and high neuroticism, and his impulsivity is a combination of high extraversion and high neuroticism. Gray suggested that the anxiety factor involves sensitivity to signals of punishment (or nonreward) and novelty (which is often a source of danger and punishment). Impulsivity, in contrast, involves sensitivity to signals of reward (or nonpunishment). The difference between Gray's and Eysenck's two factors is simply one of rotation—that is, where to draw the axes. In terms of the Washington, D.C., map in Figure 13.1, Eysenck's two orthogonal factors can be viewed as running north-south and east-west, while Gray's run northeast-southwest and northwest-southeast. The same locations can be described equally well by each system. Thus Eysenck's pure emotional stability (low neuroticism) could be described in Gray's terms as a combination of low anxiety and low impulsivity.

WHAT IS PSYCHOTICISM?

For many years Eysenck believed that the two superfactors of extraversion and neuroticism were adequate to describe the domain of traits and temperament. By 1976, however, he concluded that a third dimension would also be needed, and so he added the third superfactor, psychoticism (see Eysenck & Eysenck, 1976). Since we use the related word "psychotic" to describe severely disturbed people who are out of touch with reality, you may think that the term "psychoticism" refers to bizarre, crazy, psychotic, or abnormal behavior. While Eysenck and Eysenck believed that the trait dimension of psychoticism is in fact the underlying basis for most disorders that we label psychotic (for example, schizophrenia or bipolar affective disorder), they also believe that it includes many behaviors that are more or less normal. If the word psychoticism makes us think only of psychosis, then it may have been an unfortunate choice of term (see Block, 1977a; Eysenck & Eysenck, 1977). In this section, I will try to use words carefully. Whereas we often refer to people who score high in extraversion as extraverts, in the case of psychoticism I will refer to high-scorers as "people scoring high in psychoticism," reserving the label "psychotic" for those with a diagnosed psychosis.

Are all people who score high on psychoticism psychotic? By no means, Eysenck argued; often they may be contented and free of symptoms. What their high psychoticism score means is that they have a *latent vulnerability* to psychotic states and psychotic disorders, perhaps under high stress or in the presence of certain specific stressors. In abnormal psychology, this kind of explanation is called a *diathesis-stress model:* a psychological disorder arises from a combination of a particular predisposition (diathesis) within the person and a particular stress in the environment. Thus psychoticism would be the diathesis of the psychotic disorders, but not the disorders themselves.

Psychoticism within Normal Limits

You can get a sense of the everyday behaviors that fall within the range of "normal" psychoticism by studying some of the questions that make up this dimension (adapted from Eysenck & Eysenck, 1985, p. 84):

1. Would being in debt worry you? (scored negatively)

2. Do you prefer to go your own way rather than act by the rules?

3. Do good manners and cleanliness matter much to you? (scored negatively)

4. Do you try not to be rude to people? (scored negatively)

5. Do you like taking risks for fun?

Taken together, these items suggest three everyday ways in which psychoticism manifests itself: (1) risk-taking and indifference to planning ahead (for example, lack of concern about debt), (2) impulsive behavior unconstrained by morality or sensitivity to other people, and (3) independence or autonomy. While these may be "normal" manifestations of psychoticism, in their extreme form they involve such insensitivity to human feelings and society that they can scarcely be called normal. Thus Eysenck and Eysenck (1976) describe people high in psychoticism as being "solitary, troublesome, cruel, lacking in feeling, lacking in empathy, hostile to others, sensation-seeking and liking odd and unusual things" (p. 202).

A rather chilling study of 145 male college students by Barnes, Malamuth, and Check (1984) illustrates the point. While the men listened to audiotapes depicting either consenting heterosexual intercourse or rape, their levels of sexual arousal were monitored by self-report and physiological measurements. Men scoring high in psychoticism were more aroused by the rape story than by the nonviolent consenting sex story. For men low in psychoticism, the results were the other way around: consenting sex was arousing, but rape was not. This is not to say that every male scoring high in psychoticism is a rapist but rather that male psychoticism does embody a pattern of sexual arousal that can facilitate rape.

Positive and Negative Sides of Psychoticism

Psychoticism can also have a positive, appealing aspect. People scoring high in psychoticism are likely to strike us as "free spirits," delightful and charming in the way they so casually ignore the rules, fears, and guilt that constrain and shackle the rest of us. Like sleepwalkers, they blithely dance their way through life, somehow contriving to just miss dangers that seem obvious to us but of which they are not even aware. Sometimes we say that they are "marching to a different drummer," for they appear to hear sounds and voices we do not hear and see things we do not see. If they also have the gift of creativity or divergent thinking, then they may end up as a political hero (Joan of Arc), a musical genius (Mozart or Beethoven), a scientific revolutionary (Einstein), a gifted poet (Emily Dickinson), or a religious visionary.

Viewed in a slightly different light, however, marching to an internal drummer—to private sights and sounds not available to others—takes the person scoring high in psychoticism away from the world of everyday shared reality into a narcissistic, private world where self is at the center and other people exist only at the outer edges, if at all. Distortion is likely, and intimacy is impossible. (The introvert, in contrast, realizes that the external world exists, but finds it aversive. In this case, distortion is not so likely, and intimacy is possible.)

People scoring high in psychoticism ignore the rules and the moral constraints of organized society. In contrast to neurotics, who are often locked in an anguished rebellion against rules and morality, they are blandly indifferent: the idea of moral constraints simply doesn't occur to them. In psychoanalytic terms, they are not in rebellion against the superego but rather seem to lack superego formation. Since the moral constraints that we call superego originate as a reaction to perceived danger, especially physical danger (see the discussion in Chapters 3 and 4), people who score high in psychoticism may simply have nervous systems less sensitive to pain and danger.

Without moral constraints on their pursuit of impulse gratification and experience for its own sake, people scoring high in psychoticism often appear cruel and indifferent to human suffering. Certain kinds of criminals, for example, those who murder "for the hell of it," fit this pattern. In contrast to the extravert, who is strongly tied to other people and the social context, such people may experience other persons as no more real than screen characters in a video game. Thus the act of committing murder may not feel much different from that of pressing a button or clicking a mouse.

The negative side of psychoticism can be summarized as a profound *shallowness*: living that lacks the complexity and richness of texture that come from outer social rules, inner moral restraints, and involvement with other people.

What Makes Psychoticism Psychotic?

While psychoticism is not the same as psychosis, psychoticism is related to schizophrenia and other psychoses by way of traits such as lack of attention or awareness; or insensitivity to the knowledge, dangers, and moral code of everyday shared reality. These deficits of attention and sensitivity are often used as the distinguishing features of the psychoses. For example, schizophrenics are said to be out of touch with reality; they withdraw into catatonic states, use faulty or distorted reasoning, and express emotions that are flat or in other ways seemingly inappropriate to the situation.

A literary example. A vivid example of these characteristics can be found in the character Mersault in Albert Camus's existential novel *The Stranger* (1942/1946). The novel opens with Mersault's lack of emotion about his mother's death:

> Mother died today. Or, maybe, yesterday; I can't be sure. The telegram from the Home said, "YOUR MOTHER PASSED AWAY, FUNERAL TOMORROW. DEEP SYMPATHY." Which leaves the matter doubtful; it could have been yesterday. (p. 1)

As the novel progresses, Mersault begins an intimate relationship, commits murder, is tried, imprisoned, and sentenced to die—all with scarcely any display of emotion:

> "But, damn it all. . . . I've something really important to tell you." However, on second thoughts, I found I had nothing to say. (p. 124)
> I have never been able really to regret anything in all my life. I've always been far too much absorbed in the present moment, or the immediate future, to think back. (p. 127)
> I realized people would soon forget me once I was dead. I couldn't even say that this was hard to stomach; really, there's no idea to which one doesn't get acclimatized in time. (p. 144)
> I laid my heart open to the benign indifference of the universe. (p. 154)

Instead of feeling emotions, Mersault responds, in exaggerated fashion, to visual and auditory sensations:

> Wherever I looked I saw the same sun-drenched countryside. . . . Presently we struck a patch of freshly tarred road. A shimmer of heat played over it and one's feet squelched at every step, leaving bright black gashes. In front, the coachman's glossy black hat looked like a lump of the same sticky substance, poised above the hearse. (p. 20)
> As a matter of fact, I had great difficulty in following his remarks, as, for one thing, the office was so stiflingly hot and big flies were buzzing round and settling on my cheeks. (p. 85)

Psychosis and the world of shared everyday assumptions. The social psychologist Brown (1973) reviewed the voluminous literature on schizophrenia (the most common psychosis) and immersed himself in a group of hospitalized schizophrenics. His conclusions illustrate the role of psychoticism in psychosis. Brown argued that the essential feature of schizophrenia was an *inability to attend to, accept, or use the working assumptions that most people make without even thinking.* Thus without even thinking about it, most of us are able to ignore a "harmless" smudge mark on the wall as being of no significance. A paranoid schizophrenic, however, is driven to "explain" the mark, often with elaborate and grandiose ideas of persecution and divine power. Another example: Did you ever notice that the word "dog," spelled backward, is "god"? Perhaps you have, and dismissed the coincidence without further thought; even if you had a dog, you probably thought nothing more about it. One of the patients Brown came to know, however, could not make this simple everyday assumption. Instead, she felt she had to kill the family dog because of the blasphemy implied by the reversible spelling.

Brown's argument extends to laboratory studies of schizophrenics versus normals. For example, in one perception experiment, most people who are told to choose which of several circles is "as large as" a plate seen in the distance will pick the circle that matches the "real" size of the plate. Some schizophrenics, however, pick the circle that matches the "apparent" size of the plate on their retina. Of course in one sense they were not wrong: they did pick the circle that actually matched the retinal image. But they were simply not following the unspoken rules and assumptions that make up daily life. Philosophers (for example, Grice, 1989) call these rules "conversational implicatures"—that is, the things we take for granted (without actually saying so) in everyday social conversation and interaction.

This inability to follow implicit everyday assumptions and unspoken rules (according to Brown, the defining characteristic of schizophrenia) reflects a basic characteristic of people scoring high in psychoticism. They do not share the conceptual, moral, or emotional responses—all implied rather than explicitly stated—of our daily lives.

Distinguishing Genius from Madness

According to Eysenck, then, psychoticism is a normally distributed trait dimension that includes the essential features of the psychoses but is not the same as psychosis. Viewed in a different light, however, psychoticism may be connected to literary, artistic, political, and scientific genius. These, too, involve diverging from or violating everyday conceptual, moral, and emotional assumptions. Yet genius and psychosis are not at all the same. There may be hospitalized schizophrenics who believe they are Mozart, but they haven't written any memorable music lately.

Regression, primary process, and control. One difference between genius and psychosis is control. Geniuses can violate everyday shared assumptions—that is, can gaze at the visions of psychoticism—and then return to the "normal" world to tell the rest of us about those visions. In short, they can control their psychoticism. We may think of them as quirky, but they are not crazy. People who are truly psychotic, in contrast, cannot return so easily. They seem trapped in their private, nonshared worlds, perhaps because they cannot control their psychoticism.

Psychoanalytic theorists have distinguished genius and madness in similar terms. According to Kris (1952), creative people are distinguished by the capacity to practice *regression in the service of the ego.* (Some psychologists use the term *adaptive regression* instead.) That is, they *can* regress to primary-process thinking and primitive fantasies. Since primary-process functioning is based on the similarity or association of mental images, without the organizing principles of negation, time, or causality (Chapter 3), such regression can produce unusual analogies and new insights. While such insights are an important part of the creative process, they are not truly creative until they have been expressed. Thus genuinely creative people are also able to use more mature or developed modes of functioning to express and communicate their creative insights. These modes employ the organizational principles of time, causation, and negation—in short, Freud's secondary process. Thus in psychoanalytic terms, creativity and genius involve a deliberate and controlled alteration between primary and secondary process: a regression that is ultimately in the service of (that is, for the purpose of enhancing) ego functioning.

In terms of Eysenck's theory, we might describe the creative process as the careful use of controlled doses of psychoticism—breaking with everyday consensual reality in order to refashion that very reality.

Psychoticism in Einstein. The case of Einstein illustrates some of these points in the distinction between genius and madness. In many respects, Einstein displayed aspects of psychoticism. In physics, for example, he overturned existing consensual reality about such elementary conventional concepts as space and time. In his everyday social behavior, moreover, Einstein betrayed a continuing lack of concern with customs, manners, and respectability. Although he had close relationships, he himself spoke of a "lack of need for direct contact with other human beings" (Einstein, 1954a, p. 9). A scientific colleague wrote of his "queer mixture of great warmth and great aloofness" (Infeld, 1947, p. 338), while a biographer concluded that "he felt an intuitive sympathy with human beings in the mass; but when it came to individuals . . . he found little time or sympathy or understanding to spare" (Clark, 1971/1984, pp. 387, 53). Einstein's own reflections on his work style highlight the role of regression and recall Erikson's comment (Chapter 12) about the "survival of the child" in Einstein: "the gift of fantasy has meant more to me than my talent for absorbing positive knowledge [facts]" (Plesch, 1949, p. 207).

We think of Einstein as a genius, however, because he was highly successful at articulating and communicating his revolutionary creative insights—not only to his fellow physicists, but (rather surprisingly) to ordinary people as well. His colleague Leopold Infeld (1941) described Einstein's delivery of "a perfect lecture":

> The calmness with which Einstein spoke was striking. There was nothing of the restlessness of a scientist who, explaining the problems with which he has lived for years, assumed that they are equally familiar to the listener and proceeds quickly with his exposition. . . . Walking slowly and with dignity round the room . . . he

formed his sentences perfectly. Everything he said could have been printed as he said it and every sentence would make perfect sense. The exposition was simple, profound, and clear. (p. 255)

On the other hand, Einstein took few physical risks and had a well-developed moral sense. His psychoticism was channeled into the conceptual or intellectual domain, probably because of his intense introversion. Further, his low neuroticism freed him from the kinds of conflicts that lead many true psychotics to outbursts of antisocial rage against the bonds of conventional morality.

RECENT FACTOR STUDIES OF PERSONALITY: THE BIG FIVE

While Eysenck's three-factor theory has been widely cited in studies of traits and temperament, many personality researchers have taken a fresh look at factor-analytic studies of traits. The result is a theory of five major trait factors—popularly known as the five-factor model, or Big Five—that has in recent years become an especially popular approach to the study of traits. In 1992, for example, the *Journal of Personality* devoted an entire issue to the five-factor model.

The five-factor model originated in a paper by Tupes and Christal (1961/1992), which was later summarized and expanded by Norman (1963). Using a subset of the adjectives originally selected by Cattell (1957) from the Allport-Odbert (1936) list, Tupes and Christal asked four groups of U.S. Air Force officers and officer trainees (all male, overwhelmingly white, aged 20 to 45) to rate each other on thirty adjectives, using a 3-point scale. In addition, they reanalyzed data from four other trait-rating studies (three studies of men, one of women; all overwhelmingly white) carried out with college and graduate students. In each separate study, the same five orthogonal factors consistently emerged:[4] *surgency* (extraversion), *agreeableness* (warmth), *conscientiousness* (will), *emotional stability* (low neuroticism), and *culture* (openness to experience). This convergence of results across studies led Tupes and Christal, and later Norman, to conclude that a "highly stable structure of personal characteristics has been identified and that reasonably good measures of these characteristics are available" (Norman, 1963, p. 581). Surveying this work eighteen years later, Goldberg (1981) introduced the term "Big Five" to designate these five factors. Table 13.3 shows the names and the bipolar adjective scales used by Norman to define each factor, along with alternative names used by other researchers.

Empirical Convergence on Five Trait Factors

Since the publication of Norman's study, many other personality researchers using factor-analytic techniques with other kinds of data (descriptive phrases

---

[4]As noted above, factor names are somewhat arbitrary. Here I have used the original names used by Tupes and Christal and Norman and give other popular alternative names in parentheses.

Warren Norman, who first proposed the "Big Five" (or five-factor model) of traits on the basis of several factor-analytic studies. "The construction of more effective theories of . . . personality will be facilitated by . . . [a] well-organized vocabulary. . . . It is clear that a relatively orthogonal and highly stable structure of personal characteristics has been identified" (1963, pp. 574, 581). (Bob Kalmbach/The University of Michigan)

or sentences rather than single adjectives, self-reports as well as peer ratings) have obtained these same five factors (see the reviews by John, 1989, 1990; McCrae & John, 1992). McCrae (1989) further demonstrated that factor analyses of many traditional personality tests and questionnaires produce similar five-factor structures. Botwin and Buss (1989) also found these same five factors in people's reports about their actual behaviors, though such a result might have been expected since their list of behaviors was preselected to fit the five-factor model. Because all these different lines of research appear to produce similar results, the Big Five trait factors have become widely used (though under a variety of names, as shown in the right-hand column of Table 13.3).

To some personality psychologists, the success of the Big Five suggests that "we have truly discovered the basic dimensions of personality" (McCrae & John, 1992, p. 177). Such a conclusion is surely an overstatement, for it neglects the importance of the subjective or private elements of personality—motives (Part One of this book) and cognitions (Part Two)—as well as the contexts that shape personality and channel its expression (Part Four). Even within the domain of traits, the Big Five approach has encountered several

TABLE 13.3 THE BIG FIVE PERSONALITY TRAIT FACTORS

Original name and adjective scale labels (from Norman, 1963)	Alternative names used by other researchers
Surgency (or extraversion)	Ambition and sociability (Hogan, 1986)
Talkative (vs. silent)	Power (Peabody & Goldberg, 1989)
Frank, open (vs. secretive)	
Adventurous (vs. cautious)	
Sociable (vs. reclusive)	
Agreeableness	Friendly compliance (Digman & Inouye, 1986)
Good-natured (vs. irritable)	Likeability (Hogan, 1986)
Not jealous (vs. jealous)	Love (Peabody & Goldberg, 1989)
Mild, gentle (vs. headstrong)	
Cooperative (vs. negativistic)	
Conscientiousness	Will to achieve (Digman & Inouye, 1986)
Fussy, tidy (vs. careless)	Prudence vs. impulsivity (Hogan, 1986)
Responsible (vs. undependable)	Work (Peabody & Goldberg, 1989)
Scrupulous (vs. unscrupulous)	
Persevering (vs. quitting, fickle)	
Emotional stability	Ego strength vs. anxiety (Digman & Inouye, 1986)
Poised (vs. nervous, tense)	Adjustment (Hogan, 1986)
Calm (vs. anxious)	Neuroticism* (McCrae & Costa, 1987)
Composed (vs. excitable)	Affect (Peabody & Goldberg, 1989)
Not hypochondriacal (vs. hypochondriacal)	
Culture	Intellect (Digman & Inouye, 1986; Peabody & Goldberg, 1989)
Artistically sensitive (vs. artistically insensitive)	Intellectance (Hogan, 1986)
Intellectual (vs. unreflective, narrow)	Openness (McCrae & Costa, 1987)
Polished, refined (vs. crude, boorish)	
Imaginative (vs. simple, direct)	

*Label is the name of the opposite or low-scoring pole of the factor.

conceptual issues and measurement problems (Block, 1995; Briggs, 1989, 1992; McAdams, 1992a). Thus while the five-factor theory is a promising development, it is hardly the final word even in trait psychology.

"Bandwidth" and the hierarchical structure of traits. Five factors are scarcely enough to capture all of the trait variation shown by human beings. Rather, they are a useful set of highly abstract categories. As John (1989) put it:

> The Big Five dimensions represent the broadest level. . . . they are to personality what the categories "plant" and "animal" are to the world of natural objects—extremely useful for some initial rough distinctions but of less value for predicting specific behaviors of a particular object. (p. 268)

Each of the five factors actually includes several more specific components, variously labeled "facets" (Costa & McCrae, 1985), "categories," or "synonym clusters." These facets or categories, in turn, are composed of still more specific and narrowly defined clusters, until finally we reach the level of specific trait adjectives and phrases. All of the component elements of a trait factor may share some overlapping meanings, but each is also quite distinct from the others. For example, depression and anxiety are both components of neuroticism (or low emotional stability), but they have quite different manifestations, consequences, and implications for intervention. Even to a casual acquaintance, these distinctions are obvious; to a therapist, they would be critically important.

In selecting the appropriate level of descriptive words within the hierarchical structure of a trait, therefore, we face a trade-off between bandwidth (breadth of coverage) and fidelity (accuracy of coverage) (see also Briggs, 1989, p. 251; Cantor & Mischel, 1979b; and Mischel, 1984, pp. 293–297, on this trade-off).

Table 13.4 illustrates three different versions of the hierarchical structure of the culture or openness to experience factor (factor 5). What does it mean to say that someone scores high on this factor? From reading through the table, you can see that such people *may* be wiser, more curious, more given to fantasy, more sensitive to aesthetics, or more perceptive; but they will not neces-

TABLE 13.4 HIERARCHICAL STRUCTURE OF FACTOR 5, CULTURE

	Norman*	Goldberg (1990)	Costa & McCrae (1985)
Overall factor name	Culture	Intellect	Openness to experience
Middle-level subcategory type	Category	Synonym cluster	Facet
Subcategory examples	*Positive pole* Wisdom Originality Objectivity Knowledge Reflection Art	*Positive pole* Intellectuality Depth Insight Intelligence Creativity Curiosity Sophistication	Ideas Feelings Fantasy Aesthetics Actions Values
	Negative pole Imperceptivity	*Negative pole* Shallowness Unimaginativeness Imperceptiveness Stupidity	
Example of a constituent item in a subcategory	*"Wisdom"* Intelligent Philosophical Complex Meditative Deep	*"Intellectuality"* Contemplative Intellectual Introspective Philosophical	*"Openness/Ideas"* I often enjoy playing with theories and abstract ideas.

*As cited by Goldberg (1990, pp. 1218–1219).

sarily be all of the above. While these different words give a general sense of this factor, you can see that it includes quite a variety of types of people.

Predicting behavior from trait factors. So far, you might get the impression that psychologists working with the Big Five trait factors are mainly concerned with the results of factor analysis and debates about how many traits there are and what their structure is. While these are important current issues in trait theory, there are also many studies showing how particular trait factors are related to behavior.

A study of newly married couples by Buss (1991a) is a good example of the utility of measuring all five factors at once. After gathering trait measures, Buss asked partners to indicate (privately, of course!) their complaints about each other—things the partner did that made them angry and upset. He found that men and women scoring high on surgency (factor 1) drew complaints of being condescending from their partners. In other words, forceful and assertive people make others feel inferior; surgency thus seems to create difficulties for intimacy. People scoring low in emotional stability (factor 4) elicited complaints of jealousy, possessiveness, and dependency from their partners. Notice how each of these behaviors reflects a way in which generalized neuroticism or low emotional stability can poison an intimate relationship by eroding feelings of trust, safety, and autonomy. Finally, Buss found that people scoring low in culture (factor 5) were seen as too emotionally constricted by their partners. (This finding supports the broader label of "openness to experience" over the narrow label of "culture" or "intellect" for factor 5.)

Other recent studies have linked people's scores on the five trait factors to the tactics of influence they use (Buss, 1992b), their physical health (Smith & Williams, 1992) and mental health (Widiger & Trull, 1992), their adjustment during adolescence (Graziano & Ward, 1992), and how they go about pursuing their "personal projects" (see Chapter 10) (Little, Lecci, & Watkinson, 1992).

The Big Five versus Eysenck's Three Factors

During the late fourteenth century, two men—one in Rome, one in Avignon—claimed to be pope of the Catholic church. Each demanded obedience from the other, and each excommunicated the other from the church. No doubt the rivalry between the partisans of Eysenck and the Big Five, each claiming to have identified the fundamental dimensions of personality traits, is less intense and will be more quickly resolved. Still, a lively debate (based on the subtleties of mathematical statistics rather than theological doctrine) about the "real" number of fundamental dimensions or superfactors is still going on. For our purposes, a brief review of the arguments on each side will be enough (see Briggs, 1989; John, 1989).

There has been considerable debate about where Eysenck's three dimensions can be located or defined in terms of the Big Five map (see Costa &

McCrae, 1992; Eysenck, 1992). Eysenck prefers to squeeze the Big Five into his own three-dimensional scheme. For example, since in some analyses the adjectives defining agreeableness overlap with those defining conscientiousness and emotional stability, Eysenck and Eysenck (1985, p. 79) suggest that agreeableness is simply one manifestation of extraverted stability, while conscientiousness is a form of introverted stability.

With factor 5, the variations in its name come into play. Considering it as intellect (Goldberg's preferred name), Eysenck and Eysenck argue that it is simply intelligence considered as a personality trait rather than an ability variable (1985, p. 80). John (1990) disputes this, arguing that factor 5 is another name for low psychoticism. McCrae and Costa (1985) disagree. They argue instead that psychoticism is a combination of low agreeableness and low conscientiousness (that is to say, poor socialization) and believe that factor 5 is simply not reflected in any of Eysenck's measures.

We can leave the argument at this point. Perhaps over the next few years a consensus will emerge among the factor theorists about questions such as the relationship of each system to all of the others (often called the mapping of systems on each other) and the nature of factor 5.

Mapping Other Personality Variables onto the Big Five

Table 13.5 shows how the five factors can be used as a kind of map on which other more specific traits and personality variables can be located with respect to each other. Of course, making such a map is not the end of trait research, but rather only a good beginning, because there are many interesting personality variables in the middle and lower levels of the five-factor hierarchy—variables that deserve measurement and study in their own right. In Table 13.5 I have tried to describe and then locate several variables that are of particular and recent interest to personality psychologists (based on John, 1990; McCrae & John, 1992).

The Jungian types. According to the results of McCrae and Costa (1989), MBTI extraversion is practically identical to surgency (factor 1). Almost as strong is the relationship between the MBTI intuiting and factor 5 (culture or openness to experience). That is, intuitive types score high and sensing types score low on factor 5. Less strong are the connections between MBTI feeling and factor 2 (agreeableness), and between MBTI judging (that is, thinking and feeling, as contrasted with sensing and intuiting; see Chapter 12) and factor 3 (conscientiousness). None of the MBTI scales is related to factor 4 (emotional stability), probably because Jung based his typology on normal people. (Recall his difference with Freud, discussed in Chapter 12, about whether introversion was necessarily neurotic.)

Ego control and ego resiliency. Ego control and ego resiliency emerged as major dimensions of ego functioning in an intensive longitudinal study by

TABLE 13.5 POSSIBLE BIG FIVE "LOCATIONS" OF PERSONALITY VARIABLES

Personality variable and characterization	Big Five factor*				
	1 Surgency	2 Agreeableness	3 Conscientiousness	4 Emotional stability	5 Culture
MBTI scales:					
Extraversion (vs. introversion)	+				
Intuiting (vs. sensing)					+
Feeling (vs. thinking)		+			
Judging (vs. perceiving)			+		
Ego control:	−		+		
Containment of emotions and impulses by values and responsibility					
Ego resiliency:				+	+
Capacity for calm and insightful look at self and problems					
Shyness	−			−	
Sensation seeking:					
Adventure seeking, low inhibition	+		−	−	
Boredom susceptibility, experience seeking			−		
Hardiness:					
Enthusiastic and zestful response to change	+			+	+
Type A pattern:					
Competitive, impatient, and hostile	+	−	+	−	
Narcissism:					
Enhancement of self over others	+	−	−		

*Plus (+) and minus (−) signs indicate high and low scores on the factor, respectively.

Block and Block (1980; see also Block, 1971; Klohnen, 1994). Because ego control involves the restraint of emotions and impulses through the influence of values and responsibility, it should be associated with low scores on factor 1 (surgency) and high scores on factor 3 (conscientiousness). Ego resiliency, or the capacity to take a calm, optimistic, and insightful look at problems, should involve high scores on factors 4 (emotional stability) and 5 (culture or openness) (John, 1990, pp. 82–83).

Other variables. *Sensation seeking* (Zuckerman, 1979; see also Eysenck & Eysenck, 1985, pp. 70–75) has several different components: adventure seeking and low inhibition would be high surgency and perhaps low conscientiousness and emotional stability; while boredom susceptibility and experience seeking might be low conscientiousness (the latter would also be high openness to experience).

The *Type A pattern* of competitiveness, impatience, hostility, and being at risk for coronary heart disease (Matthews, 1982, 1988) seems to have a complex pattern involving four of the five factors: high surgency, low agreeableness, high conscientiousness, and low emotional stability.

The "self-enhancement" or entitlement component of *narcissism* (Chapter 9) should involve surgency, while the "exploitation of others" component might reflect low agreeableness and conscientiousness.

Finally, *shyness,* as discussed in connection with Figure 13.2, is a combination of low surgency and low emotional stability.

Mapping collegiate slang. The latest fashions in college slang terms for describing other people can also be located on the Big Five map. Probably each factor has its slang words, but the overwhelming proportion of slang examples from my students reflects the culture or openness to experience factor. For example:

> *Positive pole of factor 5:* awesome, bashus, cool, fly, fresh, rad, slippery, sweet, tasty
>
> *Negative pole of factor 5:* bim, bog[ue], cheesy, clueless, ditzy, doofus, dork, delbert, dweeb, fermented, geek, gump, gweeb, janey, loser, mook, narly, neb, nerd, neal [from "Neanderthal"], nimbnod, nicklehead, nob, scaggy, skanky, squid, squirrel, tonar [from "totally narly"], wimp

At least two words, "heinous" and "toasty," are especially interesting because (at the University of Michigan in 1994, anyway) they can refer to *either* pole of factor 5, depending on tone of voice and context!

Why is factor 5 so prominent in college slang, whereas in most of the factor-analytic studies reported by McCrae and John (1992), it is the *least* well represented factor? Why is it so important for you, as college students, to comment about whether other people are "awesome" or "clueless"? I can think of two explanations. First, colleges and universities are supposed to teach students to think critically, to be cultured and mature citizens, and to develop "character." In other words, colleges are institutions designed to socialize the virtues of the positive pole of factor 5 and eliminate the qualities of the negative pole. College slang trait terms might function as "markers" to indicate students' progress toward this goal. More generally, this explanation suggests that the slang terms used within any institution will reflect the purpose or mission of that institution. In other institutions, with socialization goals different from those of colleges and universities, we might find different factors emphasized in popular slang. Slang terms related to surgency (factor 1) might be especially popular in the Marine Corps.

Another explanation for the prominence of factor 5 slang among college students is that most colleges are heterogeneous institutions, like a large city to which students come from their many different "village" backgrounds.[5] Like the people of any large and heterogeneous city, therefore, students find it important to distinguish "us" (people who fit with their particular group's definition of correct style or culture) from "them" (people who don't). The large, rapidly changing, and exquisitely subtle slang trait vocabulary of factor 5 facilitates these identifications and distinctions.

Why map variables onto the five-factor model? What is the use of locating or "mapping" variables in this way? As McCrae and John (1992) and McAdams (1992a) point out, both the prediction and understanding of behavior are often more successful when specific traits, subtraits, or facets of traits are employed instead of broad general factors.

First, the five-factor structure gives us a larger framework in which we can locate and understand relationships among the many separate trait variables studied by personality psychologists. This can increase the coherence of the trait domain as a whole.

Second, the five factors provide a common, theoretically neutral language for talking about and moving between different personality concepts and variables. Consider an analogy: Many of you write term papers with personal computers, using a variety of different word processing systems. Documents created by one system usually cannot be read by another system, but in most word-processing systems they can be translated into an ASCII (American Standard Code for Information Interchange) or text-only version that can be read by another system. Similarly, if different personality trait variables can be expressed in the common five-factor language, we can "translate" from variable to variable, leading us to discover interesting similarities and contrasts. For example, a look at Table 13.5 might suggest that the Type A syndrome is a more conscientious and less adjusted form of narcissism. This translation capacity of the Big Five framework may be an important advantage in longitudinal studies, where data collected long ago with now-obsolete instruments must be compared with recent data collected with modern instruments. Translating the variables of both instruments into the ASCII of the Big Five, as it were, would make it possible to study the same traits over time, across different measures (Briggs, 1992, pp. 277–278; see Conley, 1985, as an example).

Some Cautions

While the emerging agreement on a five-factor structure of the trait domain is a promising development in personality psychology, I want to suggest some cautions. In a detailed review of the origins and development of the five-factor approach, Block (1995) has pointed out how certain characteristics of the early five-factor research—samples employed, restrictions on the adjective and

---

[5] I borrowed this analogy from John H. Finley, one of my college teachers.

questionnaire items used, and subjective interpretation of factors—affected and constrained the results of later studies. Block concluded, therefore, that some of the replicability of the five-factor structure across different studies, samples, and instruments was actually built into the studies from the outset rather than being an actual convergence within nature.

Furthermore, given the apparent success at replicating the five factors across many studies, it is easy to overlook differences in the meaning and connotations of the replicated factors from one study to the next. The conclusion that they are always the same five factors may be premature. For example, consider factor 3, named "conscientiousness" by Norman. Other researchers have labeled this factor "will to achieve," "prudence," and "work" (see the right-hand column of Table 13.3). While these labels are related, they are also quite different. The "will to achieve" (Digman & Inouye, 1986) might involve conscientiousness, but it also suggests ambition and surgency (factor 1). Further, at least three different labels have been proposed for factor 5: culture, intellect, and openness to experience. These, too, may be related; but they are also clearly different. I have friends who are very cultured and intellectual, but not particularly open to new experience. And some of my most "open" friends are not exactly cultured or intellectual (see McCrae & John, 1992, p. 197). In speaking of the Big Five, therefore, we may have to specify *which* (or whose) Big Five we are talking about.

Most important, the nature of the samples employed in the five-factor research should make us cautious about generalizing the results. Seven out of the eight groups analyzed by Tupes and Christal (1961/1992), and all five groups studied by Norman (1963), used American, English-speaking men between the ages of 18 and 45! While the race and class of these groups were not specified, we can infer that they were overwhelmingly white and middle-class. Would the same factors emerge if we studied women, people from other classes and races in our own society, or in other societies where other languages are spoken? The evidence reviewed by John (1990) and McAdams (1992a) suggests that there is some convergence across languages and cultures when the standard adjectives or items are used, but of course these adjectives were selected because they fit the five-factor model closely. The work of Yang and Bond (1990; see also Chapter 17) suggests that different factors might emerge if we *started with* a broader pool of adjectives and used ratings made by women, people of color, or poor people. Clearly, more work needs to be done here.

Finally, many traits are combinations of more than one factor (or factor subcategory). In such a combination, each component affects all the others, so the sum may be quite different from the separate components in isolation (see Hampson, 1989). Surgency, for example, plays a very different role in personality when it is combined with low agreeableness, low conscientiousness, and low emotional stability than when it is added to high agreeableness and high emotional stability. Scores on individual trait factors, taken in isolation, may not be of much use in predicting or understanding behavior. In personality (if not in geometry), the whole is often greater than the sum of its parts.

MEASURING TRAITS AT A DISTANCE

Rating the Traits of Presidents

To measure traits at a distance, researchers have adapted the observer-rating and questionnaire techniques that are used in direct studies of people. Simonton (1986), for example, studied U.S. presidents from Washington through Reagan. For each president, he first excerpted personality descriptions from standard biographies. Then he had raters read these descriptions and fill out an Adjective Check List for each president. (To protect against bias, Simonton removed identifying information as much as possible, typed the descriptions on large index cards, and put these cards in random order.) Interrater agreement on 110 of the 300 adjectives was sufficient for further analysis.

A factor analysis of the presidents' scores on these 110 adjectives produced fourteen factors, which is far more than the three or five factors discussed in this chapter. However, further examination shows that the most important factors seem familiar. Simonton labeled the two factors with the most highly loaded adjectives *moderation* and *friendliness.* The first seems close to emotional stability or low neuroticism (factor 4), while the second resembles Eysenck's extraversion and a combination of the Big Five factors surgency and agreeableness. The next three factors, in order of size, were labeled *intellectual brilliance, poise and polish* (both aspects of factor 5, culture or openness), and *Machiavellianism* (possibly low conscientiousness?). So even though Simonton found a large number of factors, we can see traces of the Eysenck and Big Five lists in his results.

These traces are even stronger in another Simonton study of presidents (1988), which asked raters to judge phrases instead of adjectives. A factor analysis of these ratings yielded five factors that correspond rather closely to the Big Five: interpersonal (agreeableness), charismatic (surgency), deliberative (conscientiousness), creative (culture or openness), and neurotic (low emotional stability). Table 13.6 presents scores for six presidents—Washington, Lincoln, Kennedy, Nixon, Carter, and Reagan—on the factors from both Simonton studies.

Filling Out Questionnaires for Presidents

Since traits are often measured by questionnaires, Winter (1990) asked three scholars of the presidency to fill out the Eysenck Personality Inventory "as if" they were each of the six U.S. presidents from Truman through Carter (excluding Ford). The exact instructions were as follows (Winter, 1990):

> When you fill out each questionnaire, try to imagine you *are* the president and so fill it out as you believe he would. That is, give the answers you believe the president would give. (p. 3)

The resulting scores indicated that the three raters agreed quite well among themselves (average interrater correlation = .85). Presidential extraver-

TABLE 13.6 ADJECTIVE FACTOR SCORES FOR SIX U.S. PRESIDENTS

	Score*					
Rated factor	Washington	Lincoln	Kennedy	Nixon	Carter	Reagan
Adjective check list ratings						
Moderation	Med	High	Med	Low	High	Med
Friendliness	Med	High	High	Low	High	High
Intellectual brilliance	Med	High	High	Med	Med	Med
Machiavellianism	Med	Med	Med	High	Med	Med
Poise and polish	High	Low	High	Med	Med	Med
Achievement drive	High	Med	High	High	Med	Med
Forcefulness	Med	Low	High	High	High	High
Wit	High	High	High	Low	Low	High
Physical attractiveness	Med	Low	High	Low	Med	High
Pettiness	Med	Low	Low	High	Med	Low
Tidiness	High	Low	Low	Med	High	Med
Conservatism	Med	Med	Low	Med	High	High
Inflexibility	Med	Low	Low	High	Low	Med
Pacifism	Med	High	Low	Low	High	Low
Modified Q-sort ratings						
Interpersonal	High	High	High	Low	Med	Med
Charismatic	Med	Med	High	Med	Med	High
Deliberative	High	Med	High	Med	Med	Med
Creative	Med	Med	High	High	Med	High
Neurotic	Med	Med	High	High	Med	Low

*Compared to all U.S. presidents; High = factor score above .50; Med = factor score between −.50 and +.50; Low = factor score below −.50.
SOURCE: Data adapted from Simonton (1986, Table 2; 1988, Table 3).

sion is related to having an active and aggressive presidential policy: for example, Truman's domestic social agenda and vigorous responses to the Soviet challenge during the early years of the Cold War, Kennedy's "New Frontier," and Johnson's military escalation in Vietnam. Presidential neuroticism is associated with having major problems and scandals: for example, Johnson's frustrations that led him to withdraw from the 1968 campaign and Nixon's handling of the Watergate scandal. Both of these results are consistent with research on these trait factors.

Figure 13.3 plots the location of each president along the two dimensions of extraversion and neuroticism. Notice that Nixon emerges as a neurotic introvert. This is consistent with many characterizations of him by close observers: "A brooding, moody man, given to long stretches of introspection. . . . A man of major talent—but a man of solitary, uncertain impulse" (White,

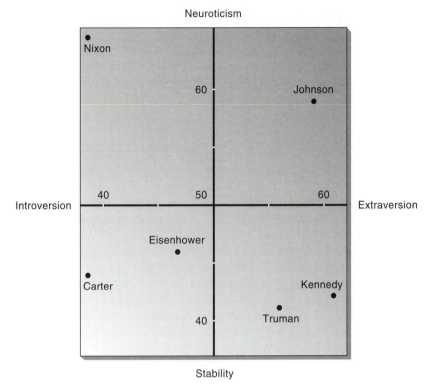

FIGURE 13.3
Plot of presidential scores on extraversion and neuroticism. (Adapted from Winter, 1990)

1961, p. 81). In fact, Nixon is said to have described himself as an "introvert in an extravert profession" (Mazlish, 1972/1973, p. 55), a self-characterization that by itself suggests neurotic conflict.

Although the number of presidents in Winter's study is small, the questionnaire-based scores correlate rather well with Simonton's ratings-based scores. For extraversion, the correlations were .69 (phrase-based) and .48 (adjective-based); for neuroticism, .63 (phrase-based) and .84 (adjective-based).[6] This convergence suggests that trait factors (at least the most prominent ones) can be measured at a distance by a variety of methods.

Coding Traits from Verbal Material

On the basis of extensive clinical research, Weintraub (1989) has developed methods of scoring interviews and other spontaneous verbal material for certain traits and defenses. For example, expressions of feeling ("I *love* music")

---

[6] Simonton's extraversion adjective factors were "forcefulness" and "friendliness"; the only adjective factor suggesting neuroticism was "pettiness."

and adverbial intensifiers ("She is *so* intelligent") are said to indicate *emotional expressiveness*. The combination of few qualifiers and many retractors ("but," "although," "however," and "nevertheless") suggests *impulsivity*. Weintraub's studies of the presidential press conferences of U.S. presidents Eisenhower through Reagan suggest that Nixon was lowest in both traits, Eisenhower was highest in expressiveness, and Reagan highest in impulsivity.

NOMOTHETIC VERSUS IDIOGRAPHIC: JENNY REVISITED

In this chapter and the previous one, we have studied examples of the idiographic and nomothetic approaches to trait description. The comparison between these two can be summarized by referring again to the case of Jenny. In Chapter 12, we presented an idiographic perspective on Jenny's traits (see especially Table 12.1). What would be her scores on the Big Five trait factors? Using a dictionary for converting adjectives to trait factors (compiled by Goldberg, 1990, Tables 1 and 3), along with a little extra help from Goldberg (personal communication, February 26, 1991), we can classify most of the twenty-six descriptive phrases from Allport's letter of recommendation to the church

TABLE 13.7 ESTIMATED SCORES OF JENNY ON THE BIG FIVE TRAIT FACTORS

1	*2*	*3*	*4*	*5*
			Emotional	
Surgency	*Agreeableness*	*Conscientiousness*	*stability*	*Culture*
Adjectives in Allport's letter of recommendation				
Positive pole traits				
Fortitude	Self-denial	Singleness	Independent	Cultivated
Courage	Kind	of purpose		Intelligent
Vivid personality	Helpful	Frugal		Bright
	Generous	Personal		Aesthetic
	Appreciative	integrity		Appreciative
	of kindness	Critical		of beauty
		of hypocrisy		Pride
Negative pole traits				
Aloof from	Critical of			
intimate	hypocrisy			
contact	Aloof from			
	intimate			
	contact			
	Austere			
	philosophy			
	of life			

TABLE 13.7 *(Continued)*

1	2	3	4	5
Surgency	Agreeableness	Conscientiousness	Emotional stability	Culture

Adjectives used by observers who read Jenny's letters

Positive pole traits

Egocentric	Appreciative	Rigid	Self-reliant	Literary
Courageous	Loyal	Scrupulous	Indomitable	Cultured
Vigorous	Affectionate	Hardworking		Poetic
Voluble	Maternal	Frugal		Intelligent
Self-dramatizing	Oversacrificial	Persistent		Proud
Expressive		Calculating		Snobbish
Ascendant		Serious		
Self-assertive		Fastidious		
Forceful		Predictable		
Witty				

Negative pole traits

Reclusive	Distrustful	Rebellious	Hypochondriacal	
Solitary	Prejudiced	Recalcitrant	Insecure	
Pessimistic	Bellicose	Whimsical	Martyr complex	
Humorless	Tactless		Self-pitying	
Despondent	Misogynous		Emotional	
Fixation on death	Selfish		Temperamental	
	Opinionated		Insecure	
	Jealous		Paranoid	
	Stubborn			
	Violent			
	Domineering			
	Autocratic			
	Sarcastic			
	Possessive			

SOURCE: Readers' descriptions from Allport (1965, pp. 193–194); classification based on groupings by Norman and Goldberg (see Goldberg, 1990, Tables 1 and 3; also Goldberg, personal communication).

home, as well as the sixty-nine adjectives used by observers who had read *Letters from Jenny* (see Chapter 12 and Allport, 1965, pp. 193–194) in terms of the five factors. The results are shown in Table 13.7.

When converted to five-factor ratings by giving one point for each adjective used, the trait description in Allport's letter and those based on observers' ratings show a moderate level of agreement, as shown in Table 13.8. The rank-order correlation between the two descriptions of Jenny, across ten scales (two poles each, of five factors), is .41. The two biggest discrepancies involve Allport's infrequent use of the negative poles of agree-

TABLE 13.8 INTERRATER CONVERGENCE ON ESTIMATED SCORES OF JENNY ON THE BIG FIVE TRAIT FACTORS

	Factor				
	1	*2*	*3*	*4*	*5*
Positive traits					
Allport's letter	3	5	4	1	6
Readers' adjectives	10	5	9	2	6
Negative traits					
Allport's letter	1	3	0	0	0
Readers' adjectives	6	14	3	8	0

ableness and emotional stability, which would be expected in a letter of recommendation. His relatively low use of surgency may be misleading, because he did refer to Jenny's effects on other people with phrases that might not be coded as surgency traits ("remarkable," "fascinating," and "appealing").

Jenny's Profile on the Big Five

Drawing on the Big Five translations of Allport's letter and the observers' ratings, we can suggest the following five-factor profile for Jenny: She was high on surgency (factor 1), conscientiousness (factor 3), and culture (factor 5); she was low (that is, negative) on agreeableness (factor 2) and emotional stability (factor 4). In simpler terms, Jenny was a dominant, conscientious, cultured woman who was often disagreeable and emotionally unstable.

Compared to the idiographic portrait in Chapter 12, this nomothetic description is certainly flatter and less vivid. It is a list of common trait words rather than a complex and detailed structural portrait. On the other hand, the nomothetic description does make it possible to locate Jenny in a standardized framework of traits. With the scores of Table 13.8, we could answer some important questions about Jenny even before we met her:

1. Will she be active or withdrawn? (Active, unless she is in one of her reclusive and aloof moods.)

2. Will she be agreeable or disagreeable? (Quite likely disagreeable.)

3. Can she be counted upon? (Yes, as long as you don't threaten her sense of independence.)

4. Will she be stable or unstable? (Unstable.)

5. Is she interesting? (Very much so!)

Whenever we meet new people, we ask questions like these. Goldberg (1981, p. 161) suggests that these are universal questions, the first things any human being wants to know about another person, because happiness, welfare, and even life itself may depend on the answers. Buss (1991b, pp. 471–473) suggests that these concerns reflect important features of the social terrain to which humans have adapted over the centuries.

A Psychology of the Stranger

For answering these elementary but essential questions, we need a vocabulary of traitlike terms that can be quickly applied on the basis of minimal cues but that will reflect broad, important dimensions of other peoples' public, enduring behavior—in other words, a language of first impressions. The five factors give us just such a language. They are a convenient vocabulary to describe people we do not know well. In McAdams's (1992a, p. 348) terms, the five factors represent a "psychology of the stranger"—the words that first come to mind, for example, when we describe ourselves or someone else to a stranger. Thus when John (1989, p. 266) asked a sample of college students to describe their own personalities, he found that the ten most commonly used words—"friendly," "caring," "intelligent," "happy," "lazy," "moody," "shy," "outgoing," "selfish," and "kind"—covered each of the Big Five factors. Norman's (1963) earliest work, however, showed that people used the same factor structure whether they were rating people they knew well or people they had barely met. Obviously, he concluded, "the 'level' or 'depth' of the contracts required to produce such results may not be very great." "Indeed," he went on, "one associate remarked that these factors sound very much like the sorts of things she sees in letters of recommendation!" (p. 581). In fact, a review of five-factor trait ratings, by Kenny, Albright, Malloy, and Kashy (1994), shows only modest increases in the level of interobserver agreement as a function of increased acquaintance with the people being rated.

With longer acquaintance, our impressions and descriptions of other people become more differentiated and subtle; they are likely to be phrased in terms of more precise and narrower traits rather than the global language of the Big Five. The five factors are probably not adequate for describing your parents, your closest friend, or yourself (to yourself, at least). It is true that when we construct a description of someone we *really* know, we may still use five to ten words and phrases, as Allport (1958, pp. 253–257) suggested and as our idiographic analysis of Jenny in Chapter 12 illustrated. However, the five to ten phrases we would use are much richer, more specific, and therefore more descriptive than are the names of the five factors.

This point can be illustrated with the Swede and Tetlock (1986) study of how Henry Kissinger described foreign leaders (see Chapter 11). Kissinger's overall five dimensions do in fact correspond approximately to the Big Five:

Professional anguish = conscientiousness (perhaps also low
emotional stability)
Ambitious patriotism = surgency
Revolutionary greatness = surgency
Intellectual sophistication = culture
Realistic friendship = agreeableness

When he described leaders he knew really well, however, Kissinger used exquisitely subtle and differentiated phrases that go well beyond the five factors. For example, he described himself as "the plumber in Kafka's novel *The Castle*," former French President Charles de Gaulle as having "the natural haughtiness of a snow-capped Alpine peak," and former President Lyndon Johnson as a "caged eagle" (Swede & Tetlock, 1986, p. 641).

At their most general level, then, nomothetic trait descriptions reflect first impressions. Scores on five traits may be an efficient way to sketch the major observable features of another person, just as a few strokes (traits) of a brush *can* serve as a brief portrait, as shown by the artist Picasso's simple sketch of the Russian choreographer Léonide Massine in the left-hand panel of Figure 13.4 (from Cooper, 1968). On the other hand, with more extensive and complex experience and information, we can make a much fuller and denser portrait, as shown by Picasso's more complex sketch of Massine in the right-hand half of the figure.

FIGURE 13.4
Two kinds of artistic "portraits" of Léonide Massine by Picasso.

*T*RAITS IN THE DESCRIPTION OF PERSONALITY

This chapter has reviewed a large body of complicated research, involving complex technical issues of psychological measurement, factor analysis, and other arcane topics. Despite the differences and disputes, one conclusion does seem clear. At least for the populations usually studied by trait researchers, there is general agreement that the domain of traits can be described by a few (perhaps three to five) major dimensions. The issues involve the precise location of the dimensions, the names of the poles of each dimension, and the usefulness of broad dimensions versus narrower, more specific traits.

In terms of the map example of Figure 13.1, we have a series of different maps for Washington, D.C. Some (Eysenck) have a fundamental direction ("north") going from the White House straight up to the top. Others (for example, Gray) rotate that fundamental direction toward the upper right of the figure (toward Baltimore) and call it "northeast." Still other maps (for example, Cattell) add extra directions based on the location of important Washington sights. Using any of these maps, we *can* find our way around the city, getting from the White House to the Vietnam Memorial or the Capitol. For certain places of interest, of course, we would consult more detailed neighborhood maps and even floor plans of particular buildings (Allport's approach). These latter are analogous to the finer-grained, more specific trait variables such as ego control, Type A pattern, and so forth. They are special places of interest in the universe of traits because they help us to explain and predict certain unique patterns of behavior and outcomes such as health or psychopathology.

In the last two chapters, we have focused on the universe of traits and trait factors as ways to describe the public observable features of personality. But these are only descriptions, not explanations, as Briggs (1992) noted. Traits may be summary names for behavioral regularities, but they may also reflect underlying psychological and physiological processes and mechanisms. That is, traits may be biological as well as social. Many personality psychologists believe that traits do ultimately have a biological basis, though they go on to argue that we are a long way from discovering that basis. We turn to this question in the next chapter.

Cooper, Douglas. (1968). *Picasso's Theatre*. NY: Abrams. The simple drawing on the left is a portion of an India-ink drawing entitled *Massine, Bakst, and Diaghilev* (original in Mme. Barsacq Collection, Paris). The complex drawing on the right is a pencil drawing entitled *Léonide Massine* (original in the Massine Collection, Paris).

14

The Biological Basis of Traits and Temperament

❖

What could be more obvious than the connection between our bodies and our personalities! Human beings are constituted so that one personality is paired with one body; any other arrangement we recognize as abnormal. When the body dies, the personality ends—at least in the form that we know it. In Chapter 9, we have already seen how people's *cognitions* about their bodies are an important part of their personalities. However, there are also more direct links between biology and personality. Since most of this research involves traits and temperament, this chapter is the appropriate place to review the evidence and take stock of what we know. We shall focus on Eysenck's three factors, because their similarity of structure among different groups and their consistency in individuals over time (Conley, 1984, 1985; McCrae & Costa, 1984, pp. 59–62) suggest a possible basis in biology. Recent work on biological bases for other, more narrowly defined variables, such as sensation seeking, will also be mentioned (see Zuckerman, 1991, for a summary).

Yet we must be careful. Throughout human history, biological and physical characteristics—as reflected in gender, race, or ethnicity—have been used to oppress. For example, women have been excluded from social, educational, and economic life on the basis of their sex. For over 400 years, blacks were enslaved because of the color of their skin, and to this day skin color continues to be a basis of individual and institutional discrimination. In World War II, millions of Jews, Gypsies, gays and lesbians, and others were exterminated by Nazi Germany, while many Japanese Americans were forced into "relocation camps" by the U.S. government. In all these cases, exclusion and oppression were justified by attributing certain personality characteristics to the oppressed group *on the basis of* their supposedly distinctive physical characteristics. (You know the stereotypes.) In MacKinnon's (1987b) terms, the forces of dominance—people who have power—construct or exaggerate the difference between themselves and others; then they use these differences to legitimize their power. Even supposedly objective scientists are not immune to this process.[1] For example, one scientist, upon learning of a study that suggested rapid evolutionary change in certain visual areas of the cat's brain, made a breathtaking jump to the topic of human racial differences (Blakeslee, 1993):

> The real surprise is the speed at which the change occurred in the cat. The idea that a part of the brain can evolve so differently in so short a time makes one wonder about different human races. Are we different in subtle ways? (p. B8)

In exploring relationships between biology and personality, then, we should examine the evidence with extra care in order to avoid merely rationalizing existing power structures.

---

[1]Thus the subtitle of Charles Darwin's first major book, *The Origin of Species* (1859/1936), is "the preservation of favored *races* in the struggle for life" (emphasis added).

BODY AND PERSONALITY IN LITERATURE AND FOLKLORE

The idea that personality has roots in biology is an ancient one. In Chapter 11, we reviewed Galen's theory of the four humors. Folk wisdom abounds in sayings such as "fat people are jolly," a stereotype that has caused a good deal of pain for people with weight problems. English literature is full of examples where personality is diagnosed or described on the basis of physical appearance. In Shakespeare's play *Julius Caesar*, for example, Caesar discussed the personality of Cassius:

> Yon Cassius has a lean and hungry look;
> He thinks too much; such men are dangerous. . . .
> Would he were fatter!. . .
> . . . He reads much;
> He is a great observer and he looks
> Quite through the deed of men; he loves no plays,
> As thou dost, Antony; he hears no music;
> Seldom he smiles. . . .
> Such men as he be never at heart's ease
> Whiles they behold a greater than themselves,
> And therefore are they very dangerous.
>
> (I, ii, 192–210)

According to Shakespeare, leanness of body is related to the following personality characteristics: reading, cynicism, lack of a sense of humor or appreciation of the arts, and jealousy.

In *The Masters*, a novel about academic politics set in the University of Cambridge, the English writer C. P. Snow (1951/1959) contrasts the personal styles of three professors in terms of their facial features:

> I watched their heads, grouped round the desk, their faces glowing with their purpose—Brown's purple-pink, rubicund [healthy, rosy complexion], keen-eyed, Chrystal's beaky, domineering, Jago's pale, worn with the excesses of emotion, his eyes intensely lit. Each of these three was seeking power, I thought—but the power each wanted was as different as they were themselves. (p. 60)

Finally, in his memoirs the economist John Kenneth Galbraith reported a conversation between himself and French President Charles de Gaulle about the psychological effects of being tall (1969/1970):

> De Gaulle began by pointing to [another guest] and asking why I had been conversing with such a short man. I said that he obviously agreed with me that the world belongs to the tall men. They are more visible, therefore their behavior is better and accordingly they are to be trusted. (p. 516)

(Galbraith and de Gaulle were each well over 6 feet 6 inches tall, so perhaps their beliefs about height and personality were self-serving.)

While these literary examples and folk wisdom are vivid and entertaining, any serious attempt to link biology and personality needs to go beyond mere association and distinguish the effects of biological factors from the effects of beliefs about and reactions to biology. To do this, we need to work out the psychophysiological mechanisms that link biology to personality.

THE EYSENCK GRAND DESIGN

Over the past forty years, Hans Eysenck set himself the goal of working out biological mechanisms underlying the three trait factors of extraversion, neuroticism, and psychoticism (see Chapter 13). Eysenck recognized that this was an ambitious, even audacious goal: at the beginning of *The Biological Basis of Personality*, for example, he likened himself to the circus acrobat who announces: "My next trick is impossible!" (1967, p. xi). His pursuit of that goal led to a series of research papers, books (for example, Eysenck, 1957, 1967; Eysenck & Eysenck, 1985), and review chapters (for example, Eysenck, 1990). We will begin with a brief example of the 1950s and 1960s experimental psychology research inspired by Eysenck's thinking, then move on to his more recent work on arousal. While the specific topics and mechanisms have changed over the years, Eysenck's basic strategies of inquiry have remained the same, and have remained controversial. To illustrate these strategies, I will discuss mainly research on extraversion, with a briefer review of neuroticism.

Strategies of Inquiry

Eysenck's search for the biological basis of extraversion proceeded along several fronts. First, he assembled laboratory studies that related extraversion to basic psychological functions such as perception, conditioning and learning, and motor performance (Eysenck, 1957, p. 28). (Many of these studies used one of Eysenck's questionnaire measures of extraversion, but in his reviews he also included research that employed related scales from other personality inventories.) Eysenck was especially interested in these basic functions because, he believed, they are controlled by basic physiological and biological factors instead of voluntary higher-order factors. If extraversion was correlated with individual differences in perception, learning, or performance, he reasoned, then extraversion must be related to these underlying physiological factors and mechanisms.

In a more controversial decision, Eysenck included studies where extraversion was measured indirectly, through differential psychiatric diagnoses or classifications. Refer back for a minute to the two-dimensional diagram of Figure 13.2. While people labeled "hysterics" and "dysthymics" (Eysenck's collective term for obsessives, depressives, and people prone to anxiety) are both high in neuroticism, they are at opposite poles on extraversion (hysterics high, obsessives low). Eysenck argued, therefore, that since hysterics and obsessives differ in average level of extraversion, they can be used as proxies or substitutes for normal (nonneurotic) extraverts and introverts. *If the two labeled groups do indeed differ only on extraversion*, then this technique may be valid; but if there are other personality differences besides level of extraversion between hysterics and dysthymics—and many psychologists believe there are—then such comparisons will produce misleading results.

Eysenck also studied the effects of certain drugs that apparently change behavior in the direction of introversion (depressants such as alcohol or barbiturates) or extraversion (stimulants such as caffeine or amphetamine). One problem with this approach is that drugs often have complex and even paradoxical effects, including effects of setting and expectations. Thus stimulants and depressants may do much more than mimic extraversion-introversion. (For example, many British people believe that a "nice cup of tea," which is full of the stimulant caffeine, helps them to relax!)

Finally, Eysenck's most controversial strategy involves the use of persons with brain damage (see Eysenck, 1957, pp. 32–34, 145–147; 1967, pp. 319–339). He observed that brain damage (and certain kinds of surgery in which brain tissue is destroyed) often changes behavior in the direction of extreme extraversion; therefore, he argued, brain-damaged patients could be considered a criterion group for high extraversion. Given the enormous complexity of the human brain, and the many and complex effects of brain damage, many personality psychologists find Eysenck's simple equation of brain damage with higher extraversion scores to be inappropriate and unwarranted.

Early Laboratory Research on Introversion and Conditioning

One landmark early study purporting to link extraversion-introversion to physiological processes was Franks's (1956) study of eye-blink conditioning. In this experiment, first participants heard a tone, and then a puff of air was directed at their eyeball. Of course they blinked. After several more tones and blinks, they eventually came to blink at the tone itself, without the air puff. This blink to the tone alone is called a *conditioned response*, equivalent to the salivation responses of Pavlov's (1927) dogs (see Chapter 15). (Franks used this procedure to study conditioning in humans because blinking in response to a puff of air in the eye is almost wholly an involuntary reflex, not affected by conscious intentions or other things an experimenter cannot control.) Franks found that dysthymics (that is, people presumed to be high in introversion) formed conditioned eye-blink responses more quickly than did hysterics (presumed to be high in extraversion). In a later study (1957), Franks replicated these results with a group of normal college students, using a questionnaire measure of extraversion-introversion.

Excitation and inhibition. Eysenck explained these results in terms of the physiological concepts of *excitation* and *inhibition*. Excitation refers to the process by which impulses are conducted within the nervous system, while inhibition refers to anything that blocks or retards the transmission of such impulses; for example, the inherent resistance of the nervous system itself, fatigue, distractions produced by other stimuli, and simple adaptation to whatever stimulus caused the impulse (as when we seem to stop hearing a regular, repeated sound). Formation of a conditioned response is facilitated by excitation and blocked by inhibition. Eysenck's original biological model (1957) held that introverts have strong excitation and weak inhibition, while extraverts have weak excitation and strong inhibition. As a result, introverts will respond more strongly to external stimuli and form connections between stimuli by conditioning quicker than extraverts. As an analogy, we could imagine that introverts' nervous systems are wired with copper (a very efficient conductor of electricity), whereas extraverts' systems are wired with lead (a less efficient conductor). The actual biological basis for such differences in excitation and inhibition might be differences at the synapse (chemical transmission of an impulse between two nerve cells), or differences in the myelin sheath (a coating of nerve fibers that speeds transmission of the impulse within the nerve cell).

Excitation, inhibition, and social behavior. Since we usually think of extraverts as "bouncy"—sociable, energetic, maybe a little impulsive—you may be surprised at Eysenck's hypotheses that they have higher levels of inhibition, and that introverts—subdued and comfortable by themselves—have higher excitation. The explanation of this apparent paradox, according to Eysenck, is that the terms "excitation" and "inhibition" in the *neural* sense mean the opposite of what they mean in the *behavioral* sense. That is, since introverts have nervous systems with stronger excitatory potential, they will be more sensitive to external stimuli (particularly the strong stimuli of punishment). Thus they have lower stimulus thresholds; over time they will develop stronger conditioned anxiety and avoidance responses. In short, they will be more controlled and better socialized. Since other people are major sources of stimulation, punishment, and neural excitation, introverts will therefore tend to avoid other people and prefer being alone. Extraverts, in contrast, have higher thresholds, are less sensitive to stimuli (including punishment stimuli), and so are less socialized and controlled. Since they have not experienced other people as a source of pain and punishment to the same extent, they are more sociable. To summarize Eysenck's early hypothesis: *high neural inhibition leads to low behavioral inhibition and high impulsivity (extraversion), while high neural excitation leads to high behavioral inhibition and low impulsivity (introversion).*

While Eysenck's 1957 theory was an impressive attempt to bring together personality data, laboratory findings, and biological principles, it was not without problems. For example, conditionability (the ease with which conditioned responses are formed) is not a unitary variable, but rather a complex function of the particular stimuli and responses and numerous peripheral factors (see Eysenck, 1965; Eysenck & Eysenck, 1985, pp. 241–246; and Mischel, 1968, p. 32).

Extraversion, Introversion, and Arousal

As knowledge of the nervous system increased and as technology improved, psychologists grew less interested in hypothetical concepts of excitation and inhibition and more interested in the concept of *activation* or *autonomic nervous system arousal* as a critical psychophysiological dimension of behavior. Eysenck revised his theory of introversion and extraversion to take account of this new interest (Strelau & Eysenck, 1987).

The nature of arousal. Arousal is not a single thing, but rather a complex phenomenon that can be approached from many different perspectives: From the subjective perspective, we can describe our state of arousal along a scale running from one extreme of "nearly asleep," through "relaxed" and "alert" to the other extreme of "clutched up" (Thayer, 1967). From the perspective of the brain, arousal ranges from synchronized large alpha waves (characteristic of sleep and relaxation) to smaller amplitude, irregular waves (characteristic of intense mental activity). Here a part of the brain called the reticular formation (ascending reticular activation system, or ARAS) plays a critical role. All nerves transmitting information from the senses to specific areas of the brain also stimulate the reticular formation along the way. In turn, the reticular formation collects and transforms this stimulation into a diffuse arousal of the entire brain—a kind of alarm clock that keeps the brain awake. Figure 14.1 illustrates this process. (Don't take this simple figure too literally; in all probability, the reticular formation is only one of several different arousal systems affecting the brain; see Eysenck, 1990, pp. 248–249.)

From the perspective of internal bodily organs, high levels of arousal mean that the sympathetic nervous system is engaged or active. Heart rate and respiration increase, the flow of blood is reduced to the digestive organs and increased to the muscles, and tiny amounts of perspiration are secreted on the skin. This increases the electrical conductivity of the skin as measured by the galvanic skin response (GSR), more recently called *electrodermal activity*, or EDA. Hair on the back of the neck stands up, and goose bumps are raised on the arms. (In cats, this latter effect, called piloerection, puffs up the fur, which makes the cat more frightening to a potential enemy.) Collectively, these changes prepare the body to respond to a threat with either fight or flight, along with inner feelings of fright. With our digestion shut down, our lungs taking in more oxygen, and our hearts pumping more blood to our muscles, we are better able to leap tall buildings (or to handle the threat in some other appropriate way, such as fighting or running away).

Finally, many psychologists have suggested that arousal is a major underlying dimension of emotion, along with a second dimension of pleasant-unpleasant (see Larsen & Diener, 1992). According to this theory, the emotion of "surprise" is a state of pleasant high arousal, whereas feeling "jittery" is unpleasant high arousal; "contentment" is pleasant low arousal, and "droopy" is unpleasant low arousal. Figure 14.2 presents a map of common emotion words as they might be located in this two-dimensional space.

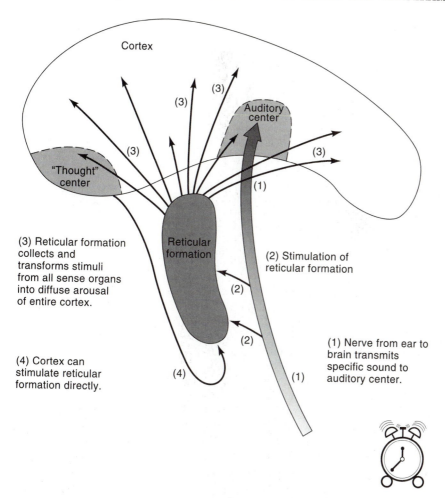

Cortex

Auditory
center

(3)

(3)

(3)

(3)

(3)

"Thought"
center

(3) Reticular formation
collects and
transforms stimuli
from all sense organs
into diffuse arousal
of entire cortex.

Reticular
formation

(1)

(2) Stimulation of
reticular formation

(2)

(2)

(4) Cortex can
stimulate reticular
formation directly.

(4)

(1)

(1) Nerve from ear to
brain transmits
specific sound to
auditory center.

Sound of the alarm clock is transmitted as information to the auditory
center (1). At the same time, it also stimulates the reticular formation (2),
which transmits this and all other stimuli it receives as diffuse
arousal to the entire cortex of the brain (3), waking it up or keeping it
awake. The reticular formation can also be stimulated by the cortex itself
(4). Thus we can be aroused by thoughts ("It's 8 A.M.; I'll be late for the
exam!") as well as by external stimuli (alarm clock).

FIGURE 14.1

The role of the reticular formation in cortical arousal.

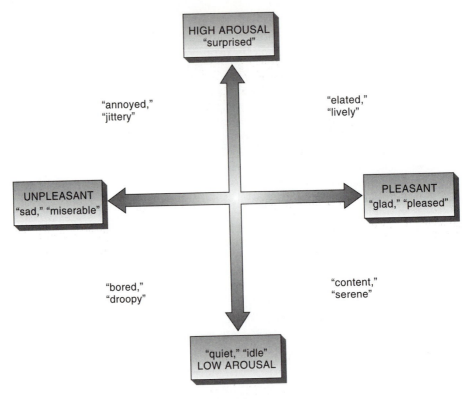

FIGURE 14.2
The dimensions of emotion. (Adapted from Larsen and Diener, 1992, p. 31)

Optimal level of arousal. A central feature of many arousal theories is the concept of an *optimal level of arousal.* Below a certain point, people's performance is sluggish and they don't feel "up" for the task at hand. Above that point, however, further arousal is too much: people's performance deteriorates and they feel "stressed out." (You will probably recognize optimal level as similar to the Yerkes-Dodson law, discussed in Chapter 2, in which level of motivation has an inverted U-shaped relation to performance.) However, the optimal level of arousal is not a simple concept. It depends on the nature of the task. Different people have different optimal levels, and even the same person has different optimal levels at different times.

Measuring arousal. In principle, arousal can be measured through any of its associated signs: self-report, brain-wave activity, or measures of sympathetic nervous system activity (heart rate, respiration, or EDA). In fact, however, matters are not so simple. Different measures of physiological arousal are not highly correlated (r's usually between .20 and .30), and there are large individual differences in the pattern of the measures (see Strelau & Eysenck, 1987, pp. 7–8). Furthermore, different researchers often use different measures of arousal, which means that their results are not always consistent with each other.

Arousal, arousability, and extraversion-introversion. Over the years, Eysenck has suggested several different ways in which the extraversion-introversion dimension might be related to arousal. First, introversion might be associated with a higher typical level of arousal, without considering the effects of any special conditions or intervention by the experimenter. Second, introversion could also be associated with having a lower optimal level of arousal, so in any given situation, introverts would be more likely than extraverts to be above their optimal level. Third, introversion might be associated with greater *arousability*—that is, a greater increase of arousal to a given stimulus. All of these possibilities converge in the following general hypothesis: *under any particular set of conditions introverts are (or become) more aroused than extraverts; consequently, they are more likely to be operating closer to their optimal level or above it.*

Laboratory tasks, arousal, and introversion-extraversion. If we assume that introverts have higher levels of arousal (or are more arousable) and then add in the Yerkes-Dodson law, that is, the inverted-U relationship between arousal and performance, we can predict several relationships between introversion-extraversion and performance under different conditions. For simple tasks, where most people are below their optimal arousal level, introverts should perform better than extraverts, because they will be at a "higher" point on the curve relating arousal to performance, as shown in Figure 14.3. For complex tasks, where most people are above their optimal level, extraverts should perform better. And on any given task, conditions that increase arousal (for example, loud noise or caffeine) should increase the performance of extraverts more (or decrease it less) than the performance of introverts. Conversely, conditions that reduce arousal should improve introverts' performance more (or hurt it less) than extraverts' performance.

Figure 14.3 illustrates these relationships. For the sake of simplicity, assume that everyone has the same optimal level of arousal and that introverts and extraverts differ only in their actual arousal level at the moment. When extraverts and introverts are below the optimal arousal level (points E_b and I_b in Figure 14.3), the greater height of I_b indicates the relatively superior performance of introverts; but when both are above optimal level (points E_a and I_a), extraverts do relatively better. Increases in arousal, represented by the arrows pointing to the right, produce relatively larger increases in performance for E_b (or relatively smaller decreases for E_a). Decreases in arousal (arrows pointing to the left) have the opposite effect.

Two studies will illustrate how the overall theory works. Geen, McCown, and Broyles (1985) found that during a learning task, extraverts chose significantly louder levels of background noise than did introverts (85 versus 65 decibels, respectively) and improved their performance with the louder

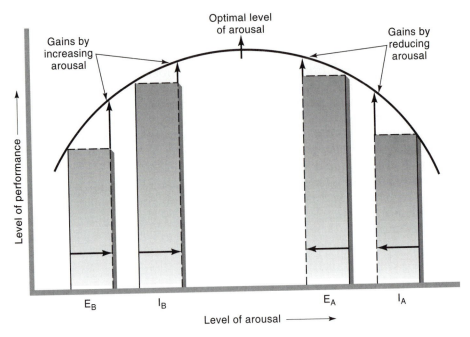

FIGURE 14.3
Introversion-extraversion, level of arousal, and performance.

noise. Introverts, in contrast, both preferred and performed better in the quieter condition. This suggests that extraverts felt the need for higher levels of arousal (by turning up the volume), whereas introverts preferred lower levels. Davies, Hockey, and Taylor (1969) conducted a "vigilance" task under two conditions. (Vigilance tasks, originally designed to simulate the job of a radar operator, typically require people to detect inconspicuous visual or auditory signals over a long period of time, typically an hour or more.) In the quiet condition (an electric fan masking most other noise), participants could press a button to hear 30 seconds of tape-recorded music and speech. As shown in Figure 14.4, extraverts requested the tape segments more often during the vigilance task. In the noisy condition (with the tape playing), participants could push a button to get 30 seconds of silence. Here introverts asked for silence more often. Perhaps these results help to explain why your (extraverted) roommate can claim to do better homework with the stereo turned up loud, while (introverted) you do your best work in a quiet, deserted library during early morning hours! Or is it the other way around?

To test aspects of Eysenck's arousal model, psychologists have carried out many other studies, involving ingenious measures of sensory thresholds, task performance, and preferred levels of arousal (see the review in Eysenck & Eysenck, 1985, chap. 9). For example, some researchers manipulated conditions that are known to increase or decrease arousal (such as intense noise, failure feedback, the presence of incentives, sleep deprivation, the time of day, electric shock, and drugs) in order to see whether these conditions also pro-

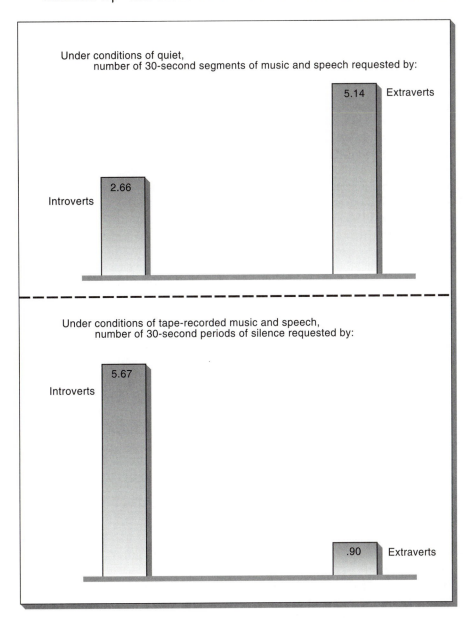

FIGURE 14.4
Performance of introverts and extraverts in a "vigilance" task. (Adapted from Davies, Hockey, and Taylor, 1969)

duced the characteristic introverted or extraverted effects on behavior and performance. While this research demonstrates considerable support for the model, there are exceptions, and the overall pattern is quite complex, depending on the precise nature of the task, other features of the situation, and other personality variables.

Effects of drugs. Some of the most intriguing predictions from Eysenck's arousal model involve the effects of different drugs and people's different preferences for them. While drugs have complex and varied effects, Eysenck has focused on the two groups of *stimulants* (caffeine, Dexedrine, amphetamine or "speed," and cocaine) or *depressants* or sedatives (alcohol, barbiturates, heroin, sodium amytal). In general, stimulants increase arousal. In terms of Figure 14.3, they move people toward the right. Depressants generally decrease arousal, moving people toward the left. A typical prediction from Eysenck's theory would run as follows: If we imagine the extreme left end of the arousal scale in Figure 14.3 as a person's threshold for sedation (the point at which the person loses consciousness), then introverts should need a relatively higher dose of any particular depressant to reach that threshold. Conversely, extraverts should need relatively more of any stimulant (for example, more coffee) to reach a given threshold of arousal toward the right end of the arousal scale. You can use Figure 14.3 to work out how different kinds of drugs should affect the performance of extraverts and introverts.

Now let us complicate matters. Assume a quiet, boring situation. Which people would use which kind of drug to reach their preferred or optimal level of arousal? How would patterns of drug use change in a crowded, bustling, and noisy situation? Many predictions of this kind, about the relation between introversion-extraversion and thresholds, performance effects, and preferences for different drugs, have been confirmed by researchers, although the results are sometimes subtle and usually complicated (see Eysenck, 1967, chap. 6; Eysenck & Eysenck, 1985, p. 229).

As suggested above, drug effects are notoriously complicated and variable—even reversed or "paradoxical" among many people. For example, alcohol is technically a depressant and not a stimulant, yet it often leads to behavior that seems quite stimulated or aroused. In such cases, moderate levels of alcohol seem to depress drinkers' inhibitions, judgment, and self-control. (As one of my professors once put it, "The superego is that part of the personality that is soluble in alcohol.") Only at much higher doses does alcohol begin to depress impulsivity, and it may have no depressant effect at all on imagination and fantasy! Even the stimulants in coffee (caffeine) and tobacco (nicotine) have variable and often paradoxical effects on some people. My father, for example, firmly believed that a cup of (*caffeinated*) coffee helped him to get to sleep at night. And many smokers say they light up a cigarette (containing the stimulant nicotine) in order to relax. Thus while drugs may have certain effects on the average, our beliefs and expectations about these effects can often override the effects themselves.

Direct measurement of arousal. With advances in psychophysiological technology, Eysenck and his colleagues have tried to relate introversion-extraversion scores to direct electroencephalography (EEG, or brain-waves) measures of arousal. As noted above, higher levels of arousal are characterized by low-amplitude, high-frequency, irregular waves. According to the model, then, introverts should tend to have more brain waves of this pattern, while extraverts should show more of the high-amplitude alpha waves. In a review of EEG research, Gale (1983) found twenty-two studies supporting this general prediction; five that contradicted it (that is, where extraverts were more aroused); and eleven studies showing no EEG differences between introverts and extraverts. Gale noted that those studies in which the testing conditions themselves were moderately arousing almost always supported Eysenck's model, whereas studies in which the testing conditions were extremely arousing or not at all arousing did not. This suggests that strong situational conditions may override or wipe out any effects of introversion-extraversion.

Essentially the same results are obtained in studies using EDA methods (measuring electrical resistance and conductance of the skin): introverts are more aroused (or more arousable) than extraverts, especially under moderately arousing experimental conditions.

The general trend of these results suggests that introverts are more sensitive to most forms of stimulation. In some studies, this greater sensitivity can even be detected at the periphery (that is, in receptor cells of sense organs such as the ear or eye and in the first few synapses leading from these receptor cells toward the brain), as well as in the reticular formation or the cortex of the brain. However, studies using cardiac (heart-rate) measures of arousal have not found consistent introvert-extravert differences (Stelmack, 1990).

Biological Aspects of Neuroticism

While Eysenck's biological research has focused mainly on extraversion-introversion, he has speculated that neuroticism is related to the "visceral brain" or *limbic system* (Eysenck, 1967, pp. 234–235). As shown in Figure 14.5, the limbic system contains a number of structures—hippocampus, amygdala, cingulum, septum, and hypothalamus—that are both interconnected and connected to the rest of the brain in exquisitely complicated ways. All of these different structures are involved in *emotion*—the expression of emotions and the regulation of emotional behavior. The amygdala, for example, is said to be "the sensory gateway to the emotions. . . involved in the assigning of emotional significance to stimuli" (Zuckerman, 1991, p. 162). The septum may play a special role in the emotion of fear, since rats with septal lesions (surgical destruction of the septum) show fewer behavioral signs of fear. In humans, electrical stimulation of the cingulum often produces emotions, while surgical removal of the cingulum reduces various expressions of emotion—neuroticism scores, observer ratings of anxiety, and in some cases physiological responses to stress (Zuckerman, 1991, pp. 158 and 153, and chap. 4 generally).

Fahrenberg (1987, p. 101) reported some indirect evidence that neuroticism is linked to limbic system activity: people who score high in neuroticism report more fatigue, stress, and disturbances of body functions and lower levels of life satisfaction. These symptoms might be expected of people whose emotional engines work overtime and get in the way of a satisfying life. The link is further supported by Gray's (1981) analysis that neuroticism acts as an

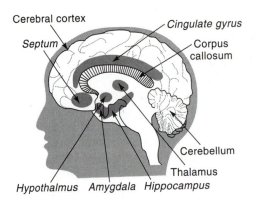

FIGURE 14.5
Diagram of the limbic system.

"amplifier" of people's characteristic emotional reactions to reward and punishment. That is, neuroticism intensifies introverts' sensitivity to punishment *and* extraverts' sensitivity to reward. Where a stable introvert would be cautious, a neurotic introvert would be paralyzed with fear; while a stable extravert would seek pleasure, a neurotic extravert would recklessly throw caution to the winds in the pursuit of the most improbable reward.

Unfortunately for the sake of Gray's model (which was based mostly on animal studies), research with humans has not shown any consistent correlation between neuroticism scores and any *direct* measures of limbic system functioning. In fact, there are no consistent relations between neuroticism and *any* other autonomic nervous system measure (Fahrenberg, 1987). Fahrenberg ended his review of this literature with an unusually blunt conclusion:

> Further use of emotionality (neuroticism) supposing a consistent psychophysiological basis would be misleading as this theoretical construct has not been sufficiently substantiated by empirical data. (p. 105)

While the hypothesis may be wrong, there are also many problems in carrying out research on the human limbic system. Limbic system activity is difficult to measure directly. Many measures are contaminated with the effects of general arousal (which is mediated by the reticular formation and therefore influenced by the person's level of introversion-extraversion). Moreover, it is difficult to design a laboratory experiment that would really engage people's neuroticism without creating a situation so stressful that it would violate ethical standards for human research. On the other hand, Fahrenberg's conclusion may be correct; as he suggested, neuroticism may represent a distinctive *labeling* of internal experience, rather than a physiologically distinctive experience itself (1987, pp. 115–117).

Eysenck and Eysenck (1985, pp. 294–299) suggest that neuroticism may affect the *efficiency* of behavior rather than its overall effectiveness. That is, people scoring high in neuroticism can often achieve the same levels of performance as more stable people, but only at a much greater cost in terms of the resources they need and the effort they spend. On a task involving the muscles, for example, high neuroticism scorers tense more muscles for a longer time than is necessary. On verbal and symbolic tasks, they use more of their processing and storage capacity; thus they have less of a reserve available for doing other things. In other words, while people scoring high in neuroticism can do one thing pretty well, their performance really breaks down when they have to do two or more things at once.

Biological Aspects of Psychoticism

We must approach studies of the biological basis of psychoticism with some caution, remembering some of the issues raised in Chapter 13 about the Eysenck psychoticism measure. It may capture some essential features of some psychoses, it may simply reflect superficial ways in which some normal people resemble some psychotics, or it may measure the predisposition among normal people to develop psychosis (for example, schizotypy, or a tendency toward schizophrenic thought but not actual schizophrenia). Recently Eysenck has even described psychoticism as "emotional independence" versus "superego control" (1990, p. 245), which raises the possibility that the scale points toward the antisocial or sociopathic personality rather than the psychotic or delusional personality. Until the nature of the psychoticism scale is clarified, we cannot be sure that its biological bases (if any) have anything to do with the biological bases of psychoses.

After reviewing the evidence on psychosis, psychoticism, and physiology, Claridge (1987) came to two conclusions. First, research on every conceivable biological aspect of only one of the psychoses—schizophrenia—has demonstrated mainly that schizophrenics are a very heterogeneous group. Differences between schizophrenics and normals emerging in one study often reverse in the next study. Indeed, these patterns of heterogeneity and conflicting results have led some theorists to question whether schizophrenia is a single entity or instead a catchall word for several quite different conditions. Second, research studies showed no distinctive physiological or arousal measures associated with psychoticism.

However, Claridge did find evidence in the literature for distinctive *patterns of covariation* of physiological measures among people scoring high and low in psychoticism (see also Eysenck, 1990, pp. 267–268). That is, the measures showed one pattern of intercorrelation among normals and people scoring low in psychoticism and quite a different pattern among schizophrenics and people scoring high in psychoticism. In other words, one important physiological feature of both psychosis and psychoticism may involve the *pattern* of relationships among variables rather than the absolute level of any particular variable. Claridge calls this difference in patterning in psychosis a "dysregulation" of the nervous system.

When I first read Claridge's 1987 article, I remembered a story that Gordon Allport told in one of my graduate school classes. Back in the early 1930s, Allport had collaborated with Philip Vernon in a study of styles of expressive movement (Allport & Vernon, 1933). Although they found some interesting patterns among different measures of expressive movement, many correlations were considerably reduced by the scores of just one person. Shortly after the study was completed, Allport told us, that person was diagnosed as schizophrenic. "Could it be," Allport went on to ask, "that the breakdown of patterns in a person's expressive movements is an early sign of the breakdown of the personality?" Claridge's review, suggesting that schizophrenia and psychoticism involve a different pattern of relationships among physiological variables, is certainly consistent with Allport's speculation.

NEUROPSYCHOPHARMACOLOGICAL MODELS

Neurochemical Pathways

In constructing arousal models of extraversion-introversion, Eysenck and his colleagues seem to have an image of the brain and nervous system as a vast electrical switchboard, wired to sense organs and muscles. In recent years, however, biopsychologists have begun to think of the brain and nervous system in more complicated ways, as a series of many different *chemically defined* neural pathways (linked networks of nerve cells). This emerging field has sometimes been given the rather forbidding name of *neuropsychopharmacology*, because it focuses on the ways in which chemicals in the nervous system act to produce effects on behavior. While the field is still in its infancy, researchers have high hopes of discovering even more basic biological foundations of personality traits.

We can grasp the general principles of neuropsychopharmacology by considering one particular neural pathway, the noradrenergic system, which is involved in arousal. (What follows is a highly simplified account, based on Zuckerman, 1991, chap. 5. If you are interested in more detail, you can consult this or a similar source.) From introductory psychology, you probably remember that impulses or "messages" are transmitted electrically within the individual nerve cell (or neuron). Between neurons, however, there is a gap, or *synapse.* Impulses are transmitted across this gap by chemicals called *neurotransmitters.* They are released by the first (presynaptic) neuron, move across the synapse, and then activate the electrical impulse again in the second (postsynaptic) neuron. While there are many different kinds of neurotransmitters, norepinephrine predominates in the noradrenergic system. Norepinephrine is constantly being produced and depleted at each synapse in the noradrenergic pathway, but over time a delicate balance must be maintained: either too much or too little norepinephrine would disrupt normal neural functioning and thus behavior. After it has been used at the synapse, therefore, norepinephrine is either recycled or else removed from the synapse by enzymes such as monoamine oxidase (MAO) and others. MAO activity, in turn, is either enhanced or blocked by other neurochemicals present in the synapse region.

Even this simple example shows the complexity of neuropsychopharmacology, because the ultimate message transmitted along the noradrenergic pathway, which at the behavioral level will result in arousal, can be affected by each of the following seven classes of neurochemical:

1. Norepinephrine (the neurotransmitter itself)

2. The many precursor chemicals involved in the manufacture of norepinephrine (and the precursors of these precursors)

3. Any chemicals that block norepinephrine

4. Chemicals involved in recycling norepinephrine

5. The MAO enzymes that remove norepinephrine

6. Precursor chemicals of MAO enzymes

7. Chemicals that block MAO enzymes (MAO inhibitors)

To add to the complexity, some substances (such as dopamine) are both neurotransmitters in their own right and also precursors to the formation of other neurotransmitters. Furthermore, most of these eight classes of chemicals can also be enhanced or blocked by various other chemicals, including both naturally occurring hormones and drugs.

Thus the overall functioning and contribution to behavior of any particular neural pathway are very complicated, since they depend on levels and interactions of so many different chemicals. Since it is difficult to measure and track many of these chemicals in people, researchers usually have to rely on measuring their traces, products, and metabolites in blood, spinal fluid, or urine. You can imagine, therefore, how hard it is to establish any firm conclusions in the field of neuropsychopharmacology!

So far as mapping detailed relations between neurochemistry and behavior traits goes, neuropsychopharmacology has only made a beginning. In the next few years we may expect more research, some advances, considerable controversy, and revised theories and models. Meanwhile, Zuckerman (1991, chap. 5, especially pp. 224–225) has summarized some important results to date, as shown in Table 14.1. For example, across different theories and studies there is agreement that the *dopamine system* enhances extraverted behavior and

TABLE 14.1 SUMMARY OF CURRENT THEORIES OF THE NEUROCHEMICAL BASIS OF TRAIT-RELATED BEHAVIORS

	Trait dimension		
Neurochemical system or pathway	*Extraversion*	*Neuroticism*	*Psychoticism*
Catecholamine systems			
Norepinephrine	Enhances	(?)	
MAO enzyme	Reduces		Reduces
Dopamine	Enhances		Enhances (?)
Indoleamine system			
Serotonin		Enhances	Reduces

SOURCE: Based on Zuckerman (1991, chap. 5 and pp. 224–225).

(possibly) psychoticism, while the *serotonin system* enhances anxiety and neuroticism and may reduce psychoticism. The role of the *norepinephrine system* is less clear, although the MAO enzyme, which removes norepinephrine from the synapse, appears to reduce both extraversion and psychoticism. But even this summary is much too simple: in all likelihood, traits and behavior are the result of complex interactions and balances among these and other neurochemical systems or pathways.

Cloninger's Theory: Dopamine, Serotonin, and Norepinephrine Pathways

Cloninger (1986, 1991) has proposed a comprehensive theory linking brain chemistry and trait factors. He begins by separating the observed factor structure of trait-related behaviors from the underlying chemical-physiological structure of traits. Because of the modifying effects of experience and the environment, he argues, they may not be the same. Rather than beginning with behavior and working inward toward physiology (as did Eysenck), Cloninger began by examining three major chemically defined pathways linking several brain structures. Each pathway is governed or modulated by a specific neurotransmitter: dopamine, serotonin, or norepinephrine. Drawing on a wide variety of studies, he proposed that each pathway is related to a fundamental brain-behavioral system and thus to a corresponding cluster of personality traits. As shown in Table 14.2, the dopamine pathway involves the behavioral activation system, which appears as *novelty-seeking* behavior. The serotonin pathway regulates behavioral inhibition, which is expressed as a tendency toward *harm-avoidance*. Finally, the norepinephrine pathway governs behavioral maintenance, or *reward-dependence*.

TABLE 14.2 CLONINGER'S THEORY OF PERSONALITY TRAITS AND CHEMICALLY DEFINED NEURAL PATHWAYS

Personality dimension	Principal neurochemical modulator	Brain system	Correlation of Tridimensional Personality Questionnaire dimension with Eysenck measure		
			Extraversion	Neuroticism	Psychoticism
Novelty seeking	Dopamine	Behavioral activation	.32	.28	.12
Harm-avoidance	Serotonin	Behavioral inhibition	−.60	.55	−.02
Reward-dependence	Norepinephrine	Behavioral maintenance	.09	.26	.02

SOURCE: Based on Cloninger (1986, 1991).

Having constructed his theory on the basis of distinct neurochemical pathways, Cloninger then developed a Tridimensional Personality Questionnaire to measure the behavioral expression of these three dimensions (Cloninger, Przybeck, & Svrakic, 1991). Although he refined the questionnaire by means of factor analysis, he was more concerned with the theoretical meaningfulness of the factors than with their strict independence or orthogonality. Therefore he employed oblique rotation (see Chapter 13), which means that the three factors are somewhat correlated. As shown in Table 14.2, all three dimensions are somewhat related to extraversion and neuroticism. In fact, the first two dimensions—novelty seeking and harm-avoidance—are similar to Gray's factors of impulsivity (neurotic extraversion, in Eysenck's terms) and anxiety (neurotic introversion), respectively (see also Figure 13.2).

Given the complexity and difficulty of relating brain functions to personality variables, progress in neuropsychopharmacology research is difficult. So far, Cloninger's work is interesting and promising, though not without its problems and critics (for example, Gray, 1987). For the moment, an attitude of interest tempered with caution seems appropriate.

A BRIEF EXCURSION: PERSONALITY AND BLOOD TYPES

One other possible biological basis of traits—blood type—deserves a brief mention. To many people, the idea that people's blood type could reflect their personality seems absurd, but this idea is taken very seriously by Eysenck. And in Japan, blood type is an established part of popular culture. For example, a magazine article containing personality sketches of teenagers might include their blood types along with their heights and weights, hobbies, fashion preferences, and favorite foods ("Teen Tokyo," 1992)—just as similar American magazine sketches might include zodiac signs. Potential lovers check on how well their blood types match, and some employers are said to recruit by blood type ("Japan's Success?" 1985, p. 45).

Table 14.3 summarizes two kinds of more formal research studies about personality traits and blood types: correlations of trait scores with blood type among individuals, and comparisons across nations of the incidence of different blood types with the average extraversion, neuroticism, and psychoticism scores of samples tested from that country (cited by Eysenck & Eysenck, 1985, pp. 109–111; and Eysenck, 1990, pp. 263–264).

Looking at the bottom of the table, you can compare these research results with the conclusions of a best-selling Japanese book, *Advice on How to Form a Good Combination of Blood Types*, by Toshitaka Nomi (see "Fate Is Not in the Stars," 1985; "Japan's Success?" 1985; Mangnall, 1984). If people that Nomi calls "creative" and "independent" can be said to be high in neuroticism and psychoticism, then there is some agreement between popular lore and Eysenck's conclusions about blood type B, but the popular description of blood type A seems to be contradicted by the research reported by Eysenck. Even if some of these connections turn out to be true, though, I know of no

TABLE 14.3 BLOOD TYPES AND ASSOCIATED PERSONALITY TRAITS

	Blood type		
A	*B*	*AB*	*O*
*Traits per individual and cross-national research**			
Low neuroticism	High neuroticism	Low extraversion	
	High psychoticism		
Traits per popular Japanese characterizations[†]			
Industrious	Creative	Two-faced	Aggressive
Image-conscious	Independent	Moody	Realistic
People-loving	Self-assertive	Seeks consensus	Astute about power
Perfectionist	Craves freedom		Cautious about making friends
Susceptible to stress			

*As cited by Eysenck and Eysenck (1985, pp. 109–111) and Eysenck (1990, pp. 263–264).
[†]Based on *Advice on How to Form a Good Combination of Blood Types,* by Toshitaka Nomi (as cited by "Fate Is Not in the Stars," 1985; "Japan's success?" 1985; Mangnall, 1984).

mechanisms that could explain them. (Remember that the four familiar types of A, B, AB, and O are only broad groupings: there are really 240 different blood types.)

SO IS THERE A BIOLOGICAL BASIS OF TRAITS?

From Excitement to Disappointment

No doubt you have observed a pattern repeated in most of the sections of this chapter. I have described research results as "complex," "subtle," "complicated and variable," "inconsistent," or even "nonexistent." Often we have seen researchers start out with high hopes, only to end up confused and even discouraged. At an early stage, for example, Eysenck and Eysenck described EEG findings about arousal and introversion-extraversion with real excitement: "If these findings can be replicated, then we are well on the way to understanding the underlying physiological basis of individual differences in extraversion" (1985, p. 227). After a few years comes a qualification—"later studies show a slightly more complicated picture" (Eysenck, 1990, p. 261)—and sometimes a retreat: "Studies within the normal population have not been successful in giving support to the theory linking N[euroticism] with psychophysiological measures of activation" (p. 266). To at least one reviewer, the whole effort has simply failed (Gormly, 1985):

> The idea that individual differences in personality are rooted in physiological structures and functioning is a bewitching one, and it is a central tenet for the modern personality theories of Eysenck. . . . Despite a myriad of empirical studies. . . . there are no data that clearly support this viewpoint. (p. 393)

Given this repeated pattern, you may wonder about the prospects for establishing any secure links between biology and personality. We must never lose sight of the complexity of the human body and especially the brain and nervous system. If you have studied other sciences, you know that most apparently simple scientific laws really conceal enormous complexity, as in subatomic physics, genetics, or physiology. It would be unreasonable, therefore, to expect things to be different with brain-personality relationships. Often confusion reigns until some scientist hits upon the right approach, as did Dimitri Mendeleyev in chemistry, with the periodic table of elements, or Gregor Mendel in genetics. Perhaps the recent focus on neurochemical pathways will turn out to be the royal road to the biological roots of personality traits, or perhaps we must wait for some other approach.

Causality between Biology and Personality

The search for the biological basis of personality usually implies that biological factors are the fundamental causes and that personality traits are the effects of these causes. Yet there is evidence that the direction of causation does not always run from biology to personality. Sometimes personality, behavior, or situational factors can bring about changes in biological factors. Often causal relations are reciprocal or circular. For example, it is possible to change people's extraversion. Turnbull (1976) found that spending three months selling books door-to-door during the summer significantly increased the extraversion scores of male college students. Other experiences that increase extraversion include practice in transcendental meditation (Turnbull & Norris, 1982) and, for male drug offenders, an extended 6- to 12-month stay in a residential therapeutic community (Wilson & Kennard, 1978).

There is also evidence from animal studies that situations and behaviors have direct effects on physiological processes. For example, levels of the male hormone testosterone seem to cause certain kinds of aggression in many species; but several studies suggest that the relationship can also work the other way around. Bernstein, Gordon, and Rose (1983) found that among monkeys, victories in fights to establish dominance led to increased testosterone levels, while defeats led to drastically lower levels. In the African cichlid fish, Davis and Fernald (1990) found that certain brain cells in the hypothalamus that are related to the production of sexual hormones grow or shrink *as a result of* whether fish grow up surrounded by same-age and same-size fish or by older and larger fish, respectively. (There were also similar differences between the two groups in size of testes, but no differences in overall size or brain size.) Further work by Francis, Soma, and Fernald (1993) demonstrates that this relationship can be experimentally manipulated and reversed in adult male fish. When they changed "dominant" fish into "nondominant" fish (and vice versa) over a four-week time span by altering the social environment, they found that the fishes' brain cells and testes changed size accordingly.

Studies of humans also demonstrate that the relationship between behavior and physiology runs in both directions. For example, Baxter and colleagues (1992) studied two groups of people suffering from obsessive-compulsive disorder (obsessive, unwanted thoughts and compulsive rituals). One group was treated with the drug Prozac, and the other group with behavior therapy. After ten weeks, most patients in each group showed reduced symptoms. Baxter and colleagues also used PET scans to study brain functioning before and after therapy. The scans were focused especially on the head of the right caudate nucleus, which is thought to be part of a brain circuit underlying obsessive-compulsive disorder. In *both* the Prozac and the behavior therapy groups, responders to treatment showed significantly less activity in the right caudate nucleus region.

The field of psychosomatic medicine provides further evidence of the reciprocal effects of personality and physiology on each other. (Recall from Chapter 5 the connections McClelland found between stressed power motivation, sympathetic nervous system functioning, and the immune system.) Mathew, Ho, Taylor, and Semchuk (1981) found that a four-week relaxation therapy treatment reduced both anxiety and MAO enzyme levels in anxiety-disorder patients. Benson's popular book, *The Relaxation Response* (1975), illustrates how meditation-like practices can affect blood pressure and health. Earlier, studies by Zimbardo (1969) and his associates showed that people's cognitions (for example, specific causal attributions) can affect appetite, pain, and a variety of other bodily functions.

Some of the most vivid human evidence for the reversibility or circularity of the biology-personality relationship comes from the study of cases of multiple personality disorder (MPD). Different "alters" (the term for the different personalities of an MPD case) show differences in autonomic nervous system activity (Putnam, 1984; Putnam, Zahn, & Post, 1990), visual acuity (Miller, 1989), and even allergic reactions (Braun, 1983). Hypnosis can also produce alterations in autonomic functioning. While many of these findings are based on case studies, the growing recognition that physiology-behavior relations are a two-way street, or even a circular pathway, should prompt more systematic and controlled research.

GENETICS AND PERSONALITY

Since our biological structures and functioning are strongly influenced by our genetic makeup, any biological basis of personality traits should also be reflected in a genetic influence on personality. Just looking at personality resemblances among family members to establish a genetic contribution to personality (or intelligence, or anything else) won't do, however, because family members share environments as well as genes. For example, I am a professor. Among my parents, my brother, my paternal aunts, uncles, and cousins (going back to my paternal grandfather), almost everyone who worked outside the home either was a teacher, was certified to be a teacher, or at least spent some time teaching. Nor is my case all that unusual; even with rapid change and social mobility, many children enter the same occupations as their parents. For me, then, teaching may "run in the family"; but this is undoubtedly due to the environment of my grandfather's household, rather than any peculiar family genes. (A generation earlier, my great-grandfather was a blacksmith!)

Measuring the Genetic Contribution to Personality

Since family members share some of the same genes and much of the same environment, how can we untangle the relative contributions of genes and environment to personality? One strategy involves studying twins. Identical twins (that is, monozygotic, or MZ, twins) develop from a single fertilized egg and so have exactly the same genes. (Strictly speaking, they have *almost* the same genes; there may be mutations after the first cell division.) Fraternal, or dyzygotic (DZ), twins, on the other hand, develop from two fertilized eggs and so have only 50 percent genetic overlap (on average), the same as any two siblings. In measuring a personality trait among pairs of twins, if we observe higher correlations among the MZ pairs than among the DZ pairs, then we might conclude that the trait in question had some genetic basis or *heritability*: the larger the difference between the MZ and DZ correlations, the larger the heritability. (The same procedures are used to estimate the genetic contribution to intelligence, schizophrenia, and any other psychological characteristic.)

Of course, there are a few technical points to keep in mind. Zygosity (that is, whether two twins are MZ or DZ) must be carefully determined with complex procedures; mere "looking alike" is not enough (see Plomin, DeFries, & McClearn, 1990, pp. 313–315). One currently preferred method is the count of fingerprint ridges (see Zuckerman, 1991, p. 101). Nevertheless, one twin study has rather surprisingly relied only on "questions concerning similarity as adults" to establish zygosity (Pederson, Plomin, McClearn, & Friberg, 1988, p. 951). And since MZ twins are always of the same sex, only same-sex DZ twins should be used for comparison (though a twin study by Tellegen, Lykken, Bouchard, Wilcox, Segal, and Rich, 1988, seems to have violated this precaution; see p. 1033). Finally, there are several different ways of calculating estimates of heritability from the patterns of correlations (see Zuckerman, 1991, chap. 3, for details).

Studies of twins reared together. Table 14.4 brings together the results of several studies of the heritability of extraversion, neuroticism, and psychoticism (based on Zuckerman, 1991, pp. 97, 102, 107, and 109). On each dimension, the correlations are between 20 and 35 points higher for identical twins than for fraternals. Depending on the method used to calculate heritability, this would give heritability estimates of between 40 and 70 percent. (Bergeman and colleagues, 1993, report heritability data on the other three of the Big Five factors: openness to experience, agreeableness, and conscientiousness.)

TABLE 14.4 HERITABILITY OF PERSONALITY TRAIT DIMENSIONS IN TWINS REARED TOGETHER IN THEIR BIRTH FAMILY

	Correlations for extraversion		Correlations for neuroticism		Correlations for psychoticism	
	MZ twins	DZ twins	MZ twins	DZ twins	MZ twins	DZ twins
Median correlations	.54	.19	.46	.22	.56	.27
Heritability estimates*	49%–54%		41%–48%		46%–59%	

*Based on different studies and calculation methods (see Zuckerman, 1991, chap. 3).
SOURCE: Based on Zuckerman (1991, pp. 97, 99).

Interpreting heritability estimates. What do the figures of Table 14.4 mean? They mean that, on the average and (only) across the populations studied, between 40 and 70 percent of variability on these dimensions is contributed by genetic factors. They do *not* mean that your own extraversion or neuroticism score is 40 to 70 percent inherited from your parents. They do *not* mean that 40 to 70 percent of the difference in extraversion, neuroticism, or psychoticism between you and someone else is genetic. Nor do they mean that any person's scores are 40 to 70 percent fixed, unchangeable, or inevitable. Heritability estimates are *only* meaningful with respect to groups—more specifically, the particular groups and particular environmental conditions studied. Change the group or environmental conditions, and the resulting heritability estimates may change.

Further—and most important—these figures do *not* mean that 40 to 70 percent of the differences between groups is based on genes. For example, samples of Australian men score quite high in psychoticism (average = 8.41) compared to samples of Spanish men (average = 3.14; see Barrett & Eysenck, 1984). While the data reported in Table 14.4 suggest that psychoticism may have a genetic component ranging as high as 50 percent, it does *not* follow that 50 percent of the Australian-Spanish male difference is due to genetic differences between Australian and Spanish males.

Why not? For one thing, genetic variation *within* human populations is much greater—perhaps up to twelve times greater—than genetic variation between populations (Tooby & Cosmides, 1990, pp. 34–35; Zuckerman, 1990, pp. 1299–1300). That is, you and a person sitting next to you in class are probably as different, genetically, as you and any particular person from the other side of the world. (What do you think might happen if Serbs and Croats, or Israelis and Arabs—or white Americans and black Americans—took that fact seriously?)

Genotype and phenotype. Even more important is the difference between *genotype* (the actual "gene") and *phenotype* (the behavior, intelligence, or other characteristic that we observe). This difference can best be explained with an analogy. Consider two fields planted with a genetically identical variety of corn. The corn in both fields should grow to the same height—but only under similar growing conditions. If one field is given adequate water and the other is not, then the corn in the first field will grow significantly taller on average, even though it is genetically identical to the corn in the second field. Now consider two fields, each planted with strains of corn that are genetically different, such that one strain normally grows 2 feet higher. If the "shorter" variety of corn is given more water and sunlight, then it may grow as tall as the "taller" variety. In other words, given only two fields of corn that are either different *or* the same in height, we cannot conclude *anything* about the role of genes. What we see—the height of corn—is only the phenotype, not necessarily the genotype. Genes contribute only *potential;* their *expression* always involves other factors.

The Australian and Spanish male psychoticism scores are also phenotypes: many other differences (history, geography, economy, and religion) undoubtedly play a role similar to that of sunlight and rainfall with corn. These differences could *completely* account for the difference in psychoticism scores, *even though* there may be a genetic component to psychoticism. We will explore this theme further in Part Four when we consider the influence of social context on personality.

Sometimes a heritability estimate of 40 to 70 percent is consistent with *no* genetic contribution at all! Consider the "trait" of hair length, as discussed by Jencks (1987; see also Jencks, 1980):

> In our society, variation in hair length is largely attributable to the fact that some people have their hair cut shorter than others. In most cases, moreover, men cut their hair shorter than women. This means that if you are born with two X chromosomes [female], your hair usually ends up longer than if you are born with an X and a Y chromosome [male]. *In a statistical sense,* therefore, the presence or absence of an X chromosome predicts much of the variation in hair length—let us say 60 percent. (p. 34, emphasis added)

Genetic factors (X versus Y chromosome) certainly do not affect hair length directly. Rather, their influence is indirect, mediated completely by the environment (customs and norms about men's and women's hair length). In this case, *despite* the "estimate" of 60 percent heritability, the environment really explains 100 percent of the variation. (In the late 1960s, men suddenly started wearing their hair longer and women wore theirs shorter. X and Y chromosomes were no obstacle to rapid change of the phenotype!) Tooby and Cosmides (1990, pp. 58–59) give a similar example regarding the trait of aggressiveness: its heritability (as estimated by the MZ-DZ comparisons) may actually be only apparent, the result of truly heritable differences in other characteristics such as *size* or muscle mass. Size is not aggressiveness, but it is relevant to the observable *expression* of aggressiveness.

If you think further about these examples, you will understand that within-population estimates of the genetic contribution to intelligence (or criminality, or sexuality) do not necessarily have anything to do with average group differences in these characteristics. But prejudiced people, from slave owners to the many avid readers of the latest "data" on race or gender differences, have always been quick to seize upon such differences to support their theories and justify their oppression of some group. This is why research on genetic and biological aspects of personality, as well as group differences in personality, should always be carried out *and interpreted* with extreme caution. (See Rushton, 1989, and Zuckerman & Brody, 1989, for a debate on studies of group differences and heritability in personality.)

The environment of twins. If you have ever known a set of identical twins, you may have read the discussion of Table 14.4 with some skepticism. Using studies of identical versus fraternal twins to make inferences about heritability requires us to make the rather strong assumption that the environments of identical twins are not more similar than the environments of same-sex fraternal twins. (This assumption is necessary because more similar environments would be an alternative explanation of the higher MZ correlations in Table 14.4.) Is such an assumption reasonable? Surely two people who look so much alike that even their parents sometimes cannot tell them apart—who may have been dressed alike as children and are treated alike by teachers and peers—have experienced more similar environments than two people who happen to be born of the same mother at the same time but do not necessarily look alike.

It is difficult to imagine how we could fully test the assumption that MZ environments are not more similar than DZ environments, since "similar" and "environment" are subtle and slippery concepts. Even so, with relatively crude measures, Loehlin and Nichols (1976, p. 51) found direct evidence that identical twins are treated more similarly than fraternals. Plomin, Chipuer, and Loehlin (1990, pp. 232–233) drew the same conclusion from internal analyses of twin study data. Moreover, identical twins are also more likely to influence each other than are fraternals (Jencks, 1987), an aspect of the "environment" that is even more difficult to measure. Still, the importance of possible greater MZ environment similarity as a source of bias in estimating heritability has been disputed (Plomin, DeFries, & McClearn, 1990, pp. 315–319).

A related problem is the fact that identical twins often maintain closer relationships with each other and interact more frequently from childhood onward (Rose, Koskenvuo, Kaprio, Sarna, & Langinvainio, 1988). Rose and associates also found that among all twins, frequency of interaction is associated with greater trait similarity. Thus the more extensive and intense social contact of MZ twins could inflate the correlation of trait scores above the actual contribution of genetic effects. (Of course the relationship may run in the opposite direction: greater "similarity," perhaps based on genetic factors, may lead to more frequent social interaction.)

Studies of twins reared apart and adoption studies. To overcome problems associated with the assumption that MZ environments are not more similar, personality researchers have studied MZ and DZ twins who were reared apart. Here the assumption is that identical twins, separated shortly after birth, will not have more similar environments than fraternal twins who are also separated shortly after birth. Hence higher trait correlations among identical twins would be uncontaminated evidence for a genetic contribution. Although this assumption seems reasonable, I know of no studies that specifically support it. We must remember that children who are raised apart from their birth family have been placed, for adoption or in a foster home, by some private or public agency. If these agencies have either deliberate or unconscious policies of matching children to environments, or selecting more similar placements for identical twins, then even these reared-apart estimates would not be free from contamination.

Moreover, even twins who were reared apart, usually spend some time together before separation. In the studies by Pederson, Plomin, McClearn, and Friberg (1988) and Tellegen and associates (1988), 48 percent and 97 percent, respectively, were separated by age 1. It is difficult to know what long-range effects this initial dose of shared environment may have had. The same considerations apply to studies comparing nontwin adopted children to their biological parents or siblings versus their adoptive parents or siblings.

Table 14.5 summarizes results of recent major studies of twins reared apart and of adoptive children compared to birth and adoptive parents and siblings. For each of the three trait dimensions, estimates of heritability are a little lower

TABLE 14.5 HERITABILITY OF PERSONALITY TRAIT DIMENSIONS IN TWINS REARED APART

	Correlations for extraversion		Correlations for neuroticism		Correlations for psychoticism	
	MZ twins	DZ twins	MZ twins	DZ twins	MZ twins	DZ twins
Twins reared together and apart						
Mean correlations						
Reared together	.63	.18	.48	.33	.43	.17
Reared apart	.32	−.02	.43	.29	.39	.11
Mean heritability estimates	40%–41%		31%–55%		23%–58%	
Studies of biological versus adoptive relations						
Heritability estimates*						
Based on parents	. . . . 22%					
Based on siblings	. . . . 26%					

*Study cited by Zuckerman (1991, p. 109) .
SOURCE: Based on Zuckerman (1991, pp. 102, 109).

than those based on twins reared together reported in Table 14.4. In explanation of these differences, Plomin, Chipuer, and Loehlin suggested that estimates from twin studies are mostly inflated by the more similar environments of identical twins (1990, pp. 228–232).

Are there any traits with little or no demonstrated genetic basis? Even with all of the cautions and reservations given above, I think there is clear evidence that the three major trait dimensions of extraversion, neuroticism, and psychoticism each have genetic components of between 20 and 50 percent. Since these heritability estimates for all three dimensions, from all three kinds of studies, are in the same range, you may wonder whether there are traits that do *not* have a genetic basis. Reviewing the evidence, Zuckerman (1991, p. 120) found that traits such as stereotyped masculinity, intolerance of ambiguity, religious orthodoxy, and intellectual interests show little heritability and much higher environmental influence. To this list Plomin, Chipuer, and Loehlin (1990, pp. 231, 240) added the following: the hostility and assertiveness aspects of Type A behavior, belief in "luck" as the cause of events, the agreeableness factor of the Big Five, and delinquency. Notice how as we move from broad trait factors or dimensions down to more specific traits and interests, the influence of genes seems to go down and the influence of environment goes up.

The environment. What exactly is the "environment"? At present, there is disagreement among behavior geneticists about whether the important aspects of the environment are those shared within the family (Rose et al., 1988), those idiosyncratic to individuals and not shared within the family (Tellegen et al., 1988), or those that involve broad cultural trends or the shared experiences of a generation (Price, Vandenberg, Iyer, & Williams, 1982). The concept of "non-shared environment" is used by behavior geneticists, though, in a special and restricted sense. Families are small-scale social systems; each member affects the other. If you have siblings, you will realize immediately that parents treat different children differently, that siblings develop patterns of interaction, and that families as a whole develop structures in which different children assume different roles. Thus the family environment will be experienced as different for each child, even though the family as a whole forms a coherent social system and environment. These different environments would be counted as "non-shared" environment effects by behavior geneticists, but they are clearly *family* environmental effects, based on the family as a unit of living and rearing.

Are Heritability Estimates Reliable?

Twin studies using subjects of different ages often give different heritability estimates. These differences are usually interpreted as showing that certain traits are under greater genetic control at one age than at another (Zuckerman, 1991, pp. 97, 99, 110–119), for reasons having to do with developmental stages and differential influence of the environment. Because of the obvious difficulty of recontacting and following up groups of twins over a period of years, however, psychologists have rarely studied the same group of twins twice. Thus the twelve-year follow-up study of forty-two pairs of twins by Dworkin, Burke, Maher, and Gottesman (1976), is one of the few longitudinal investigations of heritability spanning the years from adolescence (age 16) to adulthood (age 28). Dworkin and associates administered the Minnesota Multiphasic Personality Inventory (MMPI) and the California Personality Inventory (CPI) at both times and found that only a few variables showed significant heritability at both ages. CPI scales measuring sociability (extraversion?) and achievement, and MMPI scales measuring psychopathology (psychoticism?) showed heritability in adolescence but not adulthood. (That is, DZ twins became more similar on these variables as they got older.) CPI and MMPI scales reflecting well-being and emotional stability (low neuroticism?) showed heritability at adulthood but not adolescence. (DZ twins became less similar.) Almost half the scales showed no significant heritability at either time.

One interpretation of these results involves the concept of changing genotype-environment interactions: As we become adults, our environment changes in ways that permit fuller expression of our "genetic" neuroticism but suppress (or override) expression of our "genetic" extraversion and psychoticism. However, another interpretation is simply that these results show temporal instability, perhaps resulting from some of the methodological problems with twin studies, as discussed above. (As you might expect, behavior geneticists rarely acknowledge this latter interpretation, at least in print!)

Inconsistency among Different Heritability Estimates

The conclusion that the three major trait dimensions have some genetic basis has been challenged on other grounds. Price, Vandenberg, Iyer, and Williams (1982), for example, combined two methods of estimating heritability of personality—correlations between MZ and DZ twins and correlations among different degrees of relationship in families—by studying twins *and* their relatives (parents, cousins, spouses, offspring, etc.). Their results were different from what would be expected on the basis of research in which only twins were studied. That is, given the MZ-DZ differences, the correlations among other pairs of relatives should have been higher than they in fact were. Across the two methods, they found almost *no* simple additive genetic effects and only moderate nonadditive genetic effects (that is, complex interactions among genes) on personality. Price and colleagues concluded (1982):

> Personality traits seem to be influenced primarily by the environment, especially influences outside the home. Genetic influences, to the extent that they are indicated at all, are confounded with cultural factors. (p. 328)[2]

---

[2]Rice, Cloninger, and Reich (1980) suggest statistical models to untangle the additive genetic, cultural, environmental, and interactive effects.

What Is It That Is Inherited?

Twin studies give *estimates* of the heritability of trait dimensions, but when we say a trait is "inherited," what exactly do we mean? Often we think of traits as clusters of social behaviors, because they are usually measured with questionnaire items referring to such behaviors. But these are not what is inherited. When we say something is inherited or genetic, we can only mean that which is biologically transmitted from one generation to the next. That can only be DNA, the basic genetic material. To be precise, what is inherited is a code—a sequence of positions in a lengthy DNA strand, with each position having one of four different pairs of chemicals. In the course of development before and after birth, this code calls forth structures and hormones that, *in interaction with our environment*, develop into all the systems that regulate every aspect of our body and behavior. Only DNA—the genotype—is inherited; everything else emerges from the interaction of this inheritance with environments.

This point can be illustrated by a recent study (Plomin, Corley, DeFries, & Fulker, 1990) which purports to demonstrate a genetic contribution—perhaps 11 percent—to the amount of time young children spend watching television (see also Prescott, Johnson, & McArdle, 1991). This figure certainly does not mean that there is a "television-watching" (or "couch potato") gene. Television has only been around for a little more than fifty years, less than a microsecond in evolutionary time. However, as a complex phenotype, television watching may be an expression of certain other temperamental or trait variables such as passivity, receptivity to novel stimuli, low attention span, or even intelligence (high or low, depending on what you think of television content). However, Plomin and associates (1990) tried to identify such mediating factors and found none. They concluded that "genetic mechanisms have not as yet been uncovered for *any* complex behavioral traits, including cognitive abilities and personality" (p. 376). And so in the end even this fascinating result warns us that we really know much less than we sometimes might think about personality, biology, and genetics.

Overall, the behavior genetics of personality is a forest still shrouded in considerable fog. Researchers have moved through it along several different paths, guided by different compasses or statistical models, each involving assumptions that have not always been carefully examined. We have certainly made progress, but we are far from being out of the woods yet.

I want to suggest one additional problem with twins and adoptions, the two major ways we study heritability. Twins and adoptions are more than a mere reshuffling of genes and environments; they are also *cognitive* and *social* phenomena, associated in almost every culture with powerful beliefs, expectations, customs, stereotypes, and superstitions (see, for example, Burlingham, 1946, and Lash, 1993; and remember the story of *Cinderella*). It would be surprising if genetic effects were not modified—in some cases, perhaps, even swamped—by these powerful cognitive and cultural factors. Yet few behavior genetics researchers give serious attention to them.

PERSONALITY AND HUMAN EVOLUTION

The physiological, neuropsychopharmacological, and genetic evidence we have reviewed in this chapter points toward *some* biological influence on many trait dimensions, though the exact nature and extent of that influence is not clear. To some extent, then, these traits are part of our biological human nature. Evolutionary theory holds that the distinctive features of *physical* human nature—for example, upright posture, enlarged cerebral cortex, and capacity for language—have developed by small increments over hundreds of thousands of years because of the selective advantage they gave our ancestors. Ever since Darwin proposed the theory of evolution, scholars have tried to apply it to the social sciences, including in recent years the field of *evolutionary psychology* (D. Buss, 1984, 1991b; Tooby & Cosmides, 1990).

Evolutionary Success

To evaluate how an evolutionary perspective can contribute to an understanding of traits and personality, we must first consider the meaning of the term *selective advantage*. Charles Darwin's original phrase was "survival of the fittest," but this is misleading. What is important is not how long an individual organism lives, but how many offspring it produces, how many offspring these offspring produce, how many offspring the offspring of these offspring produce, and so on. That is, it is the genes, rather than the organism, that survive. This survival, often called "reproductive success," involves mating, conception, and birth; but for those animals (like ourselves) who invest a lot of care in our relatively few offspring, the story of reproductive success does not end with birth of offspring. The young must be nursed (among all mammals), protected, and guided until maturity; they must want to become adults; and as adults they must feel that life is worth living and offspring are worth having; then they must actually have offspring, protect them and guide them, foster in them a sense that life is worth living and offspring are worth having, and so on. As Douvan (1976) put it from the perspective of the society and parenting: "The task for all societies and all parents is to present an image of adulthood which attracts the young and makes the struggle to grow up worth it" (1976, p. 15).

Among human beings, however, the growth of the capacity for symbolic thought and therefore culture suggests the possibility of a *different definition of evolutionary success:* namely *the propagation of one's ideas, rather than one's genes.* Dawkins (1976, chap. 1) used the terms *meme* and *meme-complex* to refer to such culturally propagated ideas, as contrasted with genes:

> We were built as gene machines, created to pass on our genes. . . . But as each generation passes, the contribution of your genes is halved. It does not take long to reach negligible proportions. . . . Socrates may or may not have a gene or two alive in the world today . . . but who cares? The meme-complexes of Socrates, Leonardo, Copernicus, and Marconi are still going strong. (p. 214)

Consider the composers Mozart and Beethoven, who were among the greatest two or three musicians in the Western tradition; Vincent van Gogh, one of the greatest of modern artists; Washington and Lincoln, rated by historians as the two greatest U.S. presidents; or even Jesus and St. Paul, the founders of Christianity. These seven men have had an enormous influence on human affairs; yet they produced either no offspring or else offspring who (after one or two generations) produced no further offspring. The same is true of Helen Keller and Virginia Woolf, two of the five historical figures used in this book. Yet the *ideas* and *creations* of these people have lived on, transforming our ways of thinking and acting. Clearly, then, in thinking about human society we shall have to expand our conception of "reproductive success."

Adaptive Value of the Big Five Trait Factors

What is the evolutionary significance of human traits? One obvious hypothesis is that human traits, like human physical features, evolved because of the selective advantages they bring or the species-wide problems they solve. For example, the human tendency to be gregarious and organized into groups gives us many advantages in dealing with the forces of nature, dangerous animals, and rival groups of humans. By contributing to gregariousness and social organization, many of the Big Five trait factors (discussed in Chapter 13) would confer selective advantages on people who possessed them (see Buss, 1991b). Thus surgency (factor 1) involves the capacity to lead others, while agreeableness (factor 2) facilitates getting along with others; both are necessary for complex social organization. Conscientiousness or trustworthiness and persistent control of behavior to fit group norms (factor 3) would also confer advantages on the group if not always on the individual. The capacity to remain calm under environmental stress (emotional stability, factor 4) would be an advantage in most situations, although I suppose that in cases of sudden and extreme danger, people who are not so calm would fare better.

The selective advantages of culture (factor 5) are less clear. If "culture" means the signs and signals reflecting fundamental bonds that hold groups together, then factor 5 would be the capacity for displaying the signs and symbols of loyal group membership, whatever the group. In a time of difficulty, this could be an advantage because you would be more readily recognized as a comrade by the rest of your group, who would be more likely to come to your aid. In its more everyday sense, culture could mean learning the accumulated wisdom of the past, which would be adaptive as long as the environment has not changed too rapidly. Finally, if we consider the alternative "openness to experience" label for factor 5, it suggests a capacity for taking in and processing cues from the environment, which would certainly be advantageous.

Adaptive Value of Variation in the Big Five Trait Factors

If we look hard enough, then, we can suggest adaptive functions for most of the five factors. But wait! Remember that these five factors are *dimensions of individual difference* (like height or hair color), not *fixed characteristics of almost all humans* (like having two legs). By definition, therefore, half of the human population scores below the median on surgency, agreeableness, conscientiousness, emotional stability, and culture. If having these traits gives selective advantages, what about the low-scorers? Why have they survived? After all, physical characteristics that confer selective advantage, such as having two legs (to walk) or opposable thumbs (to grasp objects), show *almost no variation among people.* Apart from rare birth defects and accidents, every human being has two legs and opposable thumbs. These are fixed characteristics, not dimensions of difference.

Our question must be phrased more precisely: Does our evolved human psychological nature include *variation* along the five trait dimensions? What would be the selective advantages—to individuals, to groups, or to humanity as a whole—of *variation* across individuals in surgency, agreeableness, conscientiousness, emotional stability, and culture (see Buss, 1991b, pp. 473–476)?

Trait variation as "noise." One answer is that from an evolutionary perspective, variation in the Big Five traits is just evolutionary "noise," irrelevant to selective advantage. Tooby and Cosmides (1990) argue, for example, that "most *heritable* personality differences are *not* the expression of different adaptive strategies" (p. 19). The truly *adaptive* features of human nature are under complex genetic control:

> Characteristics in which individuals differ because of genetic differences are an unrepresentative subset of human . . . characteristics. . . . [They are an] almost entirely constrained variation within an encompassing, universal, adaptively organized . . . human nature. (p. 24; see also Crawford & Anderson, 1989)

More precisely, Tooby and Cosmides suggest that while the average human levels on the five factors may be adaptations that confer selective advantages, variations around their average levels—one of the main interests of the personality psychologist—are not (pp. 38–39).

Trait variation as "vestiges" or "harbingers." A second answer is that while there is no selective advantage in trait variation, certain traits do indeed confer selective advantages. Therefore, the variation that we observe simply reflects the fact that evolution works at a very slow pace. Some people—the low (or high) scorers—are vestiges or "living fossils" of our less well adapted past. If high scores on a trait factor are more adaptive than low scores (or vice versa), then over time human beings will gradually show higher (or lower) scores. Today's high (or low) scorers are an evolutionary advance guard, harbingers of what all humans will be like in the future. Stick around—say for a few hundred thousand years or so—and you will see.

The major problem with this answer is that we have little if any evidence of trait levels in the past and no way of ever getting such evidence. As far back as we can go in recorded human history—for example, to the story of Jacob and Esau or the *Characters* of Theophrastus (see Chapter 11), which is but an eye blink in evolutionary time—we find much the same trait variation that we observe today. And as for the future direction of human evolution, we cannot be sure because we are in the middle of the story and don't know (won't ever know) the end. For example, given a few different decisions by U.S. President Kennedy and Soviet Premier Khrushchev during the Cuban Missile Crisis of 1962, the entire history of humanity might have ended in a thermonuclear holocaust, an evolutionary blind alley. As Roger Brown once observed, "The smart money is on the insects for the longer run" (1965, p. 3).

Trait variation as adaptations. We can argue that a range of variation within each trait dimension is adaptive to humanity as a whole. I have outlined some of the forms this answer might take in Table 14.6. For example, social organization may require "surgent" leaders, but it also needs nonsurgent followers; thus both types would coexist in a mutually beneficial relationship. Tooby and Cosmides (1990) suggest a similar case for impulsivity.

> Impulsive individuals might need a certain number of people around to save them from their folly, while prudent individuals might need the enthusiasm of the impulsive to push them into risky but rewarding endeavors. (p. 56)

Agreeable and conscientious people may be necessary to get the routine work of a society done, but creative innovation may come from the disagreeable and lazy people who ignore social conventions and think up new and better adaptations.

It is a little harder to think of an adaptive benefit connected with low emotional stability or high neuroticism. Still, if such people are especially likely to succumb to stress, they might function as a kind of early warning system for the rest of us. They would be like the canaries that miners took into the coal mines. When the canaries died, the miners knew it was time to leave, because oxygen levels in the mine shaft were getting dangerously low, and explosive gases were building up. In a similar fashion, when people of low emotional

TABLE 14.6 POSSIBLE ADAPTIVE BENEFITS TO SOCIETY OF HIGH AND LOW SCORES ON THE FIVE TRAIT FACTORS

Trait factor	High scores	Low scores
Surgency	Leadership	Loyal followership
Agreeableness	Promotes bonding and social organization (cooperation, reciprocity)	Creativity and innovation?
Conscientiousness	Ensures that important tasks will get done	
Emotional stability	Predictability; capacity to deal with moderate levels of stress	"Early warning system" for extreme levels of stress
Culture	Signs and signals of group membership; transmission of cultural learning and adaptive "wisdom"	Innovation? Revolution?

stability show maladaptive behaviors, it may be a warning sign to the rest of society. (Perhaps this is why such people play honored, even sacred, roles in some human societies.) And if their emotional distress leads them to the barricades of revolution, it may create better conditions for all.

Finally, people scoring low in culture, like people low in agreeableness, conscientiousness, and even emotional stability, may benefit society as innovators or even revolutionaries.

If we are ingenious enough, we could probably think up a selective advantage or adaptive benefit for almost any trait. Whether such hypothetical advantages actually lead to greater reproductive success for the individual or the group in the long run, however, may be quite difficult to demonstrate. The search for functions is limited only by our imagination and persistence. For example, did you ever wonder about the function or purpose of those little buttons on the sleeve cuffs of men's dress suit jackets? Some functionalists have suggested that they serve the function of "preserving continuity with the past and . . . making certain sectors of life familiar and predictable" (Kluckhohn, 1959, p. 28).[3] Is there *any* object or custom in our culture of which that could not be said?

Trait variation and adaptive niches. A fourth answer to the question of how trait variation could confer selective advantages involves the complex interaction of individual persons with highly variable local environments that consist of complex and often interlocking niches and microniches (Tooby & Cosmides, 1990, p. 48). High scores *and* low scores, on certain traits, might each confer selective advantages in certain situations. As conditions change, moreover, the available opportunities, hazards, and niches will change, sometimes suddenly and dramatically. For the overall human group, it would be advantageous to have a pool of trait variation available so that the species can exploit and fill the changing structure of niches and microniches. Even among our remote ancestors, for example, "timid" introverts may have been well-suited for certain important tasks, such as watching the fire all night to make sure it didn't go out. Being suspectible to boredom, the "braver" extraverts would fall asleep too easily to be reliable fire-watchers! Thousands of years later, the beginning of space travel called for extraverted astronauts with traits of "the right stuff" (Wolfe, 1979).

As an analogy, we might think of the wide variations in personality among dogs. Some are surgent (German shepherds) and are preferred by dog owners in times of high social stress; others are not (cocker spaniels), and are preferred in times of low stress (Doty, Peterson, & Winter, 1991; Sales, 1973). Some are very disagreeable (pit bulls) and are preferred by disagreeable people. Some are emotionally stable (collies), while others are quite high-strung and neurotic (poodles). Yet all these different breeds of dog flourish, because the great variety of owners' preferences and purposes has created a variety of niches.

[3]Kluckhohn was quite serious and did not intend such a "function" as a joke.

Evolved pretraits and actualized traits. A final answer applies the notion of microniches further, to the individual case. What we inherit through our genes may be called *pretraits*. These are highly general nervous system and brain characteristics that are further developed and elaborated by our experiences in specific environments, so they become the actualized traits or scores on trait dimensions that we display as adults (see MacDonald, 1991). In other words, we begin life with a set of generalized neural mechanisms; experience selects and reinforces certain mechanisms that can be said to "evolve," as we grow up, into our adult traits (see Tooby and Cosmides, 1990, pp. 50–55, for illustrations of how this might happen).

This answer uses the language of evolution and selection, but as an analogy for processes of learning and development, just as Edelman (1992) and Gazzaniga (1994) use "neural Darwinism" language to describe the learning process (see also Angier, 1995). That is, from among the vast network of all possible connections among groups of neurons, certain connections are "selected" and strengthened because they give a better fit to the experienced patterns of external stimuli (see also Tooby & Cosmides, 1990, pp. 46–47). Similarly, Dawkins (1976, chap. 11) refers to both memes and genes as generalized *replicators*—ways in which information is reproduced and preserved—each involving a different medium of transmission.

The concepts of adaptation and selection, in short, do not necessarily presuppose a genetic basis. Adaptive behaviors, customs, and mechanisms can be coded by memes (learning) as well as by genes—even better, in fact, because adaptations that are learned can be quickly unlearned or relearned as conditions change, whereas organisms are often stuck with highly specific and fixed genetically based patterns (see Gould, 1977; also A. Buss, 1988; but see also D. Buss, 1991b, 1992a, who argues for genetic human inheritance of specific traits or mechanisms).

According to this last answer, the generalized capacity for modifying behavior in response to the environmental context is humanity's greatest adaptation. In Part Four, we will explore in greater detail how personality is affected and shaped by this context.

OUR TRAITS AND OUR BIOLOGICAL HERITAGE

From the time of Galen and his doctrine of the four humors, personality and biology have been linked in Western thought. With the development of the fields of neurophysiology, neuropsychopharmacology, and behavioral genetics in the twentieth century, speculation has given way to the search for specific mechanisms relating known biological functions and principles to specific, measurable personality traits. Some researchers, notably Eysenck, have proposed grand theories spanning the entire biological-psychological terrain. While they must be continually revised with the accumulation of research evidence, such theories do offer us a tantalizing vision of the ultimate goal. Other researchers are content to explore the more limited domains of specific mechanisms.

We have learned two things, so far, about the biological bases of our traits and temperament. First, many different lines of evidence establish some connections between certain traits and certain aspects of nervous system functioning. Second, the connections are more complicated, harder to establish, and in the end probably more subtle—and elegant—than we could have imagined at the start.

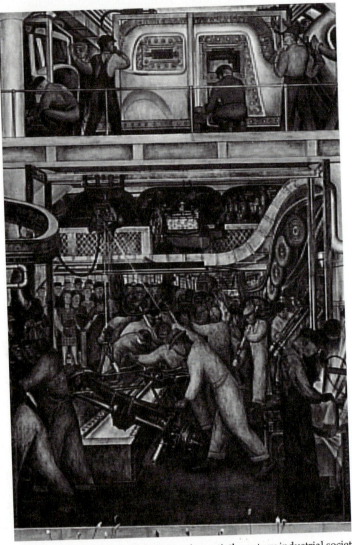

Some of the most important social contexts of twentieth-century industrial society are reflected in this portion of the south wall of Diego Rivera's frescoes at the Detroit Institute of Arts. We see the mass production of automobiles at Ford's vast River Rouge plant near Detroit, requiring coordination of machines, materials, and labor. Stratification by gender, social class, and race is apparent: middle-class tourists (at the left) observe working-class men at work; there are no women on the line, and African Americans mostly did the more grueling work of the Rouge plant's foundry, which is depicted on the north wall.

Diego M. Rivera, Mexican, 1886–1957, Detroit Industry, South Wall (detail), 1932–1933, Accession no. 33.10.S. Photo © The Detroit Institute of Arts, 1995.

PART FOUR

❖

Social Context—Situation, Social Structure, and Culture: Mischel, Erikson, and Stewart

15

Personality in its Social Context

---- ❖ ----

Up to this point, we have discussed personality as a series of elements and, ultimately, variables: motives, beliefs and values, and traits, held together by a self-schema. This makes it easy—too easy, perhaps—to think of someone's personality as being bounded by the person's skin, a "thing" that functions in isolation, following its own laws and behaving according to its essential nature. Yet for many people (for example, in India and China, or in the West before the Renaissance) it would be unusual or even impossible to think about a skin-bounded individual body without at the same time considering some larger unit—the family or kin group, tribe, neighborhood, nation, and so forth. Personalities, in short, have contexts.

Back in the time of Aristotle, people used to view the physical world as a series of individual things, each behaving according to its own nature. Thus a ball thrown into the air was believed to fall to earth because falling to earth expressed the ball's essential nature. Later, Galileo and Newton explained the ball's falling as the result of gravity, a force that depends on the relationship or *context* of the ball and the earth. Ball and earth are both part of a "comprehensive, all-embracing unity" (Lewin, 1935, p. 10). This means that to understand the ball, we must consider it in its larger context. In physical science, Galileian ways of thought have largely replaced the old Aristotelian ways, but the transformation is not complete in psychology (Lewin, 1935). In Part Four, therefore, we shall examine personality from this *contextual perspective*, the lower right-hand box in Figure 15.1, page 530.

Whatever their bases in genetics and biology, our personalities are powerfully shaped in the past and channeled in the present by their social contexts. From the social-context perspective, we could even say that people's personalities are what remains from the many and changing contexts in which they have lived. Virginia Woolf, for example, adopted such a perspective in writing about how she was influenced by her mother (1985):

> Until I was in the forties . . . the presence of my mother obsessed me. I could hear her voice, see her, imagine what she would do or say as I went about my day's doings. She was one of the invisible presences who after all play so important a part in every life. . . . Consider what immense forces society brings to play upon each of us, how that society changes from decade to decade; and also from class to class; well, if we cannot analyse these invisible presences, we know very little of [any person about whom we write]. (p. 80)

Many different kinds of social contexts affect personality. At one extreme is the social *microcontext*—the immediate features of the present situation, the simple responses or habits that we have learned in such situations from birth on, and the cumulation of such interactions that we call learning or reinforcement history. These will be discussed later in this chapter and in the next. At the other extreme is the *macrocontext* of large-scale, complex, and enduring patterns of environments. Macrocontexts can be described in terms of many different features: gender, social class, religion, race and ethnicity, nationality, culture, and history. They can also be described in terms of social-psychological mechanisms: processes of social identity, group pressure, social influence, social support, obedience, interpersonal relationships, and intragroup and intergroup relations (see Lindzey & Aronson, 1985). These two aspects of macrocontexts will be discussed in Chapter 17.

	Inner, Private, Subjective	Outer, Public, Objective
Enduring and typical across situations	COGNITIONS	TRAITS, TEMPERAMENT
Situation-dependent	MOTIVATION	SOCIAL CONTEXT Examples of variables: Habits, models, culture, class, ethnicity, gender Theorists: Mischel, Erikson, Stewart

FIGURE 15.1
The major elements of personality.

WHY SOCIAL CONTEXT?

I have called this section "social context" in order to emphasize that the environments in which our personalities develop and function are largely *social* environments. In the world of the experimental psychology laboratory, we often think of the environment as a collection of impersonal stimuli that either vary randomly or else are under the arbitrary control of an experimenter. In the real world, however, environments are not random sets of stimuli: for humans, contexts are organized packages or structures involving many other people. For example, everyone has a gender,[1] a family, a nationality (for many people, a mixture of different nationalities if they count back a few generations; perhaps also local or regional subnational identifications), a race or eth-

---

[1]More precisely, a sex *and* a gender; for a discussion of the differences between these two terms, see Deaux (1985) and Unger (1979).

nicity, and a social class or position in the society's power structure. For many people, the social context also includes a religion, institutions such as a club or college, and a workplace.

Macrocontexts, moreover, have a history, or set of collective memories and legends, often involving relationships with other similar or complementary macrocontexts. Thus every woman has a long personal history of experiences with men, and vice versa. Every worker has a personal history of bosses, and vice versa. At the society level, gender legends are as old as Adam and Eve, and labor-management legends are almost as old. Every nationality has a history of relationships with other nationalities, as the wars between the Serbs, Croats, and Bosnians in the former Yugoslavia have made tragically clear in the 1990s.

Social contexts are varied and complex. Even in one country at one time (for example, the United States in the 1990s), there are many different kinds of family, religions, nationalities or ethnic groups, and regional variations. If we then consider other cultures and other times, the variety of possible social contexts becomes truly bewildering! For some people, all the different features of context fit together; for others, the blend may not be so stable. These people experience conflicts among their different social contexts: for example, their college versus their religion, the nationality of one parent versus that of the other parent, family versus workplace, and so on. Such conflicts are especially likely during times of rapid social change and dislocation, when old contexts are destroyed and new contexts created.

Taken together, all these micro- and macrocontexts contribute to personality. Yet we are more than the sum of our social contexts, for in each person different contexts are blended together and thereby transformed into a unique personality. How contexts become internalized, blended, and transformed into personality is the theme of Part Four.

CONTEXT AND PERSONALITY: SOME EXAMPLES

Once again, we begin the study of an element of personality with several classic examples to illustrate the role and importance of that element. The most basic way in which people incorporate external microcontexts is through learning. Thus we will begin with with the experimental case study of one mechanism of learning, the classical conditioning of Little Albert (Watson & Rayner, 1920). We will then work up to the grand sweep of historical and cultural macrocontexts.

The Case of Little Albert

The Watson and Rayner study is one of the most widely cited and influential articles in the history of American psychology. At the beginning of the study, Albert B. (usually called "Little Albert" by textbook authors) was a 9-month-old infant residing at the Harriet Lane Home for Invalid Children in Baltimore, where his mother worked as a wet nurse. Watson and Rayner first established that Albert, a "stolid and unemotional" child, showed *no* fear reactions to a wide variety of stimuli, including various animals, masks (with and without hair), removal of support, and—specifically—a white rat. However, he did cry and show other signs of fear to a loud sound (produced behind his back by striking a 4-foot steel bar with a hammer). A month later, Albert again showed no fear of the rat. Now began the critical part of the study, as recounted in the laboratory notes of Watson and Rayner (1920):

1. White rat suddenly taken from the basket and presented to Albert. He began to reach for rat with left hand. Just as his hand touched the animal the bar was struck immediately behind his head. The infant jumped violently and fell forward burying his face in the mattress. He did not cry, however.
2. Just as the right hand touched the rat the bar was again struck. Again the infant jumped violently, fell forward, and began to whimper. (p. 4)

A week later, the white rat alone elicited some ambivalence in Albert. After five more pairings of rat with the loud sound, he showed definite fear responses to the rat alone:

The instant the rat was shown the baby began to cry. Almost instantly he turned sharply to the left, fell over on left side, raised himself on all fours and began to crawl away so rapidly that he was caught with difficulty before reaching the edge of the table. (p. 5)

Over the next ten days, Albert continued to show fear responses to the rat and *also* to the following objects, which in some way resembled the rat: a rabbit and a dog, a sealskin fur coat, cotton wool, Watson's hair, and a Santa Claus mask. Most of these responses persisted a month later. At *no* time, however, did Albert show fear responses to his blocks, to the experimenters or observers themselves, to the hair of the observers, or to the room and furniture in which the study was conducted.[2]

Let us look at Little Albert's experience in terms of modern learning theory. The study is often cited as the first important American experiment in *classical* or *Pavlovian conditioning,* which is one important mechanism of learning.

---

[2]I have tried to be as precise as possible in describing the Watson and Rayner study, although their own accounts of exactly what was done are not always consistent (compare Watson & Rayner, 1920, with Watson & Watson, 1921). Over the years, several details of the Little Albert story have become distorted (see Cornwell & Hobbs, 1976; Harris, 1979; Prytula, Oster, & Davis, 1977). Thus Albert did *not* show fear reactions to a toy rat, a man's beard, a fur pelt, a cat, a white furry glove, his own aunt wearing fur, his mother's fur neckpiece, or a teddy bear (Harris, 1979, p. 153). Watson and Rayner did *not* try to remove his fear by extinction or counterconditioning (though they did speculate as to how this might be done), because Albert left the hospital the day after the last conditioning session. Jones (1924), however, did use a form of counterconditioning to remove a similar fear, this time of a rabbit, in a boy named Peter. In the psychological literature, there is a small cottage industry of commentary on the Little Albert study (see also Cornwell, Hobbs, & Prytula, 1980; Creelan, 1975; Harris, 1980; Larson, 1978; LeUnes, 1983; Paul & Blumenthal, 1989; Samelson, 1980).

(Most people are familiar with Pavlov's research on dogs. If meat powder is placed on a dog's tongue, the dog will salivate. Pavlov found that when a clicking sound from a metronome immediately preceeded the meat powder, dogs eventually salivated to the sound alone. This phenomenon was labeled a conditioned response or simply "conditioning.") We can analyze Watson and Rayner's procedures in Pavlovian terms: There was *pairing* or contiguity of (1) the white rat with (2) the loud sound made by striking the steel bar. The sound was an *unconditioned stimulus* (UCS); that is, it elicited by itself the fear reaction or *unconditioned response* (UCR). The rat was a *conditioned stimulus* (CS); originally it elicited no response, but after several pairings with the UCS, it too elicited a *conditioned response* (CR) of fear. The CR is often (but not always) similar to the UCR.

In terms of a modern view of classical conditioning (Rescorla, 1988), however, Little Albert learned not a new connection between CS (rat) and CR or UCR (fear responses), but rather a *new association between CS and UCS*. The rat (CS) is now said to give "information" about the loud sound (UCS): that is, in Albert's mind white rats now go along with, or predict, loud sounds. Albert's fear CR to the rat simply confirms that this association exists.

Church (1980) suggested that the Albert study also contains elements of *instrumental* or *operant conditioning*, because—if you read Watson and Rayner's account carefully—Albert also learned a relationship between (1) his own *response* of reaching for the rat and (2) the "punishment" of the loud sound. As Watson and Rayner put it, "just as his hand touched the animal the bar was struck immediately" (p. 4). Such a learned connection, or contingency, should lead Albert to suppress his reaching-for-the-rat behavior, which is certainly what happened during the study.

Actually, the Watson and Rayner study may not show as much as its authors thought or many later psychologists believed. First, Albert's fear responses were neither as strong nor as pervasive as they seem from the way they have been described over the years since 1920. To maintain them, Watson and Rayner had to "refresh" the original conditioning (that is, they repeated the rat-sound pairing) and also carry out further conditioning (they paired the rabbit and dog with the sound). And when Albert sucked his thumb, all fear responses disappeared completely. (Watson and Rayner report that "again and again . . . we had to remove the thumb from his mouth before the conditioned response could be obtained," 1920, p. 13; see also Cornwell, Hobbs, & Prytula, 1980; Samelson, 1980.) Further, while Albert's fear generalized to some objects, it showed no sign of generalizing to other objects also present during the conditioning—for example, the laboratory room, the laboratory furniture, his own blocks, or even the rest of Watson (besides his hair).

Second, we have no real evidence that these five days' experience with the "rat = loud noise = fear" microcontext had any long-term effect on Little Albert's personality. Watson and Rayner *believed* that it would, as they confidently concluded their original paper with the following rather bizarre prediction (1920):

> The Freudians twenty years from now . . . when they come to analyze Albert's fear of a seal skin coat . . . will probably tease from him the recital of a dream which upon their analysis will show that Albert at three years of age attempted to play with the pubic hair of the mother and was scolded violently for it. . . . If the analyst has the authority and personality to put it over, Albert may be fully convinced that the dream was a true revealer of the factors which brought about his fear. (p. 14)

In fact, however, Albert left the hospital on the day after the last experimental trial, so that Watson and Rayner had no chance to follow him up. (Murray, 1973, reported an unsuccessful attempt to track Albert down.)

Finally, the essential conclusion of the study—that emotional responses can be conditioned to previously neutral stimuli—turns out to be far more limited than Watson and Rayner believed. For Watson, this study was the cornerstone of his later claim, in a popular book, that since anything could be conditioned to anything, there were no limits to the modification of human behavior (Watson, 1925):

> Give me a dozen healthy infants, well-formed, and my own specified world to bring them up in and I'll guarantee to take any one at random and train him to become any type of specialist I might select—doctor, lawyer, artist, merchant-chief and, yes, even beggar-man and thief, regardless of his talents, penchants, tendencies, abilities, vocations, and race of his ancestors. (p. 82)

In Watson's mind, the Little Albert study was a prototype of how this might be done, though in fact it was the only such study he ever carried out. As he went on to say in the above quotation,"I am going beyond my facts and I admit it." Little Albert was only a single case. In the years since 1920, there have been many failures to replicate it (Harris, 1979, p. 155; Hilgard & Marquis, 1940, pp. 293–294). In fact, "anything" *cannot* be easily conditioned to "anything else": certain objects (perhaps those that were long ago dangerous to humans) are much more successful and effective as aversive conditioned stimuli than are others (Rescorla, 1988, pp. 153–154; Schwartz, 1974; Seligman, 1970; 1971). In choosing a rat for a CS, Watson and Rayner had the good luck to get it right on their first (and only) try.

Watson was unable to follow up the Little Albert study with more systematic research because as the result of his divorce and then marriage to Rayner, he was forced to resign his position at Johns Hopkins and take up a career in advertising. As it stands, then, the Little Albert study is a vivid demonstration of the powerful effects of a short-term microcontext. However, the systematic evidence about classical and instrumental conditioning and other mechanisms of learning that have accumulated since 1920 suggests that these effects are complicated as well as powerful.

Observational Learning: Aggression toward a Bobo Doll

Microcontexts affect personality and behavior not only directly, through classical and operant conditioning, but also indirectly, through observational learning. This is obvious nowadays, but experimental psychologists did not fully accept the existence of observational learning until the 1960s; even then, some called it "vicarious operant conditioning."

The study of film-mediated aggression by Bandura, Ross, and Ross (1963) is a classic demonstration of observational learning. While playing individually with colored paper and stickers, nursery school children were exposed to one of four conditions: (1) a live adult model, working with tinker toys in the same room, who began acting aggressively toward a 5-foot inflated Bobo doll (hitting, kicking, pommeling with a mallet, and verbal aggression); (2) a film of the adult model being aggressive toward the Bobo doll; (3) a "cartoon" film, shown on a simulated television set, of a model (dressed as Herman the Cat) being aggressive toward the Bobo doll; or (4) a control condition in which the live adult model quietly assembled tinker toys and ignored the Bobo doll. Children in all conditions were then mildly frustrated by having a desirable toy taken away. They then spent twenty minutes in another room in which there were other toys (both aggressive toys such as a toy gun and darts and nonaggressive toys) and a 3-foot Bobo doll. The question of interest to Bandura, Ross, and Ross was whether the four groups would show differences in aggressive play, especially aggression toward the Bobo doll.

The results, presented in Table 15.1, show that during the twenty minutes, the three groups exposed to the aggressive model were all more aggressive toward the Bobo doll than was the fourth group. They were significantly higher in directly imitative aggressive acts (hitting, kicking, pommeling, verbal aggression similar to what the model had done). They were also higher, but not significantly so, in partially imitative aggressive acts, nonimitative aggression, and imaginary gun play. In other words, the effects of observing the model were quite specific: the children did not show higher levels of generalized aggression. Rather, they learned certain specific aggressive responses. (Undoubtedly most of the children already knew how to hit; what they learned through observation was that it was all right to hit the Bobo doll in the laboratory setting.)

TABLE 15.1 EFFECTS OF DIFFERENT KINDS OF MODELS ON CHILDREN'S AGGRESSIVE BEHAVIOR

Group	Average score			
	Directly imitative aggression	*Partially imitative aggression*	*Nonimitative aggression*	*Imaginary gun play*
Live model	21.3	20.3	34.2	7.4
Film model	16.4	26.4	34.2	14.5
"Cartoon" film model	12.0	24.7	49.7	12.7
Control	2.9	13.3	29.1	9.0

SOURCE: Adapted from Bandura, Ross, and Ross (1963). Data for boys and girls, and male and female models, are combined.

Once again, though, it is important to realize some limits of this study. All children were deliberately frustrated before being left with the toys. In other words, frustration as well as observation was necessary to produce aggression. Also, the study only assessed the immediate effects of the model on aggression toward a Bobo doll; we do not know how long these effects might last or how widely they might generalize. Finally, not every example is imitated. In the Bandura, Ross, and Ross study, for example, the models were all adults (real or cartoon), who were older, bigger and stronger, and more knowledgeable than the children. They were also apparently not punished for their aggression. Each of these model and outcome characteristics (as well as many others) can affect the extent of imitation and observational learning.

Experiments such as this one laid the foundation for extensive research demonstrating how modeling and observational learning, in addition to direct reinforcement, affect behavior and personality (Bandura, 1977b). One important question driving many studies of observational learning is whether repeated exposure to television violence makes children grow up to be more violent. (The review of evidence by Huesmann and Miller, 1994, suggests that it often does.)

Observational Learning in Real Life

An assassination and mass murders. Models and observational learning can also be studied in the macrocontext. For example, women's shelter workers know that incidents of men battering their wives increase during and after televised football games (Quindlen, 1993; see also White, Katz, & Scarborough, 1992). In the aftermath of a violent crime, commentators often suggest that the perpetrator used a television program as a model.

Berkowitz and Macaulay (1971) designed a systematic study to explore such media modeling effects. In November 1963, President John F. Kennedy was assassinated. Two days later, while being transferred from one jail to another, the alleged assassin Lee Harvey Oswald was murdered by Jack Ruby, while millions of Americans watched on live television. In July 1966, Richard Speck murdered eight nurses in Chicago. One month later, in Austin, Texas, Charles Whitman murdered his wife and mother and then took a small arsenal of weapons up to the top of the twenty-seven-story tower at the University of Texas, where he proceeded to shoot forty-five people, killing fourteen of them. These spectacular crimes were given a good deal of media coverage. To explore whether this coverage would lead others to commit crimes—whether Oswald, Ruby, Speck, and Whitman became aggressive models—Berkowitz and Macauley analyzed FBI data on violent and nonviolent crimes and offenses (homicide, rape, aggravated assault, and robbery) for the period January 1960 through December 1966. After controlling for various other influences (such as a general upward trend and seasonal variation), they found that levels of violent crime—especially aggravated assault and robbery—were significantly higher than would be expected during the months following each

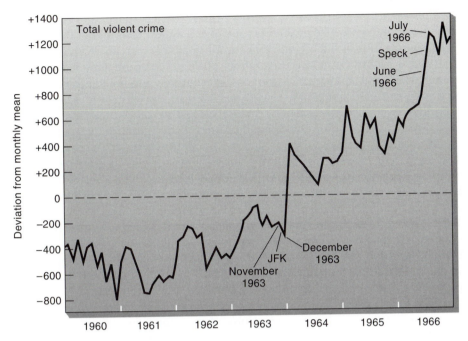

FIGURE 15.2
Levels of violent crime following the Kennedy assassination and the mass murders by
Speck and Whitman. (From Berkowitz and Macaulay, 1971, p. 250)

of the three spectacular crimes. In contrast, levels of nonviolent crime (larceny,
burglary, and manslaughter) showed no such effects. Figure 15.2 illustrates the
results for combined violent crimes.

Prize fights and suicides in the media. Other studies also suggest a general media modeling effect. For example, Marilyn Monroe's highly publicized
1962 death by (presumably) suicide was followed by a temporary 12 percent
increase in the U.S. suicide rate. Building on this example, Phillips (1979, 1983)
found a significant jump in motor vehicle deaths a few days after highly publicized suicides and significant increases in homicides a few days after heavyweight championship boxing matches.

Macrocontexts: Effects of the Internment of Japanese Americans over Two Generations

We now turn to an extended example of the effects of macrocontext, in which
family, race, ethnicity, and history combine to exert powerful effects that continue, through a variety of psychological mechanisms, to ripple down through
succeeding generations.

Concentration camps in the United States? On February 19, 1942, a little over two months after Pearl Harbor, one of the ugliest chapters in the history of ethnic relations and civil rights in the United States began. With President Roosevelt's signature on Executive Order 9066, all Japanese Americans in the western parts of California, Oregon, and Washington and the southern part of Arizona—over 110,000 people—were forced, usually with only seven days' notice, to assemble for evacuation by the U.S. Army to ten relocation camps. (The term "relocation camp" is a euphemism for concentration camp, which is the term actually used by President Roosevelt at the time; see Nagata, 1993, p. xiii.) Each camp was surrounded by barbed wire and armed guards—guards who faced inward. Over two-thirds of those interned had been born in the United States and were therefore citizens; one-third were under 15 years old; and more than one-third remained in the camps until after the war was over in 1945. (Canada established similar camps for persons of Japanese ancestry.)

Because they were allowed to bring with them only what they could carry, the internees had to sell almost all of their possessions, homes, businesses, and farms at ridiculously low prices, or else give them away—an estimated economic loss (adjusted for inflation) of between $2.5 billion and $6.2 billion (Nagata, 1993, p. 19). The internment was carried out without formal charges or trials of any kind. Constitutional procedures were ignored or suspended, and in 1944 the Supreme Court upheld the policy. (The 1990 movie *Come See the Paradise* treats the internment from the perspective of a Caucasian man married to a Japanese American woman.)

The official reason for the internment policy was "national security," to protect the western coastal areas from risks of espionage and sabotage; yet this reason is difficult to accept. Japanese Americans were *not* removed from Hawaii, which lay in a much more exposed and dangerous position militarily. Nor was there any evidence—on the Pacific coast or in Hawaii, at the time or since—of any security problem with the Japanese American community. In fact, special reports by the Navy and State Departments completed six months earlier had explicitly dismissed such potential "dangers." The army did not want to spend the time, money, and scarce resources that the evacuation required. Most disturbing of all was the fact that American-resident *aliens* from Germany and Italy (with which the United States was also at war in 1942)—let alone citizens of German or Italian descent—were not evacuated and relocated en masse.

(top) In 1942, Japanese Americans living in the West Coast were required to report for transportation to "relocation camps" for the duration of World War II. They were given only seven days notice and allowed to bring only what they could carry. (Culver Pictures)

(bottom) Most interned Japanese Americans suppressed their feelings and tried to show themselves "real Americans," as in this women's baseball game. In contrast, their children (mostly born after the war) protested the internment and worked for redress. (Culver Pictures)

It is difficult, therefore, to escape the conclusion that the Japanese American relocation policy was the result of racism and prejudice rather than any conceivable military "necessity." Is this too strong a conclusion? Here are the words of California Attorney General (later Governor) Earl Warren,[3] when asked whether there was any way to distinguish "loyal" from "disloyal" Japanese Americans (Wilson & Hosokawa, 1980):

> We believe that when we are dealing with the Caucasian race we have methods that will test the loyalty of them, and we believe that we can, in dealing with the Germans and Italians, arrive at some fairly sound conclusions because of our knowledge of the way they live in the community . . . but when we deal with the Japanese we are in an entirely different field and we cannot form any opinion that we believe to be sound. (p. 197)

An early memorandum written by General John L. DeWitt, chief of the Western Defense Command, illustrates the catch-22 racist logic: "The very fact that no sabotage has taken place to date is a disturbing and confirming indication that such action will be taken" (Wilson & Hosokawa, 1980, p. 234). The perverse imagery of racism is even more apparent in the blunt words of Colonel Karl R. Bendetsen, faced with the problem of deciding who in fact was "Japanese." "I am determined that if they have one drop of Japanese blood in them, they must go to camp" (Wilson & Hosokawa, 1980, p. 209). In fact, the internment policy was applied to people with as little as one-sixteenth Japanese ancestry—stricter even than the Nazi definition of who was a Jew.

Historical contexts of the camps. For those who experienced them, the internment camps were the focal point of a series of interlocking macrocontexts that was to affect the rest of their lives and even the lives of the next generation born well after the camps were disbanded and World War II was over. The first and most obvious macrocontext of the internment policy was *racial and ethnic stratification, discrimination, prejudice, and oppression.* Persons—all persons—of Japanese ethnicity were treated differently and subordinated, solely because of their ethnicity. To some extent ethnic discrimination and prejudice are a familiar story in human history (see Chapter 7). However, this particular ethnicity context developed out of another, broader one, the *historical situation* of growing conflict between the economic, political, and military aims of Japan and the United States since the 1920s.

But that conflict did not arise in a vacuum. In the minds of people and policymakers, many interlocking pasts were still present in 1942:

1. Japanese immigration to California in the late nineteenth and early twentieth centuries. Originally, this was encouraged by U.S. companies

---

[3]In an ironic and happier sequel to this otherwise tragic story, as Chief Justice of the United States Supreme Court a decade after the internment began, Earl Warren distinguished himself by his resolute advocacy of civil rights, as in the landmark 1953 *Brown vs. Board of Education* decision that outlawed racially segregated public schools.

as a source of cheap labor, but later it aroused Caucasian fears of a "Yellow Peril"[4] and led to discrimination and a series of restrictions on Japanese immigration and citizenship. (Not until 1952, well after the end of World War II, was it possible for Japanese immigrants to apply for citizenship.)

2. Before that there were the dramatic reforms in Japan of the post-1868 Meiji era, motivated by a desire to catch up with the West.

3. Before that there was the 1853 naval "visit" to Japan by U.S. Commodore Matthew Perry, who brought a demand for trade and diplomatic relations.

4. Before that there was Japan's policy, since the early 1600s, of expelling foreigners, ending foreign trade, and forbidding Japanese to travel abroad.

5. This Japanese policy of isolation was a reaction to the inroads that Western culture and Christian missions had made in Japan.

6. Finally, the economic-imperial and cultural-missionary expansion of the West goes back to Prince Henry the Navigator of Portugal and Christopher Columbus, and before them, to the Crusades of Christian Europe against Islam (see Wilson & Hosokawa, 1980, p. 131).

This is not a textbook in history, so we will not pursue these historical details further. I mention them to make the point that historical events—sometimes even very ancient events—shape personality. From a psychological perspective, we cannot understand the personalities of Japanese Americans without understanding the internment camp macrocontext; and we cannot understand the powerful effects of the internment on the personalities of the survivors, their children, and their children's children, without examining the historical roots. In each of us, a complex set of interlocking macrocontexts from many historical pasts lives on in the psychological present.

Effects of the camps. Recent work by Nagata (1993) has established some effects of the camps. The immediate impact on most Nisei (second-generation Japanese Americans) who were interned was a decline in self-esteem, an increase in shame, and a desire to put the camp experience behind them that was so strong that in many cases it amounted to repression and denial (Nagata, 1993, pp. 30–35, 99–102). To some extent these reactions reflect themes of fatalism and suppression of emotions prominent in Japanese culture, but they are also common among survivors of other traumas of oppression, such as rape or the Holocaust. After the war, many Nisei turned away from their Japanese heritage and tried to raise their children to be as "Ameri-

---

[4]The phrase was popularized by the German Kaiser Wilhelm II in the early years of the twentieth century, in an attempt to divert the attention of Russia from Europe to the Far East. In the United States it was picked up by the Hearst newspapers.

can" as possible. They communicated very little to their children (the Sansei, or third-generation, mostly born after the war when their parents had returned to "normal" life), a pattern that Daniels called "collective social amnesia" (1991, p. 5). It is as though the relocation camps were a shameful sign of failure at the critical and urgent task of becoming a "real American."

Nagata (1993) found, however, that the effects of the relocation on many Sansei were different. Their Nisei parents were "cryptic" and "unwilling" to talk about their camp experiences and feelings; they themselves approached the topic with "foreboding," somehow knowing "not to ask too many questions." Obviously this silence conflicted with the Sansei children's normal sense of parents as being all-powerful and in control of things. Though many Sansei grew up during the civil rights era of the 1960s, their school history books still ignored the relocation. Out of the Nisei silence, together with the Sansei sense of fulfilling disrupted parental dreams by their own educational and career accomplishments, a complex series of cross-generational family dynamics was set in motion. What the second generation wishes to forget, the third generation wants to remember and retrieve.[5] As one Nisei parent put it (Uchida, 1982):

> [Our] children, who experienced the Vietnam War, with its violent confrontations and protest marches, have asked questions about those early World War II years. Why did you let it happen? they ask of the evacuation. Why didn't you fight for your civil rights? Why did you go without protest to the concentration camps? . . . They are the generation who taught us to celebrate our ethnicity and discover our ethnic pride. (p. 147)

Compared to Sansei whose parents were not interned, Sansei with interned parents had several distinctive attitudes. First, they agreed *less* often with statements, such as the following, which reflect confidence in the United States:

> I am confident that my rights as an American citizen would not be violated in this country.

Second, they agreed *more* often with statements such as the following, which reflect a distrust of white America and preference for relationships with other Japanese Americans:

> I feel more at ease with Japanese Americans than Caucasians.

Finally, while most Sansei were in favor of financial redress for the survivors of the internment, those whose parents had been interned were even more

[5]Actually, "super-Americanism" and denial of old-world heritage are common among second-generation Americans generally; third-generation Americans often try to recapture some of the values of their ethnic past, according to the anthropologist Mead (1965, chap. 3) and the historian Hansen (1938).

strongly in favor and were also more active in working for passage of the Civil Liberties Act (finally signed into law by President Reagan in 1988), which granted $20,000 to every surviving internee.

Even though most Sansei did not experience it directly, then, the relocation affected their trust in government, their ethnic identification, and their political activism. While their achievement can be seen as a way of "redeeming" their parents' lives, their activism may also have been a symbolic way of resisting the original relocation or fighting back—a vicarious arousal of the power motive, in effect.[6] Some of these effects are easy to understand as the result of simple transmission of attitudes and values from parents to children; others suggest more complicated and ambivalent mechanisms at work. In the words of one Sansei interviewed by Nagata (1993):

> It's like a secret or maybe more like a skeleton in the closet—like a relative in the family who's retarded or alcoholic. Everyone tiptoes around it, only discussing it when someone else brings it up, like a family scandal. (p. vii)

Thus the internment camps brought together a whole series of macrocontexts, with complex and interacting effects on personality: racism, ethnicity and ethnocentrism, international relations, history, the camp environment itself, and the play of generations within the family. Psychological mechanisms of social identity (group memberships that are incorporated into the self-schema), memory, and intergroup relations play a prominent part. Although most Sansei were not even alive during the years of the internment camps, they experienced them as a vivid part of the psychological "present" of their own personalities. Similar effects have been observed among children whose parents were survivors of the Great Depression of the 1930s (Elder, Caspi, & Nguyen, 1986) or the Holocaust (H. Epstein, 1979; McClelland, 1985, pp. 328–329).

CASES IN CONTEXT: MAYA ANGELOU AND VIRGINIA WOOLF

To illustrate the effects of social context, I have chosen two cases: the African American poet and author (also actress, singer, dancer, and university professor) Maya Angelou (b. 1928) and the English novelist and essayist Virginia Woolf (1882–1941). Angelou and Woolf share gender and occupation. As children, both experienced sexual abuse. Yet they differ in race and ethnicity, nationality, precise historical period, and class background. From studying these similarities and differences, we can trace some of the many ways in which social microcontexts and macrocontexts affect personality.

---

[6]In the course of analyzing his own dreams, Freud recalled a similar experience from his childhood. Upon hearing his father's account of an earlier anti-Semitic incident, Freud experienced both vicarious feelings of humiliation and a consequent resolve to take vengeance by identifying with the Carthaginian general Hannibal, who fought against the ancient Romans (1900, IV, pp. 196–198).

Actress, poet, writer, and professor Maya Angelou. "The black female is assaulted in her tender years by all those common forces of nature at the same time that she is caught in the tripartite crossfire of masculine prejudice, white illogical hate and black lack of power" (1970, p. 231). (UPI/Bettmann)

Maya Angelou

Maya Angelou was born Marguerite Johnson in 1928. Her mother was a night-club entertainer (among many other careers) and her father a hotel doorman and later dietitian in the U.S. Navy. When she was 3, her parents separated; with her older brother Bailey, Maya was put on a train from California to Stamps, Arkansas, where she grew up with her paternal grandmother and uncle. When Maya was 8, she and Bailey spent several months in St. Louis with their mother's family, then moved back to Stamps after Maya was raped by her mother's boyfriend. After graduating from eighth grade at the top of her class, she and her brother were taken to San Francisco to live with their mother. At the age of 15 Maya secured a job as a streetcar fare collector, the first African American streetcar worker in the city. (She only got the job by waiting every day for four weeks in the company's office.) Worried about her sexual identity, she maneuvered a young man of the neighborhood into having sexual intercourse with her. As a result, she became pregnant, giving birth to her son Guy three weeks after graduating from high school.

Up to this point, Angelou's life story does not seem promising. She was intelligent and had gotten good grades in school, but (in her own words) "one would say of my life—born loser—had to be: from a broken family, raped at eight, unwed mother at sixteen" (quoted in Julianelli, 1972, p. 124). She took jobs as a waitress, cook and even mechanic in order to support herself and her son. In the 1950s she began to make appearances as a singer and dancer. She had parts in *Porgy and Bess* on a twenty-two-country tour of Europe and Africa and a New York production of Jean Genet's play, *The Blacks*. She then spent five years in Cairo and Ghana, working as a journalist, teacher, and administrator while her son attended the University of Accra in Ghana. Returning to the United States, she began an active career as a writer (poetry and prose, television and movie scripts, autobiography), director, and performer. Since 1981, she has been a professor of American Studies at Wake Forest University. She has chronicled her life through the Africa years in five volumes, beginning with *I Know Why the Caged Bird Sings* (Angelou, 1970). In 1993, U.S. President-elect Bill Clinton commissioned her to read her poem "On the Pulse of Morning" at his inauguration.

Virginia Woolf

Virginia Woolf, born Adeline Virginia Stephen in 1882, became one of the most important and innovative novelists and critics of the twentieth century. Her mother, Julia Jackson Duckworth, already had two sons and a daughter at the time of her marriage to Leslie Stephen, an eminent essayist and editor in late nineteenth-century England. In addition to her two older half-brothers and half-sister (George, Gerald, and Stella Duckworth), Virginia had one older sister (Vanessa), an older brother (Thoby), and a younger brother (Adrian).

(left) Virginia Woolf, who revolutionized the form of the modern novel. "Consider what immense forces society brings to play upon each of us, how that society changes from decade to decade; and also from class to class; well, if we cannot analyze these invisible presences, . . . how futile life-writing becomes" (1985, p. 80). (National Potrait Gallery, London)

(right) Virginia Woolf with her father, the essayist Leslie Stephen. Of him and their relationship, she later wrote: "It was like being shut up in the same cage with a wild beast. Suppose I, at fifteen, was a nervous, gibbering, little monkey, . . . he was the pacing, dangerous, morose lion; a lion who was sulky and angry and injured; and suddenly ferocious, and then very humble, and then majestic; and then lying dusty and fly pestered in a corner of the cage" (1985, p. 116). (Berg Collection, New York Public Library)

Another half-sister Laura, from her father's first marriage, lived with the family but was ultimately treated as retarded and finally institutionalized.

Though denied opportunity for a university education by barriers to women, she was educated at home by her mother and tutors. At an early age she was given free reign of her father's library, which she used to considerable advantage. After her mother's death in 1895 (Virginia was 13), she lived with her father and her older sisters. After her father's death in 1904, Virginia and Vanessa set up an apartment in the Bloomsbury section of central London. Their social-intellectual circle, beginning with brother Thoby's friends from the University of Cambridge, expanded to become the nucleus of what became known as the Bloomsbury Group, or more simply, Bloomsbury. In 1912 she married Leonard Woolf, an author and former British colonial official.

Perhaps the English-speaking world has never seen such a dazzling collection of talent and style as Bloomsbury during the early years of the twentieth century: along with Virginia and Leonard Woolf at the core were authors Lytton Strachey and E. M. Forster; art critics Clive Bell (who married Virginia's sister Vanessa) and Desmond MacCarthy; painters Roger Fry, Vanessa Bell, and Duncan Grant; and the economist John Maynard Keynes. As the literary historian Edel (1979) described the group:

> They had a passion for art; they liked the fullness of life; they knew how to relax when their day's work was done. They wrote. They painted. They decorated. They built furniture. They sat on national committees. They achieved a large fame. . . . They were damnably critical. They criticized the Establishment but, unlike most critics, they worked to improve it. They hated war. . . . People who knew them were irritated, and some found them rude and abrasive. (p. 12)

Later friends of the Woolfs included the novelists Vita Sackville-West (with whom Virginia had an affair), Hugh Walpole, and Sackville-West's statesman husband Harold Nicolson.

Beginning in 1907 with articles and reviews, Woolf's writing flowered with a first novel, *The Voyage Out*, in 1913 (published in 1917). Her reputation as a "modern" novelist soared in the 1920s and 1930s with the publication of *Mrs. Dalloway* (1925), *To the Lighthouse* (1927), and *The Waves* (1931), as well as nonfiction works such as *A Room of One's Own* (1929), *Three Guineas* (1938), and numerous essays.[7]

Ever since the death of her mother, Woolf had been subject to periods of extreme depression, often coinciding with the completion of one of her best

[7]There are some interesting connections between Woolf and Freud. The English-language *Standard Edition* of Freud's complete works is published by the Hogarth Press, which was founded by Virginia and Leonard Woolf in their basement in 1917 and run by them until her death. The translator and editor of the *Standard Edition*, James Strachey, was the brother of Bloomsbury member Lytton Strachey. While she was drawn to psychoanalytic theory, Woolf apparently had doubts: in commenting on one of Freud's interpretations, she once wrote to a friend, "We could all go on like that [making psychoanalytic interpretations] for hours; and yet these Germans think it proves something—besides their own gull-like imbecility" (Woolf, 1977, p. 134).

novels. She probably suffered from what we would now call manic depression or bipolar affective disorder. In support of this diagnosis, Caramagno (1992) has charted Woolf's mood swings over forty-six years, on the basis of the diaries and letters of both Virginia and Leonard and also the biography by Virginia's nephew, Quentin Bell.[8] On March 28, 1941, with a German invasion and occupation of England still a very real possibility after the 1940 fall of France, Woolf drowned herself by filling her pockets with stones and walking out into the River Ouse, near her country house in southeastern England.

Woolf never wrote a formal autobiography, but several autobiographical essays, collected by Jeanne Schulkind under the title *Moments of Being* (Woolf, 1985), provide a rich source of autobiographical material. They include vivid descriptions of several important early microcontexts of her life.

CHILDHOOD SEXUAL ABUSE: A TRAUMATIC EARLY SOCIAL CONTEXT

For both Virginia Woolf and Maya Angelou, childhood sexual abuse was a powerful microcontext. In each case the abuse involved broader themes of gender, social structure, culture, and history. Sexual abuse, therefore, was not just a microcontext involving sex, but rather a point of convergence for several powerful macrocontexts of personality development. In Chapter 17, we shall be referring back to these examples.

Angelou: Abuse, Rape, and Silence

When she was 8, Maya was first abused and later raped by "Mr. Freeman," her mother's boyfriend. Over three decades later, in the first volume of her autobiography, she still recalled the pain (1970):

> A breaking and entering when even the senses are torn apart. The act of rape on an eight-year-old body is a matter of the needle giving because the camel can't. The child gives, because the body can, and the mind of the violator cannot. (p. 65)

In a 1987 interview, she added that "there's not been a day since the rape 50 years ago during which I have not thought about it" (Crane, 1989, p. 175).

After the rape, Mr. Freeman warned her, "If you scream, I'm gonna kill you. And if you tell, I'm gonna kill Bailey." But Bailey and Maya's mother found out anyway and took her to the hospital. Mr. Freeman was arrested and brought to trial. While testifying, Maya was asked whether "the accused [tried] to touch you before the time he, or rather you say he, raped you?" This confronted her with a dilemma familiar to most women survivors of rape: feeling guilty and somehow responsible herself, she worried that if she dis-

---

[8]While bipolar affective disorder almost certainly involves some biochemical and genetic factors, environmental contexts also play a role, both in the appearance of the disorder itself and in the ways in which its effects are channeled, expressed, and coped with by the person.

closed the prior abuse, then people would blame her and "stone me as they had stoned the harlot in the Bible." For as long as she could, she "used silence as a retreat." Finally, she answered no, and "the lie lumped in my throat and I couldn't get air" (p. 71).

Shortly after the trial ended, a policeman came by to tell Maya and her family that Mr. Freeman had been killed. Maya immediately concluded (1970):

> I could feel the evilness flowing through my body and waiting, pent up, to rush off my tongue if I tried to open my mouth. I clamped my teeth shut, I'd hold it in. . . . If I talked to anyone else that person might die too. . . . I had to stop talking. (pp. 72–73)

This she did. For several years, Maya Angelou spoke only to her brother Bailey. They returned to Stamps: "Into this cocoon I crept" (p. 74). Gradually, under the influence of Bertha Flowers, a sensitive and perceptive older woman in Stamps, Maya came out of her cocoon and took the first steps toward a career in which spoken and written words were to play such a crucial part.

Notice how Angelou's account of the rape (see above)—a "breaking" of a child's body by the "violator," the threats of hurt and death—casts the abuse in terms that suggest power or overpowering rather than sex. This is not unique to her experience: in the modern view (see Brownmiller, 1975), rape is *generally* understood as an act of power and violence rather than an act of sex.[9] Let us examine how this experience of violent power resonated with other themes in Angelou's life.

Distrust of adults. First, the abuse reinforced an existing distrust of adults: "It was the same old quandary. I had always lived it. There was an army of adults, whose motives and movements I just couldn't understand and who made no effort to understand mine" (p. 62). For example, on an earlier occasion, she had spoken to Bailey in pig Latin, believing their father could not understand. When her father replied in pig Latin, "It didn't startle me so much as it angered. It was simply another case of the trickiness of adults where children were concerned. Another case in point of the Grownups' Betrayal" (p. 49). Even her father's manner of speaking was suspect: "He sounded more like a white man than a Negro. Maybe he was the only brown-skinned white man in the world. It would be just my luck" (p. 48).

Part of the betrayal was rooted in feelings of abandonment. One Christmas, after receiving presents from their distant parents, Maya and Bailey reflected on "the questions that neither of us wanted to ask":

---

[9]While rape involves some actions that are in other contexts "sexual," in the case of rape these acts occur—for both the rapist and the person who is raped—in a cognitive, emotional, and motivational context of violence, hurt, pain, dominance, and power rather than love or intimacy. Throughout history, rape has been associated with the systematic and deliberate oppression or conquest of ethnic and national groups (Stiglmayer, 1994; "Unspeakable," 1993). Of course, for some men (especially those high in power motivation, see Chapter 5), power and sex may be metaphors for each other. For example, Freud's disciple Otto Rank (1913) wrote an essay illustrating the use of "courtship" (rape) images in war poems about conquering cities (see also MacKinnon, 1987a, 1987b).

Why did they send us away? and What did we do so wrong? So Wrong? Why, at three and four, did we have tags put on our arms to be sent by train alone from Long Beach, California, to Stamps, Arkansas? . . . Bailey sat down beside me, and that time didn't admonish me not to cry. (p. 43)

Trust, abandonment, and the need for control. Later, when she was 15 and living in California, Maya visited her father, who took her on a day trip to Mexico. Arriving at a rather seedy country bar, he became involved in the party and seemed to abandon her:

Surely my father wouldn't allow his daughter to be ill-treated. Wouldn't he? Would he? How could he leave me in that raunchy bar and go off with his woman? Did he care what happened to me? Not a damn, I decided, and opened the flood gates for hysteria. Once the tears began, there was no stopping them. (p. 200)

Maya's desperate response—trying to assert her own control of the situation—suggests how deeply powerless she felt: when her father passed out in the back seat of his car, she decided to drive them back to California, though she had never driven a car before:

The challenge was exhilarating. It was me, Marguerite, against the elemental opposition. As I twisted the steering wheel and forced the accelerator to the floor I was controlling Mexico, and might and aloneness and inexperienced youth and Bailey Johnson, Sr., and death and insecurity, and even gravity. (pp. 202–203)

In fact, the first volume of Angelou's autobiography opens with an episode involving control, in this case Maya's desperate attempt to control her bladder during a recitation in a church pageant, and the appalling consequences of loss of control:

I tried to hold, to squeeze it back, to keep it from speeding, but when I reached the church porch I knew I'd have to let it go, or it would probably run right back up to my head and my poor head would burst like a dropped watermelon, and all the brains and spit and tongue and eyes would roll all over the place. (p. 3)

Impassivity in the face of threat. After raping her, Mr. Freeman had commanded Maya, "Don't you tell a soul." In the years of silence after his death that is exactly what she did. But her silence was also part of an impassive style—"the foam I had packed around my senses"—that she had already developed to control other external threats, her own distrust, and the sense of powerlessness. "I was called Old Lady and chided for moving and talking like winter's molasses" (pp. 48, 57). Many years later, when her son Guy was almost killed in an automobile accident in Africa, she mobilized the same reserves of impassivity (Angelou, 1986):

His assurances that he would heal and be better than new drove me into a *faithless silence.* Had I been less timid, I would have cursed God. Had I come from a different background, I would have gone further and denied His very existence. Having neither the courage nor the historical precedent, I *raged inside myself* like a blinded bull in a metal stall. (p. 4, emphases added)

For Angelou, then, silence and impassivity was one style of coping: with threat, with fear, with anything that promised pain and could not be avoided or controlled. It is her personal style, linked to many specific contexts of her own individual life; but it is also part of her broader cultural heritage. For many African American people and many women of any race, life is full of painful and uncontrollable experiences to which no response other than impassive silence is possible (or at least safe). Thus to understand Angelou fully, we shall consider these social macrocontexts of gender, race, and twenti-eth-century America in a later section below.

Woolf: Abuse within the Family

For Woolf, sexual abuse came at the hands of her half-brother Gerald, who was twelve years older (Woolf, 1985):

> There was a slab outside the dining room door for standing dishes upon. Once when I was very small Gerald Duckworth lifted me onto this, and as I sat there he began to explore my body. I can remember the feel of his hand going under my clothes; going firmly and steadily lower and lower. I remember how I hoped that he would stop; how I stiffened and wriggled as his hand approached my private parts. But it did not stop. His hand explored my private parts too. I remember resenting, disliking it. (p. 69)

Nor was this an isolated instance. In another autobiographical fragment, she painted a repellent picture of her other half-brother George, fourteen years older than herself (Woolf, 1985):

> Abnormally stupid . . . the eyes of a pig . . . inclined to fat. . . . If you pressed him further [in an argument] he would seize you in his arms and cry out that he refused to argue with those he loved. "Kiss me, kiss me, you beloved," he would vociferate; and the argument was drowned in kisses. . . . As his passions increased and his desires became more vehement . . . one felt like an unfortunate minnow shut up in the same tank with an unwieldy and turbulent whale. (p. 169)

After a dinner party, during which Virginia had committed the "impropriety" of discussing Greek philosophy at dinner, she went to bed in a state of emo-tional turmoil and disillusionment:

> Then, creaking stealthily, the door opened; treading gingerly, someone entered. "Who?" I cried. "Don't be frightened," George whispered. "And don't turn on the light, oh beloved. Beloved—" and he flung himself on my bed, and took me in his arms. (p. 177)

Effects on adult sexuality. For Woolf, some effects of this early sexual abuse were obvious and clearly described. For example, she suffered a lifelong "looking-glass shame" about her body:

> When I was six or seven, perhaps, I got into the habit of looking at my face in the glass [mirror]. But I only did this if I was sure that I was alone. I was ashamed of it. A strong feeling of guilt seemed naturally attached to it. (pp. 67–68)

Related to this abuse and shame was a dream involving mirrors:

> I dreamt that I was looking in a glass when a horrible face—the face of an animal—suddenly showed over my shoulder. I cannot be sure if this was a dream, or if it happened. Was I looking in the glass one day when something in the background moved, and seemed to me alive? I cannot be sure. But I have always remembered the other face in the glass, whether it was a dream or a fact, and that it frightened me. (p. 69)

The image of "the face of an animal" can easily be taken as a symbol for male sexual arousal, as experienced with horror and fright by a young girl. Surely such microcontexts would have long-term consequences for the girl's future attitudes and behavior regarding sex. In fact, there is clear evidence that as an adult Woolf did not particularly enjoy sexual intercourse in marriage (DeSalvo, 1989; Edel, 1979, pp. 197–199; Lehmann, 1975, p. 32; Rose, 1978, pp. 85, 255), though there is also evidence that her affair with Sackville-West was a passionate one.

Sexual abuse as power abuse. Yet such an interpretation is too pat, too simple. As with Maya Angelou's rape by Mr. Freeman, Woolf's sexual abuse from her half-brothers did not involve only—or even primarily—sex. What was really going on in the minds of Gerald and George Duckworth was *power*: they took Virginia as the object of their power; her wishes and plans and preferences were repeatedly ignored by men intent on having their way. Recall Woolf's precise words about the episode with Gerald: "I hoped that he would stop. . . . But it did not stop. . . . I remember resenting, disliking it" (p. 69). As Sackville-West put it, Woolf disliked not men's desire for sex but rather "their possessiveness and love of domination" (Caramagno, 1992, pp. 144–145).

George Duckworth insisted on having his way with her in other ways as well. He was socially ambitious and desired to ingratiate himself with the British aristocracy. After their mother's death, he arrogated to himself the "responsibility" for bringing her out into society by escorting her to numerous social functions. This involved his constant "insistence that we should go where he wished to go, and do as he wished us to do." Behind this insistence Woolf discerned a cluster of related motives: a "crude wish to dominate," "some jealousy," and "some desire to carry off the prize," as well as "some sexual urge" (p. 154). One evening Virginia came downstairs in a new green dress, "apprehensive, yet, for a new dress excites even the unskilled, elated." George reacted sharply (Woolf, 1985):

> He looked me up and down for a moment as if I were a horse brought into the show ring. Then the sullen look came into his eyes . . . the look of moral, of social, disapproval, as if he scented some kind of insurrection, of defiance of his accepted

standards. . . . He said at last: "Go and tear it up." He spoke in . . . the voice of the enraged male. . . . To my discredit, I never wore it again in George's presence. I knuckled under to his authority. (pp. 151–152)

Nor were Woolf's oppressive experiences of male power confined to her half-brothers. Her father, Leslie Stephen, was also a tyrant: "the exacting, the violent, the histrionic, the demonstrative, the self-centered, the self-pitying, the deaf, the appealing, the alternately loved and hated father" (p. 116). Leslie Stephen had always had a violent temper, but after the death of Virginia's mother and her half-sister Stella, "[Van]nessa and I were fully exposed without protection to the full blast of that strange character" (p. 107). Writing thirty-six years after her father's death, she summarized their relationship in a vivid metaphor of power:

Suppose I, at fifteen, was a nervous, gibbering, little monkey, always spitting or cracking a nut and shying the shells about, and mopping and mowing, and leaping into dark corners and then swinging in rapture across the cage, he was the pacing, dangerous, morose lion; a lion who was sulky and angry and injured; and suddenly ferocious, and then very humble, and then majestic; and then lying dusty and fly pestered in a corner of the cage. (p. 116)

Male power and Woolf's "moments of being". The theme of male power over women was a continuing theme in Woolf's experience. For example, she thought of her life as containing many "moments of being." At the time, such moments were consciously experienced and lived. Later, they became distinct and enduring memories "more real than the present moment," that were "embedded in many more moments of nonbeing. . . . in a kind of nondescript cotton wool" (pp. 67, 70). Such fragmentations of memory are a mild form of *dissociation,* in which the integrative functions of memory and identity are disturbed or altered to avoid the pain of recall (Trickett & Putnam, 1993). In reviewing her memories of childhood, Woolf identified three such moments: at least two involved a sense of helpless powerlessness and depression in the face of male power. In the first, she was fighting with her older brother Thoby (Woolf, 1985):

We were pommelling each other with our fists. Just as I raised my fist to hit him, I felt: why hurt another person? I dropped my hand instantly, and stood there, and let him beat me. I remember the feeling. It was a feeling of hopeless sadness. It was as if I became aware of something terrible; and of my own powerlessness. I slunk off alone, feeling horribly depressed. (p. 71)

Another "moment" involved a more diffuse sense of powerlessness and despair. Having heard about a neighbor's suicide:

The next thing I remember is being in the garden at night and walking on the path by the apple tree. It seemed to me that the apple tree was connected with the horror of Mr. Valpy's [a man who had lived nearby] suicide. I could not pass it. I stood there . . . in a trance of horror. I seemed to be dragged down, hopelessly, into some pit of absolute despair from which I could not escape. My body seemed paralyzed. (p. 71)

The Social Context of Sexual Abuse

Woolf and Angelou were both sexually abused and assaulted as children, and this abuse had powerful effects on their personality development. For Woolf, they involved a whole series of negative emotions—shame, powerlessness, and despair—that continued to flash out in dissociated "moments of being." We can understand them as classically conditioned emotional responses, involving some of the same mechanisms that lay behind Little Albert's conditioned fear of the white rat's furriness. Such responses of powerlessness, feelings of betrayal, depression, and dissociation are common among survivors of childhood sexual abuse (Browne & Finkelhor, 1986; Cutler & Nolen-Hoeksema, 1991; Liem, O'Toole, & James, 1992; Trickett & Putnam, 1993). In Woolf's case, these effects may have been compounded by an underlying biochemical and genetic predisposition to manic depression (see Caramagno, 1992). Yet as we shall see below, if her personality was *affected* by a predisposition to manic depression and a context of abuse and oppression, it was not completely *determined* by them. Possessed of a great intelligence and superbly skilled verbal imagination, she had the capacity to write, to transform her dissociation and depression into visionary works of literary art.

For Angelou, abuse and rape strengthened an already-existing pattern of impassive silence. This silence can be understood as an avoidance behavior learned by instrumental or operant conditioning, somewhat similar to Little Albert's withdrawal of his hand in the presence of the rat. Yet although Angelou had haunting memories of the rape, she did not become depressed or dissociative. Her later life is a story of zest and enthusiasm. Why the difference from Woolf? Underlying biochemical factors undoubtedly made some difference, but differences in the two social contexts were also important. For a girl to cope with the trauma of sexual abuse, according to Trickett and Putnam (1993), social support from other people, especially her mother, is critical. Here Angelou and Woolf had almost opposite experiences. Julia Stephen died when Virginia was 13, just as she was (presumably) trying to navigate past the critical shoals of puberty. In contrast, Angelou's brother, mother, and grandmother were all present for her after the rape. They believed her; they took her to the hospital; they comforted her; they insisted on prosecuting Mr. Freeman. In fact, as we shall see below, Maya had not one but three "mothers," each in her own way supremely gifted at encouraging her strength, pride, and confidence.

Thus for both Angelou and Woolf, early sexual abuse and later support (or lack of support) was much more than a single isolated microcontext that happened to occur in their two lives. Rather, as I suggested above, these events were part of a broader pattern of gender and culture macrocontexts. To these we now turn.

GENDER: "DIFFERENCE," POWER, AND POWERLESSNESS

In all societies, rape, sexual abuse, and violence reflect a fundamental asymmetry of gender. Overwhelmingly it is women who are abused and hurt by men. Maya Angelou had done nothing to Mr. Freeman, and Virginia Woolf had in no way provoked Gerald or George Duckworth. While all women are not necessarily raped or abused, the experience of oppression—of being, against one's will, the object of men's power—is probably shared by almost all women. Keep your eyes and ears open; watch daily life going on around you, or on television (or radio talk shows). Observe that men talk louder and longer, interrupt more, control more space by the way they sit, and engage in more controlling gestures such as condescending pats on the shoulder (see Henley, 1977; LaFrance & Mayo, 1978; Tannen, 1990). Examine the structure of institutions, especially at the very top levels. Who controls whom, in universities, corporations, the U.S. Congress, the military, and religious organizations? Who makes more money (even taking into account credentials and experience)? The answers should not be difficult to find. *Gender is a profound and recurring dimension of social inequality or stratification.*

Woolf's Struggle against Patriarchy

Virginia Woolf was well aware of the role of gender subordination in her life. After the deaths of their mother and half-sister, it was Virginia and Vanessa (not Gerald, George, or Thoby) who inherited the roles of keepers of the house and caretakers to their father. His capricious and manipulative moods alternated between an "inarticulate roar," "reproaches," and "abuse" that gave way to "groans" and plaintive appeals. Woolf and her sister experienced him as "the most oppressive stone laid upon our vitality and its struggle to live" (1985, p. 144). Yet in the midst of the oppression, she observed an important feature of his behavior: "It is notable that these scenes were never indulged in before men" (Woolf, 1985). Why not?

> Partly of course because woman was then (though gilt with an angelic surface) the slave. But that does not explain the histrionic element in these displays. . . . He needed always some woman to act before; to sympathize with him, to console him. (pp. 144–145)

In reflecting on the contrast between her brother's smooth manner in society and his tyranny at home, Woolf directly connected her personal experiences of gender subordination to a larger social context:

> The patriarchal society of the Victorian age was in full swing in our drawing room. . . . Vanessa and I . . . were only asked to admire and applaud when our male relations went through the different figures of the intellectual game. (p. 153)

In education, Woolf recognized the critical role of schools and universities in shaping men of power and the power of men. Women, of course, were mostly excluded from them. She reacted against this pattern of patriarchal privilege with an analysis of the conditions of women's subordination and proposals for how they might be overcome: through women's control of their own space and time (*A Room of One's Own*, 1929) and through higher education for women (*Three Guineas*, 1938).

Double Jeopardy: The Situation of African American Women

Body shame and racial shame. Maya Angelou, too, felt shame about her body. Sometimes she described this shame in terms of comparison between herself and her brother (1970):

> Where I was big, elbowy and grating, he was small, graceful and smooth. When I was described by our playmates as being shit color, he was lauded for his velvet-black skin. His hair fell down in black curls, and my head was covered with black steel wool. (p. 17)

Notice, though, how quickly her negative feelings focus on two characteristics—skin color and hair—that tend to differentiate black people from white. Our body images reflect our social world as well as our physical characteristics (see Chapter 9); for Angelou the body-based oppression of gender was overlaid with oppression of race and racism, a kind of double jeopardy. No wonder that Angelou cast her body feelings in terms of a racial comparison and a dream of race transformation:

> Wouldn't they be surprised when one day I woke out of my black ugly dream, and my real hair, which was long and blond, would take the place of the kinky mass that Momma wouldn't let me straighten. . . . Because I was really white and because a cruel fairy stepmother, who was understandably jealous of my beauty, had turned me into a too-big Negro girl, with nappy black hair, broad feet and a space between her teeth that would hold a number-two pencil. (p. 2)

Abuse of blacks by whites. In Maya Angelou's childhood world, African Americans were relegated to inferior jobs, homes, and schools. They were in constant danger of physical violence and verbal humiliation from whites, who controlled almost all local and national institutions of power. Earlier, for several hundred years, the white-black color line had also been the status line of master-slave.

Sometimes African Americans experienced racism in direct and simple terms of physical danger, as when a deputy sheriff would come by her grandmother's store to "tell Willie he better lay low tonight" because "some of the boys [the Ku Klux Klan] 'll be coming over here later" (1970, p. 14). Other times, the threat involved the pain of emotional humiliation, as in "the most painful and confusing experience I ever had with my grandmother." A group of white schoolgirls had gathered outside the store to mock her grandmother with derogatory imitations and obscene gestures. Angelou's immediate reaction was, understandably, rage:

> I heard their laughter crackling and popping like pine logs in a cooking stove. I suppose my lifelong paranoia was born in those cold, molasses-slow minutes. . . .

> I wanted to throw a handful of black pepper in their faces, to throw lye on them, to scream that they were dirty, scummy peckerwoods. (pp. 24–25)

Throughout the episode her grandmother, knowing that any expression of anger would have been suicidal, impassively hummed the hymn "Bread of Heaven, bread of Heaven, feed me till I want no more." After the white girls left, she changed to "Glory, glory, hallelujah, when I lay my burden down."

For African Americans, such humiliations and dangers were part of the texture of everyday life: condescending remarks by a white school official that spoiled Maya's eighth-grade school graduation ceremony (pp. 142–156); the white dentist, to whom her grandmother had loaned money, who announced when Maya had a toothache that "I don't treat nigra, colored people. . . . I'd rather stick my hand in a dog's mouth than in a nigger's" (pp. 159–160); the streetcar company's personnel office in San Francisco, where she waited every day for several weeks before being allowed to apply for a job (pp. 225–229); the constant horror of being "called out of name"—that is, of being addressed with a degrading nickname, a racial slur, or whatever name white people decided to use rather than being called by one's own name (pp. 90–93); and the everyday experience of being powerless, poor, and ragged (p. 20). Angelou's own words are the clearest description of how gender and race converge as dimensions of power and oppression:

> The Black female is assaulted in her tender years by all those common forces of nature at the same time that she is caught in the tripartite crossfire of masculine prejudice, white illogical hate and Black lack of power. (p. 231)

Of course race and ethnicity as dimensions of power and oppression are not confined to the United States, but rather appear in many times and places. For example, the ancient Greeks and Romans enslaved "barbarians," that is, people who were not Greek or Roman. In India, the conquering Aryans from the north became the higher castes of Hinduism, while the conquered Dravidians were relegated to lower-caste status. Nazi Germany planned an eastern empire based on enslaving Slavic peoples. And the many civil conflicts in Bosnia, Somalia, Rwanda, and elsewhere give abundant evidence that social macrocontexts of racism or ethnocentrism are all too alive and well.

COPING WITH OPPRESSION

Maya Angelou and Virginia Woolf were survivors, survivors both of being the object of individual people's cruel power (microcontext) and also of a world in which power and privilege were structured along the lines of gender and race (macrocontext). The theme pervades Angelou's poetry, as for example in this passage from "Still I Rise" (1978):

> You may shoot me with your words,
> You may cut me with your eyes,

You may kill me with your hatefulness,
But still, like air, I'll rise.

It is also present in her conversation, as in the following passage from an interview (Elliot, 1977/1989):

> One of the first things that a young person must internalize . . . is the understanding that although he may encounter many defeats, he must not be defeated. . . . Look at a diamond: it is the result of extreme pressure. Less pressure, it is crystal; less than that, it's coal; and less than that, it is fossilized leaves or just plain dirt. (p. 96)

Models of Coping

What were the mechanisms by which Angelou and Woolf coped with their contexts and survived? The presence of other people was certainly important, both as sources of general support and as models for specific behaviors. As Angelou put it, "the theme of my work is that, it can be rough, it can be tough but someone dares to love somebody and so we survive" (Cunningham, 1987/1989, pp. 185–186).

Models for coping (or, to use Angelou's term, "allegiances") abound in her autobiography. Her mother not only modeled having multiple careers and residences but was possessed of an indomitable spirit. Angelou recalled a critical incident of self-definition, when she was 20, in a conversation with her mother (quoted in Paterson, 1982/1989):

> We walked down the street, down Fulton Street [in San Francisco]. I'll never forget it. There was a mayonnaise and pickle factory nearby. I still remember that smell. And she said: "Baby, let me tell you something. I think you are the greatest woman I have ever met. . . . because you are intelligent and merciful. Those two things don't often go together." I walked across the street and got on the bus *in shock*. And I thought, she's not a liar, she's much too fierce to lie. She's intelligent, so maybe she sees something, maybe, just maybe. (pp. 119–120)

Later, she would speak of this incident as "one of those moments when the sky rolled back and TA-DA. TATA! It's almost as if at times like that, the whole earth holds its breath" (Manegold, 1993, p. B5).

Her mother's mother, who would often "stop speaking . . . when she was angry" (Angelou, 1970, p. 70), modeled silence and control—the "control I remember in [her] voice when she heard of a lynching" (Angelou, 1981, p. 263). Miss Kirwin, of San Francisco's George Washington High School, was "the only teacher I ever remembered" (1970, p. 184). There were also many black writers and poets and Shakespeare.

Another significant relationship involved Mrs. Bertha Flowers, "the aristocrat of Black Stamps" and "the lady who threw me my first life line" after the rape and time of being silent. She was impressive, refined, and beautiful, "throughout my life the measure of what a human being can be" (p. 77). Taking the recently traumatized Maya under her wing, Mrs. Flowers loaned her books, discussed poetry, and gave her "lessons in living." Addressing Maya's silence directly, she spoke words that Maya was to memorize over the years (Angelou, 1970):

> Now no one is going to make you talk—possibly no one can. But bear in mind, language is man's way of communicating with his fellow man and it is language alone which separates him from the lower animals. . . . Words mean more than what is set down on paper. It takes the human voice to infuse them with the shades of deeper meaning. (p. 82)

If you watched Maya Angelou on television reading "On the Pulse of Morning" at President Clinton's 1993 inaugural (see the right-hand picture on page 544), you were able to catch a glimpse of the profound influence of Mrs. Flowers, over fifty years before, at a critical turning point in Angelou's childhood.

How do models have their effect? Let us examine some of the details of these two episodes involving Maya Angelou with her mother and Mrs. Flowers. Of course, both episodes were *positive, directly rewarding experiences:* Maya's mother praised her, and Mrs. Flowers paid attention to her. Looking a little deeper, we also observe that Maya brought to these experiences a certain *readiness for a model.* For example, Maya encountered Mrs. Flowers about a year after the rape, the trial, and the death of Mr. Freeman. At that time she felt "like an old biscuit, dirty and inedible" (p. 77). Mrs. Flowers treated her as a valued human being: "I was liked, and what a difference it made. I was respected, not as Mrs. Henderson's grandchild or Bailey's sister but for just being Marguerite Johnson" (p. 85). And at the time of her mother's remark, Maya was fiercely concerned about establishing her independence and prickly about accepting the least bit of assistance from anyone else: "she knew I wouldn't take a ride from her, that I would take the streetcar, that I had to own myself" (Manegold, 1993, p. B5). In this context, her mother's words were a support, endorsement, and validation of that independence. These two examples suggest that there are critical periods when people are more likely to be receptive to the influence of a model—for example, when their self-concept is in doubt, in jeopardy, or newly established.

We are influenced by some but not all models. Some classic social psychology studies have established two characteristics of successful models, the people we do imitate and by whom we are influenced: they are perceived to be *expert,* and they are thought to be *trustworthy* (Giffin, 1967; Hovland, Janis, & Kelley, 1953). Thus to the young Maya, Mrs. Flowers radiated *prestige:* she was a source of expert knowledge about books and poetry; she was "our side's answer to the richest white woman in town" (p. 78).[10] The effect on Maya's

---

[10]Though in a poignant aside, Angelou notes the vulnerability of this prestige in the face of white racism:

> It was fortunate that I never saw her in the company of powhitefolks. For since they tend to think of their whiteness as an evenizer, I'm certain that I would have had to hear her spoken to commonly as Bertha, and my image of her would have been shattered like the unmendable Humpty-Dumpty. (1970, p. 79)

self-esteem was dramatic: "It would be safe to say that she made me proud to be Negro, just by being herself" (p. 79). And in the episode with her mother on the streets of San Francisco, quoted above, her mother's essential trustworthiness ("she's not a liar, she's much too fierce to lie") was an important reason for the powerful impact of her words.

For Virginia Woolf, her father Leslie Stephen, despite his many oppressive qualities, was also a source of reward. She recalled (Woolf, 1985):

> How proud, priggishly, I was, if he gave his little amused surprised snort, when he found me reading some book that no child of my age could understand. I was a snob no doubt, and read partly to make him think me a very clever little brat. (pp. 111–112)

Woolf's later literary career and intellectual interests reflected the strong influence of her father, her brother Thoby, and their entire social circle as models.

Less happily, Woolf's mother may also have been a model for the depressions that were to plague Woolf's adult life. Like Woolf herself, Julia was plagued with melancholy: "severe; with a background of knowledge that made her sad" (Woolf, 1985, p. 82). As further evidence of daughter-mother modeling or identification, we observe that Woolf's first major depressive breakdown in the summer of 1895 followed shortly after her mother's death and her father's resulting depression. Later, her father's death in 1904 precipitated an even more intense breakdown in Virginia, involving an exaggerated imitation of his characteristic emotions of self-accusation, irritation, and anger. These two episodes illustrate Freud's (1914) suggestion that the *loss of a loved object* is yet another cause of imitation or identification with that object. Taking the lost object as a model is a way of ensuring its presence forever.

Coping through Writing

Both Woolf and Angelou transformed their experiences of oppression through the act of writing. Angelou described this transformation in a poem, "Caged Bird," that echoed the title of the first volume of her autobiography (1983):

> But a bird that stalks
> down his narrow cage
> can seldom see through
> his bars of rage
> his wings are clipped and
> his feet are tied
> so he opens his throat to sing.

As we have seen, Woolf saw her life experience in terms of *dissociation* or splitting: the "nondescript cotton wool" punctuated by vivid "moments of being" that often involved "the sense of horror [that] held me powerless. . . . They seemed dominant; myself passive." The act of writing offered a way out of the memory of these oppressive experiences, for it provided an *explanation* that "blunts the sledge-hammer force of the blow" (1985, p. 72). For Woolf, then, writing worked to unify her dissociated experience, and in this unification she found moments of supreme happiness (Woolf, 1985):

> The rapture I get when . . . I seem to be discovering what belongs with what; making a scene come right; making a character come together. . . . That behind the cotton wool is hidden a pattern; that we—I mean all human beings—are connected with this; that the whole world is a work of art; that we are parts of the work of art. (p. 72)

Thus the experience of writing recapitulated the single *happy* "moment of being" from her childhood, when, while looking at the leaves of a plant:

> It seemed suddenly plain that the flower itself was a part of the earth; that a ring enclosed what was the flower; and that was the real flower; part earth; part flower. . . . "That is the whole," I said. (p. 71)

Made whole in this way through writing, Woolf's experience had "lost the power to hurt"; indeed, the act of writing transmuted the pain of being powerless to a "great delight" (p. 72). Thus in writing *To the Lighthouse*, she transformed her complex and ambivalent feelings of love and rage toward her father:

> I rubbed out much of his memory there too. Yet he too obsessed me for years. *Until I wrote it out,* I would find my lips moving; I would be arguing with him; raging against him; saying to myself all that I never said to him. (p. 108, emphasis added)

In 1919, after finishing her second novel, she tried to formulate her own experiences of dissociation and unification through writing as a kind of manifesto for modern novelists (Woolf, 1919/1925):

> Examine for a moment an ordinary mind on an ordinary day. The mind receives a myriad impressions—trivial, fantastic, evanescent, or engraved with the sharpness of steel. From all sides they come, an incessant shower of innumerable atoms; and as they fall, as they shape themselves into the life of Monday or Tuesday, the accent falls differently from of old. The moment of importance comes not here but there; so that, if a writer were a free man and not a slave, if he could write what he chose, not what he must . . . there would be no plot, no comedy, no tragedy, no love interest or catastrophe in the accepted style. . . . Life is not a series of gig lamps, symmetrically arranged; life is a luminous halo, a semitransparent envelope surrounding us from the beginning of consciousness to the end. Is it not the task of the novelist to convey this varying, this unknown and uncircumscribed spirit? (p. 189)

THE WIDER CONTEXT OF HISTORY AND CULTURE

I have suggested that the oppression and abuse experiences of Angelou and Woolf were parts of a macrocontext patterned along the dimensions of gender and race. Yet even this is not the end of the story. Contexts also include class, nation, and history, by themselves and in combination and relation with each other.

Virginia Woolf in Victorian and Edwardian England

Woolf once described her childhood and young adulthood in historical terms: "Two different ages confronted each other in the drawing room . . . the Victorian age and the Edwardian age" (p. 147). Some brief historical details will help us understand what she meant by this phrase. Woolf was born into a Victorian England that had already passed the high noon of worldwide empire involving assumption of imperial "responsibilities" and the "white man's burden" (a phrase of the poet and author Rudyard Kipling). Since 1880, Britain had encountered increasing economic, political, military, and cultural rivalry from Germany and the United States. At home, organized movements of labor and women began to challenge the easy assumptions of upper-class male privilege. By the dawn of the Edwardian age at the beginning of the twentieth century, then, Victorian England was in decline, at home and abroad.[11]

These economic, political, and historical events affected the British mindset. Among men of the privileged social and intellectual circles who, like Leslie Stephen, had come to adulthood at the height of Victorian power and prestige, the threats of German and American competition and social upheaval created a fascination with power and its control. The figure of Nietzsche's superman stalked the land, as social Darwinist doctrine spoke of the survival of the fittest (which to the male English leaders, of course, meant themselves). To prevent the "erosion from within of the will to rule, the willingness to wage the Darwinian struggle for the survival of the fittest" (Hobsbawm, 1987, pp. 83), therefore, these men believed that they must strive to control themselves for the task of controlling power. In this striving, women were usually perceived as a distraction or temptation; hence *men's struggle for the control of power entailed the strident assertion of male superiority over women* (p. 206).

At the national level the situation posed by Britain's relative decline could be described in symbolic terms as the English male need to ward off fears of impotence through the forceful display of male strength and prestige, specifically through the renewed exclusion and suppression of women. In reaction, women campaigned for emancipation and opportunity. These two cultural cross-currents were important contexts for Virginia Woolf's work, as we have seen; but at the same time they also shaped her personal contexts. For Leslie Stephen, male concern with impotence was made worse by the unmistakable evidence of his own personal inferiority, as he admitted to Virginia that he had "only a good second-class mind" (Woolf, 1985):

> This frustrated desire to be a man of genius, and the knowledge that he was in truth not . . . led to a great deal of despondency, and to that self-centeredness

---

[11]The story of imperial decline is a familiar one in world history. The historian Paul Kennedy analyzed the Spanish, British, German, and United States versions in his book, *The Rise and Fall of the Great Powers* (1987).

which in later life at least made him so childishly greedy for compliments, made him brood so disproportionately over his failure. (p. 110)

A sense of inferiority led to violent outbursts and self-pitying demands for attention, with a wife or daughter always expected to pick up the pieces, live with the rage, and provide the attention. For Woolf, then, the microcontext of specifically sexual abuse was but part of a larger family pattern of men oppressing women, a pattern derived from and made worse by the larger social and historical macrocontext of Victorian and Edwardian England.

Maya Angelou in the American South

For Maya Angelou, as for any other African American, the enduring legacy of slavery—from the initial "fog of dislocation" and the "ships of bondage," "arriving on the nightmare, praying for a dream," to the endless suffering and violence—was *the* macrocontext in the American South (Angelou, 1982, p. 130; 1993). As she once put it in an interview (Toppman, 1983/1989):

> The black Southerner and white Southerner are locked to the land and to history, a painful history of guilt and cruelty and ignorance. It clings to us like the moss on the trees. That's what my play ["On a Southern Journey"] is about. Two women who have gone north—one black, one white—have done very well and think they're terribly sophisticated. But once back South, they revert to old ways and stereotypes. (p. 143)

Yet she also observed that relations between the races are far from simple, even in the South—or, perhaps, especially in the South—where one finds (Angelou, 1982):

> The plum, blue, honey brown, pink and red-skinned figures who struggle against the landscapes, professing love and hiding unforgivable hate. Or professing hate and holding in tenuous control, unspeakable love. (p. 130)

Her move to wartime California at age 13, however, added another important context (1970):

> In San Francisco, for the first time, I perceived myself as part of something. Not that I identified with the newcomers, nor with the rare Black descendants of native San Franciscans, nor with the whites or even the Asians, but rather with the times and the city. I understood the arrogance of the young sailors. . . . The undertone of fear that San Francisco would be bombed which was abetted by weekly air raid warnings, and civil defense drills in school, heightened my sense of belonging. . . . I became dauntless and free of fears, intoxicated by the physical fact of San Francisco. (pp. 179–180)

In her young adult years, Angelou's social contexts expanded to include the African American literary and theatrical heritage, the civil rights movement, and the emergence of independent African nations in the early 1960s. Finally, the offer of a professorship at Wake Forest University led her to return at last to the American South. Summing up her experiences in these many contexts, she concluded (Kay, 1987/1989):

> You can never go home again, but the truth is you can never leave home, so it's all right. And yet it is innate in human nature to try to go home again, and it may in fact be what life is all about: getting back to home, back to death, and then out of death and back to life. (p. 199)

In Maya Angelou's words, we can never leave home. Our contexts are always with us, as channels for the expression of personality and as parts of personality itself. Situationalist theorists of personality took this point to an extreme, arguing that social contexts were an alternative to personality, that personality was really nothing more than the contexts of a life. We turn to this argument in the next chapter.

16

The Situationist Critique of Personality and the Responses of Personality Psychologists to It

❖

Mischel's Alternative to Traditional Conceptions of
Personality
Bandura's Self-Efficacy Theory
SUMMARY: PERSONALITY, SITUATION, AND BEHAVIOR

Tucked away in a side hall of the Ontario Science Centre in Toronto is a simple exhibit. Many small bar magnets, about 2 inches long and 1/4-inch wide, are mounted on a vertical board in the pattern of a 3-foot diameter circle (like the numbers on a large clock face), as shown in Figure 16.1. When the exhibit is turned on, the little magnets come to life, spinning around in a series of exquisitely complicated and varied movements. Some rotate very slowly, then rapidly; others spin rapidly; a few change the direction of their spin in an instant. Magnets right next to each other show completely different patterns of movement. Taken together, the different magnets seem to show almost as

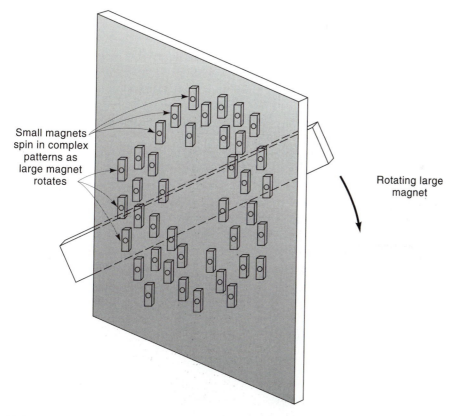

Small magnets spin in complex patterns as large magnet rotates

Rotating large magnet

FIGURE 16.1
Magnet board at the Ontario Science Centre in Toronto.

much variation as a group of people. When I first saw this exhibit, I was almost tempted to explain the striking differences in the behavior of individual magnets as the result of differences in their "personalities."

One look behind the board, however, led me to a very different understanding of the magnets. On the other side of the board, a large 3-foot bar magnet revolves like a large clock hand when the exhibit is turned on. The intricate spinning patterns of the little magnets on the other side of the board—so varied and so reminiscent of human differences—are in fact completely determined by the changing magnetic fields generated by the revolving large magnet and the many small magnets. In other words, in this case complex individual variations are completely explained by variations in the situation. The small bar magnets are all exactly the same; their different behaviors are only the result of their different locations with respect to the large moving magnet and each other.

The situationist critique of personality psychology is a lot like taking a look behind the board of the magnets exhibit: that is, *individual variability is to be explained by variations in the situation rather than differences within people.* This was the message of a 300-page book, *Personality and Assessment,* published in 1968 by personality psychologist Walter Mischel. Despite its rather unassum-

Walter Mischel, whose situationist critique challenged the usefulness of broad, general personality variables. "The traditional trait-state conceptualizations of personality, while often paying lip-service to . . . complexity and to the uniqueness of each person, in fact lead to a grossly oversimplified view that misses both the richness and the uniqueness of individual lives" (1968, p. 301). (Courtesy Walter Mischel)

ing title, the book had the impact of a bombshell on the field of personality psychology. Mischel's critical review of the field appeared devastating.[1] Obviously the field has survived: you are reading this book, and Mischel himself is still active in personality theory and research (see Mischel, 1984, 1993). Still, the issues Mischel raised and the responses of other personality psychologists are among the most important intellectual developments in the psychology of personality over the past thirty years. Because the debate focused on the importance of the situation as an alternative to personality, this is the appropriate place to tell that story.

MISCHEL'S 1968 CRITICISMS

Is Behavior Specific or General across Situations?

First, Mischel (1968) challenged the very usefulness of personality variables, because he believed they overstated the consistency of people's behavior across situations and over time:

> It is evident that the behaviors which are often construed as stable personality trait indicators actually are highly specific and depend on the details of the evoking situation and the response mode employed to measure them. (p. 37)

What evidence led Mischel to this conclusion? A study of attitudes toward authority and nonauthority figures, by Burwen and Campbell (1957), is one example. Using a variety of different procedures (interviews, TATs, adjective checklists, photo judgments, autobiographies, attitude surveys, and sociometric questionnaires), Burwen and Campbell assessed the attitudes of a sample of 155 men toward several different persons: father, boss, symbolic authority figures, peers, and symbolic peers. The idea that people have a generalized attitude toward all authority figures can be found in many personality theories. According to the Freudian concept of transference, for example, people "transfer" their attitudes toward early persons in their environment onto later persons who symbolically resemble them: for example, attitudes toward father are transferred to all later authorities. Thus many personality theories would lead us to make at least two specific predictions about the men in the Burwen and Campbell study: (1) that they would have similar attitudes toward all authority figures, and (2) that these attitudes would be similar to their attitudes toward their father.

Some of Burwen and Campbell's results are shown in Table 16.1. Each correlation coefficient is the average of the correlations between attitudes

---

[1]The depth of Mischel's effect on the field can be illustrated by the question put to him in 1990 by one of my colleagues, in the discussion after Mischel delivered a lecture at the University of Michigan: "How does it feel to be the person who almost destroyed personality?" In response, Mischel argued that his intention all along had been not to destroy personality but rather to improve it by emphasizing the individualized specificity of behavior, as he had earlier claimed in print (e.g., Mischel, 1984, pp. 278–282). Perhaps this is now clear, but for several years many personality psychologists thought otherwise.

TABLE 16.1 INTERCORRELATIONS AMONG ATTITUDES TOWARD AUTHORITY FIGURES

Authority figure	Mean correlation of attitude				
	Father	Symbolic authority	Boss	Peer	Symbolic peer
Father	.35	.12	.03	.06	.08
Symbolic authority		.15	.08	.10	.06
Boss			.09	.13	.03
Peer				.22	.07
Symbolic peer					.01

SOURCE: Adapted from Burwen and Campbell (1957, p. 26).

toward that pair of persons, across the different measures. (The correlations along the diagonal are average correlations of attitudes toward the *same* person, across the different measures.) All correlations are low, so low as to suggest that there is virtually no relationship among attitudes toward father and different authority figures, and even little consistency of attitude toward the same authority figures. For example, attitudes toward father correlated only .03 with attitudes toward boss and .06 with attitude toward peer. Most personality theories would predict father-boss correlations that were higher than this. Even attitudes toward father only intercorrelate .35 across the different measures. Overall, these results seriously challenge the notion that people have a generalized attitude toward authority and, by extension, any concept (such as transference) or personality theory (such as psychoanalysis) that presumes such a generalized attitude. Burwen and Campbell characterized their findings as "totally negative" and "so out of keeping with the general assumptions of current . . . personality psychology of all schools that they are worth some special consideration" (1957, pp. 31, 29). Mischel endorsed this conclusion.

A study of dependency in preschool children by Sears (1963; see also Sears, Rau, & Alpert, 1965) gave Mischel a second example of apparent lack of consistent behavior across situations. The results, shown in Table 16.2, show only insignificant correlations among the following five behavioral measures of dependency: *negative attention seeking,* as in disruption or aggressive activity; *positive attention seeking;* nonaggressive *touching or holding; being near,* as in following another child or a teacher; and *seeking reassurance.* (Note that the correlations for girls, above the diagonal in Table 16.2, were higher than those for boys. This suggests at least the possibility of gender differences in the cross-situational consistency of dependency, a behavior category that is undoubtedly part of the female sex-role stereotype.) From these correlations, the researchers concluded that "the evidence for a basic trait of dependency behavior is unsatisfactory for girls and clearly lacking for boys" (Sears, Rau, & Alpert, 1965, p. 42).

These and other similar results led Mischel to conclude that "it is evident that the behaviors which are often construed as stable personality trait indica-

TABLE 16.2 INTERCORRELATIONS AMONG MEASURES OF DEPENDENCY

Measures of dependency	Negative attention seeking	Seeking reassurance	Positive attention seeking	Touching and holding	Being near
			Correlations		
Negative attention seeking	—	.06	.10	.15	.37
Seeking reassurance	−.24	—	.25	.19	.26
Positive attention seeking	.23	−.11	—	.11	−.03
Touching and holding	.04	.14	−.16	—	.71
Being near	−.03	.12	−.14	.13	—

Note: Correlations for girls are above the diagonal, and correlations for boys are below.
SOURCE: Adapted from Sears (1963, p. 35).

tors are highly specific and depend on the details of the evoking situations and the response mode employed to measure them" (1968, p. 37).

Is Consistency Constructed or Real?

People's behavior is apparently less consistent across situations than we might think. Mischel suggested several reasons for our belief in the consistency of behavior: First, people's behavior may sometimes *appear* to be consistent merely because their situation has remained the same, or because of the continuing effects of some underlying factor such as occupational role, social class, or intelligence that is correlated with the behavior in question (1968, pp. 55–57, 281–287). Change people's situations, take away their jobs or money, and the apparent consistencies may evaporate.

Second, the apparent consistency of behavior may be constructed in the mind of the observer, rather than being something that exists "out there" in behavior itself (1968, chap. 3). Consider the Big Five trait factors discussed in Chapter 13 above. We have seen that in many different factor-analytic studies, observers' ratings of personality yield more or less the same five factors. On the other hand, Passini and Norman (1966) found that these same five factors also emerged when people were asked to rate *complete strangers,* on the basis of observing them for only fifteen minutes and without having any verbal interaction with them! Thus the five factors may reflect the cognitive framework or schemas that we use to organize our perceptions of other people, rather than the way traits are actually organized in people. According to this view, the Big Five are simply an informal personality theory that people carry around in their heads.

The Passini and Norman result suggests, then, that the consistency of behavior (and the broader concept of personality that we assume to be behind this consistency) are in part imposed by observers. It is easy to see how this could happen. For example, we observe that people are consistent across situations and over time in their physical appearance, sound of voice, and style of speech; hence we may expect that their behavior will be equally consistent. Perhaps our *expectation* of consistency constrains our observations, so we find what we expect. We then attribute our findings to the other person's personality rather than our own expectations (Mischel, 1968, pp. 55–59).

Do Personality Variables Really Predict Behavior?

Mischel went on to review the literature relating various personality variables to actual behavior. Typically, measures from one personality test or questionnaire are highly correlated with other tests or questionnaires, but much less highly correlated with nonquestionnaire measures of actual behavior in real life situations. Here are some examples of personality research from the 1950s and 1960s cited by Mischel (1968, pp. 78–81): (1) A major review of research on leadership success showed only a modest correlation with intelligence (median $r = .25$) and far lower relationships with personality variables. (2) Questionnaire measures of anxiety showed at best only weak correlations with physiological measures. (3) A longitudinal study of motives measured by means of the TAT showed more correlations with relevant actions than would be expected by chance, but the magnitude of the correlations was not great. (You may recall from statistics that a correlation of .30 between two variables is statistically significant—that is, would not arise by chance—if the number of cases is above forty-five. Even so, however, the amount of variation in the second variable that is accounted for or "explained" by the correlation with the first is quite small—around 9 percent according to many psychologists, although Ozer [1985] argues that such a correlation really explains 30 percent of the variance.)

Mischel's conclusion about the relation of personality variables to behavior is quite negative (Mischel, 1968):

> The magnitude of relationships obtained . . . is typically low. Indeed, the phrase "personality coefficient" might be coined to describe the correlation between .20 and .30 which is found persistently when virtually any personality dimension inferred from a questionnaire is related to almost any conceivable external criterion. . . . Generally such correlations are too low to have value for most individual assessment purposes. (pp. 77–78)

He then argued that situations, in contrast, usually have powerful effects on behavior:

> These weak associations [between personality and behavior], accounting for a trivial portion of the variance, become understandable when the enormous variation due to situationally specific variables that determine the consequences for behavior in any particular context is recognized. (p. 83)

Along these lines, Mischel quoted with approval an earlier conclusion by Endler, Hunt, and Rosenstein (1962): "The fact that a sampling of situations can contribute over 11 times the amount of variance contributed by individual differences [i.e., personality] among a sampling of [people] should give pause to clinicians, personologists, and psychometricians in general" (p. 12). (Many later writers, for example Nisbett [1980], made the same point.)

If we want to predict how people will behave in any particular situation, Mischel suggested that instead of making complex inferences about their personalities, we pay more attention to *base rates* (what most people of their age, gender, and social class do), *self-prediction* (what people say they will do), *the precise details of the situation*, and the *past* (how they have behaved in just this situation before) (1968, chap. 6). As an illustration of the power of predicting from simple measures of past behavior, Mischel cited a study by Lasky and colleagues (1959), who found that the best predictor of whether discharged psychiatric patients would wind up back in the hospital was simply the weight of their hospital file folder ($r = .61$)!

Two classic studies in which personality seemingly failed to predict important behaviors provided further illustration of Mischel's point. During World War II, Murray and his associates (OSS Assessment Staff, 1948) were employed by the U.S. Office of Strategic Services (predecessor to the CIA) to predict who would make an effective overseas spy. Murray and his colleagues developed an extensive battery of personality procedures, including interviews, objective and projective personality tests, situation tests, and individual case conferences. After the war, they went back to evaluate their predictions against the spies' actual performance. For overall performance, the correlations between assessment predictions and actual outcome ratings ranged from .08 to .53, with a median of .22; for more specific personality traits, the range was −.14 to +.53, with a median correlation of .11 (OSS Assessment Staff, 1948, pp. 423, 431). While some individual correlations were high, the overall pattern was disappointing. From this experience, the assessment staff concluded that successful personality assessments and predictions had to take into account the precise situations for which assessments and predictions were made—a point that seemed to anticipate Mischel's conclusions, two decades later, about the specificity of behavior.

After World War II, the U.S. Veterans Administration greatly expanded the field of clinical psychology in order to provide for the counseling needs of returning veterans. To improve the quality and training of clinical psychologists, Kelly and Fiske (1951) studied several hundred clinical psychology trainees in order to determine what personality characteristics were associated with rated success as a clinician. Again, they used a wide variety of methods, including autobiographies, personality tests, interviews, situation tests, and psychodrama or role playing. The results were almost an embarrassment: the two best predictors of the different measures of effectiveness as a clinical psychologist were the Miller Analogies Test (which is a measure of abstract intelligence), and the "psychologist" scale of the Strong Vocational Interest Blank (which is a measure of how similar one's interests are to those of psychologists). Even for these two variables, the median correlations with the effectiveness measures were .24 and .18, respectively (Kelly & Fiske, 1951, pp. 146,

150).[2] They were even lower for a second group of trainees assessed the following year. Other standard personality tests and ratings by experts showed virtually no relation to effectiveness. As one reviewer of the Kelly and Fiske study concluded (McNemar, 1952):

> If psychologists with ample funds and the best available personnel at their disposal cannot come up with a better solution to the prediction problem . . . the question may be asked as to whether we haven't oversold certain psychological services. (p. 860)

SKINNER AND THE EXPERIMENTAL ANALYSIS OF PERSONALITY

Mischel's 1968 book was not an isolated critique, but rather was very much in the spirit of the times. Many of his points had already been made by Vernon (1964) and Peterson (1965), and the behaviorist B. F. Skinner (1904–1990) had long argued against the use of hypothetical constructs, including personality constructs, in psychology.

From Skinner's perspective, concepts such as "personality" or "motive" are inferential constructs, connecting *situational contingencies* (what goes with what in the organism's environment) with *responses*. He argued that such constructs were unnecessary and unhelpful, since the determinants of the internal constructs themselves still needed to be explained. When this is done, the constructs will no longer be necessary. Thus for Skinner (1974), "a self or personality is at best a repertoire of behavior imparted by an organized set of contingencies" (p. 149). As for the specific variables of personality—plans, intentions, purposes, drives, needs, emotions, defenses:

> [They are] aspects of human behavior attributable to contingencies of reinforcement . . . [and] . . . to the subtle and complex relations among three things: the situation in which behavior occurs, the behavior itself, and its consequences. (p. 148)

For Skinner, then, personality simply refers to the person's prior learning or reinforcement history. Thus the traditional concepts and language of personality will be replaced by the unambiguous, objective, observable, experimentally based language of reinforcement and learning history—in Skinner's terms, the "experimental analysis of behavior." As he later put it toward the end of his life, "the greater part of human behavior must be traced to contingencies of reinforcement, especially to the very complex contingencies we call cultures" (Skinner, 1989, p. 18).

---

[2]Kelly and Fiske did not follow up the trainees long enough to measure their actual effectiveness as clinicians. Rather, they took supervisors' ratings of present and probable future effectiveness, while the trainees were still in graduate school. To my knowledge, no one has carried out a further, truly longitudinal prediction study using the Kelly and Fiske personality assessment data.

Let us see how such an analysis might be applied to some traditional personality concepts. Here is how Skinner (1974) described the Freudian concept of the ego:

> The product of the practical contingencies in daily life, necessarily involving susceptibilities to reinforcement and the punitive contingencies arranged by other people, but displaying behavior shaped and maintained by a current environment. (p. 151)

The id, in contrast, is derived from people's "innate susceptibilities to reinforcement, most of them almost necessarily in conflict with the interests of others." Finally, the superego:

> Is mainly the product of the punitive practices of a society which attempts to suppress the selfish behavior generated by biological reinforcers . . . [as] the injunctions of parents, teachers, and others become part of its repertoire." (pp. 150–151)

Level and Language of Analysis

If you think about Skinner's analyses or translations, you can probably detect the familiar Freudian concepts (see Chapter 3) behind the new names. The id as an "innate susceptibility to reinforcement" seems very similar to Freud's concept of an "instinctual endowment." The ego as "product of the practical contingencies in daily life" resembles Freud's "reality principle." And the superego as "the injunctions of parents, teachers, and others" sounds a good deal like Freud's conception of an internalized morality. Conflict among the three (intrapsychic conflict, in psychoanalytic language) is for Skinner "a person with different, possibly conflicting repertoires as the result of different, possibly conflicting, contingencies" (1974, p. 151). In principle, it is possible to translate any concept of personality into the Skinnerian language of contingencies, reinforcement schedules, and so forth, much as we might translate a word or phrase from one language to another. (Of course in psychology as in languages, translations cannot be exact, because every language has words and phrases for which there is no equivalent in the other language.) You may wonder, then, whether Skinner's experimental analysis of personality concepts and language is anything more than an exercise in translation. Skinner thought it was, because he believed that once we had a complete experimental analysis of personality concepts, we could dispense with these concepts.

Psychologists trained in the psychology of learning had made such translation attempts before (for example, Dollard & Miller, 1950; Sears, 1944). If a literary idea can be expressed (more or less) in different languages, then in principle a psychological truth should be capable of being expressed in the "languages" of different personality or learning theories. Which personality language or set of concepts is best: psychoanalysis (Chapter 3), personal constructs (Chapter 6), ordinary English (Chapter 11), the Big Five (Chapter

13), or reinforcement schedules and the experimental analysis of behavior (Chapter 16)? As you think about this question, imagine that you can speak several languages and are traveling in another country. The language you use will depend on several factors: which language you know best, which language you or your listeners prefer, and which language is best suited for the purpose at hand. The same considerations apply to the question of choosing a personality language. For some purposes, such as the analysis of a phobia (for example, the case of Little Albert described in Chapter 15), examining the person's reinforcement history might provide the simplest and most direct interpretation (see the classic psychoanalytic case of "Pearson Brack" as reanalyzed by Mischel, 1968, pp. 264–271). On the other hand, concepts such as achievement motivation (Chapter 5), authoritarianism (Chapter 7), or self-esteem may represent the most efficient way of describing other phenomena. In principle, it would be possible to analyze any of these concepts into schedules of a thousand (a million?) specific past contingencies and reinforcements, but in actual practice this is usually not realistic or useful.

As an analogy, you can think of yourself as a collection of trillions of atoms, each obeying complex laws of atomic physics and combined in structures according to the laws of chemistry. This kind of thinking is called *reductionism*. Such a reductionistic analysis is certainly true, but for purposes of getting tomorrow's assignment done, planning your life, or enjoying time with a close friend, it may not be particularly useful, meaningful, or even comfortable. As an intellectual exercise, reductionism is possible, but it is not always practical or appropriate for the task at hand.

Philosophical Assumptions of Atomism and Situationism

It is easy to think of the arguments of Skinner and Mischel simply as attacks on personality. However, a more balanced view would focus on their two underlying philosophical positions about scientific psychology and human personality. First, they advocate *atomism*, that is, the desire to break down complex entities into smaller units for purposes of analysis (just as chemists think of every substance as made up of atoms of different elements). Obviously we *can* describe either physical or personal realities in atomic ways or other ways, depending on our purposes, intellectual style, and preferences.

Second, the critiques of Mischel and Skinner reflect *situationism*, or a preference for external, situational factors over internal personality factors in understanding and predicting behavior. No one—not even the most radical behaviorist—goes so far as to suggest that behavior is a simple function of only the immediate present situation, however. Humans are not billiard balls that respond only to the forces of the immediate present moment. Past situations, stored, represented, or embodied within the person, clearly affect present behavior, whether we label these effects "reinforcement history" or "personality." Thus situationism, too, is not something that can be proved, but rather a matter of intellectual purpose, preference, and style. To understand the nature and power of Mischel's critique, then, we must see it as part of a larger philosophical and intellectual climate, the spirit of the times or *Zeitgeist*.

Overall, Mischel's book had a greater impact than Skinner's work on the field of personality psychology. Whereas Skinner had always been known as a reductionistic behaviorist whose primary research was on operant conditioning of pigeons, Mischel had been trained in clinical psychology (as a student of George Kelly, at Ohio State University) and was active in personality research; he knew personality "from the inside." In any case the 1968 publication date of *Personality and Assessment* is a convenient marker for the beginning of an era of crisis within personality psychology that was to last for almost two decades.

RESPONSES TO MISCHEL'S CRITIQUE

In the years after 1968, personality psychologists responded to Mischel's critical conclusions. Since these responses make up the philosophical and methodological framework of modern personality psychology, they are worth discussing in some detail, with examples.

Taking Another Look at the Research Literature

First, some personality psychologists went back to the original journal articles of the studies cited by Mischel to see whether they really supported the conclusions he drew from them. I will illustrate this by a re-examination of two of the most important studies that Mischel cited in order to question the cross-situational consistency of personality.

Reexamining the Burwen and Campbell study of attitudes toward authority. Consider the Burwen and Campbell (1957) study of attitudes toward authority. The results—that is, the correlation coefficients—are indeed as Mischel reported them (as shown in Table 16.1 above), but a careful reading of the original article reveals some important facts about what actually went on in the experiment, facts that were not contained in Mischel's account.

The 155 men studied by Burwen and Campbell were members of U.S. Air Force bomber crews assigned to Randolph Air Force Base (outside of San Antonio, Texas) for "crew assembly training" in preparation for action in the Korean war (1950–1953). Of these, 73 men were officers, mostly veterans of World War II, while 82 were enlisted men, mostly in their first military service. At the time of the testing (January and February, 1953), the Korean war was in its second year of stalemate. (The movie and television sitcom M*A*S*H, which you can still see on reruns, reflected some of the widespread feelings of cynicism and frustration among soldiers.) While the men were waiting for transfer to Korea, the bomber crews were required to participate in many other research studies and testing sessions besides the Burwen and Campbell study. Their participation in the study was compelled, though they were told that the data would not become part of any person's record.

Burwen and Campbell were clear about the effects of the setting and testing conditions (1957):

> The practical anonymity and mutual support of the research situation, plus more general attitudes characteristic of the impending transfer to Korea, resulted in a testing situation characterized in some cases by *perfunctory compliance* and occasional *humorous sabotage* of the test purpose. In the end, *between 10 and 15 per cent of the answer sheets had to be discarded. . . .* [In the interviews] this setting created a *guarded, deferential attitude* that was difficult to overcome. (pp. 24–25, emphases added)

If 10 to 15 percent of the answer sheets were so obviously faked or sabotaged that they had to be discarded, many of the rest were probably filled out in a haphazard way, by men who simply did not take these compulsory tasks at all seriously. In these circumstances, I doubt that a valid test of *anything*, particularly attitudes toward authority, would be possible. At the very least, the details of Burwen and Campbell's account should make us look at the correlation coefficients of Table 16.1 (and the conclusion Mischel drew from them) in a different light.

Although Burwen and Campbell used some established procedures (such as TATs, interviews, and sociometric questionnaires), most of the specific measures of attitude toward authority were newly developed for this study, which means that they have no history or established validity. (In other words, we have no way of knowing that they really measure what they purported to measure.)

All of the different sources of information about attitude toward a particular authority figure were reduced to the single dimension of favorable-unfavorable. While favorability is one important dimension of any attitude, there are others. For example, Stewart (1982; Stewart & Healy, 1992) has distinguished four different stances—receptive, autonomous, assertive, and integrated—toward authority (see Chapter 18).

Finally, we can ask whether any reasonable concept of personality really requires that people have exactly the *same* attitude toward *all* authorities. For example, Thomas Jefferson differentiated autocratic authority and democratic authority, while the socialist writers Marx and Engels distinguished the political authority of the capitalist state from the administrative authority of the state under socialism (Engels, 1873/1969). Can we therefore say that Jefferson and Engels were not "consistent" in their attitudes? Moreover, Freud's concepts of reaction formation or undoing, in which surface appearances are the opposite of deeper feelings (see Chapter 4), would suggest that highly favorable and highly unfavorable attitudes can be consistent with each other at a deeper level! The authoritarian personality, deferent to in-group authority but hostile to out-group authority, would be an example (see Chapter 7). Thus there are many theoretical reasons why we might not expect high intercorrelations among favorability ratings of different authority figures.

Because of these theoretical shortcomings and methodological flaws, the Burwen-Campbell study is really not an adequate test of whether people have generalized attitudes toward authority. (This review also suggests a caution: it is always a good idea to check carefully through original sources, rather than relying only on abstracts or summaries, which can distort the transmission of scientific findings.)

The Sears study of dependency. Recall from Table 16.2 that Sears and his colleagues found only very low positive correlations among five presumed measures of dependency behavior among girls, and essentially zero correlations among boys. They concluded that "apparently, then, these kinds of behavior do not represent aspects of a trait or any other unified behavior" (Sears, Rau, & Alpert, 1965, p. 68).

But why did Sears and associates pick these particular five behavior categories, and why did they expect high correlations among them? They apparently reasoned as follows: In young children, each of these five behaviors generally leads to greater attention (nurturance, affection, reassurance) from a parent or caretaker (Sears, 1963, pp. 30–31; Sears, Rau, & Alpert, 1965, pp. 28–32, 68). Since they all have the same effect, of eliciting nurturance, *therefore* they are all part of the same dependency action system. But any act may have many different effects. Consider negative attention seeking, which is defined by Sears, Rau, and Alpert as follows (1965):

> Getting attention by disruptive, aggressive activity with minimal provocation, defiance, or oppositional behavior; opposing and resisting direction, rules, routines, and demands by ignoring, refusing, or doing the opposite. Examples: Child skips through block corner kicking at the children's constructions. Child waves a saw threateningly by another's neck until stopped by teacher. Child hits at teacher to get her attention. (p. 300)

Each of these acts might get the nursery school teacher's attention, but the attention it gets may not be the same as the attention elicited by a child who seeks reassurance, for example by asking, "Could you help me dig in the sandbox?" And getting attention may not be the *primary* purpose of any of these acts. Most of the negative attention-seeking acts listed above are aggressive, so they could also (or instead) be categorized as aggression instead of dependency. (In fact, "negative attention seeking" showed higher correlations with another measure of "antisocial aggression" than with any of the other dependency categories; see Sears, Rau, & Alpert, 1965, p. 34).[3] Perhaps, then, the Sears results have less to do with the cross-situational stability of dependency than with the particular categories, definitions, and theoretical conceptions of the researchers.

Moreover, even if we grant that these five categories are an appropriate definition of dependency, it does not follow that they will necessarily be highly intercorrelated. If you do a lot of any one of these categories, you really don't need to do all the others in order to be high in the overall behavior system. As an analogy, consider the foods you eat at any particular meal. If you eat a lot of chicken, then you probably won't eat a lot of fish; if you eat a lot of cheese, you may eat less chicken and fish; and if you are a strict vegetarian, you may not eat any chicken, fish, or cheese. Thus you would show low "consistency" of eating behavior across these different foods. Still, the idea of a

---

[3]Double-scoring for dependency and aggression was not allowed (see Sears, Rau, & Alpert, 1965, pp. 302–303).

broad hunger motive, which might express itself alternatively in each of these different meals, is reasonable.

In more formal terms, both Sears and colleagues and Mischel assume that a behavior system can have only one internal structural logic, namely, simple, positive, and additive relationships among all component behaviors of the system. Other, more complex structures are also possible. In the meal case, for example, chicken, fish, and cheese are substitutes or *functionally equivalent alternatives* for each other. In the case of dependency, the five categories may all lead to an equivalent goal or state (the attention of a powerful other person), but the categories themselves do not thereby have to be highly intercorrelated (see also McClelland, 1975, pp. 12–13; Wittenborn, 1955). While Sears and his colleagues did recognize this possibility—that dependency might be organized on the basis of "the dynamic substitutability of one response for another"—they dismissed it as "not susceptible to test with our data" (1965, p. 69).

To take this point a bit further, there may be different *kinds* of dependency, each sharing a common effect (getting the attention of a nurturant parent or teacher) but different in certain other respects. For example, Sears and his colleagues did suggest a distinction between "mature" dependency (negative and positive attention seeking and reassurance seeking, which are all active and verbal) and "immature" dependency, which is passive and nonverbal. The same children would not necessarily score high in both kinds of dependency. Similarly, in the case of attitudes toward authority we could distinguish attitudes toward legitimate authority from attitudes toward illegitimate authority, attitudes toward benevolent authority from attitudes toward punitive authorities, and so forth.

In this connection, recall Allport's original definition of a trait as a generalized structure that is not always expressed with perfect consistency in behavior of conflicting traits and the situation (Chapter 11; see also Allport, 1931). In summary, then, personality variables have a more complicated internal structure and external context than would be revealed by a simple matrix of correlation coefficients.

Comparing Magnitudes of Situation and Personality Effects

Magnitude of effect and the statistics used to report it. Mischel's claim that situation variables have much more powerful effects on behavior than personality variables is shared by many psychologists (for example, Nisbett, 1980). This claim is difficult to test because it all depends upon which behaviors, which personality variables, and which situations we study. However, the different statistics we typically use to measure each kind of effect may contribute to the impression of the greater explanatory power of the situation. Table 16.3 illustrates how this might happen. In a typical personality research study, we relate a personality variable to some other personality or behavior variable, using the *correlation coefficient*. Correlations can vary from −1.00 (a

TABLE 16.3 PERSONALITY RESEARCH RESULTS REPORTED WITH DIFFERENT STATISTICS

| Dependent variable | "Personality" version | | "Social-psychology" version | | |
	Correlation with power motivation	Grouping on dependent variable	N	Power motivation Mean	SD
	Power motivation and office holding among male college students				
Office holding	.30	Officers	37	52.62	9.12
	(N = 73)	Nonofficers	36	46.78	9.49
	p < .01	Difference		5.84	
				t = 2.68, p <.01	
	Power motivation and power careers* among women college graduates				
Having a power career	.26	Power careers*	30	54.70	10.73
	(N = 71)	Other careers	41	49.39	9.14
	p < .05	Difference		5.31	
				t = 2.25, p <.05	
	Power motivation and power careers* among men college graduates				
Having a power career	.27	Power careers*	59	53.84	12.04
	(N = 173)	Other careers	114	48.02	8.08
	p < .001	Difference		1.85	
				t = 3.75, p < .001	

*Power careers include business executive, teacher, psychologist, clergy, and journalist.
SOURCE: Data adapted from Winter (1973, 1988).

perfect negative correlation) to +1.00 (a perfect positive correlation), but in personality research correlations are often in the range of −.30 to +.30. (Mischel's derogatory term is "personality coefficient," as discussed above.) While a correlation of .30 may be statistically significant (that is, unlikely to have arisen by chance), it seems well below the 1.00 value of a perfect relationship. Even worse, if we square the correlation coefficient to determine the variance in the second variable explained by the first, .30 drops to $(.30)^2$ or .09 (but see the objection to squaring correlations by Ozer, 1985).

In social-psychology laboratory experiments, however, we usually create two or more situations by experimental manipulation and then use the *t-test* or *analysis of variance* to evaluate the resulting differences in behavior. The larger the value of *t*, the less likely it is that the difference between conditions could have arisen by chance. The value of *t* has no upper limit. Thus in reading we tend to notice how much larger *t* is than its minimum value of zero, not how much smaller it is than its theoretical maximum value (which is infinite).

To illustrate this effect of difference in statistical presentation, Table 16.3 shows the same results—concerning the office-holding and career correlates of power motivation (from Winter, 1973, 1988)—in two different ways: in the left column by correlation coefficients, as would be done in personality research; and in the right column by *t*-tests, as would be done in a social-psychology experiment. Does the "social-psychology" (*t*-test) version seem to be a stronger or more powerful finding than the "personality" (correlation) version? Remember that the two versions are exactly equivalent: they are of exactly the same level of statistical significance and can in fact be mathematically translated into each other. As an informal experiment, I randomly distributed the correlation and the *t*-test versions of these findings to a group of personality faculty and graduate students and asked them to evaluate the significance, strength, and importance of the findings. The faculty and graduate students rated the two versions as more or less equivalent in strength and importance, but they rated the *t*-test versions as demonstrating a relatively greater role of personality versus situation in the relevant behavior. Even personality "experts," then, may be more impressed with results expressed in *t*-tests than in exactly equivalent correlations.

Magnitude of typical effects in social-psychology research. A typical "personality coefficient" in the .30 to .40 range seems small, but how small is it really, as compared with the values of *t* typically reported in studies of the effect of situations? If you have taken a statistics course, you may recall that a *t*-test tells us how likely it is that a difference between two groups (representing two situations) has arisen by chance. It does not, however, tell us the *magnitude* of the effect—that is, the variance in the behavior that is explained by the situations. For estimating the magnitude of effect, we need the statistic *eta*, which is analogous to the correlation coefficient. It is not usually reported in journal articles, but any *t* value can be converted into its equivalent correlation, or *eta*.

Funder and Ozer (1983) made these conversions for several of the most famous and widely cited demonstrations in the social-psychology literature of the power of situations: the phenomenon of cognitive dissonance (that is, attitude change brought about by advocating a counterattitude; see Festinger & Carlsmith, 1959); the effects on bystander intervention of the number of other people present, and the degree of "hurry" (Darley & Batson, 1973; Darley & Latané, 1968); and the effects of proximity of authority and proximity of victim on obedience (Milgram, 1975). From the statistics reported in the original studies, Funder and Ozer calculated effect sizes or *eta* values. As shown in Table 16.4, these range from .36 to .42—the same range that Mischel (1968) and Nisbett (1980) dismissed as "personality coefficients."

Effect size in other fields of science. The effect sizes of typical personality psychology research findings also stack up well against those in so-called hard-science fields. Rosenthal (1990) presents some interesting and provocative comparisons. For example, the Physicians' Health Study explored whether aspirin prevents heart attacks. A sample of doctors was randomly divided into two groups: one group regularly took an aspirin tablet, the other regularly took a chemically inert placebo pill that looked

TABLE 16.4 CLASSIC STUDIES ON THE EFFECTS OF SITUATIONS, EXPRESSED AS CORRELATIONS

Behavior	Situational variable	Correlation	Reference
Reported attitude	Incentive for advocating counterattitude	−.36	Festinger & Carlsmith (1959)
Bystander intervention	Number of onlookers	−.38	Darley & Latané (1968)
	"Hurry"	−.39	Darley & Batson (1973)
Obedience	Proximity of authority	.36	Milgram (1975)
	Proximity of victim	−.42	Milgram (1975)

SOURCE: Adapted from Funder and Ozer (1983, p. 110).

like aspirin. In 1987, the officials in charge of the study ended it early: the evidence that aspirin prevented heart attacks and deaths was so strong that it would have been unethical to continue giving only the placebo to half the participating doctors. In actual fact, the aspirin group had suffered only about half as many heart attacks as the placebo group. Such a difference sounds impressive, but Rosenthal observed that the *correlation coefficient* between the two variables aspirin/placebo and heart attack/no heart attack was actually only −.034. After squaring, this means that the aspirin/no aspirin variable explains only one-tenth of 1 percent of the variance in heart attacks. The correlation was significant, although the magnitude of the aspirin effect was small, because the sample was large ($N = 22,071$) and heart attacks were very infrequent ($N = 293$). Still, the effect was *important* enough to justify ending the study early so that all the participating doctors could benefit from taking aspirin.

Rosenthal analyzed results of three other important medical discoveries in terms of the correlation coefficient as a measure of effect size. Among Vietnam-era veterans, for example, service in Vietnam was associated with subsequent alcoholism ($r = .07$); the drug cyclosporine reduces the likelihood that the body will reject a transplanted organ ($r = −.19$); and the drug AZT extends the life of patients with AIDS ($r = .23$). Compared to these figures, "personality coefficients" of .30 are much more impressive! Given the complexity of the real world, we should not expect stronger relationships. Any effect—of personality, situation, aspirin, Vietnam service, or drugs such as cyclosporine and AZT—therefore exists in the context of many other important effects of many other factors.

*I*MPROVEMENTS IN PERSONALITY RESEARCH SINCE 1968

In addition to examining Mischel's evidence and reconsidering the meaning and importance of correlation coefficients and effect sizes, personality psychologists also made major conceptual and methodological improvements in personality research after Mischel's critique (see Block, 1977a).

Consistency as a Personality Variable in Its Own Right

Some people may be more consistent than others. In other words, consistency may be a variable of personality, either by itself or in combination with other variables. Consider the two traits of friendliness and conscientiousness (approximately factors 2 and 3 of the Big Five, discussed in Chapter 13). Bem and Allen (1974) first asked a sample of sixty-four men and women college students to rate their average level on each trait ("In general, how friendly and outgoing [conscientious] are you?"), then to rate how consistent they were on each trait ("How much do you vary from one situation to another in how friendly and outgoing [conscientious] you are?"). On the basis of this latter response, each participant was classified as either consistent or inconsistent on each trait. Next, Bem and Allen collected a variety of other measures relating to each trait: (1) self-ratings in over twenty specific situations, (2) ratings by mother, (3) ratings by father, (4) ratings by a peer, and (5) various behavioral measures. ("Friendly" behaviors included friendly interaction in a group discussion and spontaneous friendliness in a waiting room. "Conscientious" behaviors included returning course evaluations, doing course readings on time, and neatness of personal appearance.)

Bem and Allen's results are shown in Table 16.5. As you can see, the self-ratings of consistency on a trait are related to the actual cross-measure consistency of behaviors related to that trait. Thus people who see themselves as consistent in friendliness (whether at a high or low absolute level) show more consistency across several other measures than do those who see themselves as inconsistent in friendliness. For them, there is more consistency to friendliness ratings by others, and the measures of friendliness are more highly correlated with a standard questionnaire measure of extraversion (from the Eysenck Personality Inventory; see Chapter 12).[4] Similarly, people who see

[4]Since the EPI is a self-report questionnaire, it may be appropriate to consider only its correlations with the other, non-self-report measures. As shown in Table 16.5, these are less different, though still in the same direction.

TABLE 16.5 SELF-RATED CONSISTENCY ON FRIENDLINESS AND CONSCIENTIOUSNESS AND THE CONSISTENCY OF MEASURES

	Friendliness		Conscientiousness	
	Consistent*	Inconsistent	Consistent*	Inconsistent
Mean intercorrelation of separate measures	.57	.27	.36	.12
Mean correlation of self-report with others' reports	.57	.44	.41	.25
Mean correlation of EPI extraversion with other measures	.51	.31		

*For friendliness, measured by answer to a general question about variability on the trait; for conscientiousness, measured by self-reported variability across twenty-three specific "conscientiousness" situations.
SOURCE: Adapted from Bem and Allen (1974).

themselves as consistent across situations in conscientiousness show greater consistency across the different conscientiousness measures (especially the ratings) than do people who see themselves as inconsistent. The Bem and Allen results suggest that *trait consistency* may vary across people, with trait measures predicting behavior much better among people who are consistent on that trait.

When people undergo major life changes (college graduation, first full-time job, getting married, birth of a child, retirement, etc.), their personalities are likely to change and develop (see Cantor, 1990; Stewart, 1982). Such effects could influence the apparent consistency of personality measures. Thus Koestner, Franz, and Hellman (1991) found that TAT measures of power and intimacy motivation were quite stable over eight months among people whose lives were stable (average $r = .65$), but much less stable among people undergoing major life changes during that interval (average $r = .24$).

Individual Differences in the Explanatory Power of Situation versus Personality

The Bem and Allen results suggest that for consistent people, personality is a relatively more powerful cause of behavior than situation; for inconsistent people, however, situations may be more powerful. That is, when people are inconsistent on some trait, other factors (such as situation or other personality variables) are likely to predict behavior. Along these lines, Jenkins (1982) hypothesized that self-defining people (people scoring high in self-definition; see Stewart & Winter, 1974) would be personality-defined; that is, their behavior would be predicted by personality variables. In contrast, the behavior of low-scorers (called *socially defined* by Stewart and Winter) would be more situation-dependent. Jenkins's reasoning was that the self-definition measure reflects the tendency to define one's self rather than to be defined by other people and society. It also involves the ability to cope instrumentally with personal issues, stress, and health problems (see Stewart, 1992b). Jenkins confirmed this hypothesis in a study of women college graduates. For women scoring high in self-definition, personality variables were more powerful than situational variables in predicting achievement aspirations and behavior during the years after college. Among the socially defined low-scorers, however, social support (a situational variable) was a more powerful predictor of achievement aspirations and behavior than personality.

Analysis of longitudinal data on college-educated men from Winter, McClelland, and Stewart (1981, chap. 4), in Table 16.6, shows the same results. For self-defining men, personality as measured at the beginning of college (in this case, achievement and affiliation motivation, see Chapter 5) predicted important life outcomes ten years after college; but for socially defined men, current situation was a more powerful predictor. For example, for self-defining men, the outcomes of current income and early career success are significantly predicted by achievement motivation. That is, the success of these men is an

TABLE 16.6 PREDICTING BEHAVIOR FROM PERSONALITY AND SITUATION FOR SELF-DEFINING AND SOCIALLY DEFINED MALE COLLEGE STUDENTS

Correlations of personality and situational variables with postcollege life outcomes	Self-defining (high in self-definition, N = 39)	Socially defined (low in self-definition, N = 49)
Income level predicted by		
Achievement motivation (personality)	.45[†]	−.25
Having children (situation)	−.09	.51[‡]
Early career success predicted by		
Achievement motivation (personality)	.34[*]	.06
Having children (situation)	−.12	.57[‡]
Self-rated happiness predicted by		
Affiliation motivation (personality)	.39[*]	−.14
Having a "desirable" job[§] (situation)	.28	.42[†]

[*]$p < .05$
[†]$p < .01$
[‡]$p < .001$
[§]Self-ratings of "Overall, how frustrating is your present job?" subtracted from self-ratings of "Overall, how satisfying is your present job?"
Note: Personality was measured at age 18, during first year in college; life outcomes were measured at ages 32–33, ten years after college.

expression of their personality fourteen years earlier. For the socially defined men, in contrast, income and early success are predicted by a variable of current situation—whether they had children. In other words, their success is more of a response to the situational pressures of the traditional male family-provider role. Other differences between the two groups showed the same pattern. Among self-defining men, current happiness is related to prior levels of the affiliation motive whereas for socially defined men, happiness depends on the relative satisfactions and frustrations of the current job.

Interaction between Personality and Situation

When psychologists speak about the influence of personality on behavior, they do not mean that a person who scores high on a particular personality variable (for example, affiliation motivation or extraversion) will always act the same way in every situation (though Mischel's criticism may imply this). We do not expect that a friendly person will always be friendly to every other person, in every situation, any more than a person with a good appetite would eat all the time, everywhere. Even so, there are differences between people who are, generally, friendly (or people with a good appetite) and those who are not.

Person-situation interaction. In an early and influential paper on personality traits, Allport (1931) suggested that people's traits were only *generalized* characteristics that were expressed in *varied* behavior, according to their specific situation. Mischel's critique, thirty-seven years later, led personality psychologists to emphasize again the *joint* importance of personality and situation and to develop a variety of techniques for studying *person-situation interaction* (see Magnusson, 1981, 1990; Magnusson & Endler, 1977).

We have already presented several studies illustrating this interaction. Recall from Chapter 14 (especially Figures 14.3 and 14.4) how the relationship between introversion-extraversion and behavior depends on the complexity or arousal properties of the current situation. Two classic motivation studies, shown in Table 16.7, provide further examples. Feather (1961) found that as an initially easy task became harder, students scoring high in achievement motivation tended to persist longer than low-scorers. However, when an initially difficult task became almost impossible, achievement-motivated students showed relatively *less* persistence. Superficially, these results are not consistent in Mischel's sense: achievement motivation is associated with more persistence in one condition and less persistence in another condition. At a more abstract or general level, however, these two results are quite consistent: on tasks that are (or seem to become) of middle-level difficulty, achievement motivation predicts higher persistence; but on tasks that are at one or the other extreme of difficulty (that is, very easy or very hard), achievement motivation predicts lower persistence.

A study by Fishman (1966), mentioned in Chapter 5, illustrates how the affiliation motive interacts with situational cues. In informal discussions among well-acquainted friends, college women scoring high in affiliation motivation showed more friendly sociable interaction toward other members of the group than did women scoring low. In discussions with strangers, however, this relationship reversed: the high-scoring women showed relatively *less* friendly behavior. Thus the affiliation motive leads to friendly behavior, but not always. Under conditions of threat or uncertainty, it may actually lead to defensive retreat.

TABLE 16.7 INTERACTION OF PERSONALITY AND SITUATION AMONG COLLEGE STUDENTS

	Behavior shown	
Situation	High in motivation	Low in motivation
Persistence behavior and achievement motivation [*]		
Initially easy task becoming harder	75% showed[†]	33% showed
Initially hard task becoming almost impossible	22% showed	75% showed
Friendly behavior and affiliation motivation[‡]		
In a discussion group of close friends	36.8[§]	26.1
In a discussion group of nonfriends or strangers	23.4	25.8

[*]From Feather (1961, p. 558).
[†]Persistence above median for all participants.
[‡]From Fishman (1966, p. 159).
[§]Average number of friendly actions during a discussion.

These studies illustrate the general point that behavior is often related to personality variables *in combination with* situational variables. In such cases, the situational variables are referred to as *moderator variables*, because they moderate (or modify) the relationship between personality and behavior. For example, in Fishman's study the situational variable of group composition (friends versus strangers) is a moderator variable because it moderates or modifies the expression of the affiliation motive.

Assessing the "personality" of situations. It is difficult to know exactly what aspects of a situation will act as moderator variables for the expression of any given personality variable. Sometimes we can make predictions on the basis of theory, as for example Eysenck's prediction that introvert-extravert performance differences will reverse as the situation changes from one of low to high arousal (see Chapter 14). Sometimes we just make a lucky guess about which situational variable will act as a moderator. Bem and his colleagues (Bem, 1982; Bem & Funder, 1978) introduced a technique that could make our guesses more educated. By using the California Q-sort (see Chapter 9 and Block, 1978) to describe both the personality of people and the "personality" of situations in the same terms, they were able to construct profiles or templates of the personality characteristics relevant to the situations. Alternatively, this technique enables us to construct a profile of situations relevant to a given personality characteristic. We would predict higher correlations between the personality characteristic and relevant outcomes in these situations as compared to other situations with a different profile.

The interaction of personality and macrocontexts. The studies just cited demonstrate that personality interacts with contrived laboratory situations, or microcontexts, in predicting behavior. In real-life macrocontexts, however, these interactive effects should be even more striking. For example, consider personality variables as power motivation (Chapter 5), attributional style (Chapter 8), or surgency and conscientiousness (Chapter 13). How differently would these variables be expressed by the following two groups of people in the following two situations: (1) white 20-year-old American men storming Utah Beach during the Normandy invasion of World War II on the morning of June 6, 1944; and (2) Japanese American women in an internment camp in the middle of the desert in the state of Utah, on that same day.

So far as I know, no one has collected the data to answer that question, but Nuttall (1964) and Greene and Winter (1971) have shown that among African American males, the region of the country in which they spent their childhood had major effects on how their achievement and power motives (see Chapter 5) were expressed, at least during the 1960s. Table 16.8 summarizes the findings of both studies. Among Northern-reared males, both motives were related to a "militant" or confrontational sense of black consciousness. Among Southern-reared men, however, these two motives predicted a more accommodating, pragmatic style. The *reasons* for these differences may be the result of many factors, from history (slavery and then legalized discrimination in the

TABLE 16.8 EFFECT OF REGION OF REARING ON THE EXPRESSION OF ACHIEVEMENT AND POWER MOTIVES AMONG AFRICAN AMERICAN MEN IN THE 1960S

Motive and behavior variable	Place of rearing	
	North	South
Achievement motivation and[*]		
Self-reported feeling being victim of racial discrimination	.32 ($p < .05$)	−.31 ($p < .05$)
Militancy	.28 ($p < .10$)	−.26
Repression of hostility	.02	.38 ($p < .05$)
Power motivation and[†]		
Peer ratings of "confrontational"[‡]	.60 ($p < .01$)	−.25
Peer ratings of "pragmatic"	−.33	.58 ($p < .01$)

[*]From Nuttall (1964, p. 597).
[†]From Greene and Winter (1971, p. 325).
[‡]Combination of high ratings of "directly active within the Black community" and low ratings on "willing to work within the system."

South) to socioeconomic conditions and popular attitudes (greater societal disruption and hypocrisy in the relatively industrialized and urban North; see Lemann, 1991). These two studies date from the very beginning of the civil rights movement. Conditions have undoubtedly changed, and the findings might well be different if the studies were carried out today.

Person-situation interactions over the life course. Personality also interacts with situation over time, leading each individual to accumulate a complex series of person-situation interactions that we call the *life course.* Caspi and his associates (Caspi, Elder, & Bem, 1987, 1988) have charted life-course sequences for "explosive" and "shy" children. In their model, initial personality characteristics affect later situations. These situations, in combination with personality, have consequences for later situations, and so on. For example, at ages 8 to 10, explosive boys often had temper tantrums. As a result, they were problems for their school teachers. This impeded their academic performance, which limited their later career options. Ending up in lower-status jobs as adults, they experienced even more frustration. These jobs, in combination with their continuing bad temper, led to higher unemployment and a less stable job history. These outcomes (again in combination with their bad temper) led to unhappy marriages, inadequate parenting, and divorce. Finally, at midlife they were described by observers as "undercontrolled," "irritable," and "moody." The same general pattern of results also holds true for explosive girls, except that a history of tantrums has no effect on their job and work history. (The reason for this exception is probably that these women entered the labor force in the late 1940s, when women's career choices were largely restricted to low-level clerical and sales jobs without the possibility of advancement that could be jeopardized by irritability.)

You may be wondering whether the families of the explosive, bad-tempered children were different to start with. If these children came disproportionately from working-class (rather than middle-class) families, then the findings of Caspi and his associates may simply reflect the continuing effects of parents' education or income, rather than the effects of the child's personality or temperament. Although Caspi and colleagues do not report the relationship between children's temperament and parents' social class, they were careful to control for parental social class in their analyses. The chain of relationships described above held for children from middle-class *and* working-class origins, though they were stronger for the middle-class children. Perhaps, then, having a pleasant personality is especially important for the white-collar jobs and careers that middle-class children typically enter.

Figure 16.2, adapted from Caspi, Elder, and Bem (1987), illustrates these relationships for middle-class explosive male children. Solid lines indicate *causal paths* or relationships that are statistically significant; all other relationships are nonsignificant. (The numbers are called beta coefficients; they are

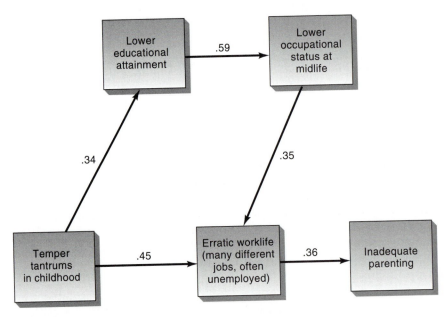

FIGURE 16.2
Direct and indirect effects of childhood temper tantrums in the life course of middle-class men. (Adapted from Caspi, Elder, and Bem, 1987, pp. 311–312. Lines indicate causal "paths" that are significant. Numbers are *beta* weights, analogous to correlations with the effects of other variables controlled.)

like correlations except that each one is controlled for the effects of all other variables.) Notice, for example, that childhood tantrums directly affect educational attainment. Notice, too, that childhood tantrums have no direct effect on midlife occupational status, but rather affect it indirectly, through educational attainment, which does have a direct effect. As Caspi and colleagues describe the meaning of this pattern, "middle-class boys with a history of childhood tantrums arrived at lower occupational status at mid-life because they truncated their formal education earlier, not because they continue to carry an ill-tempered interactional style" (1987, p. 311). But notice that childhood tantrums do have an important direct effect on erratic worklife and, via erratic worklife, an indirect effect on inadequate parenting.

In summarizing their results concerning personality and situation over the life course, Caspi and his associates suggest two underlying mechanisms. *Cumulative continuity* occurs when the consequences of behaviors (which are, themselves, the result of personality) progressively accumulate and channel a person into certain situations and environments that constrain further behaviors and so reinforce the original personality factor. For example, bad-tempered children end up with less education, which restricts them to lower-status jobs, which means that they will be more vulnerable to unemployment, which makes them more likely to be angry. *Interactional continuity* refers to the reactions from others that are evoked by a behavior (that is originally the result of personality) and serve to maintain that behavior. For example, bad-tempered children are likely to elicit anger and aggression from their peers, teachers, and parents; this anger in turns maintains and reinforces their own aggression. Both mechanisms suggest that personality and situation are not separate and opposed explanations of behavior, but rather are bound together in complex and changing relationships that may endure and evolve throughout the life course.

Personality Can Affect Situations

The basic premise of the situationist critique of personality is that behavior is largely the result of the external situation rather than of internal "personality" factors. Still, even situationists concede that behavior patterns often show some stability over time (though not as often, they argue, as personality psychologists think). They explain this stability, however, as the result of the stability of people's situations rather than the stability of their internal personality dispositions. In response, many personality psychologists turned the situationist argument on its head, arguing that *people's personality affects their situation*. The work of Caspi and his associates, by tracing how initial personality factors lead people into certain later situations, is an example. Buss (1987) formalized this perspective by specifying three ways in which personality affects situations: selection, evocation, and manipulation.

Consider *selection*, the fact that people seek out and avoid different situations selectively. Within limits, we choose the kind of college to attend, the partner with whom we want to share our life, whether to live in a large city, a small town, or a rural setting, and so forth. (The word "selection" may be a little misleading, because it implies conscious, mindful, and deliberate choice. In fact, many if not most of these selections may not be conscious, at least at the time they are made.) Once made, however, these choices have enduring effects, because they create important and enduring situations that will affect (and moderate) our behavior and personalities in the future. For example, in selecting a life partner, Buss reminds us that we are "simultaneously selecting the social acts [of the partner] to which [we] will be enduringly exposed" (1987, p. 1216).

Evocation refers to the way in which a person's action evokes or draws forth certain responses from other people. These responses in turn constitute a (new) situation that maintains that person's further behavior. Examples from everyday life include the aggressive child whose behavior evokes punishment from a teacher (the punishment serving to maintain the child's aggression) or the fussy baby whose parents, exhausted and impatient as a result of the baby's fussiness, are more "distant" and not as nurturant as they might otherwise be. At the level of societies and nations, many wars result from arms races in which each side, arming to protect itself from a feared enemy, only succeeds in provoking the enemy to arm further.

Few situations are forever fixed and unchanging; some restructuring or *manipulation* of the situation is usually possible. (By this Buss meant actually changing the situation, not merely reconstruing or reconceptualizing it in Kelly's sense, as discussed in Chapter 6.) In agriculture, for example, irrigation can make the desert bloom like a rose. Similarly, with the right kind of leadership and organization, an oppressed people can be set free. With a little knowledge and experience, you can even make a college bureaucracy work for you.

The study of boys in small groups by Merei (1949/1958) is a classic example of how people can manipulate situations. When a boy who had showed leadership in a previous group was introduced into a group of other boys that had already formed fixed traditions and patterns of leadership, that child was at first displaced as leader. His influence attempts were no longer followed. Obviously the immediate situation had overridden any of his leadership personality characteristics. Nevertheless, over time these "ex-leaders" managed, by a variety of strategies, to regain the role of leader. Because Merei's study is such a vivid example of how personality can affect situations, I will give lengthy examples of these strategies.

One such strategy was *order-giving*. As Merei (1949/1958) observed:

> Though keeping within the frame of activities he had just learned from them, and according to their rules, he told the children what to do—that is, he ordered them to do exactly what they would have done anyway. (p. 526)

Because the ex-leader only tells the group to do what they would have done anyway, they are likely to follow his orders. At the same time, this transforms the situation: the group is not only following tradition but also following orders of the ex-leader. By making this small change in the situation, the ex-leader begins to reemerge as leader.

Next, the former leaders made *small changes* and *innovations* in existing group traditions—some added ritual or faster pace—which subtly established their leadership. Here is how one boy did this:

> He tried to suggest new games but was not accepted. Then he joined their traditional game and slowly took over the leadership. . . . For example, he joined in the block game traditional with the group, but he demanded that always the red side of a block be on top. . . . The third time he was with the group he again suggested new activities. One was "hide and seek." . . . The group did not accept the suggestion and played instead another traditional game they called "acting with hats." The leader yielded, joined the "hat game" and instantly began to organize it, in the course of which he made changes so as to combine with it the hide-and-seek game he had suggested. (p. 529)

Finally, some of the former leaders *assumed ownership* of important objects, even if only to give them back again:

> The leader joining the developed group takes possession of all the objects in the room. They continue being used according to group tradition; the games played with them remain the same. . . . but all the objects "belong" to him. . . . Their play remained unchanged; the same game with the same toys. They talked of the toys as they did before—Johnny's blocks, Tom's box—but occasionally they said . . . "Tom's box belongs to Andrew" [the leader]. The owners of the objects became their users, while the right of ownership was given over, voluntarily or otherwise, to the new leader. (pp. 527–528)

During the Renaissance, the newly emerging European kings and queens used many of the same strategies to wrest land and power back from the feudal nobility!

Kinds of Data Used in Personality Research

Domains of data. In response to Mischel's critique, Block (1977a) took a careful look at different kinds or domains of data used in personality research. Borrowing terms originally introduced by Cattell, he distinguished the following: *R* data, based on observers' *ratings* of people; *S* data, based on people's own *self-report*; *L* data, drawn from *life outcomes*; and *T* data, based on people's performance on a *test* or in a *laboratory situation*. Table 16.9 gives some typical examples of these different kinds of data.

Reviewing the state of personality research, Block suggested that studies using data from the *R, S,* and *L* domains show considerable convergence of measurement as well as coherence, consistency, and continuity of personality. The literature supporting these conclusions is enormous; here I will cite only a few studies to illustrate Block's point. Block's own longitudinal studies (see also Block, 1971) show impressive correlations over time (*r*'s above .45) for *R*

TABLE 16.9 KINDS OF DATA USED IN PERSONALITY RESEARCH

Kind of data	Examples in personality research
R Ratings by others	Sociometric questionnaire, Q-sort completed by observers
S Self-report	Most personality tests and questionnaires, Q-sort completed by self
L Life outcome	Academic performance, career choice, occupational performance, marital history, health, whether a criminal record, psychiatric symptoms
T Test/situation	Performance in a single experiment or situation (e.g., measuring delay of gratification, obedience to authority, honesty, helpfulness)

SOURCE: Adapted from Block (1977a) and Cattell (1957).

data and S data, as well as considerable convergence between the same variables as measured by both kinds of data. Thus in combining the results of sixteen longitudinal studies of rated aggression (R data) in men, Olweus (1979) found that the over-time correlation coefficients averaged well above +.60, which indicated considerable stability in male aggressive behavior. For questionnaire measures of extraversion and neuroticism (S data) measured over forty-five years, Conley (1984) reported correlations above +.60, while McCrae and Costa (1984, pp. 59–62) reported correlations as high as +.85 over twelve years.

Finally, a study by Block, Block, and Keyes (1988) illustrates a very strong relationship between R data and L data. Block and associates found that "undercontrol" or low ego control (see Chapter 13; also Block & Block, 1980), as assessed by ratings of children at ages 3 to 4 (R data) significantly predicted whether those children used drugs over ten years later, in adolescence (L data)!

How can these results be reconciled with Mischel's (1968) claim that personality variables possess only low stability, consistency, and validity? Block (1977a) suggested that Mischel's conclusions were mostly drawn from studies involving T data—that is, laboratory situations focused on a single instance of some behavior presumed to reflect a personality variable. For studies using such data, Block argued, "the evidence for personality consistency [and coherence] . . . is extremely erratic, sometimes positive but often not" (1977a, p. 45). As an example, he cited one of his own studies using two different situations used to measure delay of gratification, each repeated one year apart. In the first situation, children could work for as many M&M candies as they liked before stopping to eat any, but once they ate an M&M they could not work for more. In the second situation, children were presented with a brightly wrapped "present" but had to wait ninety seconds before opening it until the experimenter finished some work. These two T measures of delay of gratification— how many candies the child worked for before eating any, and how long the child waited before opening the present—only showed weak stability over time (r's around .27) and did not correlate with each other at all (r's around −.07). Observer ratings of "is unable to delay gratification" (R data) correlated

−.47 with the present-opening measure, but were unrelated to candy eating. Apparently, then, we have two different situations purporting to measure delay of gratification. They do not correlate with each other, and only one relates to delay of gratification as measured by observers. Block concluded: "Because we have shown R data can function impressively well, the fault must lie with the insufficiencies of T data—in this case, one of the two specific situations intended to measure delay of gratification" (1977a, p. 63). Bem and Funder (1978) present an extensive analysis of the differences between these two kinds of delay of gratification experiments and suggest ways to design and select sources of T data that will overcome the problem illustrated by Block's study.

Although they may present problems, T variables do sometimes predict behavior surprisingly well. Back in the 1960s, for example, Mischel administered several specific delay-of-gratification tests to a group of preschool children. When he followed up on some of these children over ten years later (when they were high school juniors and seniors), he found a substantial correlation ($r = .34$, $p < .001$) between (1) the number of seconds they delayed before taking a marshmallow at age 4 to 5 and (2) their rated social competence in high school. Mischel's comment about this finding betrays his considerable surprise: "Sometimes even single acts *can* predict meaningful life outcomes!" (1984, p. 277).

What is the precise problem with T data? Can they be improved or rescued, or should personality psychologists consign them to the scrap heap and emphasize ratings, personality tests, and long-term life-outcome data? At the outset, we should recognize that T data are like a snapshot, reporting the outcome of one specific situation at one moment in time. What we do in any particular situation may reflect what we "can" do—the maximal expression of a behavior—rather than what we "like" to do, "prefer" to do, or "typically" do. The differences between these behaviors were illustrated in a laboratory study of dominance in college women. Klein and Willerman (1979) asked women college students to participate in a problem-solving discussion, under two different conditions: first, without any special instructions (the "typical" condition), and then under instructions to "be as dominant and assertive as you can be" (the "maximal" condition). They found that personality, role, and situational variables showed quite different relationships to observers' ratings of dominance, and total talking time, in the "typical" and "maximal" conditions.

In any *single* instance or experimental situation, then, our behavior is affected by many factors in addition to our personality; thus the relationships between any of these factors and outcomes will be rather weak and unstable. Hence it is unwise to assume that a single instance of behavior reflects much influence of personality variables. However, if we carefully select representative kinds of T data, and then aggregate results across separate occasions or instances, many of these nonpersonality factors will tend to cancel each other out, leaving a much stronger relationship between personality and the (aggregated) results.

Aggregating data. Epstein (1979, 1982, 1984) demonstrated the benefits of this kind of data aggregation when he asked students to fill out daily ratings of feelings (such as "happy-sad" or "secure-threatened") and measured certain objective behaviors (such as number of social contacts initiated or heart-rate) every day for fourteen days. Estimates of the stability (reliability) of these feeling-ratings and behaviors were quite low (typically .20 or less) when figures for just the first two days were being compared; but when the figures were based on all fourteen days (by correlating aggregated odd-number days with aggregated even-numbered days), the stability figures increased markedly (typically .70 or greater). Feelings and behaviors aggregated over the entire fourteen-day period of the study showed quite substantial correlations with standard personality tests, as shown in Table 16.10 for the extraversion and neuroticism scales of the Eysenck Personality Inventory.

Act frequency analysis. Another approach to aggregating data is the act-frequency approach developed by Buss and Craik (1983). Whereas Epstein aggregated instances of the *same* act (self-reported feeling, behavior, etc.) over successive days or other time units, the act-frequency approach aggregates instances of *different* acts, each of which is a member of a broader *category* of acts that, taken together, make up a personality disposition or variable. The logic of the act-frequency approach is that personality measures will show higher and more stable relationships to a whole class of acts (many of which are functional substitutes for each other) than to isolated individual component acts. (This recalls the discussion earlier in this chapter of chicken and cheese as functionally substitutable foods: we would expect a measure of hunger to be more highly correlated with the average consumption of chicken *and* cheese than with either by itself.)

TABLE 16.10 RELATION OF PERSONALITY MEASURES TO BEHAVIOR AGGREGATED OVER FOURTEEN DAYS

Behavior aggregated over fourteen days	Correlation with Eysenck Personality Inventory	
	Extraversion scores	*Neuroticism scores*
Self-reported feelings		
Spontaneous (vs. inhibited)	.45	
Outgoing (vs. seclusive)	.47	
Optimistic (vs. pessimistic)	.33	−.53
Calm (vs. tense)		−.50
Secure (vs. threatened)		−.41
Objectively measured behaviors		
Number of social contacts initiated	.52	
Headaches		.41
Stomach aches		.33
Range (variability) of heart rate		.37

Note: All correlations are significant at $p < .05$; correlations greater than .38 are significant at $p < .01$.
SOURCE: Adapted from Epstein (1979, Table 5).

But how do we know where to draw the category boundaries for act-frequency analysis? Which acts shall we take as expressing love, or conscientiousness, or curiosity? This is one of the central problems of the act-frequency approach (Block, 1989). We could draw boundaries on the basis of theory: psychoanalytic theory, for example, might suggest eating, talking, chewing pencils, thumb sucking, and smoking as component acts for the category of orality or oral fixation. Botwin and Buss (1989) used empirical methods to develop act categories for the Big Five trait factors (see Chapter 13), asking college students to nominate or suggest different examples of actions for each trait factor and then asking students or psychologists to rate the prototypicality (how good an example it is) of these acts.

In research that combined the approaches of Epstein and Buss, Moskowitz (1982, 1988) found that as she aggregated across instances and across acts, there were dramatic increases in the coherence and prediction for measures of dominance, dependency, and friendliness.

Multivariate Personality Research

If people's personalities and the situations in which they act are complicated, then it follows that no single variable of personality will explain very much of the variation in behavior. In an effort to increase the explanatory and predictive power of personality variables, therefore, many personality psychologists turned to *multivariate* research—that is, studying the effects of several different variables on behavior. We have already discussed simple illustrations of multivariate research: for example, the combination of power motivation and responsibility described in Chapter 5 (see Table 5.2) or the use of moderator variables earlier in this chapter.

Several further examples will illustrate the advantages of a multivariate approach. In a study of personality and interpersonal behavior, Couch (1962/1969) found that traditional personality measures showed correlations with behavior in the familiar range of .20 to .45. However, when he added in measures of three other kinds of variables—ego defenses, the perceived immediate situation, and the actual situation—these correlations increased to between .65 and .88. Alker and Owen (1977) used traditional personality scales to predict success of male soldiers in advanced Ranger forces training. They obtained a correlation of .42 with the personality measures alone, but adding in other measures based on biographical information and samples of behavior raised the correlation to .72. McClelland (1981) cited two other studies that produced similar results: In predicting the leadership performance of naval officers, Winter (1978) found that nine different variables, each by themselves, correlated in the .20 to .30 range with leadership ratings. When combined together, however, these nine variables showed a multiple correlation of .68 with leadership ratings. Boyatzis and Burruss (1977), using five variables to predict successful performance of naval alcoholism counselors, obtained a multiple correlation of .79.

These examples all involve multivariate research in which several different variables are used to predict a single outcome behavior. McClelland's research

TABLE 16.11 CORRELATION OF MULTIPLE PERSONALITY VARIABLES IN RESEARCH ON POWER MOTIVATION

	Correlation coefficients		
Relation tested between power motivation and:	*Average*	*Median*	*Range*
Individual dependent variables	.12	.12	−.02 to .32
Average score of component variables within a cluster, across eight clusters	.20	.22	.08 to .24
Average score of component variables within a cluster, with appropriate stance toward the environment score added to power motivation, across eight clusters	.38	.38	.30 to .43

SOURCE: Data taken from McClelland (1975, chap. 2).

on power motivation (1975) is multivariate in a different sense: he used multiple personality variables to predict multiple behaviors, as shown in Table 16.11. On the basis of theory and previous research, he first identified sixty-two behaviors that should be related to power motivation. In a sample of 200 adult women and men, the correlations between power motivation and any single behavior were not high. As shown in the first row of Table 16.11, they ranged from −.02 to .32, with an average $r = .12$. On theoretical grounds, McClelland then grouped the sixty-two behaviors into eight clusters and examined the correlations between people's power motivation and their average scores for the component variables of each cluster. As shown in the second row of the table, these correlations are a little higher. In other words, power motivation predicts slightly better to a whole cluster of variables than to each individual variable of the cluster. Finally, McClelland added a measure of the appropriate psychological stance toward the environment (Stewart, 1982; Stewart & Healy, 1992; see also Chapter 18 below) to the power-motivation scores. As shown in the bottom row of the table, this resulted in considerably higher correlations.

In Chapter 18, we will come back to multivariate research as a way of integrating the different elements of personality. For the present, these examples show how considering the effects of even two or three variables in personality research can raise correlation coefficients well above the .30 "personality coefficient" criticized by Mischel and others.

SOCIAL-LEARNING THEORY INCORPORATES COGNITION

Mischel's Alternative to Traditional Conceptions of Personality

While Mischel intended his 1968 book as a critical analysis of conventional theories and conceptions of personality, in one chapter (entitled "Principles of Social Learning") he proposed an alternative conception of personality that combines elements of both traditional learning theory and observational learning and modeling. This is often called social-learning theory, though its increased emphasis on cognition in recent years makes the term *cognitive social-learning theory* (or even cognitive social theory) more appropriate.

Rather than conceiving personality as a structure of broad, general, and fixed traits or other dispositions, social-learning theory views it as a series of separate, flexible components that are continually adjusting to, and being modified by, forces in the situation. In Mischel's terms, social-learning theory "seeks the determinants of behavior in the conditions that covary with the occurrence, maintenance, and change of the behavior" (1968, p. 150). You can see how Mischel's theory reflects the assumptions of atomism and situationism discussed earlier in this chapter.

Instead of treating the person's reinforcement history or learning history as a simple and homogeneous whole, however, Mischel distinguished several different mechanisms that reflect different *kinds* of learning. For example, by means of classical conditioning, different stimuli come to have different *valences* or emotion-arousing properties. Thus for Little Albert (Chapter 15), white rats and similar objects acquired negative valence, or the potential of arousing fear. (In conditioning terminology, conditioned responses are emotional reactions or valences that have generalized or transferred from the unconditioned stimulus to the associated or conditioned stimulus.[5] "Once these negative emotional reactions have been acquired," Mischel suggested, "they also constrict the person's actions toward the emotion-provoking events" (1968, p. 159)

Operant conditioning or the direct reinforcement of performance is another powerful determinant of behavior. The work of Skinner and his colleagues has demonstrated the importance of *schedules of reinforcement*. For example, actions that are always followed by reward are quickly learned, but are also quickly unlearned when the reward stops. In contrast, actions reinforced on a variable-interval schedule—sometimes rewarded but often not, and you never know which or when—are very resistent to extinction or unlearning. (Hitting a slot-machine jackpot is an example. It happens rarely and unpredictably; thus some people play the slots hour after hour, hoping the next play will be the lucky one.) In the social-learning theory view, reinforcement (reward and punishment) does not affect learning so much as it affects the *performance* of already-learned actions. Thus for reinforcement to affect a behavior, that behavior must already be in the person's repertoire of available actions. For this reason, social-learning theorists emphasize the importance of knowing the *skills* that are available in people's *behavioral repertoires*. Regardless of the reward or punishment that is at stake, people cannot perform what they cannot do.

While acknowledging the role of classical and operant conditioning, social-learning theorists usually place the greatest emphasis on *observational*

---

[5]This conception of classical or Pavlovian conditioning as producing acquired emotional valences is slightly different from Rescorla's (1988) conception, as discussed in Chapter 15.

Our personalties are often shaped by the other people we observe and take as models, as in this famous Alfred Eisenstaedt photograph of young children imitating a University of Michigan drum major. (Life Magazine © Time Warner, Inc.)

learning and modeling—hence the "social" in social-learning theory. Through observation we learn a great deal about the world, the nature of institutions and society, and how to make our way in life. We learn most skills by watching and then imitating. We imagine the consequences for ourselves of an action through observing what happens to others. We may even acquire fears through indirect or vicarious classical conditioning—for example, watching someone else get hurt in a traffic accident can make us shudder at the sight of an approaching car.

One of the most important principles of social learning is the concept of *self-administered rewards and punishments*. When by our own standards we do well, we praise ourselves for our good work; when we do badly, we can be our own worst critics. These capacities for self-reward and self-punishment free our actions from the immediate consequences of the situation. Martyrs, dying for a cause, can mobilize internal reinforcements so powerful that they literally overcome the power of the fear of death.

Finally, much of our behavior is governed by simple *rules* and *verbal instructions*, rather than by actual consequences. In the age of AIDS, for example, merely being told about the consequences of unsafe sex may be enough to bring about changes in behavior, without direct or indirect experiences of those consequences. Still, there are often differences between behaviors learned from a book and behaviors learned through actual trial and error or the experience of others. For example, who could ever learn to use a new computer software program solely on the basis of reading the manual, instead of using trial and error, or having a personal guide?

Notice how individualistic and varied—how idiographic—social-learning theory explanations of personality can be. Each person has unique stimulus valences, reinforcement history, observational experiences, significant models, and self-administered consequences. Because the development of personality is so individualized, social-learning theorists find it difficult—and not very useful—to go much beyond listing these general mechanisms to construct a "periodic table" of the elements of personality. In this respect, Mischel has followed the lead of George Kelly, his graduate school mentor at Ohio State University, who emphasized the uniqueness of each individual's construct system.

Bandura's Self-Efficacy Theory

Bandura (1977a, 1986, 1989) has developed cognitive social-learning theory into a theory of self-efficacy. For Bandura, self-efficacy or the "strength of people's convictions in their own effectiveness" (1977a, p. 193) is the major determinant of what situations they choose, how hard they try, how long they persist, and so forth. In other words, we *choose to do* and *try to do* what we *can do* well. While Bandura devotes little attention to motivation, his theory clearly follows from White's concepts of effectance and competence (Chapter 4): we want to do what we can do well. Of course our definition of "do well" may be different from other people's, and we may be wrong about what we can do; nevertheless, Bandura holds, our personal expectation of self-efficacy is the principal determinant of our behavior.

Bandura argued that reinforcement and punishment affect behavior not because they "stamp in" or "stamp out" certain behaviors in an impersonal, machine-like fashion (these were popular terms in the early learning theories of Thorndike and others). Rather, *rewards and punishments affect our cognitions about the consequences of our actions.* This difference—between reinforcement as a mechanistic principle and reinforcement as information, something that creates and modifies expectations—is the main distinction between *cognitive* social-learning theory and social-learning theory. As Bandura put it, "the mechanisms by which human behavior is acquired and regulated are increasingly formulated in terms of cognitive processes" (1977a, p. 191). In other words, even our own operant conditioning, or learning from the consequences of our own actions, is really a type of observational learning in which we are observing ourselves.

So far you may think that Bandura's theory resembles the locus-of-control variable discussed in Chapter 8. It is true that efficacy (typically defined as the "capacity for producing a desired result") is related to internal locus of control of reinforcement. Bandura's theory, however, contains a more comprehensive and sophisticated analysis of the ways in which the sense of efficacy is created and maintained (1977a, pp. 195–200). Of course, one source of efficacy expectations are the actual results of our performances (analogous to operant condi-

Albert Bandura, who elaborated social-learning theory into self-efficacy theory.
"Through their capacity to manipulate symbols and to engage in reflective thought,
people can generate novel ideas and innovative actions that transcend their past
experiences . . . [influencing] their motivation and action in efforts to realize valued
futures" (1989, p. 1182). (Courtesy Stanford University. Photo by Chuck Painter.)

tioning). Other sources include the vicarious experiences available through
observation and models. Verbal persuasion, whether from others (parent,
teacher, therapist) or our own self-instruction or insight, are a third source.
Finally, however, experiences that change our emotional state (either cognitively, through attribution, or directly, through changes in arousal or affect)
also have effects on efficacy. If, by one means or another, we come to experience a lower level of arousal, less fear, or a reduced sense of personal incompetence in the presence of a formerly feared object, then in the future our
enhanced sense of self-efficacy that results will make it possible to inhibit
avoidance and flight responses. Bandura's theory stresses that self-efficacy is
the critical mechanism at work here. *However* it is increased—through attribution retraining (Chapter 8) or mood-altering or arousal-altering drugs (Chapter
14) or desensitization (Chapter 15, footnote 2)—its characteristic effects of
increased choice, effort, and persistence will follow.

Self-efficacy theory, which is based on the sense of the self as capable of
producing desired results, also has important philosophical implications for
our conceptions of human agency and freedom (Bandura, 1989).

SUMMARY: PERSONALITY, SITUATION, AND BEHAVIOR

More than twenty-five years have passed since Mischel published his critique of personality research and assessment. What have personality psychologists learned, and how do they now think about the issues Mischel raised? Clearly, the field has survived and prospered, but the field of personality psychology as it is in the 1990s is different from what it was in the 1950s and 1960s. I would characterize the changes with three words: complexity, modesty, and theory. Today, personality psychologists recognize the complexity of their enterprise: the world is complex, people are even more complex, and so the behavior of people in the world is very complex indeed. This being so, personality psychologists should be modest about how much they claim to interpret and explain. In an effort to design concepts and methods that will be adequate to deal in at least modest ways with this complexity, personality psychologists have turned to deeper analyses of their concepts and methods, and this requires the use of theory—not necessarily the grand and sweeping theories of classical psychoanalysis or other broad theories. Rather, they carefully consider how different elements of personality combine into structures, and how these complex structures interact with the world in complex, subtle, and multiple ways.

And this world is scarcely the unitary and undifferentiated lump sometimes implied by the simple word "situation." As suggested at the beginning of Chapter 15, the world of human personality is a social world, structured along lines of gender, social class, ethnicity, religion, nationality, and history. All of these forces have their effects on personality; these are the focus of Chapter 17.

To return to the spinning magnets in Toronto's Ontario Science Centre. While the complex patterns of their spin are completely determined by their relation to each other and to the large rotating magnet, they are after all *magnets,* only spinning at all because of certain of their "dispositional" characteristics. They are made of iron; noniron bars would not move at all. Thus they spin *both* because they are iron bars *and* because they exist in a complex force field. In the next chapter, we consider the nature of the infinitely more complex human "force fields" through which we all move, every day of our lives.

17

Social Structure and Culture
As Contexts for Personality

❖

It seems impossible to think of Maya Angelou and Virginia Woolf as personalities without at the same time thinking of their social contexts—the shared context of gender and the different contexts of race, nation, social class, historical era, and occupation. Yet it is often difficult to distinguish the effects of each context or decide which context is most important.

Many personality research studies are carried out among fairly homogenous samples of college students, in relatively restricted contexts. Such studies may create a false sense that personality variables are context-free universals, always and everywhere having the same meanings and effects. However, when we broaden the people and contexts (historical, cultural and subcultural, organizational, interpersonal, and developmental), these meanings and effects often change. In reviewing findings from two representative national samples of American adults, Veroff (1983) noted such changes.

1. Over the past few decades in the United States, the nature of achievement motivation seems to have changed from "pride in task accomplishment" to a sense of "personal actualization" (effect of historical context).

2. Motives sometimes play different roles in the lives of men and women (gender context).

3. Whether people focus their power motivation on work or family depends on their social class (social class or social-structural context).

4. Achievement and affiliation motives increase, decrease, and change their meaning over the life course (developmental context).

THE DIVERSITY OF MACROCONTEXTS

Distinguishing Social Structure and Culture

In this chapter, I will try to redress this unbalanced state of personality research by taking macrocontext seriously. Since it is not possible in one chapter to discuss the effects of every context on personality, we will focus on the two broad topics of social structure and culture. They can be distinguished briefly as follows. *Social structure* involves differentiation or differences between the people in a group or society. In almost every human society or group (as well as many animal groups), power and its symbolic substitutes of prestige and wealth are unevenly distributed. In other words, certain individuals and subgroups have more power (prestige, wealth) than others. To use a geological metaphor, human groups are stratified or layered. Anything that distinguishes between those who have more power and those who have less power is a *dimension of stratification*. Examples include gender, age, social class, race, and ethnicity. This unequal distribution of power creates complex relationships between members of the society and thus has complex effects on individual personalities. Taken together, these make up the society's social structure. In contrast, *culture* refers to those characteristics (customs, practices, meanings, beliefs) that are shared by all or most members of a group.

Hegemony

A convenient word for summarizing structured patterns of relationships involving the unequal distribution of power is *hegemony*. It derives from the Greek word *hegemon*, "leader," and generally refers to the rule of one country over another or the command, influence, or predominance of some people over others. In the rest of this chapter, I will use hegemony, hegemonic relationships, power, domination, and control interchangeably to refer to *structured unequal distribution of power within a society or group*. You will know what I mean. The best clue for detecting hegemonic relationships is when the behavior of persons or groups is not reciprocal—that is, when person A acts differently toward person B than B acts toward A. For example, a boss acts differently toward a worker than the worker acts toward the boss. The same is true of parents and children, teachers and students, officers and members, coaches and players. (This does not mean that all parents or bosses or coaches are alike; there are many different styles of hegemony.) In contrast, when A and B each act the same toward the other, the relationship is likely to be mutual or equal rather than hegemonic. For example, friends do the same things, together, with each other.

SOCIAL STRUCTURE AND HEGEMONY

Gender Relations as a Prototype of Hegemony

Hegemony assumes many different forms or dimensions and is manifest in many different kinds of relationships. One of the most important and pervasive dimensions of hegemony is *gender*. Unger and Crawford (1992), for example, use power as a major organizing theme in their discussion of the psychology of women. Recall from the discussion of sexual abuse in Chapter 15 that "sexual" relations between men and women involve not only sex, but also—and perhaps even principally—power. Dworkin's claim that all sexual relations are a form of rape (1987, especially pp. 121–143) is an extreme statement of this position. While you may not agree with that view, I encourage you to consider the following examples of the many connections between gender and power or hegemony:

1. Across society as a whole, persons of one gender (men) generally have more social and economic power than persons of the other gender (women). They control more resources, make more decisions about the society as a whole, have more prestige, and enjoy more freedom and autonomy.

2. Within small groups or two-person relationships such as the family, gender is associated with patterns of dominance and deference. For example, men and women speak with different words and styles (Tannen, 1990) and use different gestures and postures (Henley, 1977; LaFrance & Mayo, 1978). You can see this in the nonreciprocal ways in which men and women often describe or address each other. Even in a social (rather than work) setting, and regardless of their relative ages, a male corporate executive might refer to his female secretary as a "girl" and call her "Mary"; she, in contrast, would describe him as a "man" and rarely address him as other than "Mr. Smith."

3. The entire pattern of hegemonic gender relationships is taught by socialization rituals and enforced by formal and informal sanctions. For example, according to a recent survey (Barringer, 1993), most American girls receive verbal and physical sexual harassment during their middle-school years. Not surprisingly, this turns out to be the very age when many girls' career aspirations and self-esteem decline (Gilligan, 1990). Rape, spouse abuse, and even homicide—*always* much more common from men to women than the other way around—can be viewed as extreme sanctions that enforce and perpetuate the hegemony by gender.[1]

These three aspects of gender relations—differential access to power, patterns of dominance and deference, and socialization and sanctions—are also present in hegemonies that are based on other dimensions of stratification.

---

[1]Psychologists have advanced different theories about the cause of gender-based hegemony. Some would agree with Freud (see Chapter 4) that the hegemony of gender relations is based on sex differences in anatomy and physiology or on characteristics derived from them, such as "reproductive strategy" (Buss & Schmitt, 1993). While some degree of gender-based hegemony may be universal (Ortner, 1974), the *nature and extent* of male dominance in any particular society varies as a function of that society's other social and economic characteristics (Stewart & Winter, 1977). This suggests that male dominance is at least to some extent constructed rather than biologically based. Feminist theorists take a variety of positions on the causes of gender-based hegemony (see Herrmann & Stewart, 1994).

Other Dimensions of Hegemony

Maya Angelou's experiences make clear that *race* is another dimension of power and domination. In the United States and most other countries, race relations are often hegemonic. Whether the particular mechanism is slavery, segregation, or merely systematic inequality, the results are similar: unequal control of resources, decisions, prestige, freedom, autonomy, and opportunities for job and political advancement; patterns of dominance and deference; and socialization and enforcement rituals such as lynching or differential sentencing (especially the death penalty) for the same crimes.

In India, the institution of *caste*—with its hereditary basis, its concerns about "pollution" by contact between castes, and its restrictions on intermarriage, eating together, and occupational opportunity—has many aspects of race relations in the United States and other Western countries. In fact, the caste system probably originated during the Aryan conquest of the Indian subcontinent thousands of years ago, in the racial differences between the conquering Aryans and the conquered Dravidians (see Srinivas, 1962). The age of European empires and *colonialism* produced a further castelike stratification of colonizers and colonized in the non-Western world.

Social class was originally defined by Karl Marx as a person's relationship to the means of production: do you own the tools (or machines) with which you work, or do you own only your own labor power? Nowadays class is the most frequently studied dimension of stratification in industrial cultures. It is measured by many variables such as occupation, level of education, and style of life. People of the upper and middle classes have economic, social, and political power over people of the working class and the so-called underclass. The structure of classes is maintained by patterns of dominance and deference (often called "manners"), which are taught to the young and often enforced by law. (Do you doubt the existence of classes in the "egalitarian" United States? Read the persuasive analyses of Domhoff, 1983, or Dye, 1990.)

There are also temporary dimensions of stratification: for example, *institutions* such as concentration camps (Bettelheim, 1943), welfare bureaucracies, prisons, and even colleges and universities (Goffman, 1961). Events such as *torture, rape,* or *violence* can also be seen as forms of dominance that may have a brief duration but long-lasting effects. In each case one person or group exercises control over another person or group.

PERSONALITY AND THE EFFECTS OF POWER AND CONTROL

The Psychological Meaning of Hegemony

For our purposes, we want to know whether all these different kinds of hegemonic relations have similar effects on personality. Can we find a common theme running through studies of the effects of gender, race, caste, class, concentration camps, torture, rape, and violence? In today's academic world, these topics are usually treated as quite different subjects, each studied by different specialists and each with its own scholarly literature. Thus there is no single, unified set of research findings. For now, we can observe parallel themes and connections among these different topics, themes having to do with the psychological meaning and effects of power.

As we have suggested, all hegemonic relationships share certain characteristics. Those on top have more material and personal *resources*—access to force, money, training for intelligence and other "social skills," freedom, safety, and health—than those on the bottom.[2] Recall, for example, the educational opportunities that were available to the men in Virginia Woolf's family but were denied to her, or the streetcar-conducting job that Maya Angelou, as a woman and an African American, attained only after a long struggle. While some of these differences may be due to factors such as the greater income and education of people on top, many are simply the result of their relative position in the hierarchy (see, for example, the discussion of social class differences in health by Adler et al., 1994, p. 20).

In contrast, people on the bottom are generally more *accountable* and *vulnerable* to others, especially to others on top. Recall from Chapter 15 the sexual abuse suffered by both Woolf and Angelou or blacks' fear of white Klan "boys" on a rampage. Angelou described her grandmother's fears and caution when dealing with white people: "she didn't cotton to the idea that whitefolks could be talked to at all without risking one's life" (1970, p. 39).

While they have a freer, safer, and more comfortable life, people on top also have more to lose. As a result, they are often more anxious about their status and threatened by change. In times of rapid change and instability, therefore, humans (and animals) at the top of status hierarchies are more vulnerable to health and psychological problems (Adler et al., 1994, p. 20). We have already seen this reversal in Woolf's account of her father's and half-brother's feelings of vulnerability. Angelou (1970) recognized it in her description of how the Great Depression of the 1930s affected blacks and whites:

> The Depression must have hit the white section of Stamps with cyclonic impact, but it seeped into the Black area slowly, like a thief with misgivings. The country had been in the throes of the Depression for two years before the Negroes in Stamps knew it. I think that everyone thought that the Depression, like everything else, was for the whitefolks, so it had nothing to do with them. (p. 41)

Woolf describes how her father—a privileged male—felt an acute sense of failure as a philosopher. While he had to conceal this in the presence of men, among women he was free to display "an illicit need for sympathy." When women such as her sister and herself did not respond to this need, he exploded in brutal rage (Woolf, 1985, pp. 145–146). Similarly, she linked her half-brother George's abusive behavior to his sense of failure in pursuit of a diplomatic career (pp. 153–154). (Recall also from Chapter 7 how threat is

---

[2]In this chapter I have deliberately tried to avoid using polite euphemisms; hence the simple terms "on top" and "on the bottom." No evaluation is intended; I hope that my sympathies are with the underdogs of our stratified world!

associated with increased authoritarian—that is, hegemonic—behavior.) Woolf's account makes clear that those who are near the edge—who are only just on top—are the most threatened.

Psychological Effects of Hegemony

The characteristics of hegemonic, dominant-subordinate relationships have certain effects on people who are in them, both those on top and those on the bottom.

Those on top. First let us consider those on top—the power holders. Kipnis (1976, chap. 9) identified several ways in which power changes those who exercise it, changes that he called the "metamorphic effects of power." For example, wielding power leads to an *exalted view of the self.* Because they observe only the sequence of I-command-and-others-obey, power holders exaggerate their own personal impact on the world. That is, they overattribute results to their own actions rather than to external causes (see Chapter 8). (To protect themselves by making the bosses feel good, people who are the targets of power often encourage these attributions through flattery.)

At the same time, wielding power also leads to a *changed view of others, especially those over whom power is exercised* (the targets of power). Power increases the distance and sense of difference between power holder and target. Because power holders believe they control the behavior of their targets, they do not pay attention to the target as an individual person (Fiske, 1993). As a result, power holders usually view targets in stereotyped terms—in extreme cases, as less than human beings. In contrast, people on the bottom usually have to pay close attention to the power holder. As Fiske notes, "secretaries know more about their bosses than vice versa; graduate students know more about their advisors than vice versa" (1993, p. 624).

As a result of these cognitive effects, Kipnis argues that wielding power leads to a *degraded moral sense.* Because they see the targets of power as less than human, power holders often feel contempt and treat them in dehumanizing, immoral ways. This effect can easily be seen during wars, when soldiers of each side refer to the enemy with derogatory slang words and treat them in brutal and dehumanizing ways. It can even be seen in brief laboratory experiments such as the Stanford Prison Experiment (Haney, Banks, & Zimbardo, 1973), in which students were randomly assigned the roles of prisoner or guard. After a few days, the pretend-guards started acting like real guards, expressing contempt for the "prisoners."

Many great writers have commented on the degrading effects of power and domination. The English essayist Lord Acton's characterization of power has entered every dictionary of quotations: "Power tends to corrupt, and absolute power corrupts absolutely. Great men are almost always bad men" (1887/1949, p. 364). A detailed description of this process of moral decay can be found in *House of the Dead* by the Russian novelist Dostoevsky (1861–1862/1961):

Anyone who has once experienced this power, this unlimited mastery of the body, blood and soul of a fellow man made of the same clay as himself . . . anyone who has experienced the power and full license to inflict the greatest humiliation upon another creature . . . will unconsciously lose the mastery of his own sensations. Tyranny is a habit; it may develop, and it does develop, at last, into a disease. . . . Blood and power intoxicate; coarseness and depravity are developed; the mind and the heart are tolerant of the most abnormal things, till at last they come to relish them. (pp. 181–182)

In this passage, Dostoevsky was referring to prison guards who tortured prisoners, but he quickly extended his point to more ordinary instances of power:

Even those who express [disgust at power] have not all been able to extinguish in themselves the lust of power. Every manufacturer, every capitalist, must feel an agreeable thrill in the thought that his workman, with all his family, is sometimes entirely dependent on him. (p. 182)

Those on the bottom. In those over whom power is wielded, hegemonic domination tends to destroy existing cognitive structures. For example, in their studies of survivors of rape and other temporary violent hegemonic relationships, Janoff-Bulman and Frieze (1983) describe how things the survivors had taken for granted—their "assumptive worlds"—are shattered. Thus ordinary people living ordinary and safe lives have a sense that the world is meaningful, that they are invulnerable to harm, and that they are good. When situations arise in which they are the object of others' power (violence, abusive relationships, even a natural disaster), these assumptions collapse. Suddenly the world is no longer meaningful, just, or safe; they themselves are not as "good" as they thought they were.

Hegemony and the Variables of Personality

From this review, we can begin to see some core patterns of personality characteristics that are associated with power and dominance. The next task is to determine whether these characteristics also apply to enduring hegemonic structures, such as social class. Unfortunately, there are few reviews of social class differences in traditional personality variables. Such studies were popular in the 1940s and 1950s (see Cohen, 1961, chaps. 3 and 5; Grey, 1969; and Honigman, 1967 for examples), but they have diminished markedly over the past thirty years. For example, the words "class" and "social class" do not even appear in the index of Pervin's recent *Handbook of Personality Theory and Research* (1990). The situation is better in the case of gender (see Ashmore, 1990, and Spence, Deaux, & Helmreich, 1985). What follows, therefore, is an exercise in translation: from the psychological meaning of hegemonic dominance relations outlined above to the traditional personality variables that *ought to* be associated with hegemonic status. I will draw on a variety of theories, empirical studies, and descriptive accounts (for example, Kahl, 1957).

Let us begin with the greater freedom, autonomy, and access to resources that are enjoyed by people on top in hegemonic relationships. These privileges should lead to an enhanced sense of internal control of outcomes, which is just what has been found among (for example) white and middle-class people (see Chapter 8). In his classic review of social stratification research in different countries, Inkeles (1960) identified the following characteristics of people from higher classes as compared to people from lower classes: greater experienced job satisfaction, more concerned that a job be interesting than that it be secure, greater happiness and satisfaction with life, and a greater belief in the possibility of changing human nature. More recently, Kohn and his colleagues (Kohn, Naoi, Schoenbach, Schooler, & Slomczynski, 1990) found that American, Japanese, and Polish men from higher social classes all had a more self-directed orientation (higher internal control and higher trust; see Chapter 8, lower authoritarianism (Chapter 7), and lower conformity. They were less anxious and more intellectually flexible, which suggests greater cognitive complexity (Chapter 6). These studies are part of a "sociological" tradition in social psychology, where social structure is viewed as a system of contingencies, opportunities, and constraints that have direct effects on personality (see House, 1981; Kohn, 1989).

What about the people on the bottom? MacKinnon (1987b) drew a direct connection between hegemony and personality: "Women value care because men have valued us according to the care we give them. . . . Women think in relational terms because our existence is defined in relation to men" (p. 39). Miller (1986) argued that a common set of stereotyped personality characteristics is applied to people in different kinds of subordinate positions (women, blacks, and people from the lower class or underclass): they are believed to be submissive, docile, dependent, lacking in initiative, unable to care for themselves, childlike, irrational, and emotional. In terms of the five trait factors of Chapter 13, these would translate into low surgency (factor 1) and perhaps low emotional stability (factor 4).

Fiske's (1993) observation that people on the bottom need to pay attention to and please higher-ups in order to survive suggests that we should add high agreeableness (factor 2) and high conscientiousness (factor 3) to this profile, but the role of factor 3, along with culture (factor 5), may be more complicated. People on top often rationalize their hegemonic position with claims that people on the bottom are "lazy," "shiftless," and "not to be trusted" (low factor 3), as well as being "ill-bred," "uncouth," and "lacking a sense of the finer things" (low factor 5).[3] Yet some people on the bottom—usually women and particularly black women—are believed to be appropriate and responsible caretakers for people on top, which implies high conscientiousness. And women, especially women of the upper classes (see Domhoff, 1983), are often assigned the role of "culture bearer," with responsibility for preserving cultural institutions, manners, and the finer things of life. (Here, though, the actual *production* and *control*

---

[3]These characteristics can also be subtle forms of resistance or sabotage on the part of people on the bottom.

of culture remains disproportionately with people—mostly men—who are on top.) Perhaps the real truth about factors 3 and 5 is that the people on top simply make up and use whatever stereotypes they need to justify their position.

While some of these characteristics of people on the bottom may reflect stereotypes, others may be *responses to pressures*, ways of surviving that become real differences in behavior and personality. Thus men could be expected to score higher on measures of aggression, task leadership, body restlessness, and filling pauses with verbal noise—all suggesting high surgency— as adaptations to their (hegemonic) gender role. In contrast, women might show more empathy, social-emotional leadership, ability at decoding nonverbal behavior, and social smiling—in short, high agreeableness—as an adaptation to their gender role. (See Ashmore, 1990, and Spence, Deaux, & Helmreich, 1985, for discussions of stereotypic and nonstereotypic differences in the case of gender.)

RESPONSES TO HEGEMONY FROM BELOW

Hegemonic relationships often look more impressive and effective than they really are. While their behavior and personalities are constrained by the power of others, people on the bottom are not helpless and without any control over their lives. Depending on their level of self-definition (Chapters 9 and 16; see also Stewart, 1992b; Stewart & Winter, 1974), they can respond in at least three different ways: *accepting, rebelling against*, or *transcending* the hegemonic relationship.[4] Each of these alternative responses involves a different constellation of personality variables. I will give examples from the literature on dominance relationships and illustrations from Maya Angelou's autobiography.

Acceptance of Hegemony: Identification with the Aggressor

Recall the experiences of the psychoanalyst Bruno Bettelheim (1943) as an inmate in a Nazi concentration camp just before World War II (see Chapter 3). Most of his fellow inmates accepted the camp regimen and obeyed the rules— understandably, since the guards possessed all the means of force and did not hesitate to use them. A few inmates went further, however, and identified with the aggressor guards. They imitated the guards' behavior, made their clothing look like guards' uniforms, and so forth. With the shattering of their own beliefs and sense of self, these inmates incorporated the guards' beliefs and values. If they themselves were "bad," they could at least become "good" by imitating the guards as much as possible. Thus identifying with (or "taking in") the feared hegemonic power offers the possibility (or at least the fantasy) of controlling it.

---

[4]This typology of alternative responses to hegemony is based on the analysis by Meier and Rudwick (1986) of Black responses to slavery and oppression, Franz and Stewart's (1994) accounts of women's lives, and Stewart and Winter's (1974) study of female responses to male definition.

This phenomenon—of people at the bottom of a hegemonic relationship forming close, even enthusiastic attachments and identifications with people on top—is not confined to concentration camps. In 1974, for example, 19-year-old Patty Hearst (heiress to the Hearst family fortune and at the time a college student) was kidnapped and held for several months by the Symbionese Liberation Army, a tiny radical group. Over the next nineteen months, she was brainwashed into considering herself part of the SLA with the revolutionary name of "Tania"; she denounced her family as "the pig Hearsts" and even participated with other SLA members in a bank robbery (Alexander, 1979).

Another name for the phenomenon of identification with the aggressor is the "Stockholm syndrome." This name originated in a 1973 bank robbery and hostage taking in Stockholm, Sweden (Ochberg & Soskis, 1982). Some of the hostages developed positive ties and a sense of gratitude to their captors. They came to see them as protectors while expressing hostility toward their rescuers.

Identification with the aggressor often occurs in long-term hegemonic relationships based on colonial status or race. For example, Mahatma Gandhi, who pioneered the use of nonviolent political protest in India, described in his autobiography a quite different earlier reaction to English colonial hegemony. As a young law student in London, he "undertook the all too impossible task of becoming an English gentleman," wearing "a chimney-pot hat" and "an evening suit made in Bond Street" and taking lessons in dancing, French, and elocution (1929/1957, p. 50).

At the beginning of her autobiography, Maya Angelou reported a daydream of acceptance of the dominant white standards and an explicit identification with whites: "Wouldn't they be surprised when one day I woke out of my ugly black dream. . . . Because I was really white" (1970, p. 2). Nor was Angelou's reaction unusual among African Americans in the early decades of the twentieth century, as shown in a classic study by Clark and Clark (1947). Black children were given a black doll and a white doll. When asked which doll was "better" and which "looks more like you," many children chose the white doll. (The results of this and other studies helped to convince the U.S. Supreme Court in 1954 that school segregation was inherently unequal.)

At the bottom of every hegemonic relationship, then, there are usually some people who cooperate with things as they are, not only out of a deep identification with the hegemonic force but also out of a conviction that this is the best way to make the most progress.

Reactance, Resistance, and Rebellion

To many people, especially those in privileged positions, identification with the aggressor is difficult to understand. Surely the "obvious" response to hegemonic power is resistance and rebellion. Psychologists call this *reactance*, the desire to restore freedom that has been taken away, reduced, or threatened (J. Brehm, 1972; S. Brehm, 1981). What could be more natural than fighting

back, meeting power with power, or at least doing the opposite of what someone else tells you to do? Yet this so-called natural desire for revenge may be
difficult for people on the bottom of a hegemonic relationship, because resistance can often be dangerous, even fatal. For example, there were numerous
slave rebellions in the Western hemisphere before slavery was finally abol-
ished (see Aptheker, 1983), but with the single exception of the overthrow of
the French colonial government of Haiti (1798–1804), all were crushed.

Still, Angelou recorded many subtle and symbolic forms of resistance. For
example, along with every other black person in Stamps, Arkansas, she
eagerly cheered the radio broadcasts of the victories of Joe Louis, the first
African American heavyweight boxing champion. Even this symbolic resistance was not without danger, however. As Angelou reminds her readers, "it
wouldn't do for a Black man and his family to be caught on a lonely country
road on a night when Joe Louis had proved that we were the strongest people
in the world" (1970, p. 115). Still, fantasied rebellion was often possible. Thus
at her eighth-grade graduation, after a particularly condescending and offensive speech by a white politician, she momentarily "wished that Gabriel
Prosser and Nat Turner [leaders of slave rebellions] had killed all whitefolks in
their beds . . . and Christopher Columbus had drowned in the *Santa Maria*"
(p. 152). And when the only dentist in Stamps humiliated her grandmother,
Angelou constructed an appealing fantasy of revenge (pp. 161–162).

The figure of the "con man," ever popular among the black storytellers of
Stamps, represents another symbolic form of rebellion:

> [Taking advantage of white ignorance, prejudice, and overconfidence,] the con
> man who could act the most stupid, won out over the powerful, arrogant white.
> . . . [They] used their intelligence to pry open the door of rejection and not only
> became wealthy but got some revenge in the bargain. (pp. 187, 190)

Another, more subtle form of resistance involves maintaining an impassive front, keeping quiet, and revealing as little as possible. Angelou used this
strategy to weave "a cat's ladder of near truths and total lies" when she was
finally permitted to apply for the job as a streetcar conductor (p. 229).

Endurance, Transcendence, and Transformation

Is there a third alternative to acceptance of hegemony or rebellion against it?
In spite of oppression, most African American people in Stamps and elsewhere endured, sustained themselves and their peers, and thus survived. For
many, the black church was a source of strength to endure and transcend.
Thus Angelou (1970) recorded the energy and sense of restoration of a revival
meeting:

> Down front to the right, Mr. and Mrs. Stewart, who only a few hours earlier had
> crumbled in our front yard, defeated by the cotton rows, now sat on the edges of
> their rickety-rackety chairs. Their faces shone with the delight of their souls. The

mean whitefolks were going to get their comeuppance. Wasn't that what the minister said, and wasn't he quoting from the words of God Himself? . . .

They basked in the righteousness of the poor and the exclusiveness of the downtrodden. (pp. 107, 110)

For black Americans as for many other people on the bottom of hegemonic relationships, the ability to endure is rooted in the power of cultural traditions and institutions—often religion, and specifically religious music. In the concentration camp, Bettelheim himself did not identify with the aggressor. Rather, he drew strength from the "cultural institution" of psychoanalysis in order to transform the camp experience into a meaningful private project: he would observe, record, and interpret what was happening around him.

These cultural institutions, moreover, often train individual leaders whose gifts for writing and interpretation make it possible to transform the hegemonic situation in new and creative ways, drawing in both the oppressor and oppressed—the top and bottom of the hegemonic structure. Thus both Gandhi and his latter-day American disciple, Martin Luther King, Jr., drew heavily on the religious and cultural traditions of the people whose cause they led, but at the same time creatively transformed these traditions (see Erikson, 1969). In the end, each was able to persuade and bring around many of his people's oppressors.

Finally, through their gifts of verbal and literary expression, Angelou and Woolf endured, transcended, and transformed their own situation and that of others.

In psychological terms, this "cultural-transformative" pattern of response to hegemonic relationships involves not so much the defense mechanism of denial as the capacity for sublimation (see Chapter 3).

PERSONALITY AND INSTITUTIONS

Complex societies are made up of many different institutions or subsocieties. Most institutions are hegemonic structures, but they also have distinctive structures, beliefs, and values that affect the personalities of their members: for example, schools, corporations, religious bodies, prisons, and the military. We shall consider briefly two such institutions: the factory and the liberal arts college.

The Factory

Factories are important, not only as sites of modern industrial production but also as powerful social institutions. As Inkeles and Smith (1974) put it:

To work in a factory means to expose oneself to its regimen for at least 8 hours a day, 5 to 6 days a week, and continuously, week in and week out, over a period of years. . . . [Production and profit constraints] all act to give the factory a firm and relatively invariant character. It does not so much adapt to men as it requires that they adapt to it. (p. 157)

Inkeles and Smith suggested several possible ways that working in a factory might affect people's personalities, especially if they come from more traditional backgrounds.

1. *Increased sense of efficacy.* Factories turn raw materials into all sorts of "new shapes and forms far exceeding the capacity of the unaided individual to do so" (p. 158). Inkeles and Smith argue that this process enhances the worker's sense of what is possible for humans to do.

2. *Greater openness to innovation.* Factories introduce new machines, techniques, and products in order to keep up with market demands.

3. *More planning and the use of time.* Careful, rational layout and scheduling are necessary in order to maximize output.

4. *Greater respect for the rights of subordinates.* Formal rules and procedures are necessary for maximum efficiency.

To determine the actual effects of factory work, as compared to more traditional economic activities, Inkeles and Smith tested large samples of factory workers and (carefully matched) nonfactory workers in Argentina, Chile, Bangladesh, India, Israel, and Nigeria. Controlling further for education and exposure to mass media, they found in each country a substantial relationship between amount of factory experience and questionnaire measures of "modernity"—themes of efficacy, openness to new experience, universalism, belief in planning, valuing punctuality, beliefs in women's rights, and so forth (see Inkeles & Smith, 1974, chaps. 5–8).

Of course this is an ideal portrait of a factory, far different from the nightmare sweatshops of the Industrial Revolution or the decaying industries of the former socialist countries. The work of Kohn and his associates (1990), cited above in connection with social class, suggests quite a different picture. Boring and oppressive factory work seems to create rigidity and a sense of distress in workers. The differences between the two studies may be the result of the different comparisons that were made (factory versus traditional work, or factory versus "modern" nonfactory work), as well as the different kinds of factories, in different economic climates, that were studied. In any case, it seems clear that factories have powerful effects on the personalities of those who work in them.

The Liberal Arts College

Most of you are or have been students in a college or university that offers some kind of liberal arts education, perhaps combined with more technical or vocational learning. American colleges and universities delight in making up fancy statements about their educational goals or "mission," and college graduates fondly recall their alma mater (the phrase is from the Latin for "nourishing mother"), but there is little firm evidence about what such institutions actually do. Apart from your learning (and likely forgetting) particular facts or concepts, what effect does a liberal arts higher education have on your personality?

After studying several different colleges and universities, Winter, McClelland, and Stewart (1981) concluded that liberal education has at least four important effects.

1. It increases the ability to do *thematic analysis* (Winter & McClelland, 1978), which is the ability to draw comparisons and contrasts within an array of confusing and complicated material (an ability that is probably related to cognitive complexity; see Chapter 6).

2. It increases *self-definition*, a cognitive style reflecting independence of thought that predicts handling stress (see Chapters 9 and 16, as well as Stewart, 1992b, and Stewart & Winter, 1974).

3. It increases the *leadership motive pattern*, a combination of high power motivation, low affiliation motivation, and self-control that is associated with effective management and the capacity to arouse loyalty and enthusiasm in subordinates (McClelland, 1975, chap. 8; McClelland & Boyatzis, 1982).

4. Finally, it increases the *maturity of adaptation to the environment* (Stewart & Healy, 1992; see also Chapter 18), that is, the ability to make quick and effective emotional adaptations to new situations.

These results may sound like a college catalog's statement of intended effects, but Winter and associates (1981, chap. 4) concluded that they also led to important real-life outcomes. In a longitudinal study of college graduates, *these four measures were better predictors of career and career satisfaction, family, organizational activity, personal happiness, and self-image ten years after college than social class background, SAT scores and grades, and current life situation combined!*

CULTURE AND PERSONALITY

If social structure refers to the patterns of relationships that create differences among people within a group, then *culture* refers to the beliefs, practices, symbols, and institutions that are shared by all and that bind the group together. While the effects of social structure on personality are transmitted through present opportunities and constraints, the effects of culture often come down from the past and are mediated or transmitted by socialization and learning (House, 1981). Obviously the two concepts are connected, for every social structure has a culture (sometimes different cultures or subcultures on each side of the hegemonic line between powerholder and target of power), and cultures can only exist within human groups that have concrete social structures.

Sometimes structural and cultural explanations compete. For example, is poverty best understood as the result of structural conditions that prevent people from realizing their goals (structural explanation), or is it the legacy of a "culture of poverty" that makes people unable to take advantage of opportunities (cultural explanation) (House, 1981, pp. 545–547)? Whatever the balance of structural and cultural influences on any particular behavior, both are major contexts for the development and expression of personality.

Is It Personality or Is It Culture? Some Examples

Getting the bed sheets right. To illustrate the role of culture in personality, I will begin with a personal example. Whenever I remake a bed, I am very careful to get the ends of the sheets put back as they were: the "head" end of the sheet at the head of the bed and the "foot" end at the foot. If someone else making the bed with me is careless about this, I get upset and even a little offended at the thought of sleeping with the "foot end" of the top sheet pulled around my neck and shoulders. To me, this was simply a little habit that I never thought much about. To my wife, it was one of my personality quirks. Over the years, it had led to a certain amount of teasing and a little exasperation.

A few years ago, however, I had an experience that led me to see this quirk in a completely different light. I was reading Schama's *The Embarrassment of Riches: An Interpretation of Dutch Culture in the Golden Age* (1987), a book about the Netherlands in the seventeenth-century. (Since all eight of my great-grandparents had emigrated to western Michigan from the Netherlands in the mid 1800s, I qualify as Dutch American.) I came to the following passage in Schama's book:

> No visitor to Holland . . . failed to notice the pains that the Dutch took to keep their streets, their houses, and themselves . . . brilliantly clean. The spick-and-span towns shone from hours of tireless sweeping, scrubbing, scraping, burnishing, mopping, rubbing and washing. (p. 375)

This I already knew, for the citizens of Holland, Michigan (near where I grew up) still sweep the streets during their annual Tulip Time festival. But Schama went on:

> Within the house, too, a cleaning regimen was followed with almost military precision. And its timetable was extraordinarily elaborate and exacting—a whole department of human activity specified in relentless detail. . . . Such were the demands of this regimen that it was laid down that *when sheets were folded it was imperative that the end used for the feet never be accidentally turned so that it could be used for the head.* (pp. 376–377, emphasis added)

I could scarcely believe what I read. Over 300 years ago, here was a whole culture—my ancestors' culture—that also kept track of the head and foot ends of sheets—even when they were on the shelf! And so my personality quirk was really a small part of a larger cultural pattern.

I have no idea how this cultural practice was transmitted to me. For example, I don't remember my parents ever saying, "You know, it's very important not to mix the head and foot ends of sheets." Perhaps I unconsciously observed my mother being careful about the sheets. I happened to mention this story to my older son, who as a child could not have been accused of keeping his room excessively neat. He replied, "Oh yes, I'd be upset too if the ends of the sheets were mixed up." I *know* I never taught him that. Later I told the story to some graduate students at Michigan, as an illustration of the effects of culture on personality. Most were amused, but one student confessed to the very same quirk—and she also had some Dutch ancestry.

Executing cats. In twentieth-century American culture we are taught to be kind to animals. If you or I went out and collected cats in order to torture and murder them, we would probably be prosecuted for cruelty to animals and maybe even sent for psychiatric evaluation. But now consider the historian Robert Darnton's story about the apprentices in one Paris printing shop in the 1730s (1984, chap. 2): First they killed their master's gray cat in a particularly gruesome fashion by smashing its spine with a steel rod. Then they collected all the cats they could find in the neighborhood and put them in bags. Some cats were simply killed by suffocation. Others were subjected to a mock trial, condemned to death, and executed by hanging on a small cat gallows. The episode became part of the folklore of that particular printing shop. Whenever the apprentices got drunk at a party, they would reenact the "great cat massacre."

Darnton makes clear that this particular episode was not an isolated instance, but rather reflected a common French practice at the time regarding cats. He traced a complex series of beliefs, symbols, and other cultural practices that lay behind this particular episode of cat-torture: tensions between masters and apprentices, a fear of witches and witchcraft, hostility toward women, and rape. (Sixty-some years later, the Paris mobs were to carry out executions on the masters themselves, including the deposed king and queen, rather than only on their cats.) To our modern sensibilities, laughing at the torture and murder of cats seems cruel and revolting, likely also a sign of some personality disorder. To the Parisian apprentices of the 1730s, however, it was an aspect of the culture.

Propaganda leaflets in the Gulf war. Among the many weapons employed by U.S.-led coalition forces in the 1991 Persian Gulf war were simple pieces of paper—propaganda leaflets designed by U.S. Army Psychological Operations personnel and air-dropped on Iraqi forces, in order to induce them to surrender. According to Parker's (1992) analysis of interviews with those Iraqi soldiers who surrendered, one of the most effective leaflets, shown in Figure 17.1, "displayed the silhouette of two soldiers—one Iraqi and one Saudi—holding hands and walking into the sunset. The sole written message was, 'In peace we will always remain hand in hand'" (p. 14; see also U.S.

FIGURE 17.1
Successful propaganda leaflet used by United States forces in the Gulf War. (From United
States Army, Fourth Psychological Operations Groups [Airborne], n.d., p. 3.)
This leaflet, with the Iraqi and Saudi Arabian flags and the Arabic caption "In peace we
will always remain hand in hand" was one of the most effective propoganda weapons
of the U.S.-led coalition forces in the 1991 Gulf War—though it had almost been
canceled in advance by U.S. generals.

Army, Fourth Psychological Operations Group, n.d., p. 3). Before it was used,
however, the leaflet was nearly canceled by the U.S. military. No doubt a picture of two men holding hands implied homosexuality to the Western mind;
and as the continuing controversy about gays and lesbians in the American
military made clear, this is a topic that arouses strong taboos and feelings
among many Americans, soldiers and civilians alike. But, as Parker notes,
"those who understood the Arab culture . . . realized that men in the Mid-
East are more likely to hold hands with other men than they are with women"
(p. 14). Here we have another example of the importance of culture as a context for the beliefs, values, motives, and traits of personality. Two men holding
hands implies something very different to an Iraqi male soldier and an American male general.

What Does It Mean to Say "It's Culture"?

In each of the three preceding examples, behaviors that could be analyzed in
terms of individual personality (concern about bedsheets, torturing cats, two
men holding hands) seem different when interpreted in terms of the cultures
in which they are embedded. The moral of each example was "It's the culture," rather than "It's [only] personality." But what do we mean when we say
that?

We might be making a statement about the *frequency or level of a particular
behavior*. This is probably the most common meaning of "It's culture." For

example, the average level of concern about the arrangement of bed sheets may be high among the Dutch but low among Americans; torture of cats was much more common in eighteenth-century France than twentieth-century America; and heterosexual Arab men often hold hands. If a behavior is common or routine in a particular culture, then that behavior is less an expression of individual personality and more an expression of culture.

Related to this meaning, the statement "It's culture" might also refer to the *origin or meaning of the behavior, or its role in personality integration and functioning.* Thus any American who is concerned with bed-sheet arrangement probably has had specific and unusual early learning experiences. In American culture, such a concern would be thought of as unusual; it might even get in the way of smooth functioning. In contrast, Dutch people with this concern have probably simply grown up in Dutch culture, where they picked up many messages about how and why bed sheets should be arranged. Such a concern would be supported by many other cultural practices, and would not be thought at all unusual; in fact, people who are careful about bed sheets would likely be viewed as "typically Dutch."

Related to these meanings, we might be making a statement about the *psychopathology* of the behavior. For example, wantonly torturing animals can be taken as a sign of psychological disturbance in twentieth-century America; in eighteenth-century Paris, however, it would not necessarily indicate pathology. A concern with bed-sheet arrangement might reflect an obsessive-compulsive style if you are an American, but not necessarily if you are Dutch.

Finally, we could turn some of these statements on their heads and argue that they indicate *differences in the "average" or "typical" personalities of the different cultures,* or even *differences in how pathological a particular culture is.* To us, the sound of a cat being tortured indicates a cruel personality at work. However, if in eighteenth-century Paris it only means that the printers' apprentices are having another party, then perhaps eighteenth-century France was a cruel (even pathologically cruel) culture. Similarly, the Dutch concern with bed-sheet arrangement may be a sign that Dutch culture itself is obsessive-compulsive, perhaps even pathologically so. Of course, this sense of the phrase "It's culture" takes our own culture as the statistical or moral norm, with any departure from it considered abnormal. We should remember that this kind of thinking can be reversed and the tables turned on us: to a seventeenth-century Dutch housewife, *we* might seem slovenly; to an Iraqi, American army officers might seem unreasonably obsessed with homosexuality.

Universalism or Localism?

If we take seriously the notion that every personality is embedded in a cultural context, then we may ask whether there is such a thing as a truly universal psychology of personality. After reading the above examples of cultural variation, you may wonder whether everything you have read about personality in this book applies to all personalities or only to the personalities of certain rather privileged groups of people in Western Europe and North America in the late twentieth century. Perhaps there are only different "local" psychologies of personality, varying according to history, culture, social class, and gender. Or perhaps these local differences are only variations within universal categories.

The debate between universalism (represented, for example, by Brown, 1991, and Buss, 1992) and localism (represented, for example, by Shweder, 1991, and Stigler, Shweder, & Herdt, 1990) is one of the most active controversies in personality and social psychology. In this book I do not propose to resolve the debate, but rather to suggest some examples of cultural variations in personality that would have to be taken into account by any universalistic theory of human personality.

VARIATION IN LEVELS OF PERSONALITY VARIABLES

The Culture and Personality Movement

Ever since the ancient Greek writer Herodotus (fifth century B.C.) described how other peoples differed from Greeks, people have speculated about how people are different across nations and cultures. In the early decades of this century, as psychologists (and especially psychoanalysts) became aware of other cultures and anthropologists became interested in psychology (especially in psychoanalysis), the field of *culture and personality* was born.[5] The guiding hypothesis of this interdisciplinary field was that each culture, through its distinctive child-rearing practices, produced adults who shared a distinctive personality pattern. Such patterns were variously called "modal personality" [that is, most common personality], "culturally required personality," or (especially in the case of industrialized nation-states) "national character."

Critics were quick to point out, however, that in most cultures neither child-rearing practices nor adult personalities are as uniform as this hypothesis suggests (Inkeles & Levinson, 1969). They also pointed out that most culture and personality studies relied on impressionistic evidence of an adult personality pattern that was presumed to be distinctive, rather than systematically gathering data on the personality characteristics of representative adult persons. In response to these criticisms, personality psychologists interested in culture broadened their framework. They considered the possibility of national *characters* or multiple modal *personalities* and examined personality determinants other than child-rearing practices.

Still, there remains the problem of distinguishing genuine cultural and national differences in personality from simple prejudice. (Remember that Adolf Hitler also had theories about the distinctive national characters of the German, Jewish, and Slavic peoples!) To overcome this problem of subjectivity and possible prejudice, personality psychologists have developed a variety of systematic methods for inferring the personality characteristics of entire populations. We shall examine some classic studies that illustrate each method.

---

[5]See Honigman (1967) for a general account of this field, Kluckhohn, Murray, and Schneider (1953) for a representative sampling of its research output, and LeVine (1982) for a recent assessment of the field.

Measuring the Personalities of Representative Samples

Measuring the personality of every person, even in a small culture, is obviously impossible, but administering personality tests to carefully selected representative *samples* may be a reasonably valid way to make inferences about the modal personalities or national characters of different cultures (or subcultural groups). In order to draw valid cross-national comparisons,[6] we must be sure that the items and the testing procedure have the same meaning, or "stimulus value," in each country, and that the people tested are equivalent in gender, age, sex, social class, and so forth. As you might imagine, the costs of doing research of this kind can mount up very quickly! Good survey research requires modern transportation, communication and census infrastructures, as well as a willingness on the part of people to answer questions from strangers. For these reasons, it is mostly carried out in advanced industrial countries. Hofstede (1980) worked around this problem by surveying over 70,000 people, in forty different countries, who were all employed by the same multinational corporation. Of course, these employees may not have been typical of the population at large in each country.

Inferring personality from survey and polling data. With these cautions in mind, we can take a look at systematic opinion polls and comparative surveys carried out in several different countries, in order to draw conclusions about cross-national personality differences. For example, in a landmark study by Almond and Verba (1963/1989), cross-section samples of about 1,000 adults in five countries (United States, Great Britain, Germany, Italy, and Mexico) were asked questions about social and political attitudes and practices. Some of the results, shown in Table 17.1, suggest that people in these five nations differ in such personality variables as sense of trust and political efficacy (similar to internal locus of control; see Chapter 8), level of social participation, and attachment to governmental institutions.

Almond and Verba argued that these factors constitute a kind of "civic culture" that democratic political structures and institutions require in order to function effectively. Their results suggest that people in the United States and Britain have higher levels of this civic culture than do Germans (who were detached from their political system but took pride in their economy) and the more alienated Italians and Mexicans (who took more pride in their country's natural beauty and culture). Remember, though, that this survey was carried out in 1959–1960 and reflects the historical conditions and philosophic and methodological concerns of those times. (For example, only fourteen years earlier Germany had lost a world war.) Given the many changes that have taken place since that time in each of these five countries, the results might be quite different today (see Almond & Verba, 1980).

---

[6]The terms "cross-national" and "cross-cultural" overlap, but I try to use "cross-national" to describe comparisons made only among Western nations, because in many ways they are all part of a single modern industrial culture.

TABLE 17.1 DIFFERENCES IN SOCIAL AND POLITICAL ATTITUDES AMONG FIVE NATIONS

	United States	Great Britain	Germany	Italy	Mexico
Sense of efficacy: "Suppose a law were being considered by [the national legislature] that you considered to be unjust or harmful. What do you think you could do?"					
Percent replying that they could do something	75	62	38	28	38
Sense of trust: "Most people can be trusted."					
Percent agreeing	55	49	19	7	30
Social participation: Type of leisure activity preferred					
Percent choosing an "outgoing" leisure activity	40	30	16	7	11
Sources of national pride: "What are the things about this country that you are most proud of?"					
Percent proud of:					
Political institutions	85	46	7	3	30
Economic system	23	10	33	3	24
Characteristics of the people	7	18	36	11	15
Contributions to the arts	1	6	11	16	9
Physical attributes of country	5	10	17	25	22

SOURCE: Taken from Almond and Verba (1963/1989, pp. 142, 213, 210, and 64).

Further, Almond and Verba also found consistent trends within each nation for the civic culture complex of attitudes and sentiments to be positively associated with social class (1963/1989, pp. 315–324, 335–336), and higher among men than women (pp. 324–335). (The effects of race and ethnicity were apparently not considered in the original study.) While these within-nation differences were not emphasized by Almond and Verba, they certainly suggest that cultures and nations are not psychologically homogeneous. People's level of civic culture depends upon their status in a hegemonic or dominance structure as well as their culture or nationality.

In recent years, the questions asked in international surveys have expanded considerably to include measures of happiness or "subjective well-being" and a wide variety of other values, attitudes, and feelings (Inglehart & Rabier, 1985; Inglehart, 1990; see also the typical results shown in Table 17.3). Such surveys usually focus on concrete, practical issues rather than personality variables, because these are usually the questions to which research funders want answers. However, Veroff, Depner, Kulka, and Douvan (1980) included a four-picture Thematic Apperception Test in nationwide interviews of over 1,000 randomly selected adult Americans in 1957 and 1976. These TATs were scored for the achievement, affiliation, and power motives (see Chapter 5). Some of the results are shown in Table 17.2. While there are no comparable data from any other country, these two studies do allow us to explore whether

TABLE 17.2 PERCENT OF AMERICANS SCORING HIGH IN TWO NATIONAL SURVEYS OF MOTIVES*

Motive	Women		Men	
	1957	1976	1957	1976
Achievement	41	60	47	53
Affiliation	48	50	58	39
Power	48	49	46	53

*High scores are those above combined 1957 and 1976 median; separate medians were used for men and women.
SOURCE: Adapted from Veroff, Depner, Kulka, and Douvan (1980, p. 1254).

the motive elements of Americans' personalities changed between 1957 and 1976. This was a lively period in the nation's history. It included the turmoil of the late 1960s, the civil rights and women's movements, the legacy of cynicism and disillusion following the Vietnam war and Watergate, and the persistent economic problems that began in the early 1970s. It would be surprising, therefore, if all these changes did *not* have personality effects!

The data in Table 17.2 suggest that between 1957 and 1976, American women showed a dramatic increase in achievement motivation. This may have been a result of the women's movement, which led to increased opportunities for women in education, business, and the professions. (Recall from Chapter 5 the connection between achievement motivation and economic performance, especially entrepreneurial performance.) On the other hand, the women's movement may have arisen and drawn energy from the already-rising achievement motivation of American women. Notice also that over the same time period, American men's power motive scores went up and their affiliation motive scores dropped. Perhaps this change is an early sign of male backlash against women's achievements (Faludi, 1991). By considering the correlates of the power and affiliation motives in Chapter 5, these changes in average motive levels could be used—as causes or effects—to explain the dramatic increases in such diverse things as divorce, violence, drug use, and even the popularity of televised sports.

Comparing personality test scores from different countries. Certain personality tests have been used so widely in so many different countries that it is possible to look at national differences in average scores. As in the case of surveys, problems of equivalence in meaning and stimulus situation are important, but some efforts can be made to overcome these. For example, each item can be translated from one language to another and then translated back into the first language to see if the original meaning of the item has been preserved. The problem of sample equivalence is much more serious, for we usually have no way of knowing how representative of its country each sample is. Lynn (1981) collected the results of studies carried out in twenty-four countries and published between 1958 and 1980 that used one or another of Eysenck's measures of extraversion, neuroticism, and psychoticism. Later, Barrett and Eysenck (1984) reported results of a more systematic and parallel study of people from twenty-five countries, which used translations of a single instrument, the Eysenck Personality Questionnaire. Some results of both studies are given in Table 17.3 on page 626.

Using Social Indicators

To get around the problems and expense of systematic cross-national surveys and personality testing, many researchers have devised alternative strategies to measure national or group differences in personality. One such approach relies on the use of social indicators. (Recall from Chapter 7 how Sales, 1973, and later Doty, Peterson, and Winter, 1991, used social indicators to measure changing levels of authoritarianism in American society.) Lynn and Hampson (1975) constructed measures of the extraversion and neuroticism trait factors for eighteen advanced industrial nations by using national "rates" of certain behaviors that are supposedly correlated with one or the other of the two factors (crime; consumption of cigarettes, caffeine, and alcohol; divorce; motor vehicle accidents; suicides; average calorie intake; and so forth). Since many of these social-indicator measures are also affected by national income, this method may be not be applicable to poorer nations.

Content Analysis of "Cultural Documents"

McClelland (1961, 1963) suggested that since many forms of written expression produced by nations or other cultural groups contain imaginative verbal material that resembles individual TAT stories, these "documents" could be scored to measure motive levels in different countries. For example, every nation with a school system uses readers to teach primary-school children to read. McClelland collected examples of such readers from forty-three countries for the period 1946–1950. He selected and translated twenty-one stories per country and then scored them for achievement, affiliation, and power motivation. These results are presented in Table 17.3 below. Along these same lines, Child, Storm, and Veroff (1958) scored motives in the folktales of fifty-two non-Western cultures. (See Winter, 1992a, for other group or national studies using documents of this kind.)

For a sample of twenty-three nations, Table 17.3 brings together the motive scores from children's readers (McClelland, 1961, pp. 461–462), the subjective well-being survey scores (Inglehart & Rabier, 1985), and the extraversion, neuroticism, and psychoticism test scores (Barrett & Eysenck, 1984; Lynn, 1981). For convenience, scores for each variable are standardized in terms of all countries that were in the original study (overall mean = 50 and standard deviation = 10). Thus a score of 45 (half a standard deviation below

TABLE 17.3 STANDARDIZED SCORES FOR NATIONAL CHARACTER PORTRAITS OF TWENTY-TWO COUNTRIES*

	Motives[†]			Cognition[‡]	Traits[§]		
	Achievement	Affiliation	Power	Subjective well-being	Extraversion	Neuroticism	Psychoticism
Australia	55	48	57		53	55	64
Bulgaria	53	48	49		50	52	44
Canada	54	57	44		61	45	30
China	53	45	58		29	50	62
France	55	47	38	39	47	53	53
Germany	52	41	58	49	49	46	58
Great Britain	46	63	45	53	48	52	41
Greece	54	56	53	27	58	67	53
Hungary	48	48	41		42	51	41
India	60	48	76		68	58	72
Iran	39	26	42		35	45	50
Ireland	54	43	51	57			
Israel	54	69	34		67	23	39
Italy	41	64	58	39	51	45	
Japan	41	57	59	36	41	60	48
Lebanon	60	55	61		58	54	
Netherlands	43	57	40	57			
Poland	35	52	38		55	55	
Spain	54	35	61	39	44	58	35
Sweden	45	53	40	61	52	26	
Syria	51	52	65		47	60	
Turkey	72	34	58		47	33	
United States	53	54	36	54	68	44	

*Scores for each variable were standardized (mean = 50, standard deviation = 10) on the total sample of countries in the original study. Scores of 45 and below can be considered low, 46–55, average, and 56 and above high.
[†]From McClelland (1961, pp. 461–462; based on stories from children's readers, 1946 to 1950).
[‡]From Inglehart and Rabier (1985, p. 12).
[§]From Barrett and Eysenck (1984, p. 618; scores for males and females averaged for each country), supplemented by Lynn (1981, p. 264).

the mean) or less can be considered low, meaning approximately the bottom third of nations; scores of 46 to 55 can be considered medium, in the middle third; and scores of 56 and above are high, in the top third. (Another way of interpreting these standardized scores is to add on a zero to the right column and think of them as SAT scores, which are also standardized scores, with a mean of 500 and a standard deviation of 100.)

Even from these few variables, you can begin to construct a portrait of the "personality" or "national character" for each country. If you have traveled or lived in one or more of these countries, you can reflect on whether your impressions and experiences fit this portrait and the scores in the table. For example, if you know Greece, you may wonder whether Greeks are as unhappy as their score on subjective well-being suggests or simply more open about admitting dissatisfactions that most people feel. Or perhaps Greek people are reluctant to speak in public (for example, to an unknown survey interviewer) about their happiness, lest it tempt the gods (or other people). Why do the less prosperous British and Dutch feel so much better off than the more prosperous French and the Germans? The possibility that high national income per capita does not produce happiness is reinforced by the data for Japan, where economic success has apparently not translated into a sense of well-being among individual Japanese people.

CULTURAL DIFFERENCES IN THE STRUCTURE AND MEANING OF PERSONALITY VARIABLES

So far our discussion of culture and personality has assumed that the familiar variables of personality described in this book are universally true, and the important questions involve different levels of these variables in different cultures and nations. But this may not be a reasonable assumption. If the meanings and structure of personality variables differ from culture to culture, then as Yang and Bond (1990) suggest, "the importation of [universalistic] instrumentation and theorizing results in an incomplete and distorted science" (p. 1093). Let us consider some examples of cultural differences in the very elements of personality themselves.

The Chinese Big Five

The research discussed in Chapter 13 suggests that we organize the domain of personality traits in terms of five factors. But who is "we"? Many if not most five-factor theorists would reply that "we" means all people. For example, John's review of cross-national studies (1990, pp. 77–78) suggests that the Dutch and German languages show the same structure of trait adjectives as English; but Dutch, German, and English are closely related languages. For non-Western languages, the picture is not so clear. A recent study of Chinese trait adjectives by Yang and Bond (1990) illustrates some of the complexities. They asked over 2,000 Chinese college and university students to rate other persons (for example, "mother," "neighbor," or "self") in terms of (1) Chinese translations of the 20 bipolar adjective scales (four for each factor) used in the original American Big Five research (the "imported" terms), and (2) 150 Chinese-language trait adjectives selected from a longer comprehensive list (the "indigenous" terms).

The five factors that emerged from a factor analysis of the imported scales closely resembled the traditional five factors found in American and European research. There were some exceptions: for example, in the ratings of "teacher" and "friend," factor 3 (conscientiousness) tended to merge into other factors. When the indigenous Chinese trait adjectives were factor-analyzed, the result was also five factors. However, these factors were quite different from the traditional Western Big Five. Table 17.4 illustrates the structure of these five indigenous factors by giving English translations of the adjectives with the highest loadings on each factor.

There is some convergence between the two sets of factors; for example, Chinese factor 1 ("social orientation") is correlated +.66 with Big Five factor 2 ("agreeableness"). On the other hand, all Big Five factors taken together are not very sensitive to Chinese factor 5 ("optimism versus neuroticism"). Yang and Bond (1990) concluded:

> Overall, the imported dimensions do a reasonable job of identifying four of the five indigenous factors. There is, however, a one-to-one correspondence for only one of these four factors. . . . Imported and indigenous instruments [are] likely to yield somewhat different theories about the local reality . . . even if they are both true. (p. 1094)

Self-as-Individual versus Self-as-Collective

As we saw in Chapter 9, the concept of self plays an essential part in personality functioning. But what is the self? In the traditional Western view, according to Markus and Kitayama (1991), the self is:

> An independent, self-contained, autonomous entity who (a) comprises a unique configuration of internal attributes (e.g., traits, abilities, motives, and values), and (b) behaves primarily as a consequence of these internal attributes. (p. 224)

Many cultures, however, have a quite different view of the self as interdependent:

> Seeing oneself as part of an encompassing social relationship and recognizing that one's behavior is determined, contingent on, and, to a large extent, organized by what [one] perceives to be the thoughts, feelings, and actions of others in the relationship. (p. 225)

This alternative conception of the self is common in many Asian cultures and among those from Asian cultural backgrounds. Thus a group-based, interrelated sense of self helped many Japanese Americans to cope with the psychological effects of being interned during World War II (Nagata, 1993; see also Chapter 15). The interrelated self is also important in Latin American and African cultures, as Markus and Kitayama point out; and in Korea, as Ryff, Lee, and Na (1993) demonstrate. Even within mainstream American culture, the interrelated sense of self can be found in such diverse groups as Quakers

TABLE 17.4 THE CHINESE BIG FIVE: FACTOR STRUCTURE OF RATINGS MADE WITH 150 CHINESE TRAIT ADJECTIVES

Factor name	Adjectives at the positive pole	Adjectives at the negative pole
1. Social orientation vs. self-centeredness	Honest	Untruthful
	Good and gentle	Selfish
	Loyal	Opportunistic
	Cordial	Sly
	Kind	Greedy
2. Competence vs. impotence	Determined	Dependent
	Resolute and firm	Fearful
	Capable	Timid
	Tactful	Childish
	Brave	Foolish
3. Expressiveness vs. conservatism	Vivacious	Old-fashioned
	Passionate	Conservative
	Straightforward	Rigid
	Humorous	Solemn
	Talkative	Awkward
4. Self-control vs. impulsiveness	Quiet and refined	Impulsive
	Cultured	Irritable
	Modest	Frivolous
	Upright and correct	Bad-tempered
	Self-possessed	Headstrong
5. Optimism vs. neuroticism	Optimistic	Moody
	Pleasant	Worrying
	Self-confident	Pessimistic
		Anxious
		Sensitive

SOURCE: Adapted from Yang and Bond (1990, p. 1091).

and many urban gangs. Lykes (1985) suggests that it is also more characteristic of women than men because of the shared experience of being at the bottom of the power hierarchy of gender. Thus individualism and the independent, individualistic self may be characteristics of people on top, rather than universal features of human nature.

Table 17.5, adapted from Markus and Kitayama (1991), lays out the differences between these two conceptions of the self in more detail. In contrasting the two, consider for example the role of other people. For the independent self, other people provide a standard of comparison against which to measure one's own performance or a source of information about how one is viewed. (Remember Cooley's concept of the self as "reflected appraisal" discussed in Chapter 9.) For the interdependent self, in contrast, other people provide the basic definition of self.

TABLE 17.5 KEY DIFFERENCES BETWEEN AN INDEPENDENT AND AN INTERDEPENDENT CONCEPTION OF SELF

Feature of self	Independent	Interdependent
Definition	Separate from social context	Connected with social context
Structure	Bounded, unitary, stable	Flexible, variable
Important features	Internal, private (abilities, thoughts, feelings)	External, public (status, roles, relationships)
Tasks	Be unique Express self Realize internal attributes Promote own goals Be direct; "Say what's on your mind"	Belong, fit in Occupy one's proper place Engage in appropriate action Promote others' goals Be indirect; "Read other's mind"
Role of others	Important for social comparison, reflected appraisal	Relationships with others in specific contexts define the self
Bases of self-esteem	Ability to express self, validate internal attributes	Ability to adjust, restrain self, maintain harmony with social context

SOURCE: Adapted from Markus and Kitayama (1991, p. 230).

Markus and Kitayama suggest replacing *self-esteem*, which they argue is primarily a Western phenomenon, based on the independent self, with the more inclusive *self-satisfaction*, a concept that reflects the sense that one is fulfilling whatever sense of self—individual or interdependent—is endorsed by one's culture. They go on to discuss how the independent-interdependent distinction affects processes of attribution, emotion, and motivation. In a later paper (Markus & Kitayama, 1992, pp. 361–362), they explore other Western personality concepts that may need modification or expansion when applied to people from other cultures and call for a close look at the concrete elements of culture—social structures, customs, laws and rules, school practices, artifacts, institutions, and myths—in relation to personality.

Personality Elements Unique to a Culture

The standard personality variables were developed in Western contexts. There may, however, be other variables that are important in certain cultures, but that never made it on the standard list because they are not important (or have been overlooked) in the West.

Amok and koro. For example, in Southeast Asia the word *amok* describes a particular pattern of destructive, maddened excitement. It may be a variable or process distinct to that part of the world, something not found in the West. On the other hand, in the last few decades the term "run amok" has made its way into American English. This suggests that "amok" is a useful descriptor of *something* in our culture, perhaps something that Western personality psychologists have overlooked. *Koro,* another term from Southeast Asia, refers to a man's belief that his penis is retracting into his abdomen. Perhaps it is a culturally specific personality variable, but perhaps such a belief (or fantasy, or worry) could also be detected in Western men who are concerned with their sexual potency. (See Berry, Poortinga, Segall, and Dasen, 1992, pp. 89–93, for more examples of such apparently unique personality elements.)

Amae in Japan. Doi (1962) has suggested that *amae* (pronounced ah-mah-yeh) is a critical concept for understanding Japanese personality. It means "depending or presuming on another's benevolence." Perhaps it could be translated as "dependency," but this would be misleading. To a Japanese person, *amae* is a consciously recognized need that continues through adulthood, whereas to most Westerners, "dependency" is something to be concealed or repressed in an adult. The sense of *amae* may be a motivational foundation for the Japanese interdependent sense of self noted by Markus and Kitayama.

Universalism versus Localism

In personality psychology, the debate between universalism and localism is focused on the issue of whether we all have one generic kind of personality or many (locally or culturally different) kinds of personalities. That is, can we best understand the nature and structure of personality as local variations of a universal human structure or as a series of local structures that have certain resemblances but are really distinct in certain fundamental ways? These questions can only be answered by extensive and sensitive studies using both kinds of theories, variables, and instruments. Such studies are just beginning. Examples can be found in Bond's (1986) review of research in China, and Church's (1987) review of research in the Philippines, as well as the more comprehensive six-volume *Handbook of Cross-Cultural Psychology* (Triandis, 1980). For the present, we must realize that just as the hegemony of white, male, Western systems of authority have started to give way to a more pluralistic, multicultural, and gender-sensitive world, so also must a "monocultural," largely American conception of personality be prepared to be modified by indigenous research and conceptions that more adequately represent the rest of the world's people.

SYNTHESIS: NATION, CULTURE, AND PERSONALITY IN THE LIVES OF WOOLF AND ANGELOU

Angelou's Personality in Black Culture

As we have seen in Chapter 15, Maya Angelou's rape, her subsequent months of silence, and her rescue by Mrs. Flowers were critical incidents in the development of her personality. Looking at Angelou's life now from a cultural perspective, we can see that these themes are not unique to her experience and personality, but rather are common in the lives of African American women over the last 150 years. They are, in short, part of a larger cultural pattern.

The threat of rape. Let us begin with rape and the pervasive threat of rape. According to Hine (1989), "one of the most remarked upon but least analyzed themes in Black women's history deals with Black women's sexual vulnerability and powerlessness as victims of rape and domestic violence" (p. 912). Hine went on to suggest that African American women's resulting concern for sexual self-preservation was, along with economic opportunity, a major motive leading them to migrate North:

> I believe that many Black women quit the South out of a desire to achieve personal autonomy and to escape both from sexual exploitation from inside and outside of their families and from the rape and threat of rape by white as well as Black males. (p. 914)

We can see this pattern in Angelou's life. After being raped by Mr. Freeman, she was sent away to Stamps from St. Louis; later, at the time of puberty, she and Bailey were sent out of the South to California.

Angelou responded to being raped with many months of silence. Her words, she felt, were "evil" and dangerous to others: "If I talked to anyone else that person might die too" (1970, p. 73). But this silence was also part of a larger cultural pattern of silence, secrecy, and disguise (Hine, 1989):

> Because of the interplay of racial animosity, class tensions, [and] gender role differentiation . . . Black women, as a rule, developed and adhered to a cult of secrecy, a culture of dissemblance, to protect the sanctity of inner aspects of their lives. . . . creating the appearance of disclosure, or openness about themselves and their feelings, while actually remaining an enigma. Only with secrecy, thus achieving a self-imposed invisibility, could ordinary Black women accrue the psychic space and harness the resources needed to hold their own in the often one-sided and mismatched resistance struggle. (p. 915)

At the institutional level, Hine suggests, this women's culture of silence and secrecy led to the founding of the National Association of Colored Women's Clubs in 1896, to counteract rape culture and the threat of rape: in the words of its first president, to "stop the ravages made by practices that sap our strength, and preclude the possibility of advancement" (Hine, 1989, p. 917). To protect and shelter young African American women, many Association members founded boarding houses, training centers, and schools—much as Mrs. Flowers rescued the young Maya with love, respect, and "lessons in living."

Fluid family living arrangements. Growing up, Maya Angelou had many mothers: her biological mother; her grandmother ("Momma"), with whom she lived the greater part of her childhood; her older brother, Bailey; Mrs. Flowers; and several school teachers. This pattern is not unusual in

African American culture, where the "mothering" function is often spread out among many people, especially grandmothers and older siblings (Joseph, 1981), with children typically experiencing a more fluid pattern of family life (Hunter & Ensminger, 1992).

The mother-daughter bond. As a result of the peculiar disruptions of slavery, the mother-daughter relationship tends to be an especially intense and largely positive one among African American women (Joseph, 1981, pp. 89–90). Instead of being caught in issues of enmeshment and separation from their mothers, African American daughters describe their mothers with respect, focusing on their qualities of strength and endurance in overcoming difficulties, and honesty in "telling it like it is." These cultural themes can be found throughout Angelou's accounts of her many "mothers," but they are especially vivid in her memory of her mother's words of praise in a San Francisco conversation when she was 20 (Paterson, 1982/1989; see also Chapter 15):

> And she said, "Baby . . . I think you are the greatest woman I have ever met. . . ." And I thought, she's not a liar, she's much too fierce to lie. . . . So maybe she sees something, maybe, just maybe. (pp. 119–120)

What Was the National Character of Virginia Woolf's England?

In Chapter 15, I suggested that the patriarchal English culture of Virginia Woolf's late nineteenth-century England was dominated by themes of *competition and decline* abroad and *social upheaval* at home, leading to a *male fascination with power and its control* and a *cult of male strength* that was set against *female weakness and temptation.* Woolf experienced these forces personally, through abuse by her father and half-brothers; and institutionally, through exclusion from the world of men.

Controlling aggression. In his study of English national character, the anthropologist Gorer (1955) identified the latter half of the nineteenth century as a critical time of change in England, a change involving the control of power and aggression.

> Up till [1850] the English were openly aggressive (John Bull, in fact) and took pleasure and pride in their truculence, their readiness to fight and to endure. . . . There was little or no guilt about the expression of aggression in the appropriate situations; and there was no doubt . . . that every English man and woman had sufficient aggression for every possible event. . . .
>   Today . . . almost any overt expression of aggression is fused with guilt. Nearly all the amusements of our forefathers [for example, public floggings, dog fights, and animal baiting] would provoke the greatest indignation . . . any form of childish aggressive behaviour is watched for and punished; and when we think of our faults we put first, and by a long way, any lapses from our standards of non-aggression, bad temper, nagging, swearing and the like. Public life is more gentle

than that reported for any other society of comparable size and industrial complexity. (p. 287)

As causes of this dramatic change, Gorer cited the development of the modern English police force, which in the years after 1856 was devoted to "preserving the peace by a uniformed group of powerful men demonstrating self-restraint" (p. 309), and also the spread of universal education. For males of the upper and upper-middle classes such as Leslie Stephen and the Duckworth brothers, this meant "public" (i.e., private) schools, which by midcentury had adopted the supposedly character-building reforms begun by Thomas Arnold at Rugby School. Through moral piety and the encouragement of sports, Arnold managed to sublimate schoolboy aggression.

Gorer suggests that while directly aggressive behaviors were thus brought under control, indirect traces of aggression can still be detected in certain characteristic English traits and interests: wit and humor, detective stories (the first Sherlock Holmes story dates from 1887), mastery and control of pets, and even the mastery of nature through gardening.[7]

Many of these themes come together in the witty operettas of W. S. Gilbert and Sir Arthur Sullivan, especially *The Pirates of Penzance* (which was first performed in 1880, two years before Virginia Woolf's birth). The band of pirates represents aggression, but an aggression already tempered with humor and good spirits (Gilbert, 1886):

A rollicking band of pirates we,
Who, tired of tossing on the sea,
Are trying their hand at a burglaree,
With weapons grim and gory. (p. 333)

The police spring up from their hiding place to capture the pirates, but are quickly overcome. Just as the pirates celebrate their triumph, however, the police sergeant announces:

Your proud triumph will not be long-lived. . . .
On your allegiance, we've a stronger claim—
We charge you yield, in Queen Victoria's name!

To this the pirate king replies:

We yield at once, with humbled mien,
Because, with all our faults, we love our Queen. (p. 337)

Public aggression, then, is overcome and the police forces reinforced by claims of morality and devotion that are personified by the powerful female

[7]Gorer himself admitted that "I have often found myself that operations such as pruning or weeding tend to be accompanied by fantasies of retaliation for humiliations, slights or annoyances" (1950, p. 292).

figure of Queen Victoria. All of the complex subplots are brought to a happy conclusion as duty prevails on all sides. (The subtitle of the operetta is "The Slave of Duty.") In fact, the pirates turn out not to be real pirates but rather men of the upper class:

> They are no members of the common throng;
> They are all noblemen who have gone wrong! (p. 337)

From pirate king to patriarch in the home. Woolf's experiences with her father and half-brothers were thus part of the broader social and cultural patterns of her time and place: specifically, the not-quite-completed control of male aggression. It was precisely during the years of Leslie Stephen's adulthood and the Duckworth brothers' youth that English male aggression was finally being brought under control. Since public behavior is much easier to control than behavior within the family (especially given the tradition that "an Englishman's home is his castle"), male aggression was probably at first driven indoors. Abetted by the sexual segregation and misogynist tradition of the public schools, it was then expressed against women, such as Virginia and her sisters. Had Virginia been born a few decades earlier, her father and brothers might have expressed their aggression in more public ways. Had she been born a few decades later, they might have been more controlled and less abusive.

The balance of power and affiliation motives. While we cannot go back in time to administer personality tests to the late Victorians, there is some independent evidence for Gorer's interpretation of English character. Following McClelland's (1961) strategy, we can look at cultural documents of the times. For example, every year the reigning British monarch delivers a speech (called the Sovereign's Speech or Speech from the Throne) to Parliament, in which she or he sets out the concerns and plans of the government. (Of course the sovereign only *reads* this speech: every word has been written by the prime minister and the Cabinet.) Thus the year-by-year series of Sovereign's Speeches can be taken as a rough measure of the changing concerns of British elite groups. Winter (1993c) examined levels of power and affiliation motivation in these speeches over the years 1603 to 1988. Figure 17.2 shows average scores for power-minus-affiliation motivation during the decades from 1840 to 1929.

Recall from Chapter 5 that the combination of high power motivation and low affiliation motivation is associated with aggression, violence, and war in international relations. The figure shows that this aggressive motive pattern was at its highest during the 1870s and 1880s, the decades before and after Virginia Woolf's birth. It declines sharply after the turn of the century, heralding a climate less saturated with male aggressive drives. In this later climate, then, Woolf could flourish as an author and critic.

Further traces of this change in English national character can be found in another kind of cultural document, the stories from English children's school readers of the 1920s, collected by McClelland (1961). By this time, the process of bringing male aggression under control should have been largely com-

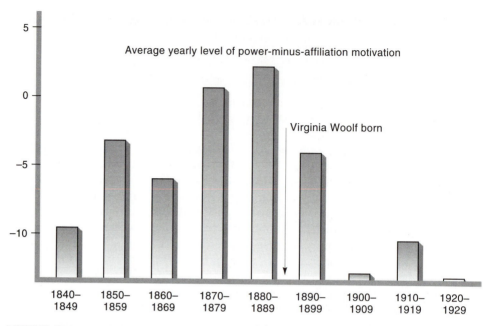

FIGURE 17.2
Average motive levels in the British sovereign's speech to Parliament by decade, 1840–1920. Data are from Winter's (1993c) study of British sovereign's speeches from 1603–1988. Power and affiliation motive scores were each standardized (mean = 50 and standard deviation = 10) on the entire sample of speeches.

pleted. And, indeed, these stories are full of human and animal characters in whom aggressive impulses are controlled and checked—by law, pity, moral teaching, and other means. Table 17.6 illustrates a typical story, "How Mr. Tortoise Helped Mr. Rabbit."

In its general outline, the story is common to many countries and eras, from Aesop to Uncle Remus; but in this version the details are elaborated in a peculiarly English way. For example, notice how Mr. Rabbit's pride at the beginning of the story gets him into trouble later, through Mr. Wolf's aggression. Later on, even though he is in captivity, Mr. Rabbit speaks up forthrightly, with all the moral assurance of an English policeman ("Now look here, it's against the law."). To our surprise, Mr. Wolf accepts the recourse to law. He thinks his aggression will be able to overturn any unfavorable verdict, but in the end he is tricked and the rule of law is triumphant. The whole story is wrapped in the imagery of an English courtroom, with a tortoise-judge lecturing all parties. If we can judge on the basis of this one story, English male aggression had been brought well under the control of law by 1920. We can still detect its traces, though—in this "policeman" version of the tortoise-and-hare tale, in Gilbert and Sullivan operettas, and in the English fondness for murder mysteries that has continued strong ever since that first appearance of Sherlock Holmes in 1887.

TABLE 17.6 STORY FROM AN ENGLISH CHILDREN'S SCHOOL READER, CIRCA 1920

How Mr. Tortoise Helped Mr. Rabbit

As Mr. Rabbit was frisking about the wood as proud as a peacock, he heard someone shouting, "Help! Help, or I'll be flattened out worse than a pancake!" Mr. Rabbit looked about and at last he saw Mr. Wolf lying on the ground with a great big rock on the top of him. Mr. Rabbit got a good strong stick, and somehow he managed to get the rock up so that Mr. Wolf could crawl out.

"Thank goodness none of my bones are broken," said Mr. Wolf, "and now, as you have been so kind, you must come home to dinner with me." And with that, Mr. Wolf grabbed Mr. Rabbit by the small of his back and began to carry him off.

"If you hurt me, I'll never again do you a good turn," said Mr. Rabbit.

"Of course you won't," said Mr. Wolf. "You won't be any more use to me till you're dead."

"Now look here, Mr. Wolf," said Mr. Rabbit, "it's against the law for folks to kill people who have done them a good turn. You ask Mr. Tortoise."

"And if he gives an opinion against me," said Mr. Wolf to himself, "I'll take him as well as Mr. Rabbit." So Mr. Wolf and Mr. Rabbit went to Mr. Tortoise, and Mr. Wolf told his side of the case and old Mr. Rabbit told his side.

"Before I can make out which of you is in the right," said Mr. Tortoise, "I must see the place where Mr. Wolf was, when Mr. Rabbit found him." So the three of them went to the spot where Mr. Wolf had been caught under the big rock.

"Now let me see, Mr. Wolf," said Mr. Tortoise, "just how you were fixed when Mr. Rabbit found you." Mr. Rabbit put the stick under the rock and lifted it up, Mr. Wolf got under it, and Mr. Rabbit dropped the rock.

"Now you were clearly in the wrong, Mr. Rabbit," said Mr. Tortoise. "You had no right whatever to go interfering with Mr. Wolf. You found him lying under the rock, and you just leave him there now, and go and mind your own business." And off Mr. Rabbit and Mr. Tortoise went laughing, and they left Mr. Wolf lying under the great heavy rock.

SOURCE: From the collection assembled by McClelland (1961), deposited at the Henry A. Murray Research Center of Radcliffe College, Cambridge, Massachusetts.

*P*ERSONALITY AND HISTORY: ARE THERE DISTINCTIVE GENERATIONS?

To understand the full context of Woolf's personality, we needed to examine her historical era as well as her nationality, race, and gender. History was critical for Woolf because it was a time of transition: male aggression was not fully brought under control by the late nineteenth century. For Angelou, history in general was important because of the oppressive legacy of slavery. Angelou's own historical time was also important, however, because her young adulthood coincided with the civil rights era in the United States and the independence struggles of the nations of Africa.

Thus personality is shaped by both the macrocontext of history in general and the particular historical era in which people are born and grow up—their generation. In the United States, for example, we speak of the Depression generation, the baby boom generation, the Vietnam generation, generation X, and so on.

Mannheim and "Generation"

The work of the sociologist Karl Mannheim (1928/1952) has inspired recent psychological studies of the relationship between people's generation and their personalities. Mannheim defined a generation in rather precise terms as those people who are born at the same point in historical time and develop a shared experience of the world, organization of beliefs, set of aims, and style. A generation's "personality" is shaped by events that occur during the critical period of its late adolescence (approximately ages 18 to 25), when everything is experienced fresh, for the first time. (Earlier events are only learned about indirectly, and later events are experienced through the lens of this critical period.) Such experiences make up the generation's "natural view of the world," a view that may differ from that of past generations and that will endure throughout the lives of the generation. The more significant the events and changes during this critical period, the greater the resulting sense of generational identity.

A recent book by Straus and Howe (1991) recasts American history from 1594 to 2069 as a series of biographies of eighteen generations. If you were born between 1961 and 1982, for example, you are of the so-called thirteenth generation (also known as generation X). You are having the unprecedented experience (for Americans) of a future that may not be better than the past. Those born after 1982 are part of the millennial generation, which means that they will come of age in the year 2000.

Personality and the Incorporation of Historical Events: Stewart's Theory

Stewart and Healy (1989) have developed a comprehensive theory to account for the different ways in which history and social events are incorporated into personality, depending on the person's age and stage of development. They agree with Mannheim that events occurring during a generation's critical period, in late adolescence, have a major impact. These are the events that people later recall as having been especially important or significant for them (see also Schuman & Scott, 1989). However, Stewart and Healy suggest that events occurring earlier and later than this critical period also have effects, though of a different kind. (Nagata's findings about the different impact of the internment camps on different generations of Japanese Americans, discussed in Chapter 15, are an example.) Stewart's theory is outlined in Table 17.7.

Stewart and Healy report data on the different effects of the women's movement of the early 1970s as an illustration of the theory. For most women

TABLE 17.7 LINKS BETWEEN SOCIAL AND HISTORICAL EVENTS AND PERSONALITY

Age when social event is first experienced	Focus or impact of the event on personality
Childhood and early adolescence	Fundamental values and expectations: "This is the way the world has always been."
Early adulthood	Opportunities, life choices, identity: "This has made me the person I am; it is a part of me."
Mature adulthood	Behavior: "Because of this, I do certain things differently, but it hasn't changed who I am."
Later adulthood	New opportunities and choices; revision of identity: "This has given me a chance to change my life, to change the way I view myself."

SOURCE: Adapted from Stewart and Healy (1989, p. 32).

born after about 1960, the changes associated with the women's movement are simply facts of life. That is, the educational, occupational, and reproductive freedom and opportunities for women are *the way the world is,* for they have no personal experience of a time when things were different. However, for women born earlier, in the late 1940s and 1950s, the women's movement often became a *central feature of their identity,* with enormous effects on life choices (career, whether and when to marry and have children, and so forth). Women born still a decade earlier (in the 1930s and early 1940s) were already settled into life patterns by the time of the women's movement. For them, the movement may have affected *behavior* (for example, getting a job or continuing to work) more than identity and personality. Finally, for older women (born in the 1920s), the advent of the women's movement may have meant some *new opportunities* (for example, employment outside the home or easier ending of an unhappy marriage) as well as *revision of earlier identities* (for example, seeking a new identity beyond "housewife").

SUMMARY: PERSONALITY IN CONTEXT

As we saw in Chapter 16, the lasting legacy of Mischel's 1968 critical analysis was the realization that personalities exist within contexts. To understand a person adequately, we must take account of the person's context. Too often, however, this context has been defined only in the narrow microcontext terms of reinforcement history, or variables that an experimenter tries to manipulate in the psychological laboratory. From the perspective of the larger world, this research (however important) gives only the microscopic perspective.

The total context of personality includes much broader forces: stage of the life cycle; gender, race, social class, and other forms of hegemony; institutions and organizations; nationality and culture; and finally the succession of generations in the ongoing flow of history. In the end, the study of human personality merges into the study of humanity itself.

18

The Integration of Personality

❖

As an organizing principle throughout this book, I have divided personality into four basic elements or components: motivation, cognition, traits and temperament, and social context (see Figure 18.1). This principle makes it possible to arrange related personality theories and personality research findings into natural groupings. I have tried to be eclectic and inclusive, fitting into this framework as many ideas and variables as possible in order to gain the fullest possible understanding of the ways in which people differ from each other.

Perhaps as you have been reading this book, you have wondered where, in the midst of all of these components and variables, the *person* can be found. Human personality is surely more than Frankenstein's monster, stitched together from many separate, ill-fitting parts! In real life, personalities are not conglomerations of individual variables; rather, people usually function as integrated wholes. In this chapter, we will explore how this comes about, how the different *elements* of personality are integrated into *individual personalities* that are unique, recognizable, and (across all people) extraordinarily variable.

	Inner, Private, Subjective	Outer, Public, Objective
Enduring and typical across situations	COGNITIONS Examples of variables: Beliefs, attitudes, values, self-concept Major Theorists: Kelly, Rogers	TRAITS, TEMPERAMENT Examples of variables: Extraversion, energy level Major Theorists: Allport, Jung, Eysenck
Situation-dependent	MOTIVATION Examples of variables: Motives, defenses, psychic structure Major Theorists: Freud, Murray, McClelland	SOCIAL CONTEXT Examples of variables: Habits, models, culture, class, ethnicity, gender Major Theorists: Mischel, Erikson, Stewart

FIGURE 18.1
The major elements of personality.

Of course we must not exaggerate the unity of personality. From a post-modern perspective, the unity of personality is something we construct rather than something that is. Thus there is no reason to require or even expect integration of the separate elements of personality or of the self. As Gergen (1991) has argued:

> There is a *population of the self*, reflecting the infusion of partial identities through social saturation. And there is the onset of a multiphrenic [that is, of multiple minds] condition, in which one begins to experience the vertigo of unlimited multiplicity. Both the populating of the self and the multiphrenic condition are significant preludes to post-modern consciousness. (p. 49, emphasis added)

However, even if we accept the postmodern emphasis on fragmentation over unity, we must still account for the considerable personality coherence and integration that human beings do display.

I believe the elements of personality can be integrated in three different ways: (1) by considering how personality develops; (2) by using multivariate research strategies, in which relevant variables are drawn from each of the different domains and then brought together to predict concrete behaviors; and finally (3) by interpreting the lives of individual persons. In this final chapter, we will examine each kind of integration in turn.

THE DEVELOPMENT OF PERSONALITY: ERIKSON'S PSYCHOSOCIAL THEORY

In considering how personality develops, we begin with Erikson's psychosocial theory. Born in Germany of Danish parents, Erik Erikson (1902–1994) spent several years as an itinerant artist. He decided to settle in Vienna after spending a summer there tutoring the children of an American psychoanalyst studying with Freud. He helped to found a progressive school for children. Invited by Anna Freud into a personal analysis, and then the practice of analysis, he became at first a child analyst. In 1933, sensing the danger of Hitler's rise to power, he moved to the United States. After participating in Henry Murray's research group at Harvard and becoming familiar with personality development among different Native American peoples, he developed into a major figure in personality theory. Erikson's best-known and most influential works include the classic *Childhood and Society* (1950/1963), psychological interpretations of the lives of Martin Luther (1958) and Gandhi (1969), and several studies of the human life cycle. We have already discussed Erikson's concept of identity in Chapters 9 and 10. However, this concluding chapter is an appropriate place for a more systematic account of his general theory, because it emphasizes the contributions of temperament, motives, cognition, *and* social context to personality development. After laying out Erikson's theory, we shall turn to a more detailed discussion of the role that each of the four elements—traits, learning, motives, and cognitions—plays in personality development.

Erik Erikson, who broadened Freud's psycho-*sexual* theory of development into a psycho-*social* approach, by considering the influence of key social relations and institutions on personality development. "Cultures . . . elaborate upon the biologically given . . . [striving for what is] workable within the body's scheme, meaningful to the particular society, and manageable for the individual ego" (1950/1963, p. 108).

Erikson modified psychoanalytic theory by giving much more weight to the role of context in personality development. His psychosocial theory is broadly integrative and emphasizes biological, cognitive, and contextual factors. For Freud, as we have seen in Chapter 3, the prime elements of personality—the libidinal motives—unfolded according to a biologically determined, context-free master plan focused on body zones or stages. For Erikson, in contrast, stages are opportunities or "potentialities for changing patterns of mutual regulation" (1950/1963, p. 69). That is, the person's changing biological capacities furnish opportunities for development, but it is the context and culture that "decide what they consider workable and insist on calling necessary. . . . Everything depends on whether the cultural environment wants to make something of it" (pp. 72, 81).

Erikson identified eight stages of the life cycle. The characteristics of each stage are shown in Table 18.1. The first four stages resemble Freud's oral, anal, phallic, and latency stages, but the emphasis has been transformed from psychosexual development to *psychosocial development*. Erikson's *epigenetic principle* suggests that each stage is affected by what happened at every previous stage. Furthermore, the manner in which each stage is resolved will affect the resolution of all later stages.

TABLE 18.1 ERIKSON'S EIGHT STAGES OF PSYCHOSOCIAL DEVELOPMENT

Significant social relations	Associated social institutions	Virtues associated with positive stage outcome	Vulnerabilities associated with negative stage outcome
Trust versus Mistrust Primary caretakers	Religion	Hope and confidence; sense of being "rooted"	Withdrawal from the world; depression; sense of despair
Autonomy versus Shame and Doubt Parents	Law and order	Will—ability to make judgments and decisions about desires and wishes	Overcontrol; defiance as a counteraction
Initiative versus Guilt Nuclear family	Adult "heroes"	Sense of purpose and direction; focused striving; ability to "play" as rehearsal for later life	Ego-paralysis; "show-off" style as an over-compensation; self-righteousness
Industry versus Inferiority Neighborhood, school	Schools, technology	Competence, sense of work quality; learning of skills and development of intelligence	Discouragement; sense of inadequacy
Identity versus Identity Diffusion Peer groups	Ideology	Fidelity, sustained loyalty in a world of contradictions	Confusion about social roles; inability to tolerate diversity
Intimacy versus Isolation Intimate partners	Pair-bonding; household	Love and mutuality; ability to overcome divisions and antagonisms	Self-absorption; intimacy blocked by regression
Generativity versus Stagnation Family; workmates	All institutions	Productiveness and creativity; capacity to nurture and mentor younger people; concern for the works and ideas of one's society	Self-absorption; self-indulgence
Integrity versus Despair	All institutions	Wisdom, acceptance of life as a meaningful whole	Fear of death; cynicism; bitterness and disgust about humanity

SOURCES: Based on Erikson (1950/1963, chap. 8; 1964, chap. 4).

According to Erikson, each stage is an opportunity for significant interaction of person and context. From this interaction, two outcomes are possible. The positive outcome of each stage is a process of *mutual regulation,* in which the person (typically the child) and the context (typically a parent) each exert control and influence on the other, while adjusting to the control and influence of the other. Even during the earliest stages, personality development is not a one-way street. The person is affected by forces in the social context, *but* the person also has effects on that context. Mutual regulation is the ideal result and leads to the formation of the virtue associated with that stage (trust, autonomy, initiative, and so forth). Where mutual regulation breaks down, both person and context become caught up in "fruitless, painful, and destructive attempts at controlling one another" (p. 68). This is the possible negative outcome of each stage, which leads to the problem or vulnerability associated with that stage (mistrust, shame and doubt, guilt, and so forth).

Erikson's theory is a broad and general account of personality development in terms of the interaction of person and context.[1] With it as a background, we now focus on the development process in terms of the specific personality elements and variables discussed in this book.

THE DEVELOPMENT OF PERSONALITY: FROM BIOLOGY TO COGNITION

For purposes of presentation, we can consider personality development as beginning with traits and temperament and proceeding to cognition. Of course this is an oversimplification of the facts of development: even very young infants have cognitions, and even adults show some change in traits over time. As a way of understanding the developmental integration of personality, however, this is a useful way to proceed.

Traits and Temperament as Physiological Endowment

Development begins, then, with traits and temperament. As discussed in Chapter 14, there is a good deal of evidence that major trait factors such as extraversion-introversion and neuroticism have physiological and genetic bases (though our understanding of the exact nature of these bases seems to change with each new wave of research). For example, among babies in the first few months of life, Kagan (1989) has found reliable individual differences in behavioral inhibition (a concept related to introversion, see Chapters 13 and 14). Let us assume that these differences are innate or genetically based and then trace how they could develop into traits such as introversion or conscientiousness.

---

[1]The universality of Erikson's chosen sequence of stages has been questioned by some (see, for example, Franz and White, 1985).

Remember that a genetic or physiological basis for any human characteristic only means that there is some DNA sequence that can lead to certain biochemical characteristics of the nervous system (see Chapter 14). Thus any genetically based differences develop into the familiar personality traits *only* in interaction with aspects of the social world (for example, other people) that are defined as important by the particular society into which the person is born. To understand these interactions and thus the true nature of the genetic inheritance of personality, we need to make several further assumptions about how the world impinges on the nervous system. The introversion-extraversion variable is an illustrative example. Introversion-extraversion may have a physiological basis in different sensory thresholds, different efficiencies of transmission in the nervous system, or different optimal levels of overall stimulation (see Chapter 14). In any case, introverts prefer lower levels of stimulation. Because the presence of other people is a major source of stimulation, introverted people will tend to develop aversion (or less attraction) to the presence of other people. These aversions constitute the familiar behaviors—low sociability or inhibition of impulse—of introversion.

Further, because much learning involves punishment (that is, large increases of aversive stimulation), people with different thresholds or different optimal levels will learn differently. Since they have lower thresholds for stimulation, introverts should be more sensitive than extraverts to punishment. They will select different situations and manipulate these situations in different ways. Thus from birth, the physiological bases of people's traits lead to differences in how the world impinges on them, and therefore how they will approach the world. In other words, traits select, are affected by, and interact with situations. Out of these interactions, people develop motives and cognitive structures. Thus for two babies of different temperament, the "same" context as measured in objective terms will not have the same effects on personality. Equally, two babies with the "same" temperament, but reared in different micro- and macrocontexts, will develop different personalities.

Encountering the Social Context: Stewart's Theory of Stances

Contexts, then, determine how traits develop and are expressed. Over the long run, contexts also become incorporated as part of personality itself. In a general way, the incorporation of contexts involves the principles and mechanisms of learning outlined in Chapters 15 and 16: classical conditioning, instrumental or operant conditioning, observational learning, and higher-order forms of learning that are guided by abstract rules, self-instruction, and self-reinforcement.

Yet people are not merely passive objects, molded and shaped by whatever context they encounter. From the beginning of life, people have *different stances or positions toward the social contexts they encounter.* These stances, in combination with the contexts themselves, regulate adaptation and personality development. Stewart and her associates (Stewart, 1982; Stewart & Healy, 1984, 1985, 1992) have developed an elaborate theory of how this works.

Table 18.2. As noted in Chapter 3, Freud's theory of psychosexual stages describes a sequence of libidinal motives, each developing in close connection with a particular body zone. During the oral stage, the child develops sucking and biting (and by extension, incorporation) motives. During the anal stage, elimination and retention (and by extension, mastery and control) emerge; during the phallic stage, intrusion and penetration, and so forth. While Erikson adopted the general Freudian sequence of stages, he conceptualized the developmental process as psychosocial rather than psychosexual, emphasizing the importance of social relationships instead of sexual motives.

In formulating her theory of stances, Stewart drew on the prior work of Freud and Erikson. For example, Erikson's emphasis on relationships is reflected in Stewart's term *stance*, which implies a position with respect to someone or something, in this case a stance toward the environment as a whole. On the other hand, Stewart's theory is different from those of both her predecessors in two important ways. First, it describes a sequence that we negotiate again after each major life change, rather than a developmental sequence that proceeds in a single direction from birth onward. Second, Stewart emphasized the emotional or *affective* aspect of relationships, using the four themes of authority, relations with others, feelings, and orientation to action (described in Table 18.2).

Stances and the mechanisms of learning. Stewart and Healy (1992) describe the sequence of stances as a continuum: at the receptive end the person is "at risk of being entirely submerged in the environment," while at the integrated end the person is "in some stable and neutral relation to the environment" (p. 442). Such a characterization suggests some parallels or analogies between the four stances and the four major mechanisms of learning—classical conditioning, instrumental conditioning, observational learning from a model, and learning of abstract rules (see Chapters 15 and 16). These connections are illustrated in Table 18.3. For example, the receptive stance involves passive attention. It should facilitate learning by classical conditioning, because all that classical conditioning requires is simple contiguity or co-occurence of stimuli. (In fact, since cognition and voluntary actions tend to interfere with the conditioning process, researchers studying classical conditioning often immobilize the subject through distraction, physical restraint or even the use of paralyzing drugs such as curare.)

In contrast, in the autonomous stance the person's own action and its consequences become important. This would facilitate instrumental conditioning, which is essentially a process of learning the consequences of one's own actions. When they adopt the assertive stance, people become especially concerned about the possibility that their own actions might fail. As a result, they should become interested in learning through the observation of other, successful models.[2] At the same time, the emotions of opposition and anger asso-

[2]Moreover, the assertive stance resembles the Freudian phallic stage, during which children resolve their Oedipus complexes and through identification develop a superego. In psychoanalytic theory, this is the original model, to which all later models are added.

TABLE 18.3 STANCES TOWARD THE ENVIRONMENT AND MECHANISMS OF SOCIAL LEARNING

Affective stance	Mechanism of social learning hypothesized to be related to it
Receptive	Classical conditioning
	Learning "what goes with what" (Rescorla, 1988)
	Picking up cues and information that are not necessarily "conscious" (i.e., that do not fit into existing schemas)
	Does not requires extensive cognitive abilities
Autonomous	Instrumental conditioning
	Active learning: picking up the consequences of one's own actions
	Likely to involve considerable nonreinforcement or punishment
Assertive	Observational learning
	Learning from (admired or feared) models
	Requires ability to attend, comprehend, and remember
Integrated	Abstract rule-based learning
	Learning guided by abstract rules and instruction, including self-instruction
	Facilitates the organization of complex sequences of behavior
	Requires the existence of abstract cognitive schemas

ciated with this stance should sharpen the distinction between admired others who are imitated out of positive feelings and hated others whose actions are avoided—in learning terms, positive versus negative models. Only at the integrated stage, when emotions are tempered and balanced, are people able to bring their highest and most sophisticated cognitive skills to bear. This makes it possible for them to learn by self-direction, abstract rules, and other complex cognitive mechanisms.

Stance and the processing of context. These affective stances have consequences for the way in which new environments are processed and incorporated as lasting structures of personality. People in the receptive stance, for example, are better at picking up information that is wholly new. Since their existing concepts have been overwhelmed by the changed context, they are able to attend to new information without trying to assimilate it to old frameworks. In contrast, people who have adopted the more mature stances (assertive and integrated) are able to reorganize, rearrange, and assimilate new information so that it fits into existing cognitive frameworks. This is a more comfortable process, but it can limit growth and may involve distortion and denial of the information.

These contrasts in the way people of different stances process the environment can be seen in the results of a study of seventy-two men who graduated in 1964 from "Ivy College" (see Winter, McClelland, & Stewart, 1981, chap. 4). During the first week of their first year in college, these men were given a TAT, which was later scored for Stewart's stance measure. In 1974, ten years after graduation, they were surveyed about the effects of Ivy College on their lives. Table 18.4 shows the striking differences in their responses, as a function of their stance at the beginning of college. Men who had entered college in the receptive stance viewed it fourteen years later as having been much more influential in their lives, especially in broad and diffuse ways such as "identity formation," than did the men who were in other stances. These men were clearly swept off their feet by Ivy College. Men who entered college in the autonomous stance, however, actually denied that Ivy had much of an effect on them! Men in the assertive stance later viewed college only in terms of how it affected their career strivings, which is consistent with the tough-minded and practical themes of this stance. Finally, men who entered college in the integrated stance later felt that Ivy College had broadened them culturally (themes of complexity and balance) but hadn't contributed to their basic sense of identity. Overall, then, the long-range effects of Ivy College were different, in ways that are quite consistent with people's stance on entering college.

Determinants of stance. What determines a person's stance toward the environment? The work of Stewart and her associates suggests three principles: First, there is a natural tendency for people to move from the receptive stance toward the integrated stance over time. After major life changes, however, most people move back to the receptive stance and then renegotiate the sequence. Finally, the greater a person's previous experience with change, the quicker this process of renegotiation after later life changes. In short, with more experience of change, we get better at managing change.

TABLE 18.4 SELF-REPORTED EFFECTS OF IVY COLLEGE ON MEN IN DIFFERENT STANCES AT THE BEGINNING OF THEIR FIRST YEAR

	Correlation with initial stance score			
	Receptive	Autonomous	Assertive	Integrated
"How strongly do you feel your experience at Ivy College has affected your present life in the following ways?"				
Average of 11 specific ways	.31[†]	.01	−.12	−.22
"How strong would you say the overall influence of your Ivy College experience has been in your own life?"				
	.25*	−.20	.08	−.14
"In what ways has Ivy College been most influential in your life? Why?"				
Identity formation (e.g., political or moral values formed, lifestyle, sense of confidence)	.27*	−.09	.08	−.31*
"Not much"	−.09	.26*	−.07	−.07
Career (choice or preparation)	−.03	.01	.15	−.13
Cultural broadening	−.27*	−.06	.11	.26*

*$p < .05$
†$p > .01$
SOURCE: Based on data collected by Winter, McClelland, and Stewart (1981, chap. 4).

Incorporating the context. Let us review the course of personality development so far. At the very beginning of life, people may be differentially sensitive to different aspects of their environment and social context. Their affective stance during any encounter with the environment, moreover, will affect what they take in from that environment and how they take it in. Thus people who have adopted different stances will not experience the same objective context in the same way; nor will this context be incorporated into their personalities in the same ways. In short, individual differences in the way people encounter social contexts and differences among the contexts themselves affect and interact with each other.

The Development of Motives

Motives present a more complicated developmental picture. First, our motives reflect our biological heritage as shaped by evolutionary forces. Without food and water, we would die; hence our hunger and thirst motives direct and energize appropriate life-sustaining behaviors. The biological heritage of social motives such as affiliation, power, and achievement is not so obvious, but with a little thought we can recognize it. Any person who did not desire and seek at least *some* contact or closeness to others of the same species (affiliation) would not stand a very good chance for survival. Similarly, the desires for having impact (power) or maintaining standards of quality (achievement) would usually confer selective advantages (see MacDonald, 1991).

Second, motives obviously involve considerable learning. Human motives are much more variable in level and modifiable in forms of expression than are the hunger or thirst instincts that we share with other animals. But if motives are learned, we must make clear how they are different from other kinds of learning.

Third, if human motives involve cognitions and associative networks (see Chapter 2), then we must establish how they are different from beliefs, attitudes, values, and other cognitions (see Chapters 6 to 8). In short, why do we consider motives to be a distinct element of personality?

McClelland's conception of motive. McClelland (1985, chaps. 4 and 5; see also Weinberger & McClelland, 1990) has outlined a conception of motive that answers all these questions at once. While this model is only tentative at the present time, it does offer an exciting integration of many diverse findings, concepts, and theories. Specifically, McClelland's theory takes account of the biological, learned, and cognitive components of motivation, while distinguishing motives from learned habits, on the one hand, and cognitions, on the other.

McClelland's theory can be characterized as a "neo-instinctive" theory. That is, it uses the model of such familiar instincts as hunger and fear as a basis for explaining complex social motives, although it also draws a sharp distinction between instincts and motives. To illustrate the theory, we can begin with a brief analysis of hunger and fear, as shown at the top of Table 18.5. Such instincts have two elements: a *response pattern* (eating, in the case of hunger; flight or fright, in the case of fear) that is aroused, set off, or "released" by a *sign stimulus* (the sight of food, for hunger; a danger stimulus, for fear). This is also called a *releasing stimulus*. For many animals, the nature of the sign stimulus and response pattern and the relation between the two are quite fixed. For example, given the sign stimulus of Niger seed, a yellow finch bird will eat. (There is some variability: yellow finches will eat other seeds too, and when they have just eaten they are less likely to eat Niger seeds.) For the fear motive: given the sign stimulus of an object moving rapidly across its visual field, a yellow finch will quickly fly away.

McClelland suggested that *in the case of human social motives, both the eliciting sign stimuli and the response patterns have evolved toward greater plasticity or modifiability.* Originally (at birth), most human response patterns exist only as diffuse emotions. And originally, each response pattern is elicited (or released) by certain relatively specific sign stimuli. With learning and experience, however, the range of eliciting stimuli broadens considerably, and the emotional responses develop into action patterns.

If emotions are the basis of human social motives, then we need to identify which emotions are "basic," in order to determine which motives are basic.

TABLE 18.5 SIGN STIMULI AND RESPONSE PATTERNS ASSOCIATED WITH INSTINCTS AND HUMAN SOCIAL MOTIVES

Instinct (or motive)	Sign stimulus	Response pattern
In the yellow finch bird		
Hunger	Sight of Niger seed	Approach, pecking, eating
Fear	Object moving across visual field	Rapid flying away
In humans		
Affiliation		
Positive	Contact (especially with another member of species)	Emotional response of joy-happiness-pleasure
Negative	Loss (of contact especially with member of species)	Emotional response of sadness-distress
Power		
Positive	Impact	Emotional response of anger-excitement
Negative	Pain	Emotional response of fear-anxiety
Achievement		
Positive	Stimuli moderately discrepant from expectations	Emotional response of interest-surprise
Negative	Stimuli greatly discrepant from expectations	Emotional response of disgust

SOURCE: Adapted from McClelland (1985, p. 125).

While in human adults emotions are complex and finely shaded, there is considerable evidence that we have only a few innate or primary emotions (Izard, 1979; Plutchik, 1980; Reeve, 1992, pp. 390–392). Psychologists do not agree on the exact number, but the list compiled by Ekman (1971) is typical: *interest* or surprise, *anger* or excitement, *joy* and happiness or pleasure, *sadness* or distress, *fear,* and *disgust.* The bottom part of Table 18.5 shows the sign stimulus that is innate (or associated at birth) with each of these emotions. (These are analogous to the examples of hunger and fear in the yellow finch.) Notice that these six emotions can be grouped into three pairs, each with a positive emotion involving the presence of a particular sign stimulus and a negative emotion involving its absence.

McClelland has suggested that these three pairs of emotions, each with its own characteristic sign stimulus, are the prototypes or origins of the three fundamental dimensions of human social motives or motivated behavior—affiliation, power, and achievement (see Chapter 5). In Table 18.5 I have labeled each pair accordingly.

The bottom part of Table 18.5 can be explained with a few examples. A parent picks up and cuddles an infant. That infant experiences the sign stimulus of contact (affiliation-positive) and responds with a smiling face and perhaps a gurgling sound. This response pattern is recognizable around the world as expressing the emotion of joy. Then the parent puts down the infant and moves away to answer the telephone. The resulting sign stimulus of loss of contact (affiliation-negative) leads to the child's emotional response pattern of distress (crying). Another example: at the house of family friend, a small child pounds on the dog with glee (power-positive sign stimulus of having impact; emotional response of excitement). But then the dog rears around and barks at the child. Suddenly this new sign stimulus of threat (power-negative) changes the emotion to fear and the child withdraws its hand in fright. (Perhaps a very bold child might retaliate by pounding the dog even harder [power-positive; emotion of excitement-tinged-with-anger].)

These examples of (presumably) innate links between sign stimuli and emotional responses reflect the earliest stages of motive development in the infant. McClelland suggests that the complex social motives of human adults are built up from these innate patterns or prototypes by processes of classical and instrumental conditioning. Figure 18.2 illustrates how this happens.

First, with experience the range of stimuli that elicit the emotional response is broadened. Although certain sign stimuli can innately release the emotional response pattern, many other stimuli can acquire such a releasing capacity through being paired with the original stimuli (classical conditioning). For example, contact with a parent innately releases the joy-happiness-pleasure response, but by classical conditioning (see Chapter 15) other stimuli (such as the sight of the parent, a picture of the parent, the parent's voice on the telephone, or a smile from anyone) can also come to elicit the same response. As the child develops, more and more stimuli come to evoke the joy-happiness-pleasure response. This *broadening of the range of stimuli that release the emotional response* is one way in which motives develop as learned behavior systems constructed on an innate base.

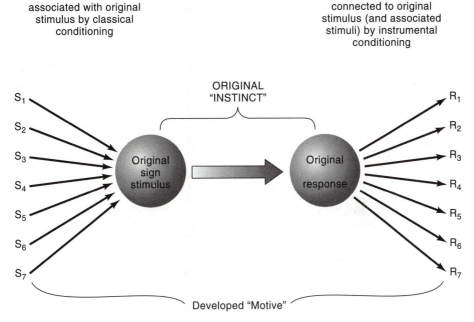

Other stimuli associated with original stimulus by classical conditioning

Other responses connected to original stimulus (and associated stimuli) by instrumental conditioning

ORIGINAL "INSTINCT"

S_1
S_2
S_3
S_4
S_5
S_6
S_7

Original sign stimulus

Original response

R_1
R_2
R_3
R_4
R_5
R_6
R_7

Developed "Motive"

FIGURE 18.2
How motives are built up from instincts through classical and instrumental conditioning. (Based on McClelland, 1985, chaps. 4 and 5).

Second, because the joy-happiness-pleasure emotional response is experienced as pleasant, the child attempts to keep it going and to make it happen again. That is, through processes of instrumental or operant conditioning (see Chapter 15) the child learns behaviors that have the consequence of bringing back the releasing stimulus, which leads to a repetition of the positive emotional response. This *learning of behaviors that keep the response going* is a second way in which motives are learned behavior systems developed on an innate base.

Individual differences in motive strength can be explained as follows. For both kinds of learning—broadening of the categories of eliciting stimuli and learned behaviors that maintain the response—many people (especially if they are in the same culture or macrocontext) will have similar experiences and therefore similar learning. In other words, for each motive, most children will form similar sets of associations between the original sign stimulus of that motive and other stimuli. Similarly, for each motive most children will learn the same kinds of behaviors to maintain or reinstate the emotional responses. However, there will also be individual differences in both kinds of learning. Some children will be exposed to a wider range of stimuli associated with physical-contact-with-parent than other children. (For example, the more physical contact there is in a family, the wider the range of other stimuli that are likely to be conditioned to it.) Thus different children will develop different patterns of "releasing" stimuli for what will develop into the affiliation motive. Similarly, different children will experience different consequences of any particular act, in terms of maintaining or terminating the positive emotional experience (joy) of the affiliation motive.

By the time the children become adults, therefore, there will be *broad individual differences in the strength of the motive, the range of cues that arouse it, and the actions associated with it.* Thus the affiliation motive, in the original form in which it appears in a human infant, is probably an evolved innate aspect of our biological heritage. As an adult social motive, however, it is a complex learned pattern of eliciting stimuli, emotional responses, and maintaining behaviors that vary greatly in strength and range across different individuals. Sometimes the range of cues and actions that can be attached to a motive system can be quite striking and unusual. Recall from Chapter 2 that for Richard Nixon, even cues of death, departure, and failure were apparently associated with physical contact and parental love.

The role of early learning and our two motive systems. Motives constitute a special element of personality, different from other elements such as learning and cognitions, because of the way in which they are learned. The available evidence suggests that motives are shaped during the period when language is available to children but not yet under their complete control (see McClelland, 1951, pp. 445–458).[3] At this relatively early stage of cognitive development, the goal states represented by motives can be verbalized (as in a TAT story) but cannot yet be manipulated with the same ease that adults have in thinking about their conscious intentions, projects, and choices (see Chapter 10, and Cantor & Zirkel, 1990).

Thus the special status of motives, and the reason for their being a separate element of personality, results from the child's primitive level of cognitive development when motives are first learned. The complex patterns of classical and instrumental conditioning involved in creating motives take place before language development is complete. They are likely to remain somewhat outside of conscious awareness and control while at the same time being saturated with emotions. They will be difficult to verbalize or modify. For example, this is how you probably "learned" about your parents, grandparents, older siblings, or your country's flag. Very likely you cannot recall such learning, and you could reverse or unlearn it only with considerable difficulty. (In contrast, as we saw in Chapter 6, Helen Keller's experience of early learning was mostly different; she developed language so rapidly and at such a late age that she was able to preserve memories of many experiences most people have forgotten because they had only a primitive verbal framework for them.)

Once language and other sophisticated cognitive structures have developed, further learning is more deliberate and conscious, less saturated with emotions, easier to control, and relatively easier to reverse if conditions

---

[3]Although motives can sometimes be changed in adulthood (see McClelland & Winter, 1969).

change. For example, consider the way in which you "learned" this year's popular movies, television shows, or musical performers. Such learning is under tight cognitive control. You can immediately alter what you have learned in response to new information.

Thus we appear to have two different systems or "tracks" of goal-directed behavior. The first system, for which I reserve the name "motives" in this book, is laid down early in life on a foundation of a few major instincts. It is saturated with emotion. It is not wholly accessible to conscious awareness or change. It tends to guide our long-term course of behavior in unconstrained or free-ranging situations. The second system originates in our highly organized perceptions of immediate situational pressures, demands, incentives, and expectations. This system is quite available to conscious awareness, can readily be altered, and influences immediate choice behavior in constrained situations (McClelland, Koestner, & Weinberger, 1989; Weinberger & McClelland, 1990). In this book, I consider this second system as part of the cognitive (rather than the motivational) element of personality. Thus I have discussed it in Chapter 10 as a motivational form of cognition.

Cognition

With the mastery of language, children acquire much greater access and control over their mental processes. After the years of childhood, therefore, personality development normally consists largely in the expansion, elaboration, and increased complexity of cognitive structures. The life story (see Chapter 9), for example, is constantly being revised (sometimes even dramatically rewritten) throughout adulthood. We have already discussed the ways in which beliefs, attitudes, values, attributions, self-schema, personal narratives, and unifying philosophies each develop according to their own principles (see Chapters 6 through 9), but a few general principles that apply to all these different kinds of variables can be mentioned here.

Principles of cognitive development. The cognitive elements of personality depend upon the more advanced and complex mechanisms of learning discussed at the end of Chapter 16: observational learning, modeling, direct instruction, and above all self-administered rewards and punishments and self-regulated rule following. For all these mechanisms, the development of language is crucial. That is why Helen Keller, before she learned language, can be said to have had only a rudimentary personality—a few general traits, many habits, and some primitive and inchoate motives. That is why even the smartest animals, who may have distinguishing individual characteristics or traits, cannot be said to have "personalities." (No doubt some pet owners will disagree with me about this.)

Skinner's behaviorist challenge to cognition. The human *capacity* to learn language evolved along with the rest of the human brain and nervous system.

Most psychologists believe that the development of language competence in individual persons is a creative process. That is, it involves learning rules and abstract principles (grammar), which permit people to generate meaningful and correct sentences that they have never heard or seen before. On the other hand, the behaviorist Skinner insisted that words—even the most complex and abstract words—are originally built up through the laws of learning, based on concrete situations, body states, and behaviors. "Cognitive processes are behavioral processes; they are things people *do*" (Skinner, 1989, p. 17; emphasis added). Skinner demonstrated these concrete origins by tracing the history of words, especially their Latin or Greek roots. (As an undergraduate at Hamilton College, he was an English major!) For example, certain words having to do with motivation originated in the description of concrete physical phenomena (Skinner, 1989):

> Because things often fall in the direction in which they lean, we say we are *inclined* to do something, or have an *inclination* to do it. If we are strongly inclined, we may even say we are *bent* on doing it. Because things also often move in the direction in which they are pulled, we say that we *tend* to do things (from the Latin *tendere*, to stretch or extend) or that our behavior expresses an intention. (p. 13)

Many words for cognitive processes have similar concrete origins:

> We say we *perceive* the world in the literal sense of taking it in (from the Latin *per* and *capere*, to take). (p. 14)
> *Contemplate*, another word for think, once meant looking at a template or plan of the stars. (p. 16)
> An *attitude* is the *position, posture,* or *pose* we take when we are about to do something. (p. 13)

Skinner's point, that the abstract language of cognition is grounded in concrete contexts and concrete effects of behavioral acts, can be illustrated with Helen Keller's recollection (from Chapter 6) of how she learned to understand the word "think" while stringing beads:

> Miss Sullivan touched my forehead and spelled with decided emphasis, "Think." In a flash I knew that the word was the name of the process that was going on in my head. This was my first conscious perception of an abstract idea. (1903b, pp. 30–31)

General Principles of Personality Development

By considering how personality develops, then, we can bring together the four elements of traits, context, motivation, and cognition. During personality development, each element affects and is in turn affected by the other elements. For example, contexts affect the development of motives and cognitions and the expression of traits and motives. People's traits, motives, and cognitions, in turn, affect how they select and modify their contexts.

Often we find that a single topic or theme plays different but related roles in connection with the development of each element of personality. Consider, for example, the theme of relationships to other people. First, the number, nature, distribution, and structural position of other people is one of the most important aspects of any person's social *context*. Second, since other people are a major source of stimulation, they will be responded to differently as a function of the person's *trait* of introversion-extraversion. Third, the goal of warm and friendly relationships with similar and comfortable others is a major *motive*. Finally, people's beliefs and values about other people and their proper relationship to them are core *cognitions*.

Two general principles of personality development emerge from this brief survey. First, there is *a general progression from biology to cognition*. Of course the biological foundations of personality continue to be important throughout our lives. With the development of personality, however, structures of categorization, meanings, and regulation are constructed upon these foundations. Often these structures are able to alter, or even override, the influence of the biological foundations. Second, over the course of personality development we move *from inner (genetic and physiological basis of traits) to outer (social context); then back again from outer to inner*, as contexts become transformed and internalized as motives and cognitions.

*I*NTEGRATING PERSONALITY THROUGH MULTIVARIATE RESEARCH

A second way of bringing the different elements of personality together is through multivariate research, in which variables from the different elements are used to predict specific behaviors and life outcomes. All personality elements and variables are somewhat arbitrary abstractions, convenient and useful for the purposes of scientific analysis. In the real world, however, people's behavior and life outcomes usually appear as unified fusions or "integrates" of many different variables. A given action can express, at the same time, a blend of many different aspects of personality. Multivariate personality research permits us to preserve and study this blended quality of behavior.

Previous Studies Using Variables from Different Personality Domains

In Chapter 16 we saw that the correlation coefficient between a personality variable and a behavioral outcome can be dramatically increased by adding additional personality variables as predictors. These increased correlations do not result from merely adding in more personality variables, however, but rather from adding in different *kinds* of personality variables (especially variables that reflect the social context or situation). We shall review several studies that illustrate this point.

Consider the results of Couch's (1962/1969) study of personality and interpersonal behavior in experimental small discussion groups, as illustrated in Table 18.6. Measures of people's personality needs (or motives) gave correlations in the range of .18 to 46 with measures of the corresponding dimension of their behavior in the group. When a measure of concealment defenses was added to the measures of needs, the correlations increased to the range of .26 to .58. Concealment defenses, such as suppression and repression (see Chapter 3), act as generalized tendencies to control, suppress, or mask the open expression of needs or wishes. They are thus a very different *kind* of variable from needs or motives. When Couch added measures of the perceived group context relevant to each need dimension, the correlations increased still further, to the range of .41 to .64. Finally, Couch added measures of the actual (that is, objectively measured) group context relevant to each need dimension. This raised the correlations to the range of .65 to .88, a level that is truly extraordinary in personality research.

Much of the success of the Couch study comes from his use of four different *kinds* of variables, added together in a theoretically coherent way. In the language of this book, needs are similar to motives, concealment defenses are an aspect of extraversion-introversion (see Eriksen & Pierce, 1969, as well as the distinction between repressing and sensitizing defense mechanisms in Chapter 3 and the discussion of extraversion in Chapter 13). The perceived context brings in cognition, and the actual context is context. An example will illustrate how these different kinds of variables (or elements) interact. First, people with a high dominance need might not act in a dominant way if that

TABLE 18.6 PREDICTING INTERPERSONAL BEHAVIOR FROM PERSONALITY NEEDS, DEFENSES, AND CONTEXT

Dimension of interpersonal behavior	Need	Need + defense	Need + defense + perceived context	Need + defense + perceived context + objective context
Dominance	.35[†]	.53[‡]	.64[‡]	.88[‡]
Positive affect	.33[†]	.32[*]	.41[†]	.66[‡]
Involvement (dominance and positive affect)	.18	.26[*]	.44[‡]	.65[‡]
Hostility (dominance and negative affect)	.46[‡]	.58[‡]	.61[‡]	.84[‡]

[*] $p < .05$
[†] $p < .01$
[‡] $p < .001$

Note: Need = measures of the personality motive relevant to the behavior dimension; defense = measures of concealment defenses; perceived context = measure of situation relevant to the behavior dimension, as perceived by the person; objective context = objective measures of the context relevant to the behavior dimension.

SOURCE: Adapted from Couch (1962/1969, p. 87).

need were controlled by defenses (suppression or repression) that concealed it. Second, any dominance need would be regulated by the person's perception of the situation or context: in the absence of likely targets, for example, even a very strong dominance need might not lead to dominant behavior. Finally, the nature of the actual behaviors directed toward the person by others (for example, asking for leadership versus ignoring) would further modify or channel the combination of need, defense, and perceived situation.

Thus in the Couch study, the actual amount of dominance behavior is an integration of the relevant need, as modified by ego defenses, along with perceptions of the situation or context, and the actual context itself. In the terms of this book, behavior is an integration of the four elements of personality.

Similarly, Winter (1978; cited by McClelland, 1981) predicted rated leadership performance among U.S. Navy officers, using nine personality variables (including measures of motivation, cognition, and traits) and one context variable (the officer's particular kind of job within the navy). The resulting multiple correlations between these personality measures and rated leadership ranged above .65.

Additive Multivariate Predictions

While the Couch and Winter studies used variables that can be loosely classified into each of the four elements of personality, longitudinal data collected by Winter, McClelland, and Stewart (1981, chap. 4) actually used several of the personality measures discussed in this book. Through a further analysis of their data, we can give an even more vivid demonstration of the predictive power of multiple personality variables drawn from each of the four domains of personality.

From the data collected on men from the Ivy College class of 1964, the following variables were developed:

Motivation (measured by a TAT at the beginning of first year in college)
   Achievement motive
   Affiliation motive
   Power motive
Cognition (measured during first year in college)
   F-scale measure of authoritarianism
   Self-definition (see Chapters 9 and 16)
Traits (constructed from an adjective self-description checklist given ten
      years after college)
   Extraversion
   Neuroticism
   Psychoticism
Context
   Characteristic stance of adaptation to the environment (measured at the
      beginning of first year in college)

Social class of family (measured at the beginning of first year in college)
Currently in a bureaucratic (versus entrepreneurial) job
Currently married (versus not)

These twelve variables were used to predict two important life outcomes measured ten years after college: *net happiness* and *sense of career fulfillment*. The men were asked how often (on a 4-point scale) they had felt each of a series of different feelings or moods in the past week. Net happiness was defined as the sum of "on top of the world feeling," "particularly excited or interested in something," "pleased about having accomplished something," and "proud at being complimented about something you did," minus the sum of "anger at something that doesn't usually bother you," "depressed or very unhappy," and "bored." The men were also asked to rate (on a 4-point scale) various characteristics of their current job. Career fulfillment was defined as the sum of ratings for the following career characteristics:

Your work is intrinsically interesting.
The social environment at work is pleasant.
You have a chance to do what you do best.
You leave work each day with good feelings.
Your supervision is competent.
Your job measures up well to the sort of job you wanted when you left college.
Your achievements have been fully recognized by your coworkers.
Overall rating of how "satisfying" the job is minus rating of how "frustrating" it is.

The results for predicting net happiness are shown in Table 18.7. The table shows, for each predictor variable, both its correlation and its regression (beta) weight, which is like a correlation coefficient but with the influence of all the other variables taken into account. (Since only six of the twelve variables showed significant relationships, Table 18.7 shows the regression results for only these six.) As can be seen from the table, in this sample of male college graduates at least one variable from each of the four elements of personality is involved in predicting happiness: the affiliation motive, low authoritarianism, low neuroticism, high psychoticism, a relatively more mature stance of adaptation to the environment, and not having a bureaucratic job. The overall multiple correlation of these six variables with net happiness is .58, which is quite high considering the crudeness of some of the measures and the fact that the different personality variables were measured at different points over a span of fourteen years. These results demonstrate the value of drawing upon the different elements of personality in order to predict an important life outcome such as happiness.

At the same time, the multivariate approach enables us to understand how "happiness" results from a fusion or integration of many different personality components. From what was been presented earlier in this book about

TABLE 18.7 PREDICTING NET HAPPINESS AMONG ADULT MEN

Predictor variable	Relation to self-rated net happiness	
	Simple correlation coefficient	Standardized regression coefficient (beta weight)
Motivation		
Affiliation motivation	.08	.21[†]
Cognition		
Authoritarianism	−.18	−.26[†]
Traits		
Neuroticism	−.34[‡]	−.39[§]
Psychoticism	.16	.24[†]
Social context		
Stance toward environment	.29[†]	.33[‡]
Having a "bureaucratic" job	−.06	−.19[*]
		Multiple $R = .58$[§]

[*] $p < .10$
[†] $p < .05$
[‡] $p < .01$
[§] $p < .001$
SOURCE: Based on data collected by Winter, McClelland, and Stewart (1981, chap. 4).

each of these six variables, you could probably construct an explanation of why that variable is associated with happiness.

Psychoticism, however, may be an exception. Why should high psychoticism scores make people happier? Recall from Chapter 13 that psychoticism, as Eysenck has defined and measured it, does not necessarily mean "psychotic." In fact, Eysenck's measure really suggests nonconformity and creativity. Even moderately high scores could signify a person who is a free spirit rather than a sociopath. (And if sociopaths are truly oblivious to punishment and other negative consequences, then they are probably quite happy!)

A word of caution: these results apply for certain only to one sample of white, well-educated, pre-middle-age American men who were last studied by Winter and associates in 1974. Remember the message of Chapter 17: Personality variables are always channeled and affected by social contexts. In a different sample, with people of a different age and under different historical conditions, different variables might predict happiness. Thus you might ponder which of these six variables would also predict happiness for someone of Maya Angelou's or Virginia Woolf's gender, race, life stage, and generation.

The results for predicting career fulfillment are given in Table 18.8. Affiliation motivation, low authoritarianism, and mature stance toward the environment predict career fulfillment in the same way that they predict net happiness; but the trait measures drop out, and marriage replaces type of career as a

TABLE 18.8 PREDICTING CAREER FULFILLMENT AMONG ADULT MEN

Predictor variable	Relation to self-rated career fulfillment	
	Simple correlation coefficient	*Standardized regression coefficient (beta weight)*
Motivation		
Affiliation motivation	.14	.20[†]
Cognition		
Authoritarianism	−.37[†]	−.37[§]
Social context		
Stance toward environment	.18	.28[‡]
Being currently married	.27[†]	.23[†]
		Multiple $R = .52$[§]

[†] $p < .05$
[‡] $p < .01$
[§] $p < .001$
SOURCE: Based on data collected by Winter, McClelland, and Stewart (1981, chap. 4).

current-context predictive variable. Again, the overall multiple correlation of .52 demonstrates the value of a multivariate research strategy.

Interactive Multivariate Predictions

So far, our demonstrations of the multivariate strategy have involved only additive effects—that is, adding the effect of each predictor variable to the effects of all others. But predictor variables can also interact with each other, such that the presence of one predictor variable completely changes the direction of the relationship between the other and the behavior or outcome. Consider the affiliation motive and extraversion-introversion. Since both involve friendly social interaction, they might have additive effects. For example, people who are high in the affiliation motive *or* who are extraverted tend to be friendly, and if they are high in both variables they would tend to be especially friendly. Now consider affiliation-motivated introverts. Because they are high on only one of the two variables, they might be a little less friendly than affiliation-motivated extraverts. This would be an additive effect. On the other hand, they might be a lot less friendly because of the conflict between their motive—to approach people—and their trait—to avoid excessive stimulation. In other words, introversion might channel the affiliation motive in a different way than extraversion does. This is what statisticians call an *interaction effect*. Another way of describing it is to say that the affiliation motive is moderated by extraversion-introversion, or that extraversion-introversion is a *moderator variable* (see Chapter 16) for the expression of the affiliation motive.

Interaction effects are easily measured with an analysis-of-variance statistical design, in which there are two or more independent predictor variables, each divided into two or more categories (women/men, black/white, middle class/working class, and so forth). However, most personality variables are continuous rather than binary (that is, they can take on any of a range of values), which means that interaction effects must be studied in a multiple-regression statistical design. While the analysis of interactions among many predictor variables is complicated and difficult to visualize, I will use some simple two-variable examples from recent research to show the nature and power of interactive effects in personality research.[4]

The affiliation motive moderated by extraversion-introversion. Let us consider the interaction between the affiliation motive and extraversion. Both variables have to do with the friendship-affiliation behavior system, but they are uncorrelated, because each involves a different element of personality. The affiliation motive has to do with friendly relations as a *goal*, while the trait of extraversion involves a friendly interactive *style* that could characterize people who are pursuing many other goals (for example, achievement, power, exploration, or dependency).

When we think about how these affiliation-related motive and trait variables interact, it is easy to imagine two of the four combinations—an affiliation-motivated extravert and an introvert low in affiliation motivation. The case of an affiliation-motivated introvert is more complicated. Such a person would "need" or "want" affection and friendship from others, but at the same time would be ill at ease in many situations where such affiliation was most likely. While this motive-trait combination would lead to discomfort or conflict, it is not an implausible one. For example, there is evidence that former president Richard Nixon was just such a person—an introvert who was also high in the affiliation motive. (This is discussed further below, in the next major section.)

The opposite combination, extraverted people who are "friendly" but who nevertheless do not seek affiliation as a goal, is also interesting. Such people would be cheery, impulsive, and friendly; popular and adept at social relationships—but they would be able to take them or leave them, depending on the situation and their other motives. In other words, they would pursue whatever goals they have in an extraverted style, with any resulting friendships and warm relations experienced as a harmless (and possibly useful) add-on, rather than a core motivational concern. They might often be surprised at the amount of friendly interaction that surrounds them. In an extreme case, they might display the hysteric style of "casual indifference" toward other people (see Shapiro, 1965). Former president Ronald Reagan may have fit this pattern. (See the motive and trait scores in Tables 5.3 and 13.6, respectively.)

---

[4]For those who want to understand and do this kind of research, I refer you to Cohen and Cohen (1983) and Aiken and West (1991) for a full discussion of the method used in the following examples.

To summarize the above discussion: Affiliation motivation combined with extraversion is quite different from affiliation motivation combined with introversion. *In each case, though, it is still recognizably affiliation motivation*, involving the goal of close relationships with other people. Thus relationships are relevant to both the trait of extraversion and the affiliation motive, but in different ways. Affiliation-motivated people want them, and extraverted people are adept and comfortable in them. In combination (both high), these two variables should predict unconflicted intimate relationships; but in opposition (one high, one low), they should predict more conflicted intimate relationships.

With their more inward focus, affiliation-motivated introverts should find relationships troublesome, conflicted, and even aversive. (In terms of the paradoxical findings of previous research on the affiliation motive, as discussed in Chapter 5, affiliation-motivated introverts would be the people who become prickly and defensive under threat, perhaps because as introverts they experience relationships as intrusive and threatening.) Thus they should show a conflicted pattern of wanting close relationships but having difficulty maintaining them, and therefore ending them.

John and associates (1993) studied these motive-trait interactions in samples of adult women graduates of "Ivy" and "Coastal" colleges. The women in each sample had been given personality tests in college and were then followed up over twenty years after college graduation. John and associates developed two life-outcome measures reflecting "conflicted affiliation": (1) marriage followed by divorce, and (2) self-reported difficulties with intimate relationships. In both samples, they found that among introverts, the affiliation motive predicted the presence of both conflicted affiliation variables. Among extraverts in both samples, however, the affiliation motive was negatively related to these same conflicted affiliation outcomes. In other words, affiliation-motivated introverts make and break relationships, while affiliation-motivated extraverts make and keep them.

Regression results involving interactions are hard to present in tables, but they can be represented by bar graphs as in Figure 18.3, which present the results for one of the two samples.

The power motive moderated by extraversion-introversion. As discussed in Chapter 5, power-motivated women and men tend to enter certain "impact" careers such as business executive, education, psychology and psychotherapy, journalism, and the clergy—careers in which they directly and legitimately influence other people (Winter, 1973, chap. 4; 1988; Winter & Stewart, 1978). Such careers should be particularly attractive to power-motivated people who are also high in extraversion, since they involve many social contacts. For power-motivated introverts (who are striving for more inwardly channeled power goals), however, such careers might actually be aversive.

In a test of this prediction, John and colleagues (1993) found significant or near-significant relationships between power motivation and impact careers, unmoderated by extraversion, in both samples. In other words, power motiva-

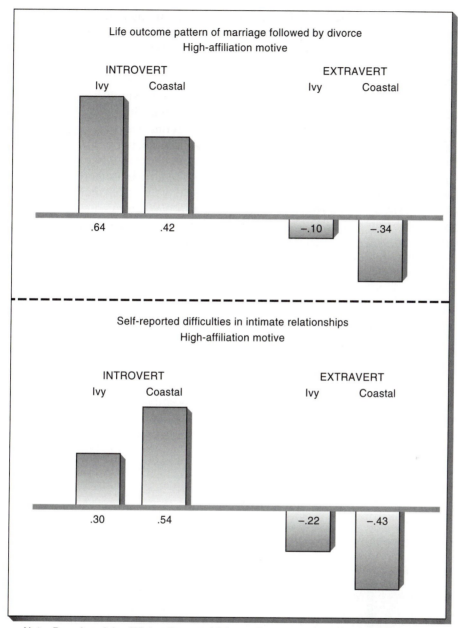

Note: Based on John, Winter, Stewart, Klohnen, Duncan, and Peterson (1993).
Values for the two outcome variables are in standardized form (mean=0 and
standard deviation=1).

FIGURE 18.3
Interaction of affiliation motive and extraversion in predicting relationship difficulty
among adult women.

tion by itself predicted having an impact career among both groups of women. In the Ivy College sample, however, the interaction of power motivation and extraversion was also significant, which means that the power motive–impact career relationship tends to reverse among introverts, as illustrated in the bar graph of Figure 18.4.

Among the Coastal College women there was no significant interaction between power motivation and extraversion-introversion. This difference is probably due to differences in career levels between the two samples. Typically, Ivy College women entered impact careers that were at the time dominated by men (for example, psychiatrist, college professor), while Coastal College women entered lower-prestige versions of the "same" career that were at the time filled by women (for example, social worker, elementary school teacher). Any person trying to enter a field traditionally dominated by another group probably has to be especially assertive, active, and energetic (that is, extraverted) and *not* quiet, reserved, shy, and silent (introverted). Thus for the Coastal women, impact careers that were traditionally female required only power motivation; among the Ivy women, in contrast, traditionally male impact careers required both power motivation (potential for impact) and

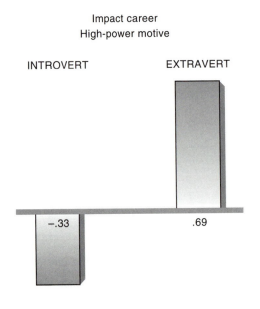

Impact career
High-power motive

INTROVERT   EXTRAVERT

−.33   .69

Note: Based on John, Winter, Stewart, Klohnen, Duncan, and Peterson (1993). Values for the outcome are in standardized form (mean=0 and standard deviation=1).

FIGURE 18.4.
Interaction of power motive and extraversion in predicting impact careers among adult women graduates of Ivy College.

extraversion (overcoming resistance and being a pathbreaker). Comparing the results from Ivy and Coastal College women gives a sense of how complicated personality research can get when it involves real-life outcomes.

The power motive in the context of social class. Life-outcome data from the Ivy College men illustrate how another macrocontext variable, social class (see Chapter 17), interacts with power motivation. As shown in Figure 18.5, power motivation is related to having an impact career only among men from middle-class backgrounds. Among upper-class men, the relationship actually reverses. The reason is probably that most impact careers are middle- or upper-middle-class careers. For upper-class men, these careers would be a step downward, hardly an incentive to someone with high power motivation.[5] As a result, their power motivation is probably expressed in other arenas than career.

---

[5]"Business executive" may be an exception, but it is a broad category that could include anything from being a director of a multinational corporation to sinecure positions for unmotivated upper-class men.

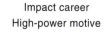

Impact career
High-power motive

MIDDLE CLASS   UPPER CLASS

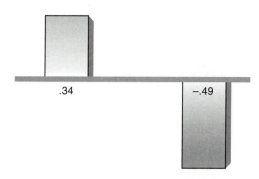

.34   −.49

Note: Data colected by Winter, McClelland, and Stewart (1981, chap.4). Values for the outcome variable are in standardized form (mean=0 and standard deviation=1).

FIGURE 18.5
Interaction of power motive and social class in predicting impact careers among adult men.

Statistical Interaction and Systemic Integration

These examples demonstrate that the multivariate research strategy increases the size of correlation coefficients between personality variables and behavioral outcomes. More important, however, they illustrate that personality is not simply a list of isolated characteristics or variables, but rather an *integrated system*. Variables may be separated out for analytic purposes, but in actual persons they function together as a system. Each variable interacts with other variables both within and outside the person; these interactions, taken together, constitute personality. Thus, for example, the separate components of affiliation motivation and introversion interact with each other and with certain features of the situation (such as the presence or absence of other people) to produce complex patterns of enduring behavior (such as gregarious friendliness or difficulty with relationships).

INTERGRATING PERSONALITY THROUGH INTERPRETATION OF INDIVIDUAL CASES

Finally, we can bring together the different elements and variables of personality by considering how they operate in the lives of particular people. In this book, I have used each of the historical cases as an example of one particular domain or element of personality: Nixon for motivation, Keller for cognition, Einstein for traits, and Angelou and Woolf for the social context. However, we can use all four personality elements to give fuller interpretations of all four cases.

Richard Nixon

For example, consider Richard Nixon. From Chapter 5, we know that he scored high on affiliation motivation. Studies by Simonton (1986) and Winter (1990) suggest that he was introverted (and probably also high in neuroticism). Mazlish (1972/1973) suggested the importance of this combination for Nixon's personality:

> Nixon himself has commented many times that he is an introvert in an extraverted profession, and there is little question that this ambivalent relationship has contributed to the puzzle of the "real" Nixon. (p. 55)

As we have seen, this combination of introversion and high affiliation motivation is likely to generate certain conflicts in the domain of interpersonal relationships. There is considerable evidence that Nixon experienced such conflicts. Though he took great pleasure in close one-on-one relationships and small groups, he was prickly and defensive when threatened (see Chapter 2). His advisers recalled both aspects:

> After meeting Nixon individually or in a small group, people usually would say that they had a new and warm feeling for him. "Isn't it too bad he doesn't come

across that warmly in an auditorium or on television," they would say. (Klein, 1980, p. 133)

One part of Richard Nixon is exceptionally considerate, exceptionally caring, sentimental, generous of spirit, kind. . . . [A second] part is angry, vindictive, ill-tempered, mean-spirited. (Price, 1977, p. 29)

A secondary analysis of data from the longitudinal study of Ivy College male graduates (Winter, McClelland, & Stewart, 1981) illustrates the effects of different elements of the Nixon personality on well-being and happiness. Among introverts, the affiliation motive is negatively related to self-reported *happiness*, while among men high in neuroticism, it is positively related to *unhappiness*, as shown in the bar graphs of Figure 18.6 on page 672. (While they reinforce each other, these two findings are not the same. Happiness and unhappiness measures are unrelated to each other and are brought about by different life experiences. Our everyday word "happiness" probably reflects the balance between these separate measures; see Ryff, 1989, p. 1070). Thus for Nixon, an introvert high in neuroticism and affiliation motivation, we would expect considerable negative affect (unhappiness) and not much positive affect (happiness). It is not surprising, therefore, that his nickname in college and law school was "Gloomy Gus" (Ambrose, 1987, p. 76) or that he was frequently given to periods of stormy rage (Ambrose, 1987; Mazlish, 1972/1973). Even the affiliative themes in his autobiography are often tinged with death and separation (see the discussion in Chapter 2).

Taking into account Nixon's traits as well as his motives is only a first step toward understanding his personality as a whole. His cognitive complexity (probably quite high), his specific beliefs, and his self-schema are also important. Finally, any interpretation of Richard Nixon's personality must pay attention to several important life contexts: growing up in southern California during the 1920s and 1930s, World War II and the status of veteran in the late 1940s and early 1950s, the American yearning for a return to normal times after that war, and the Cold War and hunt for national "enemies."

Virginia Woolf and Maya Angelou

We can also employ all four elements of personality to increase our understanding of Virginia Woolf and Maya Angelou and the similarities and differences between them. Although we do not have systematic at-a-distance data, we can make reasonable estimates of several key personality variables. In terms of Eysenck's major trait factors, Woolf was relatively introverted and high in neuroticism (see Caramagno, 1992), while Angelou is more extraverted and stable. Woolf grew up in a social context dominated by men who were worried about declines in their previously high personal and national status. In Angelou's world, however, African Americans (especially African American men) who had been at the bottom of a hegemonic structure were beginning to demand change and redress. Her world was also filled with models of powerful and compelling women. Only one man—her brother Bailey—appears consistently in her account of her early years, and he (only a year older) was more a peer than a model.

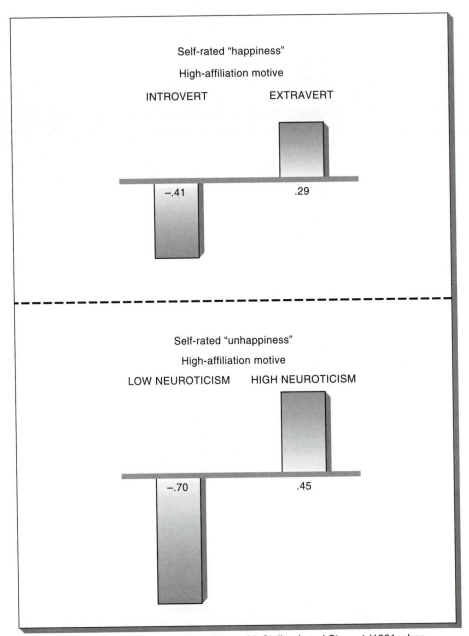

Note: Based on data collected by Winter, McClelland, and Stewart (1981, chap. 4). Values for the outcome variable are in standardized form (mean=0 and standard deviation=1).

FIGURE 18.6
Interaction of affiliation motivation extraversion, and neuroticism in predicting self-rated "happiness" and "unhappiness" among adult men.

Both women were sexually abused, and both were highly successful authors. Perhaps these differences in traits and context can help us to understand differences in the effects of that abuse and differences in the meaning and significance of their writing. There is research evidence that two long-term effects of childhood sexual abuse are depression (Cutler & Nolen-Hoeksema, 1991) and increased power motivation (Liem, O'Toole, & James, 1992). In Woolf's and Angelou's lives, we can see how these effects were channeled by other personality elements. Woolf's vulnerability to depression was further increased by her introversion, her lack of social support, and possibly also by biological factors (see Caramagno, 1992). Introversion also channeled her increased power motivation into writing—power by revolutionizing English fiction and power by analyzing the English patriarchy in essays. For Woolf, writing was a way to bring together dissociated experiences so that they no longer had "power to hurt" (1985, p. 72). Her fiction represented the inner world, "the vision in our minds," but as it actually is and not as clothed in "ill-fitting vestments" by traditional novelists (Woolf, 1919/1925, p. 188). However, Woolf's high neuroticism made it difficult for her to take satisfaction from even her best work. In the end, perhaps, her power motivation was directed even more intensely inward, and she took her own life.

As an African American woman, Angelou experienced the double jeopardy of race and gender, but she was nevertheless surrounded by powerful and generous sources of aid and comfort. Others believed and acted upon her account of being raped; she was rescued from her silence by Mrs. Flowers; she found companionship with Bailey; and she was validated by her mother's wisdom and praise. As a result, her exuberant extraversion channeled her motives into vibrant activity, innovation, movement, and change. Her writing, focused on retelling the story of her life, is upbeat, energetic, and filled with a sense of grace. In the concluding words of her poem at President Clinton's inauguration (Angelou, 1993):

> Here, on the pulse of this new day
> You may have the grace to look up and out . . .
> And say simply
> Very simply
> With hope—
> Good morning.

PERSONALITY AND THE PREDICTION OF BEHAVIOR

From the humanistic perspective, we want to use personality theory and research to interpret the whole course of people's lives. From the perspective of scientific psychology, we want to predict people's concrete acts, or even (as Murray once put it) to predict their every thought and fantasy. How close have we come to this goal?

George Bush and the Gulf War

A personal example will illustrate the opportunities and dangers of making predictions and suggest the levels of success and precision we can reasonably expect. A few years ago, along with several colleagues, I had finished a paper on the personalities of George Bush (then president of the U.S.) and Mikhail Gorbachev (then president of the former Soviet Union), using many of the at-a-distance measurement techniques described in this book (Winter, Hermann, Weintraub, & Walker, 1991b). Our description of Bush's personality is summarized in Table 18.9. Among other characteristics, we evaluated Bush as being high in affiliation and only average in power motivation. Based on past presidents with this motive pattern (see Winter, 1991a), we described Bush as a "peacemaker, concerned with development and not prone to seek political ends through violence and war" (p. 237). We also noted Bush's impulsivity and tendency to react with anger, which may also derive from his high affiliation motive (see Chapter 5).

In June 1990, we sent the paper off to a journal, where it was promptly accepted. Eight weeks later, Iraqi president Saddam Hussein invaded and annexed Kuwait, Bush proclaimed that "this shall not stand," and the long

TABLE 18.9 PERSONALITY PORTRAIT OF GEORGE BUSH

Domain	Characterization of Bush's personality
Motives	High in achievement
	High in affiliation
	Moderate in power
Cognition Beliefs	High in cognitive complexity
	High in nationalism (ethnocentrism)
	Sees events as only partly controllable
	Low in trust
	Low in self-confidence
Operational code	The world is a dangerous place
	Goals should be limited
	Conflict is an appropriate tactic
Traits	Extraverted Emotionally expressive Emphasizes people rather than task Impulsive Reacts with anger
	Moderate neuroticism Not anxious Vulnerable to indecision and depression Sensitive to criticism

SOURCE: Adapted from Winter, Hermann, Weintraub, and Walker (1991b, p. 236).

slow march to the Gulf war had begun. On January 17, 1991, this affiliation-motivated president began a devastating (if mercifully short) war. What went wrong with our predictions? Were they indeed actually wrong? After all, we had noted many aspects of Bush's personality—his distrustful nationalism, the themes of danger and conflict in his "operational code," and his tendency toward impulsive action—which are practically the script for Operation Desert Storm. And we had (successfully) predicted that Bush and Gorbachev would engage in cooperative negotiations. But what about that high affiliation motivation and the outcome of the Gulf war?

In a later follow-up article (Winter, Hermann, Weintraub, & Walker, 1991a), we reexamined the research literature about affiliation motivation and aggression:

> Under favorable and "safe" conditions, people high in affiliation and achievement motivation are indeed cooperative bargainers. Under conditions of threat, however . . . *affiliation-motivated people are the least cooperative and the most suspicious and defensive bargainers. . . .* Thus leaders with Bush's motive profile are likely to be "peaceful" only when they are comfortable—that is, when they interact with similar people whom they like. Bush's relations with Gorbachev seem to have engaged this "positive" affiliation cycle. With dissimilar people, in contrast, affiliation-motivated people distance themselves and respond with dislike. Bush and Saddam Hussein differ in culture, social class, family background, religion, language, goals, interests, and personal style. Nevertheless, Bush seems to have supported Saddam Hussein . . . up to the Iraqi invasion of Kuwait. This act, however, seems to have precipitated a dramatic decline in Bush's perceptions of Saddam Hussein's similarity (hence increased dislike and distrust) and so engaged the "negative" affiliation cycle. (pp. 459–460, emphasis in original)

According to our interpretation, then, once Saddam Hussein had been perceived as an enemy ("another Hitler," in Bush's words), Bush's high affiliation motive may actually have pushed him toward war rather than away from it. Having courted Saddam Hussein with military, economic, and intelligence assistance, Bush responded to the invasion of Kuwait with vindictive, personalized, impulsive aggression: "Hell hath no fury like an affiliation-motivated person scorned—or being double-crossed" (Winter, 1993b, p. 114). Moreover, Bush's behavior and policies during the Gulf crisis and war certainly reflected his high affiliation motivation. For example, his decision to oppose the Iraqi actions emerged only after a meeting with Britain's prime minister, Margaret Thatcher (being swayed by others is a characteristic of the affiliation motive). His policy decisions were made in consultation with only a small, intimate group of advisers. His policy itself emphasized a broad coalition of world leaders, a coalition sustained through extensive personal telephone contact.

On Predicting and Understanding Behavior

The example of George Bush and the Gulf war is useful in helping us to understand what kinds of predictions about people's behavior we can and cannot make on the basis of knowledge of their personality. After the fact, it is usually not difficult to interpret outcomes (in Bush's case, the Gulf war) in terms of personality. Could we have predicted these outcomes in June 1990? Of course not. The Iraqi invasion of Kuwait was a surprise, and certainly not predictable from any knowledge of Bush's personality. What we *can* do, however, is interpret and predict Bush's responses, given that unpredictable event. Thus while the at-a-distance personality assessment portrayed Bush as a person who is disposed to peace and rational cooperation, it could also specify the circumstances under which such a person would be likely to go to war (though I and my coauthors never thought to discuss these circumstances in our first article on Bush).

Such predictions are called contingent or *conditional predictions.* They are of the following general form: particular person X (or personality type X), under particular set of conditions Y, is likely to exhibit particular behavior Z.[6] Another name for them is if-then predictions: if conditions are X, then person Y will carry out action Z. (In contrast, absolute predictions simply predict that person Y will carry out act Z, without reference to the conditions or context.) The most successful predictions of behavior from personality—whether they are predictions about presidential foreign policy, the actions of your closest friends, or your own plans for yourself—are likely to be of this conditional, rather than absolute, variety.

Recently Mischel has developed a similar formulation, as a way of reconciling "the invariance of personality and the variability of behavior" (Mischel & Shoda, 1995, p. 246). For example, Wright and Mischel (1987, 1988) argue that almost all personality variables are really "clusters of if/then propositions" (1987, p. 1159). That is, they are "predictions about what a person would do under appropriate conditions" (p. 1161). In fact, this is also true of most scientific constructs. To use an example from Wright and Mischel: the adjective (trait?) "soluble" does not refer to a general behavior of a substance, but rather describes a specific set of situation-action tendencies—that is, dissolving when submerged in a liquid (p. 1160).

PERSONALITY: PREDICTING, UNDERSTANDING, AND LEARNING

Predicting

The psychology of personality, then, has an important but limited and contingent role in the advance prediction of the specific acts of specific individuals in specific circumstances. We cannot predict every outcome under every circumstance; but given some knowledge of personality factors and some information about the context, we can often forecast a rather narrow range of likely outcomes. This seems an appropriate goal for the psychology of personality.

[6]These conditional predictions are similar to Kelly's *propositional* constructs (Chapter 6).

Understanding

Making predictions, however, is not the only purpose of personality psychology. Sometimes it is important to understand people after the fact, even if their actions could not have been predicted in advance. Understanding is not a trivial accomplishment. Not only does it give us the sense that we know people and comprehend their actions, but it also guides our efforts to intervene, whether by therapy or by social policy.

The distinction between prediction and understanding can be illustrated with the example of Virginia Woolf's suicide. In the first few months of 1941, even the briefest personality description of Woolf would have made reference to her bouts with depression. Suicide was always a *possibility,* but it is unlikely that even the most sophisticated personality analysis could have predicted that on the specific morning of March 28, 1941, she would drown herself in the river. Even her husband Leonard was surprised by the suddenness of her 1941 depression: "but this time there were no warning symptoms of this kind. The depression struck her like a sudden blow" (L. Woolf, 1969, p. 79). By mid March he became alarmed: "one knew that at any moment she might kill herself" (p. 91). Still, during the last two days of Virginia's life, Leonard was reluctant to intervene with measures she would have found "intolerable." Afterward, he admitted that "the decision was wrong and led to the disaster" (pp. 92–93).

After the fact, Woolf's suicide can be understood in the light of familiar features of her personality and forces at work in her social context. For example, she had just finished a novel, *Between the Acts,* the kind of achievement milestone that had set off her depression in the past. As Leonard (1969) later observed:

> I am sure that what was about to happen was connected with the strain of revising the book and the black cloud which always gathered and spread over her mind whenever, a book finished, she had to face the shock of severing as it were the mental umbilical cord and send it to the printer—and finally to the reviewers and the public. (p. 79)

The Woolfs' London house and Hogarth Press offices had been destroyed the previous autumn in an air raid. On the day before her suicide, a German bomber had flown at tree-top level above the village street and dropped its bombs nearby. Virginia Woolf's final diary entry describes an awkward conversation with another woman: "Sitting there I tried to coin a few compliments. But they *perished in the icy sea* between us" (Woolf, 1984, p. 359; emphasis added). Reading this in the light of Woolf's suicide two days later, we are struck by the metaphorical reference to drowning.

Thus although an appreciation of the psychology of personality might not enable us to have predicted that Woolf would take her own life on March 28, it can enable us to understand that act—that is, to fit it into the complex mosaic of temperament, motive, belief, and context that was her personality. This is neither a trivial nor an obvious accomplishment, for it enables us to understand Woolf as a person. In the long run, understanding Woolf—even in retrospect—may help us to understand depression, suicide, literary creativity, and the destructive effects of childhood sexual abuse and gender-based hegemony. Fortified with this understanding, we can then formulate interventions and policies that combine humanity, precision, and efficiency.

Learning

Finally, the analysis and interpretation of lives enables us to learn about being human. With the aid of personality theories and research, we come to a greater understanding of human nature, of ourselves. From Nixon, for example, we can grasp the consequences of motives that conflict with traits. From Keller, we see the surpassing importance of cognition as a motive, something that is easy to underestimate when we are caught up in everyday, short-term goals. From Einstein, we realize that introversion does not necessarily mean instability and that psychoticism is not necessarily psychotic. Finally, from Angelou and Woolf, we appreciate the constraints and opportunities that context features such as gender, race, class, and history set on the development and expression of personality. We understand that severe early traumas have powerful effects, but that these effects are also variable and depend on personality and social context.

From the study of personality theories and research, then, we get a sense of what it means to be human, of what is possible. We come to recognize the structures and processes that define both our individuality as persons and also our commonality as members of groups. By learning about the range and types of personality, we come to know ourselves better.

These are the goals and accomplishments—conditional prediction, interpretive understanding, and self-reflexive learning—of a humane and scientific personality psychology as we approach the third millennium.

Abelson, R. P. (1981). Psychological status of the script concept. *American Psychologist, 36*, 715–729.

Abraham, K. (1927). *Selected papers on psychoanalysis.* London: Hogarth.

Abramson, L. Y., Seligman, M. E. P., & Teasdale, J. (1978). Learned helplessness in humans: Critique and reformulation. *Journal of Abnormal Psychology, 87,* 49–74.

Acton, Lord (J. E. E. Dalberg-Acton). (1949). Letter to Mandell Creighton, April 5, 1887. In G. Himmelfarb (Ed.), *Essays on freedom and power* (pp. 358–367). Glencoe, IL: Free Press.

Adams, J. S. (1965). Inequity in social exchange. In L. Berkowitz (Ed.), *Advances in experimental social psychology* (vol. 2, pp. 267–299). New York: Academic Press.

Adams-Webber, J., & Mancuso, J. C. (Eds.). (1983). *Applications of personal construct theory.* Toronto, New York & London: Academic Press.

Adler, A. (1927). *Understanding human nature.* New York: Greenberg.

Adler, A. (1929). *The practice and theory of individual psychology* (rev. ed.). London: Routledge & Kegan Paul.

Adler, N. E., Boyce, T., Chesny, M. A., Cohen, S., Folkman, S., Kahn, R. L., & Syme, S. L. (1994). Socioeconomic status and health: The challenge of the gradient. *American Psychologist, 49,* 15–24.

Adorno, T. W., Frenkel-Brunswik, E., Levinson, D. J., & Sanford, R. N. (1950). *The authoritarian personality.* New York: Harper & Row. Abridged paperback edition published by Norton in 1982.

Aiken, L. S., & West, S. G. (1991). *Multiple regression: Testing and interpreting interactions.* Newbury Park, CA: Sage.

Ainsworth, M. D. S. (1969). Object relations, dependency, and attachment: A theoretical review of the mother-infant relationship. *Child Development, 40,* 969–1025.

Agarwal, A., & Tripathi, L. B. (1980). Time perspective in achievement motivation. *Psychologia: An International Journal of Psychology in the Orient, 23,* 50–62.

Aldington, R. (1924). *A book of characters.* London: Routledge.

Alexander, S. (1979). *Anyone's daughter.* New York: Viking Press.

Aliotta, J. M. (1988). Social backgrounds, social motives, and participation on the U.S. Supreme Court. *Political Behavior, 10,* 267–284.

Alker, H. A., & Owen, D. W. (1977). Biographical, trait, and behavior-sampling predictions of performance in a stressful life setting. *Journal of Personality and Social Psychology, 35,* 717–723.

Allport, G. W. (1931). What is a trait of personality? *Journal of Abnormal and Social Psychology, 25,* 368–372.

Allport, G. W. (1937). *Personality: A psychological interpretation.* New York: Holt.

Allport, G. W. (1954). *The roots of prejudice.* Reading, MA: Addison-Wesley.

Allport, G. W. (1958). What units shall we employ? In G. Lindzey (Ed.), *Assessment of human motives* (pp. 239–260). New York: Holt, Rinehart & Winston.

Allport, G. W. (1960). Personality: A problem for science or for art? In *Personality and social encounter* (pp. 3–15). Boston: Beacon Press. (Original work published 1938).

Allport, G. W. (1960). The trend in motivational theory. In *Personality and social encounter* (pp. 95–109). Boston: Beacon Press. (Original work published 1953.)

Allport, G. W. (1961). *Pattern and growth in personality.* New York: Holt, Rinehart & Winston.

Allport, G. W. (1962). The general and the unique in psychological science. *Journal of Personality, 30,* 405–422. Reprinted in G. W. Allport, *The person in psychology* (pp. 81–102). Boston: Beacon Press, 1968.

Allport, G. W. (1965). *Letters from Jenny.* New York: Harcourt Brace.

Allport, G. W. (1966a). Author's note to reprint of "Is the concept of self necessary?" In C. Gordon & K. J. Gergen (Eds.), *The self in social interaction* (p. 25). New York: Holt, Rinehart & Winston.

Allport, G. W. (1966b). Traits revisited. *American Psychologist, 21,* 1–10.

Allport, G. W., & Allport, F. H. (1921). Personality traits: Their classification and measurement. *Journal of Abnormal and Social Psychology, 16,* 6–40.

Allport, G. W., & Odbert, H. S. (1936). Trait-names: A psycho-lexical study. *Psychological Monographs, 47(1)* (Whole no. 211).

Allport, G. W., & Vernon, P. E. (1933). *Studies in expressive movement.* New York: Macmillan.

Allport, G. W., Vernon, P. E., & Lindzey, G. (1960). *A study of values* (3rd ed.). Boston: Houghton Mifflin.

Almond, G. A., & Verba, S. (Eds.). (1980). *The civic culture revisited.* Boston: Little, Brown.

Almond, G. A., & Verba, S. (1989). *The civic culture: Political attitudes and democracy in five nations.* Newbury Park, CA: Sage. (Original work published 1963.)

Altemeyer, B. (1981). *Right-wing authoritarianism.* Winnipeg: University of Manitoba Press.

Altemeyer, B. (1988). *Enemies of freedom: Understanding right-wing authoritarianism.* San Francisco: Jossey-Bass.

Altemeyer, B. (1993, July). *Authoritarianism in American legislators.* Address at the annual meeting of the International Society of Political Psychology, Cambridge, MA.

Ambrose, S. E. (1987). *Nixon: The education of a politician 1913–1962.* New York: Simon & Schuster.

Ambrose, S. E. (1991). *Nixon: Ruin and recovery 1973–1990.* New York: Simon & Schuster.

Anastasi, A. (1982). *Psychological testing* (5th ed.). New York: Macmillan.

Anderson, C. A., Horowitz, L. M., & French, R. deS. (1983). Attributional style of lonely and depressed people. *Journal of Personality and Social Psychology, 45,* 127–136.

Anderson, J. W. (1990). The life of Henry A. Murray: 1893–1988. In A. I. Rabin, R. A. Zucker, R. A. Emmons, & S. Frank (Eds.), *Studying persons and lives* (pp. 304–334). New York: Springer.

Anderson, W. (Ed.). (1970). *Theophrastus: The character sketches.* Kent, OH: Kent State University Press.

Andrews, J. D. W. (1966). *The achievement motive and life style among Harvard freshmen.* Unpublished Ph.D. thesis, Harvard University.

Andrews, J. D. W. (1967). The achievement motive in two types of organizations. *Journal of Personality and Social Psychology, 6,* 163–168.

Angelou, M. (1970). *I know why the caged bird sings.* New York: Random House.

Angelou, M. (1974). *Gather together in my name.* New York: Random House.

Angelou, M. (1978). *And still I rise.* New York: Random House.

Angelou, M. (1981). *The heart of a woman.* New York: Random House.

Angelou, M. (1982, February). Why I moved back to the South. *Ebony,* pp. 130–134.

Angelou, M. (1983). *Shaker, why don't you sing?* New York: Random House.

Angelou, M. (1986). *All God's children need traveling shoes.* New York: Random House.

Angelou, M. (1993). *On the pulse of morning.* [Poem read at the inauguration of President Clinton]. New York: Random House.

Angier, N. (1995, January 3). Heredity's more than genes, new theory proposes. *New York Times,* pp. B5, B9.

Angyal, A. (1941). *Foundations for a science of personality.* New York: Commonwealth Fund.

Anonymous. (1946). Letters from Jenny. *Journal of Abnormal and Social Psychology, 41,* 315–350, 449–480.

Ansbacher, H. L., Ansbacher, A., Shiverick, D., & Shiverick, K. (1967). Lee Harvey Oswald: An Adlerian interpretation. *Journal of Individual Psychology, 23,* 24–36.

Aptheker, H. (1983). *American Negro slave revolts.* New York: International Publishers.

Ariam, S., & Siller, J. (1982). The effects of subliminal oneness stimuli in Hebrew on academic performance of Israeli high school students: Further evidence on the adaptation-enhancing effects of symbiotic fantasies in another culture using another language. *Journal of Abnormal Psychology, 91,* 343–349.

Arkes, H. R., & Garske, J. P. (1982). *Psychological theories of motivation* (2nd ed.). Monterey, CA: Brooks/Cole.

Arnold, M. B. (1962). *Story sequence analysis.* New York: Columbia University Press.

Aruffo, J. F., Coverdale, J. H., Pavlik, V. N., & Vallbona, C. (1993). AIDS knowledge in minorities: Significance of locus of control. *American Journal of Preventive Medicine, 9,* 15–20.

Ashmore, R. D. (1990). Sex, gender, and the individual. In L. Pervin (Ed.), *Handbook of personality theory and research* (pp. 486–526). New York: Guilford Press.

Atkinson, J. W. (Ed.). (1958). *Motives in fantasy, action, and society.* Princeton, NJ: Van Nostrand.

Atkinson, J. W. (1982). Motivational determinants of thematic apperception. In A. J. Stewart (Ed.), *Motivation and society* (pp. 3–40). San Francisco: Jossey-Bass.

Atkinson, J. W., & Feather, N. T. (1966). *A theory of achievement motivation.* New York: Wiley.

Atkinson, J. W., Heyns, R. W., & Veroff, J. (1954). The effect of experimental arousal of the affiliation motive on thematic apperception. *Journal of Abnormal and Social Psychology, 49,* 405–410.

Atkinson, J. W., & McClelland, D. C. (1948). The projective expression of needs. II. The effects of different intensities of the hunger drive on thematic apperception. *Journal of Experimental Psychology, 38,* 643–658.

Aubrey, E. [pseudonym of E. S. Ions]. (1980). *Sherlock Holmes in Dallas.* New York: Dodd, Mead.

Babbitt, I. L. (1977). *Rousseau and romanticism.* Austin, TX: University of Texas Press. (Original work published 1919.)

Bakan, D. (1958). *Sigmund Freud and the Jewish mystical tradition.* Princeton, NJ: Van Nostrand.

Bakan, D. (1966). *The duality of human existence.* Chicago: Rand McNally.

Balay, J., & Shevrin, H. (1988). The subliminal psychodynamic activation method: A critical review. *American Psychologist, 43,* 161–174.

Bales, R. F. (1958). Task roles and social roles in problem-solving groups. In E. E. Maccoby, T. M. Newcomb, & E. L. Hartley (Eds.), *Readings in social psychology* (3rd ed., pp. 437–447). New York: Holt, Rinehart & Winston.

Bandura, A. (1977a). Self-efficacy: Toward a unifying theory of behavioral change. *Psychological Review, 84,* 191–215.

Bandura, A. (1977b). *Social learning theory.* Englewood Cliffs, NJ: Prentice-Hall.

Bandura, A. (1986). *Social foundations of thought and action: A social-cognitive theory.* Englewood Cliffs, NJ: Prentice-Hall.

Bandura, A. (1989). Human agency in social cognitive theory. *American Psychologist, 44,* 1175–1184.

Bandura, A., Ross, D., & Ross, S. A. (1963). Imitation of film-mediated aggressive models. *Journal of Abnormal and Social Psychology, 66,* 3–11.

Bannister, D., & Mair, J. M. M. (1968). *The evaluation of personal constructs.* London & New York: Academic Press.

Barnes, G. E., Malamuth, N. M., & Cheek, J. V. P. (1984). Psychoticism and sexual arousal to rape depictions. *Personality and Individual Differences, 5,* 273–279.

Barrett, P., & Eysenck, H. J. (1984). The assessment of personality factors across 25 countries. *Personality and Individual Differences, 5,* 615–632.

Barringer, F. (1993, June 2). School hallways as a gantlet of sexual taunts. *New York Times,* p. B7.

Barzun, J. (1961). *Classic, romantic, and modern.* Garden City, NY: Doubleday. (Anchor Books.)

Baumeister, R. F., & Scher, S. J. (1988). Self-defeating behavior patterns among normal individuals: Review and analysis of common self-destructive tendencies. *Psychological Bulletin, 104,* 3–22.

Baumrind, D. (1972). An exploratory study of socialization effects on black children: Some black-white comparisons. *Child Development, 43,* 261–267.

Baxter, L. R., Jr., Schwartz, J. M., Bergman, K. S., Szuba, M. P., Guze, B. H., Mazziotta, J. C., Alazraki, A., Selin, C. E., Ferng, H.-K., Munford, P., & Phelps, M. E. (1992) Caudate glucose metabolic rate changes with both drug and behavior therapy for obsessive-compulsive disorder. *Archives of General Psychiatry, 49,* 681–689.

Beck, A. T. (1967). *Depression: Clinical, experimental, and theoretical aspects.* New York: Harper & Row.

Becker, E. (1973). *The denial of death.* New York: Free Press.

Becker, G. S. (1976). *The economic approach to human behavior.* Chicago: University of Chicago Press.

Becker, S. (1959). *Comic art in America.* New York: Simon & Schuster.

Belenky, M. F. (1978). *Conflict and development: A longitudinal study of the impact of abortion decisions on moral judgments of adolescent and adult women.* Unpublished doctoral dissertation, Harvard University.

Bell, P. A., & Byrne, D. (1978). Repression-sensitization. In H. London & J. Exner (Eds.), *Dimensions of personality* (pp. 449–485). New York: Wiley.

Bellah, R. N., Madsen, R., Sullivan, W. M., Swidler, A., & Tipton, S. M. (1985). *Habits of the heart: Individualism and commitment in American life.* Berkeley & Los Angeles: University of California Press.

Bem, D. J. (1982). Toward a response style theory of persons in situations. In M. M. Page (Ed.), *Nebraska symposium on motivation 1982* (pp. 201–231). Lincoln, NE: University of Nebraska Press.

Bem, D. J., & Allen, A. (1974). On predicting some of the people some of the time: The search for cross-situational consistencies in behavior. *Psychological Review, 81,* 506–520.

Bem, D. J., & Funder, D. C. (1978). Predicting more of the people more of the time: Assessing the personality of situations. *Psychological Review, 85,* 485–501.

Benson, H. (1975). *The relaxation response.* New York: Morrow.

Bergeman, C. S., Chipuer, H. M., Plomin, R., Pedersen, N. L., McClearn, G. E., Nesselroade, J. R., Costa, P. T., Jr., & McCrae, R. R. (1993). Genetic and environmental effects on openness to experience, agreeableness, and conscientiousness. *Journal of Personality, 61,* 159–179.

Berkowitz, L., & Macaulay, J. (1971). The contagion of criminal violence. *Sociometry, 34,* 238–260.

Berlew, D. E. (1956). *The achievement motive and the growth of Greek civilization.* Unpublished honors thesis, Wesleyan University.

Bernard, L. L. (1924). *Instinct: A study in social psychology.* New York: Holt.

Bernstein, I. S., Gordon, T. P., & Rose, R. M. (1983). The interaction of hormones, behavior, and social context in nonhuman primates. In B. B. Svare (Ed.), *Hormones and aggressive behavior* (pp. 555–561). New York: Plenum.

Berry, J. W., Poortinga, Y. H., Segall, M. H., & Dasen, P. R. (1992). *Cross-cultural psychology: Research and applications.* New York: Cambridge University Press.

Bettelheim, B. (1943). Individual and mass behavior in extreme situations. *Journal of Abnormal and Social Psychology, 38,* 417–452. Abridged version reprinted in E. Maccoby, T. Newcomb, & E. Hartley (Eds.), *Readings in social psychology* (3rd ed., pp. 300–310). New York: Holt, Rinehart & Winston, 1958.

Bettelheim, B. (1954). *Symbolic wounds.* New York: Free Press.

Bettelheim, B. (1983). *Freud and man's soul.* New York: Knopf.

Bieri, J. (1955). Cognitive complexity-simplicity and predictive behavior. *Journal of Abnormal and Social Psychology, 51,* 263–268.

Biernat, M. (1989). Motives and values to achieve: Different constructs with different effects. *Journal of Personality, 57,* 69–96.

Birch, H. G. (1945). The role of motivational factors in insightful problem-solving. *Journal of Comparative Psychology, 38,* 295–317.

Blakeslee, S. (1993, January 12). Evolution of tabby cat mapped in brain study. *New York Times,* pp. B6, B8.

Blasi, A. (1980). Bridging moral cognition and moral action: A critical review of the literature. *Psychological Bulletin, 88,* 1–45.

Blasi, A. (1983). Moral cognition and moral action: A theoretical perspective. *Developmental Review, 3,* 178–210.

Blasi, A. (1991). The self as subject in the study of personality. In D. M. Ozer, J. M. Healy, Jr., & A. J. Stewart (Eds.), *Perspectives in personality: Self and emotion* (pp. 19–37). London: Jessica Kingsley.

Block, J. (1971). *Lives through time.* Berkeley, CA: Bancroft Books.

Block, J. (1977a). Advancing the psychology of personality: Paradigmatic shift or improving the quality of research? In D. Magnusson & N. S. Endler (Eds.), *Personality at the crossroads: Current issues in interactional psychology* (pp. 37–63). Hillsdale , NJ: Erlbaum.

Block, J. (1977b). The Eysencks and psychoticism. *Journal of Abnormal Psychology, 86,* 653–654.

Block, J. (1978). *The Q-sort method in personality assesssment and psychiatric research.* Palo Alto, CA: Consulting Psychologists Press.

Block, J. (1982). Assimilation, accommodation, and the dynamics of personality development. *Child Development, 53,* 281–295.

Block, J. (1989). Critique of the act frequency approach to personality. *Journal of Personality and Social Psychology, 56,* 234–245.

Block, J. (1995). A contrarian view of the five-factor approach to personality description. *Psychological Bulletin, 117,* 187–215.

Block, J., & Block, J. H. (1951). An investigation of the relationship between intolerance of ambiguity and ethnocentrism. *Journal of Personality, 19,* 303–311.

Block, J., Block, J. H., & Keyes, S. (1988). Longitudinally foretelling drug usage in adolescence: Early childhood personality and environmental precursors. *Child Development, 59,* 336–355.

Block, J. H., & Block, J. (1980). The role of ego-control and ego-resiliency in the organization of behavior. In W. A. Collins (Ed.), *Minnesota Symposia on Child Psychology* (vol. 13, pp. 39–101). Hillsdale, NJ: Erlbaum.

Bolger, N. (1990). Coping as a personality process: A prospective study. *Journal of Personality and Social Psychology, 59,* 525–537.

Bonarius, H., Holland, R., & Rosenberg, S. (Eds.). (1981). *Personal construct theory: Recent advances in theory and practice.* New York: St. Martin's Press.

Bond, M. H. (1986). *The psychology of the Chinese people.* Hong Kong: Oxford University Press.

Bond, M. H. (1991). *Beyond the Chinese face: Insights from psychology.* Hong Kong: Oxford University Press.

Boring, E. G. (1930). A new ambiguous figure. *American Journal of Psychology, 42,* 444–445.

Bornstein, R. F. (1987). Exposure and affect: Overview and meta-analysis of research, 1968–1987. *Psychological Bulletin, 106,* 265–289.

Bose, N. K. (1953). *My days with Gandhi.* Calcutta: Nishana.

Botwin, M. D., & Buss, D. M. (1989). Structure of act-report data: Is the five-factor model of personality recaptured? *Journal of Personality and Social Psychology, 56,* 988–1001.

Bowlby, J. (1969). *Attachment and loss: I. Attachment.* New York: Basic Books.

Boyatzis, R. (1973). Affiliation motivation. In D. C. McClelland & R. S. Steele (Eds.), *Human motivation* (pp. 252–276). Morristown, NJ: General Learning Press.

Boyatzis, R. E., & Burruss, J. A. (1977). *Validation of a competency model for alcoholism counselors in the Navy.* Boston: McBer & Company.

Bradburn, N. M., & Berlew, D. E. (1961). Need for achievement in English economic growth. *Economic Development and Cultural Change, 10,* 8–20.

Braun, B. G. (1983). Psychophysiological phenomena in multiple personality and hypnosis. *American Journal of Clinical Hypnosis, 26,* 124–137.

Brayback, M. (1983). Moral judgment: Theory and research on differences between males and females. *Developmental Review, 3,* 274–291.

Brehm, J. (1972). *Responses to loss of freedom: A theory of psychological reactance.* Morristown, NJ: General Learning Press.

Brehm, S. (1981). *Psychological reactance: A theory of freedom and control.* New York: Academic Press.

Breuer, J., & Freud, S. (1955). Studies on hysteria. In J. Strachey (Ed.), *The standard edition of the complete psychological works of Sigmund Freud* (vol. 2). London: Hogarth Press. (Original work published 1893–1895.)

Briggs, S. R. (1989). The optimal level of measurement of personality constructs. In D. Buss & N. Cantor (Eds.), *Personality psychology: Recent trends and emerging directions* (pp. 246–260). New York: Springer-Verlag.

Briggs, S. R. (1992). Assessing the five-factor model of personality description. *Journal of Personality, 60,* 253–293.

Brittain, V. (1979). *Testament of youth.* London: Virago. (Original work published 1933.)

Broadhurst, P. L. (1957). Emotionality and the Yerkes-Dodson law. *Journal of Experimental Psychology, 54,* 345–352.

Brodie, F. (1981). *Richard Nixon: The shaping of his character.* New York: Norton.

Brody, B. (1970). Freud's case-load. *Psychotherapy, 7,* 8–12. Reprinted in H. M. Ruitenbeek (Ed.), *Freud as we knew him* (pp. 495–503). Detroit: Wayne State University Press, 1973.

Brody, N. (1983). *Human motivation: Commentary on goal-directed action.* New York: Academic Press.

Brome, V. (1978). *Jung: Man and myth.* London: Macmillan.

Brooks, L. (1978). Nonanalytic concept formation and memory for instances. In E. Rosch & B. B. Lloyd (Eds.), *Cognition and categorization.* Hillsdale, NJ: Erlbaum.

Brooks, V. W. (1956). *Helen Keller: Sketch for a portrait.* New York: Dutton.

Broughton, J. M. (1983). Women's rationality and men's virtues: A critique of gender dualism in Gilligan's theory of moral development. *Social Research, 50,* 598–642.

Brown, D. E. (1991). *Human universals.* Philadelphia: Temple University Press.

Brown, N. O. (1959). *Life against death.* Middletown, CT: Wesleyan University Press.

Brown, R. W. (1953). A determinant of the relationship between intolerance of ambiguity and authoritarianism. *Journal of Abnormal and Social Psychology, 48,* 469–476.

Brown, R. W. (1965). *Social psychology.* New York: Free Press.

Brown, R. W. (1973). Schizophrenia, language, and reality. *American Psychologist, 28,* 395–403.

Browne, A., & Finkelhor, D. (1986). Impact of childhood sexual abuse: A review of the research. *Psychological Bulletin, 99,* 66–77.

Brownmiller, S. (1975). *Against our will*. New York: Simon & Schuster.

Brumberg, J. J. (1988). *Fasting girls: The emergence of anorexia nervosa as a modern disease*. Cambridge, MA: Harvard University Press.

Bruner, J. S. (1956). You are your constructs. Review of G. A. Kelly, *The psychology of personal constructs*. *Contemporary Psychology, 1*, 355–357.

Bruner, J. S. (1986). *Actual minds, possible worlds*. Cambridge, MA: Harvard University Press.

Burdick, H. A., & Burnes, A. J. (1958). A test of the "strain towards symmetry" theories. *Journal of Abnormal and Social Psychology, 57*, 367–370.

Burlingham, D. T. (1946). Twins: Observations of environmental influences on their development. *Psychoanalytic Study of the Child, 2*, 61–73.

Burwen, L. S., & Campbell, D. T. (1957). The generality of attitudes toward authority and nonauthority figures. *Journal of Abnormal and Social Psychology, 54*, 24–31.

Bushan, L. I. (1969). A comparison of four Indian political groups on a measure of authoritarianism. *Journal of Social Psychology, 79*, 141–142.

Buss, A. H. (1988). *Personality: Evolutionary heritage and human distinctiveness*. Hillsdale, NJ: Erlbaum.

Buss, A. H., & Briggs, S. R. (1984). Drama and the self in social interaction. *Journal of Personality and Social Psychology, 47*, 1310–1324.

Buss, D. M. (1984). Evolutionary biology and personality psychology: Toward a conception of human nature and individual differences. *American Psychologist, 39*, 1135–1147.

Buss, D. M. (1987). Selection, evocation, and manipulation. *Journal of Personality and Social Psychology, 53*, 1214–1221.

Buss, D. M. (1991a). Conflict in married couples: Personality predictors of anger and upset. *Journal of Personality, 59*, 663–688.

Buss, D. M. (1991b). Evolutionary personality psychology. *Annual Review of Psychology, 42*, 459–491. Palo Alto, CA: Annual Reviews.

Buss, D. M. (1992a). Is there a universal human nature? Review of D. E. Brown, *Human universals*. *Contemporary Psychology, 37*, 1262–1263.

Buss, D. M. (1992b). Manipulation in close relationships: Five personality factors in interactional context. *Journal of Personality, 60*, 477–499.

Buss, D. M., & Craik, K. H. (1983). The act frequency approach to personality. *Psychological Review, 90*, 105–126.

Buss, D. M., & Schmitt, D. P. (1993). Sexual strategies theory: An evolutionary perspective on human mating. *Psycholoogical Review, 100*, 204–232.

Butler, J. M., & Haigh, G. V. (1954). Changes in the relation between self-concepts and ideal-concepts consequent upon client-centered counseling. In C. R. Rogers & R. F. Diamond (Eds.), *Psychotherapy and personality change* (pp. 55–75). Chicago: University of Chicago Press.

Butler, R. A., & Harlow, H. F. (1957). Discrimination learning and learning sets to visual exploration incentives. *Journal of Genetic Psychology, 57*, 257–264.

Byrne, D. (1961a). The repression-sensitization scale: Rationale, reliability, and validity. *Journal of Personality, 29*, 334–349.

Byrne, D. (1961b). Interpersonal attraction as a function of affiliation need and attitude similarity. *Human Relations, 14*, 283–289.

Byrne, D. (1962). Response to attitude similarity-dissimilarity as a function of affiliation need. *Journal of Personality, 30*, 164–177.

Byrne, D. (1964). Repression-sensitization as a dimension of personality. In B. Maher (Ed.), *Progress in experimental personality research* (vol. 1, pp. 169–220). New York: Academic Press.

Byrne, D., Cherry, F., Lamberth, J., & Mitchell, H. E. (1973). Husband-wife similarity in response to erotic stimuli. *Journal of Personality, 41*, 385–394.

California Task Force to Promote Self-esteem and Personal and Social Responsibility. (1990). *Toward a state of esteem*. Sacramento, CA: Bureau of Publications, California State Department of Education.

Camus, A. (1946). *The stranger*. New York: Knopf. (Original work published 1941.)

Canaday, J. (1965). *Mainstreams of modern art*. New York: Holt.

Candee, D. (1974). Ego development aspects of New Left ideology. *Journal of Personality and Social Psychology, 30*, 620–630.

Cantor, N. (1990). From thought to behavior: "Having" and "doing" in the study of personality and cognition. *American Psychologist, 45*, 735–750.

Cantor, N., & Mischel, W. (1979a). Prototypes in person perception. In L. Berkowitz (Ed.), *Advances in experimental social psychology* (vol. 12, pp. 3–52). New York: Academic Press.

Cantor, N., & Mischel, W. (1979b). Prototypicality and personality: Effects on free recall and personality impressions. *Journal of Research in Personality, 13*, 187–205.

Cantor, N., Norem, J. K., Niedenthal, P. M., Langston, C. A., & Brower, A. M. (1987). Life tasks, self-concept ideals, and cognitive strategies in a life transition. *Journal of Personality and Social Psychology, 53*, 1178–1191.

Cantor, N., & Zirkel, S. (1990). Personality, cognition, and purposive behavior. In L. Pervin (Ed.), *Handbook of personality theory and research* (pp. 135–164). New York: Guilford Press.

Caramagno, T. C. (1992). *The flight of the mind: Virginia Woolf's art and manic-depressive illness*. Berkeley: University of California Press.

Carlson, R. (1971). Where is the person in personality research? *Psychological Bulletin, 75*, 203–219.

Carlson, R. (1980). Studies of Jungian typology: II. Representations of the personal world. *Journal of Personality and Social Psychology, 38*, 801–810.

Carlson, R. (1984). What's social about social psychology? Where's the person in personality research? *Journal of Personality and Social Psychology, 47*, 1304–1309.

Carlson, R., & Levy, N. (1973). Studies of Jungian typology: I. Memory, social perception, and social action. *Journal of Personality, 41*, 559–576.

Carroll, J. S., & Payne, J. W. (1977). Judgments about crime and the criminal: A model and a method for investigating parole decisions. In B. D. Sales (Ed.), *Perspectives in law and psychology: I. The criminal justice system* (pp. 191–239). New York: Plenum.

Carter, J. (1982). *Keeping faith.* New York: Bantam Books.

Cartwright, D., & Harary, F. (1956). Structural balance: A generalization of Heider's theory. *Psychological Review, 63,* 277–293.

Carver, C. S., & Scheier, M. F. (1981). *Attention and self-regulation: A control theory approach to human behavior.* New York: Springer-Verlag.

Carver, C. S., & Scheier, M. F. (1988). *Perspectives on personality.* Boston: Allyn & Bacon.

Caspi, A., Elder, G. H., Jr., & Bem, D. J. (1987). Moving against the world: Life-course patterns of explosive children. *Developmental Psychology, 23,* 308–313.

Caspi, A., Elder, G. H., Jr., & Bem, D. J. (1988). Moving away from the world: Life-course patterns of shy children. *Developmental Psychology, 24,* 824–831.

Cattell, R. B. (1957). *Personality and motivation structure and measurement.* Yonkers, NY: World.

Chamala, S., & Crouch, B. (1977). *Patterns of adaptation and factors associated with economic success in the wool industry, northwest Queensland, 1967/68–1971/72.* Brisbane, Australia: University of Queensland Department of Agriculture.

Charme, S. L. (1984). *Meaning and myth in the study of lives: A Sartrean perspective.* Philadelphia: University of Pennsylvania Press.

Cheek, J. M. (1982). Aggregation, moderator variables, and the validity of personality tests: A peer-rating study. *Journal of Personality and Social Psychology, 43,* 1254–1269.

Cherry, F., & Byrne, D. (1977). Authoritarianism. In T. Blass (Ed.), *Personality variables in social behavior* (pp. 109–133). Hillsdale, NJ: Erlbaum.

Chesler, P. (1972). *Women and madness.* Garden City, NY: Doubleday.

Child, I. L., Storm, T., & Veroff, J. (1958). Achievement themes in folk tales related to socialization practice. In J. W. Atkinson (Ed.), *Motives in fantasy, action and society* (pp. 479–492). Princeton, NJ: Van Nostrand.

Christie, R. (1956). Eysenck's treatment of the personality of communists. *Psychological Bulletin, 53,* 411–430.

Christie, R., & Geis, F. (1970). *Studies in Machiavellianism.* New York: Academic Press.

Church, A. T. (1987). Personality research in a non-Western culture: The Philippines. *Psychological Bulletin, 102,* 272–292.

Church, R. M. (1980). The Albert study: Illustration vs. evidence. *American Psychologist, 35,* 215–216.

Chusmir, L. H., & Azevedo, A. (1992). Motivation needs of sampled Fortune-500 CEOs: Relations to organization outcomes. *Perceptual and Motor Skills, 75,* 595–612.

Claridge, G. (1987). Psychoticism and arousal. In J. Strelau & H. J. Eysenck (Eds.), *Personality dimensions and arousal* (pp. 133–150). New York: Plenum.

Clark, K., & Clark, M. P. (1947). Racial identification and preference in Negro children. In T. M. Newcomb and E. L. Hartley (Eds.), *Readings in social psychology* (pp. 169–178). New York: Holt.

Clark, R. W. (1984). *Einstein: The life and times.* New York: Avon Books. (Original work published 1971.)

Clarke, J. W. (1982). *American assassins: The darker side of politics.* Princeton, NJ: Princeton University Press.

Cloninger, C. R. (1986). A unified biosocial theory of personality and its role in the development of anxiety states. *Psychiatric Developments, 4,* 167–226.

Cloninger, C. R. (1991). Brain networks underlying personality development. In B. J. Carroll & J. E. Barrett (Eds.), *Psychopathology and the brain* (pp. 183–208). New York: Raven Press.

Cloninger, C. R., Przybeck, T. R., & Svrakic, D. M. (1991). The tridimensional personality questionnaire: U.S. normative data. *Psychological Reports, 69,* 1047–1057.

Cofer, C. N., & Appley, M. H. (1964). *Motivation: Theory and research.* New York: Wiley.

Cohen, J., & Cohen, P. (1983). *Applied multiple regression/correlation analysis for the behavioral sciences* (2nd ed.). Hillsdale, NJ: Erlbaum.

Cohen, Y. A. (1961). *Social structure and personality: A casebook.* New York: Holt, Rinehart & Winston.

Colby, A., & Damon, W. (1983). Listening to a different voice: A review of Gilligan's *In a different voice. Merrill-Palmer Quarterly, 29,* 473–481.

Colby, A., & Kohlberg, L. (1987). *The measurement of moral judgment* (2 vols.). New York: Cambridge University Press.

Colby, A., Kohlberg, L., Gibbs, J., & Lieberman, M. (1983). A longitudinal study of moral judgment. *Monographs of the Society for Research in Child Development, 48(1–2),* 1–124.

Colvin, C. R., & Block, J. (1994). Do positive illusions foster mental health? *Psychological Bulletin, 116,* 3–20.

Combs, A. W. (1947). A comparative study of motivation as revealed in Thematic Apperception stories and autobiographies. *Journal of Clinical Psychology, 3,* 65–75.

Conan Doyle, A. (1938). The sign of the four. In *The complete Sherlock Holmes* (pp. 91–173). Garden City, NY: Garden City Publishing Company. (Original work published 1893.)

Conley, J. J. (1984). Longitudinal consistency of adult personality: Self-reported psychological characteristics across 45 years. *Journal of Personality and Social Psychology, 47,* 1325–1333.

Conley, J. J. (1985). Longitudinal stability of personality traits: A multitrait-multimethod-multioccasion analysis. *Journal of Personality and Social Psychology, 49,* 1266–1282.

Conrad, H. S. (1932). The validity of personality ratings of preschool children. *Journal of Educational Psychology, 23,* 671–680.

Conte, H. R., & Plutchik, R. (1981). A circumplex model for interpersonal personality traits. *Journal of Personality and Social Psychology, 40,* 701–711.

Cooley, C. H. (1964). *Human nature and the social order* (rev. ed.). New York: Schocken Books. (Original work published 1922.)

Cooper, D. (1968). *Picasso's theatre*. New York: Abrams.

Cornwell, D., & Hobbs, S. (1976, March 18). The strange saga of Little Albert. *New Society*, pp. 602–604.

Cornwell, D., Hobbs, S., & Prytula, R. (1980). Little Albert rides again. *American Psychologist, 35*, 216–217.

Cortes, J. B., & Gatti, F. M. (1972). *Delinquency and crime: A biopsychosocial approach*. New York: Seminar Press.

Costa, P. T., Jr., & McCrae, R. R. (1985). *The NEO personality inventory manual*. Odessa, FL: Psychological Assessment Resources.

Costa, P. T., Jr., & McCrae, R. R. (1992). Four ways five factors are basic. *Personality and Individual Differences, 6*, 653–665.

Costin, F. (1968). Dogmatism and the retention of psychological misconceptions. *Educational and Psychological Measurement, 28*, 529–534.

Couch, A. S. (1969). The psychological determinants of interpersonal behavior. In K. J. Gergen & D. Marlowe (Eds.), *Personality and social behavior* (pp. 77–89). Reading, MA: Addison-Wesley. (Original work published 1962.)

Couch, A. S., & Keniston, K. (1960). Yeasayers and naysayers: Agreeing response set as a personality variable. *Journal of Abnormal and Social Psychology, 60*, 151–174.

Coulter, T. (1953). *An experimental and statistical study of the relationship of prejudice and certain personality variables*. Unpublished doctoral dissertation, University of London.

Cowan, E. L., Underberg, R. P., & Verrillo, R. T. (1958). The development and testing of an attitude to blindness scale. *Journal of Social Psychology, 48*, 297–304.

Cramer, P. (1991). *The development of defense mechanisms: Theory, research, and assessment*. New York: Springer-Verlag.

Crandall, C., & Biernat, M. (1990). The ideology of anti-fat attitudes. *Journal of Applied Social Psychology, 20*, 227–243.

Crane, T. (1989). Maya Angelou. In J. M. Elliot (Ed.), *Conversations with Maya Angelou* (pp. 173–178). Jackson, MS: University Press of Mississippi. (Original work published 1987.)

Crawford, C. B., & Anderson, J. L. (1989). Sociobiology: An environmentalist discipline? *American Psychologist, 44*, 1449–1459.

Creelan, P. (1975). Religion, language, and sexuality in J. B. Watson. *Journal of Humanistic Psychology, 15*(4), 55–78.

Crocker, J., & Major, B. (1989). Social stigma and self-esteem: The self-protective properties of stigma. *Psychological Review, 96*, 608–630.

Crosby, F. (1976). A model of egoistical relative deprivation. *Psychological Review, 83*, 85–113.

Crosby, F. (1982). *Relative deprivation and working women*. New York: Oxford University Press.

Crosby, F. J. (1993). *Juggling: The unexpected advantages of balancing career and home for women and their families*. New York: Free Press.

Crowne, D. P., & Marlowe, D. (1964). *The approval motive*. New York: Wiley.

Csikszentmihalyi, M., & Csikszentmihalyi, I. S. (Eds.). (1988). *Optimal experience: Psychological studies of flow in consciousness*. New York: Cambridge University Press.

Cummin, P. C. (1967). TAT correlates of executive performance. *Journal of Applied Psychology, 51*, 78–81.

Cummings, J. (1991). *China: A travel survival kit*. Hawthorn, Australia: Lonely Planet Publications.

Cunningham, J. (1989). The new Black man's burden. In J. M. Elliot (Ed.), *Conversations with Maya Angelou* (pp. 183–187). Jackson, MS: University Press of Mississippi. (Original work published 1987.)

Cutler, S. E., & Nolen-Hoeksema, S. (1991). Accounting for sex differences in depression through female victimization: Childhood sexual abuse. *Sex Roles, 24*, 425–438.

Daniels, R. (1991). Relocation, redress, and the report: A historical appraisal. In R. Daniels, S. C. Taylor, & H. H. L. Kitano, (Eds.), *Japanese Americans: From relocation to redress* (rev. ed., pp. 3–9). Seattle: University of Washington Press.

Dardeau, F. M. (1992). Locus-of-control and knowledge of acquired immune deficiency syndrome as predictors of AIDS-related sexual behaviors in adult populations. *Dissertation Abstracts International, 52*(8A), 2827.

Darley, J. M., & Batson, C. D. (1973). "From Jerusalem to Jericho": A study of situational and dispositional variables in helping behavior. *Journal of Personality and Social Psychology, 27*, 100–108.

Darley, J. M., & Latané, B. (1968). Bystander intervention in emergencies: Diffusion of responsibility. *Journal of Personality and Social Psychology, 8*, 377–383.

Darnton, R. (1984). *The great cat massacre and other episodes in French cultural history*. New York: Basic Books.

Darwin, C. R. (1936). *The origin of species by means of natural selection*. New York: Modern Library. (Original work published 1859.)

Davies, D. R., Hockey, G. R. J., & Taylor, A. (1969). Varied auditory stimulation, temperament differences and vigilance performance. *British Journal of Psychology, 60*, 453–457.

Davis, M. R., & Fernald, R. D. (1990). Social control of neuronal soma size. *Journal of Neurobiology, 21*, 1180–1188.

Dawes, R. M., & Smith, T. L. (1985). Attitude and opinion measurement. In G. Lindzey & E. Aronson (Eds.), *Handbook of social psychology* (3rd ed., vol. 1, pp. 509–566). New York: Random House.

Dawkins, R. (1976). *The selfish gene*. London: Oxford University Press.

Deaux, K. (1985). Sex and gender. *Annual Review of Psychology, 36*, 49–81. Palo Alto, CA: Annual Reviews.

deCharms, R. (1957). Affiliation motivation and productivity in small groups. *Journal of Abnormal and Social Psychology, 55*, 222–226.

deCharms, R. (1976). *Enhancing motivation: Change in the classroom*. New York: Irvington.

deCharms, R., Morrison, H. W., Reitman, W., & McClelland, D. C. (1955). Behavioral correlates of directly and indirectly measured achievement motivation. In D. C. McClelland (Ed.), *Studies in motivation* (pp. 414–423). New York: Appleton-Century-Crofts.

Delia, J. G., & Crockett, W. H. (1973). Social schemas, cognitive complexity, and the learning of social structures. *Journal of Personality, 41,* 413–429.

Dembo, T. (1931). Der Anger als dynamisches Problem [Anger as a dynamic problem]. *Psychologische Forschung, 15,* 1–144.

DeSalvo, L. (1989). *Virginia Woolf: The impact of childhood sexual abuse on her life and work.* Boston: Beacon Press.

Diaz, A. J. (1982). *An empirical study of the effect of CEO motives on intra-industry performance with examples drawn from US and Japanese auto manufacturers.* Unpublished honors thesis, Harvard University.

Dickinson, E. (1890). *Poems by Emily Dickinson, First series.* Boston: Roberts Brothers.

Dickinson, E. (1891). *Poems by Emily Dickinson, Second series.* Boston: Roberts Brothers.

Dickinson, E. (1896). *Poems by Emily Dickinson, Third series.* Boston: Roberts Brothers.

Dicks, H. V. (1950). Personality traits and National Socialist ideology. *Human Relations, 3,* 111–153.

Digman, J. M., & Inouye, J. (1986). Further specification of the five robust factors of personality. *Journal of Personality and Social Psychology, 50,* 116–123.

Dillehay, R. C. (1978). Authoritarianism. In H. London & J. Exner (Eds.), *Dimensions of personality* (pp. 85–127). New York: Wiley.

DiRenzo, G. J. (1967). *Personality, power and politics.* Notre Dame, IN: University of Notre Dame Press.

Doi, L. T. (1962). Amae: A key concept for understanding Japanese personality structure. In R. J. Smith and R. K. Beardsley (Eds.), *Japanese culture: Its development and characteristics* (pp. 132–139). Chicago: Aldine.

Dollard, J., & Miller, N. E. (1950). *Personality and psychotherapy.* New York: McGraw-Hill.

Domhoff, G. W. (1983). *Who rules America now?* Englewood Cliffs, NJ: Prentice-Hall.

Donley, R. E., & Winter, D. G. (1970). Measuring the motives of public officials at a distance: An exploratory study of American presidents. *Behavioral Science, 15,* 227–236.

Dostoevsky, F. (1961). *The house of the dead.* (Tr. C. Garnett) London: William Heinemann. (Original work published 1861–1862.)

Doty, R. M., Peterson, B. E., & Winter, D. G. (1991). Threat and authoritarianism in the United States, 1978–1987. *Journal of Personality and Social Psychology, 61,* 629–640.

Doty, R. M., Peterson, B. E., & Winter, D. G. (1992, July). *Authoritarianism and American students' attitudes about the Gulf war.* Paper presented at the annual meeting of the International Society of Political Psychology, San Francisco.

Douvan, E. M. (1976). What happens to parents? *The Center Magazine, 9*(3), 11–15.

Downey, G., Silver, R. C., & Wortman, C. B. (1990). Reconsidering the attribution-adjustment relation following a major negative event: Coping with the loss of a child. *Journal of Personality and Social Psychology, 59,* 925–940.

Duncan, L., Peterson, B. E., & Winter, D. G. (1994). *Authoritarianism and gender roles: Toward a psychological analysis of hegemonic relationships.* Unpublished paper, University of Michigan.

Dustin, D. S., & Davis, H. P. (1967). Authoritarianism and sanctioning behavior. *Journal of Personality and Social Psychology, 6,* 222–224.

Dutton, D. G., & Strachan, C. E. (1987). Motivational needs for power and spouse-specific assertiveness in assaultive and nonassaultive men. *Violence and Victims, 2,* 145–156.

Dweck, C. S. (1975). The role of expectations and attributions in the alleviation of learned helplessness. *Journal of Personality and Social Psychology, 31,* 674–685.

Dworkin, A. (1987). *Intercourse.* New York: Free Press.

Dworkin, R. H., Burke, B. W., Maher, B. A., & Gottesman, I. I. (1976). A longitudinal study of the genetics of personality. *Journal of Personality and Social Psychology, 34,* 510–518.

Dye, T. R. (1990). *Who's running America? The Bush era.* Englewood Cliffs, NJ: Prentice-Hall.

E. H., Dr. (1920). Zur sexuellen Natur des Lutschens [On the sexual nature of sensual sucking]. *Internationale Zeitschrift für Psychoanalyse, 6,* 164–165.

Eckhardt, W. (1965). War propaganda, welfare values, and political ideology. *Journal of Conflict Resolution, 9,* 345–358.

Eckhardt, W., & White, R. K. (1967). A test of the mirror-image hypothesis: Kennedy and Khrushchev. *Journal of Conflict Resolution, 11,* 325–332.

Edel, L. (1979). *Bloomsbury: A house of lions.* Philadelphia: Lippincott.

Edelman, G. M. (1992). *Bright air, brilliant fire: On the matter of mind.* New York: Basic Books.

Edwards, A. L. (1953). The relationship between judged desirability of a trait and the probability that the trait will be endorsed. *Journal of Applied Psychology, 37,* 90–93.

Edwards, A. L. (1970). *The measurement of personality traits by scales and inventories.* New York: Holt, Rinehart & Winston.

Ehrlich, H. J. (1978). Dogmatism. In H. London & J. Exner (Eds.), *Dimensions of personality* (pp. 129–164). New York: Wiley.

Einstein, A. (1950). *Out of my later years.* New York: Philosophical Library.

Einstein, A. (1954a). *Ideas and opinions.* New York: Crown Publishers.

Einstein, A. (1954b, November 18). Letter to the editor. *The Reporter,* p. 8.

Einstein, A. (1955, May 5). Letter to Arthur Taub. *The Reporter,* p. 6.

Einstein, A. (1979). *Autobiographical notes.* LaSalle, IL & Chicago: Open Court Publishing Company. Original work published in P. A. Schilpp, Ed., *Albert Einstein: Philosopher-scientist* (pp. 3–95). Evanston, IL: Library of Living Philosophers, 1949.

Einstein, A. (1992). *Albert Einstein/Mileva Maric—The love letters.* Princeton, NJ: Princeton University Press.

Einstein, A., & Freud, S. (1933). *Why war?* Paris: International Institute of Intellectual Cooperation, League of Nations.

Einstein puzzled by our invitations. (1930, November 23). *New York Times*, p. 13.

Eisenberg, N. (1986). *Altruistic emotion, cognition, and behavior*. Hillsdale, NJ: Erlbaum.

Ekman, P. (1971). Universals and cultural differences in facial expression of emotion. In J. K. Cole (Ed.), *Nebraska symposium on motivation 1971* (pp. 207–283). Lincoln, NE: University of Nebraska Press.

Elder, G. H. (1974). *Children of the Great Depression*. Chicago: University of Chicago Press.

Elder, G. H., Jr., Caspi, A., & Nguyen, T. (1986). Resourceful and vulnerable children: Family influence in hard times. In R. K. Silbereison, E. Eyferth, & G. Rudinger (Eds.), *Development as action in context: Problem behavior and normal youth development* (pp. 167–186). New York: Springer-Verlag.

Eliasberg, W. G., & Stuart, I. R. (1961). Authoritarian personality and the obscenity threshold. *Journal of Social Psychology, 55,* 143–151.

Elkins, S. (1959). *Slavery: A problem in American institutional and intellectual life*. Chicago: University of Chicago Press .

Elliot, J. M. (1989). Maya Angelou raps. In J. M. Elliot (Ed.), *Conversations with Maya Angelou* (pp. 86–96). Jackson, MS : University Press of Mississippi. (Original work published 1977.)

Ellis, A. (1965). Introduction: The psychology of assassination. In K. Thornley, *Oswald*. Chicago: New Classics House.

Elms, A. C. (1976). *Personality in politics*. New York: Harcourt Brace Jovanovich.

Elms, A. C., & Milgram, S. (1966). Personality characteristics associated with obedience and defiance toward authoritative command. *Journal of Research in Personality, 1,* 282–289.

Emmons, R. A. (1986). Personal strivings: An approach to personality and subjective well-being. *Journal of Personality and Social Psychology, 51,* 1058–1068.

Emmons, R. A. (1987). Narcissism: Theory and measurement. *Journal of Personality and Social Psychology, 52,* 11–17.

Emmons, R. A. (1989). The personal striving approach to personality. In L. A. Pervin (Ed.), *Goal concepts in personality and social psychology* (pp. 87–126). Hillsdale, NJ: Erlbaum.

Emmons, R., & McAdams, D. P. (1991). Personal strivings and motive dispositions: Exploring the links. *Personality and Social Psychology Bulletin, 17,* 648–654.

Empson, W. (1947). *Seven types of ambiguity* (rev. ed.). New York: New Directions. (Original work published 1930.)

Endler, N. S., Hunt, J. McV., & Rosenstein, A. J. (1962). An S-R inventory of anxiousness. *Psychological Monographs, 76* (Whole no. 536).

Engels, F. (1969). On authority. In K. Marx and F. Engels, *Selected works* (vol. 2, pp. 376–379). Moscow: Progress Publishers. (Original work published 1873.)

Entwisle, D. R. (1972). To dispel fantasies about fantasy-based measures of achievement motivation. *Psychological Bulletin, 83,* 1131–1153.

Epstein, H. (1979). *Children of the Holocaust: Conversations with sons and daughters of survivors*. New York: Putnam.

Epstein, R. (1966). Aggression toward outgroups as a function of authoritarianism and imitation of aggressive models. *Journal of Personality and Social Psychology, 3,* 574–579.

Epstein, S. (1979). The stability of behavior: I. On predicting most of the people much of the time. *Journal of Personality and Social Psychology, 37,* 1097–1126.

Epstein, S. (1982). A research paradigm for the study of personality and emotions. In M. M. Page (Ed.), *Nebraska symposium on motivation 1982* (pp. 91–154). Lincoln, NE: University of Nebraska Press.

Epstein, S. (1984). The stability of behavior across time and situations. In R. A. Zucker, J. Aronoff, & A. I. Rabin (Eds.), *Personality and the prediction of behavior* (pp. 209–268). Orlando, FL: Academic Press.

Erdelyi, M. H. (1974). A new look at the New Look: Perceptual defense and vigilance. *Psychological Review, 81,* 1–25.

Erdelyi, M. H. (1985). *Psychoanalysis: Freud's cognitive psychology*. New York: Freeman.

Eriksen, C. W., & Pierce, J. (1969). Defense mechanisms. In E. Borgatta & W. W. Lambert (Eds.), *Handbook of personality theory and research* (pp. 1007–1040). Chicago: Rand McNally.

Erikson, E. H. (1958). *Young man Luther*. New York: Norton.

Erikson, E. H. (1963). *Childhood and society* (2nd ed.). New York: Norton. (Original work published 1950.)

Erikson, E. H. (1969). *Gandhi's truth*. New York: Norton.

Erikson, E. H. (1980). *Identity and the life cycle*. New York: Norton. (Original work published 1959.)

Erikson, E. H. (1982). Psychoanalytic reflections on Einstein's centenary. In G. Holton & Y. Elkana (Eds.), *Albert Einstein: Historical and cultural perspectives* (pp. 151–173). Princeton, NJ: Princeton University Press.

Exline, R. V. (1962). Effects of need for affiliation, sex, and the sight of others upon initial communications in problem-solving groups. *Journal of Personality, 30,* 541–556.

Eysenck, H. J. (1944). Types of personality—A factorial study of 700 neurotics. *Journal of Mental Science, 90,* 851–861.

Eysenck, H. J. (1947). *Dimensions of personality*. London: Routledge & Kegan Paul.

Eysenck, H. J. (1954). *The psychology of politics*. London: Routledge & Kegan Paul.

Eysenck, H. J. (1957). *The dynamics of anxiety and hysteria*. London: Routledge & Kegan Paul.

Eysenck, H. J. (1965). Extraversion and the acquisition of eyeblink and GSR conditioned responses. *Psychological Bulletin, 63,* 258–270.

Eysenck, H. J. (1967). *The biological basis of personality*. Springfield, IL: Charles C Thomas.

Eysenck, H. J. (1990). Biological dimensions of personality. In L. Pervin (Ed.), *Handbook of personality theory and research* (pp. 244–276). New York: Guilford Press.

Eysenck, H. J. (1992). Four ways five factors are not basic. *Personality and Individual Differences, 6,* 667–673.

Eysenck, H. J., & Eysenck, M. W. (1985). *Personality and individual differences: A natural science approach.* New York: Plenum.

Eysenck, H. J., & Eysenck, S. B. G. (1969). *Personality structure and measurement.* London: Routledge & Kegan Paul.

Eysenck, H. J., & Eysenck, S. B. G. (1976). *Psychoticism as a dimension of personality.* London: Hodder & Stoughton.

Eysenck, H. J., & Eysenck, S. B. G. (1977). Block and psychoticism. *Journal of Abnormal Psychology, 86,* 651–652.

Eysenck, H. J., & Wilson, G. D. (Eds.) (1978). *The psychological basis of ideology.* Baltimore: University Park Press.

Fahrenberg, J. (1987). Concepts of activation and arousal in the theory of emotionality (neuroticism). In J. Strelau & H. J. Eysenck (Eds.), *Personality dimensions and arousal* (pp. 99–120). New York: Plenum.

Fairbairn, W. R. D. (1952). *Psychoanalytic studies of the personality.* London: Routledge & Kegan Paul.

Falbo, T., & Beck, R. C. (1979). Naive psychology and the attributional model of achievement. *Journal of Personality, 47,* 185–195.

Fallon, A. (1990). Culture in the mirror: Sociocultural determinants of body image. In T. F. Cash & T. Pruzinsky (Eds.), *Body images: Development, deviance, and change* (pp. 80–109). New York: Guilford Press.

Faludi, S. (1991). *Backlash: The undeclared war against American women.* New York: Morrow.

Fate is not in the stars but in your blood, says Toshitaka Nomi. (1985, April 25). *People,* p. 89.

Feather, N. T. (1961). The relationship of persistence at a task to expectation of success and achievement related motives. *Journal of Abnormal and Social Psychology, 63,* 552–561.

Feinstein, H. M. (1984). *Becoming William James.* Ithaca, NY: Cornell University Press.

Fenichel, O. (1945). *The psychoanalytic theory of neurosis.* New York: Norton.

Festinger, L., & Carlsmith, J. M. (1959). Cognitive consequences of forced compliance. *Journal of Abnormal and Social Psychology, 58,* 203–210.

Fineman, S. (1977). The achievement motive construct and its measurement: Where are we now? *British Journal of Psychology, 68,* 1–22.

Fisher, S. (1986). *Development and structure of the body image* (2 vols.). Hillsdale, NJ: Erlbaum.

Fisher, S., & Greenberg, R. P. (1977). *The scientific credibility of Freud's theories and therapy.* New York: Basic Books.

Fishkin, J., Keniston, K., & MacKinnon, C. (1973). Moral reasoning and political ideology. *Journal of Personality and Social Psychology, 27,* 109–119.

Fishman, D. B. (1966). Need and expectancy as determinants of affiliative behavior in small groups. *Journal of Personality and Social Psychology, 58,* 203–210.

Fiske, S. T. (1993). Controlling other people: The impact of power on stereotyping. *American Psychologist, 48,* 621–628.

Fiske, S. T., & Taylor, S. E. (1984). *Social cognition.* Reading, MA.: Addison-Wesley.

Fleeson, W. W. (1992). *Life tasks, implicit motives, and self-regulation in daily life.* Unpublished doctoral dissertation, University of Michigan.

Fleming, J. (1984). *Blacks in college: A comparative study of students' success in Black and white institutions.* San Francisco: Jossey-Bass.

Fodor, E. (1985). The power motive, group conflict, and physiological arousal. *Journal of Personality and Social Psychology, 49,* 1408–1415.

Fodor, E. (1990). The power motive and creativity of solutions to an engineering problem. *Journal of Research in Personality, 24,* 338–354.

Fodor, E. M., & Farrow, D. L. (1979). The power motive as an influence on the use of power. *Journal of Personality and Social Psychology, 37,* 2091–2097.

Fodor, E. M., & Smith, T. (1982). The power motive as an influence on group decision making. *Journal of Personality and Social Psychology, 42,* 178–185.

Foner, P. S. (Ed.). (1967). *Helen Keller: Her socialist years.* New York: International Publishers.

Forbes, H. A. (1985). *Nationalism, ethnocentrism, and critical theory.* Chicago: University of Chicago Press.

Francis, R. C., Soma, K., & Fernald, R. D. (1990). Social regulation of the brain-pituitary-gonadal axis. *Proceedings of the National Academy of Science, 99,* 7794–7798.

Frank, P. (1947). *Einstein: His life and times.* New York: Knopf.

Franklin, B. (1990). *Autobiography.* New York: Vintage Books (Library of America). (Original work published 1788.)

Franks, C. M. (1956). Conditioning and personality: A study of normal and neurotic subjects. *Journal of Abnormal and Social Psychology, 52,* 143–150.

Franks, C. M. (1957). Personality factors and the rate of conditioning. *British Journal of Psychology, 48,* 119–126.

Franz, C. & Stewart, A. J. (Eds.). (1994). *Women creating lives: Identities, resilience, and resistance.* Boulder, CO: Westview.

Franz, C. E., & White, K. M. (1985). Individuation and attachment in personality development: Extending Erikson's model. *Journal of Personality, 53,* 224–256.

Freedman, M. B., Leary, T. F., Ossorio, A. G., & Coffey, H. S. (1951). The interpersonal dimension of personality. *Journal of Personality, 20,* 143–161.

French, E. G. (1956). Motivation as a variable in work partner selection. *Journal of Abnormal and Social Psychology, 53,* 96–99.

French, E. G., & Thomas, F. H. (1958). The relationship of achievement motivation and problem-solving effectiveness. *Journal of Abnormal and Social Psychology, 56,* 45–48.

Frenkel-Brunswik, E. (1949). Intolerance of ambiguity as an emotional and perceptual personality variable. *Journal of Personality, 18,* 108–143.

Freud, A. (1946). *The ego and the mechanisms of defense.* New York: International Universities Press. (Original work published 1937.)

Freud, S. (1893). On the psychical mechanism of hysterical phenomena: A lecture. *The standard edition of the complete psychological works of Sigmund Freud* (vol. 3, pp. 25–39). London: The Hogarth Press and the Institute of Psychoanalysis.

Freud, S. (1894). The neuro-psychoses of defense. *The standard edition of the complete psychological works of Sigmund Freud* (vol. 3, pp. 41–61).

Freud, S. (1896). Further remarks on the neuro-psychoses of defense. *The standard edition of the complete psychological works of Sigmund Freud* (vol. 3, pp. 157–185).

Freud, S. (1900). *The interpretation of dreams. The standard edition of the complete psychological works of Sigmund Freud* (vol. 4–5).

Freud, S. (1901). *The psychopathology of everyday life. The standard edition of the complete psychological works of Sigmund Freud* (vol. 6).

Freud, S. (1905a). Fragment of an analysis of a case of hysteria. *The standard edition of the complete psychological works of Sigmund Freud* (vol. 7, pp. 7–122).

Freud, S. (1905b). *Jokes and their relation to the unconscious. The standard edition of the complete psychological works of Sigmund Freud* (vol. 8).

Freud, S. (1905c). *Three essays on the theory of sexuality. The standard edition of the complete psychological works of Sigmund Freud* (vol. 7, pp. 135–243).

Freud, S. (1907a). *Delusion and dream in Jensen's* Gradiva. *The standard edition of the complete psychological works of Sigmund Freud* (vol. 9, pp. 7–95).

Freud, S. (1907b). Obsessive actions and religious practices. *The standard edition of the complete psychological works of Sigmund Freud* (vol. 9, pp. 117–127).

Freud, S. (1908a). Character and anal erotism. *The standard edition of the complete psychological works of Sigmund Freud* (vol. 9, pp. 169–175).

Freud, S. (1908b). Creative writers and daydreaming. *The standard edition of the complete psychological works of Sigmund Freud* (vol. 9, pp. 143–153).

Freud, S. (1908c). On the sexual theories of children. *The standard edition of the complete psychological works of Sigmund Freud* (vol. 9, pp. 205–226).

Freud, S. (1909a). An analysis of a phobia in a five-year-old boy. *The standard edition of the complete psychological works of Sigmund Freud* (vol. 10, pp. 1–149).

Freud, S. (1909b). *Five lectures on psychoanalysis. The standard edition of the complete psychological works of Sigmund Freud* (vol. 11, pp. 7–55).

Freud, S. (1909c). Notes upon a case of obsessional neurosis. *The standard edition of the complete psychological works of Sigmund Freud* (vol. 10, pp. 158–318).

Freud, S. (1910a). *Leonardo da Vinci and a memory of his childhood. The standard edition of the complete psychological works of Sigmund Freud* (vol. 11, pp. 63–137).

Freud, S. (1910b). The psycho-analytic view of psychogenic disturbance of vision. *The standard edition of the complete psychological works of Sigmund Freud* (vol. 11, pp. 211–218).

Freud, S. (1913a). The claims of psycho-analysis to scientific interest. *The standard edition of the complete psychological works of Sigmund Freud* (vol. 13, pp. 165–190).

Freud, S. (1913b). *Totem and taboo. The standard edition of the complete psychological works of Sigmund Freud* (vol. 13, pp. 1–161).

Freud, S. (1914). Mourning and melancholia. *The standard edition of the complete psychological works of Sigmund Freud* (vol. 14, pp. 237–258).

Freud, S. (1915a). Instincts and their vicissitudes. *The standard edition of the complete psychological works of Sigmund Freud* (vol. 14, pp. 117–140).

Freud, S. (1915b). The unconscious. *The standard edition of the complete psychological works of Sigmund Freud* (vol. 14, pp. 159–204).

Freud, S. (1916). Some character types met with in psycho-analytic work. *The standard edition of the complete psychological works of Sigmund Freud* (vol. 14, pp. 309–333).

Freud, S. (1916–1917). *Introductory lectures on psychoanalysis. The standard edition of the complete psychological works of Sigmund Freud* (vol. 15–16).

Freud, S. (1920). *Beyond the pleasure principle. The standard edition of the complete psychological works of Sigmund Freud* (vol. 18, pp. 7–64).

Freud, S. (1921). *Group psychology and the analysis of the ego. The standard edition of the complete psychological works of Sigmund Freud* (vol. 18, pp. 65–143).

Freud, S. (1923). *The ego and the id. The standard edition of the complete psychological works of Sigmund Freud* (vol. 19, pp. 1–66).

Freud, S. (1924a). The dissolution of the Oedipus complex. *The standard edition of the complete psychological works of Sigmund Freud* (vol. 19, pp. 173–1179).

Freud, S. (1924b). The economic problem of masochism. *The standard edition of the complete psychological works of Sigmund Freud* (vol. 19, pp. 159–170).

Freud, S. (1925a). *An autobiographical study. The standard edition of the complete psychological works of Sigmund Freud* (vol. 20, pp. 1–74).

Freud, S. (1925b). Negation. *The standard edition of the complete psychological works of Sigmund Freud* (vol. 19, pp. 235–239).

Freud, S. (1925c). Some psychical consequences of the anatomical distinction between the sexes. *The standard edition of the complete psychological works of Sigmund Freud* (vol. 19, pp. 241–258).

Freud, S. (1927). Humour. *The standard edition of the complete psychological works of Sigmund Freud* (vol. 21, pp. 161–172).

Freud, S. (1930). *Civilization and its discontents. The standard edition of the complete psychological works of Sigmund Freud* (vol. 21, pp. 64–145).

Freud, S. (1931a). Female sexuality. *The standard edition of the complete psychological works of Sigmund Freud* (vol. 21, pp. 221–243).

Freud, S. (1931b). Libidinal types. *The standard edition of the complete psychological works of Sigmund Freud* (vol. 21, pp. 215–220).

Freud, S. (1933a). Femininity. In *New introductory lectures on psycho-analysis. The standard edition of the complete psychological works of Sigmund Freud* (vol. 22, pp. 112–135).

Freud, S. (1933b). *New introductory lectures on psycho-analysis. The standard edition of the complete psychological works of Sigmund Freud* (vol. 22, pp. 5–182).

Freud, S. (1933c). Why war? [Correspondence with Einstein]. *The standard edition of the complete psychological works of Sigmund Freud* (vol. 22, pp. 199–215).

Freud, S. (1940). *An outline of psycho-analysis. The standard edition of the complete psychological works of Sigmund Freud* (vol. 23, pp. 144–207).

Friedan, B. (1963). *The feminine mystique.* New York: Dell.

Frieze, I. H. (1976). Causal attributions and information seeking to explain success and failure. *Journal of Research in Personality, 10,* 293–305.

Frieze, I. H., & Snyder, H. N. (1980). Children's beliefs about the causes of success and failure in school settings. *Journal of Educational Psychology, 72,* 186–196.

Fromm, E. (1941). *Escape from freedom.* New York: Rinehart.

Fromm, E. (1947). *Man for himself.* New York: Holt, Rinehart & Winston.

Frye, N. (1957). *Anatomy of criticism: Four essays.* Princeton: Princeton University Press.

Funder, D. C., & Ozer, D. J. (1983). Behavior as a function of the situation. *Journal of Personality and Social Psychology, 44,* 107–112.

Galbraith, J. K. (1970). *Ambassador's journal.* New York: Signet Books. (Original work published 1969.)

Gale, A. (1983). Electroencephalographic studies of extraversion-introversion: A case study in the psychophysiology of individual differences. *Personality and Individual Differences, 4,* 371–380.

Galotti, K. M. (1989). Gender differences in self-reported moral reasoning: A review and new evidence. *Journal of Youth and Adolescence, 18,* 475–488.

Gandhi, M. K. (1957). *An autobiography: The story of my experiments with truth.* Boston: Beacon Press. (Original work published 1929.)

Gazzaniga, M. S. (1994). *Nature's mind: The biological roots of thinking, emotions, sexuality, language, and intelligence.* New York: Basic Books.

Geen, R. G., McCown, E. J., & Broyles, J. W. (1985). Effects of noise on sensitivity of introverts and extraverts to signals in a vigilance task. *Personality and Individual Differences, 6,* 237–241.

Geis, F. (1978). Machiavellianism. In H. London & J. Exner (Eds.), *Dimensions of personality* (pp. 305–363). New York: Wiley.

George, A. L. (1969). The "operational code": A neglected approach to the study of political leaders and decision-making. *International Studies Quarterly, 13,* 190–222.

George, A. L. (1987). Some uses of dynamic psychology in political biography: Case materials on Woodrow Wilson. In T. L. Crosby & G. Cocks (Eds.), *Psycho/history: Readings in the method of psychology, psychoanalysis, and history* (pp. 132–156). New Haven, CT: Yale University Press. (Original work published 1971.)

George, A. L., & George, J. (1956). *Woodrow Wilson and Colonel House.* New York: John Day.

Gerbner, G., & Gross, L. (1976). The scary world of TV's heavy viewer. *Psychology Today, 9(11),* 41–45, 89.

Gerbner, G., Gross, L., Morgan, M., & Signorelli, N. (1980). The "mainstreaming" of America. Violence profile no. 11. *Journal of Communication, 30(3),* 10–29.

Gergen, K. J. (1991). *The saturated self: Dilemmas of identity in contemporary life.* New York: Basic Books.

Gergen, K. J., & Gordon, C. (Eds.). (1968). *The self in social interaction.* New York: Holt, Rinehart & Winston.

Giffin, K. (1967). The contribution of studies of source credibility to a theory of interpersonal trust in the communication process. *Psychological Bulletin, 68,* 104–120.

Gilbert, W. S. (1886). *Original plays, Second series.* London: Chatto & Windus.

Gilligan, C. (1982). *In a different voice: Psychological theory and women's development.* Cambridge, MA: Harvard University Press.

Gilligan, C. (1990). *Making connections: The relational world of adolescent girls at Emma Willard School.* Cambridge, MA: Harvard University Press.

Gilligan, C., & Belenky, M. F. (1980). A naturalistic study of abortion decisions. In R. L. Selman & R. Yando (Eds.), *New directions for child development: Clinical-developmental psychology* (pp. 69–90). San Francisco: Jossey-Bass.

Glad, B. (Ed.). (1990). *Psychological dimensions of war.* Newbury Park, CA: Sage.

Glauber, I. P. (1958). The psychoanalysis of stuttering. In J. Eisenson (Ed.), *Stuttering: Significant theories and therapies.* New York: Harper & Row.

Goebbels, J. (1948). *The Goebbels diaries 1942–1943.* Garden City, NY: Doubleday.

Goffman, E. (1959). *The presentation of self in everyday life.* Garden City, NY: Doubleday.

Goffman, E. (1961). *Asylums: Essays on the social situation of mental patients and other inmates.* Chicago: Aldine.

Goldberg, L. R. (1981). Language and individual differences: The search for universals in personality lexicons. In L. Wheeler (Ed.), *Review of personality and social psychology* (vol. 2, pp. 141–165). Beverly Hills, CA: Sage.

Goldberg, L. R. (1990). An alternative "description of personality": The Big-Five factor structure. *Journal of Personality and Social Psychology, 59,* 1216–1229.

Goldstein, K. (1939). *The organism.* New York: American Book Co.

Goodstadt, B. E., & Hjelle, L. A. (1973). Power to the powerless: Locus of control and the use of power. *Journal of Personality and Social Psychology, 27,* 190–196.

Goodwin, D. K. (1987). *The Fitzgeralds and the Kennedys.* New York: Simon & Schuster. Paperback edition published 1988 by St. Martin's Press.

Gordon, C. (1968). Self-conceptions: Configurations of content. In C. Gordon & K. J. Gergen (Eds.), *The self in social interaction* (pp. 115–136). New York: Holt, Rinehart & Winston.

Gordon, H. C. (1954). A comparative study of dreams and responses to the TAT: A need-press analysis. *Journal of Personality, 22,* 234–253.

Gore, P. M., & Rotter, J. B. (1963). A personality correlate of social action. *Journal of Personality, 31,* 58–64.

Gorer, G. (1955). *Exploring English character.* New York: Criterion Books.

Gormly, J. (1985). The relationship between biology and personality: Only Mother Nature knows. Review of M. Myrtek, *Constitutional psychophysiology: Research in review. Contemporary Psychology, 30,* 393–394.

Gough, H. (1987). *The California Psychological Inventory: Administrator's guide.* Palo Alto, CA: Consulting Psychologists Press.

Gough, H. G., & Heilbrun, A. B., Jr. (1965). *The Adjective Check List.* Palo Alto, CA: Consulting Psychologists Press.

Gough, H., & Thorne, A. (1986). Positive, negative, and balanced shyness: Self-definitions and the reactions of others. In W. H. Jones, J. M. Cheek, & S. R. Briggs (Eds.), *Shyness: Perspectives on research and treatment* (pp. 205–225). New York: Plenum.

Gould, S. J. (1977). Biological potentiality versus biological determinism. In *Ever since Darwin: Reflections on natural history* (pp. 251–259). New York: Norton.

Gov. Lamm asserts elderly, if very ill, have "duty to die." (1984, March 29). *New York Times,* p. A16.

Graham, M. (1991). *Blood memory.* New York: Doubleday.

Gray, J. A. (1964). *Pavlov's typology.* New York: Macmillan.

Gray, J. A. (1981). A critique of Eysenck's theory of personality. In H. J. Eysenck (Ed.), *A model for personality* (pp. 246–276). New York: Springer.

Gray, J. A. (1987). Discussions arising from Cloninger, C. R.: A unified biosocial theory of personality and its role in the development of anxiety states. *Psychiatric Developments, 5,* 377–394.

Graziano, W. G., & Ward, D. (1992). Probing the Big Five in adolescence: Personality and adjustment during a developmental transition. *Journal of Personality, 60,* 425–439.

Greene, D. L., & Winter, D. G. (1971). Motives, leadership, and involvements among Black college students. *Journal of Personality, 39,* 319–332.

Greenstein, F. I. (1987). *Personality and politics: Problems of evidence, inference, and conceptualization.* Princeton, NJ: Princeton University Press. (Original work published 1969.)

Grey, A. L. (Ed.). (1969). *Class and personality in society.* New York: Atherton Press.

Grice, P. (1989). *Studies in the way of words.* Cambridge, MA: Harvard University Press.

Grupp, F. (1975, March). *The power motive within the American state bureaucracy.* Paper presented at the Yale University Conference on Psychology and Politics.

Guilford, J. P. (1959). *Personality.* New York: McGraw-Hill.

Gurin, P., Miller, A. H., & Gurin, G. (1980). Stratum identification and consciousness. *Social Psychology Quarterly, 43,* 30–47.

Haan, N., Smith, M. B., & Block, J. H. (1968). Moral reasoning of young adults: Political-social behavior, family backgrounds, and personality correlates. *Journal of Personality and Social Psychology, 10,* 183–201.

Hale, N. (1971). *Freud and the Americans.* New York: Oxford University Press.

Haley, J. (1969). *The power tactics of Jesus Christ and other essays.* New York: Grossman.

Hall, C. S., & Lindzey, G. (1978). *Theories of personality* (3rd ed.). New York: Wiley.

Hampson, S. E. (1989). Using traits to construct personality. In D. Buss & N. Cantor (Eds.), *Personality psychology: Recent trends and emerging directions* (pp. 286–293). New York: Springer-Verlag.

Hamsher, J. H., Geller, J. D., & Rotter, J. B. (1968). Interpersonal trust, internal-external control, and the Warren Commission report. *Journal of Personality and Social Psychology, 9,* 210–215.

Haney, C., Banks, C., & Zimbardo, P. (1973). Interpersonal dynamics in a simulated prison. *International Journal of Criminology and Penology, 1*(1), 69–97.

Hansen, M. (1938). *The problem of the third generation immigrant.* Rock Island, IL: Augustana College.

Hardy, K. R. (1957). Determinants of conformity and attitude change. *Journal of Abnormal and Social Psychology, 54,* 289–294.

Hare, B. R. (1977). Racial and socioeconomic variations in preadolescent area-specific and general self-esteem. *International Journal of Intercultural Relations, 1,* 31–51.

Harlow, H. F. (1958). The nature of love. *American Psychologist, 13,* 673–685.

Harlow, H. F. (1971). *Learning to love.* San Francisco: Albion.

Harris, B. (1979). Whatever happened to Little Albert? *American Psychologist, 34,* 151–160.

Harris, B. (1980). Ceremonial versus critical history of psychology. *American Psychologist, 35,* 218–219.

Harrison, F. I. (1968). Relation between home background, school success, and adolescent attitudes. *Merrill-Palmer Quarterly, 14,* 331–344.

Hartogs, R., & Freeman, L. (1965). *The two assassins.* New York: Crowell.

Harvey, J. H., Town, J. P., & Yarkin, K. L. (1981). How fundamental is "the fundamental attribution error?" *Journal of Personality and Social Psychology, 40,* 346–349.

Harvey, J. H., & Weary, G. (1981). *Perspectives on attributional processes.* Dubuque, IA: W. C. Brown.

Harvey, O. J., Hunt, D. E., & Schroder, H. M. (1961). *Conceptual systems and personality organization.* New York: Wiley.

Hassan, M. K., & Sarkar, S. N. (1975). Attitudes toward caste system as related to certain personality and sociological factors. *Indian Journal of Psychology, 50,* 313–319.

Hastie, R. (1981). Schematic principles in human memory. In E. T. Higgins, C. P. Herman, & M. P. Zanna (Eds.), *Social cognition: The Ontario symposium* (vol. 1, pp. 39–88). Hillsdale NJ: Erlbaum.

Hauser, S. T. (1976). Loevinger's model and measure of ego development: A critical review. *Psychological Bulletin, 80,* 928–955.

Heckhausen, H. (1967). *The anatomy of achievement motivation.* New York: Academic Press.

Heckhausen, H., Schmalt, H.-D., & Schneider, K. (1985). *Achievement motivation in perspective.* Orlando, FL: Academic Press.

Heider, F. (1958). *The psychology of interpersonal relations.* New York: Wiley.

Helson, R. (1977). The creative spectrum of authors of fantasy. *Journal of Personality, 45,* 310–326.

Helson, R. (1982). Critics and their texts: An approach to Jung's theory of cognition and personality. *Journal of Personality and Social Psychology, 43,* 409–418.

Helson, R. (1987). Which of those young women with creative potential became productive? II. From college to midlife. In R. Hogan & W. H. Jones (Eds.), *Perspectives in personality* (vol. 2, pp. 51–92). Guilford, CT: JAI Press.

Helson, R., & Crutchfield, R. S. (1970). Creative types in mathematics. *Journal of Personality, 38,* 177–197.

Henley, N. (1977). *Body politics: Power, sex, and nonverbal communication.* Englewood Cliffs, NJ: Prentice-Hall.

Hermann, M. G. (Ed.). (1977). *A psychological examination of political leaders.* New York: Free Press.

Hermann, M. G. (1980a). Assessing the personalities of Soviet Politburo members. *Personality and Social Psychology Bulletin, 6,* 332–352.

Hermann, M. G. (1980b). Explaining foreign policy behavior using the personal characteristics of political leaders. *International Studies Quarterly, 24,* 7–46.

Hermann, M. G. (1983). Assessing personality at a distance: A portrait of Ronald Reagan. *Mershon Center Quarterly Report, 7(6).* Columbus, OH: Mershon Center, Ohio State University.

Hermans, H. J. M. (1970). A questionnaire measure of achievement motivation. *Journal of Applied Psychology, 54,* 353–363.

Herrmann, A., & Stewart, A. J. (1994). *Theorizing feminism: Parallel trends in the humanities and social sciences.* Boulder, CO: Westview.

Hersh, S. M. (1970). *My Lai 4: A report on the massacre and its aftermath.* New York: Random House.

Hersh, S. M. (1983). *The price of power: Kissinger in the Nixon White House.* New York: Summit Books.

Higgins, E. T. (1987). Self-discrepancy: A theory relating self and affect. *Psychological Review, 94,* 319–340.

Higgins, E. T., Klein, R., & Strauman, T. (1985). Self-concept discrepancy theory: A psychological model for distinguishing among different aspects of depression and anxiety. *Social Cognition, 3,* 51–76.

Hilgard, E. R., & Marquis, D. G. (1940). *Conditioning and learning.* New York: Appleton-Century.

Hine, D. C. (1989). Rape and the inner lives of Black women in the Middle West. *Signs: Journal of Women in Culture and Society, 14,* 912–920.

Hines, K. S. (1977). *Subliminal psychodynamic activation of oral dependency conflicts in a group of hospitalized male alcoholics.* Unpublished Ph.D. thesis, Memphis State University.

Hobsbawm, E. J. (1987). *The age of empire 1875–1914.* New York: Pantheon Books.

Hochreich, D. J. (1972). Internal-external control and reaction to the My Lai courts-martial. *Journal of Applied Social Psychology, 2,* 319–325.

Hoffman, L. W. (1974). Fear of success in males and females: 1965 and 1971. *Journal of Consulting and Clinical Psychology, 42,* 353–358.

Hofstadter, R. (1967). *The paranoid style in American politics and other essays.* New York: Vintage Books.

Hofstede, G. H. (1980). *Culture's consequences: International differences in work-related values.* Beverly Hills, CA: Sage.

Hogan, R. (1986). *Hogan personality inventory.* Minneapolis, MN: National Computer System.

Hogan, R. (1987). Personality psychology: Back to basics. In J. Aronoff, A. I. Rabin, & R. A. Zucker (Eds.), *The emergence of personality* (pp. 79–104). New York: Springer.

Holland, N. (1968). *The dynamics of literary response.* New York: Oxford University Press.

Holmes, R. M. (1989). *Profiling violent crimes: An investigative tool.* Beverly Hills, CA: Sage.

Holzworth, R. J., & Pipping, C. B. (1985). Drawing a weapon: An analysis of police judgments. *Journal of Police Science and Administration, 13,* 185–194.

Homans, G. C. (1961). *Social behavior: Its elementary forms.* New York: Harcourt, Brace & World.

Honigman, J. J. (1967). *Personality in culture.* New York: Harper & Row.

Horner, M. S. (1972). Toward an understanding of achievement-related conflicts in women. *Journal of Social Issues, 28,* 157–176.

Horney, K. (1939). *New directions in psychoanalysis.* New York: Norton.

Horney, K. (1967). *Feminine psychology.* New York: Norton.

House, J. S. (1981). Social structure and personality. In M. Rosenberg & R. H. Turner (Eds.), *Social psychology: Sociological perspectives* (pp. 525–561). New York: Basic Books.

House, R. J., Spangler, W. D., & Woycke, J. (1991). Personality and charisma in the U.S. presidency: A psychological theory of leader effectiveness. *Administrative Science Quarterly, 36,* 364–396.

House of Representatives. (1979). *Report of the select committee on assassinations* (House report no. 95-1828, pt. 2). Washington, DC: Government Printing Office.

Hovland, C. I., Janis, I. L., & Kelley, H. H. (1953). *Communication and persuasion.* New Haven, CT: Yale University Press.

Hovland, C. I., & Sears, R. R. (1940). Minor studies of aggression: VI. Correlation of lynchings with economic indices. *Journal of Psychology, 9,* 301–310.

How do Americans think people get rich? (1986, December 31). *Middletown [CT] Press,* p. 1.

Huesmann, L. R., & Miller, L. S. (1994). Long-term effects of repeated exposure to media violence in childhood. In L. Huesmann (Ed.), *Aggressive behavior: Current perspectives* (pp. 153–186). New York: Plenum.

Hundal, P. S. (1971). A study of entrepreneurial motivation: Comparison of fast- and slow-progressing small-scale industrial entrepreneurs in Punjab, India. *Journal of Applied Psychology, 55,* 317–323.

Hunter, A. G., & Ensminger, M. E. (1992). Diversity and fluidity in children's living arrangements: Family transitions in an urban Afro-American community. *Journal of Marriage and the Family, 54*, 418–426.

Hurley, J. R. (1955). The Iowa Picture Interpretation Test: A multiple-choice variation for the TAT. *Journal of Consulting Psychology, 19*, 372–376.

Hyman, H. H., & Sheatsley, P. B. (1954). "The authoritarian personality"—A methodological critique. In R. Christie & M. Jahoda (Eds.), *Studies in the scope and method of "The authoritarian personality"* (pp. 50–122). Glencoe, IL: Free Press.

Ike, N. (Ed.). (1967). *Japan's decision for war: Records of the 1941 policy conferences.* Stanford, CA: Stanford University Press.

Infeld, L. (1941). *Quest: The evolution of a scientist.* New York: Doubleday, Doran.

Infeld, L. (1947). Portrait . . . Einstein. *American Scholar, 16*, 337–341.

Inglehart, R. (1990). *Culture shift in advanced industrial society.* Princeton, NJ: Princeton University Press.

Inglehart, R., & Rabier, J.-R. (1985). If you're unhappy, this must be Belgium: Well-being around the world. *Public Opinion, 8(2)*, 10–15.

Inkeles, A. (1953). Some sociological observations on culture and personality studies. In C. Kluckhohn, H. A. Murray, & Schneider, D. (Eds.), *Personality in nature, culture, and society* (pp. 577–592). New York: Knopf.

Inkeles, A. (1960). Industrial man: The relation of status to experience, perception, and value. *American Journal of Sociology, 66*, 1–31.

Inkeles, A., & Levinson, D. J. (1954). National character: The study of modal personality and sociocultural systems. In G. Lindzey (Ed.), *Handbook of social psychology* (vol. 2, pp. 977–1020). Cambridge, MA: Addison-Wesley.

Inkeles, A., & Levinson, D. J. (1969). National character. In G. Lindzey & E. Aronson (Eds.), *Handbook of social psychology* (rev. ed., vol. 4, pp. 418–506). Reading, MA: Addison-Wesley.

Inkeles, A., & Smith, D. H. (1974). *Becoming modern: Individual change in six developing countries.* Cambridge, MA: Harvard University Press.

Izard, C. E. (1979). Emotions as motivations: An evolutionary-developmental perspective. In H. E. Howe & R. A. Dienstbier (Eds.), *Nebraska symposium on motivation 1978* (pp. 163–200). Lincoln, NE: University of Nebraska Press.

Izzett, R. R. (1971). Authoritarianism and attitudes toward the Vietnam war as reflected in behavioral and self-report measures. *Journal of Personality and Social Psychology, 17*, 145–148.

Jaeckel, E. (1972). *Hitler's world view.* Middletown, CT: Wesleyan University Press.

James, W. (1890). *Principles of psychology.* New York: Henry Holt.

James, W. (1955). *Pragmatism and other essays.* New York: World Publishing Co. (Original work published 1907.)

James, W. (1962). *Psychology: Briefer course.* New York: Collier Books. (Original work published 1892.)

Janis, I. L. (1983). *Groupthink: Psychological studies of policy decisions and fiascos.* Boston: Houghton Mifflin.

Jankowicz, A. D. (1987). Whatever happened to George Kelly? Applications and implications. *American Psychologist, 42*, 481–487.

Janoff-Bulman, R., & Brickman, P. (1982). Expectations and what people learn from failure. In N. Feather (Ed.), *Expectations and actions: Expectancy-value models in psychology* (pp. 207–237). Hillsdale, NJ: Erlbaum.

Janoff-Bulman, R., & Frieze, I. (1983). A theoretical perspective for understanding reactions to victimization. *Journal of Social Issues, 39(2)*, 1–17.

Japan's success? It's in the blood. (1985, April 1). *Newsweek*, p. 45.

Jefferson, T. (1944). A bill for establishing religious freedom. In P. S. Foner (Ed.), *Basic writings of Thomas Jefferson.* New York: Wiley. (Original work published 1779.)

Jemmott, J. B., III, & Locke, S. E. (1984). Psychosocial factors, immunologic mediation, and human susceptibility to infectious diseases: How much do we know? *Psychological Bulletin, 95*, 78–108.

Jencks, C. (1968). *The academic revolution.* Garden City, NY: Doubleday.

Jencks, C. (1980). Heredity, environment, and public policy reconsidered. *American Sociological Review, 45*, 723–736.

Jencks, C. (1987, February 12). Genes and crime. *New York Review of Books*, pp. 33–41.

Jenkins, S. R. (1982). *Person-situation interaction and women's achievement-related motives.* Unpublished doctoral dissertation, Boston University.

Jenkins, S. R. (1994). Need for power and women's careers over 14 years: Structural power, job satisfaction, and motive change. *Journal of Personality and Social Psychology, 66*, 155–165.

John, O. P. (1989). Towards a taxonomy of personality descriptors. In D. Buss & N. Cantor (Eds.), *Personality psychology: Recent trends and emerging directions* (pp. 261–271). New York: Springer-Verlag.

John, O. P. (1990). The "Big Five" factor taxonomy: Dimensions of personality in the nature of language and in questionnaires. In L. Pervin (Ed.), *Handbook of personality theory and research* (pp. 66–100). New York: Guilford Press.

John, O. P., & Robins, R. W. (1994). Accuracy and bias in self-perception: Individual differences in self-enhancement and the role of narcissism. *Journal of Personality and Social Psychology, 66*, 206–219.

John, O. P., Robins, R. W., & O'Reilly, C. (1994). *Narcissists and people with self-enhancing illusions do not do better in their careers: A five-year study of M.B.A. students.* Unpublished paper, Institute of Personality and Social Research, University of California, Berkeley.

John, O. P., Winter, D. G., Stewart, A. J., Klohnen, E., Duncan, L., & Peterson, B. E. (1993). *Motives and traits: Toward an integration of two traditions in personality research.* Unpublished paper, University of California, Berkeley, and University of Michigan.

Johnston, R. A. (1955). The effects of achievement imagery on maze-learning performance. *Journal of Personality, 24*, 145–152.

Joll, J. (1968). *1914: The unspoken assumptions.* London: Weidenfeld & Nicolson.

Jones, D. F. (1969). *The need for power as a predictor of leadership and exploitation in a variety of small group settings.* Unpublished honors thesis, Wesleyan University.

Jones, E. (1949). *Hamlet and Oedipus.* New York: Norton.

Jones, E. (1953–1957). *The life and work of Sigmund Freud* (3 vols.). London: Hogarth Press.

Jones, E. E., & Nisbett, R. E. (1972). The actor and the observer: Divergent perceptions of the causes of behavior. In E. E. Jones, D. E. Kanouse, H. H. Kelley, R. E. Nisbett, S. Valins, & B. Weiner (Eds.), *Attribution: Perceiving the causes of behavior.* Morristown, NJ: General Learning Press.

Jones, M. C. (1924). A laboratory study of fear: The case of Peter. *Pedagogical Seminary, 31*, 308–315.

Joseph, G. I. (1981). Black mothers and daughters: Their roles and functions in modern American society. In G. I. Josephs and J. Lewis, *Common differences: Conflicts in black and white feminist perspectives* (pp. 75–126). Garden City, NY: Anchor/Doubleday.

Julianelli, J. (1972, November). Maya Angelou. *Harper's Bazaar,* p. 124.

Jung, C. G. (1971). A contribution to the study of psychological types. In H. Read, M. Fundham, G. Adler, & W. McGuire (Eds.), *The collected works of C. G. Jung* (vol. 6, pp. 499–509). Princeton, NJ: Princeton University Press. (Original work published 1913.)

Jung, C. G. (1971). *Psychological types.* In H. Read, M. Fundham, G. Adler, & W. McGuire (Eds.), *The collected works of C. G. Jung* (vol. 6, pp. 1–495). Princeton, NJ: Princeton University Press. (Original work published 1923.)

Jung, C. G. (1971). Psychological types. In H. Read, M. Fundham, G. Adler, & W. McGuire (Eds.), *The collected works of C. G. Jung* (vol. 6, pp. 510–523). Princeton, NJ: Princeton University Press. (Original work published 1925.)

Jung, C. G. (1971). A psychological theory of types. In H. Read, M. Fundham, G. Adler, & W. McGuire (Eds.), *The collected works of C. G. Jung* (vol. 6, pp. 524–541). Princeton, NJ: Princeton University Press. (Original work published 1931.)

Jung, C. G. (1971). Psychological typology. In H. Read, M. Fundham, G. Adler, & W. McGuire (Eds.), *The collected works of C. G. Jung* (vol. 6, pp. 542–555). Princeton, NJ: Princeton University Press. (Original work published 1936.)

Jung, C. G. (1973). The association method. In H. Read, M. Fundham, G. Adler, & W. McGuire (Eds.), *The collected works of C. G. Jung* (vol. 2, pp. 439–463). Princeton, NJ: Princeton University Press. (Original work published 1910.)

Jung, C. G. (1973). *Memories, dreams, reflections* (rev. ed.). New York: Pantheon.

Jung, C. G. (1973). On the doctrine of complexes. In H. Read, M. Fundham, G. Adler, & W. McGuire (Eds.), *The collected works of C. G. Jung* (vol. 2, pp. 598–604). Princeton, NJ: Princeton University Press. (Original work published 1913.)

Kagan, J. (1989). Temperamental contributions to social behavior. *American Psychologist, 44*, 668–674.

Kahl, J. (1957). *The American class structure.* New York: Rinehart.

Kahneman, D., Slovic, P., & Tversky, A. (1982). *Judgment under uncertainty: Heuristics and biases.* Cambridge: Cambridge University Press.

Kant, I. (1948). *The moral law: Kant's groundwork of the metaphysic of morals* (Ed. H. J. Paton). London: Hutchinson & Co. (Original work published 1785.)

Kass, L. R. (1983). The case for mortality. *American Scholar, 52*, 173–191.

Katz, J. (1967). President Kennedy's assassination: Freudian comments. *Journal of Individual Psychology, 23*, 20–23.

Kay, J. (1989). The Maya character. In J. M. Elliot (Ed.), *Conversations with Maya Angelou* (pp. 194–200). Jackson, MS: University Press of Mississippi. (Original work published 1987.)

Kazantzakes, N. (1953). *Zorba the Greek.* New York: Simon & Schuster.

Keller, H. (1894, January 4). My story. *The Youth's Companion,* pp. 3–4.

Keller, H. (1903a). *Optimism, an essay.* New York: Crowell.

Keller, H. (1903b). *The story of my life.* New York: Doubleday, Page.

Keller, H. (1908). *The world I live in.* New York: Doubleday.

Keller, H. A. (1929). *Midstream: My later life.* Garden City, NY: Doubleday.

Keller, H. (1955). *Teacher: Anne Sullivan Macy.* Garden City, NY: Doubleday.

Kelley, H. H. (1973). The processes of causal attribution. *American Psychologist, 28*, 107–128.

Kelley, V. (1994). *Leading with my heart.* New York: Simon & Schuster.

Kelly, E. L., & Fiske, D. W. (1951). *The prediction of performance in clinical psychology.* Ann Arbor, MI: University of Michigan Press.

Kelly, G. A. (1955). *The psychology of personal constructs* (2 vols.). New York: Norton.

Kennedy, J. F. (1962, March 21). News conference. *Public papers of the president of the United States: John F. Kennedy: 1962* (pp. 254–261). Washington, DC: Government Printing Office.

Kennedy, J. F. (1963, June 10). Commencement address at American University. *Public papers of the president of the United States: John F. Kennedy: 1963* (pp. 459–464). Washington, DC: Government Printing Office.

Kennedy, P. M. (1987). *The rise and fall of the great powers: Economic change and military conflict from 1500 to 2000.* New York: Random House.

Kenny, D. A., Albright, L., Malloy, T. E., & Kashy, D. A. (1994). Consensus in interpersonal perception: Acquaintance and the Big Five. *Psychological Bulletin, 116*, 245–258.

Kenrick, D. T., & Braver, S. L. (1982). Personality: Idiographic and nomothetic! A rejoinder. *Psychological Review, 87,* 88–104.

Kenrick, D. T., & Stringfield, D. O. (1980). Personality traits and the eye of the beholder: Crossing some traditional philosophical boundaries in the search for consistency in all of the people. *Psychological Review, 87,* 88–104.

Kerlinger, F., & Rokeach, M. (1966). The factorial nature of the F and D scales. *Journal of Personality and Social Psychology, 4,* 391–399.

Keynes, J. M. (1936). *The general theory of employment, interest and money.* New York: Harcourt Brace.

Kiehl, N. (1963). *Psychoanalysis, psychology and literature: A bibliography.* Madison, WI: University of Wisconsin Press.

Kiesler, D. J. (1983). The 1982 interpersonal circle: A taxonomy for complementarity in human transactions. *Psychological Review, 90,* 185–214.

Kihlstrom, J. F. (1987). The cognitive unconscious. *Science, 237,* 1445–1452.

Kihlstrom, J., & Cantor, N. (1984). Mental representations of the self. In L. Berkowitz (Ed.), *Advances in experimental social psychology* (vol. 17, pp. 1–47). New York: Academic Press.

Kinder, D. R., & Mebane, W. R., Jr. (1983). Politics and economics in everyday life. In K. R. Monroe (Ed.), *The political process and economic change* (pp. 141–180). New York: Agathon.

King, M. L., Jr. (1986). Letter from Birmingham city jail. In J. M. Washington (Ed.), *A testament of hope: The essential writings of Martin Luther King, Jr.* (pp. 289–302). San Francisco: Harper & Row. (Original work published 1963.)

Kipnis, D. (1976). *The powerholders.* Chicago: University of Chicago Press.

Kirkpatrick, I. (1964). *Mussolini: a study in power.* New York: Hawthorn Books.

Kissinger, H. (1979). *White House years.* Boston: Little, Brown.

Kissinger, H. (1982). *Years of upheaval.* Boston: Little, Brown.

Kissinger, H. (1994). *Diplomacy.* New York: Simon & Schuster.

Klein, H. G. (1980). *Making it perfectly clear.* Garden City, NY: Doubleday.

Klein, H. M., & Willerman, L. (1979). Psychological masculinity and femininity and typical and maximal dominance expression in women. *Journal of Personality and Social Psychology, 37,* 2059–2070.

Klein, M. (1948). *Contributions to psychoanalysis 1921–1945.* London: Hogarth.

Kline, P. (1972). *Fact and fantasy in Freudian theory.* London: Methuen.

Klinger, E. (1966). Fantasy need achievement as a motivational construct. *Psychological Bulletin, 66,* 291–308.

Klinger, E. (1987). Current concerns and disengagement from incentives. In F. Halisch & J. Kuhl (Eds.), *Motivation, intention and volition* (pp. 337–347). New York: Springer-Verlag.

Klohnen, E. C. (1994). *The construct of ego-resiliency: Conceptual analysis and measurement.* Unpublished paper, University of California, Berkeley.

Kluckhohn, C. K. M. (1959). *Mirror for man.* New York: Fawcett Library.

Kluckhohn, C. K. M., & Murray, H. A. (1953). Personality formation: The determinants. In C. K. M. Kluckhohn, H. A. Murray, & D. Schneider (Eds.), *Personality in nature, culture, and society* (pp. 53–67). New York: Knopf.

Kluckhohn, C. K. M., Murray, H. A., & Schneider, D. M. (1953). *Personality in nature, culture and society.* New York: Knopf.

Kluckhohn, F. R., & Strodtbeck, F. L. (1961). *Variations in value orientations.* Evanston, IL: Row, Peterson.

Knapp, R. H. (1958). *N* Achievement and aesthetic preference. In J. W. Atkinson (Ed.), *Motives in fantasy, action and society* (pp. 367–372). Princeton, NJ: Van Nostrand.

Knutson, J. (1974). *Psychological variables in political recruitment: An analysis of party activists.* Unpublished paper, Wright Institute, Berkeley, CA.

Kock, S. W. (1965). *Management and motivation.* Unpublished Ph.D. thesis, Swedish School of Economics, Helsinki.

Koestner, R., Franz, C., & Hellman, C. (1991). *Life changes and the reliability of TAT motive assessment.* Unpublished paper, Boston University.

Koestner, R., & McClelland, D. C. (1992). The affiliation motive. In C. P. Smith (Ed.), *Motivation and personality: Handbook of thematic content analysis* (pp. 205–210). New York: Cambridge University Press.

Kohlberg, L. (1963). The development of children's orientations toward a moral order: I. Sequence in the development of moral thought. *Vita Humana, 6,* 11–33.

Kohlberg, L. A. (1966). Cognitive-developmental analysis of children's sex-role concepts and attitudes. In E. E. Maccoby (Ed.), *The development of sex differences* (pp. 82–173). Stanford, CA: Stanford University Press.

Kohlberg, L. (1981–1984). *Essays on moral development* (2 vols.). New York: Harper & Row.

Kohlberg, L., Levine, C., & Hewer, A. (1983). *Moral stages: A current formulation and a response to critics. Contributions to human development* (vol. 10). Basel & New York: Karger.

Kohn, M. L. (1989). Social structure and personality: A quintessentially sociological approach to social psychology. *Social Forces, 68,* 26–33.

Kohn, M. L., Naoi, A., Schoenbach, C., Schooler, C., & Slomczynski, K. M. (1990). Position in the class structure and psychological functioning in the United States, Japan, and Poland. *American Journal of Sociology, 95,* 964–1008.

Kohut, H. (1985). *Self psychology and the humanities.* New York: Norton.

Kornadt, H.-J., Eckensberger, L. H., & Emminghaus, W. B. (1980). Cross-cultural research on motivation and its contribution to a general theory of motivation. In H. C. Triandis & W. Lonner (Eds.), *Handbook of cross-cultural psychology* (vol. 3, pp. 223–321). Boston: Allyn & Bacon.

Kornitzer, B. (1960). *The real Nixon: An intimate biography.* Chicago: Rand McNally.

Kris, E. (1952). *Psychoanalytic explorations in art.* New York: International Universities Press.

Kroeber, T. C. (1963). The coping function of the ego mechanisms. In R. W. White (Ed.), *The study of lives* (pp. 178–198). New York: Atherton.

Kuhn, M. H., & McPartland, T. A. (1954). An empirical investigation of self attitudes. *American Sociological Review, 19,* 68–76.

LaFrance, M., & Mayo, C. (1978). *Moving bodies: Nonverbal communication in social relationships.* Monterey, CA: Brooks/Cole.

Lakoff, R. (1979). Stylistic strategies within a grammar of style. *Annals of the New York Academy of Sciences, 327,* 53–80.

Lamiell, J. T. (1981). Toward an idiothetic psychology of personality. *American Psychologist, 36,* 276–289.

Langer, W. (1972). *The mind of Adolf Hitler: The secret wartime report.* New York: Basic Books.

Lansing, J. B., & Heyns, R. W. (1959). Need affiliation and frequency of four types of communication. *Journal of Abnormal and Social Psychology, 58,* 365–372.

Larsen, R. J., & Diener, E. (1992). Promises and problems with the circumplex model of emotion. *Review of Personality and Social Psychology* (vol. 13, pp. 25–59). Beverly Hills, CA: Sage.

Larson, C. A. (1978). Some further notes on the "rat-rabbit" problem and John B. Watson. *Teaching of Psychology, 5,* 35–36.

Lasch, C. L. (1979). *The culture of narcissism.* New York: Norton.

Lash, J. (1993). *Twins and the double.* London: Thames and Hudson.

Lash, J. P. (1980). *Helen and teacher: The story of Helen Keller and Anne Sullivan Macy.* New York: Delacorte Press.

Lasky, J. J., Hover, G. L., Smith, P. A., Bostian, D. W., Duffendack, S. C., & Nord, C. L. (1959). Post-hospital adjustment as predicted by psychiatric patients and by their staff. *Journal of Consulting Psychology, 23,* 213–218.

Lasswell, H. (1930). *Psychopathology and politics.* Chicago: University of Chicago Press.

Lazarus, R. S. (1982). Thoughts on the relation between cognition and emotion. *American Psychologist, 37,* 1019–1024.

Lazarus, R. S. (1985). On the primacy of cognition. *American Psychologist, 39,* 124–129.

Leavis, F. R. (1952). *The common pursuit.* London: Chatto & Windus.

Lee, V. E., & Bryk, A. S. (1986). Effects of single-sex secondary schools on student achievement and attitudes. *Journal of Educational Psychology, 78,* 381–395.

Lee, V. E., & Marks, H. M. (1990). Sustained effects of the single-sex secondary school experience on attitudes, behaviors, and values in college. *Journal of Educational Psychology, 82,* 578–592.

Leeper, R. (1935). A study of a neglected portion of the field of learning—the development of sensory organization. *Journal of Genetic Psychology, 46,* 41–75.

Lefcourt, H. M. (1976). *Locus of control: Current trends in theory and research.* Hillsdale, NJ: Erlbaum.

Lefcourt, H. M. (1981–1984). *Research with the locus of control construct* (3 vols.). New York: Academic Press.

Lehmann, J. (1975). *Virginia Woolf.* San Diego, CA: Harcourt Brace Jovanovich.

Leitner, L. M. (1985). Interview methodologies for construct elicitation: Searching for the core. In F. Epting & A. W. Landfield (Eds.), *Anticipating personal construct psychology* (pp. 292–305). Lincoln, NE: University of Nebraska Press.

Lemann, N. (1991). *The promised land: The great Black migration and how it changed America.* New York: Knopf.

Lemann, N. (1994, February). Is there a science of success? *Atlantic Monthly,* pp. 82–98.

Lessing, E. E. (1969). Racial differences in indices of ego functioning relevant to academic achievement. *Journal of Genetic Psychology, 115,* 153–167.

LeUnes, A. (1983). Little Albert from the viewpoint of abnormal psychology textbook authors. *Teaching of Psychology, 10,* 230–231.

LeVine, R. A. (1966). *Dreams and deeds: Achievement motivation in Nigeria.* Chicago: University of Chicago Press.

LeVine, R. A. (1982). *Culture, behavior and personality* (2nd ed.). Chicago: Aldine.

Levinson, D. J. (1978). *The seasons of a man's life.* New York: Knopf.

Levinson, M. H. (1950). Psychological ill health in relation to potential fascism: A study of psychiatric clinic patients. In T. W. Adorno, E. Frenkel-Brunswik, D. J. Levinson, & R. N. Sanford, *The authoritarian personality* (pp. 891–970). New York: Harper & Row.

Lewin, K. (1935). *A dynamic theory of personality.* New York: McGraw-Hill.

Lewinsohn, P. M., Steinmetz, J. L., Larson, D. W., & Franklin, J. (1981). Depression-related cognitions: Antecedent or consequence? *Journal of Abnormal Psychology, 90,* 213–219.

Liem, J. H., O'Toole, J. G., & James, J. B. (1992). The need for power in women who were sexually abused as children. *Psychology of Women Quarterly, 16,* 467–480.

Lindzey, G., & Aronson, E. (Eds.). (1985). *Handbook of social psychology* (3rd ed.). New York: Random House.

Lipset, S. M. (1963). Working class authoritarianism. In *Political man: The social bases of politics* (pp. 87–126). Garden City, NY: Doubleday (Anchor Books). (Original work published 1960.)

Little, B. R. (1989). Personal projects analysis: Trivial pursuits, magnificent obsessions, and the search for coherence. In D. Buss & N. Cantor (Eds.), *Personality psychology: Recent trends and emerging directions* (pp. 15–31). New York: Springer-Verlag.

Little, B. R., Lecci, L., & Watkinson, B. (1992). Personality and personal projects: Linking Big Five and PAC units of analysis. *Journal of Personality, 60,* 501–525.

Loehlin, J. C., & Nichols, R. C. (1976). *Heredity, environment, and personality.* Austin, TX: University of Texas Press.

Loevinger, J. (1966). The meaning and measurement of ego development. *American Psychologist, 21,* 195–206.

Loevinger, J. (1976). *Ego development: Conceptions and theories.* San Francisco: Jossey-Bass.

Loevinger, J. (1979). Construct validity of the sentence-completion test of ego development. *Applied Psychological Measurement, 3,* 281–311.

Loevinger, J. (1987). *Paradigms of personality.* New York: W. H. Freeman.

Lundy, A. (1985). The reliability of the Thematic Apperception Test. *Journal of Personality Assessment, 49,* 141–145.

Lykes, M. B. (1985). Gender and individualistic vs. collectivistic bases for notions about the self. *Journal of Personality, 53,* 356–383.

Lynn, R. (1981). Cross-cultural differences in neuroticism, extraversion and psychoticism. In R. Lynn (Ed.), *Dimensions of personality: Essays in honour of H. J. Eysenck* (pp. 263–286). Oxford, England: Pergamon Press.

Lynn, R., & Hampson, S. L. (1975). National differences in extraversion and neuroticism. *British Journal of Social and Clinical Psychology, 14,* 223–240.

McAdams, D. P. (1982). Intimacy motivation. In A. J. Stewart (Ed.), *Motivation and society* (pp. 133–171). San Francisco: Jossey-Bass.

McAdams, D. P. (1985). *Power, intimacy, and the life story.* Homewood, IL: Dorsey.

McAdams, D. P. (1990a). *The person: An introduction to personality psychology.* San Diego, CA: Harcourt Brace Jovanovich.

McAdams, D. P. (1990b). Unity and purpose in human lives: The emergence of identity as a life story. In A. I. Rabin, R. A. Zucker, R. A. Emmons, & S. Frank (Eds.), *Studying persons and lives* (pp. 148–200). New York: Springer Publishing Company.

McAdams, D. P. (1992a). The five-factor model in personality: A critical appraisal. *Journal of Personality, 60,* 329–361.

McAdams, D. P. (1992b). The intimacy motive. In C. P. Smith (Ed.), *Motivation and personality: Handbook of thematic content analysis* (pp. 224–228). New York: Cambridge University Press.

McAdams, D. P. (1993). *Stories we live by: Personal myths and the making of the self.* New York: Morrow.

McAdams, D. P., & Bryant, F. B. (1987). Intimacy motivation and subjective mental health in a nationwide sample. *Journal of Personality, 55,* 395–413.

McAdams, D. P., & Constantian, C. (1983). Intimacy and affiliation motives in daily living: An experience sampling analysis. *Journal of Personality and Social Psychology, 45,* 851–861.

McAdams, D. P., & de St. Aubin, E. (1992). A theory of generativity and its assessment through self-report, behavioral acts, and narrative themes in autobiography. *Journal of Personality and Social Psychology, 62,* 1003–1015.

McAdams, D. P., Jackson, R. J., & Kirshnit, C. (1984). Looking, laughing, and smiling in dyads as a function of intimacy motivation and reciprocity. *Journal of Personality, 52,* 261–273.

McAdams, D. P., & Ochberg, R. L. (Eds.) (1988). Psychobiography and life narratives. Special issue. *Journal of Personality, 56(1).*

McAdams, D. P., & Vaillant, G. E. (1982). Intimacy motivation and psychosocial adjustment: A longitudinal study. *Journal of Personality Assessment, 46,* 586–593.

McArthur, L. A. (1972). The how of what and why: Some determinants and consequences of causal attributions. *Journal of Personality and Social Psychology, 22,* 171–193.

McClelland, D. C. (1951). *Personality.* New York: Holt, Rinehart & Winston.

McClelland, D. C. (1961). *The achieving society.* Princeton, NJ: Van Nostrand.

McClelland, D. C. (1963). Motivational patterns in Southeast Asia with special reference to the Chinese case. *Journal of Social Issues, 19(1),* 6–19.

McClelland, D. C. (1975). *Power: The inner experience.* New York: Irvington.

McClelland, D. C. (1979). Inhibited power motivation and high blood pressure in men. *Journal of Abnormal Psychology, 88,* 182–190.

McClelland, D. C. (1980). Motive dispositions: The merits of operant and respondent measures. In L. Wheeler (Ed.), *Review of personality and social psychology* (vol. 1, pp. 10–41). Beverly Hills, CA: Sage.

McClelland, D. C. (1981). Is personality consistent? In A. I. Rabin, J. Aronoff, A. M. Barclay, & R. A. Zucker (Eds.), *Further explorations in personality* (pp. 87–113). New York: Wiley.

McClelland, D. C. (1982). The need for power, sympathetic activation, and illness. *Motivation and Emotion, 6,* 31–41.

McClelland, D. C. (1984a). Motives as sources of long-term trends in life and health. In *Motives, personality, and society: Selected papers* (pp. 343–364). New York: Praeger.

McClelland, D. C. (1984b). Summary: My view of my main contributions. In *Motives, personality, and society: Selected papers* (pp. 447–466). New York: Praeger.

McClelland, D. C. (1985). *Human motivation.* Glenview, IL: Scott, Foresman.

McClelland, D. C. (1986). Some reflections of the two psychologies of love. *Journal of Personality, 54,* 334–353.

McClelland, D. C. (1989). Motivational factors in health and disease. *American Psychologist, 44,* 675–683.

McClelland, D. C., & Atkinson, J. W. (1948). The projective expression of needs. I. The effect of different intensities of the hunger drive on perception. *Journal of Psychology, 25,* 205–232.

McClelland, D. C., Atkinson, J. W., Clark, R. A., & Lowell, E. L. (1953). *The achievement motive.* New York: Appleton-Century-Crofts.

McClelland, D. C., & Boyatzis, R. E. (1982). The leadership motive pattern and long-term success in management. *Journal of Applied Psychology, 67,* 737–743.

McClelland, D. C., & Burnham, D. H. (1976, March-April). Power is the great motivator. *Harvard Business Review,* pp. 100–110, 159–166.

McClelland, D. C., Davis, W. N., Kalin, R., & Wanner, E. (1972). *The drinking man.* New York: Free Press.

McClelland, D. C., & Franz, C. E. (1992). Motivational and other sources of work accomplishments in mid-life: A longitudinal study. *Journal of Personality, 60,* 679–707.

McClelland, D. C., & Koestner, R. (1992). The achievement motive. In C. P. Smith (Ed.), *Motivation and personality: Handbook of thematic content analysis* (pp. 143–152). New York: Cambridge University Press.

McClelland, D. C., Koestner, R., & Weinberger, J. (1989). How do self-attributed and implicit motives differ? *Psychological Review, 96,* 690–702.

McClelland, D. C., & Teague, G. (1975). Predicting risk preferences among power-related tasks. *Journal of Personality, 43,* 266–285.

McClelland, D. C., & Watson, R. I., Jr. (1973). Power motivation and risk-taking behavior. *Journal of Personality, 41,* 121–139.

McClelland, D. C., & Winter, D. G. (1969). *Motivating economic achievement.* New York: Free Press.

McCrae, R. R. (1989). Why I advocate the five-factor model: Joint factor analyses of the NEO-PI with other instruments. In D. Buss & N. Cantor (Eds.), *Personality psychology: Recent trends and emerging directions* (pp. 237–245). New York: Springer-Verlag.

McCrae, R. R., & Costa, P. T. (1984). *Emerging lives, enduring dispositions.* Boston: Little, Brown.

McCrae, R. R., & Costa, P. T. (1985). Comparison of EPI and psychoticism scales with measures of the five-factor model of personality. *Personality and Individual Differences, 6,* 587–597.

McCrae, R. R., & Costa, P. T. (1987). Validation of the five-factor model of personality across instruments and observers. *Journal of Personality and Social Psychology, 52,* 81–90.

McCrae, R. R., & Costa, P. T. (1989). Reinterpreting the Myers-Briggs Type Indicator from the perspective of the five-factor model of personality. *Journal of Personality, 57,* 17–40.

McCrae, R. R., & John, O. P. (1992). An introduction to the five-factor model and its applications. *Journal of Personality, 60,* 175–215.

MacDonald, K. (1991). A perspective on Darwinian psychology: The importance of domain-general mechanisms, plasticity, and individual differences. *Ethology and Sociobiology, 12,* 449–480.

McDougall, W. (1908). *An introduction to social psychology.* London: Methuen.

McFarland, S. G., Ageyev, V. S., & Abalakina, M. A. (1992a). The authoritarian personality in the United States and the former Soviet Union: Comparative studies. In W. F. Stone, G. Lederer, & R. Christie (Eds.), *Strength and weakness: The authoritarian personality today* (pp. 199–225). New York: Springer-Verlag.

McFarland, S. G., Ageyev, V. S., & Abalakina-Paap, M. A. (1992b). Authoritarianism in the former Soviet Union. *Journal of Personality and Social Psychology, 63,* 1004–1010.

McFarland, S. G., Ageyev, V. S., Abalakina-Paap, M. A., & Djintcharadze, N. (1993, July). *Why are Russians less authoritarian than Americans?* Paper presented at the annual meeting of the International Society of Political Psychology, Cambridge, MA.

McFarland, S. G., Ageyev, V. S., & Djintcharadze, N. (1996). Russian authoritarianism two years after Communism. *Personality and Social Psychology Bulletin., 22,* 210–217.

McGuire, W. (Ed.) (1974). *The Freud/Jung letters.* Princeton, NJ: Princeton University Press.

McGuire, W. J., & Padawer-Singer, A. (1976). Trait salience in the spontaneous self-concept. *Journal of Personality and Social Psychology, 33,* 743–754.

McKeachie, W. J. (1961). Motivation, teaching methods, and college learning. In M. R. Jones (Ed.), *Nebraska symposium on motivation 1961* (pp. 111–142). Lincoln, NE: University of Nebraska Press.

MacKinnon, C. A. (1987a). Desire and power. In *Feminism unmodified: Discourses on life and law* (pp. 46–62). Cambridge, MA: Harvard University Press.

MacKinnon, C. A. (1987b). Difference and dominance: On sex discrimination. In *Feminism unmodified: Discourses on life and law* (pp. 32–45). Cambridge, MA: Harvard University Press.

MacKinnon, D. W. (1965). Personality and the realization of creative potential. *American Psychologist, 20,* 273–281.

McMillan, P. J. (1977). *Marina and Lee.* New York: Harper & Row.

McNemar, Q. (1952). Review of *The prediction of performance in clinical psychology. Journal of Abnormal and Social Psychology, 47,* 857–860.

Macy, J. A. (1903). A supplementary account of Helen Keller's life and education. In H. Keller, *The story of my life* (pp. 281–431). New York: Doubleday, Page.

Magnusson, D. (Ed.) (1981). *Toward a psychology of situations: An interactional perspective.* Hillsdale, NJ: Erlbaum.

Magnusson, D. (1990). Personality development from an interactional perspective. In L. Pervin (Ed.), *Handbook of personality theory and research* (pp. 193–222). New York: Guilford Press.

Magnusson, D., & Endler, N. S. (1977). *Personality at the crossroads: Current issues in interactional psychology.* Hillsdale, NJ: Erlbaum.

Mahler, M. S., Pine, F., & Bergman, A. (1975). *The psychological birth of the human infant.* New York: Basic Books.

Mailer, N. (1972). *St. George and the godfather.* New York: Signet Books.

Malinowski, B. (1927). *Sex and repression in savage society.* New York: Harcourt, Brace.

Manegold, C. S. (1993, January 20). Inaugural wordsmith finds steel in the fire of memory. *New York Times,* pp. B1, B5.

Mangnall, R. C. (1984, October). Pisces out, type O in. *Psychology Today,* p. 88.

Mannheim, K. (1952). The problem of generations. In *Essays on the sociology of knowledge.* New York: Oxford University Press. (Original work published 1928.)

Mao Zedong. (1966). *Quotations from Chairman Mao Tse-Tung.* Beijing: Foreign Languages Press.

Marcia, J. E. (1966). Development and validation of ego-identity status. *Journal of Personality and Social Psychology, 3,* 551–558.

Marcia, J. E., Waterman, A. S., Matteson, D. R., Archer, S. L., & Orlofsky, J. L. (1993). *Ego identity: A handbook for psychosocial research.* New York: Springer-Verlag.

Margolis, L. (1994, August). Sex, death and kefir. *Scientific American, 271(2),* 96.

Markus, H. (1977). Self-schemata and processing information about the self. *Journal of Personality and Social Psychology, 35,* 63–78.

Markus, H. R., & Kitayama, S. (1991). Culture and the self: Implications for cognition, emotion, and motivation. *Psychological Review, 98,* 224–253.

Markus, H. R., & Kitayama, S. (1992). The what, why, and how of cultural psychology: A review of Shweder's *Thinking through cultures. Psychological Inquiry, 3,* 357–364.

Markus, H., & Nurius, P. (1986). Possible selves. *American Psychologist, 41,* 954–969.

Markus, H., & Ruvolo, A. (1989). Possible selves: Personalized representations of goals. In L. Pervin (Ed.), *Goal concepts in personality and social psychology* (pp. 211–241). Hillsdale, NJ: Erlbaum.

Markus, H., & Sentis, K. (1982). The self in social information processing. In J. Suls (Ed.), *Psychological perspectives on the self* (vol. 1, pp. 41–70). Hillsdale, NJ: Erlbaum.

Marrow, A. J. (1969). *The practical theorist: The life and work of Kurt Lewin.* New York: Basic Books.

Martin, A. (1975). *The effect of subliminal stimulation of symbiotic fantasies on weight loss in obese women receiving behavioral treatment.* Unpublished Ph.D. thesis, New York University.

Martin, N. H., & Sims, J. H. (1956, November–December). Power tactics. *Harvard Business Review* (pp. 25ff.). Reprinted in D. A. Kolb, I. M. Rubin, & J. M. McIntyre (Eds.), *Organizational psychology: A book of readings* (pp. 155–161). Englewood Cliffs, NJ: Prentice-Hall, 1971.

Masling, J. M. (Ed.). (1983–1990). *Empirical studies of psychoanalytic theories* (3 vols.). Hillsdale, NJ: Erlbaum.

Maslow, A. H. (1954). *Motivation and personality.* New York: Harper.

Maslow, A. H. (1968). *Toward a psychology of being* (2nd ed.). Princeton, NJ: Van Nostrand.

Maslow, A. H. (1970). *Motivation and personality* (2nd ed.). New York: Harper & Row.

Mason, A., & Blankenship, V. (1987). Power and affiliation motivation, stress, and abuse in intimate relationships. *Journal of Personality and Social Psychology, 52,* 203–210.

Mathew, R. J., Ho, B. T., Taylor, D. L., & Semchuk, K. M. (1981). Catecholamine and dopamine-beta-hydroxylase in anxiety. *Journal of Psychosomatic Research, 25,* 499–504.

Matthews, K. (1982). Psychological perspectives on the Type A behavior pattern. *Psychological Bulletin, 91,* 293–323.

Matthews, K. (1988). CHD and Type A behavior: Update on and alternative to the Booth-Kewley and Friedman quantitative review. *Psychological Bulletin, 104,* 373–380.

Mazlish, B. (1973). *In search of Nixon: A psychohistorical inquiry.* New York: Penguin Books. (Original work published 1972.)

Mead, G. H. (1968). The genesis of the self and social control. In C. Gordon & K. J. Gergen (Eds.), *The self in social interaction* (pp. 51–59). New York: Wiley. (Original work published 1925.)

Mead, M. (1965). *And keep your powder dry* (expanded ed.). New York: Morrow.

Meagher, S. (1967). *Accessories after the fact: The Warren Commission, the authorities, and the report.* Indianapolis: Bobbs-Merrill.

Mehrabian, A. (1969). Measures of achieving tendency. *Educational and Psychological Measurement, 29,* 445–451.

Meier, A., & Rudwick, E. (1986). *Black history and the historical profession, 1915–1980.* Urbana, IL: University of Illinois Press.

Meloen, J. D. (1990, July). *The emperor's new clothes? The authoritarianism concepts of Adorno et al. and Altemeyer tested.* Paper presented at the annual meeting of the International Society of Political Psychology, Washington, DC.

Meloen, J. D., Farnen, R., & German, D. (1993, July). *Authoritarianism, democracy and symbolic political leadership in the new world order.* Paper presented at the annual meeting of the International Society of Political Psychology, Cambridge, MA.

Meloen, J. D., Hagendoorn, L., Raaijmakers, Q., & Visser, L. (1988). Authoritarianism and the revival of political racism: Reassessments in the Netherlands of the reliability and validity of the concept of authoritarianism by Adorno et al. *Political Psychology , 9,* 413–429.

Melton, A. W. (1952). Motivation and learning. In W. S. Monroe (Ed.), *Encyclopedia of educational research.* New York: Macmillan. Reprinted in D. C. McClelland (Ed.), *Studies in motivation* (pp. 424–427). New York: Appleton-Century-Crofts, 1955 .

Merei, F. (1958). Group leadership and institutionalization. In E. E. Maccoby, T. M. Newcomb, & E. E. Hartley (Eds.), *Readings in social psychology* (3rd ed., pp. 522–532). New York: Holt, Rinehart & Winston. (Original work published 1949.)

Merydith, S. P., & Wallbrown, F. H. (1991). Reconsidering response sets, test-taking attitudes, dissimulation, self-deception, and social desirability. *Psychological Reports, 69,* 891–905.

Milbrath, L. (1986). Environmental beliefs and values. In M. G. Hermann (Ed.), *Political psychology: Contemporary issues and problems* (pp. 97–138). San Francisco: Jossey-Bass.

Milgram, S. (1963). Behavioral study of obedience. *Journal of Abnormal and Social Psychology, 67,* 371–378.

Milgram, S. (1975). *Obedience to authority.* New York: Harper & Row.

Miller, G. A. (1956). The magical number seven, plus or minus two: Some limits on our capacity for processing information. *Psychological Review, 63,* 81–97.

Miller, J. B. (1986). *Toward a new psychology of women* (2nd ed.). Boston: Beacon Press.

Miller, J. G. (1984). Culture and the development of everyday social explanation. *Journal of Personality and Social Psychology, 46,* 961–978.

Miller, N. E. (1959). Liberalization of basic S-R concepts: Extensions to conflict behavior, motivation and social learning. In S. Koch (Ed.), *Psychology: A study of a science* (vol. 2, pp. 196–292). New York: McGraw-Hill.

Miller, S. D. (1989). Optical differences in cases of multiple personality disorder. *Journal of Nervous and Mental Diseases, 177,* 480–486.

Millham, J., & Jacobson, L. I. (1978). Approval motivation. In H. London & J. Exner (Eds.), *Dimensions of personality* (pp. 365–390). New York: Wiley.

Mink, L. O. (1978). Narrative form as a cognitive instrument. In R. H. Canary & H. Kozicki (Eds.), *The writing of history: Literary form and historical understanding* (pp. 129–149). Madison, WI: University of Wisconsin Press.

Mischel, W. (1961). Delay of gratification, need for achievement, and acquiescence in another culture. *Journal of Abnormal and Social Psychology, 62,* 543–552.

Mischel, W. (1968). *Personality and assessment.* New York: Wiley.

Mischel, W. (1984). On the predictability of behavior and the structure of personality. In R. A. Zucker, J. Aronoff, & A. I. Rabin (Eds.), *Personality and the prediction of behavior* (pp. 269–305). Orlando, FL: Academic Press.

Mischel, W. (1993). *Introduction to personality* (5th ed.). Fort Worth, TX: Harcourt Brace Jovanovich.

Mischel, W., & Gilligan, C. (1964). Delay of gratification, motivation for the prohibited gratification, and responses to temptation. *Journal of Abnormal and Social Psychology, 69,* 411–417.

Mischel, W., & Shoda, Y. (1995). A cognitive-affective system theory of personality: Reconceptualizing situations, dispositions, dynamics, and invariance in personality structure. *Psychological Review, 102,* 246–268.

Monte, C. S. (1991). *Beneath the mask* (4th ed.). San Diego, CA: Harcourt Brace Jovanovich.

Morgan, C. D., & Murray, H. A. (1935). A method for examining fantasies: The Thematic Apperception Test. *Archives of Neurology and Psychiatry, 34,* 289–306.

Morgan, M. (1983). Symbolic victimization and real world fear. *Human Communication Research, 9,* 146–157.

Morris, J. L., & Fargher, K. (1974). Achievement drive and creativity as correlates of success in small business. *Australian Journal of Psychology, 26,* 217–222.

Moskowitz, D. S. (1982). Coherence and cross-situational generality in personality: A new analysis of old problems. *Journal of Personality and Social Psychology, 43,* 754–768.

Moskowitz, D. S. (1988). Cross-situational consistency in the laboratory: Dominance and friendliness. *Journal of Personality and Social Psychology, 54,* 829–839.

Munro, P. (Ed.). (1989). *U.C.L.A. Slang: A dictionary of slang words and expressions used at U.C.L.A. UCLA Occasional papers in Linguistics 8.* Los Angeles: Department of Linguistics, University of California, Los Angeles.

Murray, F. (1973). In search of Albert. . . . *Professional Psychology, 4,* 5–6.

Murray, H. A. (1933). The effects of fear upon estimates of the maliciousness of other personalities. *Journal of Social Psychology, 4,* 310–329.

Murray, H. A. (1937). Techniques for a systematic investigation of fantasy. *Journal of Psychology, 3,* 115–143.

Murray, H. A. (1938). *Explorations in personality.* New York: Oxford University Press.

Murray, H. A. (1981). E. S. Schneidman (Ed.), *Endeavors in psychology: Selections from the personology of Henry A. Murray.* New York: Harper & Row.

Murray, H. A. (1985, February). Letter to the editor. *Second Century: Radcliffe News,* p. 2. Cambridge, MA: Radcliffe College.

Murstein, B. (1963). *Theory and research in projective techniques (emphasizing the TAT).* New York: Wiley.

Myers, I. B. (1980). *Gifts differing.* Palo Alto, CA: Consulting Psychologists Press.

Nagata, D. K. (1993). *Legacy of injustice: Exploring the cross-generational effects of the Japanese American internment.* New York: Plenum.

Nails, D. (1983). Social-scientific sexism: Gilligan's mismeasure of man. *Social Research, 50,* 642–664.

Nandy, A. (1973). Motives, modernity and entrepreneurial competence. *Journal of Social Psychology, 91,* 127–136.

Narby, D. J., Cutler, B. L., & Moran, G. (1993). A meta-analysis of the association between authoritarianism and jurors' perceptions of defendant culpability. *Journal of Applied Psychology, 78,* 34–42.

Nathan, O., & Norden, H. (Eds.). (1960). *Einstein on peace.* New York: Simon & Schuster.

Nehru, J. (1948). *Nehru on Gandhi.* New York: John Day.

Neimeyer, R. A. (1985). Problems and prospects in personal construct theory. In D. Bannister (Ed.), *Issues and approaches in personal construct theory* (pp. 143–171). London: Academic Press.

Neustadt, R., & May, E. (1986). *Thinking in time: The uses of history for decision-makers.* New York: Free Press.

Nietzsche, F. (1967). *The birth of tragedy, and the case of Wagner.* New York: Vintage. (Original work published 1871.)

Nisbett, R. E. (1980). The trait construct in lay and professional psychology. In L. Festinger (Ed.), *Retrospections on social psychology* (pp. 109–130). New York: Oxford University Press.

Nisbett, R. E., & Wilson, T. D. (1977). Telling more than we can know: Verbal reports on mental processes. *Psychological Review, 84,* 231–259.

Nissen, H. W. (1930). A study of exploratory behavior in the white rat by means of the obstruction method. *Journal of Genetic Psychology, 37,* 361–376.

Nixon, R. M. (1962). *Six crises.* Garden City, NY: Doubleday.

Nixon, R. M. (1974, August 9). Remarks on departure from the White House. *Public Papers of the Presidents of the United States: Richard Nixon: 1974* (pp. 630–632). Washington, DC: Government Printing Office.

Nixon, R. M. (1978). *RN: The memoirs of Richard Nixon.* New York: Grosset & Dunlap.

Nixon, R. M. (1989). May 11, 1970 memo to H. R. Haldeman. In B. Oudes (Ed.), *From: The president: Richard*

Nixon's secret files (pp. 127–134). New York: Harper & Row.

Nixon, R. M. (1990). *In the arena: A memoir of victory, defeat, and renewal.* New York: Simon & Schuster.

Nolen-Hoeksema, S. (1987). Sex differences in unipolar depression: Evidence and theory. *Psychological Bulletin, 101,* 259–282.

Nolen-Hoeksema, S., Girgus, J. S., & Seligman, M. E. P. (1986). Learned helplessness in children: A longitudinal study of depression, achievement, and explanatory style. *Journal of Personality and Social Psychology, 51,* 435–442.

Nolen-Hoeksema, S., Girgus, J. S., & Seligman, M. E. P. (1992). Predictors and consequences of childhood depressive symptoms: A 5-year longitudinal study. *Journal of Abnormal Psychology, 101,* 405–422.

Norem, J. K., & Cantor, N. (1986). Defensive pessimism: Harnessing anxiety as motivation. *Journal of Personality and Social Psychology, 51,* 1208–1217.

Norman, W. T. (1963). Toward an adequate taxonomy of personality attributes: Replicated factor structure in peer nomination personality ratings. *Journal of Abnormal and Social Psychology, 66,* 574–583.

Nunberg, H., & Federn, E. (Eds.). (1962). *Minutes of the Vienna Psychoanalytic Society: I. 1906–1908.* New York: International Universities Press.

Nutt, P. C. (1979). Influences of decision styles on use of decision models. *Technological Forecasting and Social Change, 14,* 77–93.

Nuttall, R. L. (1964). Some correlates of high need achievement among urban northern Negroes. *Journal of Abnormal and Social Psy chology, 68,* 593–600.

Oates, J. C. (1994, May 8). The woman before Hillary. [Review of V. Kelley, *Leading with my heart.*] *New York Times Book Review,* pp. 1, 14–15.

Ochberg, F. M., & Soskis, D. A. (Eds.). (1982). *Victims of terrorism.* Boulder, CO: Westview.

Ogilvie, D. M. (1987). The undesired self: A neglected variable in personality research. *Journal of Personality and Social Psychology, 52,* 379–385.

Olweus, D. (1979). Stability of aggressive reaction patterns in males: A review. *Psychological Bulletin, 86,* 852–875.

Only spectacular crimes grab headlines in L.A. (1994, February 19). *Toronto Globe and Mail,* p. A12.

Orbovich, C. B. (1985, June). *Assessing cognitive style at a distance: Foreign policy decisionmaking in the Truman and Eisenhower administrations.* Paper presented at the annual meeting of the International Society for Political Psychology, Washington, DC.

Orpen, C. (1970). Authoritarianism in an "authoritarian" culture: The case of Afrikaans-speaking South Africa. *Journal of Social Psychology, 81,* 119–120.

Ortner, S. (1974). Is female to male as nature is to culture? In M. Z. Rosaldo & L. Lamphere (Eds.), *Woman, culture, and society* (pp. 67–87). Stanford, CA: Stanford University Press.

Osgood, C. E., Suci, G. J., & Tannenbaum, P. H. (1957). *The measurement of meaning.* Urbana, IL: University of Illinois Press.

OSS Assessment Staff. (1948). *Assessment of men.* New York: Rinehart.

Oswald, R. L. (1967). *Lee: A portrait of Lee Harvey Oswald by his brother.* New York: Coward-McCann.

Outside review criticizes F.B.I. on raid on cult. (1993, November 16). *New York Times,* p. A7.

Ovsiankina, M. (1928). Die Wiederaufnahme von unterbrochenen Handlungen [Resumption of interrupted behavior]. *Psychologische Forschung, 11,* 302–389.

Oyserman, D., & Markus, H. R. (1990). Possible selves and delinquency. *Journal of Personality and Social Psychology, 59,* 112–125.

Ozer, D. J. (1985). Correlation and the coefficient of determination. *Psychological Bulletin, 97,* 307–315.

Packer, S. (1983). *The effect of subliminally stimulating fantasies aimed at gratifying symbiotic and sanctioning aggressive strivings on assertiveness difficulties in women.* Unpublished Ph.D. thesis, New York University.

Paige, J. M. (1964). *Automated content analysis of "Letters from Jenny."* Unpublished honors thesis, Harvard University.

Paige, J. M. (1966). Letters from Jenny: An approach to the clinical analysis of personality structure by computer. In P. J. Stone, D. C. Dunphy, M. S. Smith, & D. M. Ogilvie (Eds.), *The general inquirer: A computer approach to content analysis* (pp. 431–451). Cambridge, MA: MIT Press.

Pais, A. (1993, January). Review of *Albert Einstein/Mileva Maric—The love letters. Physics Today,* p. 74

Palmatier, J. R., & Bornstein, P. H. (1980). The effects of subliminal stimulation of symbiotic merging fantasies on behavioral treatment of smokers. *Journal of Nervous and Mental Diseases, 168,* 715–720.

Parker, J. M. (1992, July). *United States Army psychological operations: Theory and practice in the Gulf war.* Paper presented at the annual meeting of the International Society of Political Psychology, San Francisco.

Parker, K. A. (1982). The effects of subliminal symbiotic stimulation on academic performance: Further evidence for the adaptation-enhancing effects of oneness fantasies. *Journal of Counseling Psychology, 29,* 19–28.

Passini, F. T., & Norman, W. T. (1966). A universal conception of personality structure? *Journal of Personality and Social Psychology, 4,* 44–49.

Paterson, J. (1989). Interview: Maya Angelou. In J. M. Elliot (Ed.), *Conversations with Maya Angelou* (pp. 115–124). Jackson, MS: University Press of Mississippi. (Original work published 1982.)

Paul, D. B., & Blumenthal, A. L. (1989). On the trail of Little Albert. *Psychological Record, 39,* 547–553.

Pavlov, I. P. (1927). *Conditioned reflexes.* London: Oxford University Press.

Peabody, D., & Goldberg, L. R. (1989). Some determinants of factor structures from personality-trait descriptors. *Journal of Personality and Social Psychology, 57,* 552–567.

Pederson, N. L., Plomin, R., McClearn, G. E., & Friberg, L. (1988). Neuroticism, extraversion, and related traits in adult twins reared apart and reared together. *Journal of Personality and Social Psychology, 55,* 950–957.

Peplau, L. A., & Perlman, D. (Eds.). (1982). *Loneliness: A sourcebook of current theory, research, and therapy.* New York: Wiley-Interscience.

Peplau, L. A., Russell, D., & Heim, M. (1979). An attributional analysis of loneliness. In I. Frieze, D. Bar-Tal, & J. S. Carroll (Eds.), *New approaches to social problems* (pp. 53–78). San Francisco: Jossey-Bass.

Perry, R. B. (1936). *The thought and character of William James* (2 vols.). Boston: Little, Brown.

Pervin, L. A. (1990). *Handbook of personality theory and research.* New York: Guilford Press.

Peterson, B. E., Doty, R. M., & Winter, D. G. (1993). Authoritarianism and attitudes toward contemporary social issues. *Personality and Social Psychology Bulletin, 19,* 174–184.

Peterson, B. E., & Stewart, A. J. (1990). Using personal and fictional documents to assess psychosocial development: A case study of Vera Brittain's generativity. *Psychology and Aging, 5,* 400–411.

Peterson, B. E., & Stewart, A. J. (1993). Generativity and social motives in young adults. *Journal of Personality and Social Psychology, 65,* 186–198.

Peterson, C. (1992). Explanatory style. In C. P. Smith (Ed.), *Motivation and personality: Handbook of thematic content analysis* (pp. 376–382. New York: Cambridge University Press.

Peterson, C., & Seligman, M. E. P. (1984a). Causal explanations as a risk factor for depression: Theory and evidence. *Psychological Review, 91,* 347–374.

Peterson, C., & Seligman, M. E. P. (1984b). *Content analysis of verbatim explanations: The CAVE technique for assessing explanatory style.* Unpublished paper, Virginia Polytechnic Institute and State University.

Peterson, C., Seligman, M. E. P., & Vaillant, G. E. (1988). Pessimistic explanatory style is a risk factor for physical illness: A thirty-five year longitudinal study. *Journal of Personality and Social Psychology, 55,* 23–27.

Peterson, D. R. (1965). Scope and generality of verbally defined personality factors. *Psychological Review, 72,* 48–59.

Pettigrew, T. F. (1958). Personality and sociocultural factors in intergroup attitudes: A cross-national comparison. *Journal of Conflict Resolution, 2,* 29–42.

Pettigrew, T., Allport, G. W., & Barnett, E. O. (1958). Binocular resolution and perception of race in South Africa. *British Journal of Psychology, 49,* 265–278.

Phares, E. J. (1976). *Locus of control in personality.* Morristown, NJ: General Learning Press.

Phares, E. J. (1978). Locus of control. In H. London & J. Exner (Eds.), *Dimensions of personality* (pp. 263–303). New York: Wiley.

Phares, E. J., & Wilson, K. G. (1972). Responsibility attribution: Role of outcome severity, situational ambiguity, and internal-external control. *Journal of Personality, 40,* 392–406.

Phillips, D. P. (1979). Suicide, motor vehicle fatalities, and the mass media: Evidence toward a theory of suggestion. *American Journal of Sociology, 84,* 1150–1174.

Phillips, D. P. (1983). The impact of mass media violence on U.S. homicides. *American Sociological Review, 48,* 560–568.

Piaget, J. (1952). *The origins of intelligence in children.* New York: International Universities Press.

Piaget, J. (1966). *The moral judgment of the child.* New York: Free Press. (Original work published 1932.)

Plesch, J. (1949). *Janos: The story of a doctor.* New York: A. A. Wyn.

Plomin, R. C., Chipuer, H. M., & Loehlin, J. C. (1990). Behavioral genetics and personality. In L. Pervin (Ed.), *Handbook of personality theory and research* (pp. 225–243). New York: Guilford Press.

Plomin, R. C., Corley, R., DeFries, J. C., & Fulker, D. W. (1990). Individual differences in television viewing in early childhood: Nature as well as nurture. *Psychological Science, 1,* 371–377.

Plomin, R., DeFries, J. C., & McClearn, G. E. (1990). *Behavioral genetics: A primer* (2nd ed.). New York: Freeman.

Plutchik, R. (1980). *Emotion: A psychoevolutionary synthesis.* New York: Harper & Row.

Plutchik, R., & Kellerman, H. (1980). *Emotion: Theories, research, and experience* (3 vols.). New York: Praeger.

Polivy, J., Herman, C. P., & Pliner, P. (1990). Perception and evaluation of body image: The meaning of body shape and size. In J. M. Olson & M. P. Zanna (Eds.), *Self-inference processes: The Ontario symposium, Volume 6* (pp. 87–114). Hillsdale, NJ: Erlbaum.

Porter, C. A., & Suedfeld, P. (1981). Integrative complexity in the correspondence of literary figures: Effects of personal and societal stress. *Journal of Personality and Social Psychology, 40,* 321–330.

Porter, E. H. (1913). *Pollyanna.* Boston: Page.

Prescott, C. A., Johnson, R. C., & McArdle, J. J. (1991). Genetic contribution to television viewing. *Psychological Science, 2,* 430–431.

Price, R. (1977). *With Nixon.* New York: Viking Press.

Price, R. A., Vandenberg, S. G., Iyer, H., & Williams, J. S. (1982). Components of variation in normal personality. *Journal of Personality and Social Psychology, 43,* 328–340.

Progoff, I. (1967). The psychology of Lee Harvey Oswald: A Jungian approach. *Journal of Individual Psychology, 23,* 37–52.

Prothro, E. T. (1952). Ethnocentrism and anti-Negro attitudes in the deep South. *Journal of Abnormal and Social Psychology, 47,* 105–108.

Prussia, G. E., Kinicki, A. J., & Bracker, J. S. (1993). Psychological and behavioral consequences of job loss: A covariance structure analysis using Weiner's (1985) attribution model. *Journal of Applied Psychology, 78,* 382–394.

Prytula, R. R., Oster, G. D., & Davis, S. F. (1977). The "rat rabbit" problem: What did John B. Watson really do? *Teaching of Psychology, 4,* 44–46.

Putnam, F. W. (1984). The psychophysiologic investigation of multiple personality disorder: A review. *Psychiatric Clinics of North America, 7(1),* 31–39.

Putnam, F. W., Zahn, T. P., & Post, R. M. (1990). Differential autonomic nervous system activity in multiple personality disorder. *Psychiatry Research, 31,* 251–260.

Pye, L. W. (1985). *Asian power and politics: The cultural dimensions of authority.* Cambridge, MA: Harvard University Press.

Pye, L. W. (1986). Political psychology in Asia. In M. G. Hermann (Ed.), *Political psychology: Contemporary issues and problems* (pp. 467–486). San Francisco: Jossey-Bass.

Pyron, B., & Kafer, J. (1967). Recall of nonsense and attitudinal rigidity. *Journal of Personality and Social Psychology, 5,* 463–466.

Quindlen, A. (1993, January 17). Time to tackle this. *New York Times,* National ed., p. E17.

Raina, T. N. A. (1974). A comparison of Indian students belonging to four political parties on a measure of authoritarianism. *Journal of Social Psychology, 92,* 311–312.

Rank, O. (1913). "Um Städten werben" ["Conquering" cities]. *Internationale Zeitschrift für ärtzliche Psychoanalyse, 1,* 50–58.

Rank, O. (1932). *Art and artist.* New York: Knopf.

Rank, O. (1936). Life fear and death fear. In *Will therapy* (pp. 119–133). New York: Knopf. (Original work published 1931.)

Rank, O. (1961). *Psychology and the soul.* New York: A. S. Barnes & Co. (Original work published 1930.)

Rank, O. (1973). *The trauma of birth.* New York: Harper & Row. (Original work published 1924.)

Rank, O. (1975). *The Don Juan legend.* (Ed. and Trans. D. G. Winter). Princeton, NJ: Princeton University Press. (Original work published 1924.)

Ransford, H. E. (1968). Isolation, powerlessness, and violence: A study of attitudes and participation in the Watts riot. *American Journal of Sociology, 73,* 581–591.

Raskin, R. N., & Hall, C. S. (1979). A narcissistic personality inventory. *Psychological Reports, 45,* 590.

Raskin, R. N., Novacek, J., & Hogan, R. (1991). Narcissistic self-esteem management. *Journal of Personality and Social Psychology, 60,* 911–918.

Raskin, R. N., & Shaw, R. (1988). Narcissism and the use of personal pronouns. *Journal of Personality, 56,* 393–404.

Reeve, J. (1992). *Understanding motivation and emotion.* Fort Worth, TX: Harcourt Brace Jovanovich.

Rehm, L. P., & O'Hara, M. W. (1979). Understanding depression. In I. Frieze, D. Bar-Tal, & J. S. Carroll (Eds.), *New approaches to social problems* (pp. 53–78). San Francisco: Jossey-Bass.

Reno approved FBI assault on compound. (1993, April 20). *San Francisco Chronicle,* pp. A1, A11.

Rescorla, R. A. (1988). Pavlovian conditioning: It isn't what you think it is. *American Psychologist, 43,* 151–160.

Ressler, R. K., & Burgess, A. W. (1985). Crime scene and profile characteristics of organized and disorganized murderers. *FBI Law Enforcement Bulletin, 54(8),* 18–25.

Rest, J. R. (1976). New approaches in the assessment of moral judgment. In T. Lickona (Ed.), *Moral development and behavior* (pp. 198–218). New York: Holt, Rinehart & Winston.

Rest, J. (1986). *Moral development: Advances in research and theory.* New York: Praeger.

Rice, J., Cloninger, C. R., & Reich, T. (1980). Analysis of behavioral traits in the presence of cultural transmission and assortative mating: Applications to IQ and SES. *Behavior Genetics, 10,* 73–92.

Richardson, L. F. (1960). *Statistics of deadly quarrels.* Pittsburgh & Chicago: Quadrangle Books.

Riesman, D., Glazer, N., & Denny, R. (1950). *The lonely crowd.* New Haven, CT: Yale University Press.

Ritchie, E., & Phares, E. J. (1969). Attitude change as a function of internal-external control and communicator status. *Journal of Personality, 37,* 429–443.

Rivera, D. L. B. (1983). *The relationship between selected personality factors and cancer.* Unpublished doctoral dissertation, University of Florida.

Robins, R. W., & John, O. P. (1993, August). *Accuracy and bias in self-perception: The role of visual perspective.* Paper presented at the annual meeting of the American Psychological Association, Toronto.

Robinson, F. G. (1992). *Love's story told: A life of Henry A. Murray.* Cambridge, MA: Harvard University Press.

Robinson, J. P., & Shaver, P. R. (1973). *Measures of social psychological attitudes.* Ann Arbor, MI: University of Michigan, Institute for Social Research.

Robinson, J. P., Shaver, P. R., & Wrightsman, L. S. (1991). *Measures of personality and social psychological attitudes.* San Diego, CA: Harcourt Brace Jovanovich.

Rogers, C. R. (1948). *Dealing with social tensions.* New York: Hinds, Hayden, & Eldredge.

Rogers, C. R. (1951). *Client-centered therapy.* Boston: Houghton Mifflin.

Rogers, C. R. (1959). A theory of therapy, personality, and interpersonal relationships, as developed in the client-centered framework. In S. Koch (Ed.), *Psychology: A study of a science* (vol. 3, pp. 184–256). New York: McGraw-Hill.

Rogers, C. R. (1963). Actualizing tendency in relation to "motives" and to consciousness. In M. R. Jones (Ed.), *Nebraska symposium on motivation 1963* (pp. 1–24). Lincoln, NE: University of Nebraska Press.

Rogers, C. R. (1966). Autobiography. In E. G. Boring & G. Lindzey (Eds.), *A history of psychology in autobiography* (vol. 5, pp. 343–384). New York: Appleton-Century-Crofts.

Rogers, C. R., & Skinner, B. F. (1956). Some issues concerning the control of human behavior: A symposium. *Science, 124,* 1057–1066.

Rogers, E. M., & Svenning, L. (1969). *Modernization among peasants: The impact of communication.* New York: Holt, Rinehart & Winston.

Rokeach, M. (1960). *The open and closed mind.* New York: Basic Books.

Rokeach, M. (1973). *The nature of human values.* New York: Free Press.

Rosch, E. (1978). Principles of categorization. In E. Rosch & B. B. Lloyd (Eds.), *Cognition and categorization* (pp. 27–48). Hillsdale, NJ: Erlbaum.

Rose, P. (1978). *Woman of letters: A life of Virginia Woolf.* New York: Oxford University Press.

Rose, R. J., Koskenvuo, M., Kaprio, J., Sarna, S., & Langinvainio, H. (1988). Shared genes, shared experiences, and similarity of personality: Data from 14,288 adult Finnish co-twins. *Journal of Personality and Social Psychology, 54,* 161–171.

Rosenberg, M. (1979). *Conceiving the self.* New York: Basic Books.

Rosenberg, M., & Pearlin, L. I. (1978). Social class and self-esteem among children and adults. *American Journal of Sociology, 84,* 53–77.

Rosenthal, R. (1990). How are we doing in soft psychology? *American Psychologist, 45,* 775–777.

Rosenzweig, S. (1938). The experimental study of repression. In H. A. Murray, *Explorations in personality* (pp. 472–498). New York: Oxford University Press.

Rosenzweig, S. (1943). An experimental study of "repression" with special reference to need-persistive and ego-defensive reactions to frustration. *Journal of Experimental Psychology, 32,* 64–74.

Ross, L. (1977). The intuitive psychologist and his shortcomings: Distortions in the attribution process. In L. Berkowitz (Ed.), *Advances in experimental social psychology* (vol. 10, pp. 173–220). New York: Academic Press.

Rothstein, D. (1966). Presidential assassination syndrome. *Archives of General Psychiatry, 15,* 260–266.

Rotter, J. B. (1966). Generalized expectancies for internal versus external control of reinforcement. *Psychological Monographs, 80(1)* (Whole no. 609).

Rozelle, R. M., & Baxter, J. C. (1975). Impression formation and danger recognition in experienced police officers. *Journal of Social Psychology, 96,* 53–63.

Rubin, J. (1981). *Dynamics of third-party intervention: Henry Kissinger in the Middle East.* New York: Praeger.

Runyan, W. McK. (1981). Why did Van Gogh cut off his ear? The problem of alternative explanations in psychobiography. *Journal of Personality and Social Psychology, 40,* 1070–1077.

Runyan, W. McK. (1983). Idiographic goals and methods in the study of lives. *Journal of Personality, 51,* 413–437.

Runyan, W. McK. (1984). *Life histories and psychobiography: Explorations in theory and method.* New York: Oxford University Press.

Runyan, W. McK. (1988). Progress in psychobiography. *Journal of Personality, 56,* 295–326.

Rushton, J. P. (1989). Race differences in behavior: A review and evolutionary analysis. *Personality and Individual Differences, 9,* 1009–1024.

Ruvolo, A., & Markus, H. (1987). *Possible selves and motivation.* Unpublished paper, Department of Psychology, University of Michigan.

Ryan, W. (1971). *Blaming the victim.* New York: Pantheon.

Ryff, C. D. (1989). Happiness is everything, or is it? Explorations on the meaning of psychological well-being. *Journal of Personality and Social Psychology, 57,* 1069–1081.

Ryff, C. D. (1995). Subjective well-being in adult life. *Current Directions in Psychological Science, 4,* 99–104.

Ryff, C. D., Lee, Y. H., & Na, K. C. (1993, November). *Through the lens of culture: Psychological well-being at midlife.* Paper presented at the Gerontological Society of America meeting, New Orleans.

Safire, W. (1975). *Before the fall: An inside view of the pre-Watergate White House.* New York: Belmont Tower Books.

Salaman, E. (1955, Septembeer 8). A talk with Einstein. *The Listener,* pp. 370–371.

Sales, S. M. (1972). Economic threat as a determinant of conversion rates in authoritarian and nonauthoritarian churches. *Journal of Personality and Social Psychology, 23,* 420–428.

Sales, S. M. (1973). Threat as a factor in authoritarianism: An analysis of archival data. *Journal of Personality and Social Psychology, 28,* 44–57.

Sales, S. M., & Friend, K. E. (1973). Success and failure as determinants of level of authoritarianism. *Behavioral Science, 18,* 163–172.

Samelson, F. (1980). J. B. Watson's Little Albert, Cyril Burt's twins, and the need for a critical science. *American Psychologist, 35,* 619–625.

Samelson, F. (1986). Authoritarianism from Berlin to Berkeley: On social psychology and history. *Journal of Social Issues, 42 (1),* 191–208.

Sampson, E. E. (1978). Personality and the location of identity. *Journal of Personality, 46,* 552–568.

Sanford, N. (1986). A personal account of the study of authoritarianism: Comment on Samelson. *Journal of Social Issues, 42(1),* 209–214.

Sartre, J. P. (1946). *Anti-Semite and Jew.* New York: Schocken Books.

Satterfield, J. M., & Seligman, M. E. P. (1994). Military aggression and risk predicted by explanatory style. *Psychological Science, 5,* 77–82.

Schama, S. (1987). *The embarrassment of riches: An interpretation of Dutch culture in the Golden Age.* New York: Knopf.

Schnackers, U., & Kleinbeck, U. (1975). Machmotiv und machtthematisches Verhalten in einem Verhandlungsspiel [Power motivation and power-related behavior in a bargaining game]. *Archiv für Psychologie, 127,* 300–319.

Schopenhauer, A. (1901). Personality, or what a man is. In *The Wisdom of life and other essays* (pp. 12–35). New York and London: Dunne. (Original work published 1851.)

Schroder, H. M., Driver, M. J., & Streufert, S. (1967). *Human information processing.* New York: Holt, Rinehart & Winston.

Schulkind, J. (1985). Introduction to V. Woolf, *Moments of being.* San Diego, CA: Harcourt Brace.

Schultz, D. P. (1969). The human subject in psychological research. *Psychological Bulletin, 72,* 214–228.

Schuman, H., & Scott, J. (1989). Generations and collective memories. *American Sociological Review, 54,* 359–381.

Schurtman, R., Palmatier, J. R., & Martin, E. S. (1982). On the activation of symbiotic gratification fantasies as an aid in the treatment of alcoholics. *International Journal of Addiction, 17,* 1157–1174.

Schwartz, B. (1974). On going back to nature: A review of Seligman and Hagen's *Biological boundaries of learning. Journal of the Experimental Analysis of Behavior, 21,* 183–198.

Schwartz, H. (1986). *Never satisfied: A cultural history of diets, fantasies, and fat.* New York: Free Press.

Scott, W. A. (1969). Attitude measurement. In G. Lindzey & E. Aronson (Eds.), *Handbook of social psychology* (2nd ed., vol. 2, pp. 204–273). Reading, MA: Addison-Wesley.

Sears, R. R. (1944). Experimental analysis of psychoanalytic phenomena. In J. McV. Hunt (Ed.), *Personality and the behavior disorders* (vol. 1, pp. 306–332). New York: Ronald Press.

Sears, R. R. (1951). *Survey of objective studies of psychoanalytic concepts.* Ann Arbor, MI: Edwards.

Sears, R. R. (1963). Dependency motivation. In M. R. Jones (Ed.), *Nebraska symposium on motivation 1963* (pp. 25–64). Lincoln, NE: University of Nebraska Press.

Sears, R. R., Rau, L., & Alpert, R. (1965). *Identification and child rearing.* Stanford, CA: Stanford University Press.

Seegmiller, R. A., & Epperson, D. L. (1987). Distinguishing thinking-feeling preferences through the content analysis of natural language. *Journal of Personality Assessment, 51,* 42–52.

Seelig, C. (1956). *Albert Einstein: A documentary biography.* London: Staples Press.

Seeman, M. (1963). Alienation and learning in a reformatory. *American Journal of Sociology, 69,* 270–284.

Seeman, M., & Evans, J. W. (1962). Alienation and learning in a hospital setting. *American Sociological Review, 27,* 772–783.

Seeman, M., & Seeman, T. E. (1983). Health behavior and personal autonomy: A longitudinal study of the sense of control in illness. *Journal of Health and Social Behavior, 24,* 144–160.

Seligman, M. E. P. (1970). On the generality of the laws of learning. *Psychological Review, 77,* 406–418.

Seligman, M. E. P. (1971). Phobias and preparedness. *Behavior Therapy, 2,* 307–320.

Seligman, M. E. P., Nolen-Hoeksema, S., Thornton, N., & Thornton, K. M. (1990). Explanatory style as a mechanism of disappointing athletic performance. *Psychological Science, 1,* 143–146.

Seligman, M. E. P., & Schulman, P. (1986). Explanatory style as a predictor of productivity and quitting among life insurance sales agents. *Journal of Personality and Social Psychology, 50,* 832–838.

Shapiro, D. (1965). *Neurotic styles.* New York: Basic Books.

Shaw, G. B. (1956). Saint Joan. In Bernard Shaw's *Saint Joan, Major Barbara, Androcles and the lion.* New York: Modern Library. (Original work published 1924.)

Shils, E. A. (1954). Authoritarianism: "Right" and "left." In R. Christie & M. Jahoda (Eds.), *Studies in the scope and method of "The Authoritarian Personality"* (pp. 24–49). Glencoe, IL: Free Press.

Shotter, J., & Gergen, K. J. (Eds.) (1989). *Texts of identity.* Beverly Hills, CA: Sage.

Shweder, R. A. (1991). *Thinking through cultures: Expeditions in cultural psychology.* Cambridge, MA: Harvard University Press.

Silverman, L. H. (1976). Psychoanalytic theory: The reports of my death are greatly exaggerated. *American Psychologist, 31,* 621–637.

Silverman, L. H., Bronstein, A., & Mendelsohn, E. (1976). The further use of the subliminal psychodynamic activation method for the experimental study of the clinical use of psychoanalysis: On the specificity of relationships between manifest psychopathology and unconscious conflict. *Psychotherapy: Theory, Research, and Practice, 13,* 2–16.

Silverman, L. H., Frank, S., & Dachinger, P. (1974). Psychoanalytic reinterpretation of the effectiveness of systematic desensitization: Experimental data bearing on the role of merging fantasies. *Journal of Abnormal Psychology, 83,* 313–318.

Silverman, L. H., Lachmann, F. M., & Milich, R. H. (1982). *The search for oneness.* New York: International Universities Press.

Silverman, L. H., Ross, D., Adler, J., & Lustig, D. (1978). A simple research paradigm for demonstrating subliminal psychodyanmic activation. *Journal of Abnormal Psychology, 87,* 341–357.

Silverman, L. H., & Weinberger, J. (1985). Mommy and I are one: Implications for psychotherapy. *American Psychologist, 40,* 1296–1308.

Simonton, D. (1986). Presidential personality: Biographical use of the Gough Adjective Check List. *Journal of Personality and Social Psychology, 51,* 149–160.

Simonton, D. (1988). Presidential style: Personality, biography, and performance. *Journal of Personality and Social Psychology, 55,* 928–936.

Simonton, D. K. (1990). *Psychology, science, and history.* New Haven, CT: Yale University Press.

Singh, N. P. (1969). *N* Achievement among successful-unsuccessful and traditional-progressive agricultural entrepreneurs of Delhi. *Journal of Social Psychology, 79,* 271–272.

Singh, S. (1979). Relation among projective and direct verbal measures of achievement motivation. *Journal of Personality Assessment, 43,* 45–49.

Singh, S., & Gupta, B. S. (1977). Motives and agricultural growth. *British Journal of Social and Clinical Psychology, 16,* 189–190.

Sinha, B. P., & Mehta, P. (1972). Farmers' need for achievement and change-proneness in acquisition of information from a farm telecast. *Rural Sociology, 37,* 417–427.

Skinner, B. F. (1974). *About behaviorism.* New York: Knopf.

Skinner, B. F. (1989). The origins of cognitive thought. *American Psychologist, 44,* 13–18.

Smelser, N. J. (1989). Self-esteem and social problems: An introduction. In A. M. Mecca, N. J. Smelser, & J. Vasconcellos (Eds.), *The social importance of self-esteem* (pp. 1–23). Berkeley: University of California Press.

Smith, C. P. (Ed.). (1992). *Motivation and personality: Handbook of thematic content analysis.* New York: Cambridge University Press.

Smith, H. (1958). *The religions of man.* New York: Harper & Row. (Perennial Library Edition, 1965).

Smith, P. B., & Bond, M. H. (1993). *Social psychology across cultures: Analysis and perspectives.* New York: Harvester & Wheatsheaf.

Smith, T. W., & Williams, P. (1992). Personality and health: Advantages and limitations of the five-factor model. *Journal of Personality, 60,* 395–423.

Snow, C. P. (1959). *The masters.* Garden City, NY: Anchor Books. (Original work published 1951.)

Snyder, M. (1987). *Public appearances, private realities: The psychology of self-monitoring.* New York: Freeman.

Snyder, M., Simpson, J. A., & Gangestad, S. (1986). Personality and sexual relations. *Journal of Personality and Social Psychology, 51,* 181–190.

Sorenson, T. C. (1965). *Kennedy*. New York: Harper & Row.

Sosis, R. H. (1974). Internal-external control and the perception of responsibility of another for an accident. *Journal of Personality and Social Psychology, 30*, 393–399.

Spalding, A. D. (1992). Psychosocial variables and disease progression in human immunodeficiency virus. *Dissertation Abstracts International, 53(3A)*, 948–949.

Spangler, W. D. (1992). Validity of questionnaire and TAT measures of need for achievement: Two meta-analyses. *Psychological Bulletin, 112*, 140–154.

Spence, D. P. (1983). Narrative persuasion. *Psychoanalysis and Contemporary Thought, 6*, 457–481.

Spence, J. T., Deaux, K., & Helmreich, R. L. (1985). Sex roles in contemporary American society. In G. Lindzey & E. Aronson (Eds.), *Handbook of social psychology* (3rd ed., vol. 2, pp. 149–178). New York: Random House.

Spielrein, S. (1912). Die Destruktion als Ursache des Werdens. [Destruction as the origin of becoming]. *Jahrbuch für psychoanalytische und psychopathologische Forschungen, 4*, 465–503.

Spranger, E. (1928). *Types of men*. [Translation of *Lebensformen*]. Halle: Max Niemeyer.

Srinivas, M. N. (1962). *Caste in modern India and other essays*. Bombay: Asia Publishing House.

St. Lawrence, J. S. (1993). African-American adolescents' knowledge, health-related attitudes, sexual behavior, and contraceptive decisions: Implications for the prevention of adolescent HIV infection. *Journal of Consulting and Clinical Psychology, 61*, 104–112.

Stafford, J. (1966). *A mother in history*. New York: Farrar, Straus, & Giroux.

Stagner, R. (1937). *Psychology of personality*. New York: McGraw-Hill.

Stagner, R. (1936). Fascist attitudes: An exploratory study. *Journal of Social Psychology, 7*, 309–319.

Stark, L. (1978). Trust. In H. London & J. Exner (Eds.), *Dimensions of personality* (pp. 561–599). New York: Wiley.

Steele, C. M. (1992, April). Race and the schooling of Black Americans. *Atlantic Monthly*, pp. 68–78.

Steele, R. S. (1982). *Freud and Jung: Conflicts of interpretation*. London: Routledge & Kegan Paul.

Steele, R. S., & Kelly, T. J. (1976). Eysenck Personality Inventory and Jungian Myers-Briggs Type Indicator correlation of extraversion-introversion. *Journal of Consulting and Clinical Psychology, 44*, 690–691.

Stefan, C., & Linder, H. B. (1985). Suicide, an experience of chaos or fatalism: Perspectives from personal construct theory. In D. Bannister (Ed.), *Issues and approaches in personal construct theory* (pp. 183–209). London: Academic Press.

Stelmack, R. M. (1990). Biological bases of extraversion: Psychophysiological evidence. *Journal of Personality, 58*, 293–311.

Stephens, W. B. (1972). *Relationship between selected personality characteristics of senior art students and their area of study*. Unpublished doctoral dissertation, University of Florida.

Stewart, A. J. (1978). A longitudinal study of coping styles in self-defining and socially defined women. *Journal of Consulting and Clinical Psychology, 46*, 1079–1084.

Stewart, A. J. (1982). The course of individual adaptation to life changes. *Journal of Personality and Social Psychology, 42*, 1100–1113.

Stewart, A. J. (1992a). Scoring manual for psychological stances toward the environment. In C. P. Smith (Ed.), *Motivation and personality: Handbook of thematic content analysis* (pp. 451–480). New York: Cambridge University Press.

Stewart, A. J. (1992b). Self-definition and social definition: Personal styles reflected in narrative style. In C. P. Smith (Ed.), *Motivation and personality: Handbook of thematic content analysis* (pp. 481–488). New York: Cambridge University Press.

Stewart, A. J. (1995, March). *Rethinking middle age: Lessons from women's lives*. Address at the annual meeting of the Eastern Psychological Association, Boston.

Stewart, A. J., & Chester, N. L. (1982). Sex differences in human social motives: Achievement, affiliation, and power. In A. J. Stewart (Ed.), *Motivation and society* (pp. 172–218). San Francisco: Jossey-Bass.

Stewart, A. J., Franz, C., & Layton, L. (1988). The changing self: Using personal documents to study lives. *Journal of Personality, 56*, 41–74.

Stewart, A. J., & Healy, J. M., Jr. (1984). Processing affective responses to life experiences: The development of the adult self. In C. Malatesta & C. Izard (Eds.), *Emotion in adult development* (pp. 277–295). Beverly Hills, CA: Sage.

Stewart, A. J., & Healy, J. M., Jr. (1985). Personality and adap-tation to change. In R. Hogan & W. Jones (Eds.), *Perspectives in personality: Theory, measurement and interpersonal dynamics* (pp. 117–144). Greenwich, CT: JAI Press.

Stewart, A. J., & Healy, J. M., Jr. (1986). The role of personality development and experience in shaping political commitment: An illustrative case. *Journal of Social Issues, 42(2)*, 11–31.

Stewart, A. J., & Healy, J. M., Jr. (1989). Linking individual development and social change. *American Psychologist, 44*, 30–42.

Stewart, A. J., & Healy, J. M., Jr. (1992). Assessing adaptation to life changes in terms of psychological stances toward the environment. In C. P. Smith (Ed.), *Motivation and personality: Handbook of thematic content analysis* (pp. 440–450). New York: Cambridge University Press.

Stewart, A. J., Lykes, M. B., & LaFrance, M. (1982). Educated women's career patterns: Separating social and developmental changes. *Journal of Social Issues, 38(1)*, 97–117.

Stewart, A. J., & Malley, J. E. (1987). Role combination in women: Mitigating agency and communion. In F. Crosby (Ed.), *Spouse, parent, worker: On gender and multiple roles* (pp. 44–62). New Haven, CT: Yale University Press.

Stewart, A. J., & Rubin, Z. (1976). The power motive in the dating couple. *Journal of Personality and Social Psychology, 34*, 305–309.

Stewart, A. J., & Salt, P. (1981). Life stress, life-styles, depression, and illness in adult women. *Journal of Personality and Social Psychology, 40*, 1063–1069.

Stewart, A. J., Sokol, M., Healy, J. M., Jr., & Chester, N. L. (1986). Longitudinal studies of psychological consequences of life changes in children and adults. *Journal of Personality and Social Psychology, 50*, 143–151.

Stewart, A. J., & Winter, D. G. (1974). Self-definition and social definition in women. *Journal of Personality, 42*, 238–259.

Stewart, A. J., & Winter, D. G. (1977). The nature and causes of female suppression. *Signs: Journal of Women in Culture and Society, 2*, 531–553.

Stigler, J. W., Shweder, R. A., & Herdt, G. (1990). *Cultural psychology: Essays in comparative human development.* New York: Cambridge University Press.

Stiglmayer, A. (Ed.). (1994). *Mass rape: The war against women in Bosnia-Herzegovina.* Lincoln, NE: University of Nebraska Press.

Stone, P. J., Dunphy, D. C., Smith, M. S., & Ogilvie, D. M. (Eds.). (1966). *The general inquirer: A computer approach to content analysis.* Cambridge, MA: MIT Press.

Stone, W. F. (1980). The myth of the left-wing authoritarian. *Political Psychology, 2(3-4)*, 3–19.

Stone, W. F., Lederer, G., & Christie, R. (Eds.). (1992). *Strength and weakness: The authoritarian personality today.* New York: Springer-Verlag.

Stone, W. F., & Schaffner, P. E. (1988). *The psychology of politics* (2nd ed.). New York: Springer-Verlag.

Stone, W. F., & Smith, L. D. (1988, July). *Left-wing authoritarianism: Yet to be demonstrated.* Paper presented at the annual meeting of the International Society of Political Psychology, Secaucus, NJ.

Storm, H. (1972). *Seven arrows.* New York: Harper & Row.

Stouffer, S. A., Suchman, E. A., DeVinney, L. C., Star, S. A., & Williams, R. M. (1949). *The American soldier: Adjustment during army life* (vol. 1). Princeton, NJ: Princeton University Press.

Strauman, T. J., & Higgins, E. T. (1987). Automatic activation of self-discrepancies and emotional syndromes: When cognitive structures influence affect. *Journal of Personality and Social Psychology, 53*, 1004–1014.

Straus, W., & Howe, N. (1991). *Generations: The history of America's future, 1584 to 2069.* New York: Morrow.

Strelau, J., & Eysenck, H. J. (Eds.). (1987). *Personality dimensions and arousal.* New York: Plenum.

Streufert, S. & Streufert, S. C. (1978). *Behavior in the complex environment.* Washington & New York: Winston-Wiley.

Strickland, B. R. (1965). The prediction of social action from a dimension of internal-external control. *Journal of Social Psychology, 66*, 353–358.

Strickland, B. R. (1977a). Approval motivation. In T. Blass (Ed.), *Personality variables in social behavior* (pp. 315–356). Hillsdale, NJ: Erlbaum.

Strickland, B. R. (1977b). Internal-external control of reinforcement. In T. Blass (Ed.), *Personality variables in social behavior* (pp. 219–279). Hillsdale, NJ: Erlbaum.

Strickland, B. R. (1978). Internal-external expectancies and health-related behaviors. *Journal of Consulting and Clinical Psychology, 46*, 1192–1211.

Strouse, J. (Ed.). (1974). *Women and analysis: Dialogues on psychoanalytic views of femininity.* New York: Grossman.

Suedfeld, P. (1964). Attitude manipulation in restricted environments: I. Conceptual structure and response to propaganda. *Journal of Abnormal and Social Psychology, 68*, 242–247.

Suedfeld, P. (1980). Indices of world tension in the Bulletin of the Atomic Scientists. *Political Psychology, 2(3-4)*, 114–123.

Suedfeld, P. (1985). APA presidential addresses: The relation of integrative complexity to historical, professional, and personal factors. *Journal of Personality and Social Psychology, 49*, 1643–1651.

Suedfeld, P., Corteen, R. S., & McCormick, C. (1986). The role of integrative complexity in military leadership: Robert E. Lee and his opponents. *Journal of Applied Social Psychology, 16*, 498–507.

Suedfeld, P., & Piedrahita. (1984). Intimations of mortality: Integrative simplification as a precursor of death. *Journal of Personality and Social Psychology, 47*, 848–852.

Suedfeld, P., & Rank, A. D. (1976). Revolutionary leaders: Long-term success as a function of changes in conceptual complexity. *Journal of Personality and Social Psychology, 34*, 169–178.

Suedfeld, P., & Tetlock, P. (1977). Integrative complexity of communications in international crises. *Journal of Conflict Resolution, 21*, 169–184.

Suedfeld, P., Tetlock, P., & Ramirez, C. (1977). War, peace, and integrative complexity. *Journal of Conflict Resolution, 21*, 427–442.

Suedfeld, P., Tetlock, P. E., & Streufert, S. (1992). Conceptual/integrative complexity. In C. P. Smith (Ed.), *Motivation and personality: Handbook of thematic content analysis* (pp. 393–400). New York: Cambridge University Press.

Suedfeld, P., & Vernon, J. (1966). Attitude manipulation in restricted environments: II. Conceptual structure and the internalization of propaganda received as a reward for compliance. *Journal of Personality and Social Psychology, 3*, 586–589.

Sugimoto, K. (1989). *Albert Einstein: A photographic biography.* New York: Schocken.

Sullivan, A. (1903). Letter, April 5, 1887. In H. Keller, *The story of my life* (pp. 316–317). New York: Doubleday, Page.

Summers, A. (1980). *Conspiracy.* New York: McGraw-Hill.

Swede, S. W., & Tetlock, P. E. (1986). Henry Kissinger's implicit theory of personality: A quantitative case study. *Journal of Personality, 54*, 617–746.

Sweeney, P. D., Anderson, K., & Bailey, S. (1986). Attributional style in depression: A meta-analytic review. *Journal of Personality and Social Psychology, 50*, 974–991.

Tabin, J. K., & Tabin, C. J. (1987). An alternative interpretation of oneness. *American Psychologist, 42*, 954–955.

Tannen, D. (1990). *You just don't understand: Women and men in conversation.* New York: Morrow.

Taylor, S. E., & Brown, J. D. (1988). Illusion and well-being: A social psychological perspective on mental health. *Psychological Bulletin, 103*, 193–210.

Taylor, S. E., Lichtman, R. R., & Wood, J. V. (1984). Attributions, beliefs about control, and adjustment to breast cancer. *Journal of Personality and Social Psychology, 46,* 489–502.

Teen Tokyo. (1992, November). *Winds* [Japan Air Lines magazine], pp. 46–53.

Tellegen, A., Lykken, D. T., Bouchard, T. J., Wilcox, K. J., Segal, N. L., & Rich, S. (1988). Personality similarity in twins reared apart and together. *Journal of Personality and Social Psychology, 54,* 1031–1039.

Temkin, O. (1981). The scientific approach to disease: Specific entity and individual sickness. In A. L. Caplan, H. T. Engelhardt, & J. J. McCartney (Eds.), *Concepts of health and disease: Interdisciplinary perspectives* (pp. 247–263). Reading, MA: Addison-Wesley.

Terhune, K. W. (1968). Motives, situation, and interpersonal conflict within prisoners' dilemma. *Journal of Personality and Social Psychology Monograph Supplement, 8*(3), pt. 2.

Tetlock, P. E. (1979). Identifying victims of groupthink from public statements of decision makers. *Journal of Personality and Social Psychology, 37,* 1314–1324.

Tetlock, P. E., Armor, D., & Peterson, R. S. (1994). The slavery debate in antebellum America: Cognitive style, value conflict, and the limits of compromise. *Journal of Personality and Social Psychology, 66,* 115–126.

Tetlock, P. E., Peterson, R. S., & Berry, J. M. (1993). Flattering and unflattering personality portraits of integratively simple and complex managers. *Journal of Personality and Social Psychology, 64,* 500–511.

Thayer, R. E. (1967). Measurement of activation through self-report. *Psychological Reports, 20,* 663–678.

Thompson, C. M. (1964). *Interpersonal psychoanalysis* (Ed. M. R. Green). New York: Basic Books.

Thompson, J. K., Penner, L. A., & Altabe, M. N. (1990). Procedures, problems, and progress in the assessment of body images. In T. F. Cash & T. Pruzinsky (Eds.), *Body images: Development, deviance, and change* (pp. 21–48). New York: Guilford Press.

Thorne, A. (1987). The press of personality: Conversations between introverts and extraverts. *Journal of Personality and Social Psychology, 53,* 718–726.

Thorne, A., & Gough, H. (1991). *Portraits of type: An MBTI research compendium.* Palo Alto, CA: Consulting Psychologists Press.

Tolman, E. C. (1932). *Purposive behavior in animals and man.* New York: Century.

Tomkins, S. (1963). Left and right: A basic dimension of ideology and personality. In R. W. White (Ed.), *A study of lives* (pp. 388–411). New York: Atherton.

Tomkins, S. S. (1978). Script theory: Differential manifification of affects. In H. E. Howe & R. A. Dienstbier (Eds.), *Nebraska symposium on motivation 1978* (pp. 201–236). Lincoln, NE: University of Nebraska Press.

Tomkins, S. S. (1987). Script theory. In J. Aronoff, A. I. Rabin, & R. A. Zucker (Eds.), *The emergence of personality* (pp. 147–217). New York: Springer.

Tooby, J., & Cosmides, L. (1990). On the universality of human nature and the uniqueness of the individual: The role of genetics and adaptation. *Journal of Personality, 58,* 17–67.

Toppman, L. (1989). Maya Angelou: The serene spirit of a survivor. In J. M. Elliot (Ed.), *Conversations with Maya Angelou* (pp. 140–145). Jackson, MS: University Press of Mississippi. (Original work published 1983.)

Triandis, H. C. (1972). *The analysis of subjective culture.* New York: Wiley-Interscience.

Triandis, H. C. (Ed.). (1980). *Handbook of cross-cultural psychology* (6 vols.). Boston: Allyn & Bacon.

Trickett, P. K., & Putnam, F. W. (1993). Impact of child sexual abuse on females: Toward a developmental psychobiological integration. *Psychological Science, 4,* 81–87.

Tupes, E. C., & Christal, R. E. (1992). Recurrent personality factors based on trait ratings. *Journal of Personality, 60,* 225–251. (Original work published 1961.)

Turnbull, A. A. (1976). Selling and the salesman: Prediction of success and personality change. *Psychological Reports, 38,* 1175–1180.

Turnbull, M. J., & Norris, H. (1982). Effects of transcendental meditation on self-identity indices and personality. *British Journal of Psychology, 73,* 57–68.

Turner, R. H., & Vanderlippe, R. H. (1958). Self-ideal congruence as an index of adjustment. *Journal of Abnormal and Social Psychology, 57,* 202–206.

Tversky, A., & Kahneman, D. (1973). Availability: A heuristic for judging frequency and probability. *Cognitive Psychology, 5,* 207–232.

Uchida, Y. (1982). *Desert exile: The uprooting of a Japanese American family.* Seattle: University of Washington Press.

Unger, R. (1979). Toward a redefinition of sex and gender. *American Psychologist, 34,* 1085–1094.

Unger, R. K., & Crawford, M. (1992). *Women and gender: A feminist psychology.* New York: McGraw-Hill.

U.S. Army. Fourth Psychological Operations Group (Airborne). (n.d.). *Leaflets of the Persian Gulf War.* Fort Bragg, NC.

United States. Warren Commission. (1964). *Report of the President's Commission on the Assassination of President John F. Kennedy.* Washington, DC: Government Printing Office.

Unspeakable. (1993, February 22). *Time,* pp. 48–50.

Vacchiano, R. B. (1977). Dogmatism. In T. Blass (Ed.), *Personality variables in social behavior* (pp. 281–314). Hillsdale , NJ: Erlbaum.

Vaillant, G. E. (1977). *Adaptation to life.* Boston: Little, Brown.

Valentine, C. W. (1963). Men of anger and men of shame: Lakalai ethnopsychology and its implications for sociological theory. *Ethnology, 2,* 441–477.

Vanwesenbeeck, I., deGraaf, R., Van Zessen, G., & Straver, C. J. (1993). Protection styles of prostitutes' clients: Intentions, behavior, and considerations in relation to AIDS. *Journal of Sex Education and Therapy, 19,* 79–92.

Varga, K. (1975). N Achievement, n Power, and the effectiveness of research and development. *Human Relations, 28,* 571–590.

Vernon, P. E. (1964). *Personality assessment: A critical survey.* New York: Wiley.

Veroff. J. (1983). Contextual determinants of personality. *Personality and Social Psychology Bulletin, 9,* 331–343.

Veroff, J. (1992). Power motivation. In C. P. Smith (Ed.), *Motivation and personality: Handbook of thematic content analysis* (pp. 278–285). New York: Cambridge University Press.

Veroff, J., Atkinson, J. W., Feld, S. C., & Gurin, G. (1960). The use of thematic apperception to assess motivation in a nationwide interview study. *Psychological Monographs, 74(12)* (Whole no. 499).

Veroff, J., Depner, C., Kulka, R., & Douvan, E. (1980). Comparison of American motives: 1957 versus 1976. *Journal of Personality and Social Psychology, 39,* 1249–1262.

Veroff, J., Douvan, E., & Kulka, A. (1981). *The inner American.* New York: Basic Books.

Wainer, H. A., & Rubin, I. M. (1969). Motivation of research and development entrepreneurs. *Journal of Applied Psychology, 53,* 178–184.

Waite, R. G. L. (1972). Afterword. In W. Langer, *The mind of Adolf Hitler: The secret wartime report* (pp. 215–238). New York: Basic Books.

Waite, R. G. L. (1977). *The psychopathic god: Adolf Hitler.* New York: Basic Books.

Walker, E. L., & Heyns, R. W. (1962). *An anatomy for conformity.* Englewood Cliffs, NJ: Prentice-Hall.

Walker, L. J. (1991). Sex differences in moral reasoning. In W. M. Kurtines & J. L. Gewirtz (Eds.), *Handbook of moral behavior and development: II. Research* (pp. 333–364). Hillsdale, NJ: Erlbaum.

Walker, S. (1984, August). *Analyzing the operational codes of U.S. presidents and secretaries of state.* Paper presented at the annual meeting of the American Psychological Association, Toronto.

Walker, S., & Falkowski, L. (1984). The operational codes of United States presidents and secretaries of state: Motivational foundations and behavioral consequences. *Political Psychology, 5,* 237–266.

Wasserstein, W. (1978). *Uncommon women and others.* New York: Avon Books.

Watson, D., & Clark, L. A. (1984). Negative affectivity: The disposition to experience aversive emotional states. *Psychological Bulletin, 96,* 465–490.

Watson, J. B. (1925). *Behaviorism.* New York: Norton.

Watson, J. B., & Rayner, R. (1920). Conditioned emotional reactions. *Journal of Experimental Psychology, 3,* 1–14.

Watson, J. B., & Watson, R. R. (1921). Studies in infant psychology. *Scientific Monthly, 13,* 493–515.

Webb, E. J., Campbell, D. T., Schwartz, R. D., & Sechrest, L. (1966). *Unobtrusive measures: Nonreactive research in the social sciences.* Chicago: Rand McNally.

Weinberger, J., & Hardaway, R. (1990). Separating science from myth in subliminal psychodynamic activation. *Clinical Psychology Review, 10,* 727–756.

Weinberger, J., & McClelland, D. C. (1990). Cognitive versus traditional motivational models: Irreconcilable or complementary? In E. T. Higgins & R. M. Sorrentino (Eds.), *Handbook of motivation and cognition* (vol. 2, pp. 562–597). New York: Guilford Press.

Weinberger, J., & McLeod, C. (1989, August). *The need to belong: A psychoanalytically-based affiliative motive in the McClelland-Atkinson tradition.* Paper presented at the annual convention of the American Psychological Association, New Orleans.

Weinberger, J., & Silverman, L. H. (1990). Testability and empirical verification of psychoanalytic dynamic propositions through subliminal psychodynamic activation. *Psychoanalytic Psychology, 7,* 299–339.

Weiner, B. (1980). *Human motivation.* New York: Holt, Rinehart & Winston.

Weiner, B. (1982). The emotional consequences of causal attributions. In M. S. Clark & S. T. Fiske (Eds.), *Affect and cognition* (pp. 185–209). Hillsdale, NJ: Erlbaum.

Weiner, B. (1985). An attributional model of achievement motivation and emotion. *Psychological Review, 92,* 548–573.

Weiner, B. (1986). Attribution, emotion, and affect. In R. M. Sorrentino & E. T. Higgins (Eds.), *Handbook of motivation and cognition: Foundations of social behavior* (vol. 1, pp. 281–312). New York: Guilford Press.

Weiner, B., Russell, D., & Lerman, D. (1978). Affective consequences of causal ascriptions. In J. H. Harvey, W. Ickes, & R. F. Kidd (Eds.), *New directions in attribution research* (vol. 2, pp. 59–90). Hillsdale, NJ: Erlbaum.

Weintraub, W. (1986). Personality portraits of American Presidents as revealed in their public statements: The Presidential news conferences of Jimmy Carter and Ronald Reagan. *Political Psychology, 7,* 285–295.

Weintraub, W. (1989). *Verbal behavior in everyday life.* New York: Springer.

Wendt, H. W. (1955). Motivation, effort, and performance. In D. C. McClelland (Ed.), *Studies in motivation* (pp. 448–459). New York: Appleton-Century-Crofts.

Werner, H. (1957). The concept of development from a comparative and organismic point of view. In D. Harris (Ed.), *The concept of development* (pp. 125–148). Minneapolis: University of Minnesota Press.

White, G. F., Katz, J., & Scarborough, K. E. (1992). The impact of professional football games upon violent assaults on women. *Violence and Victims, 7,* 157–171.

White, R. K. (1947). "Black boy": A value-analysis. *Journal of Abnormal and Social Psychology, 42,* 440–461.

White, R. K. (1949). Hitler, Roosevelt and the nature of war propaganda. *Journal of Abnormal and Social Psychology, 44,* 157–174.

White, R. K. (1951). *Value-analysis.* Ann Arbor, MI: Society for the Psychological Study of Social Issues.

White, R. K. (Ed.). (1986). *Psychology and the prevention of nuclear war.* New York: New York University Press.

White, R. W. (1959). Motivation reconsidered: The concept of competence. *Psychological Review, 66,* 297–333.

White, R. W. (1981). Exploring personality the long way: The study of lives. In A. I. Rabin, J. Aronoff, A. M. Barclay, & R. A. Zucker (Eds.), *Further explorations in personality* (pp. 3–26). New York: Wiley.

White, R. W., & Watt, N. F. (1981). *The abnormal personality* (5th ed.). New York: Wiley.

White, T. (1961). *The making of the president 1960.* New York: Atheneum.

Wicker, F. W., Lambert, F. B., Richardson, F. C., & Kahler, J. (1984). Categorical goal hierarchies and classification of human motives. *Journal of Personality, 52,* 285–305.

Widiger, T. A., & Trull, T. J. (1992). Personality and psychopathology: An application of the five-factor model. *Journal of Personality, 60,* 329–361.

Wiggins, J. S., & Broughton, R. (1985). The interpersonal circle: A structural model for the integration of personality research. In R. Hogan & W. H. Jones (Eds.), *Perspectives in personality* (vol. 1, pp. 1–47). Greenwich, CT: JAI Press.

Wilkinson, D. (1980). *Deadly quarrels: Lewis F. Richardson and the statistical study of war.* Berkeley, CA: University of California Press.

Wilkinson, R. (1972). *The broken rebel: A study in culture, politics, and authoritarian character.* New York: Harper & Row.

Willis, A. C. (1990). The relationship of health belief model variables, perceived self-efficacy, internal-external locus-of-control, and knowledge about AIDS to the practice of safer sex: A survey of community college students. *Dissertation Abstracts International, 51(6B),* 3153–3154.

Wilson, E. (1948). Is verse a dying technique? In *The triple thinkers: Twelve essays on literary subjects* (rev. ed., pp. 15–30). New York: Oxford University Press.

Wilson, R. A., & Hosokawa, B. (1980). *East to America: A history of the Japanese in the United States.* New York: Morrow.

Wilson, S., & Kennard, D. (1978). The extraverting effect of treatment in a therapeutic community for drug abusers. *British Journal of Psychiatry, 132,* 296–299.

Wimsatt, W. K., & Beardsley, M. C. (1953). The intentional fallacy. In W. K. Wimsatt (Ed.), *The verbal icon: Studies in the meaning of poetry* (pp. 3–18). Lexington: University of Kentucky Press.

Winefield, A. H., Tiggeman, M., & Winefield, H. R. (1992). Unemployment distress, reasons for job loss and causal attributions for unemployment in young people. *Journal of Occupational and Organizational Psychology, 65,* 213–218.

Wink, P. (1992). Three types of narcissism in women from college to mid-life. *Journal of Personality, 60,* 7–30.

Winter, D. G. (1973). *The power motive.* New York: Free Press.

Winter, D. G. (1978). *Navy leadership and management competencies: Convergence among tests, interviews and performance ratings.* Boston, MA: McBer.

Winter, D. G. (1980). Measuring the motive patterns of southern Africa political leaders at a distance. *Political Psychology, 2 (2),* 75–85.

Winter, D. G. (1987). Leader appeal, leader performance, and the motive profiles of leaders and followers: A study of American presidents and elections. *Journal of Personality and Social Psychology, 52,* 196–202.

Winter, D. G. (1988). The power motive in women—and men. *Journal of Personality and Social Psychology, 54,* 510–519.

Winter, D. G. (1990, July). *Presidential "scores" on the Eysenck Personality Inventory in relation to presidential behavior.* Paper presented at the annual meeting of the International Society for Political Psychology, Washington, DC.

Winter, D. G. (1991a). Measuring personality at a distance: Development of an integrated system for scoring motives in running text. In A. J. Stewart, J. M. Healy, Jr., & D. Ozer (Eds.), *Perspectives in personality: Approaches to understanding lives* (pp. 59–89). London: Jessica Kingsley Publishers.

Winter, D. G. (1991b). A motivational model of leadership: Predicting long-term management success from TAT measures of power motivation and responsibility. *Leadership Quarterly, 2,* 67–80.

Winter, D. G. (1992a). Content analysis of archival materials, personal documents, and everyday verbal productions. In C. P. Smith (Ed.), *Motivation and personality: Handbook of thematic content analysis* (pp. 110–125). New York: Cambridge University Press.

Winter, D. G. (1992b). Personality and foreign policy: A historical overview of research. In V. Harper & E. Singer (Eds.), *Personality and political psychology* (pp. 79–101). Boulder, CO: Westview Press.

Winter, D. G. (1992c). Power motivation revisited. In C. P. Smith (Ed.), *Motivation and personality: Handbook of thematic content analysis* (pp. 301–310). New York: Cambridge University Press.

Winter, D. G. (1992d). Responsibility. In C. P. Smith (Ed.), *Motivation and personality: Handbook of thematic content analysis* (pp. 500–505). New York: Cambridge University Press.

Winter, D. G. (1993a). Gordon Allport and "Letters from Jenny." In K. M. Craik, R. T. Hogan, & R. N. Wolfe (Eds.), *Fifty years of personality psychology* (pp. 147–163). New York: Plenum.

Winter, D. G. (1993b). Personality and leadership in the Gulf war. In S. A. Renshon (Ed.), *The political psychology of the Gulf war* (pp. 107–117). Pittsburgh, PA: University of Pittsburgh Press.

Winter, D. G. (1993c). Power, affiliation and war: Three tests of a motivational model. *Journal of Personality and Social Psychology, 65,* 532–545.

Winter, D. G. (1994). Presidential psychology and governing styles: A comparative psychological analysis of the 1992 presidential candidates. In S. A. Renshon (Ed.), *The Clinton presidency: Campaigning, governing, and the psychology of leadership* (pp. 113 –134). Boulder, CO: Westview.

Winter, D. G., Alpert, R., & McClelland, D. C. (1963). The classic personal style. *Journal of Abnormal and Social Psychology, 67,* 254–265.

Winter, D. G., & Barenbaum, N. B. (1985). Responsibility and the power motive in women and men. *Journal of Personality, 53,* 335–355.

Winter, D. G., & Carlson, L. (1988). Using motive scores in the psychobiographical study of an individual: The case of Richard Nixon. *Journal of Personality, 56,* 75–103.

Winter, D. G., & Healy, J. M., Jr. (1984). *Coding the motive imagery content of television programs.* Unpublished paper, Wesleyan University.

Winter, D. G., Hermann, M. G., Weintraub, W., & Walker, S. G. (1991a). The personalities of Bush and Gorbachev at a distance: Follow-up on predictions. *Political Psychology, 12,* 457–464.

Winter, D. G., Hermann, M. G., Weintraub, W., & Walker, S. G. (1991b). The personalities of Bush and Gorbachev at a distance: Procedures, portraits, and policy. *Political Psychology, 12,* 215–245.

Winter, D. G., & McClelland, D. C. (1978). Thematic analysis: An empirically derived measure of the effects of liberal arts education. *Journal of Educational Psychology, 70,* 8–16.

Winter, D. G., McClelland, D. C., & Stewart, A. J. (1981). *A new case for the liberal arts.* San Francisco: Jossey-Bass.

Winter, D. G., & Stewart, A. J. (1977a). Content analysis as a method of studying political leaders. In M. G. Hermann (Ed.), *A psychological examination of political leaders* (pp. 27–61). New York: Free Press.

Winter, D. G., & Stewart, A. J. (1977b). Power motive reliability as a function of retest instructions. *Journal of Consulting and Clinical Psychology, 45,* 436–440.

Winter, D. G., & Stewart, A. J. (1978). The power motive. In H. London & J. Exner (Eds.), *Dimensions of personality* (pp. 391–447). New York: Wiley.

Winter, D. G., Stewart, A. J., & McClelland, D. C. (1977). Husband's motives and wife's career level. *Journal of Personality and Social Psychology, 35,* 159–166.

Winter, D. G., & Wiecking, F. A. (1971). The new Puritans: Achievement and power motives of New Left radicals. *Behavioral Science, 16,* 523–530.

Winter, N. J. G. (1992, July). *The effects of the Hitler relationship on Mussolini's motive profile.* Paper presented at the annual meeting of the International Society of Political Psychology, San Francisco.

Wittenborn, J. R. (1955). The study of alternative responses by means of the correlation coefficient. *Psychological Review, 62,* 451–460.

Wittgenstein, L. (1922). *Tractatus logico-philosophicus.* London: Routledge & Kegan Paul.

Wolfe, T. (1979). *The right stuff.* New York: Farrar, Straus, & Giroux.

Woodward, C. V. (Ed.). (1974). *Responses of the presidents to charges of misconduct.* New York: Dell.

Woolf, L. (1969). *The journey not the arrival matters: An autobiography of the years 1939 to 1969.* New York: Harcourt Brace Jovanovich.

Woolf, V. (1925). Modern fiction. In *The common reader* (pp. 184–195). London: Hogarth Press. (Original work published 1919.)

Woolf, V. (1977). *A change of perspective: The letters of Virginia Woolf: III. 1923–1928.* (Ed. N. Nicolson & J. Trautman). New York: Harcourt Brace Jovanovich.

Woolf, V. (1984). *The diary of Virginia Woolf: V. 1936–1941.* Orlando, FL: Harcourt Brace Jovanovich.

Woolf, V. (1985). *Moments of being* (Ed. J. Schulkind). (2nd ed.). San Diego, CA: Harcourt Brace Jovanovich.

Wormley, W. P. (1976). *Portfolio manager preferences in an investment decision-making situation: A psychological study.* Unpublished doctoral dissertation, Harvard University.

Worrell, J., & Worrell, L. (1977). Support and opposition to the Women's Liberation Movement: Some personality and parental correlates. *Journal of Research in Personality, 11,* 10–20.

Wright, J. C., & Mischel, W. (1987). A conditional approach to dispositional constructs: The local predictability of social behavior. *Journal of Personality and Social Psychology, 53,* 1159–1177.

Wright, J. C., & Mischel, W. (1988). Conditional hedges and the intuitive psychology of traits. *Journal of Personality and Social Psychology, 55,* 454–469.

Wylie, R. C. (1974–1979). *The self-concept.* Lincoln, NE: University of Nebraska Press.

Yang, K.-S., & Bond, M. H. (1990). Exploring implicit personality theories with indigenous or imported constructs: The Chinese case. *Journal of Personality and Social Psychology, 58,* 1087–1095.

Yerkes, R. M., & Dodson, J. D. (1908). The relation of strength of stimulus to rapidity of habit formation. *Journal of Comparative and Neurological Psychology, 18,* 459–482.

Yinger, J. M. (1982). *Countercultures: The promise and peril of a world turned upside down.* New York: Free Press.

York, K. L., & John, O. P. (1992). The four faces of Eve: A typological analysis of women's personality at midlife. *Journal of Personality and Social Psychology, 63,* 494–508.

Young, P. T. (1961). *Motivation and emotion.* New York: Wiley.

Young-Bruehl, E. (1988). *Anna Freud: A biography.* New York: Summit Books.

Zaehner, R. C. (1962). *Hinduism.* London: Oxford University Press.

Zajonc, R. B. (1980). Feeling and thinking: Preferences need no inferences. *American Psychologist, 35,* 151–175.

Zajonc, R. B. (1984). On the primacy of affect. *American Psychologist, 39,* 117–123.

Zeigarnik, B. (1927). Über das Behalten von erledigten und unerledigten Handlungen [On the recall of completed and incompleted actions]. *Psychologische Forschung, 9,* 1–85.

Zeldow, P. B., Daugherty, S. R., & McAdams, D. P. (1988). Intimacy, power, and psychological well-being in medical students. *Journal of Nervous and Mental Disease, 176,* 182–187.

Zimbardo, P. G. (1969). *The cognitive control of motivation.* Glenview, IL: Scott, Foresman.

Zimbardo, P. (1977). *Shyness: What it is and what to do about it.* Reading, MA: Addison-Wesley.

Zirkel, S., & Cantor, N. (1990). Personal construal of life tasks: Those who struggle for independence. *Journal of Personality and Social Psychology, 58,* 172–185.

Zuckerman, M. (1979). *Sensation seeking: Beyond the optimal level of arousal.* Hillsdale, NJ: Erlbaum.

Zuckerman, M. (1990). Some dubious premises in research and theory on racial differences: Scientific, social, and ethical issues. *American Psychologist, 45,* 1297–1303.

Zuckerman, M. (1991). *Psychobiology of personality.* New York: Cambridge University Press.

Zuckerman, M., & Brody, N. (1989). Oysters, rabbits, and people: A critique of "race differences in behavior" by

J. P. Rushton. *Personality and Individual Differences, 9,* 1025–1033.

Zuckerman, S. (1980). *The effects of subliminal symbiotic and success-related stimuli on the school performance of high school underachievers.* Unpublished Ed.D. thesis, New York University School of Education.

Zullow, H. M. (1983). *Women, self-focused power, and anorexia nervosa.* Unpublished honors thesis, Princeton University.

Zullow, H. M. (1991). Pessimistic rumination in popular songs and newsmagazines predicts economic recession via decreased consumer optimism and spending. *Journal of Economic Psychology, 12,* 501–526.

Zullow, H. M., Oettingen, G., Peterson, C., & Seligman, M. E. P. (1988). Explanatory style and the historical record: CAVeing LBJ, East versus West Berlin, and presidential elections. *American Psychologist, 43,* 673–682.

Zullow, H. M., & Seligman, M. E. P. (1990). Pessimistic rumination predicts defeat of presidential candidates, 1900 to 1984. *Psychological Inquiry, 1(1),* 52–61.

ACKNOWLEDGMENTS

Grateful acknowledgement is made to the rights holders for permission to reproduce material from the following sources:

Excerpts beginning on p.215 from *The Authoritarian Personality* by T. W. Adorno, E. Frenkel-Brunswik, D. Levinson, and N. Sanford. Copyright (c) 1950 by the American Jewish Committee. Copyright renewed. Reprinted by permission of HarperCollins Publishers, Inc.

Excerpts from Allport, G. W.: From the Gordon Allport papers, Miscellaneous Correspondence 1930–1945, box 1: A-Bühler, Allport to Donald B. Aldrich, 26 April 1931 (Harvard University Archives, HUG4118.10). Reprinted by permission of the Harvard University Archives.

Excerpts from *Letters from Jenny* by Gordon W. Allport, copyright © 1965 by Harcourt Brace & Company and renewed 1993 by Robert P. Allport, reprinted by permission of the publisher.

Excerpts from Almond, G. A., & Verba, S.: *The Civic Culture.* Copyright © 1963 by Princeton University Press. Renewed 1991. Reprinted by permission of Princeton University Press.

Excerpts from Anderson, J. W. (1990). *The Life of Henry A. Murray: 1893–1988.* In A. Rabin, R. A. Zucker, R. A. Emmons, & S. Frank (Eds.), *Studying Persons and Lives.* Copyright 1990, Springer Publishing Company, Inc., New York 10012, as publisher. Used by permission.

Excerpts from *I Know Why the Caged Bird Sings,* by Maya Angelou. Copyright © 1969 by Maya Angelou. Reprinted by kind permission of the publishers. Random House, Inc. (Virago Press in the British Commonwealth).

Excerpts from "Still I Rise" from the collection *And Still I Rise,* by Maya Angelou. Copyright © 1978 by Maya Angelou. Reprinted by kind permission of the publishers, Random House, Inc. (Virago Press in the British Commonwealth).

Excerpts from "Caged Bird" *Shaker, Why Don't You Sing?* by Maya Angelou. Copyright © 1983 by Maya Angelou. Reprinted by kind permission of the publishers, Random House, Inc. (Virango Press in the British Commonwealth).

Excerpts from *On the Pulse of the Morning,* by Maya Angelou. Copyright © 1993 by Maya Angelou. Reprinted by kind permission of the publishers. Random House, Inc. (Virago Press in the British Commonwealth).

Excerpts from Bannister, D., & Mair, J. M. M. (1968). *The Evaluation of Personal Constructs.* San Dieg, CA: Academic Press.

Excerpts from Berkowitz, L., & Macaulay, J. (1971). The contagion of criminal violence. *Sociometry, 34,* 238–260. (American Sociological Association)

Excerpts from *The Stranger* by Albert Camus, trans. S. Gilbert Copyright 1946 and renewed 1974 by Alfred A. Knopf, Inc. Reprinted by permission of the publisher (Hamish Hamilton in the British Commonwealth).

Excerpts from Canaday, J. (1965). *Mainstreams of Modern Art.* Orlando, Fl.: Harcourt Brace & Co.

Excerpts from Carroll, J. S., & Payne, J. W. (1977). Judgments about crime and the criminal," in B. D. Sales (Ed.), *Perspectives in Law and Psychology,* Vol. 1: The Criminal Justice System, pp. 191–239. New York; Plenum Publishing Corporation.

Excerpts from Cloniger, C. R. (1991). Brain networks underlying personality development. In B. J. Carroll & J. E. Barrett (Eds.). *Psychopathology and the Brain* (pp. 183–208). New York: Raven Press.

Excerpts from Cooley, C. H. Human Nature and the social order. Reprinted with permission of Scribner, an import of Simon & Schuster, Inc., from *Human Nature and the Social Order* by Charles Horton Cooley. Copyright 1902, 1922 Charles Scribner's Sons; copyright renewed 1930 Elsie Cooley.

Excerpts from Couch, A. S. (1962/1969). The psychological determinants of interpersonal behavior. In G. S. Nielson (Ed), *Personality Research.* Reading, MA: Addison-Wesley, Reprinted with permission from Munksgaard (original publishers), Copenhagen.

Excerpts from Davies, D. R., Hockey, G. R. J., & Taylor, A. (1969). Varied auditory stimulation, temperament differences and vigilance performance. *British Journal of Psychology, 60,* 453–457.

Excerpt from *Personality Power, and Politics* by G. J. DiRenzo. ©1967 by the University of Notre Dame press. Used by permission of the publisher.

Excerpts from Dostoevsky, F. (1861–62/1961). *The House of the Dead.* Tr. Constance Garnett. London: William Heinemann, Ltd.

Excerpts from Einstein, A., *Autobiographical notes.* Reprinted from *Autobiographical Notes,* by Albert Einstein, by permission of Open Court Publishing Company, La Salle, Illinois. Copyright 1949, 1951, ©1970, and © 1979 by

The Library of Living Philosophers, Inc., and the Estate of Albert Einstein.

Excerpts from *Ideas and Opinions* by Albert Einstein. Copyright © 1954, 1982 by Crown Publishers, Inc. Reprinted by permission of Crown Publishers, Inc.

Excerpts from Eysenck, H. W., & Eysenck, M. W. (1985). *Personality and Individual Differences: A natural science approach.* New York: Plenum.

Excerpts from Foner, P. S. (Ed.) (1967). *Helen Keller: Her Socialist Years:* New York: International Publishers.

Excerpts from Freud, S. (1900). *Interpretation of Dreams.* A. W. Freud et al., by arrangement with Mark Paterson & Associates/Basic Books, Inc.

Excerpts from Sigmund Freud's letter of February 28, 1934 to Saul Rosenzweig. Mark Paterson Associates, 10 Brook Street, Wivenhoe, Essex CO7 9DS, England

Excerpts from Gilligan, C. (1982). *In a Different Voice.* Cambridge, MA: Harvard University Press.

Excerpts from Hine, D. C. (1989). Rape and the inner lives of Black women in the Middle West. *Signs: Journal of Women in Culture and Society,* vol. 14, pp. 912–920. University of Chicago Press. © 1989 by Darlene Clark Hine.

Excerpts from Jencks, C. (1987, February 12). Genes and crime. *New York Review of Books,* pp. 34–41. Reprinted with permission from The New York Review of Books. Copyright © 1987, Nyrev, Inc.

Excerpts from Jung, *C. G. Collected Works of C. G. Jung.* Copyright © 1971 by Princeton University Press. Reprinted by permission of Princeton University Press. (Routledge in the United Kingdom).

Excerpts from Keller, H. (1955). *Teacher: Anne Sullivan Macy.* New York: Doubleday Publishers.

Excerpts from Kinder, D. R., & Mebane, W. R., Jr. (1983). Politics and economics in everyday life. In K. R. Monroe (ed.), *The Political Process and Economic Change,* pp. 141–180. New York: Agathon. Adapted by permission of Agathon Press, Bronx, New York.

Excerpts from Knutson, J. (1974). *Psychological variables in political recruitment: An analysis of party activists.* Unpublished paper, Wright Institute, Berkeley, CA. By permission of Dr. Leslie K. Knutson.

Excerpts from Kohlberg, L. (1963). The development of children's orientations toward a moral order. I. Sequence in the development of moral thought. *Vita Humana, 6,* 11–33. S. Karger, AG, Basel, Switzerland.

Excerpts on pp. 16–17 from Langer, W. (1972). *The Mind of Adolph Hitler: The Secret Wartime Report.* New York: Basic Books, Inc.

Excerpts from Larsen, R. J., & Diener, E. *Review of Personality and Social Psychology,* Vol. 13, pp. 25–59, copyright © 1992 by Sage Publications, Inc. Reprinted by permission of Sage Publications, Inc.

Excerpts from Lash, J. (1980). *Helen and Teacher.* New York: Delacorte Press.

Excerpts from McClelland, D. C. (1985). *Human motivation.* Glenview, Il: Scott, Foresman.

Excerpts from McFarland, S. G., Ageyev, V. S., & Abalakina, M. A. (1992). The authoritarian personality in the United States and the former Soviet Union: Comparative studies. In W. F. Stone, G. Lederer, & R. Christie (Eds), *Strength and weakness: The Authoritarian*

Personality Today (pp. 199–225). New York: Springer-Verlag.

Excerpts from McFarland, S., Ageyev, V. S., & Djintcharadze, N. (1996). Russian authoritarianism two years after Communism. *Personality and Social Psychology Buletin, 22,* 210–217.

Excerpts from Merei, F. (1949/1958). Group leadership and institutionalization. Originally published in *Human Relations* (Plenum Publishing Corporation).

Two pictures illustrating Milton's "L'Allegro" and "Il Penseroso" reproduced by permission of the Special Collections Library, University of Michigan.

Excerpts from Mischel, W. (1968). *Personality and Assessment.* New York: Wiley.

Excerpts from Nixon, R. (1978). *RN: The Memoirs of Richard Nixon.* Reprinted by permission of Warner Books/New York (Sidgwick & Jackson in the U.K.) from RN: *The Memories of Richard Nixon.* Copyright (c) 1978 by Richard Nixon.

Excerpts from Paterson, K. (1982, September). Interview with Maya Angelou. Courtesy *Vogue.* Copyright © 1982 by the Conde Nast Publications, Inc.

Excerpts from Ressler, R. K., & Burgess, A. W. (1985). Crime scene and profile characteristics of organized and disorganized murderers. Reprinted from the *FBI Law Enforcement Bulletin,* August 1985 issue.

Excerpts from Rogers, C. R. (1959). A Theory of Therapy, Personality, and Interpersonal Relationships, as Developed in the Client-Centered Framework. In S. Koch (Ed.), *Psychology: A Study of a Science* (vol. 3, pp. 184–256). Reproduced with permission of McGraw-Hill, Inc.

Excerpts from Rosenberg, M. (1979). *Conceiving the self.* New York: Basic Books.

Excerpts from Rogers, C. R., & Skinner, B. F. (1956). Some issues concerning the control of human behavior; A symposium. Excerpted with permission from *SCIENCE,* vol. 124, pp. 1057–1066. Copyright 1956 American Association for the Advancement of Science.

Excerpts from Schama, S. (1987). *The Embarrassment of Riches: An Interpretation of Dutch Culture in the Golden Age.* New York: Alfred A. Knopf, Inc.

Excerpts from Sears, R. R. (1963). Dependency motivation. Reprinted from the *1963 Nebraska Symposium of Motivation* by permission of the University of Nebraska Press. Copyright © 1963 by the University of Nebraska Press. Copyright (c) renewed 1991 by the University of Nebraska Press

Excerpts from Shaw, Bernard (1924). *Saint Joan.* The Society of Author's [London] on behalf of the Bernard Shaw Estate.

Excerpts from *About Behaviorism* by B. F. Skinner, Copyright (c) 1974 by B. F. Skinner. Reprinted by permission of Alfred A. Knopf, Inc. (Jonathan Cape, as publisher, in the British Commonwealth).

Excerpts from Suedfeld, P., & Piedrahita (1984). Intimations of mortality: Integrative simplification as a precursor of death. *Journal of Personality and Social Psychology, 47,* 848–852. Copyright © 1984 by the American Psychological Association. Reprinted with permission.

Excerpts from Suedfeld, P., Corteen, R. S., & McCormick, C. (1986). The role of integrative complexity in military leadership: Robert E. Lee and his opponents. *Journal of Applied Social Psychology, 16,* 498–507.

Material from Thorne, A., & Gough, H. (1991). *Portraits of type: An MBTI research compendium.* Modified and reproduced by special permission of the Publisher, Consulting Psychologists Press, Inc., Palo Alto, CA 94303 from *Portraits of Types: An MBTI Research Compendium* by Thorne and H. Gough. Copyright 1991 by Consulting Psychologists Press, Inc. All rights reserved. Further reproduction is prohibited without the Publisher's written consent.

Excerpts from Wasserstein, W. (1978). *Uncommon women and others.*

Excerpts from *Moments of Being* by Virginia Woolf, copyright 1976 by Quentin Bell and Angelica Garnett, reprinted by permission of Harcourt Brace & Company (Hogarth Press in the British Commonwealth).

Excerpts from Zuckerman, M. (1991). *Psychobiology of Personality,* New York: Cambridge University Press. Reprinted with permission of the Cambridge University Press and the author.

Excerpts from Seligman, M. E. P., & Schulman, P. (1986). Explanatory style as a predictor of productivity and quitting among life insurance sales agents. *Journal of Personality and Social Psychology, 50,* 832–838.

Excerpts from Peterson, C., Seligman, M. E. P., & Vaillant, G. E. (1988). Pessimistic explanatory style is a risk factor for physical illness: A thirty-five year longitudinal study. *Journal of Personality and Social Psychology, 55,* 23–27.

Excerpts from Allport, G. W. (1966b). Traits revisited. *American Psychologist, 21,* 1–10.

Excerpts from Crosby, F. (1976). A model of egoistical relative deprivation, *Psychological Review, 83,* 85–113.

Excerpts from Winter, D. G. (1987). Leader appeal, leader performance, and the motive profiles of leaders and followers: A study of American presidents and electrons. *Journal of Personality and Social Psychology, 52,* 196–202.

Excerpts from Sales, S. M. (1972). Economic threat as a determinant of conversion rates in authoritarian and nonauthoritarian churches. *Journal of Personality and Social Psychology, 23,* 420–428.

Excerpts from Markus, H., & Nurius, P. (1986). Possible selves. *American Psychologist, 41,* 954–969.

Excerpts from Thorne, A. (1987). The press of personality; Conversations between introverts and extraverts. *Journal of Personality and Social Psychology, 53,* 718–726.

Excerpts from Bandura, A., Ross, D., & Ross, S. A. (1963). Imitation of film-mediated aggressive models. *Journal of Abnormal and Social Psychology, 66,* 3–11.

Excerpts from Funder, D. C., & Ozer, D. J. (1983). Behavior as a function of the situation. *Journal of Personality and Social Psychology, 44,* 107–112.

Excerpts from Bern, D. J. & Allen, A. (1974). On predicting some of the people some of the time: The search for cross-situational consistencies in behavior. *Psychological Review, 81,* 506–520.

Excerpts from Nuttall, R. (1964). Some correlates of high need for Achievement among urban Northern Negroes. *Journal of Abnormal and Social Psychology, 68,* 593–600.

Excerpts from Epstein, S. (1979). The stability of behavior; I. On predicting most of the people much of the time. *Journal of Personality and Social Psychology, 37.* 1097–1126).

Excerpts from Veroff, J., Depner C., Kulka, R., & Douvan, E. (1980). Comparison of American motives; 1957 versus 1976. *Journal of Personality and Social Psychology, 39,* 1249–1262.

Excerpts from Yang, K. S., & Bond, M. H. (1990). Exploring implicit personality theories with indigenous or imported constructs: The Chinese case. *Journal of Personality and Social Psychology, 58,* 1087–1095.

Excerpts from Markus, H. R., & Kitayama, S. (1991). Culture and the self. Implications for cognition, emotion, and motivation. *Psychological Review, 98.* 224–253.

Excerpts from Stewart, A. J., & Healy, J. M., Jr. (1989). Linking individual development and social change. *American Psychologist, 44,* 30–42.

Excerpts from Stewart, A. J. (1982). The course of individual adaptation to life changes. *Journal of Personality and Social Psychology, 42,* 1100–1113.

Excerpts from Winter, D. G., & Barenbaum, N. B. (1985). Responsibility and the power motive in women and men. *Journal of Personality, 53:2,* pp. 335–355. Table 5 (p. 350). Copyright Duke University Press, 1985. Reprinted with permission.

Excerpts from Winter, D. G., & Carlson, L. (1988). Using motive scores in the psychobiographical study of an individual: The case of Richard Nixon, *Journal of Personality, 56:1,* pp. 75–103. Tables 1 (modified by later standardization data) and 5 (pp. 80 and 93). Copyright Duke University Press, 1988. Reprinted with permission.

Excerpts from Swede, S. W., & Tetlock, P. E. (1986). Henry Kissinger's implicit theory of personality; A quantitative case study. *Journal of Personality, 54:4,* pp. 617–646. Materials from Tables 3 and 4 (pp. 626–627 and 634–635) rearranged into a table. Copyright Duke University Press, 1986. Reprinted with permission.

Excerpts from Greene, D. L., & Winter, D. G. (1971). Motives, leadership, and involvements among Black college students. *Journal of Personality, 39:3,* pp. 319–332. Table 4 (p. 327), Copyright Duke University Press, 1971. Reprinted with permission.

Excerpts from Tooby, J., & Cosmides, L. (1990). On the universality of human nature and the uniqueness of the individual: The role of genetics and adaptation. *Journal of Personality, 58:1,* pp. 17–67. Material from pp. 24, 56. Copyright Duke University Press, 1990. Reprinted with permission.

Excerpts from Peterson, B. E., Doty, R. M., & Winter, D. G. (1993). Authoritarianism and attitudes toward contemporary social issues. *Personality and Social Psychology Bulletin, 19,* 174–184.

Excerpts from Peterson, C., & Seligman, M. E. P. (1984). *Content analysis of verbatim explanations: The CAVE technique for assessing explanatory style.* Unpublished paper, Virginia Polytechnic Institute and State University.

Excerpts from Anderson, W. (Ed.). (1970). *Theophrastus: The character sketches*. Kent, OH: Kent State University Press.

Excerpts from Simonton, D. (1986). Presidential personality: Biographical use of the Gough Adjective Check List. *Journal of Personality and Social Psychology, 5,* 149–160.

Excerpts from Simonton, D. (1988). Presidential style: Personality, biography, and performance, *Journal of Personality and Social Psychology, 55,* 928–936.

Excerpts from Winter, D. G., Hermann, M. G., Weintraub, W., & Walker, S. G. (1991). The personalities of Bush and Gorbachev at a distance: Procedures, portraits, and policy. *Political Psychology, 12,* 215–245.

Excerpts from Winter, D. G., Hermann, M. G., Weintraub, W., & Walker, S. G. (1991). The personalities of Bush and Gorbachev at a distance: Follow-up on predictions. *Political Psychology, 12,* 457–464.

Excerpts from Caspi, A., Elder, G. H., Jr., & Bem, D. J. (1987). Moving against the world: Life-course patterns of explosive children. *Developmental Psychology, 23,* 308–313.

Excerpts from Altemeyer, B. *Authoritarianism in American Legislators.* Unpublished paper.

Excerpts from Toppman, L. Interview with Maya Angelou. Originally published in *The Charlotte Observer.*

Excerpts from Steele, C. (1992, April). Race and the schooling of Black Americans. *The Atlantic,* pp. 68–78. (c) 1992 Claude Steele, as first published in *The Atlantic Monthly.*